Greenwich Readers : 4

Policy Issues in the European Union

to Deniz, Süha and Sema

Policy Issues in the European Union

A Reader in the Political Economy of European Integration

edited by

MEHMET UGUR

LECTURER IN ECONOMICS AND EUROPEAN STUDIES
UNIVERSITY OF GREENWICH

Greenwich University Press

First published in 1995 by
Greenwich University Press
Unit 42
Dartford Trade Park
Hawley Road
Dartford
Kent DA1 1PF
United Kingdom

A CIP catalogue record for this book is available from the British Library

ISBN 1 874529 38 8

Designed and produced for Greenwich University Press by
Angela Allwright and Kirsten Brown.

Printed in Great Britain by The Bath Press, Avon.

Contents

Policy Issues in the European Union: Introduction

Cohan (1992: 199) has stated recently that publications on the European Community offer more choice than studies on major Western European countries such as France, Germany, or even Britain. If anything, the abundance is now more evident. In addition to the proliferation of textbooks on the economics and politics of the European Union (EU) [El-Agraa (1990), Hitiris (1991), Tsoukalis (1993), Nugent (1991), Sbragia (1992), Pinder (1991)], there is now a new tendency to assume a European perspective in various disciplines [see, for example, Burda and Wyplosz (1993), Crouch (1993), and Andersen & Eliassen (1993)]. From a sociology of knowledge point of view, I can only agree with Cohan that what is important is not the proliferation *per se*, but the way in which the products of scholarly activity are packaged. To some extent I am worried about the message implicit in this type of packaging; namely, the presentation of the EU or Europe as an essentially non-problematic entity. I think no one would deny the legitimacy of taking the EU or Europe as a subject of scholarly research. What should be questioned, however, is the extent to which the idea of Europe associated with the campaign of relaunching European integration from the mid-1980s onwards seems to be internalised without a critical evaluation. One would venture to assert that the environment created by the discourse on the 'cost of non-Europe' [see Commission (1988)] has generated a process of convergence in the patterns of marketing research output. In other words, we observe — at least to some extent — the vindication of Hotelling's analysis on convergence [see Hotelling (1929)]. Given the demand generated by the marketing of a new idea of 'Europe', publishers (and consequently researchers) are caught in a process of approximating their products in order to avoid the loss of the marginal reader.

This tendency is both a result and contributing factor to the ascendance of essentially an empirical orientation in the study of European integration [for comments on this trend, see Halland Matlary (1994): 3]. We seem to be heading towards the peak of a phase characterised by concerns about partial aspects of European integration, which itself is still an unresolved theoretical issue due to the shortcomings of the preceding phase of theorisation. The contentious nature of the issue under investigation is observed not only at the political level where the actors involved — because of differences in assumptions, conceptions and priorities — have been eager to shape the European Union in their own image, but also at the theoretical level where social scientists from different disciplines have been attempting to conceptualise an intricate entity whose complexity is exacerbated by the combination of intergovernmental and supranational characteristics. Drawing attention to the difficulties faced by social scientists, Puchala (1972) long ago described the attempts at theorising European integration in terms of a story about an experiment that involved an elephant and blind subjects. As the subjects described the object in terms of the part they happened to touch, descriptions proved to be too diverse to be manageable.

One aim of this book is to draw the reader's attention to the fact that the legitimate study of European integration in terms of policy issues should not be detached from attempts at developing a general picture about the whole process of policy-making. To the extent that this objective is served, the student will become more aware of the ongoing debate on European integration and be better able to take the preliminary steps towards exercising an informed intervention into this debate in terms of either research or realisation of functional tasks. Secondly, this book is interested mostly in drawing the reader's attention to the complexity of the phenomenon under investigation — an aspect most often concealed *not* necessarily by the findings of the research but by the *convergent patterns* of packaging its results. One way of ensuring that this message is conveyed has been to select articles that make the Reader an interdisciplinary text, reflecting different methods of investigation and generating further questions. It is hoped that these properties will encourage the reader to develop his/her own critical assessment and synthesis. The other way has been to ensure that the selected articles reflect the interaction between national and European levels with respect to the specific policy issues under investigation. Although this interaction is only implicitly dealt with in some articles, it is treated explicitly in others. The article by Nugent and the emphasis placed on this issue here should keep the reader's attention alive and enable him/her to avoid the pitfall of considering the European Union as a single entity whose complexity is pointed to only when the policy output proves to be below what is expected.

The interdisciplinary nature of the Reader is reflected in its inclusion of articles from a variety of disciplines utilizing different methods of investigation. On the one hand, it offers articles based on econometric testing as is the case in Chapters 2 and 15. On the other hand, it also contains articles focusing on the political process involved in a specific policy area which, essentially, is economic in nature. Chapter 10 by Wise and Gibb, Chapter 12 by Keating, and Chapters 16 and 17 by Callovi and Ugur can be considered in this category. The remaining chapters reflect a combination of both methods, with the structure serving two purposes. At the practical level, it makes the book accessible to a wide range of students without necessarily compromising on rigour. In terms of intellectual considerations, it draws the student's attention to the relative merits of different research methods and the way in which this feature is linked to the aspects of the issue that the authors are trying to address — hence dissipating any prejudgment about the supremacy of a given methodology or discipline in its analysis of European integration.

The Reader is organised into five parts and one free-standing article. Chapter 1, by Nugent, is an introductory free-standing article that highlights the general aspects of the policy-making process in the European Union (EU). This chapter is especially significant in the sense that it provides the student with a brief account of the multiplicity of issues and actors involved in the policy-making process. It highlights the following points: the inputs from national levels into the policy-making process; the relationship between the extent of national input and the nature of the policy issue; the multiplicity of committees through which a certain decision is processed; and the linkages and 'package deals' that form the framework within which differences in interest are reconciled. What the student would, I hope, find interesting in Nugent's analysis is the careful balance struck between the intergovernmental and supranational features of the European Union. If this hope is proved to be not too optimistic, the student would be relatively well-equipped to dig deeper in order to unearth the dynamics behind the general stance of the policy under investigation. These dynamics could relate, for example, to national-EU level interactions, interest group politics, established economic policy preferences, and inter-institutional bargaining, etc. For readers with an interest in this direction, the following further reading can be recommended: Siedentopf and Ziller (1988), Keohane and Hoffmann (1991), and Sbragia (1992).

The main body of the Reader is organised into five parts. The first four parts cover policy areas where the EU already possesses, or is in the process of acquiring, a substantial degree of competence. The final part, on the other hand, is devoted to some policy issues for which EU competence is either limited or has proved to be more problematic. This organisation implicitly suggests that EU competence is related to the nature of the policy issue/area under consideration. Without going into a detailed discussion of this relationship, it suffices to indicate that the more the policy issue/area is divisible and transparent the more competence is delegated to the European Union. Further analysis on this issue can be found in Ugur (1994). Policy issues/areas such as immigration from third countries, because of their link with national identity and the way in which the member states utilise them in their legitimation functions, are less divisible and transparent. Consequently, EU competence in these areas is limited as they are less amenable to the trade-offs and package deals that constitute the essential characteristics of the EU policy-making process.

Part I is devoted to some microeconomic policy issues. The article by Demekas *et al.* provides an overall review of the literature on the implications of the Common Agricultural Policy for EU consumers, member states and third countries. Demekas *et al.* not only introduce the student to the body of literature on the implications of the Common Agricultural Policy (CAP), but also draw his/her attention to both the merits and limits of the methodology utilised. Although the findings assessed by Demekas *et al.* come up with strong suggestions about the cost of the CAP to various economic actors, they also reveal that the CAP is essentially beneficial for the EU's associated partners within the framework of Lomé conventions and other preferential trade agreements. This conclusion, however, should be considered in conjunction with the chapter by Stevens on the EU-Third World relations. When one considers not only the agricultural sector but also other sectors of the associated countries' economies, the benefits of having preferential links with the EU have to be qualified to a large extent — a reminder that partial results cannot and should not be generalised.

Although the Treaty of Rome did not provide for an industrial policy, the EU has developed a substantial degree of competence in this area. There are some indications in Price's article as to why it proved feasible for the EU to develop such clout in the area of industrial policy. One of the factors that facilitated this process of acquired influence has been the organised interest of European corporations [for an analysis of how producers benefit from having an EU industrial policy, see Nielsen *et al.* (1992 108-113)]. Another aspect of the article by Price is its appeal to a wide readership. This aspect, however, is not the major reason for its inclusion in this Reader. Its inclusion is related more to the fact that it attempts to investigate the EU industrial policy in the context of the debate on recent contributions to trade theory in international economics. Because of its provision of theoretical criteria against which the EU's industrial policy is analysed, the article by Price enables the reader to thread confidently. This is both in terms of the clarity of the framework within which the issue is discussed and also in terms of the criteria against which policy outcomes can be assessed.

One significant conclusion to be derived from Price's analysis is that the desirability of an EU industrial policy hinges on the balance between the benefits of supporting 'strategic industries' and the cost of rent-seeking behaviour on the part of European corporations. The significance of this conclusion, in my opinion, is due to the fact that it may generate new research questions that focus on the desirability of industrial policy from an internal rather than external perspective. Such a new research agenda may contribute to the correction of two types of bias in the public debate on EU industrial policy: the over-emphasis on external implications inspired by thorny trade issues between the EU and other industrialised countries, and the tendency to see the EU industrial policy as an essentially non-problematic solution to competitiveness problems of European industry.

In contrast to industrial policy, the Treaty of Rome *has* provided for comprehensive rules concerning competition policy. Despite this Treaty-based competence, however, the European Union's role has remained quite limited until after the adoption of the Single European Act in 1986. There may be two different explanations as to why the launch of the Single Market project has stimulated interest in an EU-wide competition policy: the neo-functionalist explanation and the convergence thesis.

According to the former, a structural process of 'spill-over' compels the actors to integrate new policy areas in order to realise the original task of establishing a common market (Haas 1964; 1968). The EU and its member states, according to this explanation, must have come to realise that the establishment of a single market could not be realised without having binding common rules about competition. Otherwise divergent national policies in this area would generate distortions, unfair competition, and consequently protectionism which eventually undermines the efforts towards creating a single market. In the absence of EU-wide competition rules, two possibilities exist. First, member states with well-established national competition policies will be forced to change existing legislation and evolve towards the level of the least-regulated country. This option, however, may not be attractive because of established national traditions and political compromises based upon them. Secondly, member states with comprehensive rules on competition will impose protectionist measures to curtail the superficially-acquired competitive edge by companies in the least regulated member states. This option may be politically feasible as far as the domestic constituency is concerned, but it runs against the objective of establishing a single market. The way out of the impasse is to integrate this policy area and ensure that the integration process is not derailed.

The alternative view criticises the former for being teleological and raises some significant questions. According to this view, the 'spill-over' thesis provides neither a time-scale nor a meaningful sequence of events that would help us predict the likely trajectory of European integration. What the alternative view offers instead is the degree of primordial convergence between national policies as a basis for integration in a certain policy area [see Sandholtz and Zysman (1989) and Ugur (1994): 20-30]. In this perspective, the revival of interest in competition policy and the advent of the single market are heavily dependent on a general trend in Western Europe that is characterised by misgivings about the effectiveness of creating 'National-champions' — i.e. nursing large national companies that would compete against foreign ills with the support of the state. What we observe at national levels is a process in which national governments gradually distance themselves from the idea of national champions in favour of 'Eurochampions' [see Tsoukalis (1993): 99-116].

Creating Euro-champions, however, requires some sort of European framework that is also linked with the general drive of the industrial policy examined by Price; namely, the encouragement of EU-wide co-operation between high-tech corporations. The revival of Commission activity under articles 85, 86, 90, 92 and 93 from the mid-1980s onwards and the adoption of Regulation 4064/89 in December 1989 can be seen as steps towards creating such a regulatory framework. The article by Bishop takes the reader through this process and points out the essentially unfinished agenda in this policy area. Although the new regulation provides the Commission with substantial powers, there are still problems lying ahead. The 'one-stop shop' in merger regulation may be superior to the ambiguity associated with articles 85 and 86, but it raises the question of how to strike a balance between 'national interests' and EU preferences. The regulation compels the Commission to consult national authorities both through their relevant ministries and their representatives in the advisory committee, but it is not clear what the outcome of such consultations would be if the merger under investigation involves companies from several member states with diverging views on the desirability of the merger. Also, how can the Commission, which is in need of member state support because of its limited resources, ensure co-operation by a member state that is keen to see a merger go ahead? These are some of the issues that must be addressed if the EU's competition policy is to function efficiently and effectively.

Another area where the EU has acquired a significant degree of competence has been environmental policy. The article by Vogel introduces the reader to the stages through which this competence has been consolidated. Vogel's article suggests that two factors have been at play in this process: the linkage between market integration and environmental policy, and the increased significance of environmental issues on the political agenda of the member states due to electoral pressure. As a result, the EU has now over 600 regulations and directives concerning environmental issues. Although Vogel does not attempt to conceal his inclination to consider this outcome as a positive achievement, he is also aware of the limitations and problems lying ahead. For example, he agrees that most of the legislation represents a compromise at the lowest common denominator — even though member states willing to introduce stricter environmental regulations are allowed to do so. Also, the increase in the amount of EU legislation raises the issue of implementation and control, for which the Commission is not well equipped. The establishment of a European Environment Agency for controlling implementation could be a solution, but intergovernmental wrangling about its location since the European Council decision of 1989 has proved to be — as usual — a stumbling block.

Part II of the Reader deals with some macroeconomic policy issues in the European Union. The article by Tsoukalis examines the stages through which the debate on economic and monetary union has evolved, leading to the three-stage formula of the Maastricht Treaty. As a close observer of European monetary integration and early contributor to the literature on this issue [see Tsoukalis (1977)], Tsoukalis offers a good overview of the debate between the monetarist and economist views subscribed to, respectively, by France and Germany. The interesting aspect of this debate is that not only was it the major issue during earlier attempts at monetary union, but also that it proved to be the framework within which the monetary union section of the Maastricht Treaty was negotiated. As it was the case with the SNAKE and European Monetary System (EMS) experiments, the three-stage monetary union envisaged in the Maastricht Treaty was also formulated on the basis of a compromise between these two views. This compromise is based on two principles: a final date by which monetary union will be achieved (the monetarist demand) and strict convergence criteria that would reduce the risk of bailing out inflation-prone countries (the economist demand). Tsoukalis also introduces the reader to other issues related to monetary integration in Europe: the credibility of the EMS, the issue of asymmetry in the system, and the institutional arrangements and macroeconomic policy co-ordination associated with the creation of a single currency.

Following the overview presented by Tsoukalis, Gros and Thygesen focus on a specific issue in European monetary integration: the implications of European monetary integration for national fiscal policy. The main question that Gros and Thygesen address is whether binding fiscal rules are necessary in a monetary union. Evaluating the pros and cons, they come to the conclusion that some sort of rules are necessary. They also suggest that the rules provided for in the Maastricht Treaty (3% of GDP for budget deficit, 60% of GDP for government debt) and the procedures through which the diverging countries will be asked to take corrective action are appropriate. Gros and Thygesen are, nevertheless, aware of the difficulties involved in implementing these rules. First, there are practical difficulties that stem from estimation and simulation procedures. Secondly, there are substantive problems as it is difficult to ascertain *a priori* the extent of spill-over from national fiscal policies and the disciplinary effects of monetary union. One further complication is caused by the fact that, in the absence of an EU-wide shock absorbing mechanism, national fiscal policy remains as the only policy option that can be referred to when dealing with adverse shocks.

While Gros and Thygesen grapple with the issue of how binding fiscal rules can be justified, the article by Westaway highlights the dynamics that would force EU member states to harmonize their fiscal systems even without a monetary union. Westaway's analysis is implicitly neo-functionalist in the sense that it points out the structural exigencies that would generate spill-overs. His reference point is the single market, the completion of which would push member states to harmonize their value added tax, excise duties and corporate taxation. Although the logic of Westaway's analysis is convincing, his article does not address adequately the question of why discrepancies still prevail in the three areas that he examines. Having said that, however, it must be acknowledged that the article remains a good source of information on the interaction between national and Union levels — an aspect of the EU policy-making that this Reader attempts to highlight.

The political economy of distribution in the European Union is an interesting area of study for two reasons. First, the amount of resources earmarked for distributive purposes is closely related to the nature of the polity that characterises the EU. Despite its supranational dimension and some European orientation of the citizens, the EU's legitimacy is still essentially dependent on the member states' delegation of authority. In this type of polity, resources for (re)distributive purposes tend to be low as cleavages between the constituent units act as an obstacle to the development of a feeling of solidarity. Also, in such a setting, redistributive decision-making tends to be problematic as contributor members will be reluctant to contribute while the recipient members will try to increase their share. This tension has been clearly observable in the area of regional policy and it has been described by some students of European integration as "pork barrel politics" [see Wallace (1983)]. A similar problem is likely to haunt the area of social policy as the redistributive dimension begins to assume some significance through the European Social Fund.

The second reason why I find the distributive policy-making of the EU interesting is the dynamics that could generate potentially significant political consequences for the domestic politics of the member states even though the amount of resources is relatively small. Currently, resources devoted to regional development and social assistance is about 30% of the EU budget which, in turn, constitutes about 1.2% of the EU GDP. Nevertheless, this amount can still cause a redirection of attention towards the EU and away from the member states. The proliferation of regional lobbies in Brussels and the creation of the Assembly of the Regions by the Maastricht Treaty are some indicators of this process. This is understandable because, given the limited resources, depressed regions are compelled to compete with their counterparts both within and outside the member states in which they are located. The European Commission, as the impartial umpire and the holder of the purse, is the level at which this rivalry has to be fought. This redirection of attention has two types of implication for the territorial politics of the member states. On the one hand, it causes some concern about the possibility of weakening central authority control over the regions. On the other hand, however, it may enable the national governments to enhance such control as the regions are compelled to strike alliances with their central authorities to increase the country's share of the cake. This is the major issue addressed by Keating in Chapter 12. The reader will also find Keating's article highly informative about other aspects of the EU's regional policy. The article by Armstrong complements Keating's contribution in the sense that it takes the reader through the stages of development in EU regional policy. Armstrong provides a comprehensive account of the 1984 reforms of the European regional development Fund (ERDF) and comments on the implications of these reforms for the competence of the EU in this area.

Because of its impact on the orientation and loyalty of the European citizens, EU social policy possesses similar characteristics. Wise and Gibb try to examine the extent to which the Social Charter may contribute to the emergence of a comprehensive EU social policy which could increase the loyalty shift. Their analysis of developments between 1989 and 1992 leads them to derive two interrelated conclusions. First, the debate surrounding the Social Charter and the limited amount of legislation derived from it suggest that we can speak of an emerging consensus about the need to have a social dimension to the single market — with the notable exception of the United Kingdom. Secondly, the nature of this social dimension, however, is still too vague and its clarification depends on the outcome of the struggle between 'economic' and 'social' visions of the single market and the political forces that they represent. The article by Majone confirms the many-sidedness of the social dimension, but goes further into the investigation of the extent to which an EU social policy is feasible. This approach is complementary to that of Wise and Gibb in the sense that it calls on the reader to consider not only the various aspects of the existing policy-making process, but also the principles upon which a social policy can be erected. Majone rejects the feasibility of an EU *social policy* in the strict sense, but concedes the feasibility and desirability of *social regulation* — a concept that is distinct from yet closely related to social policy. If one is asked to identify the merit of Majone's contribution, the answer would most probably be its attempt to dissipate the teleological vagueness surrounding the literature produced or inspired by the European Commission.

External relations is the policy area examined in **Part IV**. Given the global tendency towards formal or informal regionalisation of international trade [see Anderson and Blackhurst (1993)] and the establishment of the single market, recent research on the EU's external relations assumes a new dimension. Whereas in the past the EU's external relations were generally examined from the perspective of their contribution to the emergence of the EU as a civilian power [see Twitchet (1976) and Shlaim and Yannopoulos (1976)], recent work concentrates on the EU's place in the international trading system and the significance of its trading arrangements with various country groupings [see Hine (1985), Greenaway (1990), and Brown (1988)]. The three articles in this part of the Reader reflect this orientation in the sense that they examine the EU's external relations with different country groupings and comment on the implications of the single market for EU's trading partners in general.

The article by Holmes and Smith begins with a brief review of the EU's trade policy and its position within the GATT system. But then it moves on to examine the responses of the EU to developments in the US and Japan on the one hand, and the convergence as well as divergence between the interests of each player on the other. Although this approach reduces the space that can be devoted to a thorough examination of a limited number of issues, this shortcoming is compensated for by the authors' ability to draw the reader's attention to the multi-dimensional feature of US-Japan and EU relations. The following article by Stevens takes the reader through the myriad of preferential trade and association agreements between the EU and less developed countries (LDCs). There are two trends that can be observed in the EU's trade with these countries: their share in EU trade (import and export) is declining; and the share of primary products in EU imports is losing ground to manufactures. Both of these trends are not good news for the EU's least developed trading partners. Even the African-Caribbean-Pacific countries (ACP) who are linked to the EU with preferential association agreements — are faced with similar problems. If one reason for this is the low income elasticity of the LDC exports, the other and more worrying reason is the EU's quantitative or seasonal restrictions. One interesting point made by Stevens is the dilemma faced by EU policy-makers in this area: while externalities of economic backwardness in less developed countries (immigration, political instability, environmental issues, etc.) require further EU input into their economic development, the tendency in the member states and the EU to protect traditional industries (textiles, footwear, ceramics, etc.) is limiting the extent to which the EU can pursue such a course of action.

Langhammer's article tries to develop a scenario for the developing countries' relations with the EU after the single market. He indicates that the positive income effect on developing country exports to the EU will outweigh the negative effect of trade diversion over a period of five years. Yet here again the finding suggests that the group who are most likely to benefit from the income effect are the middle-income countries whose exports are characterised by higher income elasticities. For the low-income countries, the way out is to accelerate the restructuring of their economies and diversify their exports — a recommendation that brings the issue of the EU's contribution to this process back again. Langhammer envisages that, for this group of countries, the EU should increase the level of resource transfer rather than repeating the tune of preferential trade — a tune that becomes increasingly irritating given the maintenance of quantitative restrictions. At a less sophisticated level, however, Langhammer also looks at the implications for developing country foreign exchange earnings from services. As a result of liberalisation in this sector following the single market, he suggests that there may be some scope for increased earnings from tourism as prices/wages tend to equalise in the single market, hence reducing demand for resorts in southern members of the EU. In aviation and maritime transport, however, the developing countries are not in a position to benefit because of the strength of European organised interests in these sectors and the possible tendency of the European operators to merge and exploit economies of scale.

The final part of the Reader is devoted to an area that is highly neglected in textbooks catering for similar needs. This neglect can be contrasted with the attention devoted to intra-EU freedom of movement and the EU's external trade relations. The two articles in this part come up with a common conclusion: the lack of EU competence in the area of third-country immigration is due to political rather than economic reasons. The article by Callovi provides an insider's view as to how political considerations proved to be decisive in this area. Frustrated by the member states' reluctance to concede to Commission arguments that immigration issues are inextricably linked to the completion of the single market, Callovi observes that immigration is a policy area where nationalism tends to survive not for technical reasons but as a result of political culture. The article by Ugur tries to explain why and how political factors have prevented integration in this area in contrast to the fairly integrated and liberal stance with respect to intra-EU freedom of movement. Ugur explains this dichotomy in terms of deliberate attempts to create 'insider' and 'outsider' groups so that the non-transparent, non-divisible nature of the immigration issue does not emerge as an obstacle to labour market integration within the EU. What is involved here is granting priority and reciprocal rights to European migrants in order to (i) avoid political alienation during periods of unemployment and (ii) contribute to the emergence of an insider identity defined on the basis of excluding third country immigrants — i.e. the outsiders.

I hope that the paragraphs above have been successful in providing the reader with (i) a clear and balanced assessment of what he/she should expect of this book, and (ii) an acceptable justification for pooling together a number of articles expected to enable him/her to develop an informed opinion about the political economy of European integration and to exercise confident intervention into the current public debate on the issue. Having said this, however, I am fully aware that the proof of the pudding is in eating it. The judgment of the reader, therefore, is far more important than what one's expectations were at the moment of making his/her decision to embark on such an undertaking.

Mehmet Ugur
Autumn 1994

References

Andersen, S.S. & Eliassen, K.A. (eds.) (1993) *Making Policy in Europe: The Europification of National Policy-making* (London, Sage Publications).

Anderson, K and Blackhurst, R. (eds.) (1993) *Regional Integration and the Global Trading System* (London, Harvester & Wheatsheaf).

Brown, D.K. (1990) 'Trade Preferences for Developing Countries: A Survey of Results' in *Journal of Development Studies*, vol. 24, no. 3, 1988.

Burda, M. and Wyplosz, C. (1993) *Macroeconomics: A European Text* (Oxford, Oxford University Press).

Cohan, A S. (1991) 'Eurotexts and Eurothought: Changing Approaches to the Study of the European Community' in *Review of International Studies*, vol. 17, no. 2, April, pp. 193-200.

Commission of the EC (1988) *Studies on the Economics of Integration: Research on the 'Cost of Non-Europe'. Vols. 1-3* (Luxembourg, Office for Official Publications).

Crouch, C. (1993) *Industrial Relations and European State Traditions* (Oxford, Clarendon Press).

El-Agraa, A.M. (ed.) (1990) *Economics of the European Community* (3rd ed.) (Hemel Hempstead, Philip Allan).

Greenaway, D. (1990) *Implications of the EC 1992 Programme for Outside Countries* (Nottingham, Centre for Research in Economic Development, University of Nottingham).

Haaland Matlary, J. (1994) 'Integration Theory and International Relations Theory: What Does the Elephant Look Like Today and How Should It Be Studied?' (Paper submitted to 2nd ECSA-World Conference on Federalism, Subsidiarity and Democracy in the European Union. Brussels, 5-6 May).

Haas, E.B. (1964) *Beyond the Nation State* (Stanford, Stanford University Press).

Haas, E.B. (1968) *The Uniting of Europe* (2nd ed.) (Stanford, Stanford University Press).

Hine, R.C. (1985) *The Political Economy of European Trade: An Introduction to the Trade Policies of the EEC* (London, Harvester & Wheatsheaf).

Hitiris, T. (1991) *European Community Economics* (2nd ed.) (London, Harvester & Wheatsheaf).

Hotelling, H. (1929) 'Stability in Competition' in *Economic Journal*, vol. 39, pp. 41-57.

Keohane, R.O. and Hoffmann, S. (eds.) (1991) *The New European Community: Decision-Making and Institutional Change* (Boulder, Westview Press).

Nugent, N. (1994) *The Government and Politics of the European Community* (3rd ed.) (London, Macmillan).

Pinder, J. (1991) *European Community: The Building of a Union* (Oxford, Oxford University Press).

Puchala, D. (1972) 'Of Blind Men, Elephants, and International Integration', *Journal of Common Market Studies*, vol. 10, no. 3, March, pp. 267-84.

Sandholtz, W. and Zysman, J. (1989) '1992: Recasting the European Bargain' in *World Politics*, vol. 42, no. 1, October.

Sbragia, A.M. (ed) (1992) *Europolitics: Institutions and Policymaking in the 'New' European Community* (Washington D.C., The Brookings Institution).

Shlaim, A. and Yannopoulos, G.N. (eds.) (1976) *The EEC and the Mediterranean Countries* (Cambridge, Cambridge University Press).

Siedentopf, H. and Ziller, J. (eds.) (1988) *Making European Policies Work: The Implementation of Community Legislation in the Member States. Vol. 1 — Synthesis* (London, Sage).

Tsoukalis, L. (1993) *The New European Economy: The Politics and Economics of Integration* (2nd ed.) (Oxford, Oxford University Press).

Tsoukalis, L. (1977) *The Politics and Economics of European Monetary Integration* (London, Allen & Unwin).

Twitchet, K.J. (ed.) (1976) *Europe and the World: The External Relations of the Common Market* (London, Europa Publications).

Ugur, M. (1994) 'Integration Theory Revisited: State-Society Relations as Key for Understanding European Integration'. (Paper submitted to 2nd World-ECSA Conference on Federalism, Subsidiarity and Democracy in the European Union. Brussels, 5-6 May).

Wallace, H. (1983) 'The Establishment of the Regional Fund: Common Policy or Pork Barrel' in H. Wallace *et al* (eds.), *Policy-making in the European Community* (2nd ed.) (London, John Wiley & Sons).

Publisher's note

The contents of the readings in this anthology have been reproduced as they appear in the publications from which they are taken. In the majority of cases footnotes and bibliographic material are included, the exceptions being where they are of excessive length. Photographs have not been reproduced.

1.   Policy Processes

Neil Nugent

Variations in EU processes

There can hardly be said to be a 'standard' or a 'typical' EU policy-making or decision-making process. A multiplicity of actors interact with one another via a myriad of channels.

The actors

There are three main sets of actors: those associated with the EU institutions, with the member governments, and with Euro and national interests. As has been shown in previous chapters, each of these has responsibilities to fulfil and roles to perform. But so variable and fluid are EU policy processes that the nature of the responsibilities and roles may differ considerably according to circumstances. For instance, in one set of circumstances an actor may be anxious to play an active role and may have the power — legal and /or political — to do so. In a second set of circumstances it may not wish to be actively involved, perhaps because it has no particular interests at stake or because prominence may be politically damaging. And, in a third set of circumstances, it may wish for a leading part but not be able to attain it because of a lack of appropriate power resources.

The channels

The channels vary in four principal respects.

In their complexity and exhaustiveness. Some types of decisions are made fairly quickly by a relatively small number of people using procedures that are easy to operate. By contrast, others are the subject of complex and exhaustive processes in which many different sorts of actors attempt to determine and shape outcomes.

In the relative importance of EU level processes and member state-level processes and in the links between the two levels. One of the EU's major structural difficulties is that it is multi-layered and there are often no clear lines of authority or of hierarchy between the different layers or levels.

In their levels of seniority. This is seen in the many different forums in which the member states meet: Heads of Government in the European Council; Ministers in the Council of Ministers; Permanent Representatives and their deputies in COREPER; (Committee of Permanent Representatives); senior officials and national experts in working parties, management and regulatory committees, and expert groups.

Neil Nugent: 'Policy Processes' from *THE GOVERNMENT AND POLITICS OF THE EUROPEAN COMMUNITY* (Macmillan, 1994; 3rd ed), pp. 297-338. © Neil Nugent 1991, 1994. Reprinted by permission of The Macmillan Press Limited and Duke University Press.

In their degrees of formality and structure. By their very nature the fixed and set piece occasions of EU policy processes — such as meetings of the Council of Ministers, plenary sessions of the EP (European Parliament), Council of Ministers/EP delegation meetings called to resolve legislative and budgetary differences — tend to be formal and structured. Partly because of this, they are often, in themselves, not very well equipped to produce the trading, the concessions, and the compromises that are so often necessary to build majorities, create agreements, and further progress. As a result they have come to be supported by a vast network of informal and unstructured channels between EU actors. Examples of such channels are everywhere and range from the after dinner discussions that are held at European Council meetings to the continuous rounds of soundings, telephone calls, lunches, lobbying opportunities, and pre-meetings that are such a part of EU life in Brussels, Strasbourg, Luxembourg and national capitals.

Factors determining EU policy processes

The central point made in the pervious section — that EU policy-making and decision-making processes are multi-faceted in nature - is illustrated in some detail in Chapters 12, 13 and 14 on the budget, agricultural policy, and external relations. Taken together, these chapters demonstrate how difficult it is to generalise about how the EU functions.

It would, of course, be expected that, as in individual states, there would be some differences between EU processes in different policy arenas. What is distinctive about the EU, however, is the sheer range and complexity of its processes: a host of actors, operating within the context of numerous EU and national-level institutions, interact with one another on the basis of an array of different decision-making rules and procedures.

In trying to bring an overall perspective to the complexity of EU processes a number of factors can be identified as being especially important in determining the particular mix of actors and channels which are to be found in any particualr context.

The Treaty base

In treaty terms, the EU is based on the Treaty on European Union. As was shown in Chapter 3, the TEU is made up of several components — Common Provisions, the Treaties of the three European Communities, Provisions on a Common Foreign and Security Policy (CFSP), Provisions on Cooperation in the Fields of Justice and Home Affairs (JHA), and a series of protocols and declarations.

One of the most important things these component parts of the TEU do is to set out several different decision-making procedures and to specify the circumstances in which they are to be used. As a result, the TEU is of fundamental importance in shaping the nature of the EU's policy processes and in determining the powers exercised by institutions and actors within the processes. To give just a few examples of the variety of policy-making and decision-making procedures set down in the TEU (these are all explained at length elsewhere in the book — either below or in other chapter):

- There are four 'standard' procedures for 'non-administrative' legislation: the consultation, cooperation, co-decision, and assent procedures. Key points of difference between these procedures include: (1) the EP can exercise veto powers under the co-decision and assent procedures but cannot do so under the consultation and cooperation procedures; and (2) there are single readings in the Council and the EP under the consultation and assent procedures, two readings under the cooperation procedure, and potentially three readings — or, perhaps more accurately, two readings and a third voting stage — under the co-decision procedure.

- External trade agreements negotiated under Article 113 of the EC Treaty have their own special procedure, under which the Commission and the Council decide and the EP, at best, is able only to offer advice.

- The annual budget has its own arrangements, under which the Council and the EP are joint budgetary authorities.

- Under the Agreement on Social Policy concluded between the member states with the exception of the United Kingdom — via the consultation or cooperation procedures — by eleven member states.

- The CFSP and JHA pillars set out largely, though not wholly, intergovernmental frameworks which enable non-legislative decisions of various sorts to be taken. Under both pillars the Council is given considerable room for manoeuvre to decide whether or not it needs to consult the EP. In broad terms, major decisions under both pillars require unanimity in the Council and consultation with the EP, whilst operational and procedural decisions can usually be taken by qualified majority vote if the Council so decides and without consultation with the EP. Whether or not the EP is consulted, the Council must keep it regularly informed of developments under the two pillars.

The proposed status of the matter under consideration

As a general rule, procedures tend to be more fixed when EU law is envisaged than when it is not. They are fixed most obviously by the Treaties, but also by Court interpretations (for example, the obligation that the Council must wait upon EP opinions before giving Commission proposals legislative status) and by conventions (for example, the understanding that when a member state has genuine difficulties the matter will not normally be rushed and an effort will be made to reach a compromise even when majority voting is permissible).

Where a law is being made, Commission legislation is usually subject to much less review and discussion than Council legislation. The reason for this is that Commission legislation is normally of an administrative kind, more technical than political. Much of it, indeed, consists of updates, applications or amendments to already existing legislation — usually in the sphere of external trade or the CAP (Common Agricultural Policy). As a result, Commission legislation, prior to being introduced, is often only fully discussed by appropriate officials in the Commission, and perhaps by national officials in a management or regulatory committee. Council legislation, on the other hand, because of its normally broader scope, is usually subject to one of the legislative procedures identified above and, as such, becomes the subject of representations and pressures from many interests, is assessed by the EP and the ESC (Economic and Social

Committee), and is scrutinised in detail in national capitals and Council forums in Brussels.

Where policy activity does not involve law making, considerable discretion is available to key decision-makers, especially governments, as to what policy processes will be used and who will be permitted to participate. A common procedure when states wish the EU to do something, but do not wish for it necessarily to involve making new law, (which may be because there is no agreement on what the law should be or because, as with foreign policy pronouncements, law is inappropriate), is to issue Council resolutions, declarations, or agreements. These can be as vague or as precise as the Council wishes them to be. Often, resolutions and the like can have a very useful policy impact, even if it is just to keep dialogue going but, because they are not legal instruments, they are not normally as subject as most Council legislation to examination and challenge by other EU institutions and actors.

The degree of generality or specificity of the policy issue

At the generality end of the scale, EU policy-making may consist of little more than exchanges of ideas between interested parties to see whether there is common ground for policy coordination, for the setting of priorities, or for possible legislation. Such exchanges and discussions take place at many different levels on an almost continuous basis, but the most important, in the sense that their initiatives are the ones most likely to be followed up, are those which involve *les grands messieurs* of the Commission and the member states.

Far removed from *grands tours d'horizon* by *les grands messieurs* is the daily grind of preparing and drafting the mass of highly detailed and technical regulations that make up the great bulk of the EU's legislative output. Senior EU figures, especially ministers, are not normally directly involved in the processes which lead to such legislation. There may be a requirement that they give the legislation their formal approval, but it is Commission officials, aided in appropriate cases by national officials, who do the basic work.

The newness, importance, controversiality or political sensitivity of the issue in question

The more these characteristics apply, and the perception of the extent to which they do may vary — what may be a technical question for one may be politically charged for another — the more complex policy processes are likely to be. If, for example, it seems likely that a proposal for a Council directive on some aspect of animal welfare will cause significant difficulties for farmers, it is probable that the accompanying decision-making process will display all or most of the following features: particularly extensive pre-proposal consultations by the Commission; the raising of voices from many sectional and promotional interest groups; very careful examination of the proposal by the EP and the ESC; long and exhaustive negotiations in the Council; considerable activity and manoeuvring on the fringes of formal meetings, and in between the meetings; and, overall, much delay and many alterations en route to the (possible) eventual adoption of the proposal.

The balance of policy responsibilities between EU and national levels

Where there has been a significant transfer of responsibilities to the EC — as, for example, with agricultural, commercial and competition policies — EU level processes are naturally very important. In such policy spheres, EU institutions — and the Commission in particular — have many tasks to perform: monitoring developments, making adjustments, ensuring existing policies and programmes are replaced when necessary, and so on. On the other hand, where the EU's policy role is at best supplementary to that of the member states — education policy and health policy are examples — most significant policy and decision-making activity continues to be channelled through the customary national procedures, and policy activity at EU level may be very limited in scope.

Circumstances and the perceptions of circumstances

This is seemingly rather vague, but it refers to the crucially important fact that policy development and decision-making processes in the EU are closely related to prevailing political and economic circumstances, to the perceptions by key actors — especially states — of their needs in the circumstances, and to perceptions of the potential of the EU to act as a problem solving organisation in regard to the circumstances. Do the advantages of acting at EU level, as opposed to national levels, and of acting in the EU in a particular way as opposed to another way, outweigh the disadvantages?

It is best to explain this point about circumstances with a specific example. Steel will be taken because it shows in a particularly clear manner how changing circumstances may bring about related changes in EU processes.

As was explained in Chapter 2, the Treaty of Paris gave considerable powers to the High Authority (later Commission). Until the mid-1970s these powers were used primarily to liberalise the market, with the High Authority/Commission expending much of its time and energy attempting to ensure that internal barriers were removed and cartels were eliminated. From 1974, however, market conditions began to deteriorate as a result of falling internal and external demand, reduced profit margins, and cost increases. This led the Commission to look more towards its hitherto largely neglected interventionist powers. Initially a largely voluntarist path was preferred, but when this proved to be ineffective a stronger approach was taken. By the end of 1980 an assortment of highly *dirigiste* policy instruments, some of which were mandatory, were in place. These included common external positions in the form of price agreements and export restraint agreements, strict controls on national subsidies, restrictions on the investment decisions of individual firms, and compulsory quotas (which became possible following the declaration by the Council of a 'manifest crisis' in October 1980).

The emphasis of EU steel policy thus switched between 1974-80, from promoting the freedom and efficiency of the market, to managing the market. This switch had very important implications for steel policy and decision-making processes. Four of these implications are particularly worth noting. First, there was now more policy responsibility and activity at ECSC level than previously. As a result of this, the overall policy picture as regards steel became a complicated mixture of Community and national processes, with not all of them pulling in the same direction. Second, the assumption by the Community of new and important policy powers, many of which had direct distributional consequences, inevitably created tensions in the Council. At the same time, it also resulted in the Council, as a collective body, taking greater care to ensure that on key decisions the Commission acted under its direction. (Although this did not stop governments from using the Commission as a useful device for deflecting the blame for necessary, but unpopular, decisions away from themselves.) Third, the Commission, notwithstanding its obligation to work within a Council-approved framework, extended its roles and functions in several important respects: as an initiator and proposer of policy; as a mediator amongst national and corporate interests (by, for example, putting together complicated production quota packages for the different types of steel product); as the Community's external negotiator (the Treaty of Paris did not establish a customs union and it was not until the late 1970s that the states began to adopt common external positions); and as a decision-maker (the Commission assumed more powers to act directly — for example, on investment aids subsidies). Fourth, non-institutional and non-governmental interests inevitably sought to become much more involved in decision-making as the Community developed policies with a very obvious and very direct impact on output, prices, profits, and employment. A striking illustration of this was the way in which EUROFER — the European Confederation of Iron and Steel Industries, which represents about 60 per cent of Community steel capacity — negotiated with the Commission on production quotas.

The steel crisis of the late 1970s/early 1980s thus significantly altered the nature of the Community's decision-making processes as regards steel. A consequence of this was that when, in the 1990s, the European steel industry faced another major crisis — characterised by falling demand, depressed prices, and many plants working below capacity — these processes again came into play: with the Commission bringing forth a package of restructuring measures which the Council, after long drawn-out negotiations — in which the Italian, Spanish, and German governments were especially prominent in seeking to build in protections for their steel industries — eventually agreed to in December 1993. An important aspect of the 1993 restructuring package was that it was not imposed in the manner of the 'manifest crisis' measures of the late 1970s/early 1980s, but was based more on a dialogue between the Commission and steel producers: a dialogue in which the steel industry played a central part in identifying capacity productions — though not as many as the Commission wanted — and in which the Commission offered 'compensations' in the form of financial aid, temporary subsidies, and increased tariffs and tight quotas on steel imports from Eastern and Central Europe. In an attempt to ensure that the scheme was effective — which was problematical given its semi-voluntaristic nature — the Council increased the monitoring and implementing powers of the Commission.

The making of EU legislation

Having established that there are considerable variations in EU policy and decision-making processes, it is necessary now to look at common, shared, and recurring features. For, except in the narrowest of senses, not every policy is formulated nor every decision taken, in a manner that is unique to it alone.

This is no more clearly seen than in relation to the making of EU legislation. Most legislation takes one of three 'set routes':

1. Administrative/management/regulatory/implementing legislation is issued mainly in the form of Commission regulations and decisions. The basic work on this type of legislation is undertaken by officials in the relevant Directorate General. Commissioners themselves are only involved in the making of such legislation when it is not straightforward or someone requests they take a look.

    National officials usually have the opportunity to voice their comments in a committee, but whether they have the power to stop legislation to which they object depends on which committee procedure applies. As was explained in Chapter 4, the Commission is in a much stronger position when it works through advisory committees than it is when it works through management, and even more so regulatory, committees.

    When this type of legislation is issued as Council legislation, it naturally results in national officials playing a more active role, and formal ministerial approval is required.

2. Much of the legislation that is enacted in connection with the EU's external economic policies is based on agreements with third countries and is, therefore, subject to special decision-making procedures. These procedures are described in Chapter 14. Amongst their distinctive features are: the Commission usually acts as the EU's main negotiator in economic negotiations with third countries; the Council seeks to control and monitor what the Commission does during negotiations; the EP does not normally exercise much influence — except, where cooperation and association agreements are proposed; most legislation produced as a result of negotiations, including virtually all legislation which is intended to establish the principles of a legal framework, is enacted in the form of Council regulations and decisions and therefore requires formal ministerial approval.

3. Most of what remains consists of legislation that is deemed to require examination via one of the EU's full legislative procedures. There are no hard and fast rules for deciding when proposals fall into this category, but, in general, they are those that are thought to be significant or concerned with establishing principles. The broader in scope they are, the more likely they are to be in the form of directives.

    Because of its obvious importance, this full legislative process needs to be examined here. However, since much of the detail of how the EU institutions exercise their particular legislative responsibilities has already been set out in Part 2, a comprehensive account is not attempted in what follows. Attention is restricted to highlighting the principal features of the legislative procedures.

Since the TEU entered into force there have been four different legislative procedures: the consultation, cooperation, co-decision, and assent procedures. There are also two major internal variations to these procedures: (1) Under the consultation, co-decision, and assent procedures, qualified majority voting rules apply in the Council when legislation is being made under certain Treaty articles, whereas unanimity is required under other articles. (2) Under the consultation and cooperation procedures, legislation is made by, and for, only eleven member states (the United Kingdom being excluded) when the TEU Protocol and Agreement on Social Policy is being used.

Descriptions of the EU's legislative procedures now follow. Diagrammatic representations of the consultation and cooperation procedures are given in Figure 1 (p. 14) and of the co-decision procedures in Figure 2 (p. 16). A listing of the Treaty articles under which the procedures apply, and of the policy spheres which they cover, is given in Table 1 (pp. 18-21).

The consultation procedure

Initiation. The starting point of a legislative proposal is when somebody somewhere suggests that the EU should act on a matter. Most likely this will be the Commission, or the EP: the Council: the Commission because it is the only body with the authority formally to table a legislative proposal, and because, too, of its special expertise in, and responsibility for, EU affairs; the Council because of its political weight, its position as the natural conduit for national claims and interests, and its power under Article 152 (EC) to request the Commission 'to undertake any studies the Council considers desirable for the attainment of the common objectives, and to submit to it any appropriate proposals'; and the EP because of the desire of MEPs to be active and because under Article 138b of the EC Treaty (which was newly created by the TEU) 'The European Parilament may, acting by a majority of its members, request the Commission to submit any appropriate proposals on matters on which it considers that a Community act is required for the purpose of implementing this Treaty'.

Beyond the Commission, the Council, and the EP there are many other possible sources of EU legislation, but little progress can be made unless the Commission decides to take the issue up and draft proposals. Many circumstances may result in it deciding to do so, but often it is very difficult, in looking at specific proposals, to discover just why the Commission decided to act and to identify precisely from where the initiative originated. For example, a Commission proposal that may seem to be a response to a Council request may, on inspection, be traced back beyond the Council to a national pressure group influencing a minister, who then gradually and informally introduced the issue into the Council as an option to be considered. Similarly, a Commission proposal may seem to be a response to an EP request or to representations from European-wide interests, but in fact the Commission may itself have dropped hints to the EP or to interests that they should look at the matter, (thus reinforcing the Commission's own position *vis-à-vis* the Council).

Preparation of a text. Once it has been decided to produce a proposal (a decision that is usually taken at a senior level within the most relevant Directorate General), a text is prepared. The standard way in which this is done is as follows: officials in the appropriate DG write an initial draft; the draft is passed upwards through superiors; as it is passed upwards the draft is discussed with all DGs and specialised Commission services which have an interest; when all directly involved Commission interests have given their approval, the draft is sent to the *cabinet* of the Commissioner responsible for the subject; the *cabinet,* which may or may not have been involved in informal discussion with Commission officials as the proposal was being drafted, may or may not attempt to persuade Commission officials to re-work the draft before submitting it to the Commissioner for approval; when the Commissioner is satisfied, he asks the Secretariat General to submit the draft to the College of Commissioners; the draft is scrutinised, and possibly amended, by the *chefs des cabinets* at their weekly meeting; if the draft is judged to be uncontroversial the Commissioners may adopt it by written procedure; if it is controversial the Commissioners may, after debate, accept it, reject it, amend it, or refer it back to the relevant DG for further consideration.

In preparing a text officials usually find themselves the focus of attention from many directions. Knowing that the Commission's thinking is probably at its most flexible at this preliminary stage, and knowing, too, that once a proposal is formalised it is more difficult to change, interested parties use whatever means they can to press their views. Four factors most affect the extent to which the Commission is prepared to listen to outside interests at this pre-proposal stage. First, what contacts and channels have already been regularised in the sector and what ways of proceeding have proved to be effective in the past? Second, what political considerations arise and how important is it to incorporate different sectional and national views from the outset? Third, what degree of technical knowledge and outside expertise is called for? Fourth, how do the relevant Commission officials prefer to work?

Assuming, as it is normally reasonable to do, Commission receptivity, there are several ways in which 'external' views may be brought to the attention of those drafting a proposal. The Commission itself may request a report, perhaps from a university or a research institute. Interest groups may submit briefing documents. Professional lobbyists, politicians, and officials from the Permanent Representations may press preferences in informal meetings. EP committees and ESC sections may be sounded out. And use may be made of the extensive advisory committee system that clusters around the Commission.

There is, therefore, no standard consultative pattern or procedure. An important consequence of this is that governmental involvement in the preparation of Commission texts varies considerably. Indeed, not only is there a variation in involvement, but there is a variation in knowledge of Commission intentions. Sometimes, governments are fully aware of Commission thinking, because national officials have been formally consulted in committees of experts. Sometimes, sectional interests represented on consultative committees will let their governments know what is going on. Sometimes, governments will be abreast of developments as a result of having tapped sources within the Commission, most probably through officials in their Permanent Representations. But, sometimes, governments are not aware of proposals until they are published.

The time that elapses between the decision to initiate a proposal and the publication by the Commission of its text naturally depends on a number of factors: (1) is there any urgency? (2) how keen is the Commission to press ahead? (3) how widespread are the consultations? (4) does the Commission want the prior support of all key actors? (5) is there a consensus within the Commission itself? Not surprisingly periods of over a year are common.

The opinions of the European Parliament and the Economic and Social Committee. On publication, the Commission's text is submitted to the Council of Ministers, which in turn refers it to the EP and, where appropriate, to the ESC, for their opinions.

The EP is by far the more influential of the two bodies. Though it does not have the full legislative powers of national parliaments it has enough weaponry in its arsenal to ensure that its views are at least taken into consideration, particularly by the Commission. Its representational claims are one source of its influence. The quality of its arguments and its suggestions are another. And it has the power of delay, by virtue of the requirement that Parliament's opinion must be known before the proposal can be formally adopted by the Council.

As was shown in Chapter 7, most of the detailed work undertaken by the EP on proposed legislation is handled by its specialised committees and, to a lesser extent, by its political groups. Both the committees and the groups advise MEPs how to vote in plenary.

The usual way in which plenaries act to bring influence to bear is to vote on amendments to the Commission's proposal, but not to vote on the draft legislative resolution — which constitutes the EP's opinion — until the Commission states, as it is obliged to do, whether or not it will change its text to incorporate the amendments that have been approved by the EP. If the amendments are accepted by the Commission a favourable opinion is issued, and the amended text becomes the text that the Council considers. If all or some of the amendments are not accepted, the EP can attempt to exert pressure by not issuing an opinion and referring the proposal back to the committee responsible. A reference back can also be made if the whole proposal is judged to be unacceptable. Witholding of an opinion does not, it should be emphasised, give the EP the power of veto, because it is legally obliged to issue opinions and the Court, in several judgments, has referred to the duty of loyal cooperation between the EU institutions. What the witholding of opinions does do, however, is to give the EP the often useful bargaining and pressurising tool of the power of delay.

For the reasons which were outlined in Chapter 7, and which are considered further below, it is difficult to estimate with any precision the impact the EP has on EU legislation. In general terms, however, it can be said that the record in the context of the consultation procedure is mixed:

- On the 'positive' side the Commission is normally sympathetic to the EP's views and accepts about three-quarters of its amendments. The Council is less sympathetic and accepts considerably less than half of the amendments, but that still means that many EP amendments, on many different policy matters, find their way into the final legislative texts.

- On the 'negative' side, there are three main points to be made. First, there is not much the EP can do if the Council rejects its opinion. The best it can normally hope for is a conciliation meeting with the Council (not to be confused with a Conciliation Committee meeting under the co-decision procedure), but such meetings do not usually achieve much — mainly because the Council has no wish to re-open questions which may put at risk its own, often exhaustively negotiated, agreements. Second, the Council sometimes takes a decision 'in principle' or 'subject to Parliament's opinion', before the opinion has even been delivered. In such circumstances the EP's views, once known, are unlikely to result in the Council habving second thoughts. Third, it is quite possible for the text of proposals to be changed after the EP has issued its opinion. There is some safeguard against the potential implications of this insofar as the Court of Justice has indicated that the Council should refer a legislative proposal back to the EP if it (the Council) substantially amends the proposal after the EP has issued its opinion. In practice, however, the question of what constitutes a substantial amendment is open to interpretation, and references back do not always occur.

* * * *

The ESC is, generally, not so well placed as the EP to examine legislative proposals. As was explained in Chapter 9, a major reason for this is that its formal powers are not as great: while it must be consulted on draft legislation in many policy spheres, consultation is only optional in some. Furthermore, when it is consulted, the Council or the Commission may lay down a very tight timetable, can go ahead if no opinion is issued by a specified date, and cannot be frustrated by delays if the ESC wants changes to the text. Other sources of weakness include the part-time capacity of its members, the personal rather than representational nature of much of its membership, and the perception by many interests that advisory committees and direct forms of lobbying are more effective channels of influence.

As a result of these weaknesses the ESC's influence over EU legislation is considerably less that that of the EP. Nonetheless, some note is taken of its opinion, though exactly how much is impossible to say, for even when ESC views do appear to have been taken into account, closer inspection often reveals that the really decisive influence has probably come from elsewhere. For example, a Council directive concerned with the implementation of the principle of equal treatment for men and women in occupational social security schemes, which was listed in the 1986 ESC Annual Report as being influenced 'to a large extent' by an ESC opinion, was also the subject of strong representations by sectional interests and member governments. In the 1987 Annual Report, a similar claim was made for a Council directive on the legal protection of original topographies of semi-conductor products, but on this very same proposal the EP made much the same claim and suggested that the Council had accepted eight of the twelve amendments it had adopted.

Decision-making in the Council. As has just been noted, the Council does not necessarily wait on the EP or the ESC before proceeding with a proposal. Indeed, governments may begin preparing their positions for the Council, and informal discussions and deliberations may even take place within the Council itself, before the formal referral from the Commission.

The standard procedure in the Council is for the proposal to be referred initially to a working party of national representatives for detailed examination. The representatives have two principal tasks: on the one hand, to ensure that the interests of their country are safeguarded; on the other, to try to reach an agreement on a text. Inevitably these two responsibilities do not always coincide, with the consequence that working party deliberations can he highly protracted. Progress depends on many factors: the controversiality of the proposal; the extent to which it benefits or damages states differentially; the number of countries, especially large countries, pressing for progress; the enthusiasm and competence of the Presidency; the tactical skills of the national representatives and their capacity to trade disputed points (both of which are dependent on personal abilities and the sort of briefs laid down for representatives by their governments); and the flexibility of the Commission in agreeing to change its text.

Once a working party has gone as far as it can with a proposal — which can mean reaching a general agreement, agreeing on most points but with reservations entered by some countries on particular points, or very little agreement at all on the main issues — reference is made upwards to COREPER or, in the case of agriculture, to the Special Committee on Agriculture (SCA). At this level, the Permanent Representatives (in COREPER II), their deputies (in COREPER I), or senior agriculture officials (in the SCA) concern themselves not so much with the technical details of a proposal as with its policy and, to some extent its political, implications. So far as is possible differences left over from the working party are sorted out. Where this cannot be done, bases for possible agreement may be identified, and the proposal is then either referred back to the working party for further detailed consideration, or forwarded to the ministers for political resolution.

All proposals must be formally approved by the ministers. Those that have been agreed at a lower level of the Council machinery are placed on the ministers' agenda as 'A' points and are normally quickly ratified. Where, however, outstanding problems and differences have to be considered a number of things can happen. One is that the political authority that ministers carry, and the preparatory work undertaken by officials prior to ministerial meetings, may clear the way for an agreed settlement: perhaps reached quickly over lunch, perhaps hammered out in long and frequently adjourned Council sessions. A second, and increasingly utilised, possibility is that a vote is taken where the Treaty article(s) on which the proposal is based so allows. This does not mean that the traditional preference for proceeding by consensus no longer applies, but it does mean that it is not quite the obstacle it formerly was. A third possibility is that no agreement can be reached, a vote is not possible under the Treaties or is not judged to be appropriate, or if a vote is judged to be possible and appropriate no qualified majority exists. This may lead to the proposal being referred back down the Council machinery, being referred back to the Commission accompanied with a request for changes to the existing text, or being referred to a future meeting in the hope that shifts will take place in the meantime and the basis of a solution will be found.

As is shown in figure 1, under the consultation procedure the decision-making process at EU level ends with the Council's adoption of a text.

The cooperation procedure

The cooperation procedure was created by the SEA. There were two main reasons for establishing the procedure.

First, to increase the efficiency, and more especially the speed, of decision-making processes. This was achieved by permitting qualified majority voting in the Council of Ministers wherever decisions were subject to the procedure. Then EEC Treaty articles were made subject to the procedure, the most important of which enabled the procedure to be used in respect of the Single European Market (SEM) programme. Under the TEU, most SEM legislation was 'transferred' from the cooperation procedure to the co-decision procedure.

Second, to respond to pressures for more powers to be given to the EP. This was achived by introducing a two reading stage for legislation, and increasing the EP's leverage — though not to the point of giving it a veto — over the Council at second reading.

Under the EC Treaty as revised by the TEU, the cooperation procedure is not actually referred to as such in the Treaty, but rather as the Article 189c procedure. This is because the stages of the procedure are set out in Article 189c. Whatever name, however, is given to it, it is clear — as Figure 1 shows — that the route taken by legislative proposals which are subject to the procedure is much more complex than the route taken by proposals which are subject to the consultation procedure.

The main stages of the cooperation procedure are as follows:

EP first reading. After the Commission has published its proposal, the EP examines the text and issues an opinion. The process by which the examination is conducted is broadly similar to the process of examination under the consultation procedure.

Council first reading. After obtaining the EP's opinion the Council does not, as in the consultation procedure, take a final decision on the proposal, but rather adopts, by a qualified majority vote if need be, what is known as its common position. As is the practice on single reading proposals, unanimity is required for any amendments with which the Commission does not agree. The Council and the Commission must inform the EP of the reasons for the common position and the Commission must explain its own position. (The Commission, of course, can alter its text at any time, and is likely to have done so after the EP's first reading in order to incorporate at least some EP amendments.)

EP second reading. What the Council does at its second reading depends on what has happened at the EP second reading. Taking, in turn, the four options available to the EP that have just been outlined. The EP has three months to take one of four courses of action:

1. It can approve the common position.

2. It can reject the common position by an absolute majority of all members.

3. It can amend the common position by an absolute majority of all members.

4. It can choose, or fail, to act in none of the three ways just listed.

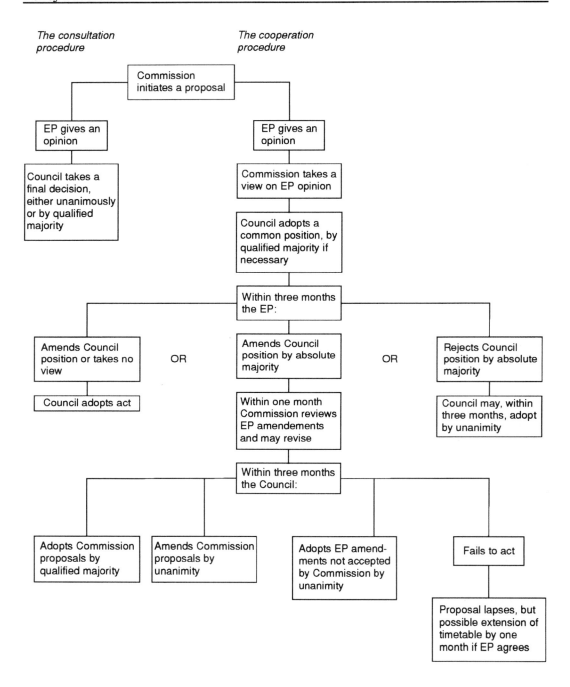

Figure 1   The consultation and cooperation (Art. 189c) procedures.

1.   In the event of EP approval of the common position, the Council may adopt the common position as a legislative act.

2.   In the event of EP rejection of the common position by an absolute majority, the Council can adopt the proposal only by acting unanimously within three months.

3.   In the event of EP amendment of the common position by an absolute majority, the Commission must decide within one month whether or not it wishes to incorporate the amendments into the version of the text that is referred back to the Council. If they are incorporated, the Council can approve them by a qualified majority or reject them by unanimity; if they are not incorporated the Council can only approve them by acting unanimously. Whether they are incorporated or not, all EP amendments not accepted by the Commission must be forwarded to the Council. If the Council does nothing within three months of receiving the re-examined text from the Commission, the proposal is deemed not to have been adopted.

4.   In the event of the EP not acting in any of the three above ways, the Council may adopt the proposal in accordance with the common position.

The co-decision procedure

The co-decision procedure was created by the TEU in a new Article 189b of the EC Treaty. Like the cooperation procedure, it is referred to in the Treaty by reference to the Article which sets out its provisions.

Just as the cooperation procedure extended the consultation procedure, so does the co-decision procedure extend the cooperation procedure. It does so, most crucially, by giving to the EP the right to veto proposals which are subject to the procedure. Before such a veto is exercised, however, there are ample opportunities under the procedure for the Council and the EP to resolve such differences as there are between them.

The various stages of the highly complex processes which constitute the co-decision making procedure are set out in Figure 2. The key features are as follows:

EP first reading. This is as under the consultation and cooperation procedures.

Council first reading. This is as under the cooperation procedure, except that in adopting its common position the Council must act by unanimity when taking decisions on cultural matters and on research and development multi-annual framework programmes (this unanimity requirement also applies to these two policy areas in respect of subsequent stages of the co-decision procedure).

EP second reading. The EP has three months to do one of the following:

(1) Approve the common position.
(2) Take no action.
(3) Indicate, by an absolute majority of its component members, that it intends to reject the common position.
(4) Propose amendments to the common position by an absolute majority of its component members.

If either (1) or (2) applies, the Council adopts the proposal in accordance with the common position.

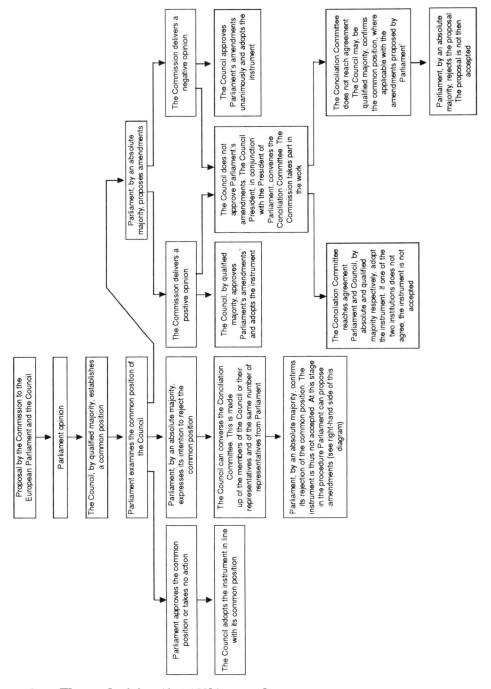

Figure 2   **The co-decision (Art 189b) procedure**.
Source: adapted from European Documentation *European Union*, Office for
Official Publications of the European Communities (1993).

Notes to Figure 2:
[1] The Council acts unanimously if its recommendation differs from that made be the Commission.
NB: (a) Each stage of the procedure is subject to time-limits which run from the moment a common position is adopted.
(b) Proposals can be adopted very quickly under the procedure if the Commission, the EP, and the Council are in agreement. Where there is disagreement, the procedure lasts a maximum of 13 months, calculated from the date of the adoption of the Council's common position.

Council second reading. In the event of the EP indicating that it intends to reject the common position, the Council may convene a meeting of the Conciliation Committee which is provided for under the co-decision procedure to explain further its position. The EP must then decide whether it wishes to confirm its rejection of the common position by an absolute majority of its member, in which case the proposal fails, or to propose amendments.

In the event of the EP proposing amendments to the common position — either directly as its second reading or following a meeting of the Conciliation Committee — the Council may decide, within three months, to accept them and adopt the proposal. In making its decisions on EP amendments, the Council acts by qualified majority vote if the Commission gives them its approval, but by unanimity if it does not. If the Council does not accept the amendments, the President of the Council, in agreement with the President of the EP, convenes a meeting of the Conciliation Committee.

The Conciliation Committee. The Committee is composed of an equal number of Council and EP representatives. (The exact composition of the Committee does, of course, vary between conciliation cases — although the EP's Rules of Procedures make provision for three MEPs to be appointed as permanent members of successive delegations for a period of twelve months). The Conciliation Committee has six weeks to try and approve a joint text.

Council and EP third readings. These are not full readings in the sense that the details of proposals are examined again, but they are the third occasion on which proposals may be considered by the two institutions. Article 189b provides a succinct description of what happens at this stage:

> If, within six weeks of its being convened, the Conciliation Committee approves a joint text, the European Parliament, acting by an absolute majority of the votes cast, and the Council, acting by a qualified majority, shall have a period of six weeks from that approval in which to adopt the act in question in accordance with the joint text. If one of the two institutions fails to approve the proposed act, it shall be deemed not to have been adopted.

> Where the Conciliation Committee does not approve a joint text, the proposed act shall be deemed not to have been adopted unless the Council, acting by a qualified majority within six weeks of expiry of the period granted to the Conciliation Committee, confirms the common position to which it agreed before the conciliation procedure was initiated, possibly with amendments proposed by the European Parliament. In this case, the act in question shall be finally adopted unless the European Parliament, within six weeks of the date of confirmation by the Council, rejects the text by an absolute majority of its component members, in which case the proposed act shall be deemed not to have been adopted.

Table 1   The application of the EU's decision-making procedures.

(Qualified majority voting rules apply in the Council of Ministers except where an asterisk indicates that unanimity is required.)

The consultation procedure

Articles of EC Treaty	*Policy sphere covered*
8b*	Rights to stand and vote in municipal and European Parliament (EP) elections
8e*	Citizenship of the Union — strengthen provisions of the Treaty. (Subject to ratification by the Member States.)
43	Agriculture
54	Freedom of establishment — drawing up of a general programme.
56	Freedom of establishment — implementing measures during transitional period.
57*	Self-employed persons — law governing the professions.
75*	Transport. (Only where decisions 'would be liable to have a serious effect on the standard of living and on employment in certain areas and on the operation of transport facilities'.)
87	Implementation of competition principles.
94	Implementation of rules on state aids.
99*	Indirect taxation.
100*	Harmonisation legislation concerned with 'the establishment or functioning of the common market'. (Derogations from this article mean that, in practice, it mainly applies to provisions relating to fiscal matters, to the free movement of persons, and to the rights and interests of employed persons. See also the co-decision procedure, Article 100a.)
100c	Visas for nationals of non-Member States. (Unanimity required until 31 December 1995; qualified majority voting thereafter.)
104-109	Various aspects of EMU and the movement to EMU. (A mixture of unanimity and qualified majority voting rules.)
130*	Industry.
130b*	Economic and social cohesion outside the framework of the structural funds.
130i	Research and technological development — adoption of specific programmes
130o*	Research and technological development — establishment of joint undertakings.
130s*	Environment — provisions of a fiscal nature, measures concerning town and country planning, measures concerned with energy sources and energy supply.

Table 1 (continued)   **The application of the EU's decision-making procedures.**

201*	Community's own resources. (Subject to ratification by the Member States.)
209*	Making of financial regulations.
228	Certain types of international agreements. (A mixture of unanimity and qualified majority voting rules apply.)
235*	This is the notorious 'catch-all' provision. It empowers the Council to take 'the appropriate measures' if 'action by the Community should prove necessary to attain, in the course of the operation of the common market, one of the objectives of the Community and this Treaty has not provided the necessary powers'.

Under the Agreement on Social Policy concluded betweeen the member states with the exception of the United Kingdom, the consultation procedure (with unanimity in the Council) applies in the following areas:

- social security and social protection of workers;

- protection of workers who are made unemployed;

- representation and collective defence of the interests of workers and employers;

- conditions of employment for third-country nationals residing in the Community;

- financial contributions for promotion of employment and job creation.

The cooperation procedure (the Article 189c procedure)

Articles of EC Treaty	*Policy sphere covered*
6	Discrimination on the grounds of nationality.
75	Common transport policy.
103-105	Various aspects of EMU and the movement towards EMU.
118a	Health and safety of workers
125	European Social Fund (ESF) — implementing decisions.
127	Vocational training — implementing decisions.
129d	Trans-European networks — implementing decisions.
130c	European Regional Development Fund (ERDF) — implementing decisions.
130o	Research and Technological development — implementation of programmes.
130s	Environment — action to achieve objectives set out in The Treaty on European Union, and implementation of general action programmes.
130w	Development Cooperation — adoption of measures to further the objectives set out in The Treaty on European Union.

Table 1 (continued)   *The application of the EU's decision-making procedures.*

Under the Agreement on Social Policy concluded between eleven member states, with the exception of the United Kingdom, the cooperation procedure applies in the following fields;

- improvement in particular of the working environment to protect worker's health and safety;

- working conditions;

- the information and consultation of workers;

- equality between men and women with regard to labour market opportunities and treatment at work;

- the integration of persons excluded from the labour market.

The co-decision procedure (the Article 189b procedure)

Articles of EC Treaty	Policy sphere covered
49	Free movement of workers.
54	Freedom of establishment — implementation of general programme.
56	Freedom of establishment — special treatment of foreign nationals.
57	Mutual recognition of formal qualifications.
57	Self-employed persons.
100a	Harmonisation for the purpose of completing the internal market.
100b	National laws affecting the operation of the internal market.
126	Education, vocational training and youth (incentive measures only).
128*	Culture.
129	Public health (incentive measures only).
129a	Consumer protection.
129d	Trans-European networks (guidelines).
130*	Research and technological development — adoption of multi-annual framework programme.
130s	Environment — adoption of general action programmes.

The assent procedure

Articles of EC Treaty	Policy sphere covered
8a*	Citizenship of the Union — adoption of provisions designed to promote the right to move and reside freely within the territory of the Member States.
105*	Supervisory tasks of the European Central Bank (ECB).

Table 1 (continued) **The application of the EU's decision-making procedures.**

106	Amendment of the Statute of the European System of Central Banks (ESCB).
130d*	The Structural Funds — definition of the tasks, priority objectives, organisation, and general rules. Establishment of Cohesion Fund.
138*	Elections to EP in accordance with a uniform procedure in all Member States. (Without prejudice to national ratification procedures.)
228	Certain types of agreements with non-member states or groups of states — association agreements; cooperation agreements; agreements having important budgetary implications; and agreements amending an act adopted under Article 189b. (A mixture of unanimity and qualified majority voting rules apply.)

Under Article O of the TEU accessions to the Union require the assent of the EP acting by an absolute majority of its component members.

This third reading stage clearly allows for the possibility of unilateral action by the Council if the EP cannot muster an absolute majority to reject a Council decision to proceed with a proposal after a failure to agree on a joint text in the Conciliation Committee. In the Rules of Procedure which it adopted just before the TEU entered into force in late 1993, the EP sought to head off this posssibility of unilateral Council action. It did so by providing: 1) in the event of no agreement being reached on a joint text within the Conciliation Committee, the EP President shall invite the Commission to withdraw its proposal and shall invite the Council not to adopt the proposal; 2) in the event of the Council deciding to proceed with the proposal, the President of the Council shall be invited to justify the Council's actions before the EP in plenary session, and the EP shall automatically vote on a motion to reject the proposal.

Periods of three months and six weeks referred to in the procedure may be prolonged for a limited period by common accord of the Council and the EP.

Legislation made under the co-decision procedure is made jointly under the names of the European Parliament and the Council of Ministers.

The assent procedure

The assent procedure, which was first established by the SEA, is simple in form: it specifies that certain types of decisions must be approved by the EP — in some cases by a majority of the votes cast, in others by an absolute majority of the EP's component members. The assent procedure, which is a single reading procedure, does not allow for the EP to make amendments.

Under the TEU the scope of the assent procedure was widened considerably, from its SEA remit of accessions to the EC and association agreements with third countries, to matters as diverse as citizenship and EMU-related issues. The roles and powers of the

EU institutions under the procedure, and particularly of the Commission and the Council, now vary considerably. So, for example, where decision-making under the procedure involves the preparation of detailed proposals (as in relation to the Structural Funds under Article 130d of the EC Treaty) or complex negotiations with third countries (as in relation to association and cooperation agreements under Article 228 of the EC Treaty) then the Commission is in a very strong position to influence and shape outcomes — especially if, as is the case in some instances, qualified majority voting rules apply in the Council. Where, however, unanimity is required in the Council and matters of political principle are of crucial importance — as, for example, in regard to citizenship issues (Article 8a, EC) and the devising of a uniform electoral procedure for EP elections (Article 138, EC) — then the Commission is much less favourably placed and the views of the national governments, and of the Council collectively, are critical.

As for the EP, it might be thought that, because under the assent procedure it can only pronounce on final proposals, and cannot table amendments, it would be confined to a rather limited confirmatory/ withholding role. To some extent it indeed is, but not completely, because by having the power to say 'No' to proposals, the EP also has the power to indicate to what it would say 'Yes'. Almost as soon as the procedure first came into operation in 1987 this power was being used — to put pressure on the human rights records of third countries who had signed association and cooperation agreements with the EC, and to put pressure on the Commission and the Council to amend and change the terms of some of these agreements.

Implications of the SEA and TEU reforms for the EU institutions

The procedures established by the SEA (cooperation and assent procedures) and TEU (co-decision procedure) have had many implications, in terms of both functioning and influence, for the institutions which have to operate them. The main implications are these:

- The institutions are now working much more closely with one another than they used to. At a broad level this is seen in increased numbers of inter-institutional meetings of various sorts, and in the practice — which began in 1988 — by which the Commission discusses and agrees its annual legislative programme and timetable with the EP. At more specific levels it is seen in conciliation meetings under the cooperation procedure and in meetings of the Conciliation Committee under the co-decision procedure.

- When presenting legislative proposals, the Commission has to ensure that it is using the correct legal base — that is to say, correct Treaty article — for this determines which procedure applies. Normally the matter is straightforward and there is no argument, but sometimes disputes do arise; is, for example, an internal market proposal with environmental aspects to be based on Article 100a of the EC Treaty (which covers most internal market matters and which provides for the co-decision procedure to apply) or Article 130s of the EC Treaty (which covers most environmental matters and which provides for the cooperation procedure to apply)? Where there is room for argument, the institutions frequently have different preferences: (1) The Commission — because it wishes to see its proposals adopted, if possible without being amended too much — usually prefers to use a procedure where qualified majority voting rules apply in the Council and where the EP does not have a veto. (2) The Council also usually prefers a procedure under which the EP does not have a veto, whilst national governments which are concerned about the implications of particular policy proposals are also likely to prefer a procedure where unanimity is required in the Council. (3) The EP, which is naturally anxious to maximise its position, prefers those procedures which give it a veto and which permit qualified majority voting in the Council. Knowing that many subjects where the legal base is open to possible dispute are politically sensitive, knowing that the Legal Services Departments of the Council and the EP will thoroughly examine each legal base, and knowing too that its decisions on the legal base are subject to challenge in the Court of Justice, the Commission necessarily acts with great care. The taking of care does not, however, always satisfy everyone: the Council, the EP, and individual governments have all at times been aggrieved, the Council has changed some legal bases, and there have been references to the Court.

- The Commission has a more difficult task under the cooperation and co-decision procedures that it has under the consultation procedure, in exercising its judgement as to whether, and if so at what stage, it should amend its text so as to get proposals through in a reasonably acceptable form. At the second reading stage, in particular, a delicate balance may have to be struck: between, on the one hand, being sufficiently sympathetic to EP amendments so as not to upset MEPs too much, and, on the other hand, being aware that a revised text might break up a majority attained in the Council at first reading.

- Decision-making in the Council has been speeded up. This is partly accounted for by the provisions for the Council qualified majority voting and partly by the timetable limitations which come into effect under the cooperation and co-decision procedures after the Council has agreed its common position. Decisions on particular proposals can still be delayed by the Council's preference — whatever the legal position — for decision-making by consensus but, overall, decision-making in policy areas now subject to the cooperation and co-decision procedures is much quicker than it was before the procedures applied.

- Under the cooperation procedure the Council has the problem of having to be unanimous not just at one legislative stage but at two, if it wishes to avoid incorporating Commission accepted EP amendments into the final text. Moreover, since amendments at the EP second reading require the support of an absolute majority of MEPs and are therefore hardly the reflection of minority interests, the EP — theoretically at least — has a reasonable chance of finding the only ally it needs when the Council holds its second reading. To try and get round this problem one thing the Council sometimes does at its first reading, on proposals where the EP appears likely to cause 'difficulties' at its second reading, is to take time to see if unanimity can be achieved: if it can — and that may be possible only after considerable horse-trading and compromising — the EP is very unlikely to be able to divide the Council and prevent unanimity at the second reading.

- The EP has had to adjust its working methods in several ways: (1) MEPs, and especially *rapporteurs* and committee chairmen, have had to develop a fuller grasp of the technical implications of Commission proposals. (2) The texts embodying Parliament's opinions have had to become more substantial and detailed documents. (3) There is pressure, especially on the group whips, to muster absolute majorities at second readings under the cooperation procedure and at second and third readings under the co-decision procedure, and — under the assent procedure — sometimes to muster majorities and sometimes to prevent them from being mustered. (When such majorities are desired and are clearly not going to be achieved there are sometimes references back to committees. There have been instances of an absolute majority having been declared on a show of hands when there have been less than 260 in the Chamber — in such instances there has been little opposition to the proposal in question, or opponents have been too slow to call for a roll-call vote.) (4) As noted in previous paragraphs, there is much more liaising and negotiating to be done with the Commission and the Council.

- Regarding the distribution of power between the institutions, the EP is the most obvious beneficiary of the SEA and TEU reforms, for it is placed in a much more advantageous position to pressurise the Commission and the Council to accept its views. Even under the cooperation procedure, where it does not have veto powers, it is able to act in ways to adopt strategies which enable it to have significant policy inputs: EP committees prepare detailed and 'sensible' reports on Commission proposals; the increased channels of communication the EP has with the Commission and the Council are exploited; and legislative proposals are occasionally rejected and are frequently amended by an absolute majority vote at second reading.

EU legislation after adoption

What happens to proposals after they are adopted as EU legislation, what use is made of them, and how they are applied, varies considerably. Many of these variations are considered on an individual basis in other chapters but it will be useful to briefly pull the more important variations together here so as to give an indication of the overall picture. The more significant of the variations are as follows:

- Whereas regulations and most decisions do not require any measures to be taken at national level before they apply, directives do not assume legislative force until after they have been incorporated into national law by the appropriate national authorities. The member states themselves determine which are the appropriate national authorities in their case, and by what process the incorporation is to be made. As a result the mechanisms by which directives are incorporated at national level varies between member states according to both differing national legislative procedures and differing perceptions of how important particular directives are judged to be. The general pattern, however, is for incorporation to be achieved either by attaching appropriate administrative measures to existing primary or secondary legislation, introducing new secondary legislation, or adding new clauses to already planned primary legislation. States are given anything from a few months to a few years to effect the incorporation — the final date being specified in the directives —

24

and are obliged to notify the Commission of the national legislation, regulations, or administrative provisions they have adopted to give formal effect to each directive.

- Much Council legislation needs to be supplemented by implementing legislation so as to fit it to particular circumstances and keep it up to date. Indeed, on a quantitative basis, the vast bulk of EU legislation is implementing legislation — issued usually in the form of Commission regulations.

- Some Council and European Parliament and Council legislation needs to be followed up not just with implementing legislation, but with further 'policy' legislation. This is most obviously the case in respect of 'framework' legislation, which is legislation that lays down general principles for an area of activity and basic rules which states have to follow, but which needs usually to be complemented by more narrowly focused legislation that covers in a reasonably detailed manner policies/issues/initiatives that fall within the remit of the framework. An example of framework legislation is the *Council Directive of 12 June 1989 on the introduction of measures to encourage improvements in the safety and health of workers at work* (89/391/EEC). That this legislation was intended to be a base and a focus for further legislation is seen in Article 16 of the Directive which states: 'The Council acting on a proposal from the Commission, based on 118a of the Treaty, shall adopt individual Directives, *inter alia,* in the areas listed in the Annex'.

- Legislation which also requires further measures, but measures which are very different in character to those that have just been outlined, is the 'new approach' legislation that constitutes an important part of the SEM programme. Under the 'new approach', the EU does not try to harmonise all the specifications and technical standards of marketed goods, as it formerly did, but confines itself to producing relatively short texts which lay down 'essential requirements' — in particular, requirements relating to health and safety matters, and consumer and environmental protection. As long as member states conform to the 'essential requirements' they can have their own national standards, which are subject to mutual recognition by other states, but the intention is that national standards are replaced as quickly as possible by European standards which are agreed by European standards bodies. The main such bodies are the European Committee for Standardisation (CEN) and the European Committee for Electrotechnical Standardisation (CENELEC). Both CEN and CENELEC include EFTA as well as EU countries amongst their membership, and both use weighted voting procedures for the taking of final decisions on standards. Once European standards are agreed EU states must adopt them within a fixed time limit, and within the same time limit must remove all conflicting national standards.

- Issues arising in connection with the implementation of EU legislation were well aired in Chapter 4 in the examination of the Commission's executive and legal guardianship functions. Attention here will, therefore, be restricted to just a few key points on the two main problem areas:

1. Regarding the incorporation of directives into national law, the Commission has — as was noted above — to be informed of the measures member states take. It

therefore has a reasonably good picture of what is happening. Notwithstanding this, however, some states have a considerably better record of incorporating directives than do others (the United Kingdom, Denmark, and Germany have the best records). In consequence, there are variations between the states in terms of the speed at which, and extent to which, directives are applied, and variations too in terms of the frequency with which states are subject to Commission and Court action for non/incomplete/incorrect incorporation of EU law (see Table 2).

2. Regarding the application of EU legislation, responsibilties are shared between EU authorities and national authorities. The main EU authorities are the various DGs that are responsible for particular policies, DGXX (Financial Control), the Commission's anti-fraud unit, the Court of Auditors, and the EP's Budgetary Control Committee. The national authorities are the numerous agencies and officials whose responsibility it is to collect excise duties, to read tachographs, to monitor fishing catches, to check that beef for which payments are made is of the quality that is claimed, etc.

In very broad terms the division of responsibilities between the two levels as regards day-to-day policy implementation is that the Commission oversees and the national authorities do most of the 'front line' work. This means that the Commission needs to move carefully and, assuming it does not wish to stoke up national resentments, must negotiate and discuss implementing problems with national authorities rather than rush them to Court. (An indication of the extent to which it does this is given in Table 2.)

Despite however (although in some respects it might be argued because of) the range of agencies which have some responsibility for policy implementation and implementation control, it is evident that all is not well with the application of some EU policies. The problem is partly one of fraud — the Commission's anti-fraud unit estimates that fraud accounts for 10-20 per cent of the EU budget. The problem is also, however, partly one of irregularities: that is to say, not of deliberate deception but of incorrect understanding and application of EU law. Doubtless the control mechanisms and administrative procedures, could be improved — not least in respect of flows of information between the Commission and the national agencies. But the fact is that with the Commission being unable to do very much direct surveillance of its own because of limited powers and limited resources, and with much EU legislation being so complicated that it is barely comprehensible even to the expert, it will probably never be possible to ensure that all laws are fully, properly and uniformly implemented.

Characteristic features of EU policy processes

A number of general features are characteristic of much EU policy and decision-making. They include compromises and linkages, difficulties in effecting radical change, tactical manoeuvring, and variable speeds.

Compromises and linkages

The diversity of competing interests across the twelve member states, coupled with the nature of the EU's decision-making system, means that successful policy development is usually heavily dependent on key actors, especially governments, being prepared to compromise. If they are not so prepared, effective decision-making can be very difficult.

As part of the process wherein compromises provide the bases for agreements, deals are frequently formulated in which different, and sometimes seemingly unrelated, policy issues are linked. Linking issues together in 'package deals' can open the door to agreements by ensuring that there are prizes for everybody and not, as might be the case when only a specific issue is taken, for just a few.

The European Council has been instrumental in formulating some of the EU's grander compromises and linked deals. For example, in 1984, at the Fontainebleau summit, it put together the package that included increasing the EU's budget revenue, decreasing the UK's budgetary contribution, and establishing budgetary discipline guidelines. And at Edinburgh, in 1992, it pulled together an agreement on a range of matters that had been causing considerable difficulties, including the Delors II budgetary proposals, financial aid to the EU's poorer countries, the opening of enlargement negotiations, and the application of the subsidiarity principle.

One of the reasons the European Council has become involved in the construction of overarching deals of the kind just described is that other EU institutions and actors, and EU processes as a whole, are ill-adapted to linking different policy areas and constructing complex package deals. The Foreign Ministers have a theoretical potential in this regard but, in practice, they tend not to have the political authority or status to impose global solutions on sectoral Councils. As for the sectoral Councils, they do not normally become involved in discussions beyond their immediate policy concern, and they certainly do not have the effective means — except perhaps occasionally in joint Councils — of linking difficulties in their own areas with difficulties being experienced by other ministers elsewhere.

Table 2
Infringement proceedings classified by member state, stage reached and legal basis.

Member State	Stage of the infringement proceeding	1990 Directives			Treaties and Regulations
		No measures notified	Not properly incorporated	Not properly applied	
Belgium	FN	26	11	16	15
	RO	18	7	6	2
	RCJ	6	2	2	3
Denmark	FN	22	1	6	7
	RO	1		3	1
	RCJ			2	1
Germany	FN	18	2	18	23
	RO	7	3	5	6
	RCJ		1	1	3
Greece	FN	78	2	26	14
	RO	36	2	5	12
	RCJ	4	1	1	4
Spain	FN	73	7	19	15
	RO	1	3	7	4
	RCJ			3	
France	FN	31	3	18	24
	RO	9	2	1	6
	RCJ		4		2
Ireland	FN	36	6	3	7
	RO	12	2	1	2
	RCJ	2		1	
Italy	FN	55	12	28	16
	RO	35	5	16	6
	RCJ	16	1	5	3
Luxemburg	FN	38	1	2	2
	RO	8	1	4	2
	RCJ	3			1
Netherlands	FN	40	13	2	6
	RO	10	3	4	3
	RCJ		1		1
Portugal	FN	147	7	16	8
	RO	3	1	3	5
	RCJ				2
United Kingdom	FN	26	2	10	6
	RO	1	2	1	2
	RCJ			1	1

Key: FN: Formal Notice
RO: Reasoned Opinion
RCJ: Reference to the Court of Justice

These different stages are explained in Chapter 4 [of *THE GOVERNMENT AND POLITICS OF THE EUROPEAN COMMUNITY*]

Table 2 (Continued)
Infringement proceedings classified by member state, stage reached and legal basis.

1991 Directives				1992 Directives			
No measures notified	Not properly incorporated	Not properly applied	Treaties and Regulations	No measures notified	Not properly incorporated	Not properly applied	Treaties and Regulations
49	5	7	10	84	1	15	10
22		9	15	13	1	2	6
3	3	1	1	2		1	3
34	1	4	13	39		2	4
1		1	1	2			2
		1					
36	1	12	11	77	6	10	4
6		4	3	4	2	5	7
		1		1	1	3	
34	19	18	17	93	4	7	8
37	2	5	4	13		7	10
2		2	5	1	1	1	1
41	9	12	17	89	2	16	20
18	3	5	4	20	3	4	12
		2		1	1	2	1
30	2	8	14	66	3	25	17
4	1	4	6	2			8
1	1	1	1			1	
46	1	8	4	79	3	5	1
22	2	2	1	12			1
2		1		8		1	
56	3	31	25	87	4	26	20
40	5	23	8	10	1	13	16
15	3	6		5	1	4	1
35	19	4	6	90	1	5	1
29	2	2	2	13	1		7
3			1	10	1	1	2
39	2	12	9	61	1	6	5
14	2	4	3	7	2	5	2
5	1		1	5			
64	1	11	10	88	6	14	8
79		3	2	18	1	2	1
2						1	
40	7	1	15	82	2	9	4
7		2	2	12			1
						2	1

Source: Adapted from the *Tenth Annual Report to the European Parliament on Commission Monitoring of the Application of Community Law — 1992. Official Journal of the European Communities*, C233 (30 August 1993).

29

Much EU policy-making and decision-making thus tends to be rather compartmentalised, and it is within, rather than across, policy compartments that the trading, bargaining, linkaging and compromising that is so characteristic of EU processes are mainly to be found. At Council working party level, trading may consist of little more than an official conceding a point on line 8 of a proposed legal instrument in exchange for support received on line 3. At ministerial level, it may result in a wide-ranging and interconnected package, such as is agreed annually between Agriculture Ministers to make up the farm price settlement.

Difficulties in effecting radical change

Partly as a consequence of the prevalence of compromise, much EU policy-making and decision-making displays a deep gradualism and incrementalism. It is just not possible for the Commission, the Council Presidency, a national government, or anyone else, to initiate a clear and comprehensive policy proposal incorporating bold new plans and significant departures from the *status quo,* and expect it to be accepted without being modified significantly — which usually means being watered down. Ambitious proposals customarily find themselves being smothered with modifications, escape clauses, and long transitional periods before full implementation.

The obstacles to innovation and radical change are powerful, and stem from a range of different national and idelogical positions and perspectives. Moreover, some of the obstacles have increased in force over the years. They have done so for four principal reasons. First, the way forward is not as clear as it was in the 1960s when specific Treaty obligations were being honoured and 'negative integration' (that is the dismantling of barriers and the encouragement of trade liberalisation) was generally accepted as the main policy priority. Second, international economic uncertainties have made states — some much more than others — cautious about ceding too many decision-making powers to the EU. The uncertainties have also exacerbated the pre-existing tension between an EU founded on an essentially liberal model of integration and states that have traditionally sought to regulate economic life by intervention. Third, the EU has become more politically and ideologically heterogeneous. This is partly because of enlargement and partly because the broad Keynesian consensus on social and economic policy that existed in most Western European countries until the mid-1970s has been called into question by high rates of inflation, high unemployment and low economic growth. Finally, policy development has inevitably created and attracted interests which have a stake in the *status quo.* This is most obviously the case in agriculture, where Commission proposals for reform invariably produce protests from powerful sectional groups and from electorally sensitive governments.

All this is not to suggest that change and reform are not possible. On the contrary, there clearly have been major integrationist advances, of both an institutional and policy kind, since the mid-1980s. These changes have been driven by a range of external and internal factors, and have been guided and shaped by complex interactions between EU and national level political forces. (These factors and forces are discussed extensively elsewhere in this book, notably in Chapter 3.) The identification of obstacles to change does not, therefore, preclude it occurring, but what it does do is to suggest that since just about any policy innovation is likely to meet with at least some resistance from some quarter(s), bold initiatives are always likely to be weakened and/or checked.

Tactical manoeuvring

Tactical manoeuvring and jockeying for positions are universal characteristics of policy-making and decision-making processes. However, they are especially apparent in the EU as a result of the multiplicity of its actors and channels and the diversity of its interests.

It is not possible to attempt a comprehensive catalogue of tactical options here, but a sample of the questions that often have to be considered by one category of key EU actors — national representatives in the Council — will serve to give a flavour of the intricacies and potential importance of tactical considerations:

- Can a coalition be built to create a positive majority or a negative minority? If so, should it be done via bilateral meetings or in a EU forum?

- Is it necessary to make an intervention for domestic political purposes? (Although Council meetings are not open to the public or the media, most of what goes on, especially in ministerial meetings, gets reported back — either through unofficial channels or through formally minuted national objections to Council decisions.)

- Is it possible to disguise an opposition to a proposal by 'hiding' behind another state?

- Should concessions be made in a working party or in COREPER to ensure progress, or should they be held back until the ministers meet in the hope that this will be seen as conciliatory and helpful — with the consequences that it might reap dividends on another occasion?

- How is the necessary balance to be struck between being seen to be tough in the defence of the national interest and being seen to be European minded and ready to compromise? (Often, on a particular issue, some states have a vested interest in an agreement being reached, whilst the interests of others are best served by the absence of any agreement and, as a result, the absence of EU obligations.)

Variable speeds

EU processes are often criticised for being cumbersome and slow. Unquestionably they can be, but it should be recognised that they are not always so. Procedures exist that allow certain types of decisions to be made as and when they are necessary. So, farm price and budgetary decisions are made (more or less) according to a predetermined annual timetable; Commission legislation can be issued almost immediately; and Council regulations and decisions can be pushed through via urgent procedures if the circumstances require it.

As for 'standard EU legislation', the introduction of new legislative processes under the SEA and the TEU has greatly speeded up decision-making. The key element is usually whether qualified majority voting rules apply in the Council, for if they do ministers are not normally prepared to wait — as they must if unanimity is required — for everyone to agree to all aspects of a proposal. Rather is it customary to give a state which objects strongly to a proposal time to adjust to the majority view — perhaps with encouragement via compromises and derogations — and then proceed to a vote.

Decision-making is likely to be at its slowest when a proposal creates difficulties of principle for a state or states, and this is combined with a decision-making process which is not subject to the dictates of a timetable and in which qualifying majority voting cannot be used in the Council. In such circumstances the Council's decision-making capacity is weak and it can be very difficult for progress to be made. There may not even be much of a concerted attempt to force progress if it is felt that the minority state(s) genuinely has considerable difficulties with the proposal, for governments tend to be very sensitive to the needs of one another — not least because they are aware that they themselves may be in a minority one day.

The efficiency of EU policy processes

The EU lacks a fixed, central authoritative point where general priorities can be set out and choices between competing options can be made. In other words, there is no adequate framework or mechanism for determining and implementing an overall policy view in which the requirements of agriculture, industry, the environment and so on, are weighed and evaluated in relation to one another and in relation to resources. The Commission, it is true, attempts to set general priorities but it does not itself have the decision-making power to carry them through. In the Council of Ministers, the sectoral Councils do not link up with one another in a wholly satisfactory manner, and although incoming Presidencies do set priorities, these are essentially short-term in nature and in most policy sectors are not part of a properly integrated long-term programme. As for the European Council, it has had some limited success in co-ordinating policies, notably at the 1988 Brussels summit when a five year reference framework for expenditure was agreed, but it has never attempted to set out anything like a comprehensive EU policy programme.

Within individual policy sectors, there are, as has been shown, many obstacles to coherent and properly ordered policy development. For example, resistance by states to what they regard as an excessive transfer of powers to the EU has undoubtably resulted in many policy spheres being less integrated and comprehensive in their approach than is — from a policy efficiency perspective — ideally desirable. Regional policy, industrial policy, environmental policy, and policy on social security systems are examples of policy areas where policy responsibilities are shared between the EU and the states, where frequently the activities of the two levels are not properly coordinated, and sometimes are not even mutually complementary.

EU policy thus tends not to be the outcome of a rational model of decision-making. That is to say, policy is not normally made via a procedure in which problems are identified, objectives are set, all possible alternatives for achieving the goals are carefully evaluated, and the best alternatives are then adopted and proceeded with. Rather other models of decision-making are often more useful for highlighting key features of EU processes. For example:

- The *political interests* model of decision-making draws attention to the interaction of competing interests in the EU, to the variable power exercised by these interests in different decision-making situations, and to the ways in which decisional outcomes are frequently a consequence of bargains and compromises between interests.

- *Political elite models* highlight the considerable concentrations of power, at official and political levels, that exist across the EU's decision-making processes. Concentrations are especially marked in areas such as monetary policy and foreign policy, where processes are more secret and more closed than they are, for example, in steel or agriculture. Political elite models also draw attention to the absence of mechanisms available to EU citizens for exercising direct accountability over EU decision-makers.

- The *organisational process* model of decision-making emphasises how the rules and understandings via which EU decisions are made do much to shape the nature of the decisions themselves. The organisational processes, that is to say, are not neutral. So where, to use Jacques Delors' phrase, policy can only 'make progress twelve abreast', and where every conceivable national, regional and sectional interest is entitled to be consulted before policy can be developed, progress is frequently slow and outcomes are often little more than lowest common denominators. Where, on the other hand, processes are more streamlined — and permit, for example, majority voting in the Council of Ministers, or the Commission to disburse funds directly — then decision-making is likely to be more decisive and, perhaps, more coherent.

Having identified weaknesses in the quality of EU policy and decision-making processes, some re-balancing is now in order lest the impression be left of a system that is wholly and uniquely disordered and undemocratic. There are three main points to be made.

The first point is that, in many respects, EU policy and decision-making processes are not so different from national processes. That is not to say that differences do not exist. The international nature of the EU, for example, makes for more diverse and more powerful opposition to its initiatives than customarily exists within states. It is also the case that EU decision-makers are less directly accountable than are national decision-makers to those who are subject to their decisions: the power of the European Council, the Council of Ministers, and the Commission, on the one hand, and the comparative weakness of the EP on the other, does make, as many have observed, for a 'democratic deficit' in the EU. Another difference is that the EU's institutions, taken collectively, are much weaker than their national counterparts. But recognition of these and other differences should not obscure similarities of type — if not perhaps intensity — between EU and national processes: political interest, political elite, and organisational process models of decision-making can throw light on features of the latter, as well as the former. So, for example, in all member states, especially those where there are coalition governments (which is the norm in most EU states), political accommodations are an everyday occurrence and policy trimming is common. Furthermore, in those countries where there is a considerable geographical decentralisation of power as, for example, there is in Germany, tensions between levels of government over who does what, and who pays for what, are by no means unusual. In short, many of the EU's decision-making 'problems' — such as the prevalance of incrementalism, and of policy slippages — are by no means unknown in national political systems.

The second point is that not all EU policy and decision-making processes are completely a matter of cobbling together deals which can satisfy the current complexion of political forces. These certainly are crucially important features, but they do not amount to the complete picture. In recent years, greater efforts have been made, especially by the Commission, to initiate rather than just to react, to look to the medium-term rather than just tomorrow, and to pull at least some of the pieces together into coordinated programmes.

At the level of overarching policy coordination, progress in the direction of more forward-looking and more coordinated policy planning has, it must be said, been only modest. But there have been some potentially significant developments. One important example of such a development is seen in the Commission's 1987 document *The Single Act: a new frontier,* which made recommendations for dealing with what it saw to be the EU's central priorities over the period up to 1992. The programme outlined in the document became the subject of exhaustive Council and European Council negotiations. These negotiations led, at the 1988 Brussels summit, to a package deal which, though the outcome of the usual political trading, did at least address, in an interlinking five year financial programme, some, though by no means all, of the EU's most pressing problems. Similar proceedings occurred in 1992 when the 1988 package needed to be renewed. On this second occassion the Commission's proposals were presented in its document *From the Single Act to Maastricht and Beyond: the Means to Match Our Ambitions*, and the final deal, on a new medium-term financial programme, was concluded at the December 1992 Edinburgh summit.

Below the level of overarching policy coordination, within certain policy sectors clear medium to long-term policy objectives and rounded programmes are to be found. These are drawn up by the Commission, usually in consultation with appropriate consultative committees and committees of experts, and have to be approved by the Council. They appear in various forms. For example: White Papers (the best known of which is still the 1985 White Paper which contained detailed proposals for the completion of the internal market); communications (such as *The Development and Future of the CAP*, which was published in 1991, approved — with modifications — by the Council in 1992, and which set out proposals for major reforms of the financing of agriculture); framework legislation and programmes (for example, the major overhaul of the Structural Funds which was set out in Council Regulation (EEC) No. 2052/88 of 24 June 1988); and action programmes.

It is worth saying a little about action programmes to illustrate how, within specified fields of activity, a measure of coordinated development over a planned medium-term period is possible. Action programmes vary in nature, from the broad and general to the highly specific. The broad and general typically include measures for improving the monitoring and supervision of existing legislation, ideas for new legislation, running a pilot scheme, and spending programmes. Such an action programme, aimed at improving 'equal opportunities for girls and boys in education' was approved by the Education Ministers in June 1985. The ten point programme was rather modest, as it had to be to attract the support of those governments which are not especially committed to such concerns and/or have little national legislation in the sphere themselves, but the provisions were not without significance. They included: educational and vocational guidance to be provided as a service to all pupils to encourage girls and boys to diversify their career choices; opening schools to working life and the outside world; eradicating persistent stereotypes from school textbooks, teaching materials in general, and guidance and assessment materials; and special measures to help the underprivileged. By contrast with the broad and general action programmes, the specific action programmes are naturally much more specialised in their areas of concern and tighter in their provisions. Examples are the ECSC social research programmes on which matters as safety in mines and industrial hygiene, which are given appropriations for a given period and which provide up to about 60 per cent of the costs of approved research projects.

The third, and final, 'rebalancing' point to be made about EU processes is that critical judgments about how the EU functions ought to be placed in the context of the considerable degree of cooperation and integration that has been achieved. There is no comparable international development where individual states have voluntarily transferred so many policy responsibilities to a collective organisation of states and, in so doing, have surrendered so much of their national sovereignty. It is hardly surprising, given the enormity of the exercise, that pressures and desires for cooperation and integration should so often be challenged, and held in check, by caution, uncertainties, conflicts, and competition.

Part I

Microeconomic Policy Issues

2. The Effects of the Common Agricultural Policy of the European Community: A Survey of the Literature

Dimitrios G. Demekas, Kasper Bartholdy, Sanjeev Gupta, Leslie Lipschitz and Thomas Mayer

This survey deals with the costs and benefits of the common agricultural policy for EC Member States and the effects of the CAP on world markets and the well-being of the Community's trading partners. It presents and discusses recent empirical literature that attempts to estimate quantitatively the domestic and international effects of the CAP. The 'domestic effects' are the welfare gains and losses of producers, consumers and taxpayers, the effects on other sectors and the deadweight costs to the economy as a whole. The 'international effects' are the effects on world commodity prices, the volume and pattern of international agricultural trade and the welfare of the rest of the world. The impact the CAP has on the stability of world commodity prices is also included in this category.

In order to compare and evaluate the empirical evidence, section 1 discusses the development of the conceptual framework for the welfare analysis of price support and its limitations. Section 2 presents the evidence in five categories: domestic welfare, level of world prices, international trade, welfare of non-EC countries, and stability of world prices. Section 3 is a discussion of the conclusions and their relevance to the current debate about agricultural policy reforms.

1. The theory

Although the structure of the CAP is complicated, for the large majority of products the basic method of implementation is through price support. This is achieved by a variety of instruments, such as intervention purchases, market withdrawals, export restitutions, minimum import prices and import levies.[1] Other price support devices (e.g. deficiency payments) and non-price support instruments (storage aids, input subsidies, voluntary export restraint (VER) agreements with non-Member States, etc.) are also used, but on a more limited scale.

The simplest way to examine the effects of price support on domestic welfare is the single-good partial equilibrium analysis.

Dimitrios G. Demekas, Kasper Bartholdy, Sanjeev Gupta, Leslie Lipschitz and Thomas Mayer: 'The Effects of the Common Agricultural Policy of the European Community: A Survey of the Literature'. *JOURNAL OF COMMON MARKET STUDIES* (Dec 1988), Vol XXVII, No. 2., pp. 113-145. Reprinted with minor modifications from *THE COMMON AGRICULTURAL POLICY OF THE EUROPEAN COMMUNITY — PRINCIPLES AND CONSEQUENCES*, Occasional Paper No. 12 (Washington, DC: International Monetary Fund, 1988).

Figure 1
The Economics of Price Support: The Single Country Case

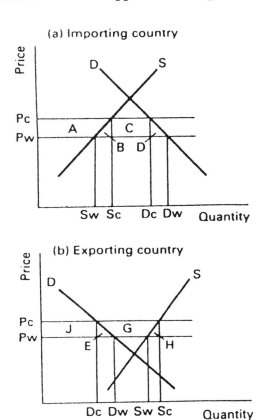

(a) Importing country

(b) Exporting country

Figure 1, panel (a) illustrates the case of a small importing country. If the world price is P_w but the domestic price is maintained at P_c by a tariff, production is at S_c, consumption at D_c and the difference is imports. Reducing consumption below and increasing production above what they would be if the world price prevailed, entails a consumer loss of A + B + C + D, a producer gain of A and an incresae in government revenue of C. The net welfare loss (or, alternatively, the net welfare gain of liberalizing) is B + D. Price support in an exporting country by means of an export subsidy is illustrated in panel (b). Here the consumer loss is J + E, the government expenditure E + G + H, and the producer gain J + E + G; by subtraction the net welfare loss is E + H.

This simple domestic welfare analysis treats the EC as a single entity. In order to examine the country-specific effects of the CAP, the previous analysis has to be modified in three ways. First, it has to allow for intra-EC commodity trade (Buckwell *et al.*, 1982, pp. 30-9). Some of the imports of an importing country will now originate in other Community members and, therefore, be priced at the CAP support level. Consequently, part of the tariff revenue C will now be forgone. Similarly, part of the government expenditure for subsidies in an exporting country will now be avoided, since the gain to producers is generated directly by sales to other Community members at the high protected prices.

Second, the analysis has to capture the function of the so-called agrimonetary system of the EC. The Monetary Compensatory Amounts (MCAs) that came into effect in the early 1970s to protect farmers from national currency fluctuations, essentially allow Member States to maintain domestic prices different from the common CAP support levels. Importers in a country with a domestic price lower than P_c can be thought of as paying P_c at the border for imports from other members and then getting a subsidy to allow these imports to compete in the domestic market. Exporters in that country must pay a tax on their exports in order not to undermine the higher prices in the rest of the Community. The situation in a member country which maintains a domestic price higher than P_c is the opposite.

Third, the principle of common financing, which means that the Community is collectively responsible for paying the subsidies for (and receiving the tariff revenue generated by) all products covered by the CAP, requires that additional transfers between the EC and members' budgets be taken into account.

Even after introducing these additional considerations to make the model capture the supranational character of the CAP, the partial equilibrium analysis still retains its simplicity. Its usefulness is limited, however, by the strong assumption that underlie it.[2] In what follows, the main difficulties of assessing the effects of price support by means of the partial equilibrium model are outlined, and ways of dealing with these difficulties are discussed.

1. The analysis of price support, even when amended to take into account the intra-EC transfers mentioned above, is designed to capture the effects of one specific policy. There are, however, many different CAP price support instruments, not all of which have the same effect. Deficiency payments, for example, differ from export subsidies in that, as consumers pay the world price, there are no consumer losses. Non-tariff barriers or variable import levels do not generate the same revenues as *ad valorem* tariffs. These differences are very hard to capture empirically.

2. The analysis in Figure I implicitly assumes that the country is a price-taker in the world market. This 'small country' assumption means that, no matter what the level of domestic protection is, the world price remains unaffected. The welfare effects of price support can then be accurately measured with reference to that world price. It also means that these effects are limited to the home country; there is no room for international repercussions. This is clearly unsatisfactory in the case of the CAP; the EC is large enough to influence world markets.

3. Partial equilibrium analysis assumes that the prices of all other goods remain constant. This means that substitutability and complementarity in consumption and production between the goods studied and other commodities is ignored. In order to correct this shortcoming, one has to model the interactions between markets for different goods explicitly. The choice of the relevant group of goods is, however, a difficult task, since the chain of substitution can extend from

commodities very close to the one studied (e g. different varieties of wheat) to non-agricultural goods.

4. The preceding discussion also assumes that all demand is final. This is obviously not true for many agricultural products. The demand for those products has to be derived from the cost function of the food industry. Moreover, many commodities use other agricultural products as inputs: beef, for example, requires animal feed. The true degree of protection for beef, therefore, is captured by the effective, rather than the nominal rate.

5. Price support policies in agriculture, especially in cases like the CAP where a wide range of commodities is covered, can have a considerable effect on total employment and the allocation of capital and labour. This, in turn, affects other sectors of the economy. The size and direction of the effects depends mainly on relative factor intensities and the policies implemented in the other sectors. Such interactions can exert a significant influence on the actual welfare gains or losses from agricultural policies.

6. Because of the range of coverage of policies like the CAP, macroeconomic considerations also enter the picture. Changes in the price support policies for many commodities can have sizeable effects on the external balance of the economy and, consequently, the exchange rate and/or the relative price of tradables and non-tradables. Either could then shift the supply and demand curves in Figure I endogenously.

7. Externalities and market distortions if present, represent the greatest challenge to the welfare analysis of price support policies. Even if they are absent from the agricultural sectors proper, but exist elsewhere, externalities and distortions can affect the calculation of welfare costs and benefits in a variety of ways. Empirical work has shied away from these problems by routinely postulating perfectly competitive structures, full information and complete markets.

These shortcomings of the simple partial equilibrium model have prompted analytical efforts in several directions. First in order to simplify the empirical question at hand and take care of the problem raised in point (1) above most researchers convert all sorts of price-support instruments into tariff equivalents (nominal or effective, as the case may be). Alternative policy options are then described in terms of changing this notional rate of protection without specifying how exactly this is to be done. Harling (1983) and Valdes and Zietz (1980) discuss at length the methods of calculating tariff equivalents and the ensuing problems.

Second 'large country' effects, substitution of agricultural commodities in production and consumption, and backward and forward linkages with other sectors are incorporated in the analysis by applying partial equilibrium techniques in a multi-country multi-sector framework. This approach is used extensively in evaluating policies such as the CAP, which affect many agricultural commodities simultaneously. Trouble spots (2) to (4) from the previous list are dealt with in this way.

Multi-country multi-commodity models differ fundamentally from the simple analysis in Figure I in one respect: the world price loses its meaning as a reference point for the measurement of the welfare costs of protection. Since the home country is 'large' a change in domestic policies will affect the world price. The effects of the policy must be estimated with respect to what the world price would be, had the policy been absent. The calculation of that hypothetical price requires formulating demand and supply functions for the country(ies) and commodity(ies) involved and solving the system at a notional, unobserved equilibrium. This is called counterfactual analysis.

Counterfactual analysis is necessary for the effects of domestic policies on international trade and other countries to be addresssed. Once counterfactual world equilibria have been computed, the resulting prices and trade flows can be compared with the actual ones and the distortions implied by the existing policies can be demonstrated. Moreover, the effects of the policies on the real income of other countries can also be calculated. Multicountry multi-sector partial equilibrium models that use counterfactual analysis to estimate both domestic and international effects of price support can get quite complicated.

Probably the most advanced model in this category is that of Tyers, used by the World Bank in the 1986 World Development Report.[3] It incorporates seven agricultural commodities and 30 countries or country groups. The intersectoral links are captured hy cross-elasticities in both supply and demand. Supply is represented by a mechanism of 'partial adjustment' of production to prices (Nerlove, 1958). It models government action explicitly by using 'transmission elasticities' which determine what proportion of a world price shock is passed through to domestic producers and consumers. It includes stockholding behaviour endogenously, and it estimates welfare effects on consumers and producers, and changes in government budgets and stockholders' profits. Finally, it is dynamic in nature, in the sense that it allows for differences in the short- and long-run effects of a shock or policy change.

Even a model of such sophistication, however, is essentially limited by the constraints of partial equilibrium methodology. Computable General Equilibrium (CGE) models make one further step and bring non-agricultural sectors, factor markets and the macroeconomy into the picture. Thus, the problems raised above in points (5) and (6) are addressed directly in CGE models.

CGE world models are essentially higher-dimensional analogues of the traditional two-sector Heckscher-Ohlin international trade model. Each region has a production function with primary and intermediate inputs and demand functions derived from utility maximization. The Armington heterogeneity assumption, which postulates that similar goods from different countries are imperfect substitutes, is usually made to account for the cross-hauling of goods observed in international trade. The countries are constrained by their total factor endowments. The balance of payments, or parts of it, is modelled explicitly and constrained by an external condition. A global general equilibrium is characterized by a set of international prices for all goods and factors such that: (i) all markets clear; (ii) the zero-profit conditions are met in all industries; and (iii) the external accounts of each country satisfy the constraints.[4]

The issues raised earlier in point (7) are not dealt with successfully in either advanced partial equilibrium or general equilibrium analysis. Externalities, in particular, are hard to handle because market prices do not reflect the true social valuations of different activities.

The discussion so far has focused on different ways of measuring the effects that price support policies have on domestic welfare, international trade and the welfare of other countries. Such policies in large countries or regions, however, have other effects as well. One that has attracted a considerable amount of attention is the effect on the stability of international commodity prices.

Price instability, especially in agricultural markets, has long been an issue of concern. The conventional view is that policies that insulate domestic markets from international price movements tend to increase world price instability. This happens because, if a country does not let its domestic consumption accommodate, for example, a world production shortfall, the consumption of everybody else must fall disproportionately. To ration the reduced world output, world prices must rise by more. This, in turn, causes farmers' incomes to fluctuate. Farmers with utility functions with the usual convexity properties react with aversion to risk in their supply decisions and, in this way, affect the economy as a whole. Moreover, the poorer the country whose commodities are affected, the more undesirable these fluctuations are, for two reasons: first, because farmers there tend to be relatively more numerous and impoverished; second because owing to the reduced access to insurance markets, they are more vulnerable to income fluctuations.

This view is not completely accurate for two reasons. First, it is unclear whether all price support measures increase instability, or whether they increase it to the same extent. Bale and Lutz (1978 and 1979b) show that some policy instruments have no impact on world price stability, while others transfer different degrees of instability from one country to another.[5] Second, world prices in theory can be stabilized even if most countries insulate their markets, as long as countries or private individuals operating in the free market hold big enough stocks. The issue is, ultimately, an empirical one.

In order to measure empirically how much the insulation of particular domestic markets adds to price instability in the world, the partial or general equilibrium models used need to be modified to take into account price fluctuations. This is done by introducing stochastic supply and demand shocks in the models (see, for example, Tyers and Anderson, 1986) and observing how the specific policies change the variance of prices.

A final methodological point that ought to be mentioned has to do with the scope of counterfactual equilibrium analysis. There is no hard and fast rule for the choice of the appropriate counterfactual 'base case'; it depends on what the specific question addressed is. If the focus is on a cost-benefit analysis of the CAP, then the free trade competitive equilibrium is the obvious choice. If, on the other hand, the objective is an evaluation of an alternative policy package (such as maintaining unchanged nominal support prices for a certain period of time, reducing protection of some communities or across the board, etc.), then this is the appropriate counterfactual. The first option has the additional advantage of being conceptually simple and familiar. The second is obviously more interesting from a policy-maker's point of view, but requires a detailed spelling out of the components of the alternative policy package.[6]

Table 1
Welfare Effects of the CAP on the EC Members
(1980 US$b per year)

Source	Commodity (ies)	Country (ies)	Model structure[a]	Effects on					
				Year	Con-sumers (a)	Tax-payers (b)	Total		
							Pro-ducers (c)	Absolute	Relative (d)
Koester and Schmitz (1982)	Sugar	EC-9	PE	1978-79				-0.40	
Morris (1980)	Main CAP commodities	EC-9	PE	1978	-43.5	-10.7	38.6	-15.6	-0.53% of EC-9 GDP transfer ratio of 1.40[c]
Thomson and Harvey (1981)	All CAP commodities	EC-9	PE	1980[b]					Transfer ratio of 1.77[c]
Australia Bureau of Agricultural Economics (1985)	All CAP commodities	EC-9	PE	1978	-35.4	-18.1	44.1	-9.4	-0.48% of EC-9 GDP transfer ratio of 1.21[c]
		EC-10	PE	1983	-25.6	-20.8	39.7	-6.7	-0.32% of EC-10 GDP transfer ratio of 1.17[c]
Buckwell *et al.* (1982)	All CAP commodities	EC-9	PE	1980	-34.6	-11.5	30.7	-15.4	-0.55% of EC-9 GDP transfer ratio of 1.5[c]
Tyers (1985)	Rice, wheat coarse grains, ruminant and non-ruminant meat	EC-9	PE	1980	-44.0	-0.9	13.9	-31.0[d]	-1.1% of EC-9 GDP transfer ratio 3.23
Tyers and Anderson (1986a)	Rice, wheat coarse grains ruminant and non-ruminant meat, dairy, sugar	EC-10	PE	1985[c]	-49.0	-2.2	27.2	-24.1[d]	-1.3% of EC-10 GDP or transfer ratio 1.88[c]

Table 1 (continued)
Welfare Effects of the CAP on the EC Members
(1980 US$b per year).

Burniaux and Waelbroeck (1985)	All CAP commodities	EC-10	GE	1995					-2.7% of EC-10 GDP
Tyers and Anderson (1987a, b)	Rice, wheat coarse grains ruminant and non-ruminant meat, dairy, sugar	EC-12	PE	1980-82	-42.3	-0.9	36.4	-6.8[e]	-0.27% of EC-12 GDP transfer ratio of 1.19
OECD (1987)	All CAP commodities	EC-9	PE	1979-81	-27.8				

[a] PE - Partial equilibrium (single- or multi-sector); GE: General equilibrium.

[b] The Thomson and Harvey (1981) results are for 1980 but their model used data from 1975 for calibration.

[c] The transfer ratio is defined as the cost of the economy of increasing farmers' income by 1 unit; in other words columns $\frac{(a) + (b)}{(c)}$

[d] Results are for 1985, but the model is calibrated to data from 1980-82.

[e] includes change in net government revenue and profits from storage.

EC-9 comprises Belgium, Denmark, France, the Federal Republic of Germany, Ireland, Italy, Luxembourg, the Netherlands and the United Kingdom.

For all these studies except OECD (1987) the free-trade equilibrium is the basis of measurement.

2. The evidence

Effects of the CAP on EC members

This section presents a survey of recent empirical literature on the domestic effects of the CAP. Most studies treat the Community as one entity, although some provide estimates of the effects on a country-by-country basis. Most also provide a breakdown of the total welfare cost into consumer and taxpayer (or government) loss and producer benefit. Table 1 summarizes the evidence from all the existing studies that report results in a comparable form. Also presented and discussed are studies that focus on different aspects of the domestic effects of the CAP or that formulate their questions in a different way. The cost estimates in columns (a) to (d) are all converted into 1980 US dollars.

All but one of the studies presented are multi-sector models, covering all or most of the CAP commodities. Koester and Schmitz (1982) is the only exception. They examine the effects of the EC Sugar Protocol (a mixed system of price support and quotas) on LDCs, intra-EC transfers and Community welfare. The welfare costs are calculated with a free trade counterfactual world price as the reference point, which was taken to be equal to 38 per cent of the EC support price. This counterfactual world price was arrived at by a series of computations of free trade counterfactual equilibria under different assumptions about demand and supply elasticities in the Community and the rest of the world. However, no exact information about the elasticities was available and, in addition, the computed counterfactual equilibria were very sensitive to the elasticity values. The welfare calculations, therefore, do not seem very reliable.

Morris (1980) estimates the effects of price support for the main CAP commodities (the exceptions being wine, tobacco, fruit and vegetables). A serious drawback of this study is that the counterfactual free trade prices do not come out of a demand and supply system, but are instead postulated *ad hoc*. Since these counterfactual prices are not listed in the study, it is impossible to tell *a priori* whether the paper tends to over- or underestimate the welfare costs.

Thomson and Harvey's (1981) paper models the markets for 16 groups of agricultural commodities. Their interaction is captured by a set of cross-elasticities. The study evaluates the CAP with respect to its stated objectives and does not address the wider social costs. The closest one which could come to a measure of overall efficiency is the transfer ratio of 1.77. The transfer ratio is the cost to the economy of an increase in farmers' income by one unit.

A very comprehensive study of agricultural protection in the EC is that by the Australian Bureau of Agricultural Economics (Bureau of Agricultural Economics, 1985). They treat the Community as one country, but distinguish between different commodities, as do Thomson and Harvey (1981), and make adjustments to account for their interaction. They consider the CAP together with national price support policies and provide yearly estimates of the costs for the 1971-83 period. In table 1 estimates are reported for 1978, when, according to the study, the costs of agricultural support peaked, and 1983. Their results imply significant costs from the operation of price support mechanisms: around 0.3 per cent of total EC-10 GDP, equivalent to roughly one-third of Greece's GDP, was wasted in 1983. In per capita terms, this means approximately US$25.

Probably the most often quoted study of the effects of the CAP is the monograph by Buckwell *et al.* (1982). As with the previous two studies, they model explicitly many countries and markets, with the interaction between commodities captured by cross-elasticities. An important advantage of this paper is that it takes into account intra-EC transfers resulting from Community preference schemes, the common financing of the CAP and MCAs. Their estimate of the consumers' loss is comparable to that of the Bureau of Agricultural Economics, but that of the taxpayers is smaller, possibly because of the inclusion of the intra-EC transfers mentioned above. The total cost estimate, however, is larger than that of the Bureau. The reason for this is probably the fact that Buckwell *et al.* model the structure of the agricultural sector in greater detail and, therefore, are more accurate in their estimation of the producers' benefit.

Tyers (1985) and Tyers and Anderson (1986, 1987a, 1987b) use different versions of the same model to estimate the costs of the CAP alone and of the CAP plus domestic policies respectively. The basic model is discussed in Section 1 of this article. In comparison to the previous studies, there seem to be several advantages in the analytical framework used by Tyers and Anderson. First, the international policy interactions are better captured, because the degree of disaggregation is higher (24 countries and country groups in the 1985 Tyers paper and 30 in the 1986 Tyers and Anderson paper). Second, government behaviour is incorporated in the model and assumed to be different in the short and the long run. Third, stockholding behaviour is modelled explicitly.

The estimates presented in the studies are for different years (1980 for the Tyers, 1980-82 and 1985 for the Tyers and Anderson studies)[7] and different country groups (EC-9 to EC-12) and for varying degrees of disaggregation of the rest of the world. In the two earlier studies, the total cost estimate is significantly higher than in any other partial equilibrium study: it is 1.1 per cent of EC-9 GDP in 1980 in the Tyers study and 1.3 per cent of EC-10 GDP in 1985 in the Tyers and Anderson paper. The implied transfer ratio in the latter study is 1.88. In their 1987 study, however, the authors estimate total costs at only 0.3 per cent of EC-12 GNP and the transfer ratio at 1.2. The discrepancy with the earlier studies seems to reflect in part a change in the measurement of the welfare effects. While the model used in this and earlier studies by the same authors is non-linear, in the earlier studies linear approximations to supply and compensated demand curves were used to measure the welfare effects. The areas which emerge from such approximations are accurate only for small changes in domestic prices — in the case of the EC, however, the price changes were in fact very large. In the 1987 studies the areas under non-linear curves were measured, which resulted in some cases in substantially smaller welfare effects. In addition, the 1987 study assumes a much lower degree of transmission of world market price changes to domestic price changes.

The long-run transmission elasticities for the EC, for example, range between 0 and 0.76 depending on the particular commodity.[8] As a consequence of the higher degree of insulation of prices in the EC and other countries and geographical regions, trade liberalization in the EC has a larger impact on world market prices. This is reflected in the significantly larger increases in agricultural world market prices as a result of trade liberalization in industrial countries in the 1987 study as compared with the earlier studies (see below). Consequently, the gains from liberalization, which depend on the counterfactual world market prices, are much smaller.

The studies by Spencer (1985) and Burniaux and Waelbroeck (1985) are general equilibrium models. Spencer (1985) has a very simple CGE model with nine countries (eight in the EC, with Belgium and Luxembourg lumped together, and the rest of the world) and two goods (agriculture and non-agriculture) produced with two factors of production. He calculates that 0.9 per cent of EC-9 GDP is lost as a result of the CAP.

Burniaux and Waelbroeck (1985) use a more sophisticated CGE framework, which includes nine regions and separately models production and consumption in the urban and rural areas of each (see Burniaux and Waelbroeck, 1985, Appendix). As in the Tyers and Anderson (1986) model, different degrees of insulation of the domestic market are captured by price transmission equations. The paper distinguishes between more and less 'flexible' regions; the US and the Latin America, for example, are assumed to insulate their domestic markets less than oil-exporting countries and Europe.

The Burniaux and Waelbroeck model calculates the long-run effects of a policy change today, subject to growth rate forecasts for the regions under consideration. Dismantling the CAP in 1985, according to the model, generates a gain in real income equal to 2.7 per cent of EC GDP in 1995. This result is somewhat surprising, compared with the other studies presented here, but can be explained by the assumption fed into the model. Burniaux and Waelbroeck, unlike other studies, assume that international commodity prices, even if nothing else changes, will be decreasing continuously until 1995. Agricultural protection in the EC with variable import levies, which maintain domestic commodity prices unchanged, is obviously bound to look increasingly expensive against this background. Nevertheless, this scenario is not unreasonable, especially if the commodity price trends of the last 30 years continue in the future.

Finally, the results from a recently released OECD study (1987a) can be construed to be based on a simple 'partial' equilibrium approach, which implicitly assumes inelastic demand for agricultural products in the EC for estimating costs to the consumers. The expenditures incurred by both the national and the EC authorities on agriculture, on the other hand, are taken in the study to represent the costs to the taxpayer. The OECD study estimates the costs of agricultural policy in the EC to the consumers at about US$28 billion in 1980 prices (or about 1.8 per cent of EC-9 GDP). The total cost (to the consumers and taxpayers) of this policy is estimated at 2.8 per cent of GDP; the annual average costs are estimated at ecu 11,437 per holding and ecu 7,465 per agricultural worker during the period 1979-81.[9]

The diversity of the methodologies used makes it difficult to summarize the evidence presented in table 1. In general, though, the estimates of the welfare costs of the CAP seem to fall into two zones: a 'low' one, with net losses ranging from 0.32 per cent to 0.55 per cent of EC GDP (Morris, 1980; Bureau of Agricultural Economics, 1985; Buckwell et al., 1982, Tyers and Anderson, 1987a, b), and a 'high' one, with net losses at around 1 per cent or more of EC GDP (Tyers, 1985; Tyers and Anderson, 1986; Spencer, 1985, Burniaux and Waelbroeck, 1985). The Thompson and Harvey study also belongs to the latter group by virtue of their estimate of the transfer ratio, which is comparable to that of Tyers and Anderson (1986).

Although it is impossible to judge the validity of these figures without some idea of the 'true' costs, it is worth noting that the studies that produce estimates in the 'high' zone use generally superior methodology and a higher level of disaggregation. To the extent that this is a valid criterion for evaluating empirical work, it can be concluded that these studies are probably more accurate in estimating the welfare costs of the CAP.

The remaining part of this section discusses briefly a few studies that focus on different, distributional or country-specific, effects of the CAP and are not included in table 1. Harling and Thompson (1985) use a partial equilibrium model to estimate the costs of intervention in the poultry industry for, among other countries, Germany and the United Kingdom. They find that in 1975-77 the resulting deadweight losses were of the order of US$10.5 million for these two countries together.

Bale and Lutz (1979a and 1981) calculated the costs of price support for wheat, maize, sugar and beef in selected countries. They use a very simple partial equilibrium model and report a net welfare loss of US$737.3 million for France, US$1,112.4 million for Germany and US$112.4 million for the United Kingdom.

The paper by Buckwell *et al.* provides estimates of the welfare costs by country. They are summarized in Table 2. The transfer ratio, which can be thought of as a broad measure of policy efficiency, is 1.50 for the Community as a whole. It is highest in the UK (2.07), Italy (1.87) and Germany (1.8). It is less than unity in the Netherlands, Ireland and Denmark, indicating that these countries benefit from the inter-country redistribution of income caused by the CAP (see Buckwell *et al.*, 1982, pp. 90-134; and Koester and Tangermann, 1986, p. 63).

Table 2
Welfare Effects of the CAP by Country in 1980 (US$m).

Country	Consumers	Taxpayers	Producers	Net	Transfer ratio
EC-9	-34,580	-11,494	30,686	-15,388	1.50
Germany	-12,555	-3,769	9,045	-7,279	1.80
France	-7,482	-2,836	7,237	-3,081	1.42
Italy	-5,379	-1,253	3,539	-3,093	1.87
Netherlands	-1,597	-697	3,081	787	0.74
Belgium/Luxembourg	-1,440	-544	1,624	-320	1.22
United Kingdom	-5,174	-1,995	3,461	-3,708	2.07
Ireland	-320	-99	965	546	0.43
Denmark	-635	-302	1,736	799	0.54

Sources: Buckwell *et al.* (1982), pp. 90-134, and staff calculations.

This ranking of the gainers from the CAP is similar to the one in Spencer (1986). He uses a general equilibrium model to evaluate which countries would do better outside the CAP, and by how much. It turns out that Ireland would be the only clear loser, with Denmark gaining the least. The only notable difference between Buckwell *et al.* and Spencer is the Netherlands: in the former study the less than unity transfer ratio indicates that the country is benefiting, whereas in the latter the Netherlands appears to be losing from the operation of the CAP.

Greece also appears to gain a very small amount, around 5-10 million ECU per year, from participating in the CAP (see Georgakopoulos, 1986; Georgakopoulos and Paschos, 1985). This result, however, should be interpreted with care, since it is not derived from a full counterfactual analysis.

Breckling *et al.* (1987) use a simple general equilibrium model to appraise the economy-wide effects of the CAP for four EC members: Germany, France, Italy and the United Kingdom. They conclude that the costs of agricultural price support extend beyond the traditional welfare losses. Specifically, for all countries taken together, manufacturing industries (excluding food processing) lose between 1.1 and 2.5 per cent of potential gross output and between 4.4 and 6.2 per cent of exports and total employment is reduced by around 1 per cent (or 860,000 jobs). Unemployment increases universally in these countries as non-agricultural sectors are relatively intensive employers of labour. The job loss is more in the United Kingdom and Germany followed by Italy and France. This is the result of slower growth of labour-intensive non-agricultural sectors in the former countries. However, the results suggest that despite the emerging unemployment, France is a net beneficiary of the CAP in view of its large rural sector and EC transfers under the applicable common policy. These results are broadly confirmed in a later study by Stoeckel and Breckling (1988), which uses the same model. The authors find that national and supranational protection of the agricultural sector in the four countries under investigation, reduce real aggregate income by 1.5 per cent and cause a loss of about four million jobs.

Despite the budgetary and welfare burden of the CAP, the agricultural lobby has resisted attempts to liberalize and is, instead, stepping up pressure to reinforce the CAP (Koester, 1985; Gerken, 1986; von Witzke, 1986). This movement away from liberalization is apparently accelerated by demands for more equal distribution of the CAP benefits between Member States. Josling (1979) discusses the CAP in the light of the expansion of the EC in Southern Europe and concludes that the wider range of commodities and the shifting political balance within the Community will increase the domestic costs, exacerbate the budgetary problems and amplify the international effects of agricultural protection. In the same vein, Koester (1977) argues that as long as it is possible for member countries to supra-nationalize costs of national agricultural support, the prospects for a CAP reform are poor. This argument may be questionable at a time of acute budgetary crisis.

Effects of the CAP on international trade

This section discusses the evidence on the effects the CAP has on the level of prices and the volume and pattern of world trade in agricultural commodities. Since the policies that apply to different products vary widely, the estimated effects for each of the most important commodities covered by the CAP are presented separately. These commodities are: wheat, coarse grains (barley, maize, rye, oats, millet and sorghum), rice, ruminant meat (beef and veal), non-ruminant meat (pork, poultry, etc.) sugar and dairy products. Table 3 presents the estimated effects of a hypothetical abolition of the CAP on the international prices of the above commodities. Each of the studies reviewed calculates a counterfactual world trade equilibrium with a completely liberalized EC market for the commodities in question and then compares the resulting counterfactual prices with the actual world prices.

The estimates show that abolition of the CAP would significantly increase the world prices of all the commodities examined. In other words, the CAP exerts a powerful downward pressure on the actual price level. Roughly speaking, the effect is stronger on dairy products, grains and ruminant meat and weaker on sugar and rice. This result is to be expected, since the former category of products is afforded greater effective protection than the latter (see Sampson and Yeats, 1977; Koester and Tangermann, 1986, p. 71).

All the estimates reported in Table 3 come from partial equilibrium models. There are considerable differences between the estimated price effects for each commodity, which can be, to a large extent, traced back to the differences in the methodology and the data used in each study. First of all, models that cover only a few commodities and/or do not take into account market interaction, tend to predict higher counterfactual prices and, therefore, overestimate the effects on world markets of price support in the CAP. If only a few isolated markets are liberalized, then the pressure from the other, still protected, markets will spill over via commodity substitution and the observed effects will be amplified. The first four studies listed in table 3 share this characteristic. The Koester and Valdes paper in particular, although it examines many products, does not take into account cross-effects and uses, essentially, a single-commodity approach.[10]

A second element that accounts for differences between estimated effects, even if the methodology is similar, is the data used. This explains partially why the results of the four other papers (Anderson and Tyers, 1984; Tyers and Anderson, 1986, 1987b, and Matthews, 1985a), which are all multi-commodity models and examine the effects of a generalized liberalization on individual commodity prices, are so diverse. Anderson and Tyers (1984) probably overestimate the degree of protection in the Community by using the official intervention prices as the appropriate domestic market prices (Koester and Tangermann, 1986, p. 74). Due to the existing surplus stocks, however, EC market prices are generally lower than the intervention prices (see the information provided in Commission of the European Communities, 1986, Statistical Appendix). Matthews, on the other hand, underestimates the degree of protection in the Community, because he uses the EC cif price as the appropriate world price. As the Community is a net exporter of many of these commodities, however, the fob price or the price in major foreign parts should be used.

A third factor that affects crucially the outcome of counterfactual experiments is the values of the parameters used. For example, the higher the domestic demand elasticity, the stronger the domestic reaction to liberalization and the larger the final effect on the world price will be. Tyers (1985) and Anderson and Tyers (1984) use EC demand elasticities between -0.5 and -0.7 (Tyers,1985, Appendix), whereas Matthews postulates a value of -0.4 for all commodities (Matthews, 1985a, p. 115). The former range of values is based on a more detailed survey of the relevant empirical literature. Also, as mentioned above, the difference in 'transmission elasticities' between the more recent Tyers and Anderson studies influences the results.

Finally, the last significant cause of deviations between the estimates of different models is the varying degree of country and commodity coverage and differences in the base period. The Tyers and Anderson papers (1986,1987b) are by far the most detailed in that respect, modelling seven commodity and 30 country groups. Unfortunately it is impossible to tell *a priori* whether a greater degree of disaggregation tends to generate larger or smaller effects.

Table 3
Effects of the CAP on International Prices (% change in world market prices following complete liberalization).

Source[a]	EC-concept	Base year	Wheat	Coarse grains	Rice	Ruminant meat	Non-ruminant meat	Sugar	Dairy
Koester and Schmitz (1982)	EC-9	1979						12.0	
Koester (1982)	EC-9	1975-77	9.6	14.3[b]					
Koester and Valdes (1984)	EC-9	1980	4.6			10.5[c]	5.9[d]	9.7	28.3[e]
Sarris and Freebairn (1983)	EC-9	1978-80	9.2						
Anderson and Tyers (1984)[f]	EC-9	1980	13.0	16.0	5.0	17.0	1.0		
Tyers and Anderson (1986)	EC-10	1985[g]	0.7	2.5	0.7	9.5	1.7	2.6	11.8
Matthews (1985a)	EC-10	1978-82	0.7	2.9[b]	0.1	4.5[h]	3.6[d]	6.0	10.5[e]
Tyers and Anderson (1987b)	EC-12	1980-82	6.0	5.0	3.0	18.0	4.0	7.0	25.0

[a]All studies cited base their results on partial equilibrium analysis.

[b]Reported figure refers to barley only.

[c]Reported figure refers to beef only.

[d]Average of estimated effect on the prices of pork and poultry.

[e]Reported figure refers to butter only.

[f]Same results also reported in Tyers (1985).

[g]Results for 1985, but the model is calibrated to data from 1980-82.

[h]Average of estimated effect on the prices of beef and mutton.

The OECD has produced a comprehensive partial equilibrium study on the effects of agricultural protection in the world (OECD, 1987). Although the emphasis is on multilateral liberalization, they report some estimates of the effect on world prices of a unilateral liberalization in the Community. Their counterfactual, however, is not the free trade equilibrium, but a 10 per cent across-the-board reduction in nominal protection of all commodities. They calculate that this partial liberalization in the EC increases the world prices of most commodities from 0.55 per cent, in the case of sugar, to 2.81 per cent in the case of milk. In the case of grains, however, prices actually fall a little following the hypothetical CAP reform, owing to decreased demand for grains by livestock producers.

The calculated counterfactual prices are important, first, because they give some idea of the degree of distortion in world agricultural markets that is due to the CAP and, second, because they provide the basis for the estimation of the effects of liberalization on the pattern and volume of world trade. Changes in the pattern and volume of trade, of course, have little importance in and of themselves. Calculating them, however, is a necessary step in assessing the effects the CAP had on the real income of Europe's trading partners. For that reason we present and discuss some of the empirical work on this issue very briefly.

Table 4 highlights the main results. Abolition of the CAP increases total commodity trade by a considerable amount. This is caused basically by a large increase in EC net imports, prompted by lower consumer and higher producer prices. The effect is stronger in the most heavily protected sectors, such as wheat, grains and dairy products. The reported effects would be much larger if they were expressed in value, rather than volume, terms.

Table 4
Effects of the CAP on World Trade^a (change in volume following complete liberalization, in millions of tons).

	EC-concept	Base year	Net imports to the EC	Net imports to developed countries (including EC)	Net imports to less developed countries	Total volume traded
Wheat						
Koester (1982)	EC-9	1975-77		-8.5	-3.4	18.6
Anderson and Tyers (1984)	EC-9	1980	14.7			
Tyers (1985)	EC-9	1980	14.7			12.3
Tyers and Anderson (1986)	EC-10	1985^b	-2.4	0.2	0.2	0.0
Tyers and Anderson (1987b)	EC-12	1980-82		4.5	-4.9	-4.0
Coarse grains						
Koester (1982)	EC-9	1975-77		-10.0^c	-5.3^c	68.5^c
Anderson & Tyers (1984)	EC-9	1980	26.0			
Tyers (1985)	EC-9	1980	26.0			23.2
Tyers and Anderson (1986)	EC-10	1985^b	5.9	3.0	-3.3	4.0
Tyers and Anderson (1987b)	EC-12	1980-82		4.0	2.3	0.0
Rice						
Anderson & Tyers (1984)	EC-9	1980	-0.2			
Tyers (1985)	EC-9	1980	-0.2			
Tyers and Anderson (1986)	EC-10	1985^b	0.1	0.1	-0.1	0.0
Tyers and Anderson (1987b)	EC-12	1980-82		3.8	-4.0	-1.0
Ruminant meat						
Anderson and Tyers (1984)	EC-9	1980	3.0			
Tyers (1985)	EC-9	1980	3.0			2.7
Tyers and Anderson (1986)	EC-10	1985^b	5.3	3.2	-2.6	107.0
Tyers and Anderson (1987b)	EC-12	1980-82		5.6	-2.9	58.0
Non-ruminant meat						
Anderson and Tyers (1984)	EC-9	1980	-2.0			
Tyers (1985)	EC-9	1980	-2.0			2.0
Tyers and Anderson (1986)	EC-10	1985^b	-0.5	0.0	-0.0	3.0
Tyers and Anderson (1987b)	EC-12	1980-82		1.7	-0.7	-6.0
Sugar						
Tyers and Anderson (1986)	EC-10	1985^b	3.0	2.8	-2.6	-5.0
Tyers and Anderson (1987b)	EC-12	1980-82		2.3	-2.9	0.0
Dairy						
Tyers and Anderson (1986)	EC-10	1985^b	38.8	29.7	-19.6	34.0
Tyers and Anderson (1987b)	EC-12	1980-82		14.0	-22.0	17.0

^{a}All studies cited base their results on partial equilibrium analysis.

^{b}Results for 1985, but the model is calibrated to data from 1980-82.

^{c}Reported figure refers to barley and maize only.

The results of studies cited in table 4 are influenced by the estimated post-liberalization counterfactual prices and the coverage and grouping of countries. Koester (1982), for example, includes in the Developed Countries group all the centrally planned economies, which form a separate group in Tyers and Anderson (1986). The only surprising result, which cannot be explained by these factors, is the negative change in EC net imports of wheat that Tyers and Anderson (1986) report. Given that the Community is a net exporter of wheat, this means that abolishing the CAP will lead to an increase in net wheat exports. Unfortunately the authors do not comment on this counterintuitive conclusion.

The net trade effects of the CAP on other trading partners are also discussed in other studies, which are not comparable to the ones reported in table 4 because in those, authors conduct a different counterfactual experiment, or use a different taxonomy for reporting their quantitative results, or do not provide quantitative results at all. Sarris (1983) calculates the effects of EC enlargement in Southern Europe on international trade in fruit and vegetables. He estimates that including Greece, Spain and Portugal under the CAP umbrella increases the value of net imports (or reduces the value of net exports) of the other major producing countries by approximately US$ 116.6 million (in 1980 prices) . Tangermann (1978 and 1981) discusses the possible effects of reforming the CAP on the trade flows between developed and less developed countries. He concludes that, since the CAP protects mostly temperate products, the EC imports from other temperate/developed countries will increase as a result of reducing price support. The effect on trade with LDCs, however, is ambiguous. The producers of such commodities there will have an incentive to increase their production but, on the other hand, they will also have to compete with other exporters. The final outcome depends crucially on the supply elasticities. Finally, Mackel et al. (1984) focus on, among other things, the effect of the CAP on trade in commodities that are not protected in the EC. They argue that the CAP has increased imports of substitute products to the EC, like manioc and soya and that, therefore, a liberalization will harm producers of such commodities.

Empirical research on the impact of the CAP on international commodity trade, far from being in unequivocal agreement, has reached some common conclusions regarding at least the direction of the effects. First, the CAP has a significant depressing effect on world prices. Second, as a result of this, trade flows are severely distorted: EC exports are artificially boosted at the expense of net exports of other countries. Third, this distortion keeps the volume of world trade at a lower level than it would otherwise be. Fourth, these effects are generally more significant for the products that are heavily protected in the Community, such as wheat, coarse grains, ruminant meat and dairy products.

Effects of the CAP on the welfare of non-EC countries

The influence the CAP exerts on international trade means that the real incomes of all trading partners are eventually affected. The conventional view, popular with Community officials, is that a unilateral liberalization in the EC will benefit the exporters and harm the importers of temperate zone products by increasing their prices. Consequently, given that most LDCs import temperate zone commodities, the CAP actually constitutes a transfer of income from EC consumers and taxpayers to poor countries via cheaper international food prices. Furthermore, the concessionary character of the Lomé Convention means that a liberalization, which would imply an abolition of those agreements as well, would be even more detrimental to the LDC group. The data in table 5 seem to support this view. The table presents the effects that a hypothetical liberalization has on the welfare of two broad groups: the non-EC developed countries and the less developed countries.

The models reviewed in table 5 are all partial equilibrium and the degree of commodity and country coverage varies, but two facts stand out. First, the size of the total effect on each of the two country groups is not large compared to GDP or total export earnings. Second, less developed countries as a group stand to lose from an abolition of the CAP, while the effect on developed countries is ambiguous.

Differences in the estimated size of the effects can be generally traced back to commodity coverage or the data used. The figures reported by Koester (1982) and Koester and Schmitz (1982) are expectedly lower than the rest, since these studies cover only cereals and sugar respectively. Therefore, although the estimated effect on the world price of the individual commodities may be higher, as discussed in the previous section, the total welfare effect is small. Matthews (1985a) also reports a small estimate of LDC loss for two reasons: (1), mentioned earlier, because he underestimates the degree of protection in the Community; (2) because he uses smaller domestic supply elasticities than other studies. The higher the LDC supply elasticity assumed, the stronger the supply response to increasing world prices and the more likely the realization of gains from increased exports. Matthews uses a supply elasticity of 0.4 for all countries (Matthews, 1985a, p. 115), whereas Koester (1982), Anderson and Tyers (1984) and Tyers (1985) use elasticities in the neighbourhood of unity (Koester, 1982, p. 27; Tyers, 1985, Appendix). Extensive empirical research has shown that long-run supply elasticities in LDCs vary widely according to the specific product, but are generally rather low, fluctuating between 0.1 and 0.3 for grains and 0.2 and 0.5 for rice (see Bale and Lutz, 1979b; Scandizzo and Bruce, 1980; and the references therein).

Anderson and Tyers (1984) conduct a different counterfactual experiment. They calculate the impact of a 2 per cent annual reduction in EC support prices from 1981 to 1990. Their results are difficult to interpret because, although the final effect of the phased reduction of the support prices will be significant, it is unclear how close it will be to that of a complete liberalization.

Tyers and Anderson (1986, 1987a) have the highest degree of disaggregation, and the most detailed model among the ones in the table, and report in both studies the highest welfare loss for less developed countries from abolishing the CAP.[11] In their 1986 study, Tyers and Anderson found that even non-EC developed countries lose because the increase in grain prices as a result of liberalization diminishes the welfare of producers of livestock as they have to pay higher input prices.

Table 5
Effects of the CAP on the Welfare of Non-EC Countries
(change in real income following liberalization (US$b).

Source	Commodity (ies)	EC-concept	Model structure	Base year	Non-EC developed countries[a]	Less developed countries
Koester (1982)	Wheat, coarse grains	EC-9	PE	1979	0.9[b]	-0.5
Koester and Schmitz (1982)	Sugar	EC-9	PE	1979		-2.3
Anderson and Tyers (1984)	Wheat, rice, coarse grains, ruminant and non-ruminant meat	EC-9	PE	1981[c]	-1.5	-3.7
Tyers (1985)	Wheat, rice, coarse grains, ruminant and non-ruminant meat	EC-9	PE	1980	0.4	-1.8
Matthews (1985b)	Wheat, rice, coarse grains, ruminant and non-ruminant meat, sugar, oil, seeds, dairy	EC-10	PE	1978-82		-0.5
Tyers and Anderson (1986a)	Wheat, rice, coarse grains, ruminant and non-ruminant meat, sugar, dairy	EC-10	PE	1985[d]	-4.1	-5.9
Tyers and Anderson (1987)	Wheat, rice, coarse grains, ruminant and non-ruminant meat, sugar, dairy	EC-12	PE	1980-82	0.1	-10.5

[a]Australia, Canada, Japan, New Zealand, and the United States.

[b]Koester's developed countries group also includes Austria, Switzerland and the Nordic countries.

[c]Anderson and Tyers estimate the final effects in 1990 of a 2 per cent year reduction in CAP support prices from 1981 to 1990.

[d]Results for 1985, but the model is calibrated to data from 1980-92.

Table 5 may lead one to believe that, no matter what the sign is for each group, the effect of the CAP is essentially small. Reporting only net effects for two large country groups, however, conceals the distribution of gains or losses among individual countries. The information that can be pieced together about this is quite interesting. First of all, the small net gain (or the net loss) in the developed countries group is entirely due to the heavy losses of Japan. The rest of the countries in the group all register gains or very small losses (see Tyers, 1985; Tyers and Anderson, 1986). Second, the distribution of the effect within the LDC group is also very varied, depending basically on whether the country is a net exporter or importer of temperate zone commodities. For some of the countries the gains or losses are significant. Argentina, for example, appears to gain around US$200 million per year, while Korea and Pakistan each lose US$300 million (Tyers and Anderson, 1986, p. 59) from a liberalization of EC agriculture. Moreover, if liberalization implies abolition of the Lomé Conventions, it is possible that the LDC signatories will lose even more than the rest of the group. Given, however, that agricultural commodities and, in particular, temperate zone products are a very small portion of the goods that receive preferential treatment under the Conventions, the effects of abolishing the Lomé agreements is likely to be small compared to the effect of a CAP liberalization.

The evidence supporting the conventional view that most LDCs actually benefit from the operation of the CAP tends to be discounted by some researchers. They argue that the fact that LDCs are net importers of temperate zone commodities is due to protectionist policies such as the CAP in developed countries, which depress international prices and make agricultural exports unprofitable. Abolishing such policies, therefore, may imply costs for LDCs in the short run, but in the long run increased prices will stimulate agricultural production and exports, the pattern of trade will change and LDCs will realize important gains. Counterfactual analysis, which uses econometrically estimated supply elasticities, fails to capture this potential 'switching' effect and, consequently, measures only the short-run losses. This argument is very appealing to the proponents of unilateral liberalization, who also point out that it is only under the CAP regime that the Community has turned into a net exporter of many temperate commodities (Bureau of Agricultural Economics, 1985, p. 129). It has, however, two important drawbacks. First, the lack of reliable long-run supply elasticity estimates makes it impossible to measure the potential 'switching' effect accurately. Second, it is not supported by the existing evidence on agricultural policies in developing countries. If they actually believed in the harmful effects of the present low level of international prices and in their dynamic comparative advantage as commodity producers, they would subsidize agriculture to stimulate domestic production. Many LDCs, however, especially in Africa, actually tax agriculture (Koester and Tangermann, 1986, p. 78).

Another argument that has been voiced against the estimates in table 5 has to do with the limitations of the partial equilibrium methodology. A unilateral liberalization in the Community will affect non-agricultural sectors and factor markets and have repercussions on commodity trade. In order to capture these secondary effects, a general equilibrium model must be used.

Burniaux and Waelbroeck (1985) use a CGE to calculate how a liberalization of trade in agricultural commodities in the Community in 1985 would affect the welfare of LDCs in 1995; the results are quite striking. They estimate that total LDC real income would be higher by 2.9 per cent if the CAP were abolished. This is explained by the strong assumption that, even with no change in the CAP, foreign exchange shortages in LDCs will oblige them to rely more and more on agricultural exports. Thus the 'switching' occurs even with no policy change in the Community. It is obvious then that an abolition of the CAP, which raises world prices, benefits the LDCs.

Loo and Tower (1988) use a four-sector general equilibrium model, which they calibrate for six 'typical' developing countries, to investigate the effects of a 10 per cent increase in agricultural prices on world markets assumed to result from trade liberalization in industrial countries. They find that LDCs would gain about US$26 billion in 1985 prices as a result of the assumed increase in world market prices for agricultural commodities.[12] This gain could be split between the developing and industrial countries in various ways. With developing country real income unchanged, the benefit to the industrial countries from agricultural liberalization in terms of a reduction in the amount of aid they need to supply would amount to a real income gain of over US$16 billion. Alternatively, the developing countries could reduce their external public debt by 2.8 per cent on average, with reductions for the poorest countries of up to 4.8 per cent.

These results basically reflect three effects of higher agricultural world market prices on developing countries. First, there is a change in the terms of trade which affects real incomes. This effect is positive for countries which are net exporters of agricultural products, but negative for others which are net importers. Second, there is a gain in efficiency for most developing countries as resources are shifted from relatively inefficient non-agricultural sectors to agriculture. Third, as a result of resource allocation in favour of agriculture, there is an increase in government tax revenue (which allows a reduction in average tax rates) since many developing countries tax agriculture and subsidize certain non-agricultural sectors. The paper by Loo and Tower suggests that the second and third effects may well dominate any terms of trade losses that developing countries may incur as a result of a liberalization of agricultural trade in industrial countries.

Matthews (1985b) makes an additional argument in favour of substantial gains by LDCs from a unilateral liberalization in the EC. If, for example, EC real income rose as a result of a more efficient allocation of resources after liberalization, the LDCs would gain indirectly from the increased demand for their exports by the Community and by other developed countries whose agricultural export earnings would also have risen. This argument is convincing in qualitative terms. Many past studies do not take account of these secondary effects on global welfare and, therefore, probably underestimate the gains from liberalization. It is far from clear, however, that these secondary effects would be quantitatively significant.

To summarize, the empirical literature surveyed in this section seems to point to a few unambiguous conclusions. First, agricultural price support in the Community is not necessarily harmful to all, or even most, non-EC countries. A unilateral liberalization would benefit some of Europe's trading partners and harm others. In particular, current net importers of temperate zone commodities would lose, whereas current or potential net exporters would gain. Since most LDCs are current net importers, they stand to lose as a group from an abolition of the CAP, at least in the short run. The important issue is, who will be able to adjust domestic production and consumption patterns so as to take advantage of the higher world prices in the longer run?

Second, although the size of the effect on broad groups of countries is small, the distribution of gains and losses is far from uniform. Countries that are heavily dependent on temperate commodity imports because of climate and geography (e.g. Japan) or because they are poor, appear to benefit significantly from the operation of the CAP.

Finally, the above results should be interpreted with some caution. It is important to keep in mind that the gains from unilateral liberalization predicted with partial equilibrium models probably have some degree of downward bias built in, because they do not take into account secondary repercussions in non-agricultural sectors.

Effects of the CAP on international price stability

Conventional wisdom holds that countries or regions that insulate their domestic markets increase world price instability. As was discussed in section 1 of this article, this is not necessarily true. The question is essentially an empirical one. Empirical research on the effects of the CAP on price stability have given an affirmative answer: all the studies reviewed here agree that the CAP exerts a significant destabilizing influence on world commodity prices. Table 6 summarizes some of the evidence.

The impact of policies on price stability is estimated with the help of counterfactual analysis. A measure of variability is defined first, and then the price variability at the counterfactual non-CAP equilibrium is calculated and compared to actual price variability. Most studies introduce random supply and demand shocks, calculate the corresponding counterfactual equilibria and then use either the standard deviation or the coefficient of variation of the resulting distribution of prices to measure variability.[13] Table 6 presents the calculated share of world price variability due to the CAP; in other words, the decrease in variability that would obtain if the CAP were abolished. The destabilizing effect is strongest in the wheat, coarse grains and dairy products sectors.

Comparing the EC agricultural policies with price support schemes in other countries reveals that the CAP is the most important destabilizing factor in the world markets. Sarris and Freebairn (1983) estimate that the CAP alone accounts for more than half of the excess variability of the price of wheat over its global free trade level. Blandford (1983) calculates 'transmission coefficients' that show the extent to which changes in trade rather than in domestic consumption are used to stabilize the domestic market, and concludes that the Community transmits a larger absolute amount of domestic variability in grain to the world market than any other group of countries. Of all the ways in which price support can affect world price stability mentioned earlier, two are most important for the destabilizing effect of the CAP. First, the CAP relies heavily on variable tariffs, which not only protect the domestic agricultural sector, but insulate domestic consumers from world price variations (Matthews, 1985a, p. 211). Second, protection reduces the incentive for private stock-building, which implies wider price fluctuations. The latter effect could be avoided by government-sponsored stockpiling. Koester, however, finds evidence that in some years EC stocks increased when world market prices were extremely high, thereby actually amplifiying world price variability (Koester, 1982, pp. 53-65).

Table 6
Effects of the CAP on International Price Stability
(% share of variability of the world price due to the CAP).

Source[a]	EC-concept	Base year	Measure of variation used[b]	Wheat	Coarse grains	Rice	Ruminant meat	Non-ruminant meat	Dairy products	Sugar
Svedberg (1981)	EC-6	1967-72	D		7.0[c]					
Sarris and Freebairn (1983)	EC-9	1978-80	SD	19.8						
Schmitz and Koester (1984)	EC-10	1982	CV							8.5
Anderson and Tyers (1984)	EC-9	1980	CV	50.0	33.0	12.1	25.0	0.0		
Tyers (1985)	EC-9	1980	SD	44.0	24.0	6.0	11.0	7.0		
Tyers and Anderson (1986)	EC-10	1985	CV	24.0	5.0	9.6	16.7	22.0	60.0	5.0
Tyers and Anderson (1987a)	EC-12	1980-82	CV	32.8	15.1	15.8	37.4	0.0	50.0	22.2

[a]All the studies cited base their results on partial equilibrium analysis.

[b]D: Change in the price level following a 5 per cent production shortfall; SD: standard deviation; CV: coefficient of variation.

[c]The reported figure applies to a price index for wheat and coarse grains.

Section 2 discussed briefly why price stability is considered important from a welfare point of view, especially for developing countries. Unfortunately, there are no empirical estimates of the welfare losses caused by the destabilizing effects of the CAP. Given the size of the effects, though, it may well be the case that a liberalization would benefit Europe's trading partners significantly by reducing world price variability.

3. Concluding remarks

The article has been concerned with two different but related aspects of the Common Agricultural Policy of the EC: the domestic effects on the welfare of EC members, and the effects on international commodity trade and, consequently, on the welfare of the rest of the world.

Recent empirical literature that has been surveyed addresses these two issues by means of various tools, ranging from single-sector partial equilibrium models to general equilibrium models of the global economy. The differences in methodology, data used, country and commodity coverage and degree of disaggregation are considerable, and so are the differences in the quantitative estimates. A good understanding of the theoretical premises and the modelling details of each study is, therefore, necessary in order to put the reported results in perspective and compare them.

Each approach has its relative merits. The attraction of partial equilibrium models is their simplicity, which means that greater effort can be devoted to collecting data and capturing the pecularities of the sector(s) represented. On the other hand, inter-sectoral links are ignored, which in turn means that not all of the effects of agricultural policies are covered. General equilibrium models are more comprehensive in that sense, but they are more demanding both analytically and in terms of data requirements. Overall, however, general equilibrium models are preferable in that they reveal the effects of agricultural price support on other sectors and on the macroeconomy. These effects are both important for policy purposes and, in the case of the CAP, significant in size. Without a general equilibrium model it is difficult to capture the secondary repercussions that liberalization has on the world economy via factor and other product markets. Ignoring these effects may cause systematic underestimation of the gains from liberalization.

Empirical research on the domestic effects of the CAP has reached some unequivocal conclusions. First, the CAP redistributes large amounts of income to farmers, primarily from consumers and secondarily from taxpayers. This transfer is economically inefficient, in that it incurs a deadweight loss. The mean estimate of this loss is around 1 per cent of the Community's GDP.

Second, the distribution of this loss between countries is not uniform. Most countries, however, stand to lose. The heaviest loser appears to be the United Kingdom, followed by Italy and Germany. France probably also registers small losses. The clear gainer is Ireland, while the evidence on Denmark and the Netherlands is ambiguous.

Third, other than the deadweight loss that the whole economy suffers, other sectors incur costs because of the CAP as well. In particular, subsidizing agricultural production means discriminating against industry and services, diverting resources away from them and reducing their exports. This kind of cost has not attracted enough attention, mainly because it requires general equilibrium modelling. Quantification of inter-sectoral effects is, therefore, an important area for future research.

The economy-wide and sectoral losses are by no means the only costs of the CAP. Agricultural price support, especially of such magnitude, generates wasteful rent-seeking and lobbying and distorts investment. These costs are difficult to estimate, but they mean that the traditional welfare calculations, even if they include inter-sectoral repercussions, underestimate the true social costs of operating the CAP.

With regard to the international effects of the CAP, empirical research has come to some interesting conclusions. By encouraging domestic production and raising consumer prices, especially in products with low income elasticity, the CAP has artificially reduced EC consumption and boosted production, turning Europe into a net exporter of most temperate zone commodities. This increase in the EC commodity surplus depresses and destabilizes world prices and makes production in other countries less profitable. The pattern of world trade is, in this way, severely distorted. This effect is more evident in the sectors that are relatively more heavily protected, like wheat, coarse grains, ruminant meat and dairy products.

The distortionary effects of the CAP affect the welfare of the Community's trading partners. Generally speaking, net exporters of temperate zone commodities lose, while net importers gain. Since most LDCs are net importers, less developed countries as a group appear to benefit from the operation of the CAP, at least in the short run, through an improvement in their terms of trade.

This result, although it is confirmed by most existing studies, should be treated with caution. First of all, it conceals the distribution of losses and gains across countries, which is far from uniform. Second, it is derived mostly from partial equilibrium models, which ignore secondary repercussions on welfare via the non-agricultural markets; the available general equilibrium studies show that ignoring these repercussions leads to systematic underestimation of the costs of the distortion. Third, it may be relevant only in the short run; if many developing countries were able to take advantage of higher commodity prices and switch from being net importers to net exporters, the result would prove incorrect over the longer run. Fourth, it ignores the cost of increased price instability, which is probably more detrimental to poor than to rich countries.

It is hard to express these qualifications quantitively. However, even if the majority of LDCs actually gained from the CAP, this gain would be very small compared with the welfare losses in the EC. It would be easy for the Community to compensate the losers from a unilateral liberalization and still realize substantial benefits.[14] From a world welfare point of view, of course, there is an even better alternative than a unilateral liberalization-cum-compensation scheme: that of a multilateral reduction of protection in agricultural markets. All existing evidence strongly suggests that moves towards freer trade that involve more, rather than fewer, trading partners would spread the benefits more uniformly. In other words, the optimal response of the losers from a unilateral liberalization is to liberalize their markets as well.[15]

Notes

1   Some of the secondary objectives of the CAP, such as improving the quality of food consumed, improving the distribution of income within the agricultural sector, protecting small family farms and preserving rural life styles and the natural environment, create the need for a different family of instruments that generally go under the name of guidance expenditure.

2   For a discussion of the partial equilibrium welfare analysis and its advantages, see Corden (1957); Corden (1971); Harberger (1959); Johnson (1960); Currie et al. (1971). For a discussion of its limitations, in particular with respect to analysing agricultural price support in the EC, see Buckwell et al. (1982); Valdes and Zietz (1980); Matthews (1985a); Wingers (1987).

3   See Tyers and Anderson, 1986 and also Tyers and Anderson, 1987a, 1987b; earlier versions of the same model are used in Anderson and Tyers, 1984, Chisholm and Tyers, 1985, and Tyers, 1985.

4   The basic structure of CGE models is discussed in detail in Whalley (1984), Whalley (1985a) ch.3 and Winters (1987). Whalley (1985b) outlines some of the methodological problems that applied general equilibrium analysis still faces.

5   The effect of domestic policies on international price stability is also analysed in Bale and Lutz (1979b), Blandford (1983) and Berck and Schmitz (1984). Koester (1982) compares alternative price support policy packages with their (de)stabilizing properties.

6   Buckwell et al. (1982) ch. 3, Bureau of Agricultural Economics (1985) ch. 6 and Whalley (1985a) ch. 3, offer a brief discussion of the problems of counterfactual equilibrium analysis.

7   Note, however, that both in the 1986 and 1987 studies the base period for the estimates was 1980-82. The results reported for 1985 are merely 'scaled up' results for 1980-82 and do not

take into account the major macroeconomic and supplu shocks which occurred between 1980 and 1985.

8 A value of 0 implies no pass through of changes in the world prices to the domestic prices; a value of 1 implies complete pass through.

9 These are the 'gross' costs of the CAP and not comparable with the 'net' costs, or deadweight losses, reported in table 1.

10 Tyers (1985) and Matthews (1985a) estimate the effects of liberalization in a multi-commodity model with and without cross-effects. In both studies the models without cross-effects produce estimates 20-100 per cent higher than the models with cross-effects. This difference is most noticeable in coarse grains, wheat and non-ruminant meat, where the removal of channels for market interaction roughly doubles the calculated effects of liberalization.

11 In line with the estimated larger price effects of liberalization. the authors report a higher loss to LDCs in their more recent study.

12 In order to assess the effects of the CAP alone the results reported by Loo and Tower (1988) could be scaled using estimates of the effects of the CAP on agricultural world market prices provided in table 3.

13 The choice of the measure is important: the standard deviation, for example, depends on the level of the mean (in this case the price level) and, therefore, even if prices remain equally stable after liberalization, the standard deviation will be different. Koester (1982), pp 53-4, discusses at length the different measures of variability. It turns out that even the coefficient of variation is not unbiased. Koester suggests correcting the coefficient of variation by the explanatory power of the trend regression to obtain a better measure of variability.

14 It is worth noting that, even by the most pessimistic estimate, the LDC losses from a unilateral liberalization in the EC are only around 70 per cent of the official development assistance actually disbursed in 1985 by the seven largest EC members, excluding Greece, Ireland and Luxembourg (in 1980 US$; see IBRD, 1986, Statistical Appendix).

15 OECD (1982) discusses the issue of multilateral liberalization in detail. There is also a large body of empirical evidence on this: Chisholm & Tyers (1985); Tyers & Anderson (1986); Whalley (1984); Whalley (1985a); IBRD (1986) and the references therein.

References

Anderson, K. and Tyers, R. (1984) 'European Community Grain and Meat Policies: Effects on International Prices, Trade and Welfare', *European Review of Agricultural Economics* (Amsterdam) 11, pp. 367-94.

Bale, M. D. and Lutz, E. (1978) *Trade Restrictions and International Price Instability,* (Washington DC: International Bank for Reconstruction and Development) Staff Working Paper No. 303.

Bale, M. D.and Lutz, E. (1979a), *Price Distortions in Agriculture and their Effects: An International Comparison*, (Washington DC: International Bank for Reconstruction and Development) Staff Working Paper No. 359.

Bale, M. D. and Lutz, E. (1979b) 'The Effects of Trade Intervention on International Price Instability', *American Journal of Agricultural Economics,* 61, 4, pp. 512-16.

Bale, M. D. and Lutz, E. (1981) 'Price Distortions in Agriculture and Their Effects: An International Comparison', *American Journal of Agricultural Economics,* 63, 1, pp. 8-22.

Berck, P. and Schmitz, A. (1984) 'Price Supports in the Context of International Trade', in C. G. Storey, A. Schmitz and A. H. Sarris, *International Agricultural Trade,* (Boulder, Colorado: Westview Press).

Blandford, D. (1983) 'Instability in World Grain Markets', *Journal of Agricultural Economics,* 34, 3, pp. 379-95.

Breckling, J., Thorpe, S. and Stoeckel, A. (1987) *Effects of EC Agricultural Policies, A General Equilibrium Approach: Initial Results* (Canberra, Australia: Bureau of Agricultural Economics and Centre for International Economics).

Buckwell, A. E., Harvey, D. R., Thompson, K.J. and Parton, K. A. (1982) *The Costs of the Common Agricultural Policy,* (London: Croom Helm).

Bureau of Agricultural Economics (1985) *Agricultural Policies in the European Community,* (Canberra, Australia: Bureau of Agricultural Economics). Policy Monograph 2.

Burniaux,J.-M. and Waelbroeck, J. (1985) 'The Impact of the CAP on Developing Countries: A General Equilibrium Analysis', in C. Stevens, and J. Verloren van Themaat, eds., *Pressure Groups, Policies and Development,* (London: Hodder & Stoughton).

Chisholm, T. and Tyers, R. (1985) 'Agricultural Protection and Market Insulation Policies: Applications of a Dynamic Multisectoral Model', in J. Piggot, and J. Whalley, eds., *New Developments in Applied General Equilibrium Analysis,* (Cambridge: Cambridge University Press).

Commission of the European Communities (1986) *The Situation on the Agricultural Markets -1986 Report* (Report from the Commission to the Council), COM(86) 700 final, (Brussels: Commission of the European Communities).

Commission of the European Communities (1987), *Proposal on the Prices for Agricultural Products and on Related Measures (1978/88),* I, March 4, (Brussels: Commission of the European Communities).

Commission des Communautés Européennes (1984) *Dépense publiques en faveur de l'agriculture.* Etude p. 229 (Brussels: Commission of the European Communities). November.

Corden, W. M. (1957) 'The Calculation of the Cost of Protection', *Economic Record,* Melbourne, 33, pp. 29-51.

Corden, W. M. (1971), *The Theory of Protection,* (Oxford: Clarendon Press).

Currie, J. M., Martin, J. A. and Schmitz, A. (1971) 'The Concept of Economic Surplus and its Use in Economic Analysis', *Economic Journal,* (London: Cambridge University Press 81, pp. 741-99)

Georgakopoulos, T. A. (1986) 'Greece in the European Communities: A View of the Economic Impact of Accession', *Royal Bank of Scotland Review* (Edinburgh) 150, pp. 29-40.

Georgakopoulos, T. A. and Paschos, P. G. (1985) 'Greek Agriculture and the CAP', *European Review of Agricultural Economics* (Amsterdam) 12, pp. 247-62.

Gerken, E., (1986) *The Determinants of European Agricultural Trade Interference* (Kiel: Kiel Institute of World Economics). Working Paper No. 254.

Harberger, A. C. (1959) 'Using the Resources at Hand More Efficiently', *American Economic Review,* (Nashville) 49, pp. 134-46.

Harling, K.F. (1983) 'Agricultural Protectionism in Developed Countries: Analysis of Systems of Intervention', *European Review of Agricultural Economics* (Amsterdam) 10, pp. 223-47.

Harling, K.F. and Thompson, R. L. (1985) 'Government Intervention in Poultry Industries: A Cross-Country Comparison', *American Journal of Agricultural Economics,* 67, 3, pp. 243-9.

Harris, S., Swinbank, A. and Wilkinson, C., (1983) *The Food and Farm Policies of the European Community* (Chichester: Wiley).

International Bank for Reconstruction and Development (1986) *World Development Report 1986* (Oxford University Press and World Bank, Washington DC).

Johnson, H. G. (1960) 'The Cost of Protection and the Scientific Tariff', *Journal of Political Economy,* (Chicago: University of Chicago Press), 68, pp. 327-45.

Josling, T. E. (1979) 'Questions for Farm Policy in an Enlarged European Community', *The World Economy,* (Washington, DC: World Bank) 2, 3, pp. 343-62.

Koester, U. (1977) 'The Redistributional Effects of the Common Agricultural Financial System', *European Review of Agricultural Economics* (Amsterdam) 4, pp. 321-45.

Koester U. (1982), *Policy Options for the Grain Economy of the European Community: Implications for Developing Countries* (Washington DC: International Food Policy Research Institute), Research Report 35.

Koester, U. (1985) 'Agricultural Market Intervention and International Trade', *European Review of Agricultural Economics* (Amsterdam) 12, pp. 87-103.

Koester, U. and Bale, M. D. (1984) *The Common Agricultural Policy of the European Community* (Washington DC: International Bank for Reconstruction and Development) Staff Working Paper No. 630.

Koester, U. and Schmitz, P. M. (1982) 'The EC Sugar Market Policy and Developing Countries', *European Review of Agricultural Economics* (Amsterdam) 9, pp. 183-204.

Koester, U. and Tangermann, S. (1986) *European Agricultural Policies and International Agriculture* (Washington DC: International Bank for Reconstruction and Development) background paper for the International Bank for Reconstruction and Development, World Development Report 1986.

Koester, U. and Valdes, A., (1984) 'Reform of the CAP — Impact on the Third World', *Food Policy,* 9, 20, pp. 94-8.

Loo, T. and Tower, E. (1988) 'Agricultural Protectionism and the Less Developed Countries: The Relationship between Agricultural Prices, Debt Servicing Capacities and the Need for Development Air' (Washington, DC) paper presented at the Conference on Agricultural Policies and the Non-farm Economy, 26-27 May.

Mackel, C., Marsh, J. and Revell, B. (1984) 'The Common Agricultural Policy', *Third World Quarterly,* 6, 1, pp. 131-46.

Matthews, A. (1985a) *The Common Agricultural Policy and the Less Developed Countries* (Dublin: Gill and Macmillan).

Matthews, A. (1985b), 'The CAP and Developing Countries: A Review of the Evidence', in C. Stevens and J. Verloren van Themaat, eds., *Pressure Groups, Policies and Development* (London: Hodder & Stoughton).

Morris, C. N. (1980) 'The Common Agricultural Policy', *Fiscal Studies,* 1, 2, pp. 15-35.

Nerlove, M. (1958) *The Dynamics of Supply: Estimation of Farmers' Response to Price,* (Baltimore: Johns Hopkins University Press).

Organization for Economic Cooperation and Development (1982) *Problems of Agricultural Trade* (Paris: OECD).

Organization for Economic Cooperation and Development (1987) *National Policies and Agricultural Trade* (Paris: OECD).

Sampson, G. P. and Yeats, A. J. (1977) 'An Evaluation of the Common Agricultural Policy as a Barrier Facing Agricultural Exports to the European Economic Community', *American Journal of Agricultural Economics*, 59, 1, pp. 99-106.

Sarris, A. H. (1983) 'European Community Enlargement and World Trade in Fruits and Vegetables', *American Journal of Agricultural Economics*, 65, 2, pp. 235-46.

Sarris, A. H. and Freebairn, J. (1983) 'Endogenous Price Policies and International Wheat Prices', *American Journal of Agricultural Economics*, 65, 2, pp. 21-24.

Scandizzo, P. and Bruce, P. (1980) *Methodologies for Measuring Agricultural Price Intervention Effects*, (Washington, DC: World Bank) Internatitonal Bank for Reconstruction and Development. Staff Working Paper No. 394.

Schmitz, P. M. and Koester, U. (1984) 'The Sugar Market Policy of the European Community and the Stability of World Market Prices for Sugar', in C. G. Storey, A. Schmitz and A. H. Sarris. *International Agricultural Trade* (Boulder, Colorado: Westview Press).

Spencer, J., (1985) 'The European Economic Community: General Equilibrium Computations and the Economic Implications of Membership', in J. Piggot and J. Whalley, eds. *New Developments in Applied General Equilibrium Analysis* (Cambridge: Cambridge University Press) .

Spencer, J. (1986) 'Trade Liberalization through Tariff Cuts and the European Economic Community: A General Equilibrium Evaluation, in T. N. Srinivasan and J. Whalley, eds., *General Equilibrium Trade Policy Modeling,* (Cambridge, MA: MIT Press).

Stoeckel, A. and Breckling, J. (1988) 'Some Economy-wide Effects of Agricultural Policies in the European Community: A General Equilibrium Study', paper presented at the Conference on Agricultural Policies and the Non-farm Economy (Washington, DC) 26-27 May.

Svedberg, P. (1981) 'EEC Variable Import Levies and the Stability of International Grain Markets', *Indian Journal of Agricultural Economics* (Bombay) 36, 1, pp. 58-66.

Tangermann, S. (1978) 'Agricultural Trade Relations between the EC and Temperate Food Exporting Countries', *European Review of Agricultural Economics* (Amsterdam) 5, pp. 201-19

Tangermann, S. (1981) 'Policies of European Community and Agricultural Trade with Developing Countries', in G. Johnson and A, Maunder, eds., *Rural Change, Proceedings of the Seventeenth International Conference of Agricultural Economists* (Aldershot: Gower).

Thomson, K. J. and Harvey, D. R. (1981) 'The Efficiency of the Common Agricultural Policy', *European Review of Agricultural Economics* (Amsterdam) 8, pp. 57-83

Traill, B., (1982) 'The Effect of Price Support Policies on Agricultural Investment, Employment, Farm Incomes and Land Values in the U. K.', *Journal of Agricultural Economics* 33, 3, pp. 369-85.

Tyers, R. (1985) 'International Impacts of Protection: Model Structure and Results for EC Agricultural Policy', *Journal of Policy Modeling* 7, 2, pp. 219-52.

Tyers, R. and Anderson, K. (1986) *Distortions in World Food Markets: A Quantitative Assessment* background paper for the World Bank World Development Report 1986, (Washington DC: World Bank).

Tyers, R. and Anderson, K. (1987a) *Liberalizing OECD Agricultural Policies in the Uruguay Round: Effects on Trade and Welfare* (Canberra: Australian National University) Working Paper in Trade and Development No. 87/10.

Tyers, R. and Anderson, K. (1987b), 'Global Interactions and Trade Liberalization in Agriculture', *Economic Policies and World Agriculture*.

Valdes, A. and Zietz, J. (1980) *Agricultural Protection in OECD Countries: Its Cost to Less-Developed Countries* (Washington, DC: International Food Policy Research Institute) Research Report 21.

Whalley, J. (1984) 'The North-South Debate and the Terms of Trade: An Applied General Equilibrium Approach', *Review of Economics and Statistics* (Amsterdam) 66, pp. 224-34.

Whalley, J. (1985a) *Trade Liberalization Among Major World Trading Areas* (Cambridge, MA: MIT Press).

Whalley, J. (1985b), 'Hidden Challenges in Recent Applied General Equilibrium Exercises', in J. Piggot and J. Whalley, eds., *New Developments in Applied General Equilibrium Analysis* (Cambridge: Cambridge University Press).

Winters, A., (1987) 'The Economic Consequences of Agricultural Support: a Survey', *OECD Economic Studies*, 9, pp. 7-54.

Witzke, H., von (1986) 'Endogenous Supranational Policy Decisions: The Common Agricultural Policy of the European Community', *Public Choice*, 48, pp. 157-74.

3. Competition and Industrial Policies with Emphasis on Industrial Policy

V. Curzon Price

This chapter will be divided into four main sections. The first will address definitional problems. The second will discuss the intellectual foundations for industrial policy. The third will review the development of industrial policy in the European Community, from the early 1970s to this day. The fourth will attempt to evaluate this historical and current experience in the light of what might be termed the 'theory' of industrial policy presented in the second section.

1. What is industrial policy?

Professors Bayliss and El-Agraa, authors of the previous chapter, on 'Competition and industrial policy', define industrial policy thus: 'Industrial policy embraces all acts and policies of the state in relation to industry', adding that it can be either positive (to the extent that the state wishes to influence industry) or negative (to the extent that it might be the industrial policy of the state to *minimise* intervention in industry) — see El-Agraa (1992: 137-155).

This, it seems to me, is an excellent starting point for our discussion. It shows, for instance, what a very broad spectrum of state acts (or non-acts) can be covered by the term 'industrial policy'. Indeed, the ground covered implicitly by such a definition is so extensive that a whole book would be insufficient to do it justice, let alone a mere chapter. Our immediate task, therefore, is to reduce 'industrial policy' to manageable proportions.

As much of what follows will be concerned with state intervention in industry, and indeed that is what is usually understood by industrial policy, we shall reserve the terms 'positive' and 'negative' for (infrequently) qualifying such interventions, and use words like 'market-oriented' or 'non-interventionist' to describe the policy of minimising attempts by the state to affect industry. Thus, while conceding the point made by Bayliss and El-Agraa, we shall in this chapter narrow the sense of the term 'industrial policy' to cover only proactive state policies.

Another way to reduce the field to manageable proportions is to look at the level of generality of the policy under discussion. Thus, while it is true that the rate of interest affects investment, hence industry, few people would hold that monetary policy is a subset of industrial policy. The same would hold for social policy, or environmental policy, or even regional policy (in its purest form). These broad, general policies, as long as they do not discriminate explicitly between industries, do not affect the allocation of resources between industries *as their primary purpose*. That they may well affect inter-industrial allocation as a secondary result is obvious: thus capital-intensive

V. Curzon Price: 'Competition and Industrial Policies with Emphasis on Industrial Policy' from *ECONOMICS OF THE EUROPEAN COMMUNITY* (3rd edition), edited by AM El-Agraa (Philip Allan, 1990). pp. 159-186.

operations will be more penalised by a tight monetary policy than labour-intensive ones; or polluting industries will be more affected by stiff anti-pollution norms than 'clean' business activities. But the general legal or policy framework is established to fulfil a particular purpose, and the pattern of industrial allocation falls into place behind it — in principle without the need for central direction.

We therefore propose to limit the term 'industrial policy' to mean any state measure designed primarily to affect the allocation of resources *between* economic activities, in other words, to impose a new direction on pure market structures. For instance, any public policy to support the steel or clothing industry, whatever the form of the support, would qualify as 'industrial policy' under this definition, since resources would be encouraged to stay on in these sectors despite market signals to the contrary. Similarly, any public policy to support, say, aeronautics, telecommunications, electronics and so forth (usually known as 'high-tech' activities) would also qualify as 'industrial policy' since, by implication, more resources would be drawn into these sectors than would be the case without the policy — and, indeed, that would be its exact purpose. One might wish to use terms such as 'forward looking' and 'backward looking', or 'positive' or 'negative' (or, if one were writing for the press, 'sunrise' and 'sunset') policies to qualify these two examples; but the main point to remember is that both of them aim to affect the allocation of resources between sectors, whether broadly or narrowly defined.

It is also worth noting that in both the examples just given, the aim of the policy is to *encourage* the 'target' activity — whatever one might think about its future prospects. In fact, there are very few examples of state intervention to explicitly penalise or run down an industry, although of course, any action to promote a particular economic activity implicitly discourages all other non-aided activities. This is no accident. The Prince, after all, wants to be loved and is most unlikely to want to make enemies by obviously selecting the victims of his policies. He will far prefer to make friends by selecting the beneficiaries. But, in principle, the term 'industrial policy', to be logically consistent, would have to cover any action by the state to help *or penalise* any particular economic activity relative to any other.

In addition, although this widens our field of investigation, I would argue that agricultural policy is a subset of industrial policy because it affects the allocation of resources between identifiable categories of business activities. The term 'industrial' is in fact retained only because it has entered into common usage: it would be much clearer if one called what we are talking about 'resource allocation policy' — a precise but unlovely term. But it goes without saving that a policy to help or hinder certain service activities, for instance, would also qualify as an 'industrial policy'. In fact, the conventional threefold division of the economy into agricultural, industrial and service activities is a statistical artefact, with no satisfactory *economic* definition of any of these three types of economic activity.

There are some borderline cases in deciding on what to include, or not, in our definition of industrial policy. For instance, competition policy (known in the United States as anti-trust policy) — see El-Agraa (1992: 137-155) — could perhaps be included. It attempts to affect the internal structure of industries by controlling mergers, joint ventures and minority acquisitions and by attempting to prevent cartels. In principle, since its main purpose is to promote competition rather than to affect the intersectoral allocation of resources, it falls outside our definition. However, to the extent that the authorities wielding the weapon of competition policy possess a certain amount of discretion, they may well practise an implicit industrial policy. For instance, they may close their eyes to a 'restructuring' cartel in the chemical industry, or, alternatively, pick on a large foreign multinational for close investigation. Either of these options would affect the allocation of national resources between sectors. Similarly, anti-dumping regulations would not normally fit our definition of industrial policy, because their main purpose is to promote 'fair' competition in *all* sectors exposed to the dangers of international competition. Since there is no reason to believe that dumping would affect some industries more than others, the sectors coming under anti-dumping investigation would tend to be purely random. If, however, there is an abnormal concentration of anti-dumping cases in, say, the textile or electronic sectors, one might begin to wonder whether an implicit industrial policy is not at work.

Another form of borderline case exists at the level of generality of the policy. Earlier, I suggested that agricultural policy was a form of industrial policy, which implies that some very general policies might qualify. Although this is purely a matter of taste, I would argue in favour of reserving for 'industrial policy' only truly microeconomic policies. And there is, incidentally, no problem when it comes to agricultural policy because if one looks carefully at what it actually does, one sees clearly that different segments are treated very differently — see El-Agraa (1992: 187-217).

It is clear that industrial policy also includes state action to discriminate between economic actors *within* a given sector (micro-microeconomic policy), as for instance happens when one motor car manufacturer gets a huge subsidy in the form of a write-off of accumulated debt, while competitors get nothing. This kind of favouritism, however, is hard to justify on any grounds save those of straightforward political expediency, which may make it hard for it to qualify for the term 'policy'. Other policies, such as regional policy, employment policy or social policy may have to be called in to help.

A brief word is needed on the *instruments* industrial policy. The favoured instruments of state intervention, whether forward or backward looking, are subsidies and protection from foreign competition. Both instruments are easy to aim at the desired target — the sector selected for preferential treatment. There is much overlap between these two, and it is not even very clear whether the distinction can be maintained at all. For instance, a public procurement policy to 'buy national' at twice the price and half the quality of a foreign competitor is *both* a form of hidden subsidy *and* a clear non-tariff barrier against foreign competition. Also, any protective barrier, whether tariff or non-tariff in nature, against foreign competition permits local firms to raise their prices, which means that they enjoy a hidden subsidy which does not even transit through government coffers, but is transferred directly to producers from consumers. This makes the point that both protection and subsidisation can take many forms: what one is looking for is evidence that the policy instrument, explicitly or implicitly, discriminates between sectors, or between firms within a sector.

On the question of whether direct or indirect (i.e. tariff) subsidisation is to be preferred, trade theorists of the 1960s and 1970s came out clearly in favour of direct subsidies, arguing that tariffs caused distortions on the consumer side of the equation, which direct subsidies avoided. After practical experience of widespread subsidisation of industry from the mid-1970s to the mid-1980s in Western Europe, and observing the sheer ingenuity of governments in covering their tracks, the advantages of subsidies over tariffs are today much less obvious.

It is worth noting that both the policy instruments just described are *indirect*. They are aimed by the state at private industry in order to modify the market's allocation of resources. But of course there is a continuum here too, running from the most 'market-friendly' instruments (those operating through the price mechanism) to the most heavy-handed (operating through the use of permits, licences and open state pressure to do this or that). At the end of this spectrum lies outright nationalisation and/or state planning of the economy. In this chapter we shall be limiting ourselves to industrial policy in a market economy.

2. Industrial policy: for and against

Historically speaking, economists have devoted a great deal of thought to the theme of international trade and were inevitably led to ask why nations practised discriminatory protection, thus favouring some industries and penalising others. Most if not all the work to date on why governments practise industrial policy has therefore in fact already been done by the trade theorists. It just needs transposing to the slightly broader framework implied by 'industrial policy' as opposed to 'trade policy' (for instance by including non-traded goods and services in the analysis), and shedding some (but not all) of its expressly mercantilist overtones.

Since this is a very well-charted area, I shall do no more than list the traditional reasons advanced for protection which are relevant to the industrial policy debate, referring the reader to any number of excellent texts or more detailed analyses of the pros and cons — see *inter alia,* Corden (1965; 1971), Hindley (1974), Johnson (1971), Kreinin (1979) and *Oxford Review of Economic Policy* (1987); a comprehensive review is provided in El-Agraa (1989). This will allow us to concentrate on two new theoretical developments of greater relevance to the contemporary discussion on industrial policy: the 'new trade theory' on the one hand, and the theory of rent seeking and public choice on the other.

Traditional arguments for state intervention in industry can be divided into three broad categories: there are respectable economic arguments (1-5); false economic arguments (6 and 7); and non-economic arguments (8 and 9).

2.1 Market failure

A case for government action can be made whenever an instance of market failure can be spotted. Two problems nevertheless remain. First, instances of market failure can usually be traced to some kind of previous public policy (a wage rigidity here, a capital market imperfection there), in which case one is not confronted with a genuine *market* failure, but rather a policy-induced *domestic distortion* (see next point); secondly, government action is not costless (see below), which implies that it may be better to live with market imperfections than to attempt to circumvent them with government intervention.

2.2 Domestic distortions

In a second best world of political and social constraints, with numerous public policies affecting every aspect of economic life, we are certainly far removed from the welfare optimum described by Pareto. In these circumstances reducing or eliminating government intervention in one segment of the economy might increase the total quantum of distortion in the entire economy and thus reduce welfare. Take, for instance, a reasonably uniform VAT system, covering all goods and services. This is in itself a source of inefficiency, since it places a barrier between producers and consumers. We then decide to eliminate this barrier for one set of goods — say children's clothes. This brings about a distortion in resource allocation which could well be worse than the initial distortion caused by the uniform VAT system. One cannot tell in advance and must let common sense (illuminated by standard economic theory) guide us. Applied to the question of industrial policy, one could, for example, argue that domestic distortions arising from tax and institutional structures are such that industry, collectively, fails to invest enough in research and development. Rather than unravel the whole complex of measures causing this failure, it might be more practical simply to find ways of subsidising extra investment of R&D (always remembering, however, that every government policy has its cost).

2.3 Infant industries

This is by far the oldest and most popular of the (economic) arguments for subsidisation and/or protection. Even in its traditional formulation, it appeals to such concepts as economies of scale and positive externalities. Thus, it asserts that an industry below optimum size will not generate around itself the necessary physical infrastructure, intellectual and managerial resources, network of suppliers and subcontractors, financing capabilities, etc., and will therefore operate indefinitely above its potential long-run average cost curve. An initial subsidy, on the other hand, could allow it to achieve the 'critical' size and thus bridge the gap with its world-scale competitors, after which subsidies would no longer be needed.

Essentially, this is an argument about obtuse capital markets, which cannot see the potential for such a profitable business, refuse to lend the money to achieve the optimum scale and make it necessary for the government to step in (i.e. it is a particular instance of the market-failure/domestic distortion argument above — see El-Agraa (1983; 1984; 1989).

That this notion has validity may be inferred from the example of Japan and other East Asian countries, which have succeeded in creating efficient world-scale industries with the help of protection, government guidance and various forms of subsidisation — in other words, industrial policy. One should, however, resist jumping to the conclusion that the Japanese example 'proves' that industrial policy works: it is impossible to say how the Japanese economy would have evolved without state intervention — it might, after all, have grown even quicker. More tellingly, even if industrial policies *have* helped Japan, South Korea and Taiwan to grow more quickly than market forces alone would have achieved, it is still not clear that industrial policies will always help a country to develop. In fact, the risk of failure is at least as high as in any normal business venture, and probably much higher.

The pitfalls are all too easy to spot. How does one select the industries to be promoted (the so-called 'specification problem')? How does one wean them from support once they have grown up? How does one stop the process of selection from becoming politicised? The economic landscape is littered with examples of infant industries which have never fulfilled their promise. It is easy to 'target' this or that economic sector for special treatment — but it is difficult to make money in competitive world markets. And this is the acid test of whether or not the infant has 'grown up' — see El-Agraa (1983; 1984; 1989).

2.4 Positive externalities

The infant industry argument for state intervention can be buttressed by an appeal to positive externalities, that is, inappropriate returns (i.e. benefits to the economy at large for which the firm producing them cannot make us pay). Thus it may be argued that support for, say the aeronautical industry will generate a large pool of skilled engineers to which other industrial sectors will also have access — because they cannot be indentured exclusively to the aeronautical industry. In these circumstances, one could argue in favour of supporting the aeronautical industry, even if it operated at a loss. because of the indirect benefits accruing to employers of engineers in the rest of the economy. Left to its own devices, the aeronautical industry would not reach the 'right' size because the whole cost of training specialised engineers could not be recovered, since some benefit would accrue to firms which had not spent a penny on training and could not be forced to contribute.

The Apollo space programme is often credited with having generated many industrial spin-off benefits, especially in the field of electronics and miniaturisation. Countless firms (and not just American ones) sprang up to take advantage of licensed technology at a fraction of the cost of developing it for themselves. Before jumping to the conclusion that we should all rush off and support a man-to-Mars programme, however, it must be remembered that if the positive externalities could be spotted in advance, the market would finance them (the engineers would borrow to study, the technicians would borrow to do the research and take out patents). In reality, positive externalities are rare. Either they have been spotted, and then it is worth something to someone to appropriate them, or they have yet to be discovered, and we are back to the old problem of how to select the economic sector which will generate the best externalities (the 'specification problem'). At the frontiers of knowledge (and this is where we often are in the externalities debate) it is very difficult to avoid costly mistakes.

2.5 Public goods

This argument states that people derive pleasure from the knowledge that their country is active in some 'strategic' branches of industry. Since this pleasure adds to national welfare, but cannot be appropriated by the producer of, say, cars, or ships, or steel, state intervention in support of the desired activities is justified, even if they operate at a loss. Since there is no way of measuring the intensity of this pleasure, or even of ascertaining that it really exists at all, this argument needs to be treated with caution. It will most often be found in the policy statements of important lobbies, which can be relied upon to argue that their industry is 'strategic' and its continued good health in the national interest. In fact, this argument comes very close to belonging to the next group of justifications for industrial policy.

In this and previous arguments in favour of state intervention, a common theme is that there is a hierarchy of economic activities which anyone of reasonable intelligence can establish, but which the market refuses to endorse because it is too concerned with short-term profits, or even with profits *tout court*. Yet very few economists would agree that such a hierarchy in fact exists, the only hierarchy worth retaining being that which measures the efficiency of a particular allocation of resources in terms of its ability to cover its costs and attract new resources into the business, i.e. profits. Economists tend to argue that today's pattern of profits (or lack thereof) are reliable *signals* for the future allocation of resources and while not necessarily rejecting arguments for active state intervention, challenge its proponents to provide a better system of establishing a hierarchy of economic activities. Since it is logically impossible to subsidise all activities at once choices have to be made and hierarchies established.

2.6 Employment

Subsidisation of declining industries in order to prevent unemployment is one of the least respectable arguments for state intervention but one of the most frequently used in practice (but not always admitted to). In terms of straightforward general-equilibrium economics, it is simply wrong to argue that a subsidy can reduce unemployment. The subsidy has to come from somewhere, and the non-subsidised sectors of the economy 'pay' (in terms of lost investment opportunities, fewer new jobs, lost market share and higher taxes) for every job 'saved' in the subsidised areas. And there is a strong presumption that the jobs 'saved' in the declining sectors will be less numerous, will pay less well and will have a dimmer future than those lost in the non-subsidised sectors.

Sheer political expediency and the fact that the jobs at risk in the stricken industries were highly visible, often regionally concentrated and industrially focused, explain why governments in Western Europe resorted to numerous bail-outs from 1975-85. But wholesale subsidisation of loss-making industries in the end shocked the voting and working public, who did not need general-equilibrium theories to see that this was make-believe economics and the worst abuses were gradually reversed — see El-Agraa (1984).

2.7 Balance of payments

The public has been taught to worry about the balance of payments, so mercantilistic arguments in favour of reducing imports and/or increasing exports always get a good hearing. Import substitution used to be considered a sensible guide for industrial policy, since it not only resolved the specification problem (one just had to run one's eye down the list of imports and select those products on which much foreign exchange was spent and which also looked easy to make) but, as an added bonus, it 'helped' the balance of payments. Practical application of these notions has since discredited them completely, not least because *import substitution does not 'improve' the balance of payments*. Again, reference to a general-equilibrium framework of analysis will quickly confirm that resources drawn into import substitution have to come from somewhere, and if the aim of the government is really to reduce imports, then they will come from the export sector, and exports will fall by at least as much as imports. Export promotion, if carefully managed, might prove a sounder policy, not for balance of payments reasons, but as a general method of enlarging the traded-goods sector if it is deemed 'too small' (see the second best argument above).

Mercantilist arguments take many forms, among the most prevalent at present being calls for sectoral reciprocity. Thus the European automobile industry argues that it is willing to face (fairly) free competition from Japanese cars on condition Japan opens its own markets to European automobiles. Since Japan, in its eyes, remains protectionist, restrictions on Japanese automobiles are justified. On the face of it, nothing sounds more reasonable. But such bilateral/sectoral arguments are unfounded in both fact and theory; here is not the place to expand on this theme — on the threat to multinational trade of 'strict' reciprocity, see Curzon and Curzon Price (1989).

Balance of payments and employment arguments together form an unbeatable combination, as in the furious 'local content' debate over the definition of what is a 'European' and what a 'Japanese' automobile. In fact, both are pseudo-economic arguments masking special pleading by powerful interest groups (see below).

2.8 National defence

This is the most noble of the non-economic justifications for industrial policy, but we know that as an argument it is frequently abused. In principle, the problem of specifying *what* should be produced, by *whom, how* and *for whom* (the 'specification problem' referred to above) is resolved politically, since the state and the military are delegated to make the necessary choices for us. But as there is no market for national defence, what is 'essential' is largely a matter of opinion, varies over time and runs the danger of becoming politicised. Note, however, that the argument is not based on the 'public goods' nature of defence (see 2.5) but on a perceived need for a degree of self-sufficiency. In an increasingly interdependent world economy, the plausibility of the national defence argument is reduced daily.

2.9 Other non-economic objectives

Besides defence, many other socio-political objectives may be pursued via industrial policy: for example, regional development, income redistribution, environmental protection, zoning (land-use) policies and even, perhaps, something as hard to specify as 'European unity'. While economics is of no use in judging whether these *ends* are valid or not (these being collective value judgements, to be decided upon by the political process) economic analysis can be applied to the *means*. Generally speaking, the shortest and most direct route is to be favoured: if raising incomes in poorer regions is the *end*, the best *means* would be a cheque through the post. Landing a poor region like Calabria with a loss-making steel mill is not necessarily a kindness in the long run. Making European industry (or agriculture for that matter) bear the burden of European political integration is also hard on industry and not necessarily good for 'Europe'.

3. The 'new trade theory' and its relevance to industrial policy

The 'new trade theory' was developed in the 1980s in response to the observed fact that two-thirds of world trade took place between developed countries and that most of this was of an 'intra-industry' nature. From this observation flowed a series of hypotheses explaining trade flows on the basis of imperfect competition; duopolistic competition (Brander 1981); oligopolistic competition (Brander and Spencer 1984); monopolistic competition (Helpman 1981 and Lancaster 1980); and declining marginal costs (Krugman 1979; 1983). The policy implications of this new approach were to add a *strategic* dimension to the economic case for state intervention in industry.

In a world where technology is paramount and very costly to produce, dynamic economies of scale (learning-curve effects) may determine where a particular economic activity is located, rather than traditional factor endowments. Comparative advantage becomes man made, hence subject to policy. The case of Japan is frequently cited: for example, microprocessors having been identified in the early 1980s as 'strategic', government direction under MITI (Ministry of Trade and Industry) did the rest, not so much by making large funds available to firms in the industry, but by a specifically Japanese combination of consensus and emulation. The point is that the 'first mover' has an advantage, since he is the first to travel down the learning curve, which is related to *accumulated* experience. Also, the larger his initial market, the faster he will travel down the learning curve, since sheer repetition is also important. Time and market size are therefore of the essence and will allow the 'first mover' to reap monopoly rents, which in turn will allow him to invest in the next cycle of technological innovation and so on.

It is easy to see that we have here a good case for state intervention in either of two cases:

1. If one can spot a strategic new industry for the future, possessing the above characteristics, one should seriously consider supporting it, in order to gain 'first mover' advantages.

2. If others have developed a man-made comparative advantage in an industry and are enjoying monopoly rents, another state might be able to share those rents if it developed its own industry in competition. At the very least, it could ensure, through competition, that the 'prime mover' shared his lower unit costs arising from the learning-curve effect.

Case 1 suffers from the specification problem already outlined: it is not that easy to foretell the future and as Kierzkowski (1987) warns: 'New industrial .. policy towards "strategic" industries would involve many policy misses, just like betting on horses'. Case 2 is altogether more attractive. It proposes, in essence, to speed up the Schumpeterian process of creative destruction, spreading the benefits of technological innovation throughout the world in the form of lower prices and lower monopoly rents. The example most frequently cited is that of the European Airbus, which exists only thanks to subsidies, but which presumably has held down the price of Boeings and DC-10s.

4. Problems with the new strategic industrial policy

We shall select two which strike us as being particularly noteworthy.

4.1 A typical prisoner's dilemma

When discussing strategic industrial policy, we are cumulating two levels of imperfect competition: firstly, the industry itself possesses the attributes of imperfect competition: economies of scale, tendency towards monopoly or at least oligopoly, etc.; secondly, state intervention is proposed not, as is customary, to limit the negative effects of imperfect competition via anti-trust legislation, but to actively promote a rival monopoly *because it is reacting to a monopoly in another country.* In fact, implicit in the whole discussion is the idea that if state industrial policy produces home country monopoly that is fine. Rivalry therefore takes the form of competition between different countries' industrial policies and the final outcome may be negative for all players.

A good parallel can be found in the world of sport. If A takes anabolic steroids, and her rivals do not, she is bound to win. If her rivals take anabolic steroids and she does not, she is bound to lose. So everybody takes them, the race is as indeterminate as ever, but everybody's health is impaired.

In the world of strategic industrial policy, if all major players consider that telecommunications are 'strategic', the world as a whole may end up investing far too much in this particular activity and duplicating efforts uselessly. If there is a case to be made for strategic industrial policy in terms of consumer welfare (scale economies, lower average unit costs, etc.), then it is more a case for *global* industrial policy at an international level, than for national industrial policy at a local level.

4.2 The problem of rent seeking

The case for state intervention has not been the same since 1967, when Tullock (1967) took a new look at the economics of rents derived from the artificial scarcity caused by tariffs, and suggested that entrepreneurs might compete for them as enthusiastically as they searched for other (more productive) ways of making profits. This apparently simple alternative approach opened up a broad new avenue for economic investigation. Until then, economists had treated transfers between members of the same community as 'neutral' or, if they worried about the distribution effects of tariffs, they did so in terms of the illegitimacy of using community indifference curves to assess 'national' welfare, both of which were effective conversation stoppers.

Tullock's approach, on the other hand, suggested that economic agents had an incentive to waste resources lobbying the state for artificial scarcity rents. These rents could therefore no longer be considered 'neutral', since part of them — and under certain constrained circumstances *all* of them — would be 'dissipated' by the competing rent seekers. In short, this constituted a substantial hidden cost of state intervention — see *inter alia,* Kreuger (1974).

Rent seeking is part of normal profit-seeking entrepreneurial behaviour; it becomes wasteful only when phoney, state-contrived rents are being competed for, and it is in this sense that the term is generally used (and will be used here). Rent seeking can take many forms: lobbying for tariff or non-tariff protection from import competition is a subtle form, usually well-accepted by the general public, especially if presented as being in the national interest (see above). Lobbying for outright subsidies, or a tax break, is rather more obvious and needs a stronger case (perhaps in terms of 'strategic' industrial policy, or a good non-economic objective like employment — see the case of steel discussed below). Obtaining the right to speak to one's direct competitors (something normally frowned upon under most anti-trust laws) can prove to be a well-disguised source of rent. Finally, a good domestic regulation, properly inspired by the industry which the regulation is supposed to constrain, can become a powerful barrier to entry, thus ensuring a permanent flow of rents to the established members of the group: see *inter alia*, Stigler (1971) and El-Agraa (1989).

All this puts microeconomic state intervention in the economy in a new, rather cynical, light. At the very least, every state intervention must be evaluated for:

1. The open and hidden rents that it generates.
2. The private resources wastefully devoted to obtaining them.
3. The incentive that they provide to other economic agents to waste another round of resources in order to obtain similiar rents for themselves.

5. Conclusion

If any general conclusion is to be drawn from this brief summary of the intellectual case for state intervention in the economy it is this: it is not enough to demonstrate market failure to justify government action. The direct and indirect costs of government action may be far greater than the original market imperfection. This is not to say that no industrial policy is the best policy, but to make a plea for very close scrutiny of what is advanced under this banner.

6. Industrial policy in the EC

6.1 *The early years*

The Treaty of Rome does not provide for a 'Common Industrial Policy' in the same way as it provides, for instance, for a Common Agricultural Policy, a Common Transport Policy and a Common Social Policy. It does not even provide for a 'Common Regional Policy'. This is no accident. Common policies were necessary between the member nations only in sectors where extensive state intervention by all members made it necessary to avoid wholesale distortions and policy wars. Where these loomed, the founding fathers elevated the problem to Community level and a 'common' policy was born. Where potential problems could be covered up (transport) or where state intervention was sporadic, individualistic or insignificant, there was no need for a common policy.

Articles 92-94 (aids granted by states) were deemed to be sufficient to cope with such problems, and gave the Commission powers of supervision to ensure that state aids did not distort competitive conditions. It was, however, some time before the Commission developed these powers into a 'policy' (see below), since the role of gendarme was not an easy one to assume when the miscreants were member states. And even then the policy was still only one of supervision and control. The Commission had to wait until the 1980s for a proactive industrial policy with a budget to match.

Nevertheless, in one area state intervention was already extensive in the 1960s and threatened the stability of the nascent common market: the regional aid policies of various member states. To persuade member states to agree on guidelines for regional aid was therefore a first priority. The process started in 1968 and by 1971 the Council of Ministers agreed to a series of rules which defined:

1. The difference between 'central' and 'peripheral' regions.
2. The establishment of aid 'ceilings' depending on the classification of the region.
3. Methods of ensuring the transparency of aids.
4. *Ex post* notification of regional aids to the Commission, which was then entrusted with their evaluation in the light of the preceding guidelines — see EC Commission (1972).

The first of the Community's 'common policies' not based specifically on the Treaty of Rome was born.

On the whole, however, the 1960s and early 1970s were good years and there was little excuse for state intervention: the only sectors in trouble (if the Commission's *First Report on Competition Policy* is any indication) were shipbuilding, textiles and films, and the Commission limited itself to exhortations to keep national aids within rather vague 'guidelines'. General aid schemes to promote investment and new industries were generally approved of and dowries for industrial weddings in the French electronics industry (Machines Bull and CII) were agreed to without difficulty.

In fact, in the 1960s and early 1970s the term 'industrial policy' was either not in use at all or subsumed under the generic term 'completion of the internal market' (see, for instance, Toulemon 1972) and considered to include the elimination of non-tariff barriers, the reduction of discrimination in government purchasing and the creation of a harmonised legal, fiscal and financial environment for European industry. In a word, industrial policy took the form of an *absence* or reduction of state intervention. True, it was felt that a Community science and research programme would be sensible; but the lack of cooperation on nuclear energy in the Euratom framework had proved disappointing — and the Commission had been told in no uncertain terms by General de Gaulle in 1965 not to overstep its limits.

6.2 The 1970s

By contrast, the 1970s and early 1980s saw interesting developments on several fronts. The Community matured, increased its membership, but above all experienced several years of unprecedented recession, industrial restructuring, high rates of unemployment and inflation, and low growth. Member states found that their traditional methods of macroeconomic demand management were useless in these circumstances: if they fought inflation with restrictive policies, unemployment figures deteriorated, while if they tried to combat unemployment with expansionary policies, inflation took off. They reacted with a ragbag of microeconomic measures: wage 'policies' (i.e. controls, price controls, credit controls, import controls — anything which might appear to manage the situation, however briefly — none of which worked. Firms continued to fail, unemployment continued to rise. Finally, wholesale direct subsidisation of loss-making industries became the only answer. For this most member states did not have to set up new machinery — they just used pre-existing general aid schemes, increased the funds available and extended their scope.

This was extremely dangerous for the future of the EC. Not only had the internal market not been completed by the mid-1970s, but what had been achieved was now under direct threat from the fatal combination of reinforced non-tariff protection between member states (frequently based on technical barriers) and subsidisation. To begin with the Commission did not appreciate the extent of the danger:

> [It] concluded that Member States, in an attempt to protect employment, were justified in boosting investment by granting firms financial benefits (in the form of tax deductions or low-interest loans) on an automatic or quasi-general basis for a limited period. Similarly, it agreed to financial aid being granted to ensure the survival of firms which have run into difficulties, thereby avoiding redundancies. (EC Commission, 1976, para. 133)

Thus plain operating subsidies were permitted to safeguard employment, subject to two criteria: that capacity should not be increased and that subsidies should 'benefit firms which are basically sound' (EC Commission 1976, para. 134). The logical inconsistency of this last criterion was quite lost on the Commission. It was obviously confident that it could, without difficulty, distinguish between sound and unsound firms. In fact, the market normally does this quite simply: if firms are 'basically sound' then they can raise money in the market; if they need subsidies because they have failed to find lenders. then the market has judged them unsound. In the event, the Commission would inevitably be approving aids to unsound firms, no matter how the definition was stretched and twisted — unless, of course, it invented its own (non-market) definition of 'soundness'.

On the enforcement front, member states agreed to prior notification of all general aid schemes and to concurrent or *ex post* notification 'of the more important specific cases where aid is granted'.

The list of sectors 'in difficulty', which until then had been limited essentially to shipbuilding and textiles, expanded to include motor cars, paper and board, machine tools, steel, synthetic fibres, clocks and watches and chemicals. The number of subsidy schemes notified to the Commission rose from a mere handful in the early 1970s to well over a hundred a year at the end of the decade (see Table 1). The race for subsidisation was in full swing.

Finally waking up to the danger, the Commission and Council in April 1978 decided to take a less lenient view of subsidies to preserve employment (EC Commission 1979, 173-4), putting more emphasis on the 'need to restore competitiveness' and to face up to worldwide competition'. The change in policy emerges quite clearly from Table 1, which lists the number of 'positions' taken by the Commission on state subsidies, dividing them into those to which no objection was raised — and the others. The rate of 'objections' (column 6) fell from about one-third in the early 1970s to a mere 12-14 per cent in 1977-9, but rose again to over 40 per cent thereafter. The number of 'final negative decisions' (where member states were told to withdraw the subsidy scheme altogether) was negligible throughout the 1970s (although the cases reviewed increased substantially), but rose significantly in the 1980s.

Table 1
Accumulated data on state subsidies 1970-87[a]

1	2	3	4	5	6
				Of which	Objections/
	Total	No		final negative	no objections
Year	positions	objection	Objection	decision	(col. 4/col. 3)
1970	21	15	6	1	0.29
1971	18	11	7	3	0.39
1972	35	24	11	3	0.31
1973	22	15	7	4	0.32
1974	35	20	15	—	0.43
1975	45	29	16	2	0.35
1976	47	33	14	2	0.30
1977	112	99	13	1	0.12
1978	137	118	19	—	0.14
1979	133	79	54	3	0.14
1980	105	72	33	2	0.31
1981	141	79	62	14	0.43
1982	233	104	129	13	0.55
1983	195	101	94	21	0.48
1984	314	201	113	21	0.36
1985	178	102	76	7	0.43
1986	181	98	83	10	0.46
1987*	274	205	69	10	0.25

Note
a According to the *17th Report on Competition Policy*, 'The increase in the total number of notifications (in 1987) is not considered to represent any significant change in the trend of the total value of State aids granted in Member States. It reflects the increasing efficiency of Commission policy in controlling such aids' (para. 174).

Source: EC Commission, *Reports on Competition Policy*, various years.

The final test of the effectiveness of the Commission in containing the subsidy crisis, and the willingness of the member states to submit to common guidelines is whether the Commission can force the member states to recover subsidies granted illegally. This has been ordered in 22 cases (see Table 2), of which have been subject to appeals to the European Court of Justice.

Table 2
Repayment of subsidies ordered by the Commission (cumulative data up to 1987).

	Cases	Amounts involved (million ECU)
Belgium	10	300
France	5	565
W. Germany	4	14
Netherlands	2	118
United Kingdom	1	2

Source: EC Commission (1986) *Seventeenth Report on Competition Policy*, para. 173, Brussels and Luxemburg.

Steel

Steel became a special case partly because the crisis in this sector proved both excessively deep and widespread (major steel producers in the Community lost some $3 billion in 1977 and the same again in 1978; at a time when a ton of raw steel cost about $250, firms like Sacilor and BSC were losing between $46 and $78 per ton — see *Financial Times,* 5 July 1978), and partly because Community policy was governed by the Treaty of Paris which, by some embarrassing oversight, prohibited specific state subsidies to steel firms without any possibility of derogation (Article 67).

Viscount Etienne Davignon, then EC Commissioner for Industrial Affairs, after consultation with the main firms in the industry, set up a stream of 'voluntary' quotas and 'guideline' prices in May 1977 in accordance with Article 57 of the Treaty of Paris (the qualifying adjectives were necessary because Article 65 of the Treaty of Paris, like Article 67, did not permit agreements between firms, in particular those which fixed prices and/or restricted production).

This first attempt to manage the steel sector in the EC did not prove successful because imports disrupted the guideline prices, forcing Community firms to break the guidelines themselves. In January 1978 the Commission accordingly introduced a minimum price for steel imports and negotiated a series of voluntary export restraints with its principal external suppliers. This worked for a time, but as small steel producers in Northern Italy refused to respect the voluntary quota system, and as the demand for steel continued to fall, discipline in the steel market evaporated. The London *Economist* (8 November 1980, p. 56) described conditions as 'chaotic' as steel firms 'resorted to frantic price-cutting to grab a share of the shrinking market'; losses amounted to $20 million a day. Finally, the Commission invoked the emergency provisions of Article 58 of the Treaty of Paris and introduced compulsory production quotas as from October 1980.

In the meantime, the Commission introduced a code for aids to the steel industry in February 1980 in view of 'the need for all aid to steel to be subject to a coherent Community discipline' (EC Commission 1980, para. 194). It insisted on prior notification of all subsidies on 'a genuine contribution to the restructuring of the industry' (the intensity of the aid being proportional to the amount of restructuring), on the minimisation of distortions of competition — and on 'complete transparency'.

Table 3
Subsidies and capacity cuts in the Community steel industry 1980-6.

	Accumulated subsidies since 1980 (million ECU)	% of total	Accumulated capacity cuts (million tonnes)	% of total
Belgium	4,259	11.0	3.4	11.0
W. Germany	4,522	11.5	6.7	21.0
France	9,222	23.6	6.1	19.7
Italy	13,893	35.5	7.2	23.0
United Kingdom	5,768	14.7	5.4	17.4
Other	1,438	3.7	2.3	7.9
Total	39,102	100.0	31.1	100.0

Source: EC Commission (1986) *Fifteenth Report on Competition Policy,* Brussels and Luxemburg.

Six years and 40 billion ECU later the Community's steel industry had cut capacity by 18 per cent (see Tables 3 and 4). Despite the Commission's attempts to prevent distortions of competition, it is quite clear from the record that Italian and French steel producers received between four and four and a half times as much help as German steel firms (Table 4) and that the latter, although by far the most efficient of the EC's steel producers, had had to cut capacity by almost as much as the notoriously inefficient state-owned Italian steel industry.

In the meantime, the Community's steel-using industries, such as automobiles and shipbuilding, were forced to contribute indirectly to subsidising the steel industry via higher prices, due to the artificial scarcity created by import restrictions and production quotas.

Little wonder that the European steel industry has been most reluctant to accept the gradual unwinding of the Davignon Plan and that it still benefits from voluntary export restrictions from competitive world suppliers — a classic case of rent seeking.

Table 4
Relative rates of subsidisation and capacity reductions.

	Accumulated cuts as % 1980 capacity	Accumulated subsidies per tonne of 1980 capacity (ECU)
Belgium	21.4	266
W. Germany	13.0	87
France	22.9	343
Italy	19.8	383
United Kingdom	23.8	250
EC average	18.1	227

Source: EC Commission (1986) *Fifteenth Report on Competition Policy.* Brussels and Luxemburg.

Synthetic fibres

An account of these dark days would be incomplete without a brief reference to the development of the Community's policy towards the synthetic fibres industry, since it prompted a novel interpretation of Article 85 (cartels) and cleared the legal ground for horizontal agreements between firms to reduce 'structural overcapacity'.

In parallel with the problem of over-capacity which developed in the steel industry, a similar crisis emerged in the synthetic fibre sector in the latter 1970s. Believing that something like the Davignon Steel Plan was called for, the directorate-general for industrial affairs in 1978 sponsored an agreement between the Community's eleven principal fibre producers to share out the existing market according to the pattern of deliveries in 1976 (see *Financial Times,* 23 June 1978). Any loss in demand would be shared equally, as well as any growth, an exception being made for Italy on the grounds that because it was a late starter, it had a 'right' to a larger share.

This agreement was no more and no less than a good, old-fashioned crisis cartel, for which the Treaty of Rome did not provide. Article 85(3) permitted only cartels which contributed 'to improving the production or distribution of goods or to promoting technical or economic progress'. The competition directorate of the Commission duly condemned the agreement among synthetic fibre producers, enjoining them to either discontinue their arrangement or modify it to meet the terms of Article 85(3). In particular, producers were asked to eliminate the quota system (EC Commission, 1979, para. 42).

What was the industry to do? One Commission directorate told them to set up a cartel, another told them to dismantle it! The lack of agreement within the Commission on the question of (temporary) 'crisis cartels' was obvious. The synthetic fibre cartel continued (shorn of its most blatant quota clauses) in a legal twilight until 1982, when the Commission produced its 'policy' on the matter.

The statement on the application of competition rules to agreements aimed at reducing 'structural overcapacity' reads as follows:

> The Commission may be able to condone agreements in restraint of competition which relate to a sector as a whole, provided they are aimed solely at achieving a coordinated reduction of overcapacity and do not otherwise restrict free decision-making by the firms involved. The necessary structural reorganization must not be achieved by unsuitable means such as price-fixing or quota agreements, nor should it be hampered by State aids which lead to artificial preservation of surplus capacity. (EC Commission 1983, para. 39)

The synthetic fibre producers duly sought and obtained exemption for their less structured agreement to cut capacity in 1984 (EC Commission 1985e, para 81-2).

The case is interesting, for it shows among other things that the generally accommodating stance of the Commission towards state subsidies during the crisis years was essentially extended also to firms. It also shows the degree of latitude which the Commission enjoys in the interpretation of the Treaty of Rome. Thus (remembering that exemptions to the prohibition of cartels under Article 85 hinge on strict *economic* criteria, in particular on improvements to production), the Commission justified its new policy towards crisis cartels on the following grounds: 'production can be considered to be improved if the reductions in capacity are likely in the long run to increase profitability and restore competitiveness'.

If *concerted* reductions in capacity are deemed to improve production, we are some way from the original meaning of Article 85. The rent-seeking interest of the industrial groups concerned is obvious: managed, or coordinated, reductions in capacity mean that all firms in the industry share out the agony 'equitably' — not on the basis of efficiency. They are spared the full implications of previous errors of judgement, while the efficient go unrewarded... Is it not a 'fatal conceit' (see Hayek, 1989) that the Commission should believe that it can enforce anything like competitive conditions on an oligopolistic industry, once it has allowed it to form an 'agreement in restraint of competition' (to use its own words)?

In fact, the less said about this whole disastrous decade the better. The Commission should have upheld competitive market principles at Community level much more forcefully, instead of accommodating member states' inglorious capitulation before political pressure from special interest groups and adding its own brand of *clientelisme* at European level. The end result, by mid-1985, was a palpable loss of competitiveness of European industry and loss of confidence in the future: the word 'Eurosclerosis' (attributable to Herbert Giersch) was on every lip.

6.3 The 1980s and beyond

So much has happened since those dark days (not so long ago) that it is difficult to know where to start. The adoption of the Commission's White Paper on completing the internal market in June 1985, the signing and later ratification of the Single European Act (SEA) in 1986 and 1987, have changed the Community entirely.

If we were to return to the Bayliss/El-Agraa definition of industrial policy (see above), we would have to discuss the entire single-market programme, since it is a grand (positive) industrial policy in its own right — a huge exercise in the withdrawal of the state from intra-European frontiers and many other spheres of the European economy (but this is not necessary since the penultimate chapter is devoted to this). For this very reason we took a more restrictive view of industrial policy.

Let it nevertheless be said that the main reason why the single market, as a concept, has fired people's imagination and awakened the 'animal spirits' of entrepreneurs is that a major restructuring of the European economy is under way, fuelled by competition and market forces. State intervention at the EC level to guide this process is therefore our subject. Whereas in the 1970s the Commission tried to limit and coordinate subsidies to dying industries, in the 1980s and beyond it sees its task as encouraging and coordinating subsidies to 'high-tech' industries. This is not to say that the problem of subsidies to declining industries has gone away, nor that aid to research and development was absent in the 1970s, but just to point out that there has been a radical shift in emphasis since 1985.

We shall not discuss regional, agricultural or social policy since these are tackled elsewhere in the book, although it should be remembered that each of these is entrusted with softening the impact of the radical restructuring of European industry implied by the single market. We shall instead concentrate on the Community's drive to promote new, technology-intensive sectors.

7. Development of the Commission's policy towards R&D

7.1 Commission's attitude to private joint ventures in R&D

From its inception, the Community's competition policy has favoured cooperative research and development by the private sector, as well as state support for private R&D. And indeed, as Articles 85-94 of the Treaty of Rome make quite clear, positive benefits are expected to flow from the direct and indirect help implied in R&D subsidies and the pooling of private R&D efforts.

Already in 1968 the Commission had established guidelines for the application of Article 85, which allowed agreements between firms (evens large ones) for the exclusive purpose of developing joint R&D, providing the cooperation did not extend downstream to actual production and on condition that the results of the R&D were freely available at least to members of the consortium, and preferably to outsiders as well on a licensing basis (EC Commission, 1972, paras 31-2).

In December 1984 the Commission adopted a 'block exemption' regulation for R&D agreements between firms which defined a new, more favourable policy. In particular, the adoption of the 'block exemption' approach meant that cooperative R&D agreements, in principle, no longer needed to be individually notified to the Commission, on condition that they met the terms of the 'block exemption'. Secondly, the exemption also applied to R&D agreements which provided for the joint exploitation of the results. This meant that cooperation could now extend to the manufacturing stage (but not marketing).

This represented a considerable shift in policy for which European industry had been asking for some time, on the grounds that it made little sense to pool R&D resources if, once they were successful, competition between the members of the pool wiped out all potential monopolistic rents: under such circumstances, firms would prefer not to pool R&D resources at all, but take the risk of going it alone — see Jacquemin (1988).

7.2 *The Eureka initiative*

The modification of Commission policy coincided with the adoption of the Eureka (European Research Cooperation Agency) intiative by the then ten member states of the EC as well as Spain, Portugal, Austria, Finland, Norway, Sweden and Switzerland. Eureka was launched in April 1985 by President Miterrand as a European response to President Reagan's Star Wars (or what is technically referred to as Strategic Defence Initiative — SDI) initiative. It involved public support (in the form of subsidies) for substantial cooperative ventures between European firms to develop and launch new, high-technology products (i.e. beyond the R&D stage). As Eureka is not a Community body, but a pan-European one (even including Turkey in some projects), and as it has appropriated for itself the sphere of high-visibility, high-technology, variable-geometry, inter-state cooperation (like Arianespace or Airbus), there is palpable disapproval on the part of the Commission. By some appalling accident this industrial policy plum has escaped its portfolio. In June 1988 the Commission accordingly made several proposals to reinforce its supervision of Eureka projects (see EC Commission, 1988a, para. 352), but it is not yet clear whether this takeover bid has been successful. The easy launching of the Eureka project by seventeen countries, its light institutional and bureaucratic structure (just a small secretariat), its immediate popularity with industry and the bypassing of the EC are all part of an interesting chapter in the broader story of European industrial policy which regretfully cannot be fitted into the scope of this chapter.

7.3 *Commission's attitude to state subsidies for R&D*

In the meantime the Commission adopted a 'Framework on State aids for research and development' (which had been some time in the making) in 1986, which again emphasised its favourable attitude towards such help but warned of the dangers of fruitless duplication of effort and hence the need for proper coordination by the Commission. It therefore called for the notification of all subsidies in excess of 20 million ECU. A good part of the increase in the number of subsidies investigated by the Commission in 1987 (see Table 1) was due to the adoption of this new framework. But part was also due to the general increase in state support for R&D, in particular collaborative R&D in the context of the Eureka initiative.

8. A real EC industrial policy at last

Despite clear advantages of pooling research efforts at a European level in areas where the costs obviously exceeded the ability of any single country, or company, to defray, member states have been traditionally hesitant to relinquish such an important instrument of policy to the Community (hence, in fact, Eureka). Their loss would be the Commission's gain, and this was tolerable only under the most extreme duress.

Thus, until the first energy crisis in the mid-1970s, the Community's industrial research activities were kept on very short rations.[1] Programmes. such as they were, had to be based on Article 235 of the Treaty of Rome[2] and it is significant that it was not until the crucial Hague meeting of heads of state or government in December 1969 that the member states confirmed their readiness 'to coordinate and promote industrial research and development in the principal pacemaking sectors, in particular by means of common programmes, and to supply the financial means for these purposes' (The Hague Summit Communiqué, 1-2 December 1969, point 9). Even then, non-repayable 'free' money available for R&D under the EC did not amount to more than 235 million EUA for the entire period 1974-9. According to Mr Daniel Strasser, at the time Director-General for Budgets, who was in a good position to judge the situation: 'The term "industrial policy" is a euphemism. Community achievements to date in this [industrial policy, R&D] field are so limited that they would scarcely deserve a mention were it not for the ECSC's role in the steel industry' — see Strasser (1981) — (to which we have already alluded).

Since failures are sometimes as revealing as achievements, it may be worth recalling briefly the fate of the Commission's 1977 proposal to research, develop, build and market a large civil transport aircraft, on the grounds that no one member state could carry out such a project on its own because of its cost. The Commission proposed that individual R&D subsidies in this area should be pooled and replaced by Community financing for all four phases (see Strasser 1981, p. 256). The Commission would then manage the project, of course in constant collaboration with the member states. Despite the obvious logic of the proposal, it was never adopted. Instead, the member states preferred the variable-geometry method of Airbus Industrie.

As the technological weaknesses of European industry became more and more apparent, however, it became harder for governments to maintain their go-it-alone attitudes. In one particular area — information technology — industrial pressure for a pooling of resources became particularly insistent. Twelve prominent firms active in the information technology sector (Bull, CGE, Thomson from France, AEG, Nixdorf, Siemens from Germany, GEC. ICL, Plessey from the United Kingdom, Olivetti and Stet from Italy and Philips from the Netherlands) formed 'The Round Table' and effectively lobbied the Commission and their respective national governments for the adoption of a European Programme for Research in Information Technology (subsequently known as ESPRIT). ESPRIT was proposed by the Commission in May 1983 and adopted unanimously by the Council of Ministers in February 1984.

The motivations behind this move were, in the words of the ESPRIT Review Board:

> The undiminished poor competitiveness of the European IT industry in the face of increasing market penetration from the US and Japan. The importance of economies of scale and the ensuing need for the European IT industry to act together in a collaborative manner in innovative technologies without restraining competition (ESPRIT Review Board, 1985. p. 1)

ESPRIT was in many ways a trail blazer: it established a pattern for creating an industrial policy partnership between the Community, the member states and industry which has since been used in many other fields. Very briefly, the Community would call for projects from industry. These would have to emanate from two or more firms from two or more countries in the EC and they would have to fit the broad terms of reference agreed to after much consultation by the Council of Ministers. The Community would finance half the cost of the project, while the other half would come from national sources, including private companies participating in the research. In fact, a substantial private sector contribution was considered necessary to guarantee both commitment on the part of industry and a correct allocation of public resources. Finally, it was always made very clear that only pre-competitive R&D fell within ESPRIT's terms of reference.

The reason for this limitation was quite clear: cooperation between European firms was to be encouraged, but not to the point where it might constitute a threat to competition. It is to be remembered, however, that the Commission's block exemption on R&D agreements between firms was at this very moment in the process of being revised in order to permit joint production of the fruits of joint R&D projects. What the Commission refused to do was in fact to *subsidise* joint production activities.

There was a very simple reason for this: to avoid being accused by the United States of subsidising industry. The more general the programme and the further removed it was from the market-place, the easier it was to refute such objections. Indeed, the Community, to this day, is at pains to point out that it does not operate any industrial policy as such, only a series of R&DT (research and technological development) programmes. 'Industrial policy' is a bad phrase.

The first phase of ESPRIT (1984-8) covered R&DT projects amounting to 1,500 million ECU, half financed by the Community. Calls for proposals produced almost a thousand projects, of which 240 were approved by the Commission after consultation with the Round Table representatives. A mid-term review, published in 1985, confirmed that industry was very enthusiastic about the programme, wanted more money, more coverage and was anxious that continuity should be assured. Respondents to the review's questionnaire added that they would have liked fewer but larger projects and that 'ESPRIT alone is not sufficient': in particular, they argued that the programme should be extended to cover prototype development, production engineering, manufacture and marketing (ESPRIT Review Board, 1985, p. 37). ESPRIT projects should be 'more focused' (coded language for actual manufacturing subsidies) -naturally enough! The rent-seeking instinct, once stimulated, expands to cover the ground available.

By now other European industries had awoken to the fact that if financial support for joint R&D was available for the information technology sector, it might also be forthcoming for other sectors as well. One can only speculate on the industrial representations being made at all levels of Community decision-taking structures in the early 1980s, but they must have been considerable, for in 1983 the Council of Ministers adopted what is now called the 'First Framework Programme' for Community R&D policy, running from 1984-7. The purpose of this programme was to integrate all Community aid to R&D into a single, coherent (it was hoped) system, capable of ensuring continuity beyond twelve months. It included all past aid to nuclear and non-nuclear energy, but added research in raw materials, recycling of industrial waste, wood, basic research in industrial technologies, high-temperature materials, metrology, agriculture, the environment, health and safety and science and technology for development (see *inter alia* EC Commission, 1984, paras 552-83). This first Framework Programme was given an overall budget of 3,750 million ECU over 4 years.

In the meantime, an important institutional change in the European industrial policy scene occurred in 1987 with the ratification of the SEA, Title VI of which was devoted to technological research and development. Under its terms the Community's sphere of action was significantly enhanced by comparison with the Treaty of Rome. The Commission was urged to coordinate member states' R&D programmes (Article 130H); the Council, the Parliament and the Commission together were urged to establish a 'multiannual framework programme' for Community R&D (Article 130I); in broad terms, they were to establish (subject to unanimous Council vote) both priority areas and the degree of Community financial support for each of the specific programmes decided upon; specific programmes could be decided upon by qualified majority vote; finally, the Community could initiate technological cooperation agreements with third countries or international organisations (i.e. coordination with Eureka was provided for) (Article 130N).

This modification of the Treaty of Rome has put the Community's proactive industrial policy on a firm legal footing for the first time. It institutes a three-stage decision-making process: the Council, acting unanimously, decides (on the basis of a proposal from the Commission) on the broad allocation of resources in the 'multiannual framework programme' (lasting four years), specific programmes are then decided upon by qualified majority vote (again on the basis of proposals from the Commission), then actual projects are finally selected by the Commission, acting in concert with industry and national civil servants.

A second Framework Programme, running from 1987 to 1991, was duly adopted and provided with a budget of 6,480 million ECU over four years. Its scope has been expanded to include medical research on AIDS, radiation protection and occupational medicine, pollution and climatology (greenhouse effect), pre-standardisation research (to establish European norms and standards more easily) and biotechnology.

9. The two Framework Programmes in greater detail

By now it is not easy to summarise the content of the Community's R&DT programmes, so wide-ranging have they become. This section nevertheless will attempt to list in a comprehensive manner the main projects in order to show where resources are being allocated.

9.1 *Information technologies*

These are covered by the ESPRIT programme already referred to. This is now in its second stage. ESPRIT II, running from 1988-93, has a budget of 3,200 million ECU (double the sum allocated to ESPRIT I), half of which is financed by the EC.

Participation by EFTA countries is expected to raise the total of public funding beyond this amount.

Information technologies (of which there are many)[3] are clearly being aggressively targeted by the Community. The ESPRIT budget is by far the largest of all the programmes receiving Community support. The strategic importance of the sector is constantly stressed in the Commission's documentation. For instance: 'Japan currently dominates the world market for domestic electronics with 60% of production, a field where Europe has a persistent trade deficit of about 8 billion ECU per year; while the USA maintains its long-standing strength in data-processing' (EC Commission, 1989d, para. 11). Information technologies are also seen to be 'pervasive' — 'seeping deeply and broadly into the economic and social fabric of all industrial countries' *(ibid.,* para. 21). The interaction between different spheres of scientific and technical knowledge is also stressed, suggesting that one thing leads to another in these high-technology areas. Thus 'in the aerospace industry, for example, electronics, materials, optical technologies and hydrodynamics have to be engineered together into new design and operating systems' *(ibid.,* para. 23). Finally, 'a growing interaction and proximity between more basic and applied R&D' is noted, suggesting that drawing the line between pre-competitive and applied research and development of new products is becoming difficult. (This may be to prepare us for the next stage in the development of the Community's industrial policy, downstream towards production and marketing.)

There is no doubt, therefore, that in information technologies the Community is convinced that it has 'picked a winner': it certainly seems to meet the criterion of strategic importance for the European economy, as well as excessive cost for any single player. One would, however, be happier with the programme were it not so obviously dominated by the twelve firms forming the Round Table, which are all represented on the supervisory board selecting the deserving projects.

9.2 Thermonuclear fusion

The Joint European Torus (JET) programme (current phase 1988-92, budget 745 million ECU) is a 'prime example of the benefits of European cooperation: the Twelve are making spectacular progress towards harnessing fusion energy' (EC Commission, 1988b; 6). This is good to know. However, a great deal more work still has to be done and the earliest practical application of the research is not expected before 2025.

This is a field which will typically be ignored by the market because the pay-off is too far ahead and risky, and the current costs enormous. Furthermore, the costs far exceed what a small European country such as France, Germany or Britain would care to devote, individually, to such a risky project. The JET programme thus meets two criteria for Community action: market failure and suboptimal investment by nations acting individually. It can perhaps be agreed that this is a 'prime example' of what is best tackled collectively at a European level rather than individually at the nation state level: i.e. the principle of subsidiarity is respected.

9.3 Telecommunications

Research and development in advanced communications for Europe (RACE: current phase 1987-91, budget 550 million ECU), 'is designed to ensure that the advanced telecommunications infrastructure which will "irrigate" Europe in the XXIst century is put in place'. The objective: sound, images and data to be freely transmitted throughout Europe (it is hoped at reasonable cost). The means: coordination of national PTT's policies and specifications, standardisation to guarantee compatibility — and recognition that 'no one European country on its own is big enough to face up to international competition'. Here is another winner: strategic, pervasive, too much for any single country — a clear candidate for Community action.

9.4 Traditional industries

Basic research in industrial technologies for Europe (BRITE: current phase 1988-92, budget 439.5 million ECU) aims to rejuvenate traditional sectors by applying new technologies. BRITE I (1985-8) was so successful that its budget had to be increased in mid-stream. Some 215 projects, each involving firms from at least two EC member states, were thus financed. Enthusiasm for BRITE shines through even the driest Commission prose:

> it has enabled transfrontier industrial alliances to be consolidated and fresh ones to be forged, the gap between industry and universities to be bridged and multidisciplinary exchanges to be promoted ... BRITE meets a real need. The participants feel that without Community funds 85% of the projects would never even have seen the light of day (*ibid.*, p. 9).

One feels the need for an exclamation mark. But is this area 'strategic'? Is there a clear case of market failure? If so, is it beyond the purse of national governments to correct? Is there not a hint of rent seeking in industry's enthusiasm for the BRITE programme? Questions, questions...

9.5 Biotechnology

As far as the biotechnology action programme (BAP: current phase 1985-9, budget 75 million ECU) is concerned, the strategic nature of the sector is not in doubt for the Commission:

> with programmed bacteria, enzymes and microorganisms serving mankind many things are at stake in the biotechnological revolution: improving the competitiveness of agriculture and industry and the quality of life and ultimately resolving the burning issues of our time: disease. malnutrition, pollution, genetic equation, etc. . . the last technological revolution of the century is in full swing (*ibid.. p.* 11).

Since we are here at the interface between industry and agriculture, BAP is not alone in taking up the challenge: it can rely on the European Collaborative Linkage of Agriculture and Industry through Research (ECLAIR: 1988-93, budget 80 million ECU) for some help in resolving the burning issues of our time. Without a doubt, another winner.

9.6 Science

A plan to stimulate the international cooperation and interchange needed by European research scientists (no acronym, just 'Science': 1988-92, budget 167 million ECU) has been adopted as a 'simple means of improving the level of European research to a truly spectacular extent and of stemming the brain drain' (*ibid.*, p. 13). By the end of the first plan (1985-8) over 3,000 European scientists belonging to 1,000 teams had taken part in 400 joint projects. By 1992 it is expected that 7,000-8,000 researchers will be thus involved.

Why not? Basic science is a public good which needs public funding. Encouraging free trade in scientific ideas is surely beneficial. The only question is the cost-benefit ratio. While the cost is clear enough, one has to take on trust the 'truly spectacular' benefit.

9.7 Road safety

Dedicated road infrastructure for vehicle safety in Europe (DRIVE: 1988-90, 60 million ECU), aims to use the innovations emerging from the ESPRIT, RACE and EUREKA programmes in order to reduce deaths (55,000 a year) and injuries (1.7 million) on European roads. DRIVE is also expected to make a major contribution to the European integrated road transport environment (IRTE), to link up with the PROMETHEUS project (the 'intelligent car'), etc. The possibilities are infinite (*ibid.*, p. 14).

The reference to Europe's appalling death toll makes it almost immoral to question the usefulness of DRIVE, but as it aims to reduce some of the strong negative externalities associated with one of our most important industries perhaps it should be financed by a tax on driving, or on the automobile industry itself, rather than out of general taxation. Unless the automobile industry were to object, of course . . .

9.8 Learning technologies

Developing European learning through technological advance (DELTA: pilot phase 18 months, budget 20 million ECU), is 'tackling head on one of the social ills of our century: unemployment' (*ibid.*, p. 15). It aims to investigate advanced technology (distance learning techniques) for educating, training and retraining.

Why not? The appeal to the social ill of unemployment makes this project irresistible. Besides, anything which speeds up the flow of information and improves the level of education is a good thing . But is the sector strategic ? Is it beyond the purse of individual governments to support? The direct beneficiaries will be the computer, IT and telecommunications industries, and we can be sure that DELTA's pilot phase will be deemed a great success.

9.9 Unconventional energy

Joint opportunities for unconventional or long-term energy supply (JOULE: 1989-92, budget 122 million ECU) aims to ensure more secure energy supplies while at the same time respecting the environment. The oil crisis is 'now just a bad memory but the Twelve are still on their guard' (*ibid.*, p. 16). Universities and industries will be partners in joint research projects, which will tackle, *inter alia*, the rational use of energy and energy-saving devices, wind power, photovoltaic, solar and geothermal energy, etc.

Enthusiasts for industrial policy have, ever since 1973, always claimed that market failure permeates the whole energy scene, but especially the area of unconventional (renewable and ecological) new sources of energy. Perhaps this is so. Perhaps we need to support all this at a European level to avoid wasteful duplication of effort. Who knows? One thing is sure: the market has discovered for itself most if not all currently efficient forms of energy saving, and new sources of energy as well — and for the remainder, avoids this area like the plague as being too removed from market realities. Our fearless leaders have therefore assumed these risks on our behalf.

9.10 Food science

Food-linked agro-industrial research (FLAIR: 1989-93, 25 million ECU) aims to promote the food industry's competitiveness and to improve the quality of the foodstuffs available to the single European market of 320 million citizens (ibid., p. 17). FLAIR is concerned with the processing-distribution-consumer part of the food chain and therefore complements the ECLAIR programme.

One must assume that the Common Agricultural Policy, ECLAIR and FLAIR are all part of the same strategic policy to support the farm sector and its close ally, the agro-industrial sector. It would be surprising if they were not on our list.

9.11 X-ray examination of research

The Community programme in the field of strategic analysis, forecasting and evaluation in matters of research and technology (MONITOR: 1988-92, 22 million ECU) aims to research research. The Commission puts it this way:

> The Community is stepping up its research activities in order to remain in control of its future. Even so there is a need to detect the new paths emerging from the work in progress, to make an accurate evaluation of the medium-term impact of the programmes and to endeavour to look far ahead into the future. For the sake of effectiveness. (ibid., p. 18)

Oh fatal conceit ... but we wish you luck in remaining in control of the future, in being able to detect new paths, in evaluating accurately the medium-term impact of all your good works, in looking far ahead into the future.

At this point, the reader will forgive us if we sign off before describing in any detail:

1. Advanced informatics in medicine (AIM: pilot phase, 20 million ECU).
2. Action programme of the Community in education and training for technology (COMETT: 1986-9, 45 million ECU).
3. European action scheme for the mobility of university students (ERASMUS: 1987-90, 85 million ECU).
4. Measures to encourage the development of the audiovisual industry (MEDIA: pilot phase 1988-9, 5.5 million ECU).

In the pipeline as future Commission proposals are:

1. Promoting European HDTV ('Are the Twelve going to lose the high-definition television battle which they are fighting against the Japanese? No . . says the Commission' (*ibid.*, p. 26)), but there is no budget as yet.
2. Space EC/ESA cooperation.
3. Aeronautics, i.e. the pooling of research talents to support Airbus.

Is this a trickle or a flood? Where is it leading us?

10. Conclusion

There is no doubt that the Community's industrial policy has come a long way in a short time. It has switched from being essentially backward looking in the 1970s to being resolutely forward looking in the 1980s and beyond. It has graduated from having a mainly coordinating and supervising function in the 1970s to possessing its own resources for fostering its own ideas in the 1980s (while still maintaining the traditional coordinating and supervising roles). It has gained legitimacy since its explicit inclusion in the 1987 Single European Act. In short, the Community's industrial policy has arrived.

The driving force behind this rapid development of EC industrial policy is the single-market project. While recognising the need for the single market, our governments and industrialists are very worried that US and Japanese firms will run off with most of the opportunities it offers. They recognise Europe's relative backwardness, especially in high-technology industries, and the fact that there are, as yet, no truly 'European' firms, but French, German, Italian firms, limited by national perspectives. Encouraging transnational inter-firm cooperation and supporting high-technology research and development are therefore the general aims of the policies outlined above. There is even a considerable sense of urgency in the whole programme: after all, the single market is not far off and there is a long way to go.

This is why certain industries are lobbying, additionally, for special local-content rules, for a buy-European public procurement policy, for strong action against international dumping, for protection of European firms against foreign takeovers, for careful scrutiny of Japanese greenfield direct investments, for 'strict reciprocity' in foreign markets or else for Community subsidisation programmes that go beyond the pre-competitive stage and so on. And it would be naive to think that they will not get most of what they are asking for.

As will by now be clear, I approach this whole complex with mixed feelings. If the Krugman-Brander-Spencer theories are correct, the Community is right to support certain 'strategic' industries. Perhaps information technologies *are* strategic. I would be the first to admit the possibility. What is more worrying, however, is the feeling that the Community's industrial policy is already in the process of being hijacked by rent-seeking special interest groups. The sheer number of projects, the rapid increase in funds available, the unbelievably wide spread of industries deemed to be 'strategic' are not encouraging symptoms. If we add in the subtle non-tariff barriers being called for daily by powerful interest groups, one wonders how long the Community's general trade and industrial policy can remain clean.

If the single market is used to shield our large corporations from global competition few of the much-vaunted economies of scale will in fact be realised. Nurturing national champions did not produce world-scale competitive industries in the past, and nurturing European champions behind tariff and non-tariff barriers will not do so in the future. A protectionist single market would simply repeat our old mistakes at a higher level.

It cannot be said often enough that the sheer size of one's domestic market is not the only, or even the main ingredient in economic growth and prosperity, otherwise Switzerland and Sweden would not be among the world's wealthiest countries, Taiwan and Korea would not be among its fastest growing and China. India and Brazil would not be among its poorest. The only long-term method of ensuring continued viability of one's industries, year after year, is to make sure that they are constantly exposed to world-scale competition *and have access* to knowledge, goods, capital and people from abroad: in other words, to have as open a trade and industrial policy as possible.

This leads me to a modest plea: the programmes described above are aimed at *European* industry. They may sometimes include firms from EFTA countries, if the latter contribute to the project financially. They may even sometimes include 'European firms of foreign parentage', as the current expression goes, because it is difficult to exclude them on any but the most mercantilistic and sectarian grounds. But they do not include non-European firms. Fair enough, one might say. After all, one is talking about European tax payers' money. But I would make a case for supporting new technologies from wherever they may come, encouraging European firms to seek out partners in the United States, Japan, wherever they can find the best fit, in their view. In the long run this would make better use of the European tax payers' money than forcing European firms to look for European technologies among European partners. In fact, the world is already too global for such a limited approach. In short, if we must have an industrial policy, let us have an open one. The single market requires no less if it is to yield its full potential.

Notes

1. Joint energy research under the aegis of Euratom ran into difficulties as a result of Franco-German rivalry, both countries possessing strong nuclear power industries and being most unwilling to pool R&D efforts. Euratom's Joint Research Centre (JRC) was accordingly starved of resources. Today it runs four establishments (Ispra in Italy, Karlsruhe in Germany, Petten in the Netherlands and Geel in Belgium). These are the Community's 'own' laboratories. Except for this one instance. the Community acts indirectly, supporting existing institutions in the member states rather than creating its own.

2. 'If actions by the Community should prove necessary to attain, in the course of the operation of the common market, one of the objectives of the Community and this Treaty has not provided the necessary powers, the Council shall, acting unanimously on a proposal from the Commission and after consulting the Assembly, take the appropriate measures.'

3. Interested readers may consult 1989 *ESPRIT Workprogramme,* Commission of the European Communities, 1989c, which lists 48 'A-type' projects 'Which usually require large

resources, both human and financial, and considerable infrastructure'. B-type projects are too numerous to list.

Bibliography

Brander J. (1981) 'Intra-industry trade in identical commodities', *Journal of International Economics, vol. 11.*

Brander, J. and Spencer. B. (1984) 'Tariff protection and imperfect competition', in H. Kierzkowski (ed.), *Monopolistic Competition and International Trade,* Oxford University Press.

Commission of the European Communities (1972) *First Report on Competition Policy.*

Commission of the European Communities (1976) *Fifth Report on Competition — EEC.*

Commission of the European Communities (1979) *Eighth Report on Competition Policy.*

Commission of the European Communities (1980) *Tenth Report on Competition Policy.*

Commission of the European Communities (1983) *Twelfth Report on Competition Policy.*

Commission of the European Communities (1984) *Eighteenth General Report on the Activities of the European Communities.*

Commission of the European Communities (1988a) *22nd General Report of the Activities of the European Communities.*

Commission of the European Communities (1988b) *Community R&TD Programmes,* special issue.

Corden. W. M. (1965) 'Recent developments in the theory of international trade', *Special Papers in International Finance, Princeton University Press.*

Curzon, G. and Curzon Price, V. (1989) 'The GATT, non-discrimination principles and the rise of "material reciprocity" in international trade', mimeo, Collège de Bruges.

El-Agraa. A. M. (1983) *The Theory of International Trade.* Croom Helm.

El-Agraa, A. M. (1984) *Trade Theory and Policy: Some topical issues,* Macmillan

El-Agraa, A. M. (1989) *International Trade.* Macmillan and St Martin's.

El-Agraa, A.M. (ed.) (1992) *Economics of the European Community,* Philip Allan (third edition).

ESPRIT Review Board (1985) *The Mid-term Review of ESPRIT,* EC Commission.

Hayek. F. A. (1989) *The Fatal Conceit,* University of Chicago Press.

Helpman. E. (1981) 'International trade in the presence of product differentiation, economies of scale and monopolistic competition', *Journal of International Economics,* vol. 11.

Hindley, B. (1974) *Theory of International Trade,* Weidenfeld & Nicolson.

Jacquemin. A. P. (1988) 'Cooperative agreements in R&D and European antitrust policy', *European Economic Review,* vol . 32.

Johnson, H G. (1971) *Aspects of the Theory of Tariffs,* Allen & Unwin.

Kierzkowski, H. (1987) 'Recent advances in international trade theory', *Oxford Review of Economic Policy,* vol. 3. no. 1.

Kreinin, M.E. (1979) *International Economics: a policy approach,* Harcourt Brace Jovanovich (also subsequent editions).

Kreuger, A. O. (1974) 'The political economy of the rent-seeking society', *American Economic Review*, vol. 64.

Krugmann, P.R. (1979) 'Increasing returns, monopolistic competition and international trade', *Journal of International Economics,* vol. 9.

Krugman. P. R. (1983) 'New theories of trade among industrial countries', *AER Papers and Proceedings,* May.

Lancaster, K. (1980) 'Intra-industry trade under monopolistic competition', *Journal of International Economics. vol.* 10.

Oxford Review of Economic Policy (1987), vol. 3, no. 1

Stigler, G. J. (1971) 'The theory of economic regulation', *Bell Journal of Economics and Management Science,* vol. 2.

Strasser, D. (1981) 'The finances of Europe', *The European Perspectives Series,* EC Commission.

Toulemon. R. (1972) 'Etat d'avancement des travaux en matière de politique industrielle dans la Communauté, paper presented to the conference organised by the European Communities on 'Industrie et sociéte dans la Communauté Européenne', Venice.

Tullock, G. (1967) 'The welfare costs of tariffs, monopolies and theft', *Western Economic Journal,* vol 5.

4. European or National? The Community's New Merger Regulation

Matthew Bishop

1. Introduction

Since September 1990, mergers taking place in the European Community (EC) have been regulated under a new merger regulation. After sixteen years of unsuccessful negotiations, undertaken with varying degrees of enthusiasm and occasional hostility, the EC member states agreed, in December 1989, to this new system of community-wide merger regulation, based around the Competition Directorate of the European Commission. The negotiation of this regulation raised questions reaching to the heart of current debates about the future economic and political development of the Community, and particularly issues of national sovereignty. These questions will continue to be debated. A central plank of the new merger regulation is to be reassessed in the years to 1994.

The new merger regulation has, however, been broadly welcomed, and its practice mostly uncontroversial. UK Trade Minister, John Redwood, called the regulation 'very important . . . providing more certainty for companies about who exactly is determining the fate of their mergers'. Leon Brittan, the European Commissioner responsible for competition policy, emphasized the link between merger control and the single market programme, and that the European Community has 'for the first time a single framework in which take-overs and mergers with a Community dimension can be dealt with, recognizing the importance of maintaining fair competition throughout the single market'. Less optimistically, however, there are fears that, in the words of one City lawyer, 'the regulation will remove many of the uncertainties which have bedevilled merger control in the Community . . . only to replace them with a new set of uncertainties'. The political controversy surrounding the first merger to be vetoed by the European Commission, in October 1991, reinforces these concerns.

This chapter describes the previous system of merger control (Section 2), examines and compares the new merger regulation (Section 3), and discusses the implications of these changes, both for businesses and for national merger authorities (Section 4). The conclusions are set out in Section 5.

In particular, the regulation sought to introduce a 'one-stop shop'. This aimed to end 'double jeopardy' — the considerable uncertainty facing businesses about whether a potential merger would be investigated by national or European merger regulators — or both. The new regulation tackles this problem by referring only the very largest cross-border mergers to the European Commission, whilst relying on the various merger control authorities within the member states to regulate the remainder.

I focus on three key issues. First, and as there is a broad consensus on this point, briefly, on what criteria should mergers be approved or prohibited? Second, how should responsibility for regulating mergers be allocated between the Commission and member states? Third, how can merger regulation in the Community be undertaken most efficiently?

Discussion of the first of these issues is built on an important assumption about the economic rationale for merger control: that it should concentrate on establishing and preserving competitive market structures. The reasons for this assumption are summarized briefly below (for a more detailed discussion see, for example, Fairburn and Geroski, in *European Mergers and Merger Policy*).

Advocates of a merger will generally cite one of three major benefits. Merger can reduce costs by enabling companies to exploit economies of scale and scope. Efficiency can be increased by replacing poor management through a competitive market for corporate control. Merger can enable two companies that are performing poorly against foreign rivals to form a 'national champion', able to compete internationally. Each of these arguments has some validity. However, economists recognize that mergers can have both beneficial and detrimental effects on companies and society. In particular, merger can have a large anti-competitive effect. Merging companies can gain market power, thus both reducing the pressure on them to be efficient, and allowing them to raise prices. It is not appropriate, therefore, to adopt a generalized stance either pro or anti mergers *per se*. Any merger will have both the possibility of benefits and of anti-competitive costs. Merger authorities inevitably face a pragmatic assessment of the relative size of these costs and benefits.

This raises a number of problems. First, the anticipated gains from mergers are likely to be overstated by the merging companies (or the acquirer, in the event of hostile take-over). This is the natural consequence of normal managerial and political motivation. Management may claim that a merger will bring forth economies of scale and scope, the replacement of inefficient management with superior skills, or the advantages of being an effective international competitor. However, they will be equally attracted by the market power and protection from competition that might accompany such benefits. Similarly, politicians may value the increased political influence deriving from 'national champion' arguments. Second, regulators have to choose between spotting potential anti-competitive behaviour in advance — with the risk that a merger might be wrongly opposed, and the benefits unnecessarily forgone — or allowing a merger to proceed, but reversing it if the merged firm behaves anti-competitively in practice. Experience has shown that regulating market structure (i.e. stopping mergers that might lead to anti-competitive behaviour) is often more effective than conduct regulation (penalizing actual anti-competitive behaviour). This is discussed in detail in Kay and Vickers (1988).

In view of the problems described above, I argue, and assume throughout this discussion, that proposed mergers promising scale economies in return for reduced competition should be treated with considerable scepticism. Although the possibility of such mergers should not be ruled out entirely, the claims of competition should be presumed superior until clearly proven otherwise.

The second area of concern — whether regulation should be undertaken at the national or European level — goes to the heart of debates about sovereignty and the future development of the European Community. I build my argument on the principle of subsidiarity — that activities should be carried out at the 'lowest' efficient level (on a hierarchy rising from the individual citizen, through local and national governments, to transnational authorities), a principle fundamental to the Community. I conclude that subsidiarity provides a powerful rationale for regulation of cross-border mergers by the European Commission in preference to member states. However, I question whether the new regulation will properly allocate mergers between state and European level. The size of the companies merging may not be a good indicator of the consequences for the Community of their merger.

The third issue — efficiency of regulation — centres on the new regulation's introduction of clearer procedures and explicit timetables. At the heart of these changes is the allocation of each merger to one, and no more than one, competition authority — the 'one-stop shop'. I suggest, however, that the 'one-stop shop' may be seriously flawed. Although the previous system of multiple regulation was undoubtedly unpopular, I suggest that it was uncertainty about merger procedure that posed the most serious problems facing companies considering merger, rather than the existence of several regulators. The proposed increase in the jurisdiction of the Commission raises legitimate fears of over centralization and regulatory capture. There is considerable doubt about the ability of the Commission's Competition Directorate to meet the timetables it has been set, purely because of the volume of work likely to be required, and the low staffing levels in that particular section of the Commission. Yet, at the same time, the new regulation relies on the extremely varied national merger regulations for controlling all but the largest mergers. As many of these smaller mergers will have some impact on the competitiveness of Community markets, I conclude that the new regulation is itself in need of further modification, though not in the manner presently favoured by many in the Community.

In the discussion throughout the chapter I refer to mergers in a broad sense, embracing the wide variety of legal arrangements within and throughout the European Community that are covered by merger control legislation. These legal arrangements control the general process by which broadly independent companies come under some, or an increasing, degree of common control. The most common examples are friendly merger, friendly acquisition of one company by another, and hostile/contested take-over. However, when I describe a particular set of merger regulations in detail, I provide a more precise definition of the mergers covered by those regulations.

I also note in passing that the absence of a consistent Community legal framework means that friendly mergers across national borders presents extreme practical difficulties. Thus, most cross-border arrangements will involve one company acquiring a majority shareholding in another, with both companies remaining legally independent. This would change were the Community directives on company law harmonization within the European Community to be implemented.

2. Articles 85 and 86

When the European Community's founding document, the Treaty of Rome, was drafted, no mention was made of mergers — largely because the mergers taking place at, and prior to, that time had little economic impact. There was, therefore, no explicit provision for merger regulation in the Community. This did not prevent the European Commission exerting some control over mergers, however, and, from 1972, when it opposed the merger of Continental Can and Thomassen Drijver,[1] the Commission's influence steadily grew. By the late 1980s, a framework for the control of mergers and acquisitions had emerged, developed incrementally from changing legal interpretations of Articles 85 and 86 of the Treaty of Rome.

Much of this legal debate took place informally, outside the courts — as throughout the 1970s and 1980s, the Commission only ever took one formal decision to prohibit a merger, and that decision was subsequently overturned. Instead, the Commission, when approached, would indicate to the companies which were proposing to merge the decision it would most likely take, were a formal decision to be necessary. On the occasions when the Commission has suggested informally that it would oppose a merger, the companies concerned have generally regarded this as a sufficient deterrent, declining to subject the Commission's informal 'decision' to judicial examination. It is not surprising, therefore, that the procedures emerging from this informal, 'quasi-judicial' process have been complex, somewhat unpredictable, and driven largely by legal rather than economic requirements.

After 1972, the Commission mostly relied on Article 86 in regulating mergers; Article 85 was only considered relevant to mergers after 1987, and there remained considerable controversy as to its precise meaning and application to mergers. I therefore begin my analysis of the previous merger control regime by examining the scope and implications of Article 86.

Article 86

Article 86 states that 'any abuse by one or more undertakings of a dominant position within the common market or in a substantial part of it shall be prohibited as incompatible with the common market in so far as it may affect trade between member states'.

Article 86 was first interpreted as applying to mergers in 1972, when Continental Can sought to merge with a subsidiary of a Dutch can producer, Thomassen Drijver. From then on, the Commission focused on three key areas in deciding whether or not Article 86 applied to a particular merger — market definition, existence of dominance, and abuse of dominance. Each area is examined in turn.

In defining the relevant market, the European Commission took account of all closely substitutable products — both from the perspective of the consumer and the producer. In assessing substitutes, the Commission considered both actual and potential competition. For instance, a proposed merger between Pont-a-Mousson and Stanton & Staveley (1974), which would have given the combined company more than a 50 per cent share in the Community market for ductile iron pipes, was allowed to proceed because there was significant competition from, among other alternatives, concrete, steel, and plastic piping. Equally, on some occasions, a manufacturer may have a large market share — and appear dominant — because other companies choose not to enter the market. Such companies might, however, enter that market should the incumbent company seek to abuse its position by raising prices. The Commission also stressed the importance of accurately defining the relevant geographical market.

The meaning of 'dominant position' was best defined, in the 1978 judgement on the United Brands refusal to supply Olesen, as 'a position of economic strength enjoyed by an undertaking which enables it to prevent effective competition being maintained in the relevant market by giving to it the power to behave to an appreciable extent independently of its competitors, customers and ultimately of its consumers'. In assessing this, the Commission emphasized the importance of market share. A market share of 40 per cent or more justified an initial presumption of dominance, and a market share of more than 80 per cent was taken as sufficient proof of a dominant position. The Commission also took account of the existence of potential entrants, barriers to entry, technological superiority, pricing behaviour, and ownership of important vertical assets.

Demonstrating actual abuse of dominant position proved a substantial and difficult task — particularly as the Commission initially employed a very tight definition of abuse. Abuse, it was held, occurred when the only companies remaining in the market were those whose behaviour depended on the dominant company. Subsequently, the investigation of Hoffmann-La Roche's customer loyalty rebate scheme resulted in the adoption of a modified definition. This focused on action which has 'the effect of hindering the maintenance of the degree of competition still existing in the market or the growth of that competition', and suggests that any merger with a significant impact on the structure of competition in any Community market could technically be an abuse, if either company involved already has a dominant position in any Community market.

Article 86 provided good criteria with which the Commission could regulate mergers. However, the procedures associated with Article 86 were inadequate in terms of the process by which the Commission became aware of mergers, the extended timetable within which the Commission operated, and the resulting uncertainty regarding their intentions. Most strikingly, although the European Commission had enormous powers to frustrate and prohibit mergers, Article 86 did not require companies involved in mergers to notify the Commission before a merger was completed. Instead, the Commission had to rely for its information on newspaper reports, complaints from customers or rival companies, or voluntary self-notification by the companies involved in merger.

Article 86 also failed to provide any effective formal mechanism for assessing proposed mergers in advance. There was some provision for 'interim measures' to delay merger pending investigation — but this required the Commission to demonstrate that a merger was 'likely to cause serious and irreparable damage to the party seeking its adoption, or which is intolerable for the public interest'. This requirement was strictly applied, and the use of interim measures rarely even threatened, not least because the

Commission was reluctant for investigations to become a regular part of the defensive armoury of any firm faced with hostile acquisition.

The absence of prior control reflected the powers available to the Commission, and the need to demonstrate actual rather than potential abuse of a dominant position. In cases where a completed merger was found to violate Article 86, the Commission could order the sale of any shares and assets, such that competition was completely restored. (Thus, it is argued, powers to control a merger in advance were unnecessary, as the Commission could remedy the situation afterwards.) There was also no procedure for declaring a merger null. Article 86 could technically be applied only to completed mergers. Because the costs of merger are substantial, there is great advantage to knowing in advance whether a merger will be allowed to continue. Thus, in the mid-1980s the Commission began to show greater interest in the use of prior controls. However, this interest failed to produce any significant changes.

There was no time limit within which the Commission had to either begin or complete an investigation. Thus, some mergers were not investigated until some years after they were completed — for instance, the Commission's investigation of the proposed merger between Berisford and British Sugar (1982) was not called for until sixteen months after the merger had been cleared by the UK's Monopolies and Mergers Commission (MMC). The lack of a comprehensive notification procedure also resulted, inevitably, in some inconsistency in the treatment of mergers that are basically similar.

Companies became more and more dissatisfied with this pervasive uncertainty about how the Commission would treat any proposed merger; and in such an environment companies considering merger were often discouraged from doing so. To combat this negative bias, an informal procedure for advance vetting of mergers grew up. Many companies proposing to merge sought clarification in advance, consulting the Commission informally prior to proceeding with a merger, and obtaining a non-binding (but usually accurate) opinion on whether the Commission would be likely to investigate the merger if it were completed. Thus, although the Commission could not prevent an undesirable merger in advance, companies were, in practice, unlikely to proceed with a merger if they were aware that it was likely to be ruled out by the Commission.

Likewise, an informal system of sanctions against undesirable mergers evolved. The Commission's formal powers, although far-reaching, were difficult to enforce and suffered from various bureaucratic disadvantages. These included, for example, numerous lengthy internal procedures such as translating all documents into nine languages. The informal options available to the Commission include writing letters of warning, setting out changes in the composition of the mergers that the merging companies would need to make if they were to avoid formal proceedings, and press releases stating the Commission's detailed objections to a particular merger. However, the reliance on informal procedures had the notable disadvantage that mergers could be called off on a preliminary view, rather than on a thorough investigation of the facts. Obviously, if a company disagreed with an informal decision, it could proceed with merger and put the decision to test in the courts. However, the costs, both financial and in time, made such an action impractical.

Article 85

Article 85 focuses specifically on anti-competitive agreements rather than market positions. It treats as being 'inconsistent with the common market', 'all agreements between undertakings, decisions by associates of undertakings and concerted practices which may have as their objective or effect the prevention or distortion of competition within the common market'.

For an agreement to fall under Article 85 it must both involve competitors and have an impact on the commercial conduct of *either* party. Such agreements include the acquisition of legal or *de facto* control over a competitor; provision for commercial co-operation; creation of a specific structure likely to be used for such co-operation; the possibility of the investing company increasing its influence over its competitor and perhaps to take control later; relationships between parties outside the community (global co-operation); rights of representation on the board of the company; special voting rights; and pre-emption and option rights.

Until relatively recently, Article 85 was not thought to apply to mergers, as it was assumed to refer only to companies that remained fully independent after an agreement was reached. However, this view changed in 1987 following the European Commission's investigation into the acquisition of a minority shareholding in Rothmans by Philip Morris. Although this was not itself a merger, and both companies remained independent, the Commission's summing up of the investigation implied a much broader role for Article 85 than was either necessary to deal with the issues raised by the Rothmans/Philip Morris case or had been previously assumed.

Article 85 was not applied to mergers before 1987 for two main reasons. It was assumed that, first, Article 85 could not apply to permanent changes in the structure of undertakings, and, second, it could not apply to simple changes in the ownership of property. The Rothmans/Philip Morris decision indicated that, whilst taking an equity stake in a competitor does not automatically constitute conduct restricting competition, it may have some influence on the 'commercial conduct of the companies in question so as to restrict or distort competition'. Thus, some mergers will, of themselves, fall within the scope of Article 85.

The precise circumstances in which Article 85 applied to mergers was never satisfactorily resolved. Article 85 certainly covered mergers to which the owners of both companies agreed; and to voluntary transfers of shares that could lead to restrictions on competition. Whether a takeover was agreed or hostile was not thought to be important in this context; more complex were the tricky legal questions about whether individuals selling shares should be treated in the same way as companies and institutions selling shares (see Reynolds (1989)) for a discussion).

These difficulties indicate why Article 85 was never applied, and was only crucial to the outcome of one case, the proposed acquisition, in 1988, of the Irish Distillers Group by a consortium involving Grand Metropolitan and Allied Lyons (although it was also used informally to persuade GEC/Siemens to modify the conditions of their acquisition of Plessey). In this case, the Commission threatened to take interim measures under Article 85 and this threat was sufficient to deter the bidders from their original plans.

However, there is little doubt that if the new merger regulations had not been agreed, Article 85 would have come to play a far more prominent role in Community merger control.

Article 85, unlike Article 86, had a formal procedure for notifying agreements. Agreements covered by Article 85 had to be notified to the Commission if the parties involved wished to obtain official exemption from the oversight of the Article or avoid certain fines. However, this requirement applied to a variety of potential infringements of the Article, including some but not all mergers. It was not, therefore, a comprehensive system of merger notification — although the increasing application of Article 85 to share transfers provided companies considering merger with a strong incentive to notify the Commission voluntarily. Notification under Article 85 could take place after the implementation of an agreement, thus the Commission could not always exercise prior control. As with Article 86, competitors of merging companies could also notify the Commission of potential infringements of Article 85.

Article 85, unlike Article 86, did give the Commission powers, exercised through the relevant national courts, to nullify an agreement. This presented few problems when a merger was being assessed in advance. However, nullifying a merger agreement after a merger has taken place poses difficult practical questions. Nullification implies the restoration of the situation that existed prior to the agreement. Yet, restoring share ownership to thousands or millions of former shareholders would have been an immense task, complicated by technical uncertainties about whether Article 85 actually applied to individual shareholders (see Reynolds (1989)). The Commission might instead have considered limiting the voting rights attached to shares as a more practical alternative to restoring ownership, had the new regulations not been agreed.

At its discretion, the Commission was able to exempt agreements from further investigation under Article 85. However, such an exemption had to be for a fixed time period — and this obviously presented problems in situations of permanent structural change such as mergers. Companies may be deterred from merger if they are uncertain about how long it would be allowed to continue. One solution here might have been to offer extremely long exemptions, similar to leaseholdings in the UK property market.

Problems with Articles 86 and 85

The absence of merger control from the Treaty of Rome clearly did not prevent the evolution of a workable Community system of merger control. However, despite achieving a number of notable results, particularly in the latter years of the 1980s, the system that emerged contained a number of serious flaws.

First, the inability to vet mergers before they took place increased the costs that would have been incurred by companies had the European Commission finally ruled against a merger. Once completed, the costs of unravelling a merger far exceed the costs of not implementing the merger in the first place.

Second, although once referred to the Commission, a merger would be evaluated on broad economic criteria, the process by which mergers were referred was founded on a somewhat unsatisfactory series of legal precedents. The most critical divergence between the legal and economic approaches lay in the treatment of dominant position. Article 86 focused on the abuse of dominant position — regulating the conduct of companies — whilst economists are increasingly concerned to regulate market structure (see Kay and Vickers (1988). This is because the kinds of market structure in which a dominant position can exist are relatively familiar, whilst actual instances of abuse of any dominant position are notoriously difficult to prove (the Commission's 'dawn raids' on companies, in the hope of finding incriminating documentation, illustrate these problems well). Article 86 failed, however, to prohibit the creation of dominant position, only its abuse. Article 85, which did regulate structure, was too limited in scope to overcome the inadequacies, in this respect, of Article 86.

Third, the Commission had no power to positively approve a merger under Article 86 (although some approval by using exemptions was allowed under Article 85), casting doubt on a merger's long-term viability. In particular, in cases in which the Commission had no objection to a merger, it would simply take no further action. Thus, it would remain open to a national authority to prohibit the merger — the normal hierarchy of authority between the Community and member states would in practice (though not in theory) fail to apply. This contrasts sharply with cases in which the Commission decided to prohibit a merger. On these occasions, national authorities did not, however, have the power to approve a merger that the Commission had disallowed (although it should be emphasized here that this is only accepted practice: such hierarchies of power have never been tested fully in the courts). Uncertainty also arose from the lack of any time limit within which the Commission had to decide whether to investigate a merger, and by the failure to create any clear procedure for deciding whether a merger should be investigated by national or Community authorities. This 'double jeopardy' — the risk that a merger would be investigated by two or more regulatory bodies, national or European — provided one of the strongest motivations for the new merger regulation.

Fourthly, the informal system of regulation that developed may have generated a degree of inequality in the treatment of relatively similar mergers. For instance, proposed mergers involving BA, British Sugar, and Pilkington, among others, were attacked by the Commission, whilst others of similar magnitude, such as Electrolux/Zanussi, Alfa Romeo/ Fiat, and Philips/Grundig were not. As Reynolds (1989) succinctly observes, 'there seems no logical reason for this' — although more cynical observers might detect a markedly higher success rate for merging companies with aspirations to become 'European Champions'. Also, it led to decisions being taken on the basis of less than rigorous analysis. An informal decision would be provided relatively quickly following a fairly superficial treatment of the issues. The large number of informal decisions also limited the extent to which the Commission's decisions were subject to rigorous scrutiny in the courts.

Finally, as Articles 86 and 85 grew in importance, the number of referrals (particularly under Article 85) increased rapidly. Without the new merger regulation, the growing role of the Commission in merger regulation would probably have exacerbated this effect, with its accompanying administrative difficulties. An increasing number of companies would have sought informal approval from the Commission, despite having no legal obligation to do so, simply because of the uncertainties surrounding the

Commission's powers and intentions in the field of merger regulation. Together, these defects present a powerful argument for improved Community merger regulation. It is to the new regulation that I now turn.

3. The new european merger regulation

As I have seen, prior to 1990 the European Community had no formal system of merger regulation. The Community's founding document, the Treaty of Rome, makes no mention of mergers and, despite the proposal of a merger regulation in 1973, little progress was made in formalizing merger control until 1987, when the original 1973 Directive was revived by then Competition Commissioner, Peter Sutherland. After substantial amendment, the new regulation was approved in December 1989, to come into force in the autumn of 1990. The key elements of the new regulation are outlined below.

The new merger regulation makes a clear division of responsibility for merger control between the European Commission and national governmental bodies. All mergers of companies with a combined world-wide turnover of more than 5 billion Ecus (£3.5 billion) will be scrutinized solely by the European Commission, subject only to two qualifications. First, each company (or at least two companies if more are involved) must have a turnover within the Community of more than 250 million Ecus. Second, a merger is exempt from Community control if either company generates two-thirds or more of turnover within one member state. Council of Ministers minutes also indicate that mergers with combined turnover of between 2 billion and 5 billion Ecus may be investigated by the Commission, but only at the request of a relevant member state. However, this right is not part of the body of the regulation. Mergers meeting these criteria must be notified to the Commission no later than one week after the conclusion of the merger agreement.

The member states have agreed to reassess the 5 billion Ecus turnover threshold within four years, with a view to reducing the threshold to 2 billion Ecus. This lower threshold was discussed extensively during the negotiations of the new regulations. However, it was opposed by, among others, the UK, and because of the need for a unanimous vote, a higher threshold satisfying the UK had to be agreed. When the threshold is reassessed, only a qualified majority will be necessary to bring about a change; thus, a lower threshold stands a greater chance of being adopted.

The definition of mergers covered by these notification criteria includes all concentrations resulting from the merger of two or more previously independent undertakings and the acquisition of direct or indirect control of a previously independent undertaking by another undertaking, or by one or more persons already controlling at least one undertaking. The creation of a joint venture performing on a lasting basis all the functions of an autonomous economic entity (and which does not involve the co-ordination of the competitive behaviour between the parties to the joint venture or between either party and the joint venture) also falls within the definition. (Distinguishing between these different types of joint venture is clearly a complex task — and is directly addressed by the Commission in a Commission Notice setting out examples of various types of joint ventures.) Joint ventures not falling within the regulation's definition of concentration may, none the less, be subject to scrutiny under Articles 85 and 86.

Once notified of a merger, the Commission has six weeks in which to decide whether to initiate proceedings. If it decides not to proceed, letters stating that the merger is compatible with the common market are issued to the undertakings concerned, and the relevant authorities in the member states. If the Commission decides that there is a prima-facie case for further investigation, it has a maximum further four months in which to investigate the merger, at the end of which it must declare whether or not the merger is compatible with the common market.

Investigation may include the examination of books and other business records, making copies of all or part of such records; and entering premises, land, or means of transport of the undertakings concerned. However, the purpose of the investigation must be specified in advance in writing, and the relevant national merger authority informed. The Commission is also required to consult with the undertakings involved throughout the investigation process, since it can only object to a merger if the investigated companies have first been able to comment on the detail of the objections cited. Throughout an investigation, the Commission works with the relevant national authorities, communicating with them and, where appropriate, employing their skills. The national authorities are kept informed throughout the investigation; some investigations are carried out by member authorities working with Commission officials, and the opinions of these authorities must be sought throughout. Before any final decision is taken to prohibit a merger, the Commission must also consult an advisory committee on concentrations comprised of one or twos representatives of each member state. The Commission is required to take 'the utmost account' of the advisory committee's opinion of its decision; indeed, the advisory committee may require the publication of its opinion along with the Commission's final decision.

Member states are not able to overrule decisions reached by the European Commission, unless given specific permission to do so by the Commission. However, member states may intervene where a concentration threatens public security, the plurality of the media, or the security of financial services. Also, the European Commission has agreed to waive any right to investigate mergers falling beneath the notification threshold that may have followed in the past from the application of Articles 85 and 86. Such decisions are now entirely under the jurisdiction of the relevant member states.

In exceptional cases, a member state may argue that a particular merger under investigation by the Commission, whilst having no undesirable impact within the European Community as a whole, restricts competition in a distinct market *within* that state's borders. If the Commission so wishes, it may allow the relevant national authorities three weeks in which to judge whether the merger does have such an effect.

The new regulation makes no presumption either for or against mergers. Rather, the Commission will find a merger to be incompatible with the common market only if it has both a 'community dimension and creates or strengthens a dominant position in the common market, or a substantial part of it'. When deciding whether a dominant position exists, the Commission must take account of various factors, including:

1. market position and economic and financial power of the firms concerned;
2. the possibilities of choice of suppliers and consumers;
3. access to supplies or markets;
4. the structure of the markets affected, having regard to actual and potential, domestic, European, and international competition;
5. barriers to entry (legal or *de facto*);
6. the trend of supply and demand for the goods or services concerned.

The definition of a market will in no way he assumed to correspond to either national or Community geographical borders, unless this is indicated by the analysis above.

Mergers which, because of the market share of the firms concerned, are unlikely to impede effective competition are presumed to be compatible with the common market; this presumption exists in particular where the merging firms do not have a market share of over 25 per cent in the common market as a whole or in any substantial part of it.

There are a number of sanctions and powers available to the Commission if it finds a merger to be incompatible with the common market. If the merger is still at the proposal stage, the Commission may decide to prohibit it, or, in the event of a completed merger, require the breaking up of the undertakings such that competition is adequately restored. Lesser measures, such as requiring modifications to a merger arrangement, are also available. In addition, the Commission may fine undertakings up to 10 per cent of annual turnover for failure to abide by the Commission's ruling on merger, or to implement agreed modifications. The Commission may also impose lesser fines of up to 50,000 Ecus for incorrect notification or non-notification of a merger; for the supply of incorrect or misleading information in notification or during investigation; for the failure to supply requested information; or for the refusal to submit to investigation. Delays in meeting Commission requests may also be penalized by fines of up to 100,000 Ecus a day.

The new regulation clearly represents a significant change from the previous regime. I now consider the differences in depth, and assess the likely effectiveness of the new controls. Before turning to the fine details of the new regulations, however, I first examine the context in which they will operate, and which will more than anything determine their success or failure — the evolution of strong European institutions and their relationship with sovereign states.

4. Subsidiarity, centralization, and the new merger regulation

How should the task of regulating European mergers be divided between the European Commission and the member states? Deciding which mergers should be assessed by the Commission and which by national merger authorities provoked fierce debate. Some member states, including the UK and West Germany, preferred the Commission to vet only the very few largest cross-border mergers (if it had to have any role whatsoever), with national regulators assessing the remainder. Other member states want the Commission to have far greater authority. This conflict reflects both differences between the existing merger regulations operated by the member states; the political debate between centralists and federalists in the European Community; and genuine differences of economic interest.

It would clearly be possible, if administratively and financially costly, for the European Community's merger regulation to be entirely centralized in Brussels — or entirely decentralized to the member states. However, the Community's fundamental commitment to the principle of subsidiarity suggests I look for a decentralized solution where possible.

Subsidiarity is the principle that decisions should he taken at the 'lowest' possible level — by all those (or their representatives) affected by the decision, and by no one who will be unaffected by the decision. The most clear statement of this principle in the context of the Community to date came in a report by the European Parliament (1990):

> The principle of subsidiarity implies that the (Community) will be required to perform those tasks which can be carried out more effectively by the institutions of the (Community) than by the Member States acting independently, because of their importance or effects or for reasons of more effective implementation. The Community therefore intervenes only in a subsidiary capacity and in accordance with a principle . . . whereby each level is granted powers only because these cannot, given their nature and scope, be exercised efficiently and effectively at any other level.

This definition is vague about precisely which tasks should be undertaken by the Community — grounds of 'importance' could easily become a catch-all justification for centralization, for example — and the definition will no doubt be improved over time. However, I am able to make the presumption that merger regulation should be carried out by national regulatory authorities, unless it can be shown that they will not perform this task adequately. I can also demonstrate that using the most decentralized definition of subsidiarity suggested by the European Parliament there is strong justification for Community regulation of certain large mergers. This decentralized approach, 'assigns to the Community level only those tasks the dimension or effects of which extend beyond national frontiers'.[2]

In applying the principle of subsidiarity to merger control in the European Community, the lowest practical level at which merger regulation can be exercised is by regulators appointed by member governments — such as the MMC, or the West German Federal Cartel Office — and the highest level is the European Commission. Clearly, using my decentralized definition, there should be no objection to a national merger authority regulating a merger involving two domestic firms with no international trade effects. There is no way in which the decision reached by the regulator in those circumstances can give the country concerned an unfair advantage over another member state — although the regulator's decision may clearly be to the disadvantage of its own national population. Although the Commission might be able to regulate such mergers more efficiently, I argue that the inadequacy of domestic institutions, when this has no clear cross-border repercussions, is a matter for the domestic electorate at the ballot box; the Commission should play no part in such decisions, regardless of how poor it considers those decisions to have been.

Where mergers concern companies involved in cross-border trade, there is potential for opportunism by the regulator on behalf of its narrow national interest. For example, a domestic company may have an opportunity to strengthen its international competitiveness by reducing domestic competition through merger. If the domestic regulator is able to allow such a merger, it may benefit its own citizens — workers, shareholders, taxpayers — at the expense of those in the other nations in which the newly merged firm will operate.[3] In other words, there are costs to the merger that arise outside the jurisdiction of the regulator — they are 'externalized'. The solution to this problem is to 'internalize' these costs by ensuring that the regulator's jurisdiction extends to the entire market in which the merging companies operate, so that the regulator is indifferent between the residents of different countries. This notion of 'equal treatment' is the vital difference between national and European level regulation, as many national regulators already base their decisions on technical criteria similar to those of the Commission, yet can reach very different conclusions.

There are, in theory at least, three ways in which such 'equal treatment' regulation of cross-border mergers could be achieved, and these vary greatly in efficiency. First, each country affected by a merger could be given the right to veto the merger and would be able to carry out its own independent investigation and decision procedures. This has obvious potential inefficiencies because of duplication.

Second, the various states concerned could negotiate bilateral or multilateral agreements to delegate the regulatory task to one member authority. Obviously, this carries the risk that a particular merger would be regulated in the interests of the regulating nation. However, this risk could be minimized by regularly rotating the regulatory responsibility. The greater the number of national markets affected, however, the more complex the process of negotiating workable bilateral arrangements becomes.

A third, and more practical, option is for all the nations affected to delegate regulation to a single authority (preferably one that is already operational) with jurisdiction over the market(s) concerned — in this case, the obvious institution is the European Commission. This avoids the unnecessary duplication of resources, and removes much of the considerable uncertainty within the business community regarding regulatory intentions and procedures that often arises in merger.

Thus, I conclude that *there is a strong justification for Community regulation of all mergers significantly affecting more than one member state.* However, national authorities should be free to regulate in whatever way they wish all mergers with solely domestic impact.

Recognizing that there is a strong case for Community-level merger regulation of cross-border mergers should not, however, be confused with support for wholesale centralization of merger control in Brussels. I have already seen that one of the most often used arguments for the new regulation was that it would allow a 'one-stop shop'. That a 'one-stop shop' is desirable seems to have been widely accepted, almost without question. It is somewhat ironic that legislation designed to promote competition should fail to be alert to the dangers of monopoly for a regulator as much as any other organization. Indeed, the history of regulation, both at the national and Community level, suggests that there are significant benefits to be gained from 'competition' amongst regulators, much as in the rest of the economy. The lack of such a competitive element in the new regulation may prove to be a serious weakness.

One of the few strengths of the Community's previous merger control regime was the element of 'competition' that existed between the national authorities. Under that regime, a number of mergers — such as those between British Airways and British Caledonian, GEC/Siemens and Plessey — were better regulated because of the 'conflict' between national authorities and the Commission, although the costs arising from this 'double jeopardy' should not be underestimated.

An initial investigation of the British Airways/British Caledonian case by the MMC resulted in the terms of the merger being modified, with British Airways forfeiting rights to fly on certain routes. However, the European Commission was not satisfied with this outcome, and investigated the merger for itself. Its findings led it to require further changes to the merger arrangements, including the forfeit of additional routes. (Less satisfactory, however, was the unnecessary duplication of resources during the simultaneous MMC and European Commission investigations of the Minorco/Consolidated Goldfields merger; the MMC concluded that the merger should be prohibited, and the European Commission reached the same conclusion a fortnight later.)

Furthermore, a degree of 'competition' between regulators can be an important safeguard against regulatory capture — regulators acting on behalf of the companies they are supposed to be regulating (see Kay and Vickers (1988)). It can also minimize the extent to which competitive advantage is conferred arbitrarily on a merged company through differences between national and European regulations.

It is clear that competition between regulators is, by definition, virtually incompatible with the 'one-stop shop'. This need not mean, however, that all of the benefits of 'competition' between regulators must be lost in the new system. The value of European-level regulation is that decisions should not be biased in favour of one country against another; however, the European Commission has no advantages over national authorities in terms of access to information, informal cultural access to management, or staffing. In all of these areas, national authorities are better placed than the Commission. Thus, a division of roles might offer a better way forward — national regulators collecting information, with the Commission setting the terms of the investigation and being responsible for taking the final decision.

The separation of roles might be even more effective were the Commission to delegate initial decisions to a national authority (selecting one of the authorities of the countries concerned), and concern itself primarily with monitoring national decisions, overturning them only when necessary. Also, the emphasis on subsidiarity would be further strengthened by allowing countries affected by a merger to veto any Commission involvement by unanimous agreement amongst themselves as to the appropriate decision. (It would be surprising if such a right were exercised in other than exceptional circumstances.)

Fears about the 'one-stop shop', and suggestions that the roles of Commission and member states be distinct yet in tension are no mere theoretical niceties. It is vital that a wholesale centralization of the merger regulation process to Brussels is avoided. In addition to substantial administrative inefficiencies, it would forfeit the limited but important benefits of the remaining potential for competition between regulators, so increasing the risk that companies will concentrate their considerable lobbying resources on, and succeed in, 'capturing' the Commission. Add to this the inevitable subjectivity involved in merger regulation (how to define a market, how to measure the degree of competition, and so on), and it becomes clear that a 'captured' regulator could be a considerable asset to a company contemplating or, indeed, seeking to avoid, merger.

Having outlined the principles on which merger regulation should be based, and the issues relevant in determining whether merger regulation should occur at the national or European level, I now consider the implications of the new merger regulation in detail.

Implications for the new regulation

It is immediately apparent that in all three areas of concern— the criteria by which mergers are regulated, the allocation of regulatory responsibility between member states and the European Commission, and efficiency— the new regulation has considerable advantages over the previous *ad hoc* system. First, much of the procedural uncertainty has been removed. There is now a formal notification system, an explicit and binding timetable, and the ability to approve acceptable mergers. Second, the need for European-level regulation of mergers with a significant impact on Community markets has been explicitly recognized.

Third, the criteria on which merger regulation will be based, though still inevitably subject to some discretion, now firmly emphasizes getting market structures right, rather than relying on controlling the conduct of the companies operating within these markets. Superficially attractive, but, as the discussion above indicated, ultimately spurious, arguments about economies of scale and the creation of 'European Champions' have been firmly rejected. (However, there is a disturbing vagueness in allowing the Commission to take account of likely 'technical and economic progress' in reaching its decision; already industrialists in areas of high technology change can be heard justifying mergers between the large European companies in order to ensure European success in the 'global markets of the future'. The UK experience of the 1960s' mergers provides a salutary warning.) Significantly, the creation of a dominant position is now sufficient grounds for prohibition of a merger, whereas previously a dominant position had to be 'abused'.

In terms of efficiency, a more serious criticism has been made (see earlier discussion) of the limited opportunity for 'competition between regulators' that has followed from the commitment to a 'one-stop shop'. The Commission is obliged to consult national authorities during investigations, and to give substantial weight to the advisory committee comprising representatives of the states whose companies are involved. This is welcome, as far as it goes — and might arguably be strengthened by the oversight of the member states. However, if the interests of different states in a particular merger vary, this scrutiny is unlikely to be effective, thus allowing the Commission a relatively free hand. It is, therefore, likely that the Commission will itself undertake the bulk of the practical work involved in an investigation — much of which could comfortably be delegated to the national authorities (so according more closely with the spirit of subsidiarity).

This will impose severe limitations on the Commission's relatively small competition staff. Indeed, there are legitimate fears that the practical demands of regulating the forty to fifty proposed mergers per year that the Commission expects may be such as to cause considerable delays. If these fears are only partially realized, one of the major advantages of the new system — its speed and predictability — may be undermined.

Fears of regulatory capture are not without basis. In October 1991, the Commission blocked a French/Italian acquisition of de Havilland, a Canadian aircraft manufacturer. Although the decision made sense on competition grounds, it provoked a fierce political row within the Commission, and might well have been voted down on the casting vote of the (French) president of the Commission, Mr Delors, who in the end abstained. One way to reduce the potential for political fudging and the promotion of 'European Champions' by stealth would be to delegate the regulatory function to an independent European Merger Office, along similar lines to the German Federal Cartel Office. With a clear mandate to promote competition, such an independent body would not prevent political interference but, by requiring the Commission to publicly overturn an unpalatable decision, it would make such interference more obvious and thus a more painful option for the Commissioners. Equally worrying problems arise with regard to the allocation of responsibility for regulating particular mergers. The Commission has voluntarily abandoned its rights to investigate certain cross-border mergers falling beneath the referral turnover threshold — many of which it would previously have been able to investigate under Articles 86 and 85. The Community has already acknowledged this potential weakness by committing itself to reassessing the threshold, with the probability of lowering the threshold to 2 billion Ecus. However, this problem highlights more fundamental problems with the turnover referral threshold.

In the discussion above, I observed that the basis for prohibiting merger should be the presence of an anti-competitive effect. Yet, mergers are to be referred to the Commission primarily on the basis of absolute size, rather than market structure. It is quite conceivable that there will be many mergers which have a significant anti-competitive impact, affecting more than one country, that will not be investigated by the Commission because the combined turnover is too small. Such mergers will thus be subject only to regulation by national merger authorities. To the extent that national regulations differ, and whilst acknowledging that some countries may choose to delegate an investigation to the Commission, many essentially similar mergers may receive arbitrarily different treatment. This may undermine some aspects of the single market.

The likely size of this problem is presently unclear, though it may be considerable. Previously the Commission would have been able to intervene in cases where inadequate national regulation allowed a merger to proceed to the detriment of the Community as a whole. Now it is unable to do so. One possible solution is to reduce the referral threshold to a level at which it embraces all conceivable mergers that might create a 25 per cent share in the common market or any substantial part thereof. This is the direction in which the Community appears to be moving. However, with the proposed reduction in the referral threshold, this would vastly increase the number of referrals to the Commission, presenting significant administrative difficulties, and strengthening fears of overcentralization.

Similar criticisms can be made of the exemption from Community merger regulation of mergers involving a company that generates two-thirds of its turnover in one member state. This exemption might allow, for example, a country to prevent foreign entry into its domestic markets by approving mergers giving domestic companies substantial market power. Although the exemption appears to accord with the principle of subsidiarity, involving, for example, only domestic producers with no international trade, it would in fact impose an external cost on the foreign companies unable to enter the national market. Thus, it should in principle be regulated by the Commission.

Another challenge for the Commission will be dealing with the competition implications of deals that remove potential competitors rather than actual competitors from the market. It is quite likely that cross-border mergers will connect firms in similar industries, serving different geographical markets. It may be that in such a merger, the number of actual competitors in either market is unchanged. Each market was dominated by one firm, and each market will still be dominated by one firm, even though it will now be the same firm whereas before it would not have been. This is an issue that has already been raised in the UK with respect to mergers between water companies, and also in the defence sector. The belief is that firms in different geographical markets but within the same industry hold a pro-competitive presence because they represent credible potential entrants to the market.

The degree to which potential competition should be considered a factor in preventing mergers is complicated, and involves weighing up the effectiveness of the potential competition in the absence of a merger. Many firms would maintain the only way that they can be effective is to merge, and this was an argument voiced in the case or Nestlé's take-over of Rowntree. The new regulation does require the Commission to look at potential competition. It will find that, to the extent that the single market/'1992' programme removes barriers to cross-border entry, potential competition will increase. It may well be that many mergers that would previously have been considered 'anti-competitive' will in future be deemed acceptable because of the greater number of potential competitors. The new merger regulation may thus have considerably less impact than is currently envisaged. The Commission should also make clear its attitudes to mergers between companies that meet the reference criteria in terms of turnover within the Community, but which are both registered outside the Community.

Finally, by allowing solely national jurisdiction over mergers in sectors where a concentration is considered threatening to public security, the plurality of the media, or the security of financial services, the regulation prevents the Commission from overseeing the restructuring of some of the most important areas of current and potential merger activity. In both cases, ending the exemptions from Community regulation would greatly increase the number of mergers referred to the Commission, and thus the administrative burden.

There are, then, a number of potential weaknesses in an otherwise attractive system. The extent to which these weaknesses will undermine the regulation will only become apparent when it is operational. However, the weaknesses do not lie in the fundamental principles underlying the regulation, and there is every probability that they will not present insuperable difficulties.

5. Conclusions

The new European Community merger regulation represents considerable progress from the *ad hoc* regime which preceded it. Mergers will now be regulated on clear economic criteria, designed to ensure a competitive single market. Many of the uncertainties associated with the earlier regimes will be removed.

Some criticism of the new regime is based on doubts about whether the 'one-stop shop' principle of merger control will actually be achieved. By the end of 1991, it appeared to be working fairly smoothly; however, the early 1990s have been a relatively quiet period of merger activity. Even so, this is not quite the essence of the matter as the threshold level of 5 billion Ecus does not capture all mergers which might have anti-competitive effects on Community markets with borders extending beyond a particular state. Indeed, the exemptions based on domestic turnover, and for certain industrial sectors, may mean that the European Commission regulates only a very few mergers. Yet the solution favoured by many in the Community — simply lowering the threshold — is a recipe for bureaucratic overload and inefficiency, presenting substantial difficulties as well as risking failure to meet the Community's commitment to subsidiarity.

The need is not for a clear demarcation between Community and national merger policies but for greater integration between them — which would, incidentally, require the development of merger policies in the many Community states which currently have weak provision. There is in reality no distinction between mergers with a Community dimension and those without — indeed the notion that there is itself contradicts the single market concept. There are mergers where local issues are most important, others where national and international issues are critical, and some which raise issues at all levels. There are some cases as the regulation acknowledges — where local and Community arguments point in different directions, and others — as the regulation does not acknowledge — where competition between different regulatory authorities ensures more effective scrutiny.

I would like to see an outcome in which the Commission (or an independent delegate body) worked closely with national competition agencies and subcontracted much of its work to them. The issue has not developed in this way because the regulation is the product of a battle for authority between Brussels and — particularly — London and

Bonn, and a battle for content between — particularly — Bonn and London on one axis and Paris and Rome on another. As the Community matures, I hope that the regulation will evolve in ways which reflect the needs of economics more than those of diplomacy.

Helpful comments on an earlier draft by Stephen Kon of S. J. Berwin & Co., Evan Davis, Paul Geroski, John Kay, and David Thompson are gratefully acknowledged. The usual disclaimer applies.

Notes

1 For details and discussion of the cases cited in this chapter see e.g Euromoney (1989), Kluwer (1988), the annual reports of the Organization for Economic Co-operation and Development Committee on Competition and Law, or Reynolds (1989).

2 This contrasts with a more centralized alternative 'based on the idea that the states will transfer to a higher level only those tasks which are essential and which will be better accomplished at Community level than by the states acting individually'.

3 Assuming, of course, that this benefit exceeds the cost resulting from reduced domestic competition — something that is assumed more often than it is achieved.

References

Euromoney (1989) 'The regulations governing mergers and acquisitions across the European Community', *International Financial Law Review.*

European Parliament (1990) 'Report by Giscard d'Estaing on the principle of subsidiarity' .

Fairburn, J. A., and Kay, J. A (1989) *Mergers and Merger Policy,* Oxford: Oxford University Press.

Kay, J. A, and Vickers, J. S. (1988) 'Regulatory reform in Britain', *Economic Policy*, No.7.

Kluwer (1988), 'Merger Control in the EC'

OECD (annual) 'Competition policy in OECD countries', annual report on the OECD Committee on Competition Law and Policy.

Reynolds, M. J. (1989) 'Application of Articles 85 and 86 to mergers', paper given to 8th Annual Conference, International Anti-Trust Law.

5. The Making of EC Environmental Policy
David Vogel

Environmental regulation under the Treaty of Rome

While the word "environment" does not appear in the 1957 Treaty of Rome which established the European Community, during the mid-1960s the Community began to recognize that the establishment of a common market also required the enactment of common environmental regulations. The EC adopted its first environmental Directive in 1967: it established standards for classifying, packaging and labeling dangerous substances. Three years later the Council approved a Directive on automotive emissions. In October 1972, at the Paris Summit, the EC Heads of State issued a communique stating that economic expansion was "not an end in itself", and that economic growth should be linked to the "improvement in living and working conditions of life of the citizens of the EC" — a phrase that was taken from the Preamble to the Treaty of Rome (Freestone 1991: 135). The summit called upon the Commission to draw up a Community environmental policy and authorized the European Commission to establish a separate administrative body or directorate whose responsibilities included environmental protection.

The following year, the Council of Ministers adopted the EC's first official environmental programme. Based on Article 2 of the Treaty of Rome, which defined one of the Community's objectives as the promotion of "a harmonious development of economic activities", the EC's "action plan" stated that "major aspects of environmental policy in individual countries must no longer be planned or implemented in isolation... and national policies should be harmonized within the community" (O'Riordan 1979: 249).

The plan stated that the EC's environmental policy would be guided by three objectives or principles (Briggs 1986: 110-111). The first was to reduce and prevent pollution both by "developing protective measures" and by requiring that the "polluter pay". The second principle was that both national and Community regulations should seek to protect the environment as well as improve the quality of life. Thirdly, the Community pledged its support for international initiatives to address environmental problems that could not be adequately addressed on either a regional or national basis.

The Community's Second Environmental Action Programme, adopted in 1977, restated and extended these aims. It also stressed the need for additional research and data collection, and expressed the EC's intention to develop a system of environmental impact assessment. The Community's Third Programme, which was approved in 1983, reflected the growth of concern about unemployment and resource depletion: it emphasized the role of environmental regulation in both preserving scarce resources for future use and "creating employment by developing environmentally compatible

David Vogel: 'The Making of EC Environmental Policy' from *MAKING POLICY IN EUROPE*, edited by S. Sven Anderson and Kjell A. Elliason (London: Sage Publications, 1993), pp. 115-131. Reprinted by permission of Sage Publications Ltd.

industries and technologies" (Briggs 1986: 110-111). It also shifted the Community's priorities from pollution reduction to pollution prevention.

Each of these three action plans was accompanied by a steady expansion in the scope of Community environmental regulations. Between the early 1970s and the mid-1980s, the Community issued 120 Regulations and Directives. A Regulation is directly applicable to all member states and thus automatically becomes part of national law. A Directive establishes a framework for national policies; it only becomes effective after member states have enacted legislation implementing it. Directives generally specify the result to be achieved, leaving it up to national authorities to determine the means and mechanisms of implementation. Most EC environmental rules take the form of Directives.

The EC's environmental policies enacted during this fifteen-year period covered a wide range of areas: the regulation of air, water, noise pollution and waste disposal, the prevention of accidents, safety requirements for chemicals, environmental impact assessment as well as wildlife and habitat protection. The EC's efforts to improve water quality were particularly important: the so-called "bathing water Directive" established uniform standards for bathing water, drinking water and shellfish waters, while another group of Directives limited the discharge of various toxins and chemicals into Community waters. The Sixth Amendment to the Framework Directive on Dangerous Substances, adopted in 1979, established a Community-wide system for the screening of new chemicals.

In addition, the EC addressed a number of global environmental problems. It ratified the Washington Convention on Trade in Endangered Species (CITIS), and the Bonn Convention on the conservation of migratory species; it also banned all imports of seals and seal-pups. Thus by the mid-1980s, most important aspects of both national and international environmental policy had been addressed, in one form or other, at the Community level (Haigh 1989). And in many critical areas of environmental policy-making Brussels had come to play as important a role as the nation-state.

The growth of EC environmental regulation during the 1970s was due to a number of factors. An important role was played by political developments in Europe. EC environmental policy was in part a response to the increase in public concern about environmental issues that took place throughout the entire industrialized world during the late 1960s and early 1970s. A survey taken in the (then) nine EC member states in 1973 reported that "pollution was cited as the most important problem, ahead of inflation, poverty and unemployment" (Liberatore 1991: 289). At the same time, environmental organizations became more politically active in a number of European countries, and most national governments significantly expanded and strengthened the scope of their own regulatory controls over industry.

In order to preserve their legitimacy, EC institutions attempted to respond to these new political forces and public pressures by enacting environmental regulations as well. EC environmental policy represented a way for Community officials to address the "democratic deficit": the gap between the Community's power and its lack of accountability to the electorate of its member states. At the same time, environmental policy-making provided a way for officials in Brussels to preserve the momentum of European integration, which in many other respects had stagnated during the 1970s. Indeed, the steady pace of environmental regulations, Directives and decisions enacted during this period stands in sharp contrast to the "political vicissitudes, budgetary crises, and recurrent waves of Europessimism of the 1970s and early 1980s" (Majone 1991: 95).

Economic considerations also contributed to the expansion of EC environmental regulation. The steady expansion of national environmental regulations posed a potentially serious threat to both the creation and maintenance of a common market. If nations were allowed to adopt their own product standards, such as for chemical safety or automobile emissions, nations with stricter environmental standards would be likely to attempt to "protect" both their citizens and their industries by excluding goods produced in member states with weaker regulatory requirements. Consequently, the free flow of goods within the EC would be impaired.

In the case of production standards, nations that had adopted more stringent pollution controls than other member states would find the goods produced by their industries at a competitive disadvantage. They would therefore be forced to choose between excluding goods produced by member states with weaker regulatory requirements or lowering their own standards to those of other EC member states. The former threatened economic integration; the latter made national regulatory policies hostage to those of the least strict member state.

A third motivation for EC environmental policy was geographic. The twelve Member States of the EC comprise a large land-area — roughly 1.6 million square kilometers — and encompass a considerable diversity of climate and topography. Certainly, the environmental problems of nations on the periphery of the Community, such as Greece and the Netherlands, have little in common and their national environmental policies do not affect the citizens of the other. However, a number of member states are physically close to one another and the quality of their physical environment, as well as the health of their population, is significantly affected by the environmental policies of their neighbours. For example, the Rhine flows west through three EC member states, namely Germany, France and the Netherlands; accordingly the quality of Dutch water is largely determined by the severity of German and French pollution controls. On the other hand, because winds in Europe travel from west to east, the air quality in northern Europe is affected by industrial emissions from Britain. As one journalist observed, "Environmental regulations are among the world's toughest in ... West Germany and the Netherlands. But that does little good when winds waft Britain's loosely regulated power-plant fumes and their product, acid rain, eastward" (Diehl 1988: 1). Equally important, industrial accidents do not respect national boundaries.

A number of important EC environmental initiatives reflect the high degree of physical interdependence of the Community. For example, the "Seveso Directive" was adopted in 1982 following a major industrial accident in Italy that unleashed large quantities of the chemical dioxin into the atmosphere. It addressed the issue of accident prevention and required industries to prepare safety reports and emergency response plans. The EC's Directive on the Conservation of Wild Birds, adopted in 1979, required member states "to preserve, maintain or re-establish a sufficient diversity and area of habitats for birds", many of which migrated across national boundaries (Haigh 1989: 288). And following the disclosure that 41 drums of waste from Seveso which had been lost in transit had been found in the French countryside, a Directive was approved that established a system for controlling and regulating the collection and disposal of hazardous wastes moving across frontiers.

For all these reasons — political, economic and geographic — the Community attempted to harmonize a wide range of national environmental regulations. Not surprisingly, this effort led to considerable conflict between those nations which favoured stricter environmental standards and those which did not. The former, most notably Germany, Denmark and the Netherlands, were relatively affluent and had strong domestic environmental movements. Other nations, such as the UK, France and Italy, had weaker environmental pressure-groups and their industries were less willing or able to absorb the costs of stricter environmental controls. Still others, such as Greece and Spain, were even less interested in Community air and water quality standards. Not only were they relatively poor, but they were physically distant from the "core" of the EC and thus unaffected by acid rain emissions or the quality of the EC's major rivers. Further complicating agreement was the requirement of the Treaty of Rome that all Directives be approved unanimously.

Thus it took the Community five years before it could reach agreement on a Directive reducing emissions of sulphur dioxide (Haigh and Baldock 1989: 32-35). The positions of the member states fell into four groups. West Germany, the Netherlands and Denmark were prepared to spend substantial sums on retrofitting their existing plants. However, both Britain and Italy, which were less affluent and whose power plants burned considerable quantities of coal, were not. France and Belgium were relatively indifferent to sulphur emission standards since they relied heavily on nuclear power. Most of the remaining nations were not interested in the Directive since they were not affected by acid rain in the first place.

The Large Combustion Directive, which was finally approved in June 1988, advanced a rather complex formula to reconcile these differences. Emissions of SO_2 would be reduced in three stages — 1993,1998 and 2003 — while NOX emissions would be reduced in two stages. In addition, the percentage reductions of each pollutant for each stage varied by country. Thus Belgium, Germany, France, the Netherlands and Luxembourg were required to reduce their SO_2 emissions by 40 percent by 1993. On the other hand, Spain was not required to reduce its emissions at all while Portugal was permitted to increase its emissions.

The form of pollution control also led to disputes among the member states. For example, most nations favoured uniform emission standards for water pollutants, since that would impose roughly similar costs on firms throughout the EC. The British, however, argued that since their rapidly flowing rivers could absorb relatively large amounts of pollution without impairing water quality, uniform emission standards were inappropriate; they instead favored water *quality* standards. "As one British official put it, Italy economically benefits from the amount of sunshine it receives each year. Why should not our industry be able to take similar advantage of our long coastline. . . and rapidly flowing waters?"' (Vogel 1989: 103). Once again the result was a complex compromise: the emissions of highly hazardous substances would be controlled by uniform emission standards, while less dangerous substances would be regulated by water quality standards.

Notwithstanding the steady growth of EC environmental regulation, the legal basis of EC environmental policy remained somewhat tenuous. Most Community environmental policy could be justified under Article 100 of the Treaty, which authorized the harmonization of all national regulations that directly affected the functioning or establishment of a common market. However in a number of cases, the link between EC environmental regulations and the common market was less clear.

What, for example, did establishing EC standards for drinking or bathing water quality have to do with economic integration? Why should the Community require the member states to protect wild birds? To justify its environmental regulations in these areas, the EC was forced to rely upon Article 235 of the Treaty, which authorized legislation not envisaged elsewhere if it was "necessary to attain . . . one of the objectives of the Community" (Freestone 1991: 136). Since the Preamble to the Treaty of Rome had declared that improving the "living and working conditions of life of the citizens of the EC" was a legitimate Community objective, it presumably followed that the EC could legislate on any aspect of the environment that it chose. Not surprisingly, this somewhat strained legal defence was not entirely persuasive (Close 1978: 461-468).

Moreover the Treaty of Rome, by not explicitly mentioning environmental protection, provided EC policy-makers with no framework for balancing environmental protection with other EC goals, the most important of which was obviously the creation of the common market itself. For virtually any level of environmental regulation was compatible with increased economic integration, providing that it was decided at the Community level. Accordingly, many observers argued that the requirements of a number of EC Directives tended to reflect the "least common denominator" and that therefore the Community had, in effect, subordinated environmental goals to the creation of a common market.

The Single European Act

On 1 July 1987, the Treaty of Rome was revised by the Single European Act (SEA). While the most important purpose of this amendment to the Community's constitution was to facilitate the creation of a single European market, it also introduced a number of important changes into Community environmental policy and policy-making.

Most important, Article 100A of the SEA explicitly recognized the improvement of environmental quality as a legitimate Community objective in its own right. This meant that EC environmental policies need no longer be justified in terms of their contribution to economic integration. The EC now had a firm constitutional basis for regulating any aspect of the environment. Even more important, the SEA stated that in harmonizing national regulations, "the Commission . . . will take as a base a high level of [environmental] protection". This explicitly linked harmonization with the improvement of environmental quality, rather than with, as under the Treaty of Rome, simply economic integration.

Article 130R further declared that "environmental protection requirements shall be a component of the Community's other policies" (Kramer 1987: 651). This provision accorded environmental protection an unusually high priority among the Community's objectives, since no other EC goal was granted a commensurate provision. In practical terms, it strengthened the hands of the Commission's Environmental Directorate (DG XI) in its conflicts with those Directorates whose focus was essentially economic.

To reassure those member states who feared that harmonization would require them to relax existing national regulations, both Article 100A and 130T explicitly granted member states the right to maintain or introduce national environmental standards stricter than those approved by Brussels, provided they did not constitute a form of "hidden protectionism" and were otherwise compatible with the Treaty of Rome (Kramer 1987: 681). The determination as to whether or not a national regulation that affected the completion of the internal market created an open or disguised barrier to trade was left up to the European Court of Justice (Vandermeersch 1987: 559-588).

The Single European Act also facilitated the adoption of environmental regulations by the Council. Prior to 1987, all Community legislation had to be approved unaminously. Legislation approved under Article 130, the SEA's environmental article, still required unanimity. However, the SEA permitted Directives approved under Article 100A — which provides for the approximation of laws concerned with the functioning of the common market — to be approved by a "qualified majority," defined as 54 of 76 votes. This provided an alternative means for enacting environmental legislation, one which deprived any single member state of the power to block approval. In fact, virtually all environmental Directives enacted since the passage of the SEA have been based on 100A.

The Single European Act also expanded the role of the European Parliament, which has generally been more supportive of stricter environmental standards than the Council, in shaping Community legislation. For ten articles of the EC Treaty, the SEA established a "cooperation procedure" under which Parliament has the right to propose amendments to legislation approved by the Council of Ministers. If the Commission chooses to retain these amendments, then the Council must then either reject them unanimously or adopt them by a qualified majority.

The SEA also contributed to the strengthening of EC environmental policy in another, more indirect, way. A primary purpose of the new Community treaty was to accelerate the move toward the creation of a single internal market — a goal which had been formally outlined in a Commission White Paper issued a few years earlier. However, Community officials recognized that the removal of all barriers to intra-Community trade by the end of 1992 was also likely to exacerbate Europe's environmental problems. A 1989 report entitled, *"1992" the Environmental Dimension*, examined some of the adverse environmental consequences of the completion of the internal market. The most important of these would be a dramatic increase in transportation, which would significantly increase emissions of both sulphur dioxide and nitrogen oxides. In addition, by accelerating intra-community trade, economic integration increased the exposure of member states to the import of environmental "bads" such as toxic and hazardous wastes from other member states. Thus the Community's renewed commitment to economic integration made the strengthening of EC environmental standards even more urgent.

The strengthening of environmental protection within the Community's constitution both reflected and reinforced the public's growing concern with environmental issues that took place throughout Europe during the latter part of the 1980s. Stimulated in part by the Soviets' Chernobyl disaster and a massive chemical spill of toxins into the River Rhine that destroyed a half million fish in four countries — both of which occurred in 1986 — environmental issues moved rapidly to a prominent position on the political agenda in a number of EC Member States. The *Washington Post* observed:

> Dead seals in the North Sea, a chemical fire on the Loire, killer algae off the coast of Sweden, contaminated drinking water in Cornwall (England). A drumbeat of emergencies has intensified the environmental debate this year in Europe, where public concern about pollution has never been higher. (Herman 1988: 19)

A poll taken in December 1986 reported that 52 percent of the German electorate regarded environment quality as the most important issue facing their nation (Kirkland 1988: 118). In 1987, the German Green Party received 8.3 percent of the votes cast for the Bundestag and increased their number of seats in the legislative body of the Federal Republic to 42. More significantly, in European Parliament elections held in June 1989, Europe's Green parties captured an additional seventeen seats, bringing their total representation to 37 and making them among the biggest "winners" of the first "European" election held after the enactment of the SEA. An EC official publication observed in 1990 that

> Major disasters [and] global problems like ozone depletion and the greenhouse effect, and quality of life issues such as drinking water and air pollution have all contributed in recent years to a "greening" of European public opinion, to a widening consensus in favour of cleaner and more sustainable economic growth. (*Environmental Policy* 1990: 5).

A survey published by the EC in 1989 reported "strong support for a common EC-wide approach to environmental protection" (Environmental Policy 1990:5).

Since the passage of the SEA, the "momentum for environmental protection [has] accelerated dramatically" (Sbragia 1992: 4). Between 1989 and 1991, the EC enacted more environmental legislation than in the previous twenty years combined. "It now has over 450 regulations in effect and is adding new ones at a rate of about 100 a year" (Bromberg 1992: 5). Not only have many EC standards been significantly strengthened — in some cases approaching American ones — but the EC has also come to play a leadership role in the making of global environmental policy. One example concerns the protection of the ozone layer. In 1987, 31 nations, including the EC, signed the Montreal Protocols in which they pledged to reduce the production of chlorofluorocarbons by 50 percent by the end of the century. However, in March 1989, the EC went a step further, announcing that its member states had agreed to cut production of this chemical by 85 percent as soon as possible and to eliminate production entirely by the year 2000.

The EC's most recent Environmental Action Programme has established four priorities: the preservation of the ozone layer, mitigation of the greenhouse effect, comprehensive regulation of hazardous wastes and fighting tropical deforestation. In 1989, the European Council voted to create a European Environmental Agency, though to date this agency has not been established due to disagreement over where it will be located. Its purpose is to serve as a central information clearing house and a coordinator for national centres of environmental monitoring and evaluation.

However, as the scope of Community regulations has grown, the problem of enforcing them has become more acute. The increased number of Community regulations not only makes the monitoring of their enforcement more difficult, but also more urgent, since significant variations in national compliance threaten to disadvantage industries in some EC member states. The Community itself has no police or enforcement powers. It only knows of a violation if someone complains to it. If it finds the complaint is justified, its final legal recourse is to sue the member state in the European Court. This, however, is a time-consuming procedure; an average of 50 months elapses between the arrival of a complaint and a ruling from the court. The problem of enforcement is further complicated by the fact that while EC Directives are intended to bind national governments, in many countries it is local governmental officials who are responsible for enforcing them.

As of May 1991, the EC had a backlog of 372 cases of noncompliance with environmental Directives and Regulations ("Dirty Dozen...", *The Economist* 1991: 52). Three-quarters of its disciplinary proceedings concerned four areas of environmental law: birds, bathing water, drinking water, and environmental impact assessments. While the Commission received more complaints about the UK than any other country, this reflected not so much the relative lack of British compliance as the eagerness of British environmental groups to complain to Brussels. In some of the Latin countries, public distrust of government bureaucracies discourages people from complaining in the first place. Spain and Italy had the poorest record of compliance with the decisions of the European Court; the former does not even have an Environment Ministry.

In February 1990, the EC Commissioner in charge of environmental protection publicly complained about unsatisfactory member state implementation of the Community's environmental Directives (Wagerbaum 1990: 465). In June 1990, the European Council acknowledged the extent of the enforcement problem by adopting a "Declaration on the Environmental Imperative," which stated that "Community environmental legislation will only be effective if it is fully implemented and enforced by the Member States" (Wagerbaum 1990: 455). The following month, 130 members of the European Parliament proposed the establishment of a committee on the transposition and application of Community environmental legislation.

A number of suggestions have been advanced for improving national compliance with Community Directives. One is to allow citizens to sue their own governments in national courts; presently the ability of citizens to file such suits is determined by national rather than EC laws. Another is to provide the newly established European Environment Agency with the resources to monitor national compliance, thus freeing the Commission from having to rely upon citizen complaints to determine if its Directives are being enforced. A third is to create a Community "ombudsman". To date, none of these proposals has been adopted, but this may well change in the near future.

Integration and regulation

The Treaty on European Union, signed at Maastricht in February 1992, further expanded the Community's legal competence in the area of environmental regulation. Article 130R added another objective to the Community's environmental policy, namely the promotion of "measures at the international level to deal with regional or global environmental problems". Article 130S permitted the Community to adopt "measures concerning town and country planning, land use ... and management of water resources" as well as measures "significantly affecting a member state's choice between different energy sources and the general structure of its energy supply" (Archer and Butler 1992: 116). Finally, Article 130T confirmed the language of the Single European Act which stated that the Community legislation shall not prevent any member state from either "maintaining or introducing more stringent protective measures (provided they were) compatible with this Treaty" (Archer and Butler 1992: 116).

Notwithstanding the ongoing debate over the Maastricht Treaty, it is clear that at least in the area of environmental regulation, the Community is already a federal structure. While implementation remains primarily in the hands of national and local authorities, the role of the Community in formulating environmental rules and regulations has steadily expanded. Not only is Brussels making policy in more and more areas that were formerly decided at either the national or the local level, but the growing importance of international environmental agreements has provided the EC with an additional regulatory role. In areas such as the protection of endangered species, the protection of the ozone layer, and global warming, the EC both negotiates on behalf of its member states and is responsible for assuring their compliance.

At the same time, tension between Brussels and the member states appears to be increasing. The most important source of this tension appears to be between the EC's interest in harmonizing national regulatory standards in order to prevent them from serving as non-tariff barriers, and the persistent efforts of a few member states with strong green movements, most notably Germany, the Netherlands and Denmark, in enacting regulations that are stricter than those of the EC itself.

Through the mid-1980s, many Community environmental regulations functioned as much as a ceiling as a floor. This was notably the case with respect to automobile emissions, without doubt the most contentious area of Community environmental regulation during the last two decades. The various Community Directives on the lead content of gasoline enacted during the 1970s and the first half of the 1980s specified both minimum and maximum standards. Likewise, the Luxembourg Compromise on automobile emissions, adopted in 1987, both allowed member states to set lower emission levels than those specified in the Directive, and refused to permit any member state to exclude any vehicles that complied with the emission standards of the Directive.

Thus the Community, while attempting to respond to growing public pressures for stricter environmental standards, was equally determined to prevent environmental regulation from interfering with economic integration. When faced with a tension between the two, it chose the latter over the former, much to the frustration of Germany, which wanted to impose both stricter standards on its own vehicles and restrict the import of automobiles from member states with laxer national standards.

In contrast, the Small Car Directive, adopted in 1989 after long and protracted negotiations, succeeded in reconciling stricter environmental standards and economic integration: it significantly strengthened the EC's automobile emission standards, most notably by requiring small as well as large vehicles to be equipped with catalytic convertors, and at the same time made these standards uniform. This Directive represented a major victory for European environmental pressure-groups, as well as an important step forward for European integration; it meant that EC environmental standards no longer simply reflected the lowest common denominator among the member states, but instead could serve as a vehicle for the gradual tightening of regulatory standards.

However, the basic national divisions that have plagued EC environmental regulation from the outset have persisted. Germany, Denmark and the Netherlands continue to insist on their right to establish stricter environmental standards than those established by the EC, even if, or in some cases, because, these regulations serve as trade barriers; however strict the EC's standards, they want to go a step further. On the other hand, Britain, France and Italy continue to place a greater priority on integration: they do not want member states to be allowed to enact environmental regulations that will make it more difficult for their industries to market their products throughout the Community.

The 1988 decision of the European Court in Commission of the *European Communities* v. *Denmark* represents an important development in this ongoing dispute between central EC institutions and various member states. The Court upheld the legality of the most important provisions of a Danish bottle recycling law, even though this legislation made it more difficult for non-Danish bottles to gain access to the Danish market. This decision marked the first time that the Court had sanctioned a trade barrier on environmental grounds — even though the Court had previously sustained a number of trade barriers for other reasons, primarily having to do with health and safety. It now upheld a national regulation that clearly interfered with the free movement of goods in the Community on the grounds that such interference was necessary to achieve the environmental goals of a member state. This decision thus represented an important victory for regulation over integration.

While "it will take further cases to show exactly where the European Court draws the line between greenery and trade" ("Freedom ...", *The Economist* 1989: 22) the political impact of the Danish bottle case has already been felt. In 1989, the German government enacted legislation requiring a compulsory deposit on all plastic and glass bottles. The Commission decided not to challenge the German scheme — although it did demand one relatively minor modification in it: the German government could not require that the deposits only be collected by retail stores. However, two years later, in April 1991, the German government approved a far more ambitious and sweeping recycling law — one "tougher than anything introduced in any other country" ("A Wall of Waste", *The Economist* 1991: 73). The objective of the German law was to reduce the amount of waste going into landfill and incineration. Beginning on 1 December 1992, all companies were required to take back and recycle all packaging used during transport, or pay another firm to do so. As of 1 April 1992, the law also covered "secondary" packaging, such as gift wrapping and boxes. On 1 January 1993, all packaging, including sweet and butter wrappers, will be included as well.

The Economist noted "the ferocity of the new obligation is extraordinary. When fully implemented, it will require a level of recycling that not even the most environmentally conscious middle-class community in any western nation has achieved" ("A Wall of Waste", *The Economist* 1991: 73). Ninety percent of all glass and metals as well as 80 percent of paper, board and plastics must be recycled. Incineration, for whatever reason, is not permitted. The German Environmental Ministry subsequently announced that it planned to extend the recycling requirement to the manufacturers of automobiles and electronic goods.

Not surprisingly, the European packaging industry was "irate", arguing that the German law crossed "the indistinct line between national environmental protection and protection of a more reprehensible sort" ("Free Trade's Green Hurdle", *The Economist* 1991: 61). Importers specifically complained to the EC that the packaging law included a provision, inserted at the last minute, requiring that only 28 per cent of all beer and soft drinks containers can be disposable. "Packagers claim that this clause was inserted for the benefit of small brewers in politically sensitive Bavaria, who will find it easier to collect and refill the empties" ("Free Trade's Green Hurdle", *The Economist* 1991: 61). They also charged that the provision requiring companies to collect their used packaging for recycling would discourage retailers from stocking imported goods.

Britain's Industry Council for Packaging and the Environment contended that the rules "restrict the free movement of goods into Germany" ("Free Trade's Green Hurdle", *The Economist* 1991: 61). Eucofel, a European trade association representing fruit and vegetable shippers, complained its member firms were unable to recycle the wooden crates in which most of the fruits and vegetables imported into Germany were shipped. One firm stated it was told by its German distributor to use "biodegradable" nails in its crates.

Not surprisingly, a number of non-German firms "complained vociferously" to the EC (Thornhill 1991). Nonetheless, fearful of being labelled "anti-green", the Commission has hesitated to take Germany to the European Court. Instead the EC has attempted to produce its own packaging Directive. But harmonizing national recycling laws has proven extremely difficult as both the degree of public enthusiasm for recycling, as well as the existence of the necessary infrastructure to accomplish it, varies considerably among the EC's member states. However, whatever standards the EC ultimately decides on, they are likely to be laxer than Germany's. This in turn will present the Community with a difficult political and legal problem. If the German law is allowed to stand, industries from member states such as the UK will be outraged. But if the German law is declared unconstitutional, both German industry, which has already invested substantial resources in complying with their nation's packaging requirements, as well as the German environmental movement, will be upset. In short, the making of EC environmental policy is likely to remain highly contentious.

Conclusion

The creation of the single European market is an ongoing process. Not only was it not concluded at the end of 1992; it might *never* be concluded. One important reason is that the regulatory agenda is constantly changing. As new environmental issues emerge, many will present additional potential obstacles for intra-Community trade that could not have been anticipated at the time of the White Paper. As long as both the priority placed on environmental protection and the competitive impact of regulation on industries in different countries varies across the EC, some member states will attempt to enact regulations that in turn will be perceived by other member states as non-tariff barriers. The opportunities are endless: as soon as one kind of regulation is harmonized, another source of contention among the member states or between the member states and Brussels emerge. 1992 was not so much a date as a moving target. And it is a goal whose achievement has been made more difficult by the emergence of environmental protection as a highly visible area of public policy making at both the national and Community level.

The tension between economic integration and environmental regulation can be resolved in one of three ways: first, the ability of member states to impose their own, stricter national environmental regulations can be restricted by Brussels in the interests of economic integration; second, the two can be reconciled by the enactment of strict, harmonized standards; and third, member states can be allowed to establish stricter national environmental laws, even if they interfere with the free movement of goods within the EC.

Clearly the Commission, along with nations such as the UK and France, favours the second alternative. And undoubtedly, an increasing number of environmental regulations will be harmonized. Indeed, to some extent the enactment of stricter laws by the various member states can be seen as part of the dynamic of Community policy-making: these laws help place additional pressure on Brussels to establish stricter, Commmunity-wide standards. But there are also important counter-pressures pushing in the direction of the third alternative. As the principle of subsidiarity assumes increasing importance in the negotiations surrounding the interpretation and ratifaction of the Maastricht Treaty, member states may well be allowed additional opportunities to establish their own environmental standards. How far the EC can or will allow this tendency to go is unclear, especially if these standards interfere with intra-Community trade. What is predictable is continual tension between environmental regulation and integration.

Finally, it is important to place the making of EC environmental policy in a broader, global context. Just as there has been a substantial expansion of the role of the Community in the making of European environmental policy, so are a growing number of national environmental regulations being harmonized at the global level. Yet at the same time, international economic integration is increasingly being threatened by the enactment of national environmental regulations which serve, either intentionally or inadvertently, as trade barriers. In this sense, the challenge faced by the EC is similar to that faced by the GATT: when, and under what circumstances should nations be permitted to restrict trade in the interests of protecting or improving environmental quality? Likewise, many of the disputes over environmental regulations between Canada and the United States under the North American Free Trade Agreement are strikingly similar to those of the EC; the province of Ontario has recently enacted recycling legislation that is similiar to Denmark's, much to the outrage of American bottlers who claim that it violates the terrms of NAFTA. In short, the challenges the EC will face in formulating environmental policy in the 1990s are not unique to it.

References

Archer, C. and Butler, F. (1992) *The European Community: Structure and Process*. New York: St. Martin's Press.

Briggs, D. (1986) 'Environmental Problems and Policies in the European Community', in C. Park (ed.) *Environmental Policies: An International Review*. London: Croom Helm.

Bromberg, Elizabeth (1992) 'European Community Environmental Policy: The Role of the European Parliament', Eighth Annual Conference of Europeanists, Chicago.

Close, G. (1978) 'Harmonization of Laws: Use or Abuse of the Powers Under the EEC Treaty', *European Law Review* 3: 461-468.

Diehl, J.(1988) 'Choking on Their Own Development', *Washington Post National Weekly Edition*, June 4:9.

Economist (1989) 'Freedom to be Cleaner than the Rest', October, 14 p. 21-24.

Economist (1991) 'A Wall of Waste', November, 30 p. 73.

Economist (1991) 'Free Trade's Green Hurdle', June 15, p. 61.

Environmental Policy in the European Community (1990). 4th edn. Luxembourg: Office of Official Publications on the European Communities.

Freestone, D. (1991) 'European Community Environmental Policy and Law', *Journal of Law and Society*, 18: 135-154.

Haigh, N. (1989) *EEC Environmental Policy and Britain, 2nd edn*. Harlow: Longman.

Haigh, N. and Baldock, D. (1989) 'Environmental Policy and 1992'. London: Institute for European Environmental Policy.

Herman, Robin (1988) 'An Ecological Epiphany', *Washington Post National Weekly Edition,* December 5-11 p.19.

Kramer, L. (1987) 'The Single European Act and Environmental Protection: Reflections on Several New Provisions in Community Law', *Common Market Law Review* 24:659-688.

Majone, G. (1991) 'Cross-national Sources of Regulatory Policymaking in Europe and the United States', *Journal of Public Policy* 11:79-106.

O'Riordan, Timothy (1979) 'Role of Environmental Quality Objectives: The Politics of Pollution Control' in O'Riordan and D'Arge (eds) *Progress in Resource Management and Environmental Planning*, Vol. 1. New York: Wiley.

Thornhill, J. (1991) "Repackaged, Recycled, Restricted", *Financial Times,* December 6, p.17.

Vandermeersch, D. (1987) 'The Single European Act and the Environmental Policy of the European Community', *European Law Review* 12:407-429.

Vogel, David (1989) *National Styles of Regulation*. Ithaca: Cornell University Press.

Wagerbaum, Rolf (1990) 'The European Community's Policies on Implementation of Environmental Directives', *Fordham International Law Journal* 14:455-477.

Part II

Macroeconomic Policy Issues

6. Economic and Monetary Union

Loukas Tsoukalis

The process of 1992 had little, if anything, to do directly with macroeconomic policies. It was basically a supply-side programme intended to eliminate the remaining NTBs in the intra-EC movement of goods, services and factors of production. However, in the Commission's analysis and strategy on the internal market, macroeconomic policies occupied a central role. A co-ordinated expansion had been originally advocated in order to take advantage of the new margin of manoeuvre expected to be created by the completion of the internal market through reduced inflation and public sector deficits (Commission of the EC, 1988; see also Tsoukalis, 1993: 77-98) Soon, as the internal market programme gathered momentum, the Commission appeared ready to go much further. It was no longer a question of co-ordination of macroeconomic policies; instead, economic and monetary union (EMU) was presented as the next logical step after the completion of the internal market.

Thus EMU has come to be seen as the post-1992 stage of economic integration, and this was ceremoniously confirmed with the treaty revision agreed at Maastricht in December 1991. Preliminary discussions, which led to the intergovernmental conference, had started earlier in 1988; yet another indication of the sea change that had taken place in Western Europe in a relatively short period of time. By then, the internal market was already taken for granted and the debate became centred on the next step; a step which would, however, have even wider political and economic ramifications.

European integration has already extended beyond trade; and the 1992 process represents both a quantitative and qualitative shift towards the creation of a regional economic system. Yet EMU is something very different. In terms of national sovereignty, the stakes are infinitely higher, and this is clearly recognized by all participants. Unlike the White Paper of 1985, the plans for the creation of EMU could not be camouflaged as a technical matter with limited political consequences. Money is, after all, at the heart of national sovereignty.

EMU already has a long and chequered history which may teach us a few lessons about its prospects for the future. Yet, history is not usually repeated, and the economic and political environment of the 1990s in Europe is very different from that prevailing when earlier attempts were made towards this goal. The decision to proceed towards a complete EMU before the end of the decade, backed up by a host of institutional and other measures which should be introduced in the meantime, guarantees that this issue will occupy a prominent, if not the most prominent, place on the European agenda for several years to come. Developments in this area will also largely determine the shape of the European economic system.

Loukas Tsoukalis: 'Economic and Monetary Union' from *THE NEW EUROPEAN ECONOMY: THE POLITICS AND ECONOMICS OF EUROPEAN INTEGRATION* (Oxford University Press, 2nd revised edition, 1993), pp. 175-227. © Loukas Tsoukalis 1993. Reprinted by permission of Oxford University Press.

Werner, Emu, and the Snake

Although the main emphasis in the Rome Treaty was on the creation of a common market, with the progressive elimination of barriers for the free movement of goods, services, persons, and capital, there was at least some, albeit rather hesitant, recognition of the importance of macroeconomic policies, and monetary policy in particular, in the context of a common market. Article 2 referred to the task of 'progressively approximating the economic policies of Member States'. In Title II of the original treaty, we find references to the main objectives of macroeconomic policy, and the balance of payments in particular. The achievement of those objectives would be facilitated by the co-ordination of economic policies, the ways and means of which remained to be defined. Specific provisions were made only as regards monetary policy; hence the creation of the Monetary Committee. The treaty also referred to the exchange rate as a matter of common concern. The possibility of mutual aid in the case of balance of payments difficulties was envisaged as well as the progressive elimination of exchange controls to the extent necessary for the proper functioning of the common market.

There was clearly no intention to set up a regional currency bloc. The Bretton Woods system provided the international framework and the US dollar the undisputed monetary standard. On the other hand, limited capital mobility allowed European governments a reasonably wide margin of manoeuvre in terms of monetary policy (hence the caution expressed in the articles of the treaty regarding capital movements). European regional integration was basically about trade in goods. Macroeconomic policies, and monetary policy in particular, remained the concern of national governments subject to the constraints imposed by the international monetary system.

During the 1960s, there was much talk about regional co-operation, but little concrete action. The central country of the Bretton Woods system, namely the United States, proved no longer willing or able to provide the public good of monetary stability, and this led to some discussions between the, by now, much more confident Europeans about alternatives, including closer regional co-operation. There was also some resentment about the asymmetrical nature of the international system, which was, however, combined with different degrees of economic and political vulnerability to US pressure. At best, the intra-European discussions of the 1960s helped to prepare the ground for subsequent plans for regional co-operation, while also leading to the expansion of the small infrastructure of committees at the EEC level. The creation of the CAP, based on common prices, was closely related to the perceived need for exchange rate stability. But this was in little doubt until 1968.

EMU was part of the new package deal agreed at the Hague summit of 1969. Growing trade interpenetration, largely the result of tariff liberalization measures, had reduced the effectiveness of autonomous economic policies; hence the new attraction of co-ordination procedures and joint action. The Six had proved unable both to insulate themselves from international monetary instability and to pursue a common policy in international fora. The events of 1968-9 provided clear evidence of this failure. This in turn endangered one of the main pillars of the EEC construction, namely the CAP. Thus the political decision to extend and deepen the process of integration led the Six, almost naturally, into the area of macroeconomic activity. And they decided to go all the way, committing themselves to the creation of an EMU which would replace the customs union as the main goal of the new decade. Money was also a means to an end, and the end was political union. This function of monetary union was widely recognized and aptly summarized by the French: 'la voie royale vers l'union politique'.

However, important divisions soon became apparent as regards the priorities and the strategy to be employed in order to achieve the final goal. Those divisions, which had their origins in an earlier debate provoked by the Commission memorandum of 1968 (better known as the first Barre plan) and the alternative proposals put forward at the time by the German Minister of Economics, Mr Schiller, dominated the discussions inside the high-level group which was entrusted with the preparation of a report on the establishment of EMU. This group was chaired by the Prime Minister of Luxembourg, Mr Werner.

The main conflict was between 'economists' and 'monetarists' and was based on the strategy to be adopted during the transitional period in order to achieve a sufficient harmonization of national economic policies which were seen as the main precondition for the elimination of payments imbalances (Tsoukalis, 1977). More specifically, the crucial difference was whether the Community would move towards the irrevocable fixity of parities and the elimination of margins of fluctuation before the system of economic policy co-ordination had proved its effectiveness.

The 'monetarists', represented by France, Belgium, and Luxembourg, stressed the importance of the exchange rate discipline and the need to strengthen the 'monetary personality' of the EC in international fora. They also, presumably, would have liked to pass the adjustment burden on to surplus countries and thus face them with the choice of either financing the deficits of others or accepting a higher rate of inflation. This would in turn have largely depended on provisions for the financing of payments imbalances. It was precisely this choice that the potential surplus countries, namely the Federal Republic of Germany and the Netherlands, would have liked to avoid. Hence the insistence of the 'economists' on policy co-ordination, the results of which were, apparently, expected to be close to their own set of policy preferences, as a necessary condition for progress on the exchange rate front. What the 'economists' in fact implied was the convergence of the inflation rates of other countries to their own. There was a certain degree of ambivalence and confusion on both sides, and also some double-talk.

The debate between 'economists' and 'monetarists' did not touch upon the big question of the economic feasibility of EMU within the relatively short time-scale envisaged. The harmonization of policy preferences was considered as the main precondition for the elimination of payments imbalances, thus ignoring basically the various factors behind different wage and price trends as well as productivity levels between member countries. Turning the realization of EMU into a question of political will, the Community ran the risk of neglecting the possible economic costs associated with the abandonment of a major policy instrument such as the exchange rate. Furthermore, the difference between 'economists' and 'monetarists' was only partly a reflection of fundamentally different approaches to the establishment of EMU. It also served as an ideological cloak for different short-term interests of individual countries. The 'short-termism' of some governments became clearer through their subsequent actions.

The final report of the Werner group was submitted in October 1970 (Werner, 1970). A complete EMU was to be achieved in three stages within an overall period of ten years. The final objective was defined in terms of an irrevocable fixity of exchange rates, the elimination of margins of fluctuation, and the free circulation of goods, services, persons, and capital. The creation of EMU would require the transfer of a wide range of decision-making powers from the national to the EC level. All principal decisions on monetary policy, ranging from questions of internal liquidity and interest rates to exchange rates and the management of reserves, would have to be centralized. Quantitative medium-term objectives would be jointly fixed and projections would be revised periodically.

With respect to fiscal policy, the Werner group argued that an agreement would have to be reached on the margins within which the main national budgets aggregates would be held and on the method of financing deficits or utilizing surpluses. Fiscal harmonization and co-operation in structural and regional policies were also mentioned as objectives. The creation of two main institutions of the Community was envisaged, namely 'the centre of decision for economic policy' and the 'Community system for the central banks'.

The final report was based on a consensus among its members, regarding the ultimate objective, and a compromise, couched in somewhat vague terms, between 'economists' and 'monetarists' about the intermediate stages. The compromise was embodied in the strategy of parallelism between economic policy co-ordination and monetary integration, with the Werner group concentrating mainly on the measures to be adopted during the first of three stages before reaching the "Elysian harmony"[1] of a complete EMU.

The fragility of the compromise and the political commitment of several countries to the final objective was soon to be exposed by the dramatic deterioration of the international economic environment. One of the few concrete decisions was to narrow the intra-EC margins of fluctuation from 1.5 to 1.2 per cent on either side of the parity; a decision, however, which was never implemented. This small, first step on the road towards monetary union took Bretton Woods and fixed exchange rates against the dollar for granted. This proved to be one of the biggest weaknesses of the European strategy. Massive capital inflows and the US policy of 'benign neglect' ('unbenign' would, perhaps, be a more accurate term) showed once again the extreme fragility of EC unity and of only recently concluded agreements. Faced with the Nixon measures of August 1971, the Six suddenly forgot the objective of EMU and produced instead an impressive variety of national exchange rate regimes ranging from independent floating to 'pivot rates' and a two-tier market.

The Smithsonian agreement of December 1971 created only a short-lived illusion of a new international order. The Six hastened to build their regional system on its foundations; and, not very surprisingly, it soon crumbled. The 'snake in the tunnel', created in March 1972, represented a new attempt to narrow intra-EC margins of fluctuation to 2.25 per cent, instead of the 4.5 per cent resulting from the application of the Smithsonian agreement.

The snake would therefore consist of the EC currencies jointly moving inside the dollar tunnel, that is the 2.25 per cent bands on either side of their parity against the US currency. Wide margins of fluctuation of intra-EC exchange rates were generally considered as incompatible with the functioning of the common market and the CAP. The birth of the snake was accompanied by rules for joint intervention in the exchange markets and provisions for very short-term credit between central banks for the financing of those interventions. As part of the strategy of parallelism, a steering committee was also set up for the more effective co-ordination of economic policies.

The continued instability in exchange markets caused the progressive mutilation of the snake, thus creating further unhappiness in the European monetary zoo. Sterling and the punt left the EC exchange rate arrangement in July 1972, soon to be followed by the Danish krone which subsequently returned to the fold. Only a few months after the Paris summit of October 1972, which reiterated the political commitment to a complete EMU by the end of the decade, the lira was floated and then the remaining currencies of the snake decided to make virtue out of necessity by accepting a joint float against the dollar. The snake had, therefore, lost its tunnel and would from then on have to wriggle its way into the open space. The final exit scene was reserved for the French franc which left the snake in January 1974, while a subsequent attempt to return did not last for very long (July 1975-March 1976).

In the following years, the snake was little more than a Deutschmark (DM) zone. The Benelux countries and Denmark remained in it recognizing the importance of stable exchange rates for their small and open economies and the relative weight of their trade relations with the Federal Republic. It was rather ironical (or was it just an illustration of the short-term considerations which had prevailed in national attitudes towards EMU?) that the core countries of the 'economist' group had chosen to remain in the regional exchange rate system, while France, the leader of the 'monetarists', had been forced to leave. The snake was hardly a Community system, with almost half of the EC members staying outside it, while a number of other Western European countries (Austria, Norway and Sweden) became associate members of the DM-zone.

The most common criticism made against any system of fixed exchange rates, with limited amounts of liquidity to finance payments deficits, used to be that the burden of adjustment is likely to fall on the deficit countries, thus creating a deflationary bias in the system. For Germany, the snake contributed towards a certain undervaluation of the DM, while at the same time it did not impose any additional constraints in the conduct of German monetary policy. For the smaller countries, the corresponding appreciation of their currencies against the DM seemed to be offset by the greater stability of the exchange rate and the increased credibility of their economic policies. Concentrating on the Danish experience, Thygesen (1979) did not find any convincing evidence of deflationary bias. On the other hand, the snake did not lead to any serious co-ordination on the external monetary front, except for one-way co-ordination on the basis of German policies. It was, undoubtedly, an asymmetrical system.

In the attempt to preserve stable intra-EC exchange rates, in the midst of the general upheaval which characterized the early 1970s, Community countries increasingly resorted to capital controls, despite the declared objective of a complete liberalization of capital movements which was supposed to be an integral part of EMU. Furthermore, there was neither uniform action nor even some form of broad agreement on this subject. The question of capital controls produced very different responses on behalf of individual member countries. This continued to be true until the end of the decade when Germany, Britain, and the Netherlands were the only countries of the enlarged EC with virtually no restrictions imposed on international capital flows. On the other hand, no attempt was made to discriminate in favour of intra-EC movements, probably recognizing the futility of such an attempt in view of the permeability of national frontiers.

The combination of an unfavourable international environment, divergent national policies, a half-baked economic strategy, and a very weak political commitment ensured the quick death of EMU. The latter became the biggest non-event of the 1970s. With the benefit of hindsight, it can be argued that the ambitious initiative, originally intended to transform radically the economic and political map of Western Europe, had been taken at the highest level without much thought of its wider implications. It certainly did not survive the test of time and economic adversity.

Monetary stability and the EMS

Despite the serious setbacks suffered in the attempt to move towards an EMU in the 1970s, interest in the subject never disappeared. The mini-snake was generally considered as only a temporary arrangement which would be improved and extended when the economic conditions became more favourable. Various plans were put forward which served to keep interest alive and also prepare the ground for a new political initiative. The aim of official plans was usually to design a more flexible exchange rate system which would incorporate all EC currencies. On the other hand, many proposals originating from professional economists and academics concentrated on the creation and development of a European parallel currency (Fratianni and Peeters, 1978). Finally, a proposal put forward by the President of the Commission, Mr Jenkins, in October 1977 acted as the catalyst for the relaunching of monetary integration. And this in turn led to the establishment of the EMS in March 1979.

The EMS was the product of an initiative taken by Chancellor Schmidt, against the advice, if not the outright opposition, of his central bank. This was later presented as a joint Franco-German initiative, something which was becoming increasingly a regular pattern in EC affairs. It could have been an arrangement among the Big Three to which the other EC countries would have been invited to join. But Britain, once again, decided to stay out (Ludlow, 1982).

The creation of the EMS was seen, first and foremost, as a means of reducing exchange rate instability among EC currencies. Despite the agnosticism expressed by many academic economists on the subject, exchange rate instability was believed by most political leaders and businessmen in Western Europe to have deleterious effects on the real economy, and more precisely on trade, investment, and growth. Our understanding of those effects has improved considerably since then, even though econometric evidence still remains inadequate (Krugman, 1989).

Concern about the proper functioning of the common market was combined with the desire to preserve the system of common agricultural prices. On the other hand, the initiative for the creation of the EMS was linked to the expectation that there would be no substantial reform of the international monetary system and hence no prospect of a return to some form of exchange rate stability in the near future. The construction of a regional system was, therefore, seen as a second- or third-best solution.

Exchange rate stability was to be backed by an increased convergence between national economies, with the emphasis clearly placed on inflation rates. The EMS was considered as an important instrument in the fight against inflation, and its creation meant an implicit acceptance of German policy priorities by the other EC countries. The experience of the 1970s was seen as validating the uncompromising anti-inflationary stance combined with the strong currency option adopted by the Federal Republic. The EMS was also intended as a European defensive mechanism against US 'benign neglect' as regards the dollar, and, more generally, what was perceived to be a political vacuum in Washington at the time of the Carter Administration; evens though it was never made very clear how the EMS could perform such a role. It was also seen as a means of strengthening Europe economically and politically through closer co-operation at a time when US leadership was seen as waning. Once again, monetary integration was partly used as an instrument for political ends.

The EMS was intended as a system of fixed but adjustable exchange rates. One of the novelties of the system was the European Currency Unit (ECU) consisting of fixed amounts of each EC currency, including those not participating in the exchange rate mechanism (ERM). Provision was made for the revision of these amounts every five years. Two revisions have already taken place in 1984 and 1989, and they also led to the inclusion of the currencies of the three new EC members (Table 1). The relative weights of each currency are a function of the economic and trade weight of the country concerned, with a clear tilt towards the stronger currencies (see relative weight of the Deutschmark and the Dutch guilder).

Each EC currency has a central rate defined in ECUs. Central rates in ECUs are then used to establish a grid of bilateral exchange rates. The margins of fluctuation around those bilateral rates were set at 2.25 per cent, with the exception of the lira which was allowed to operate within wider margins of 6 per cent and sterling which stayed completely out of the ERM. Central bank interventions were compulsory and unlimited, when currencies reached the limit of their permitted margins of fluctuation. Central rates could be changed only by common consent.

Table 1
Composition of the ECU.

Currency	13 March 1979		17 September 1984		21 September 1989	
	1	2	1	2	1	2
Deutschmark	0.828	33.00	0.719	32.00	0.6242	30.53
French franc	1.15	19.80	1.31	19.00	1.332	19.43
Netherlands guilder	0.286	10.50	0.256	10.10	0.2198	9.54
Belgian and Luxembourg franc	3.80	9.50	3.85	8.50	3.431	7.83
Italian lira	109.0	9.50	140.00	10.20	151.8	9.92
Danish krone	0.217	3.00	0.219	2.70	0.1976	2.53
Irish punt	0.00759	1.10	0.008781	1.20	0.008552	1.12
Pound sterling	0.0885	13.60	0.0878	15.00	0.08784	12.06
Greek drachma	—	—	1.15	1.30	1.44	0.77
Spanish peseta	—	—	—	—	6.885	5.18
Portuguese escudo	—	—	—	—	1.393	0.78

Note: Column 1 indicates the number of national currency units in each ECU while column 2 gives the percentage weight of each currency in the ECU basket.

Source: Eurostat.

Against the deposit of 20 per cent of gold and dollar reserves held by participating central banks, which took the form of three-month revolving swaps, the European Monetary Co-operation Fund (EMCF) issued ECUs in return. Those ECUs were therefore intended to serve as an official reserve asset, although subject to many restrictions which could qualify them basically as a non-negotiable instrument of credit. ECUs would also serve as a denominator for market interventions arising from the operation of the ERM and as a means of settlement between the monetary authorities of the EC. This in turn meant a sharing of the exchange risk between creditor and debtor countries. Exactly the same applied to the credit mechanisms of the EMS.

Another novelty of the EMS was the so-called divergence indicator intended to provide a certain degree of symmetry in the adjustment burden between appreciating and depreciating currencies and an automatic mechanism for triggering consultations before the intervention limits were reached. The device would make it possible to locate the position and the movement of an EMS currency relative to the EC average represented by the ECU. There was a so-called 'presumption to act', when the divergence threshold was reached. The creation of the divergence indicator also suggested that, at least initially, policy convergence (including the convergence of inflation rates) was expected to be towards the EC average, instead of the best performance which was later adopted as the target.

Very short-term credit facilities, in unlimited amounts, were to be granted to each other by participating central banks, through the EMCF, in order to permit intervention in EC currencies. Provisions were also made for other credit facilities, building on the already existing short-term monetary support and the medium-term financial assistance mechanism of the snake. In principle as a means of fostering economic convergence and in practice as a carrot to lure the economically weaker countries into participating in the ERM, provision was made for the granting of subsidized loans by EC institutions and the European Investment Bank.

Thus the EMS was built on the existing snake with some important novel features intended to ensure the enlargement of its membership and the smoother functioning of the exchange-rate mechanism. It was based on a political compromise between Germany which feared the effects of prolonged international monetary instability and an excessive revaluation of the DM, resulting from the continuous sinking of the dollar in exchange markets, and France and Italy which saw their participation in the EMS as an integral part of an anti-inflation strategy. All three also shared the broader political objectives associated with the EMS, namely support for European unification and the strengthening of Europe's identity in relations with the United States. It was clearly a decision of high politics. Writing about Italy, de Cecco (1989: 90) argued, with some element of exaggeration, that '[to] be in favour of the EMS meant to be in favour of freedom and of Western civilization'!

The other members of the old snake, countries with small and highly open economies and hence little prospect of independent monetary policies, were only too happy to see an extension of the area in which stable exchange relations applied. As for Ireland, the decision to join the ERM was partly a function of the side-payments offered and the attraction of the external discipline on monetary policy and partly an expression of political independence against Britain. The latter was a totally different case. The fear of deflationary pressures, stemming largely from the traumatic experience with earlier attempts under the Bretton Woods system to keep the exchange rate of sterling fixed, were combined with strong opposition to the political objectives behind the EMS. Thus, Britain stayed out of the ERM for more than eleven years, limiting its participation to the other, much less constraining manifestations of the new system.

At the time of writing, after the thirteenth birthday of the EMS, there is little doubt about the success of the system. It has survived against the odds and the expectations of most professional economists and central bankers who had greeted its birth with considerable scepticism, if not sheer cynicism, drawing largely from the earlier experience in regional monetary integration. Furthermore, it has expanded its membership, acting as a major source of attraction for non-EC members as well, and it has also acted as a launching board for the renewed attempts to create a complete EMU.

The EMS has been generally described as a zone of monetary stability, and this is linked to both exchange rates and inflation rates. Short-term volatility of bilateral exchange rates has been substantially reduced. This is true when a comparison is made with the pre-EMS experience of participating currencies or with the experience of other major currencies, including sterling for the period it stayed outside the system. The greater stability in nominal exchange rates has been achieved through a convergence of inflation rates, the gearing of the interest rate towards the exchange rate target, joint interventions in the exchange markets, capital controls and the increased credibility of the system; the mix of all those factors having changed considerably over the years. Stability does not, however, mean rigidity. During the first thirteen years of the EMS, there were twelve realignments, five of which involved more than two currencies (Table 2). They soon became a matter of genuinely collective decisions, while the element of drama, which had often accompanied the negotiations leading to the early realignments, gradually disappeared.

It is very difficult to generalize for the whole period, since the EMS has experienced major changes both in terms of the general macroeconomic environment and its own operating rules. Three different phases in the history of the EMS can be distinguished (see also Ungerer *et al.*, 1990; Gros and Thygesen, 1992). The first phase ended with the realignment of March 1983. It was a turbulent period, marked by frequent realignments of exchange rates and wide policy divergence (also manifested in terms of inflation rates — see Fig. 1). This suggested that the consensus on which the creation of the EMS had been based was rather flimsy. But after all, both parents of the EMS (Chancellor Schmidt and President Giscard d'Estaing) had left the political stage before the end of 1982.

The second phase was one of consolidation, and it ended with the realignment of January 1987. There were few realignments during this period, usually involving small changes in the central rates and only a few currencies. It was also the period of increasing price convergence downwards. Following the ill-fated attempt by the French socialists to apply Keynesianism in one country in 1982-3, exchange rate stability was based on a convergence of economic preferences, which was in turn reinforced by the operation of the system. Most countries participating in the ERM reached the lowest levels in terms of inflation rates between 1986 and 1987; since then there has been a shift upwards which was initially linked to the economic boom.

The third phase has been characterized by a remarkable stability of exchange rates, which could be, perhaps, also described as rigidity. For more than five years, there has been no realignment of exchange rates, with the exception of a small repositioning of the lira, which was announced in January 1990, together with the decision to reduce the margins of fluctuation to 2.25 per cent. It had been preceded by the most important so far modification of the operating rules of the system (see below, for a discussion of the Basle-Nyborg agreement of 1987). The stability of exchange rates has been based essentially on the continued convergence of inflation rates, even though there has been an upward shift in recent years, and the increased credibility of the system in exchange markets.

During the third phase, there has also been a gradual extension of ERM membership, a sure sign of the success of the system.[2] Having brought down the rate of inflation and in search of a credible exchange rate target and an external discipline, Spain joined in June 1989, with a 6 per cent margin of fluctuation. Later, it was the turn of the real heretics to take the oath of allegiance to the true faith. After a long internal debate, in which arguments about the petrocurrency status of sterling and the role of London as an international financial centre had been used interchangeably with political arguments about the loss of national sovereignty, the UK finally decided to join the ERM in October 1990, also with a 6 per cent margin of flutuation. It was followed by Portugal in April 1992, thus leaving only the Greek drachma outside the ERM. In all cases, the decision to join was based on a combination of economic and political considerations: the search for a stable anchor for the exchange rate and an external discipline for monetary policy, offering further proof of one's commitment to Europe, and a desire not to be left out of an increasingly important part of regional integration. High inflation rates still prevented Greece from joining the club.

Table 2
EMS Realignments: Changes in Central Rates
(% change: minus sign (-) denotes a devaluation)

Currency	24 Sept 1979	30 Nov 1979	23 Mar 1981	5 Oct 1981	22 Feb 1982	14 June 1982	21 Mar 1983	22 July 1985	7 April 1986	4 Aug 1986	12 Jan 1987	8 Jan[a] 1990
Deutschmark	2.0			5.5		4.25	5.5	2.0	3.0		3.0	
French franc				-3.0		-5.75	-2.5	2.0	-3.0			
Netherlands guilder				5.5		4.25	3.5	2.0	3.0		3.0	
Belgian and Luxembourg franc					-8.5			1.5	2.0	1.0		2.0
Italian lira			-6.0	-3.0			-2.75	-2.5	-6.2			-3.0
Danish krone	-2.9	-4.8			-3.0			2.5	2.0	1.0		
Irish punt								-3.5	2.0	-8.0		
Spanish peseta[b]												
Pound sterling[c]												
Portuguese escudo[d]												

[a]On this date the Italian lira moved from fluctuation bands of ±6% around its central rate to narrow fluctuation bands of ±2.25%.

[b]The peseta joined the ERM on 19 June 1989 with a fluctuation band of ±6% around its central rates.

[c]The pound entered the ERM on 8 Oct. 1990 with a fluctuation band of ±6% around its central rates.

[d]The escudo entered the ERM on 6 April 1992 with a fluctuation band of ±6% around its central rates.

Source: Eurostat

Figure 1
(a) Price Deflator Private Consumption in EC-12, 1979-1991.
(b) Price Deflator Private Consumption in EC-12, 1979-1991.

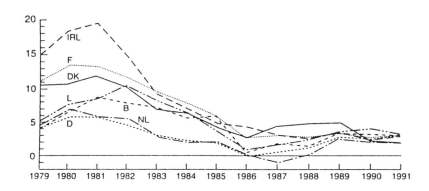

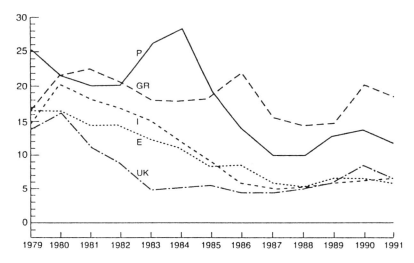

There were three other important events which marked the latter part of the third phase in the history of the EMS. One was the liberalization of capital movements; the second was the decision to proceed to a complete EMU, with the first stage starting in July 1990 and linked precisely to capital liberalization; and the third was the unification of Germany, with profound effects on the German economy and also indirectly on the other members of the system. The combination of all three may suggest that the EMS had already entered a new phase; but it is still early to judge. This subject will be discussed further below.

Figure 2
Bilateral exchange rates of the US Dollar and the Yen against the ECU, 1980-1991.

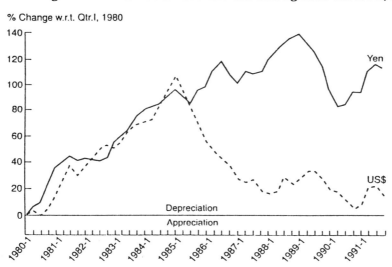

The reduction of short-term volatility and the avoidance of substantial long-term misalignment have not applied to exchange relations with major currencies outside the ERM. This is particularly true of the exchange rate of the ECU with the dollar (Fig. 2). Thus, the EMS did not provide the insulation against external instability which some Europeans had hoped for, although the centrifugal effects of the dollar gyrations on intra-ERM exchange rates seem to have been reduced in recent years. Until the Plaza agreement of 1985, there had been no serious attempt at policy co-ordination at the international level. The gross overvaluation of the dollar during the first half of the 1980s, seen in the beginning as a sign of national virility by President Reagan and several members of his Administration, and its disastrous effects on the US external trade balance finally brought about a change in US attitudes. The experience since then suggests that the conversion to the virtues of international economic co-operation and the joint management of exchange rates was neither deep nor long-lasting; but this applies virtually to all parties concerned, which is a further sign of the limitations of international policy co-ordination. Nevertheless, the Plaza agreement marked a turning-point at least in terms of the prevailing exchange rate fashion, since even the Anglo-Americans appeared ready then to abandon their earlier theological attachment to free floating (Funabashi, 1988).

Intra-ERM exchange rate stability is closely linked to price convergence. This convergence started with a time-lag in 1983 and it was downwards until 1986-7, when there was again some acceleration in inflation rates (Fig. 1). On the basis of the experience of recent years, there are three distinct groups of countries inside the EC. The first group comprises the seven original members of the narrow band of the ERM, which have experienced the highest degree of convergence and the lowest rates of inflation. The second group consists of the countries with the longest history in the wider band of the ERM, namely Spain, the UK and Italy which accepted the discipline of the narrower margins of fluctuation in 1990 despite the continued divergence in terms of inflation rates. The remaining two countries, namely Portugal and Greece, have continued all along with double digit rates of inflation.

Figure 3
(a) **Real Effective Exchange Rates (relative to 19 other industrialized countries), 1979-1991.**
(Nominal effective exchange rates adjusted for GDP deflator; 1979 = 100)
Source: Commission of the EC.
(b) **Real Effective Exchange Rates (relative to 19 other industrialized countries), 1979-1991.**
(Nominal effective exchange rates adjusted for GDP deflator; 1979 = 100)
Source: Commission of the EC.

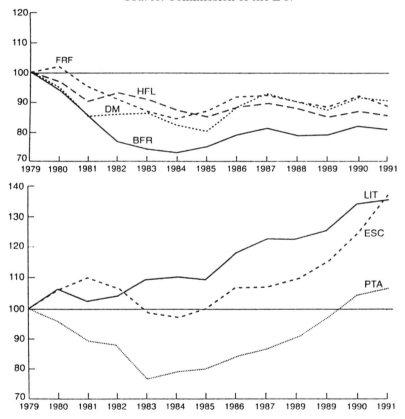

To the extent that exchange rate changes have not compensated fully for price and/or wage differentials during this period, this has had inevitably an effect on the external competitiveness of the countries concerned. Although major misalignments have been avoided in most cases, exchange rates have been used, especially since 1983, as an important anti-inflationary instrument, with realignments compensating only partially for inflation differentials. This has, therefore, led to the progressive overvaluation in real terms of the more rapidly inflating currencies (Fig. 3). Measurements of competitiveness of the different ERM currencies vary depending on the indicator used (consumer prices, unit labour costs etc; see also Ungerer *et al.,* 1990; de Grauwe and Gros, 1991). However, whatever the indicator used, the lira stands out in terms of its cumulative overvaluation which in turn raises questions about the sustainability of a policy which has relied largely on the exchange rate as an anti-inflation instrument. But this is, to a large extent, also true of the currencies of other southern European countries, such as the peseta and the escudo which had stayed for long outside the ERM. This in turn suggests that the exchange rate has been used more widely as an anti-inflation instrument. The counterpart to this overvaluation has been the gain in competitiveness of other countries, and especially the Benelux countries (Fig. 3).

There has been much discussion about the link between membership of the ERM and price convergence. After all, inflation rates of most industrialized countries, including non-EC countries of Western Europe, followed a very similar path during the same period. How much of the inflation experience inside the EC can be attributed to the operation of the ERM? The EC Commission (1991: 199), among many others, has argued that '[D]uring the 1980s, the EMS was a powerful engine for disinflation in the Community.' This statement is very difficult to prove econometrically, although there is more than circumstantial evidence to indicate that participation in the exchange rate mechanism served, at least for a large part of the period under consideration, as an important additional instrument in the fight against inflation; and this seems to be particularly true of France, Italy and Ireland. Participation in the ERM acted as an external constraint on domestic monetary policies, while the exchange rate has also been used, as shown above, as an instrument of disinflation. With growing price convergence and the increased credibility of the system, there has been in recent years a significant convergence of both short- and long-term interest rates in the countries of the original narrow band of the ERM (for long-term interest rates, see Fig. 4). This subject will be discussed in more detail below in connection with the asymmetrical nature of the system.

On the other hand, there is little evidence of convergence in the case of budgetary policies. To the extent that such a convergence has taken place, it has been the result of autonomous decisions leading to a reduction of public sector deficits in several member countries for a large part of the 1980s and not the product of an effective co-ordination of national fiscal policies within the EC. In fact, the mechanism set up for the co-ordination of policies and based on the 1974 Council Decision on convergence, itself a product of the old days of Keynesian 'fine tuning' (see also Mortensen, 1990), never worked properly: it was strong on procedure and weak on implementation. Council deliberations often resembled the dialogue of the deaf, with each minister expounding at length on the virtues of his country's policies, without the slightest inclination of modifying them for the 'general good'. Linked to the first stage of EMU, a new co-ordination framework was created with the Council Decision of April 1990. Multilateral surveillance is likely to acquire new teeth, mainly because of the various criteria established at Maastricht for the participation of member countries in the final stage of EMU.

Although the objective of monetary stability, both external and internal, has been largely achieved, even though fiscal policies have hardly converged, other objectives initially associated with the creation of the EMS have been only partially or not at all fulfilled. For example, the balance sheet on the development of a common currency has been mixed, at best. The official ECU has remained underdeveloped and under-utilized. The problem partly lies with the various restrictions imposed on its use and particularly with its non-permanent character, being still based on the three-month revolving swaps of foreign reserves held by EC central banks. On the other hand, the role of the ECU as a basket of currencies has led to a somewhat unexpected development, namely the creation of ECU-denominated instruments in the financial markets. There was rapid growth during the first half of the 1980s, which later slowed down as the uncertainty in terms of intra-ERM exchange rates was reduced and hence also the attraction of the basket.

Figure 4
(a) Nominal Long-term Interest Rates in the EC, 1979-1991.
(b) Nominal Long-term Interest Rate in the EC, 1979-1991.
Source: Commission of the EC, 1991.

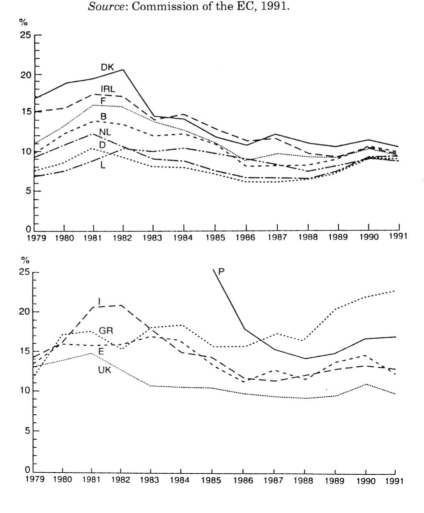

The transition to the second stage of the EMS, which had been envisaged in the original agreement, never materialized. The system continued to operate for many years on the basis of transitional structures and arrangements, although it was legitimized as an integral part of the Community system through the SEA. A few years later, it provided, however, the basis for plans and eventually for the new articles of the treaty referring to the establishment of EMU. The first stage of the latter started in July 1990, and the EMS constituted, without any doubt, the central pillar around which the new edifice started to be constructed.

Changing asymmetry

Despite special provisions, such as the creation of the divergence indicator, the EMS has operated in an asymmetrical fashion, thus following the earlier example of the snake. The degree and nature of the asymmetry have changed over time and so has the assessment of its effects, which has also been a function of the economic paradigm used to analyse those effects. After all, this is hardly a topic on which economists would be expected to agree.

As with the snake, the asymmetry inside the system, and more precisely the ERM, relates to the central role of the Deutschmark. The Delors report on EMU (Committee for the Study of Economic and Monetary Union, 1989: 12) explicitly referred to the German currency as the 'anchor' of the system, to which other currencies were pegged. The source of the asymmetry is dual: the German low propensity to inflate, at least before unification, and the international role of the DM. The former, combined with the economic weight of the country and the priority attached by the other EC partners to exchange rate stability and the fight against inflation, enabled Germany for many years to set the monetary standard for the other countries. On the other hand, the increasingly important role of the DM as an international reserve currency has placed the German central bank in a key position with respect to the external monetary policy of the EMS as a whole.

No realignment of ERM central parities in the first thirteen years of the system ever involved a depreciation of the DM in relation to any other currency (see Fig. 5 for the evolution of bilateral DM rates of the original member currencies of the ERM). Fig. 5 also gives some indication of the margin of manoeuvre used by other countries *vis-à-vis* Germany, ranging from the Netherlands at one extreme, with an almost complete alignment on German monetary policy, to Italy and France which for several years made repeated use of currency realignments as well as foreign exchange interventions and capital controls, at the other.

Asymmetry in a system of fixed (even if periodically adjustable) exchange rates is linked with the unequal distribution of the burden of intervention and adjustment and also of influence in the setting of policy priorities. The asymmetry in the EMS has manifested itself in different ways, and it reached the highest point during the second phase between 1983 and 1987. Before that, there had been little policy convergence and frequent currency realignments; hence relative symmetry being combined with monetary instability. We shall concentrate here on the experience of the second phase, and then we shall go on to examine the main changes which have happened since then.

Figure 5
Bilateral DM Rates of 6 ERM Currencies, 1980-1992
(Price of DM in terms of each of the 6 ERM currencies; the exchange rates are monthly averages).
Source: Deutsche Bundesbank.

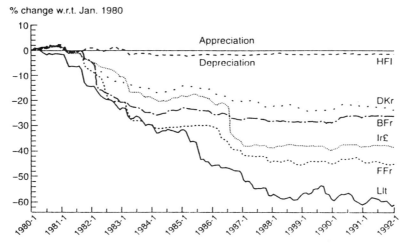

Especially after the March 1983 realignment, most central bank interventions in the exchange markets were taking place inside the permitted margins of fluctuation. The aim of intra-marginal interventions was to strengthen market confidence in the stability of existing bilateral rates and thus avoid the development of crisis situations. The heavy reliance on intra-marginal interventions had a number of important consequences. First of all, the burden of supporting the exchange rate system rested disproportionately on the shoulders of the countries with the weaker currencies. Furthermore, the very short-term credit facility, which could be triggered off automatically only as a result of marginal interventions, fell increasingly into disuse: and this also had a negative effect on the use of the ECU in the credit mechanism. The recourse to intra-marginal interventions also meant that the threshold of the divergence indicator was rarely reached, thus contributing to what had already appeared as the inoperational nature of this new mechanism. Therefore, the attempt made with the EMS to design rules which would guarantee a certain degree of symmetry between strong and weak currencies proved almost totally ineffective.

The asymmetry in foreign exchange interventions was also manifested in the implicit division of labour between the German and the other central banks in the system, with the latter intervening mainly in order to support intra-ERM exchange rates, while the former concentrated on exchange relations with third currencies, and most notably the US dollar. This division of labour was also reflected in the holding of foreign currencies by EC central banks; the Bundesbank holding only relatively small amounts of other EC currencies.

Another manifestation of asymmetry in the EMS was through the interdependence of interest rates in different national markets. Short-term interest rates have been consistently used as a key instrument in the exchange rate policy of participating countries. There is strong evidence to suggest that in times of crisis in the past, usually preceding realignments, the burden of adjustment was borne mainly by France, Italy and the smaller countries, with capital controls being used to insulate domestic interest rates from the effects of foreign exchange speculation. According to Giavazzi and Giovannini (1989: 75): 'the data on interest rates suggest that only Germany sets monetary policy independently. Italy and France can either accommodate German monetary policies perfectly or decouple domestic and foreign interest rates, at least temporarily, by resorting to capital controls.'

This is also confirmed by the fact that, more often than not, interest rate changes initiated by the Bundesbank for domestic stabilization purposes were followed almost immediately by many other European central banks, including those of countries not even participating in the ERM. There was little doubt among central bankers as to who was the leader in the European game. Although there is evidence to suggest that, even at the peak of the asymmetry inside the EMS, German monetary policy did not remain completely unaffected by policies pursued in the other countries, the distribution of influence was undoubtedly highly unequal (Gros and Thygesen, 1992).

Is asymmetry necessarily bad, at least from an economic point of view? Giavazzi and Giovannini (1989: 63), for example, argued that 'the EMS reproduces the historical experiences of fixed exchange rate regimes'. The literature on fixed exchange rates refers to the so-called N-1 problem which means that in a group of N countries (and currencies) there can only be N-1 policies that can be set independently. In the EMS, as with the Bretton Woods system earlier, the centre country retains the ability to set its monetary policy independently, while the other countries peg to its currency.

There are two sides to the asymmetrical nature of the EMS. On the one hand, it can be argued that countries with a higher propensity to inflation, such as France, Italy, and Ireland, borrowed credibility by pegging their currencies to the DM and they consequently reduced the output loss resulting from disinflationary policies. This is the alleged advantage of 'tying one's hands' to the DM anchor (Giavazzi and Pagano, 1988). Participation in the ERM is also supposed to have strengthened the commitment of national authorities to non-inflationary policies. The latter, softer version of the argument is perhaps more plausible. Participation in the ERM introduced an external discipline and thus reinforced the hand of institutions and interest groups inside a country fighting for less inflationary policies. This largely explains the popularity of the system with most central bankers, which is contrary to their earlier expectations. The Banca d'Italia is the best example in this respect. However, faced with the profligacy of the domestic political class and an inflexible labour market, the Italian central bank has also experienced the serious limitations of an anti-inflation strategy based almost entirely on the exchange rate and monetary policy.

The advantage of 'tying one's hands': as with most arguments in economics, there is also the other hand. The asymmetry of the EMS has also been seen as leading to a deflationary bias in the system (de Grauwe, 1987; Wyplosz, 1990). The early years of the EMS coincided with the worst and longest recession of the post-war period in Western Europe, which saw unemployment rates reach unprecedented levels. Until the mid-1980s, growth rates of the participating countries were significantly below those enjoyed by their main outside competitors, and intra-EMS trade remained stagnant, thus raising doubts about the beneficial effects of exchange rate stability on trade.

The criticism referring to the deflationary bias of the EMS relates to the more general debate of the early and mid-1980s in Western Europe regarding the causes of low growth. The latter was usually attributed either to supply-side factors, as part of the notorious 'Euro-sclerosis', or to the restrictive policies pursued by European governments during this period. In different terms, the debate was largely about how much of the unemployment in Western Europe could be attributed to classical or Keynesian factors and thus whether there was room for macroeconomic expansion.

The combination of low inflation and a large trade surplus, coupled with its central position in the EMS and the economic weight of the country, made Germany the natural candidate for the adoption of reflationary measures. As the progressive devaluation of the US dollar after 1985 started eliminating one of the main factors behind Western Europe's modest export-led growth, the pressures for the so-called two-handed approach mounted (Commission, 1985 ; Dreze *et al.*, 1987). This piece of Euro-jargon meant that supply-side measures aiming at greater flexibility of labour and product markets and the attempt to bring down real wages and salaries should be complemented by a co-ordinated expansion of fiscal policies; a unilateral expansion being excluded because of large import leakages in a system of fixed exchange rates. With inflation rates having already reached historically low levels, some of the participating countries started then to adopt a less benign view of German leadership. But the crisis in the EMS was at least temporarily averted as a result of changes in the rules and the dramatic improvement in the economic environment.

Following strong pressures, mainly from France and Italy, an agreement was reached in September 1987 (the so-called Basle-Nyborg agreement) aiming at a partial correction of the asymmetrical nature of the system. It referred to a 'presumption' that loans of EC currencies would be available through the EMCF for the financing of intra-marginal interventions. It also announced the extension of the very short-term credit facility and the use of ECUs for the settlement of debts as well as the intention of central bankers to achieve a closer co-ordination of interest rates. Although they have not completely eliminated the asymmetry, those measures have led to a more equitable distribution of the burden of intervention between different countries. As a counterpart to the extension of credit facilities, participating countries also expressed the intention to make realignments of central parities as infrequent and as small as possible, while also making explicit their intention not to compensate fully for inflation differentials. This intention has been confirmed by the development and the further strengthening of the EMS in the third phase.

The change of operating rules in September 1987 was accompanied by a largely unexpected improvement of the economic *conjoncture*. This was due to exogenous factors such as the decline in oil prices, the relaxation of monetary policies in the aftermath of the 1987 stock exchange crash (the effects of which on consumption were grossly exaggerated), and the 1992 effect. This led to the relaxation of tension inside the EMS, which lasted for some time. But other important developments have happened since then, which have had a major impact on the functioning of the system. One such development has been the liberalization of capital movements, as part of the internal market programme. Higher capital mobility, combined with no currency realignments, has imposed much tighter constraints on the monetary policy of individual countries, while at the same time loosening further the link between the exchange rate and the current account. This is exemplified in the case of countries such as Italy and Spain which have been able to attract for years large inflows of capital through high nominal interest rates; at least as long as ERM central parities remained credible. One consequence of the large capital inflows was that the peseta stayed for long at the upper end of its permitted margin of fluctuation, leading to complaints about the upward pressure exerted on the interest rates of partner countries. Giavazzi and Spaventa (1990) wrote about the new EMS in which the monetary standard would be effectively set by the weaker members.

Figure 6
Germany's Trade Surpluses with EC-12 and World, 1979-90.
Note: excluding Eastern Germany
Source: OECD

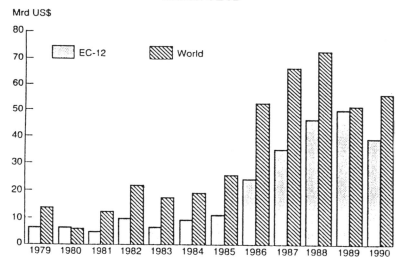

And then came German unification, the early effects of which preceded the actual event. Rapidly growing public expenditure in the new *Länder* led to high budget deficits in Germany and the acceleration of inflation. The burden of the stabilization effort fell then almost entirely on monetary policy, and this led to higher interest rates in Germany and also indirectly in the other countries of the narrow band of the ERM. This coincided with the end of the economic boom, when the anticipation effect of 1992 also started petering out. In times of recession and growing unemployment, high interest rates, seen as imposed by the German policy-mix, were strongly resented by Germany's partners. And this led to renewed tension in the system. The effect of the German policy-mix was, however, attenuated (for how long?), because the weakening of the DM in exchange markets, coupled with the increased credibility of the system, allowed the other members of the ERM to reduce progressively their nominal interest rate differentials with resepct to the Deutschmark.

On the other hand, the rapid expansion of domestic demand in unified Germany brought about a large increase in imports, which helped to reverse the previous trend of steadily growing trade surpluses for Germany (Fig. 6). Those surpluses had been seen in the past as one of the prizes gained by the leading country, linked at least partially with the overvaluation of some currencies inside the EMS. According to the EC Commission (1991a:8), the positive impact of German unification through trade on the rate of growth of the other EC countries was estimated to be around 0.5 percentage points for 1990 and 1991. This should be, therefore, set against the negative impact of high interest rates (see also Siebert, 1991; Atkinson *et al.*, 1992). The overall economic effect of German unification on different EC countries varied, depending among other things on their competitiveness and the size of their public debt.

The weakness of the DM, linked to the acceleration of German inflation which by 1991 was higher than that of several members of the ERM, raised questions about the continued role of the DM as the anchor of the system, and hence also about the continued asymmetry inside the EMS. Would this prove to be a short-term aberration or would it, instead, lead to a more symmetrical system based on a 'more explicit co-ordination of policies with Community-wide considerations' (EC Commission, 1991: 198)?

The success of the EMS has been based on a consensus about exchange rate stability and disinflation, which was centred for several years around German monetary policy. Is asymmetry the inevitable price to pay for monetary stability? Views have varied on this subject, and the leading role of Germany has not been always accepted with equanimity by the other members of the system, especially in times of low growth. The asymmetrical nature of the EMS has been both modified and attenuated in recent years. In fact, there may be question of a more fundamental change being brought about by a combination of factors, such as the progressive convergence of inflation rates, the increased credibility of the system, the liberalization of capital movements and the destabilizing effects of German unification. In the intervening period leading to the final stage of EMU, the system may come under further strain as markets anticipate the last realignment before the irrevocable fixing of parities.

EMU is back on the stage: the politics of economic fundamentals

In the late 1980s, EMU came back with a vengeance on the European agenda, and it very quickly reached the most prominent place. It was in many respects a repetition of what had happened twenty years earlier, although this time there is a reasonable chance that the final outcome will be different. EMU was generally presented as the logical continuation of the internal market programme, the next target to aim for in the long process of economic and political unification of Europe. The decision to proceed with monetary integration would help to sustain business confidence, a major factor behind the boom of the late 1980s, which started showing signs of petering out; hence also the urgency for a political commitment to the next stage of integration while the 'Euro-euphoria' still lasted. Monetary union would be the final and irrevocable confirmation of the reality of the single European market and the European economy.

A common currency was seen as the means of welding national economies together, and also the means of accelerating the movement towards political union. The developments in Eastern Europe in 1989 and German reunification provided a powerful catalyst which rapidly brought EMU back to the centre of the stage. Those developments called for a stronger Community on the European scene and also a Community which would provide a stable and secure framework for larger Germany; and money once again provided the instrument.

Proposals for EMU were directly linked to the 1992 process. Although mentioned in the SEA, no binding commitment had been undertaken in the latest revision of the treaties for the realization of EMU. Yet the increase in trade and economic interdependence, which would inevitably result from the completion of the internal market, should be expected to reduce further the effectiveness of the exchange rate as an instrument for the correction of payments imbalances. Furthermore, the very concept of the internal market was, arguably, difficult to reconcile with the considerable transaction costs involved in converting between different currencies and the uncertainty associated with changes in exchange rates. Thus exchange rates were presented as another NTB to be eliminated. On the other hand, unlike previous occasions, CAP considerations did not seem to play an important role. The exchange rate stability already achieved through the EMS and the diminishing importance of agriculture in European integration had helped to sever the link between EMU and the CAP.

The positive balance sheet of the EMS and the considerable experience and knowledge which central banks had acquired in the joint management of exchange rates were important additional factors. Gone was the old enthusiasm for independent floating, as a means of achieving national monetary independence, and also the belief in the 'efficiency' of exchange markets (Allsopp and Chrystal, 1989); although, with the exception of Britain and, to a lesser extent, Germany, such enthusiasm had never been very pronounced in the open economies of Western Europe. The transition from the EMS to EMU also had a major significance for countries such as France and Italy, because the creation of common institutions would lead to a shift from the existing German-centred system to new forms of collective management. Proposals for EMU were at least partly driven by the search for greater symmetry. Hence the considerable scepticism shown by the central bankers in Frankfurt.

As far as interest in EMU is concerned, the most important aspect of the internal market was, undoubtedly, the decision to liberalize capital movements. Padoa-Schioppa (1988) talked about the 'inconsistent quartet' of economic objectives. It includes free trade, free capital movements, fixed exchange rates, and monetary autonomy. His conclusion was that since the EC countries have committed themselves to the first three objectives, through the internal market, the EMS, and the decision to liberalize capital movements, monetary autonomy would also have to give way, moving gradually from an effective co-ordination of national policies to the centralization of monetary policy at EC level. This is also the main argument on which the EC Commission strategy was later based; another example of the Commission trying to make full use of functional spill-over.

Padoa-Schioppa's argument assumes, first of all, that EC countries are fully committed to the other three objectives, which has not always been true in the past. Thus, while Britain opted for most of the 1980s for free capital movements and monetary autonomy, at the expense of exchange rate stability, France and Italy concentrated during this period on the latter objective, while sacrificing free capital movements and part of their monetary sovereignty in the process. Wider margins of fluctuation and more frequent realignments inside the ERM could have been a possible compromise in the search for politically acceptable trade-offs between the four above-mentioned objectives. On the other hand, the fear of destabilizing speculation was clearly the most important factor behind the safeguard clause included in the directive on the liberalization of capital movements, although it remains to be seen whether capital controls could be effectively re-applied in cases of emergency.

Earlier initiatives in the field of European monetary integration had been largely motivated by external preoccupations: the instability of the dollar and US policies of 'unbenign neglect' serving as powerful federalizing factors in Europe. This was not true of the various initiatives which finally led to the new treaty provisions for the establishment of EMU; or, at least, not to the same extent as in the past. True, the reform of the international monetary system was not on the cards and the lack of unity of European countries remained an important factor behind the continuing asymmetry in the international system. But this asymmetry was now less evident, the Bush Administration did not adopt the aggressive stance of its predecessor, and intra-ERM exchange rates appeared to be less vulnerable to the gyrations of the dollar. Perhaps less preoccupation with external factors was also a sign of the new collective confidence of the Europeans.

The main driving force for the relaunching of monetary union came from Brussels and Paris, with EMU representing the flagship of the European strategy of both the EC Commission and the French Government for the 1990s. There was also strong support from Italy, Belgium, and, with some qualification, from Spain. Initially, Germany showed little enthusiasm; the Government and the central bank were happy with the *status quo* and any move towards monetary union was perceived, quite rightly, as leading to an erosion of Germany's independence in the monetary field. What later tipped the balance was the perceived need to reaffirm the country's commitment to European integration in the wake of reunification. This is how the matter was presented in Paris and Brussels. Thus the German decision to proceed with EMU was fundamentally political, as it was, indeed, in most other member countries. Once a Franco-German agreement had been reached on the subject of EMU, the process appeared almost unstoppable; thus becoming a repetition of earlier patterns of European decision-making. The Dutch shared much of the economic scepticism of the Germans, but their margin of manoeuvre was extremely limited. The main concern of the small and less developed economies was to link EMU to more substantial budgetary transfers and to avoid an institutionalization of two or more tiers in the Community. As for Britain, it remained the only country ready to question in public the desirability and feasibility of EMU, both on economic and political grounds. However, drawing some lessons from the earlier stages of European integration, the British Government, even under Mrs Thatcher, made a conscious effort to remain in the negotiating game.

In terms of decision-making, the approach to EMU bears considerable resemblance to earlier European initiatives and especially the one which had led some years ago to the adoption of the internal market programme. The gradual build-up of momentum, the steady expansion of the political support base through coalition building, and the isolation of opponents have been combined with an effective marketing campaign addressed primarily to opinion leaders and the business community. Functional spill-over was also successfully mixed with high politics and the appeal to 'Euro-sentiment'; a recipe which had proved quite powerful in the past.

In June 1988 the European Council of Hanover set up the 'Committee for the Study of Economic and Monetary Union', under the chairmanship of the President of the Commission, Mr Delors. This decision was taken only a few months after the adoption of the directive on capital liberalization, and the two were directly linked. The committee included all governors or presidents of EC central banks plus a few independent experts; its unanimous report was submitted in April 1989 (Committee for the Study of Economic and Monetary Union, 1989). There were many similarities with the Werner report which had appeared almost twenty years earlier, something which should come as no surprise since the briefs of the two committees were virtually identical. The final objective in terms of monetary union remained the same, namely complete liberalization of capital movements, the irrevocable fixity of intra-EC exchange rates, coupled with the elimination of margins of fluctuation (and possibly the replacement of national currencies by a single currency), and the centralization of monetary policy. The Delors report was, however, more explicit about the necessary transfer of powers to the level of the union and the institutional changes required.

In fact, the central bankers, constituting the large majority in the committee, appeared only too keen on stressing the full economic and institutional implications of EMU to their political masters. They called for a system of binding rules governing the size and the financing of national budget deficits and referred to the need to determine the overall stance of fiscal policy at the EC level, with decisions taken on a majority basis. The disciplinary influence of market forces on national budgetary policies was not deemed to be sufficient on its own. Much emphasis was also placed on the independence of the new institution which would be in charge of monetary policy for the union. This consensus on the question of independence of the future European central bank reflected not only the composition of the committee but also the leadership role and the prestige enjoyed by the Deutsche Bundesbank which had provided the role model.

As for the intermediate stages, the strategy of parallelism seemed to have survived the long time separating the publication of the Werner and the Delors reports. In the latter, the major institutional changes and the application of the new treaty rules were reserved for the second stage of EMU. On the other hand, it stressed that 'the decision to enter upon the first stage should be a decision to embark on the entire process' (p.31); certainly, not the right message for the faint-hearted.

The Delors report set the EMU ball rolling; and it did roll very fast indeed. On the basis of the report, a decision was taken at the Madrid European Council of June 1989 to proceed to the first stage of EMU on 1 July 1990 which coincided with the complete liberalization of capital movements in eight members of the Community. This was followed by the decision reached at the European Council in Strasbourg in December of the same year to call for a new intergovernmental conference to prepare the necessary treaty revisions for a complete EMU. Both decisions were taken unanimously, despite the expressed opposition of the UK and the persisting differences on important aspects of EMU and the nature of the transitional period among the other members. In a subsequent meeting of the European Council, the date for the second stage of EMU was fixed for 1994, thus following one year after the expected completion of the internal market. Before the official opening of the new intergovernmental conference in December 1990, a great deal of the preparatory work had already been done in the context of the Committee of the Governors of Central Banks and the Monetary Committee. This included the draft statutes of the European Central Bank. The Commission had also published a major study of the potential costs and benefits of EMU, very much along the lines of the Cecchini report (Commission of the EC, 1990). Furthermore, between the publication of the Delors report and the opening of the intergovernmental conference, important changes had taken place inside the ERM, with two more currencies joining (the peseta and sterling) with a 6 per cent margin of fluctuation, while the margin for the lira had been reduced to 2.25 per cent.

Thus, money was once again at the centre of European high politics and, even more so than with the ERM, commitment to monetary union was almost indistinguishable from the more general commitment to European unification. It was certainly not a coincidence that the other intergovernmental conference on political union was running concurrently with that on EMU. But economic fundamentals do not always conform to high political priorities. From an economic point of view, the discussion on the desirability of the final objective essentially boils down to a comparison of the benefits of monetary union with the costs of forgoing the exchange rate as an instrument of economic policy (Commission of the EC, 1990; see also Allsopp and Chrystal, 1989). A corollary to this question would be to compare the effectiveness of the exchange rate to other alternative instruments of policy geared towards economic adjustment and changes in the real competitiveness of national economies which, presumably, will continue to be needed for some time.

The benefits of monetary union are linked to the elimination of foreign exchange transaction costs and the factor of uncertainty associated with exchange rate fluctuations. According to the Commission's study, these direct benefits would be relatively small, although, as with the earlier work on the internal market, the dynamic gains were expected to be much larger and more difficult to quantify. The creation of a single currency (the emphasis had already shifted towards the creation of a single currency as the final objective as opposed to the retention of national currencies linked through irrevocably fixed exchange rates) would secure further the credibility of the internal market and the gains associated with its completion; 'one market' and now 'one money'. The Commission's study also talked in terms of the benefits from a lower average rate of inflation which would be expected to result from EMU. However, this would obviously depend on the policy stance and the credibility of the new European Central Bank, which would be, of course, one of the crucial questions for the future. On the other hand, the adoption of the ECU as an international currency, thus replacing and eventually extending the international role of the Deutschmark, was supposed to bring seigniorage gains resulting from the readiness of outsiders to hold the new currency. An international currency would also be accompanied with gains in prestige and political power, associated with a common monetary policy *vis-à-vis* the rest of the world. However, the Commission's expectations regarding the gains from the future international role of the ECU appeared to be somewhat vague and also exaggerated (Goodhart, 1993).

The relative effectiveness of the exchange rate instrument at the national level and the possible costs resulting from an irrevocable fixity of intra-EC exchange rates (and/or the adoption of a common currency) remain big questions on which there are as many views as there are economists. Many would agree about the limited effectiveness of the exchange rate because of large trade interdependence, the decisive importance of financial transactions in determining the price in exchange markets, and the limited 'efficiency' of those markets. The experience with floating exchange rates has not been particularly encouraging, in view of frequent 'overshooting' and the persistent misalignment of currencies. An increasingly fashionable paradigm in the economics profession stresses the relative ineffectiveness of the exchange rate and links this to inflation which is basically seen as a credibility problem (Mortensen, 1990; Gros and Thygesen, 1992). However, still only a minority of economists would go as far as arguing the complete ineffectiveness of the exchange rate, even for a small and open economy such as Belgium which has, for example, made a limited but apparently successful use of this instrument in the context of the ERM (the franc was devalued by 8.5 per cent in February 1982).

Very few would also argue that the EC is already an optimum currency area. This is a concept which became very popular in the literature during the 1960s when economists looked for factors which could act as near substitutes for the exchange rate instrument (Mundell, 1961; McKinnon, 1963; see also Krugman, 1990); such factors also being, usually, good indicators of the degree of economic integration inside the potential currency area. That means that economic integration inside the EC has not yet reached the level where capital and especially labour mobility could act as near substitutes for changes in the exchange rate; or that wage and price movements in different countries correspond to changes in productivity rates so as to make exchange rate realignments redundant; or even that the EC economy is sufficiently homogeneous so that different countries and regions are not frequently subject to asymmetric external shocks. But is this true of the United States or even Italy, and if not, are those countries optimum currency areas?

There is still a long distance to cover in the Community in terms of economic convergence which, interestingly enough, means very different things to different people. Thus, when the Germans talk about convergence, they invariably mean convergence of inflation rates, while the Greeks, the Irish, and the Portuguese are more interested in the convergence of income levels. The experience of the EMS in terms of both internal and external monetary stability has been positive. However, in terms of real economic variables, the experience has been mixed. The EC could be approaching fast the uncomfortable state in which, while national wages and prices still have a life of their own, being a function of history, political institutions, social traditions, and labour power among other factors, and while the need for adjustment differs considerably from one country to the other, the effectiveness of the exchange rate becomes increasingly curtailed, even before the instrument is politically banished. This could become even more uncomfortable if the move towards monetary union is not accompanied by a corresponding convergence in some of the economic fundamentals. The loss of the exchange rate instrument, coupled with a continuing need for real adjustment, could turn countries into depressed regions; and other factors, such as labour mobility and interregional budgetary transfers, would remain too weak to act as effective substitutes.

A comparison has been sometimes drawn between EMU at the European level and monetary union between West and East Germany, although the differences between the two are quite substantial. German monetary union led, at least in the early years, to a major decline in production in the Eastern *Länder* and a large increase in unemployment. The shock of unification in the East was, however, attenuated by substantial budgetary transfers from the West (and only to a much lesser extent through private investment flows). Wage convergence proceeded much faster than convergence in productivity rates, and this threatened to jeopardize the economic prospects of the new *Länder*. At the same time, labour mobility was high, thus adding to the pressure for wage convergence (see also, Siebert, 1991). Thus, on the one hand, public transfers and labour mobility helped significantly to ease the burden of adjustment for what used to be the German Democratic Republic; and in this respect, German monetary union is likely to be very different from European EMU. On the other hand, the state of the former centrally planned economy and the artificially high exchange rate, adopted for political reasons, made the scale of economic adjustment very large. Though the German experience could serve as a warning sign of some of the problems lying ahead, the qualitative differences with European EMU should not be underestimated.

Of course, in the discussion about EMU, some differentiation is needed with respect to individual countries. The attachment to stable, although not necessarily fixed irrevocably, exchange rates is usually closely related to the openness of an economy to international trade. In the case of the EC, the readiness of individual countries to accept the implications of a monetary union should also be a function of the relative importance of intra-regional trade. A broad distinction can be drawn between small and big countries in the EC as regards their openness to international trade (Table 3). The Benelux countries and Ireland on the one hand and the Big Four on the other (the German economy — the data only refer to West Germany — being significantly more open than the other three) fit nicely into those two categories. By comparison, Greece and Spain are still relatively closed economies (at least in terms of trade in goods, since the inclusion of services would significantly modify this picture), while Denmark and Portugal find themselves in between the two groups. As for the importance of intra-EC trade, this is relatively more pronounced in the case of the Benelux countries and Ireland, although differences between member countries have gradually diminished over the years. Intra-EC trade now represents on average 60 per cent of total trade for member countries (ranging from 50 per cent for the UK to 72 per cent for Belgium-Luxembourg and Ireland).

On the other hand, the Community does not start from zero on the road to EMU. The use of the exchange rate is already severely curtailed in the context of the ERM. In fact, the lack of currency realignments for several years, combined with capital liberalization, has brought the system very close to a *de facto* monetary union, without some of the benefits. The question, however, remains whether this situation can be sustainable for long, even though there has been significant convergence of inflation rates among most of its members. In the aftermath of the Maastricht decisions, the costs and risks associated with an irrevocable fixity of exchange rates would appear to be much bigger for Britain than for the Netherlands, and certainly even bigger for Greece and Portugal. We shall return to this subject when we discuss the transition to the final stage of EMU.

Table 3
Openness of EC Economies, 1960-1990
(Average of imports and exports of goods as a percentage of GDP;[a] intra-EC is given as a % of total trade).

	1960-7		1968-72		1973-9		1980-4		1985-90	
	World	Intra-EC	World	Intra-EC	World	Intra-EC	World	Intra-EC	World	Intra-EC
Belgium and Luxembourg	37.5	64.8	42.8	71.2	48.9	71.2	61.5	67.0	60.8	71.7
Denmark	27.0	52.3	23.4	46.7	25.3	48.2	29.1	49.1	26.7	50.8
Germany	15.9	44.8	17.6	50.9	20.4	50.3	24.8	50.5	24.9	53.1
Greece	12.7	50.6	12.7	53.4	17.6	47.3	19.5	48.1	20.8	60.5
Spain	8.1	47.8	9.2	44.4	11.2	41.3	14.4	39.3	14.4	56.0
France	11.0	45.8	12.5	57.2	16.6	55.0	18.9	53.9	18.6	61.9
Ireland	33.6	72.2	35.3	71.6	45.8	74.3	50.1	73.1	52.0	72.2
Italy	11.7	42.9	13.1	49.5	18.4	48.7	19.4	46.1	16.9	55.0
Netherlands	37.7	62.7	36.4	67.8	40.6	65.9	47.8	64.1	49.0	67.8
Portugal	19.8	48.3	20.3	49.6	22.2	50.2	30.1	50.1	32.5	65.1
United Kingdom	16.0	26.7	16.7	31.2	22.3	37.9	21.6	44.1	21.0	49.9
EC-12	8.8	45.0	8.3	51.9	10.2	52.6	11.5	52.2	9.8	59.8

[a]Figures for world trade as a % of GDP have been calculated by inserting country data for imports and exports of goods (SITC categories 0-9) in the formula:

$$\frac{\frac{1}{2}\Sigma\,(x+m)}{GDP}\,\times\,100$$

For the Member States, these figures include intra-Community trade; for EC-12, intra-Community trade has been excluded.

Source: Eurostat.

To the old familiar arguments about the flexibility of labour markets and trade union militancy, Dornbush (1988; see also Commission of the EC, 1990) has added the argument about seigniorage as an important means of financing large public debts in some countries. The gains from seigniorage are mainly a function of the rate of inflation, the amount of cash transactions and the reserve requirements for commercial banks; and those gains could not be easily replaced by increased tax revenues because of political and institutional constraints. This argument is relevant for some EC members. According to the Commission's study on EMU, the revenue effects through seigniorage exceeded in 1988 2 per cent of GDP in both Greece and Portugal, and 1 per cent in Italy and Spain. Thus, the transition to low inflation rates for the southern European countries could be both painful and long.

Define virtue and achieve it later

During the intergovernmental conference, the economic and political desirability of EMU was not seriously put in question. This matter was supposed to have been already settled. The political decision had been taken at the highest level, and only the British were ready to express their economic and political doubts in public. The other doubters, and they did seem to exist inside the governments and central banks of several member countries, preferred to concentrate on specific problems, instead of challenging the main principles and objectives. Thus, the negotiations revolved around other issues which could be grouped together into three main categories: the institutional framework of the union, and especially the role and statutes of the European central bank; the balance between the monetary and the fiscal arm of the union; and the nature and length of the transitional period leading to a complete EMU, including the criteria for participating in the final stage. The influence of Germany on the overall package agreed at Maastricht was decisive.

We shall start by examining the transitional arrangements before the final stage. The French wanted a firm commitment about a date for the final stage, which would tie the others, and especially the Germans, to the objective of a complete EMU. The Germans, from their side, wanted to delay any serious transfer of powers to central institutions which, once created, should be as close as possible to the German model. They also insisted on strict rules for the admission of countries to the final stage, consistent with the old 'economist' line that economic convergence should precede monetary union. The economically weaker members stressed the link between EMU and cohesion (read budgetary transfers), while also favouring loose criteria for admission to the final stage, which might allow them to sneak in. As for the British, they refused any firm commitment about the final stage, which they could not apparently sell at home.

The final compromise was essentially based on a French timetable and German conditions. The first stage, which had already started in July 1990, was meant as a consolidation of the *status quo*. This should include the liberalization of capital movements and the inclusion of all currencies in the narrow band of the ERM. Economic convergence should be promoted on the basis of multiannual programmes for each member country to be discussed in the context of the Council Decision of 1990 on multilateral surveillance. The second stage was planned to start on 1 January 1994. Although monetary policy will remain the exclusive responsibility of national authorities, a new institution will be created, the European Monetary Institute (EMI), which will prepare the way for the future European Central Bank (ECB) by further strengthening the co-ordination of national monetary policies. It remains, however, to be seen whether the setting up of the EMI, which is intended to have only a short spell of life, will constitute an important qualitative change to the co-ordination mechanisms already existing in the Community. During the second stage, member countries will also be expected to take the necessary legal steps to ensure the independence of national central banks, wherever this independence does not already exist.

The crucial part of the transitional arrangements referred to the conditions to be fulfilled for the beginning of the third and final stage which will include the irrevocable fixity of exchange rates and the adoption of a single currency as well the creation of a European System of Central Banks (ESCB), with the ECB in its centre. The first attempt will be made before the end of 1996, the European Council deciding by qualified majority and on the basis of reports from the Commission and the EMI whether a majority of member countries fulfil the conditions for being admitted to the third stage. A qualified majority decision about whether there is a majority fit to enjoy the fruits of paradise (and EMU): this will be a rather uncommon case in international and even domestic politics.

In fact, the authors of the new treaty went further. It was stipulated that the third stage will start on 1 January 1999 at the latest, irrespective of how many member countries are found to fulfil the necessary conditions; again the European Council deciding on each case and on the basis of qualified majority. Those failing the tests will remain in derogation and, to all intents and purposes, they will be excluded from the new institutional framework. Their case will, however, be examined at least every two years. There were two further complications: the UK refused to commit itself in advance to participating in the final stage of EMU, with an 'opt out' protocol which left the decision for a future government and parliament, while Denmark chose a softer version of 'opting out', thus referring to the possibility of a referendum prior to its participation in the final stage.

The conditions for admission to the final stage, otherwise known as convergence criteria, were quite explicit and they concentrated exclusively on monetary variables. The first referred to a sustainable price performance, defined as a rate of inflation which should not exceed that of the best performing member countries by more than 1.5 percentage points. The second related to national budgets: actual or planned deficit should not exceed 3 per cent of GDP, while the accumulated public debt should not be above 60 per cent of GDP. With respect to this criterion, the wording of the new Article 104C of the treaty left some margin of manoeuvre by allowing for exceptional and temporary deficits and also for government debts that may exceed the 60 per cent ratio as long as they have been declining 'substantially and continuously'. Exchange rate stability was the third criterion: the national currency must have remained within the narrow band of the ERM for at least two years prior to the decision about the final stage, without any devaluation and without any severe tension. The fourth criterion was meant to ensure that the exchange rate stability is not based on excessively high interest rates; thus, the average nominal interest rate on long-term government bonds should not exceed that of the three best performing member states by more than two percentage points.

Thus, the treaty on European Union and the attached protocols went into considerable technical detail on the subject of EMU. As the price for accepting a firm commitment about the date of the final stage, the Germans had insisted on the application of strict convergence criteria before any country were to be admitted to the final stage. In this respect, they also had the support of the Dutch. The crucial question is how much convergence in terms of inflation or budgetary policies is required before the irrevocable fixity of exchange rates; and there can be no single answer from economists. The criteria adopted in the treaty can be, perhaps, treated as too mechanistic and arbitrary; it remains to be seen how much convergence will be achieved in the intervening period and how flexible an interpretation is given to those criteria, when the European Council decision is taken.

It is also interesting that only monetary variables were used for the convergence criteria, which may be seen as a further confirmation of the prevailing economic paradigm that there is no real trade-off between price stability on the one hand and growth and employment on the other. Gros and Thygesen (1992) raise a pertinent question: can a temporary fall in inflation achieved at the expense of high unemployment be sustainable, since the disinflationary policy is apparently not credible in labour markets? On the other hand, a strict application of the convergence criteria, when the time of judgement comes, risks leaving outside the gates of paradise several member countries, including some who belong to the old 'core' group of the EC. Is that exclusion politically realistic, and if so, what would be the implications for the internal balance of the Community? Since a further enlargement of the EC is likely to have taken place before the beginning of the final stage of EMU, it is also worth noting that some of the present candidates for accession are closer to fulfilling the conditions for membership in the final stage than several of the existing members of the EC.

In terms of inflation, we have already referred to three groups of countries in the EC on the basis of the experience of recent years (Fig. 1): the original members of the narrow band of the ERM on the one end, and Portugal and Greece on the other. In terms of budgetary policies, the situation appears somewhat differentiated. Belgium, Italy, Greece, and Ireland (although steadily improving its debt situation in recent years) are still way above the 60 per cent public debt target in terms of GDP (Fig. 7). As for current deficits, Greece and Italy form a group of their own. The budget deficits of those two countries have been persistently above 10 per cent of GDP for several years. The adjustment effort required for those countries in order to meet the two budgetary criteria set in the new treaty will therefore be more than considerable. For Greece and Italy, it may, indeed, necessitate major political and institutional reforms which are long overdue.

With respect to exchange rate stability, what will count will be the performance of each currency over a period of two years prior to the final decision. Judging from the experience so far in terms of internal and external monetary stability, the countries of the original narrow band of the ERM start with a distinct advantage. The situation is not very different in terms of long-term interest rates, the fourth criterion set out in the Maastricht treaty. As already explained before, convergence of inflation rates and exchange rate stability have been accompanied by a progressive narrowing of interest rate differentials (see Fig. 4). In this respect, the UK is closer to the countries of the original narrow band than either Italy or Spain.

Figure 7
(a) Gross Public Debt in EC Member States, 1979-1991
(Percentage of GDP at market prices)
(b) Gross Public Debt in EC Members State, 1979-1991
(Percentage of GDP at market prices).
Source: Commission of the EC.

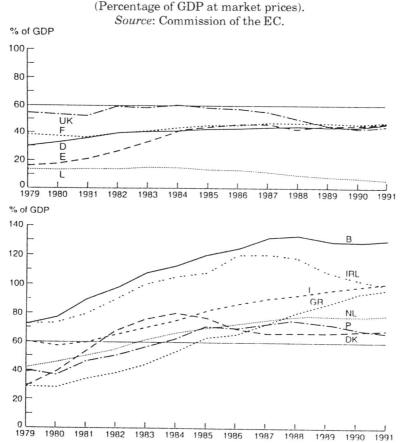

In 1992 only France, Luxembourg and Denmark (with a small question mark in terms of its public debt) would have fulfilled all four convergence criteria, the irony being that Germany, the country which had insisted all along for raising the standards for admission, would have been excluded for failing both the inflation and the budget deficit criteria. Should reunification be treated as a temporary exogenous shock and what conclusions should be drawn about the future application of rather mechanistic rules? Both the snake and the EMS have contributed to the institutionalization of a variable speed Europe, although it could be argued that the EMS experience in particular suggests that an initial central core can act as a powerful pole of attraction towards which other countries try to converge. It is difficult to predict whether the same will happen with EMU. If the Community continues moving along in different speeds, this will inevitably have serious repercussions for the model of integration as a whole. Leaving aside the political problems which may be raised with respect to the future participation of the UK, even countries such as Belgium and Italy will have a hard time in meeting all criteria before the end of the decade. Will national political systems be able to deliver the goods under peer pressure and the threat of exclusion or will the final stage start with only a limited number of members? A third scenario would involve a more flexible application of rules.

On the other hand, EC negotiators have opted for a relatively long transitional period before the final stage, with no substantial institutional changes taking place in between. Considerations of economic convergence, as a pre-condition for monetary union, were happily married with the natural instinct of politicians and lesser mortals to postpone difficult decisions. 'God, give me virtue (and EMU), but not yet.' In the intermediate period, there may be uncertainty and instability in exchange markets, as agents try to anticipate the last realignment inside the ERM, which, according to the rules, cannot take place later than the end of 1996, at least for those who would like to be with the first group in entering the final stage (or 1994, if an early agreement were to be reached for the transition to the final stage). Will EMU, therefore, destabilize the EMS? And how certain is it that EMU will happen as planned? In view of the length of the transitional period and the importance of decisions which will need to be taken some years from now, economic and political realities prevailing at the time are likely to count more than any treaty obligations; hence another element of uncertainty.

The institutional framework of the union constituted a major part of the whole debate around EMU and the negotiations which took place in the context of the intergovernmental conference. In fact, the debate went much further by establishing a direct link between EMU and political union, the latter aiming among other things at the strengthening of central political institutions, although with relatively limited success in the end. Only the UK opposed the institutional approach to EMU, and proposed instead a market approach which was based on a plan for competing currencies and later on another one for the creation of a parallel currency. But those proposals had, in the end, little effect on the negotiations.

The new treaty created the ESCB which will be based on a federal structure, composed of the ECB and the national central banks. The latter will operate in accordance with the guidelines and instructions of the ECB. The primary objective of the new monetary institution will be to maintain price stability. It will be responsible for the conduct of monetary policy for the union as a whole and for foreign exchange operations. It will also hold and manage the foreign reserves of the member states; and provisions have been made for the transfer of part of those reserves to the ECB. The treaty and the attached protocol on the statute of the ESCB and the ECB refer explicitly to the political independence of the new institution, thus following the German model. This will be true with respect to domestic monetary policy. In terms of exchange rate policy *vis-à-vis* third currencies, the Council of Ministers will also be expected to play an important role in setting the guidelines.

The ECB, the seat of which is supposed to be decided before the end of 1992, will be governed by a six-member Executive Board, appointed for eight years by the heads of state or government of member countries, and a Governing Council consisting of the members of the Executive Board and the governors of the national central banks. To ensure the independence of the ESCB, national legislations regulating the operation of national central banks are also expected to be changed accordingly. Thus, the entry into the third stage of EMU will imply not only the transfer of monetary powers from the national to the European level, but also a significant change in relations between political authorities and central banks.

The emphasis on price stability as the primary objective of the ESCB and the political independence of the new monetary institution is consistent with the prevailing idea that there is no trade-off between inflation and growth, not to mention unemployment. The Commission's study took a clear stance on this issue: 'The old theory that there is a trade-off between high inflation and low unemployment is now unsupported as a matter of theory or empirical analysis, except for short-run periods' (Commission of the EC. 1990: 22). Although the short-run may be a long time in politics, the statement did, in fact, represent a fairly broad political consensus at the time, which cannot, however, be treated as completely irreversible. But the problem goes much further: can there be a central bank without a corresponding political authority? There is hardly any historical precedent for that. Given the fragmentation and the relatively underdeveloped nature of political power in the nascent European economy, a reality which does not seem likely to change drastically in the foreseeable future, the independence of the ESCB and the ECB will be even greater in real terms.

This also brings us back to the old question of the link between economic and monetary union. It is not at all surprising that this question proved difficult for both the Werner and the Delors committees to answer. The strategy of parallelism was adopted as a compromise for the intermediate stages leading to a complete EMU, while both committees opted for a close economic union as the necessary counterpart to the centralization of monetary policies, the unhindered mobility of capital, and the irrevocable fixity of exchange rates. But this is exactly the point which provoked the strongest reactions from member states. It is interesting that, while there had been a whole debate about the alleged deflationary bias of the EMS, the Delors report concentrated on the need to control the size and financing of national budget deficits, thus implying a fear of excessively expansionary policies and hence inflationary tendencies inside the monetary union. The rather restrictive approach adopted by the Delors committee, as regards the national margin of manoeuvre in the area of fiscal policy, was also very different from the attitude expressed in the earlier Padoa-Schioppa report, where the authors referred to the experience of other federal systems which usually impose no strict controls on state budgets and where 'the effective restraint ... is the sanction of the market (Padoa-Schioppa, 1987: 85).

The new treaty did not create any new institution for the co-ordination of fiscal policies. It did, however, make provisions aiming at the strengthening of the existing mechanisms and more particularly the elimination of excessive public deficits. The monetization of deficits will not be permitted within the monetary union, nor will there be any 'bailing out' of national, regional, or local authorities by the EC. The ceilings of 3 per cent for public deficits and 60 per cent for public debt in terms of GDP, adopted as part of the convergence criteria for admission into the third stage, will also be used in general as reference values for the assessment of national budgetary policies in the context of multilateral surveillance.

On the basis of reports prepared by the Commission, which is therefore given the role of a watchdog, the ECOFIN Council (Economics and Finance Ministers) will examine the policies of individual member countries. A whole series of measures will be available to the Council in order to exert pressure on profligate members, ranging from public recommendations to the imposition of fines. In between, the Council may resort to other measures, always adopted on the basis of qualified majority votes, such as requiring the EIB to reconsider its lending policy to the particular member country and asking the latter to make non-interest bearing deposits with the Community. Assuming strict implementation, those provisions will represent a major constraint on the spending and taxation powers of national parliaments, which will be added to the constraints imposed by tax harmonization, either explicit or through the market.

The long experience of fiscal laxity in some countries and the evident inability of financial markets (see, for example, the international debt crisis of the early 1980s) to act as effective and efficient constraints on sovereign actors can be used as arguments in favour of some central discipline on national deficit financing. The treaty provisions are aimed essentially against 'free riders' in the future monetary union. But there can be some doubts both about the desirability and the effectiveness of the specific provisions. Furthermore, there is nothing in the treaty to prevent a deflationary bias resulting from excessively contractionary policies (Melitz, 1991). What is at stake is about who and how will determine the macroeconomic priorities for the European Community as a whole. In the words of Lamfalussy, in the annex to the Delors report (Lamfalussy, 1989: 101):

> The combination of a small Community budget with large, independently determined national budgets leads to the conclusion that, in the absence of fiscal co-ordination, the global fiscal policy of the EMU would be the accidental outcome of decisions taken by the Member States. There would simply be no Community-wide macroeconomic fiscal policy.

The reconciliation of different national priorities, themselves a function of history, economic development, and demography among other factors, requires a political system which is much closer to a federation than a system of intergovernmental co-operation. And the EC does not appear ready as yet to give birth to such a system.

The decentralized nature of EC fiscal policy will also have implications for the representation of Community interests in international fora. Until now, the Big Four of the EC, plus the Commission, have participated in the Group of Seven (G-7) within which the leading industrialized countries have tried, albeit with limited success, to co-ordinate their economic policies. In a future EMU, the President of the ECB will be able to speak on behalf of the Community with respect to monetary policy; but what about fiscal policy? The problems experienced by US Administrations in the past in terms of being able to commit themselves and eventually deliver the goods in international policy co-ordination will pale into insignificance compared with those to be faced by Community representatives in the future.

Another very important aspect of the economic counterpart of monetary union will be the size of the common budget and the amount of internal transfers through taxes and expenditure. In existing federal systems, interregional transfers, largely of an automatic nature, play a major redistributive role, thus reducing internal disparities (Eichengreen, 1990; Commission, 1990). The difference between the EC budget and central budgets in those federal systems is simply enormous, and this situation is unlikely to change dramatically in the foreseeable future, despite the efforts made by the economically weaker countries and the Commission itself (see also Tsoukalis, 1993; 227-77). This is a very similar argument to the one developed above: monetary union requires a much more developed European political system to be effectively managed. Could countries abandon completely the exchange rate instrument without the compensating effects of an effective transfer system and without even a high degree of labour mobility? The result could be a large increase in regional disparities and the creation of more depressed regions.

The EC countries have committed themselves to the establishment of an EMU before the end of the decade; and, unlike the 1970s, this commitment is now backed by a new treaty which defines in some detail the final stage, including the institutional framework. Yet, the political courage shown in the definition of the final stage of EMU has not been entirely matched by treaty provisions for the intermediate stages nor by the length of the transitional period. The big decisions have been left for later; and five or seven years is a very long time in politics.

On the other hand, the new treaty has left several important questions unanswered; or at least, the answers provided are not entirely convincing. They refer to the costs and benefits of EMU in a Community which is still characterized by a high degree of economic diversity and relatively limited political cohesion; and also in a Community where political institutions fall far short of economic ambitions. This problem could be tackled more effectively in the new intergovernmental conference planned for 1996. EMU constitutes a long-term and, perhaps also, a high-risk strategy in which wider political objectives have always counted more than strict economic ones. But this is not very different from the overall approach towards European integration during the last four decades.

Notes

1. This was a term used at the time by Mr Schiller, the German Minister of Economics.

2. For an analysis of the three southern European countries and Britain in relation to the EMS, see relevant chapters in de Grauwe and Papademos (1990). For a very critical approach, see also Walters (1990).

References

Allsopp, Christopher, and Chrystal, K. Alec (1989) 'Exchange rate policy in the 1990s', *Oxford Review of Economic Policy,* Autumn.

Atkinson, Anthony *et al.* (1992) *La Désinflation Compétitive, Le Mark et les Politiques Budgétaires en Europe*. Paris: Seuil.

Commission of the EC (1985) 'Annual Economic Report, 1985-86', *European Economy*, 26, November.

Commision of the EC (1988a) 'The economics of 1992', *European Economy*, 35, March.

Commission of the EC (1988) 'Creation of a European financial area', *European Economy*, 36, May.

Commission of the EC (1990) 'One market, one money', *European Economy*, 44, October.

Commission of the EC (1991) 'Annual economic report 1991-92', *European Economy*, 50, December.

Committee for the Study of Economic and Monetary Union (Delors report) (1989) *Report on Economic and Monetary Union in the European Community*. Luxembourg: Office for Official Publications of the European Communities.

de Cecco, Marcello (1989) 'The European Monetary System and National Interests'. In P. Guerrieri and P.C. Padoan (eds.), *The Political Economy of European Integration*. Hemel Hempstead: Harvester Wheatsheaf.

de Grauwe, Paul (1987) 'International trade and economic growth in the European Monetary System', *European Economic Review,* 31.

de Grauwe, Paul and Gros, Daniel (1991) 'Convergence and divergence in the Community's economy on the eve of Economic and Monetary Union'. In P. Ludlow (ed.), *Setting European Community Priorities 1991-92*. London: Brassey's/Centre for European Policy Studies.

Dornbusch, Rudiger (1988) 'The European Monetary System, the dollar and the yen'. In F. Giavazzi, S. Micossi, and M. Miller (eds.), *The European Monetary System*. Cambridge: Cambridge University Press.

Drèze, Jacques, *et al.* (1987) *The Two-Handed Growth Strategy for Europe: Autonomy Through Flexible Cooperation*. Brussels: Centre for European; Policy Studies Paper No. 34.

Eichengreen, Barry (1990) 'One money for Europe: lessons from the US currency union', *Economic Policy,* 10, April.

Fratianni, Michele, and Peeters, Theo (eds.) (1978) *One Money for Europe*. London: Macmillan.

Funabashi, Yoichi (1988) *Managing the Dollar: From the Plaza to the Louvre*. Washington DC: Institute for International Economics.

Giavazzi, Francesco, and Giovannini, Alberto (1989) *Limiting Exchange Rate Flexibility: The European Monetary System*. Cambridge, Mass.: MIT Press.

Giavazzi, F., and Pagano, M. (1988) 'The advantage of tying one's hand: EMS discipline and central bank credibility', *European Economic Review,* 32.

Giavazzi, Francesco, and Spaventa, Luigi (1990) *The 'New' EMS*. CEPR Discussion Paper No. 369.

Goodhart, Charles (1993) 'The external dimension of EMU'. In L. Tsoukalis (ed.), *Europe and Global Economic Interdependence*. Brussels: Presses Interuniversitaires Européennes for the College of Europe and the Hellenic Centre for European Studies.

Gros, Daniel and Thygesen, Niels (1992) *European Monetary Integration: From the European Monetary System Towards Monetary Union*. London: Longmans.

Krugman, Paul (1989) *Exchange Rate Instability*. Cambridge, Mass.: MIT Press.

Krugman, Paul (1990) 'Policy problems of a monetary union'. In P. de Grauwe, and L. Papademos (eds.), *The European Monetary System in the 1990's*. London: Longman for CEPS and the Bank of Greece.

Lamfalussy, A. (1989) 'Macro-coordination of fiscal policies in an economic and monetary union in Europe'. In Committee for the Study of Economic and Monetary Union, *Report on Economic and Monetary Union in the European Community*. Luxembourg: Office for Official Publications of the European Communities.

Ludlow, Peter (1982) *The Making of the European Monetary System*. London: Butterworths.

McKinnon, Ronald (1963) 'Optimum currency areas', *American Economic Review* 53.

Mortensen, Jorgen (1990) *Federalism vs. Co-ordination: Macroeconomic Policy in the European Community*. Brussels: Centre for European Policy Studies, CEPS Paper No. 47.

Mundell, Robert (1961) 'A theory of optimum currency areas', *American Economic Review 51*.

OECD, Main Economic Indicators, various issues. Paris.
(1987), *The Future of Migration*. Paris: OECD.
(1989), *OECD Economic Surveys: Spain*. Paris: OECD.
(1990), OECD *Economic Surveys: Greece*. Paris: OECD.
(1991), *OECD Economic Surveys*: Ireland. Paris: OECD

Padoa-Schioppa, T. *et al.* (1987) *Efficiency, Stability and Equity*. Oxford: Oxford University Press.

Padoa-Schippa, T (1988) 'The European Monetary System: a long-term view'. In F. Giavazzi, S. Micossi, and M. Miller, (eds.), *The European Monetary System*. Cambridge: Cambridge University Press.

Siebert, Horst (1991) 'German unification: the economics of transition', *Economic Policy,* October.

Thygesen, Niels (1979) 'The emerging European Monetary System: precursors, first steps and policy options', *Bulletin of the National Bank of Belgium*, April.

Tsoukalis, Loukas (1977), *The Politics and Economics of European Monetary Integration. London*: Allen and Unwin.

Tsoukalis, Loukas (1993) *The New European Economy: The Politics and Economics of Integration*. Oxford: Oxford University Press.

Ungerer, Horst *et al.* (1990) *The European Monetary System: Developments and Perspectives*. Washington DC: International Monetary Fund, Occasional Paper, No. 73.

Werner Report (1970) 'Report to the Council and the Commission on the realization by stages of Economic and Monetary Union in the Community', Supplement to *Bulletin of the EC*, 3.

Wyplosz, Charles (1990) 'Macro-economic implications of 1992'. In J. Dermine (ed.), *European Banking in the 1990s*. Oxford: Blackwell.

175

7. The Relationship between Economic and Monetary Integration: EMU and National Fiscal Policy

Daniel Gros and Niels Thygesen

As emphasized repeatedly, this book concentrates on monetary integration in spite of the fact that *economic and monetary* union is on the agenda of the Community. The focus on monetary union is justified by the fact that there is much less debate about the implications of economic union (in its narrow sense of a unified market). The creation of the Community in 1957 already had the aim of creating 'a common market'. In this sense the movement towards economic union predates the movement towards monetary union.

The wide agreement on the desirability of an economic union derives from the microeconomic gains a wider and truly unified market yields. However, there is much less agreement on the implications of EMU for fiscal policy in general although EMU will affect almost all aspects of fiscal policy.[1] For example, as already emphasized in chapter 7, the loss of the exchange-rate instrument implies that national governments might have to turn to a more active use of fiscal policy. Moreover, as discussed in chapter 5, an EMU committed to price stability has further implications for national budgets since inflation affects tax revenues and the value of expenditures. Finally, EMU will also increase the mobility of the tax base in a number of areas (e.g., capital income taxation and corporate taxation) and will therefore raise the issue of tax competition.

The purpose of this chapter is not to provide a survey of all the fiscal issues raised by EMU. Instead it concentrates on the issues that are closely related to the monetary and macroeconomic aspects that are the overall subject of investigation of this book. There are two broad issues in this area, both of which have become an integral part of the debate on EMU: the need for 'binding guidelines' for national fiscal policy and the desirability of some fiscal shock absorber at the Community level.

This chapter is therefore organized as follows: before going into the discussion about fiscal policy in EMU it first introduces briefly, in section 1, the concept of economic union and discusses the issue of 'parallelism', i.e., the desirability of parallel progress between the monetary and non-monetary aspects of the process of unification. Section 2 then discusses the most contentious issue in the entire EMU debate, i.e., the alleged need for binding guidelines for national fiscal policy in EMU that was sparked off by the Delors Report. Section 3 continues with an aspect of this issue that is often neglected, namely the practical difficulties that arise in the implementation of the guidelines. Section 4 then turns to the issue of whether a fiscal shock absorber mechanism is needed at the Community level to offset the effects of country specific shocks.

Daniel Gros and Niels Thygesen: 'The Relationship between Economic and Monetary Integration: EMU and National Fiscal Policy' from *EUROPEAN MONETARY INTEGRATION: FROM THE EUROPEAN MONETARY SYSTEM TO EUROPEAN MONETARY UNION* (Longman, 1992). pp. 269-291.

Since chapter 5 has already addressed the issues that arise in the transition towards EMU, this chapter concentrates on EMU in its final form,[2] assuming throughout that for political reasons the Community remains at the 'pre-federal' stage (McDougall (1977)), i.e., that the budget of the Community will not exceed 2 - 2.5 per cent of GDP and that most competences in the fiscal area will remain at the national level. This limit on the size of the EC budget is a further reason why we do not discuss fiscal mechanisms to redistribute income. Moreover, the politically motivated limit on Community competences in the fiscal area means that there is no need to discuss the vast literature on fiscal federalism which analyses the optimal distribution of economic policy competencies between the federal and sub-federal (i.e., national) level in a variety of fields (regulation of industry and labour markets, provision of public goods, etc.).[3]

1. What is economic union?

There is no precise and universally agreed definition of economic union. However, since the publication of the Delors Report its definition has been widely used. Paragraph 25 of the Delors Report lists, somewhat arbitrarily, four basic components that form the core of the economic dimension of unification:

(1) the single market within which persons, goods, services and capital can move freely;

(2) competition policy and others measures aimed at strengthening market mechanisms;

(3) common policies aimed at structural change and regional development; and

(4) macroeconomic policy coordination including binding rules for budgetary policies.

The first two components are part of the definition of economic union generally accepted by economists. Progress in these two areas seems assured since the internal market programme is well on schedule. It is also beyond doubt that the creation of a single market with an authority to enforce competitive structures yields economic benefits.

It is also becoming increasingly accepted that the initial legislative programme for 1992 is not sufficient to ensure the aim of a perfectly integrated market.[4] The original internal market programme did not contain provisions for common policies in those areas where an intervention by the Community is justified by the existence of important international external effects. Examples of these additional areas for common policy-making are network infrastructures or research and development, see Emerson *et al.* (1991), chapter 3 for more detail. EMU should make it easier to perfect the original internal market programme in this way. However, these elements are uncontroversial and of only limited significance relative to the other components of economic union.

The third component of the Delors Report's definition of economic union is difficult to assess purely on efficiency grounds. It must be based on considerations such as income distribution that relate more to equity than efficiency. These issues are dealt with in the literature on fiscal federalism, see Van Rompuy, Abrahams and Heremans (1990) for a survey.[5] These issues are not discussed here, mainly because they are not linked to the primary focus of this book, namely monetary integration.

The fourth component required to achieve an economic union in the vision of the Delors Report is coordination of national budgetary policies, going well beyond voluntary efforts on the part of each participant. While it is apparent that irrevocably fixed exchange rates (or a common currency) require a common institutional framework to manage the common monetary policy, there is a wide divergence of views as to whether that needs to be paralleled in the fiscal sphere by giving a collective body the authority to intervene in national budgetary policies in a binding way. Both economic and political objections can be raised to this interpretation of parallelism.[6] The economic ones are discussed in some detail below.

As will be described in chapter 10, the Delors Report stresses that 'economic and monetary union form two integral parts of a single whole and would therefore have to be implemented in parallel'.[7] This view has been widely accepted, and, if it is interpreted as a statement about the final stage, it can be defended on the ground that the benefits from a monetary union discussed in the previous chapter can be reaped only if there are no non-monetary barriers to trade within the area.

However, since it is impossible to measure and compare precisely the degree of monetary and economic integration, it is very difficult to assess whether the progress that will actually be taking place can be regarded as parallel or not. In contrast, the endpoints of both areas of unification, namely monetary union and economic union can be more readily defined. Parallelism should therefore be mainly understood as the idea that the economic benefits of economic and monetary integration reinforce each other so that the full benefits of monetary *and* economic union exceed the benefits that derive from integration in only one of these two areas.

There is, however, one controversial issue, which should not be included in this broad interpretation of parallelism although it links directly the economic and monetary aspects of integration. This is the issue of binding guidelines for national fiscal policy to which we now turn.

2. Does a stable monetary union require binding guidelines for fiscal policy?

The economic rationale for binding guidelines for fiscal policy is that, whatever the exchange-rate regime, there are international externalities to a country's budgetary policies. In a regime where exchange rates are either flexible or where governments occasionally resort to realignments, important elements of those externalities are deflected into movements in the currency of the initiating country. To this extent the consequences of budgetary expansion fall primarily on the country itself as domestic investment is in part crowded out by a mixture of higher interest rates at home and an appreciation of the currency.[8] However, as exchange rates are increasingly fixed these external effects become potentially more important.

The general economic[9] objection is that this sort of intervention in national policy-making would he superfluous in an EMU, since the fixed exchange-rate system, underpinned by a common monetary policy, would adequately constrain budgetary policies. There are therefore serious economic arguments on both sides.[10]

In the lively academic (and political) debate that has developed since the publication of the Delors Report three broad sets of arguments for imposing binding guidelines can be distinguished which are now discussed in turn.

In the following discussion it is assumed throughout that the guidelines would in practice be asymmetric, i.e., that there would only be upper limits for deficits. Although this is not always explicitly stated in the Delors Report it seems natural to assume since it is difficult to see how the Community could bring effective pressure on a country to spend more and thus to increase its deficit.

2.1 The EC needs to achieve a proper policy mix in the EMU

This argument is based on the view that national demand management via fiscal policy has spill-over effects because a fiscal stimulus in one member country leads to an increase in demand for the products of other countries as well. Chapter 4 discussed one variant of the widespread view that in the absence of proper coordination these spill-over effects lead to a deflationary bias in a fixed exchange-rate system if countries are concerned about their current-account position and/or capital mobility is limited. Under EMU national current accounts should no longer be a cause for concern so that this particular issue should not arise.[11]

However, chapter 4 also emphasized that the magnitude and sign of the spill-over effects are very difficult to determine because there are other effects (besides the direct demand spill-over) that go in the opposite direction (see Van der Ploeg (1991) for a survey). The extraordinary swing in German fiscal policy (from approximate balance in 1989 to a deficit of 5 per cent of GDP starting with the second half of 1990) is a good illustration of this problem. It has been estimated that the direct demand impulse coming from German unification led to additional imports from the Community of about 30 billion ecu per annum (almost 1 per cent of the GDP of the EC minus Germany). At the same time the increase in German interest rates spread throughout the EMS and led to higher interest rates in the Community which tended to depress demand. It is therefore not clear whether all of Germany's partners in the EC actually benefit from this expansionary German fiscal policy.

This particular example illustrates the theoretical difficulties in determining the magnitude and even the sign of the spill-over effects. In many cases it is therefore impossible to determine a priori whether the appropriate response in a given situation is one of fiscal expansion or the contrary. In principle one could use macroeconomic models to solve this theoretical indeterminacy. However, the existing models differ considerably in their estimates of the spill-over effects. In general they suggest that they are rather small in absolute terms, i.e., less than one tenth of the home country effects, and are often negative. Table 2.1, adapted from Emerson et al. (1991) illustrates this point.

This table shows that the demand spill-overs are often close or equal to zero and that spill-overs in terms of inflation might be more important. However, even the latter appear to vary in sign; French fiscal expansion leads to lower inflation in Italy and the United Kingdom, whereas the opposite is true for German fiscal policy.

These results cannot constitute a reliable guide because they are based on models that were estimated with data from the 1970s and 1980s. The common currency and other constraints on national policy implicit in EMU will alter radically some fundamental macroeconomic relationships, e.g., the wage-price link or the elasticity of the demand for (intra-EMU) exports. It will therefore remain very difficult for some time to come to estimate reliably the spill-over effects of national fiscal policy under EMU.

Uncertainty about the sign and magnitude of the cross-country spillovers can have serious consequences. Indeed, some calculations of the welfare gains from international policy coordination based on the major existing macroeconomic models of international interaction show that the gains from policy coordination are ambiguous.[12] The basic point of this research is that coordination based on the wrong model can be welfare-reducing. Given that the true model will never be found this implies that the welfare gains from fiscal policy coordination predicted by many models will always remain elusive.

Table 2.1   **Spillover effect of a rise in government expenditure by 2% of GDP.**

	Country originating the policy:	
	Germany	France
GDP:		
Germany	1.6	-0.16
France	0	1.6
Italy	0	-0.08
United Kingdom	-0.02	-0.1
Inflation:		
Germany	2.0	0
France	0.16	3.66
Italy	0.1	-0.34
United Kingdom	0.1	-0.14

Source: Emerson *et al.* (1991), table 5.5.

For those that regard these conceptual problems as solvable the case for fiscal policy coordination rests on the fact that the European Community is very different from large federal states. The EC budget, presently little more than 1 per cent of the combined GDP of member states, is too small to exert any significant stabilization function. For the foreseeable future, influence over the aggregate budgetary stance can come only via decisions on national budgets.[13] Large federal states permit themselves to be more relaxed about budgetary policies of regional governments because a federal budget of typically 20-30 per cent of GDP provides ample potential leverage. When imbalances in the policy mix appear, they are not due to insufficient centralization of budgetary authority. Recent experience in the United States provides a striking illustration of this point. The US Federal government has run a large deficit throughout much of the 1980s while the aggregate position of the fifty states has been in small surplus.

Even if the central EC budget is too small to achieve the proper policy mix, there are two practical objections to the alleged need for a central EC authority to impose 'effective upper limits on budget deficits of individual member countries of the Community'[14] in order get the right aggregate policy mix: (a) there is no logical reason for its influence to be asymmetrical, i.e., directed only at excessive deficits, and (b) it is not obvious that binding rules are required.[15]

(a) The policy mix may become inappropriate because national budgetary policies are in the aggregate too restrictive. Such a situation would be characterized by a rising current-account surplus for the EMU area as a whole (or by a reduction of an area deficit regarded as globally appropriate). Another illustration of national fiscal policies becoming too restrictive in the aggregate could be upward pressure on the exchange rate of the union through a rising current-account surplus, which is then countered by monetary expansion, considered inappropriate in a perspective of long-term price stability. It was often argued that there were distortions of this type in the policy mix in the EMS during the mid 1980s, when most member countries pursued budgetary consolidation while monetary growth accelerated. Situations of this type cannot be ruled out in the future and could not be addressed by asymmetric rules that limit only deficits.

(b) Across-the-board proportional adjustments of budgetary balances would be difficult to justify solely with reference to the argument on the appropriate policy mix. They might well be recommended as appropriate and they will become increasingly logical as EMU deepens integration. But, given the major differences between national budget positions that can be expected to persist for any foreseeable time, they would be difficult to justify.[16] A differentiated judgement would be required that takes into account the position of individual member states with regard to their public debt and internal conjunctural position.

There are further arguments against the view that Community-led joint demand management through national budgetary balances is desirable. For example, one might actually see a virtue in the capacity of EMU to reduce the need for discretionary coordination of non-monetary policies. That would be desirable, both because of past failures to get to grips with such coordination between the EMS countries and at the global level, and because of the inherent difficulties and arbitrariness of the exercise.

Finally it should not be overlooked that EMU will provide a reason for more divergence in national fiscal policy since, as discussed in chapter 7, fiscal policy will be the only remaining major policy tool for reacting to nationally differentiated shocks. In the case of major shocks exceptions to the guidelines may have to be made on a discretionary basis. This cautions against writing any specific norms into the Treaty framework for EMU.

2.2 Union-wide interest-rate effects of national deficits

The economic basis for this argument are spill-over effects of a different nature from those deriving from the demand management aspects discussed above. Excessive budget deficits in any one country have often led in the past to a risk premium required by investors to hold assets denominated in the currency in question because of the anticipation that it would become more attractive for politicians to monetize large deficits and allow the currency to depreciate than to undertake the difficult task of fiscal consolidation. With exchange rates at least potentially flexible, the risk premium and the wealth losses imposed on domestic asset holders and on those (including the government) who have borrowed in foreign currencies would be borne by the country itself.[17] However, with credibly fixed exchange rates, investors might require a risk premium on assets denominated in any of the currencies of the entire area or in the single currency when that has been introduced.[18] These union-wide interest-rate effects are undesirable because even a country with a sound fiscal position would have to pay the higher interest rate.

Economic integration and monetary unification increase the transmission of the interest-rate effects of national budgetary policies. It follows that in order to discourage free-riding on partner countries the imposition of some central authority becomes more necessary under EMU than in the present, more decentralized system.

This issue can be important in practice because some individual member states have budget deficits that are large relative to the entire economy of the EMU area (and much larger than those of single states in most existing federations, such as the United States or Switzerland). A deficit of 10 per cent of GDP in a large member state corresponds to more than 1 per cent of collective GDP and to more than 5 per cent of EC net savings. Borrowing by a large member state, as recently observed in Italy, is in a different category from that of even the biggest private firms or public enterprises. The absorption of a substantial part of EC savings by large and persistent public deficits would raise political pressures for correction of undesired externalities that affect other member states. While this line of reasoning may apply only to the actions of large member states, 'binding rules' would have to apply potentially to all. Though the international system and the EC has traditionally been more tolerant of imbalances in small than in large industrial countries, there could hardly be positive discrimination in favour of the former in a new mandatory system.

In this view the authority to set 'binding rules' could therefore serve to prevent more improvised and brutal pressures for adjustments coming from financial markets or political pressures by other member states late in a process of divergence.

2.3 EMU could bring fiscal laxity

This argument for binding guidelines is based on the fear that launching an EMU without any mandatory budgetary coordination could encourage an excessively lax aggregate fiscal stance. Some who favour the rigid locking of exchange rates in EMU over the present arrangements do so because the financing of external deficits becomes more automatic and the potential effects of fiscal policy more predictable and possibly larger within the borders of the initiating country. This is the counterpart to the argument discussed in the previous sub-section: there will be less crowding out of fiscal expansion through higher interest rates at home and less need for concern with external imbalance. A policy-adviser could find good arguments for concluding that ambitions in fiscal policy can be raised once exchange rates are fully fixed. A policy-maker, no longer confronted with pressures on the currency or from large reserve flows, might more readily follow the advice.

This attitude, if widespread (and if consciously adopted by several member states) would, indeed, create a bias towards budgetary laxity. Such a bias may anyway be observable in the transitory stages, as greater homogeneity of national tax regimes is approached through lower indirect and direct taxes in high-tax countries rather than by tax increases elsewhere. Given the starting point of major differences in national budgetary stance and the likely further sources of divergence in the 1990s, there is no scope for encouraging licence in budgetary policy. Furthermore, if fiscal laxity did follow EMU, the other two arguments above would both be reinforced.

This argument would not be conclusive if alternative disciplining mechanisms were to emerge so as to prevent an excessively lax aggregate fiscal stance. Participation in EMU would eliminate the escape route of devaluation and surprise inflation which has in the past occasionally reduced the real value of public debt. Participation in a fully integrated European financial area opens captive national markets for public debt where governments have been able in the past to finance deficits at below-market interest rates through high reserve requirements on bank deposits and compulsory minimum holdings of government debt. With these privileges gone, financial markets would be in a position to undertake a straight professional evaluation of the varying degrees of creditworthiness of national governments. Those persisting in rapid issues of debt would face rising borrowing costs and some outright rationing of credit, possibly linked to a downgrading of their credit rating.[19]

There is little evidence, however, that such mechanisms, even if they are allowed to develop fully, would provide adequate constraints on budgetary divergence. The experience of large federal states suggests that the sanction of an inferior credit rating is of minor importance. Within Canada, where the divergence in budgetary stance and in indebtedness is wider than in other federations, the range of borrowing costs spans less than 50 basis points. Within the United States borrowing costs show a similar lack of sensitivity to the budgetary policies of states which tend anyway to be fairly uniform. And global financial markets at first had difficulties in assessing properly the credit risks attached to Third World sovereign borrowers, then in 1982 reacted sharply and almost indiscriminately as the prospects for debtors worsened. Even New York city, which almost went bankrupt in the mid 1970s, did not have to pay a large premium until its credit was cut off almost completely.

This episode, as well as the experience with bank lending to LDCs suggests that financial markets do not operate with smoothly increasing risk premia. The fundamental reason for this *modus operandi* of financial markets lies in the adverse selection effect of higher interest rates as suggested by Stiglitz and Weiss (1981). The crucial point of this analysis is that borrowers always have better information about their own financial position. Banks (or creditors in general) will therefore be reluctant to lend to borrowers offering to pay very high interest rates since they can expect that only borrowers who are in fact very bad risks accept high interest rates. This is why credit (especially bank loan) markets are not characterized by smooth supply curves of credit that are only a function of the interest rate. The spread between bad and good borrowers is usually rather low and, beyond a certain interest rate, credit is just cut off. Financial markets might therefore exercise very little discipline until a certain threshold has been reached. Beyond this point the unavailability of any further funds would precipitate at least a liquidity crisis for the government concerned.

Stiglitz and Weiss (1981) also show that a small reduction in the quantity of credit available can in some cases cause extensive credit rationing. A small tightening of credit conditions by the European Central Bank could thus, at times, push a member country into a liquidity crisis. Under these circumstances the ECB would probably not be able to refuse to provide some 'temporary' financing. The absence of a more graduated discipline means therefore that it is likely that a funding crisis can undermine a tight monetary stance.

Could financial markets be induced to apply a more graduated discipline to the borrowing by member states in an EMU? That is possible as some observers have argued, see, e.g., Bishop *et al.* (1989). One would expect financial markets to discriminate more between member countries than between Canadian provinces which for more than a century have been part of a monetary union. But financial markets might still primarily interpret the formation of EMU as an upgrading of the creditworthiness of weak members; Bishop (1991) reports that already the differences between the interest rates paid by different member governments appear to be insufficient to account for the differences in risk that arise from the different debt burdens. If this is the case now it is difficult to see how the situation could change radically with EMU, even if the central authorities of the EMU were to state explicitly, as they appear determined to do, that they would not provide bail-out facilities (an 'umbrella') for member states. Participation in the EMU could therefore effectively protect deficit spending from market pressures. Binding guidelines could be viewed as a necessary correction to 'free-riding' that would be difficult to avoid through a mere statement of the Community that it would not bail out member states.

The evidence reported in Grilli, Masciandro and Tabellini (1991), which shows that an independent central bank can produce, on average, lower inflation even in the context of lax fiscal behaviour, is not conclusive evidence to the contrary since this result only indicates that an independent central bank can mitigate, not eliminate, the inflationary impact of excessive fiscal deficits. Recent research indicates, moreover, that even if financial markets provide adequate discipline there might be external effects of national budgetary policies. In Alogoskoufis and van der Ploeg (1990) it is argued that the level of public debt in one country can influence the rate of growth in other countries because there are international economies of scale. A high debt abroad would tend to reduce the amount of domestic savings available for domestic investment and hence domestic growth. This implies that member countries would have the right, even on purely economic grounds, to be concerned about excessive debts in their partner countries in

EMU. It is apparent that this line of reasoning would provide an argument for guidelines on public debts, rather than deficits.

3. Practical problems in implementing binding guidelines

Even those who accept the arguments in favour of mandatory budgetary coordination and share the view that financial markets will not provide a substitute discipline have doubts about how the proposal would be implemented and enforced. In principle, the 1974 Decision on convergence, which was revised in 1990, provides the Community with a tool to organize macroeconomic coordination if this is deemed desirable. Although the 1974 Decision was never used to achieve effective coordination this implies that in principle there is no need for further legislative action to ensure the proper amount of coordination of fiscal policy in short-run demand management terms.

However, the 1974 Decision would not be useful in addressing the more long-run issues discussed above that provide the more urgent reason for imposing the 'upper limits on budget deficits' mentioned in the Delors Report. The challenge is therefore to provide an operational guideline for budgetary policy for some Community oversight over national fiscal policy.

During the transition towards EMU the most logical approach would be to intervene in a country's policy only if it became a threat to the fixed exchange-rate system. That will not, however, provide a clear operational criterion: the ECOFIN Council would be guided by its collective concern whether a government could fulfil its commitment to fully fixed exchange rates without recourse to monetary financing, which would, in principle, be excluded in an EMU — but the Council will be reluctant to voice such doubts explicitly in public.

Any permanent guidelines would therefore have to be as objective as possible so that there is little room for interpretation and for political pressures to relax them in specific cases. Especially if they are to be backed up by sanctions they would have to be as justifiable as possible. Four related operational concepts have been proposed to solve this problem.

3.1 Ceilings on the deficit relative to GDP

The simplest type of rule, hinted at in the Delors Report, is to relate the maximum permissible deficit directly to GDP. However, that could be too crude a measure, as one would want to relate the ceiling also to the private savings-investment balance of the country; for this reason alone it would be impossible to apply uniformly. The Delors Report itself hints at this in saying (para, 30) that 'the situation of each country might have to be taken into consideration'. Could other generally applicable rules be envisaged?

References to the absence of federally imposed constraints on state deficits in the United States often omit to point out that a large number of states have adopted 'balanced budget amendments'.[20] This is just a particular version of a uniform ceiling on the deficit. It would be too rigorous in a Community with wide differences in budgetary positions and public debt/GDP ratios ranging from 35 per cent in France to 128 per cent in Belgium (disregarding Luxembourg with only 9 per cent), see table 5.4.4 in chapter

5. Allowance would, at a minimum, have to be made for the equally wide differences in the net costs of debt servicing which these differences in debt impose on national governments.

Reference to the US experience might be particularly misleading if one takes into account that there the problem is that the federal administration and Congress have tended not to follow their own guidelines (i.e., the Gramm-Rudman-Hollings Act of 1985 which aims at reducing the federal deficit) whereas the states in general adhere to their own restrictions and run mostly balanced budgets over the medium run. In contrast, in the Community the federal level (i.e., the Commission, Parliament and the Council) has always adhered to the provision in the Treaty for the EC budget to be balanced. The problem for the Community is therefore in some sense the opposite of that of the US, namely excessive state (national) deficits instead of an excessive federal deficit.[21]

3.2 Ceilings on the primary deficit (relative to GDP)

The simplest way of making an allowance for differences in national situations would be to set *a rule for the primary deficit*, i.e., the deficit net of interest payments. If monetary financing is excluded (see chapter 5 for estimates of the residual amount available under a financially integrated, low-inflation EMU) and nominal interest rates correspond approximately to the growth of nominal incomes in the participating countries, the primary deficit relative to GDP would fully determine public debt accumulation relative to GDP. A conceivable formulation of a rule, provided these (rather strong) assumptions are roughly met, would be to aim for a primary deficit of zero, implying a stable level of debt relative to GDP.[22]

3.3 Ceilings based on an assessment of long-run sustainability

However, at present interest rates exceed growth rates of GDP and even a primary deficit of zero would therefore not be sufficient to stop the debt/GDP ratio from rising. Gros and Thygesen (1992: 161-202) provided some estimates of the primary *surplus* needed in member countries to achieve a stable debt level relative to GDP.

In principle, one could therefore determine analytically a sustainable trend of public debt and derive the implications for the maximum primary deficit compatible with such a trend.[23] But there are two objections to such a procedure:

1. The rule would appear to be too lax. In 1988 most member countries had a primary surplus large enough to imply a gradual reduction in the debt burden relative to GDP (see table 3.1 below and Gros and Thygesen (1992: 161-202) for more detail). Only four problem countries have to undertake a fiscal adjustment to stabilize their debt ratio. An EMU would not want to be seen to encourage relaxation of the efforts of the majority, efforts that are certainly necessary in those countries where debt amounts to more than 100 per cent of GDP.

2. The estimates would be surrounded by a very considerable margin of uncertainty, leaving much room for divergent interpretations by EC and national authorities. Chapter 5 provided two estimates of the adjustment needed to stabilize debt to GDP ratios that come from two respected

international institutions, the OECD and the Commission. Table 3.1 uses these data, but shows only the *differences* between the data provided by these two institutions. This table shows that it is indeed very difficult to judge whether fiscal policy is sustainable or not because this judgement has to rely on a number of assumptions.

Table 3.1 shows that all the factors that are used to calculate the usual indicator of sustainability are difficult to determine with any precision. Even the debt/GDP ratio, that is the basic ingredient in these calculations, is measured differently by these two international organizations because the OECD data refer to net public debt whereas the EC data refer to the gross debt of general government. As can be seen from the first column of the table this leads to the result that the EC estimates of the debt/GDP ratios for Denmark and Germany are 40 and 21 percentage points higher than the estimates provided by the OECD. Given that it is not clear *a priori* whether the sustainability criterion should be based on net or gross debt it is difficult to determine objectively even the starting point for any subsequent assessment of the sustainability of a particular fiscal situation.

Table 3.1   The need for fiscal adjustment: discrepancies between OECD and EC data.

| | debt/GDP | Interest rate minus growth rate | Adjustment in Fiscal Deficit needed to: | | |
			Primary balance	Stablilize debt/GDP	Achieve convergence in debt/GDP in 10 yrs
	(1)	(2)	(3)	(4)	(5)
Belgium	6.1	-1.2	-1.8	0.45	0.21
Denmark	40.4	-4.4	0.9	-1.11	2.08
Germany	21.1	0.0	0.2	0.22	1.48
Greece	7.2	-0.4	-4.3	4.13	4.00
Spain	14.5	-1.9	-2.5	2.16	2.76
France	8.1	-1.7	-0.2	-0.03	0.13
Ireland	-17.7	-2.6	1.9	-5.35	-7.97
Italy	4.6	-2.2	-1.2	-0.81	-1.20
Netherlands	21.2	-0.9	1.3	-1.39	-0.12
United Kingdom	11.40	-2.50	1.9	-2.49	-2.20

Note: No entries for Luxembourg and Portugal because they are not covered by the OECD.

Source: OECD (1990) and table 5.3 in Emerson *et al.* (1991).

A further important factor in assessing sustainability is the difference between the interest rate and the growth rate of GDP. The OECD uses growth rates and actual long-term market rates of interest whereas the EC just assumes that real interest rates will exceed real growth rates by 2 percentage points for most member countries in the long run. This leads to further important differences as can be seen from column (2) of the table. To some extent these differences in underlying assumptions offset each other, but columns (4) and (5) of the table show that very large differences remain regarding the magnitude of the fiscal adjustment needed to attain a sustainable fiscal position. In the case of Ireland the OECD estimate of the necessary adjustment is 5.35 per cent of GDP larger than that of the EC. Conversely, in the case of Greece, the OECD estimate of the necessary fiscal adjustment is 4 per cent of GDP lower than that of the EC.

An even more serious problem arises if one considers only the deficits and debts reported by the EC. In theory the reported deficits should account for the observed changes in debt levels, at least over the long run. However, this is not the whole case as shown in table 3.2 below.

Table 3.2 Discrepancy between reported deficits and changes in debt levels.

	Averages over 1981-1989:		
	theoretical change in debt/GDP	actual change in debt/GDP	discrepancy[a]
Belgium	2.0	5.2	3.2
Denmark	-2.0	2.4	4.4
Germany	0.1	1.1	1.0
Greece	3.6	6.1	2.5
Spain	0.3	2.7	2.4
France	-0.1	1.2	1.3
Ireland	0.3	2.5	2.2
Italy	2.5	4.2	1.7
Netherlands	3.2	3.2	-0.0
UK	-2.9	-1.1	1.8

Note:

[a]Difference between actual reported changes in debt levels and the change in debt that would have resulted from the reported deficits.

Source: Commission of the European Communities (1990).

This table shows that public debts can increase substantially more than one would expect from the reported deficits. For example, between 1981 and 1989 the Belgian public debt/GDP ratio increased by more than 50 percentage points (i.e., 5.2 times ten) but this was over 30 percentage points (3.2 times ten) more than one would expect given the deficits reported over these ten years. Discrepancies on a similar scale are reported for Greece and, somewhat surprisingly, Denmark. The Netherlands appear to be the only country where there is no discrepancy, on average, between the reported deficit and the actual behaviour of the debt to GDP ratio.

These data suggest that, assuming the published data about public debt are credible, the official fiscal accounts data are of little value since the debt/GDP ratio can increase considerably even if the officially reported deficits would suggest that it should be stable (this is the case of Spain) or even fall (this is the case of Denmark). Temporary deviations from the accounting relationship that links debts to deficits are certainly understandable, but the discrepancies over the ten-year averages found here suggest that the problem is more fundamental.

Except for extreme cases it would therefore always be difficult to find an objective indicator of sustainability that would eliminate the need for discretionary judgement and would therefore also minimize the room for political interference.

3.4 Ceilings on the current balance: the 'golden rule'

Finally it has also been suggested that the so-called 'golden rule' might be used as a guideline. Under this approach the overall public deficit would not be allowed to exceed investment expenditures which is equivalent to the prescription that current receipts (taxes and social security contributions) have to match fully current expenditures. This approach would have to distinguish between current public expenditure (e.g., salaries to civil servants or social security transfers) and public investment (e.g., infrastructure investment or capital transfers) along the lines of the German constitution that rules out any deficit on current expenditure by forbidding deficits that exceed public investment.

While such a rule might have some theoretical appeal it would be even more difficult to implement than the ones discussed so far since the distinction between current and capital expenditure is always to a large extent arbitrary. Moreover, since not all public investment can be assumed to increase future tax revenues (for example investment to protect the environment), the theoretical case for constraining only the current deficit is weak.

The distinction between current and investment expenditure is crucial for one important part of total expenditure, namely interest payments on the public debt, which amount to over 10 per cent of GDP in some member countries. At present the accounting practices of all member countries classify interest payments as current expenditure. However, this classification becomes particularly doubtful when inflation is high because high inflation leads to high nominal interest rates, which compensate for the loss of purchasing power of the principal. It follows that under high inflation rates a large part of interest payments really represent capital transfers.

From an economic point of view it would be preferable to correct for this artificial increase in current expenditure by splitting total interest payments into two parts: one part represents the inflation capital adjustment (which is equal to the inflation rate times the value of the debt), and the remainder represents the true current interest expenditures, i.e., real interest payments. Only with zero inflation would all interest expenditures consist of the latter, current part.

Table 3.3 shows therefore two measures of public gross savings (i.e., current income minus current expenditure). The first column contains the uncorrected measure obtained with the usual accounting procedures. According to this measure six member countries do not obey the golden rule. The second column shows the inflation adjustment to current expenditures. The third column in this table then shows gross savings adjusted for the effect of inflation on current expenditures. It is striking that once this adjustment is made all member countries appear to follow the golden rule.

Table 3.3   Alternative measures of government savings.

	Gross savings	Inflation adjustment	Inflation adjusted savings
Belgium	-3.8	4.3	0.5
Denmark	0.9	1.9	2.8
Germany	0.3	1.6	1.9
Greece	-14.7	18.6	3.9
Spain	2.8	3.3	6.1
France	2.3	1.3	3.6
Ireland	-1.2	2.1	0.9
Italy	-5.6	7.2	1.6
Luxembourg	8.3	0.2	8.5
Netherlands	-1.4	2.3	0.9
Portugal	-2.4	9.4	7.4
UK	2.5	3.3	5.8
EC12 average	-0.2	3.4	3.2

Source: Commission of the European Communities (1990). All data refers to 1990 and is in per cent of GDP. The inflation adjustment is equal to the inflation rate times the debt/GDP ratio.

Since the last column represents (approximately) the gross savings that would be measured with zero inflation under current accounting practices it follows that the golden rule cannot be expected to become very stringent once an EMU with stable prices has been established.

The decisive objection against the golden rule is therefore that it would simply be too lax. Even some of the countries that are clearly in a fiscal position that is not sustainable in the long run would at present not be affected by such a rule. It might, however, still be useful to retain the basic idea underlying the golden rule, i.e., that it matters whether the government has a deficit because it spends on public investment or whether the deficit is caused by excessive public consumption and transfer payments (Figure 3.1).

Concern about the 'quality' of government expenditure is justified by the fact that in many cases fiscal adjustment efforts start by cutting public investment, which does not have the same powerful political constituencies as transfer payments. Figure 3.1 illustrates this by displaying the inflation-adjusted public sector balance (as per cent of GDP) against spending on public investment (also as per cent of GDP). If all member countries were to obey strictly the golden rule all observations should be on line with a slope equal to minus one. However, the data clearly show that the association between the overall public sector balance and spending on public investment is not negative as required by the golden rule. The data suggest, on the contrary, that, for the political economy reasons outlined above, countries that have less budgetary difficulties invest more.

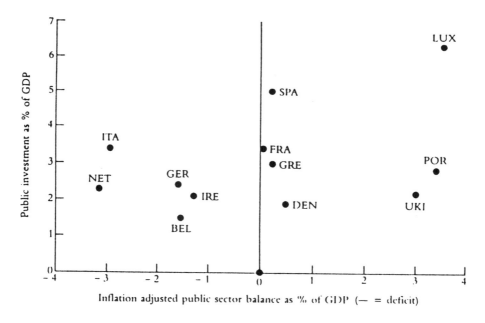

Figure 3.1   A Golden rule? (Inflation adjusted public sector deficits and public investment.)

The need to take the 'quality' of public spending into account provides therefore another reason to be sceptical about the usefulness of general guidelines for fiscal policy.

4. Fiscal shock absorbers

As discussed in chapter 7 national fiscal policy might become more important under EMU because it remains the only policy instrument that can be used by national authorities to react to outside shocks especially if labour mobility is too low to mitigate unemployment. As long as these shocks are temporary and therefore average out over the long run this would appear to pose no problem since national governments should be able to rely on the capital market to finance temporary deficits. However, it has been argued, e.g., Eichengreen (1990), that even national governments sometimes do not have sufficient access to financial markets (especially when they already have a large debt outstanding) implying that the Community should help member countries to weather the impact of adverse shocks. Although this could be done in principle through assistance to member governments (along the lines of the German *Finanzausgleich*) the debate has focused on ways by which the Community aid could be channelled directly to individuals.

Proponents of the point of view that some 'fiscal shock absorber' is needed agree that any Community mechanism would have to be as automatic and 'invisible' as possible and that its purpose would not be to equalize income levels, but to provide insurance against country-specific shocks. Assistance that involves a large discretionary element would be subject to 'bureaucratic capture' and would pose obvious moral hazard problems. This is why it has been suggested (Eichengreen (1990), Bean *et al.* (1990)) that the Community should finance a part of national unemployment insurance schemes and receive also a corresponding part of the contributions. Countries with above-average unemployment would then receive a transfer from countries with below-average unemployment. Payments to the unemployed in the former would in effect be financed by contributions from those employed in the latter. Such a scheme would be automatic in the sense that no specific decisions concerning the direction and the magnitude of the transfers need to be taken once the system has been established.

The argument for a Community unemployment insurance scheme has often been made with reference to the United States where there is some reinsurance at the federal level. However, as reported by Von Hagen (1991), in practice, the federal reinsurance scheme has not been used for some time, so that *de facto* in the United States unemployment insurance is organized and financed exclusively at the state level.

Other proposals for some Community fiscal shock absorber mechanism refer to the MacDougall report which documented that in most existing federations the federal budget redistributes income across regions and thus offsets at least part of the interregional differences in income. For the United States, MacDougall (1977) and Sachs and Sala-i-Martin (1989) estimate that the federal budget offsets about 30 to 40 per cent of the differences in income per capita across states because poorer states contribute on average lower income tax and receive higher social security payments. It has therefore been argued (Eichengreen (1990)) that because labour markets seem to be less flexible in the Community the need for a fiscal shock absorber is even greater in the Community than in the United States where migration in response to unfavourable economic shocks can be quite substantial.

However, the argument that a stable EMU needs such an automatic fiscal equalization scheme seems to be based on a misreading of the US experience. The results referred to above imply that federal fiscal systems offset about 30 to 40 per cent of the difference in the *level* of income per capita. However, this does not automatically imply that these mechanisms also provide an insurance against *shocks,* i.e., changes in income. The level effect found by Sachs and Sala-i-Martin (1989) implies that, at each point in time, individuals in a state with an income per capita 1,000 dollars lower than the average, pay about 300 dollars less in income taxes and receive about 100 dollars more in direct payments.

Von Hagen (1991) obtains different results by looking at changes in income. He finds that a fall in income per capita by 1 per cent reduces federal income tax also by 1 per cent. Since the federal income tax accounts only for 8 per cent of income this implies that if income per capita goes up from 1,000 to 1,010 dollars the federal income tax goes from 80 to 80.8 dollars; the offset is thus only 80 cents over 10 dollars, or 8 per cent.[25] Moreover, in the regressions reported by Von Hagen (1991) direct federal payments to households do not react at all significantly to *variations* in state income per capita. Gros and Jones (1991) find a level effect in the sense that inviduals in a state with a per capital income of 1,000 dollars above the average pay about 240 dollars more in federal income tax and federal social security contributions. However, year-on-year changes in income do not seem to cause significant changes in taxes or social security contributions. Moreover, neither the level nor the changes in federal transfers are correlated with income. These results suggest that the automatic insurance provided by the US tax and social security system is much more limited than sometimes claimed.

All in all, it is therefore difficult to rest the case for some Community shock absorber on the US experience. For those favouring such a policy on efficiency (as opposed to equity) grounds it would therefore be imperative to spell out in more detail why capital markets do not allow national governments to weather temporary adverse shocks by borrowing on the capital market. The distinction between transitory and permanent shocks is crucial in this area because permanent shocks could, of course, not be financed forever and would thus require adjustment in real wages and/or migration. However, it is difficult to see how the Community could provide insurance against permanent country-specific shocks without addressing directly the issue of income redistribution.

5. Binding guidelines in the Intergovernmental Conference on EMU

We have dealt more superficially with the economic aspects of integration, in part because it is more difficult to determine what they imply. Our discussion of budgetary rules in an EMU, the most controversial part of the recommendations in the Delors Report, concluded that while there are spill-over effects of national budgetary policies in an EMU it would be difficult to formulate and implement rules regarding short-run demand management. However, concerns about the systemic stability of EMU can justify more interference in budgetary policies, especially when public debt or deficits threaten to become unsustainable or 'excessive'.

The considerations about the practical difficulties in implementing binding guidelines suggest that substantial allowances for differences in initial national situations have to be made to make general rules a useful tool for improving the average quality of budgetary policies in the Community. One is led, inevitably, towards the consideration of more discretionary methods of formulating the collectively agreed budgetary guidelines. This implies that a recommendation which a qualified majority in the ECOFIN Council could agree to address to a participant would constitute a 'rule' in the sense that non-compliance with it would trigger some form of sanction on the part of the Community. Such a procedure is envisaged in the Treaty revision relating to EMU (Art. 104C).

However, there is little reason to think that the ECOFIN Council would use such authority frequently and vigorously; the past history of the Community clearly suggests that this is more than unlikely. The Council has never been demanding, for example, in administering its medium-term financial support system. Nor has the EC Commission, with which the initiative to implement the guidelines would rest, shown any eagerness in the past to use the authority which it has had since 1974 to issue recommendations to a member state; in nearly sixteen years it has only acted once.[26] The challenge in EMU is to encourage the Council and the Commission to be less cautious in confronting national policy-making than they have been in the past.

Whatever the form of binding rules adopted, one element to keep under observation is that the binding guidelines should not apply to budget forecasts. They would have to trigger corrective actions as a function not only of planned, but primarily of *actual budget out-turns*. Although this may seem self-evident it needs to be emphasized because this was not the case in the US. [27]

Finally, as regards the time horizon for the budgetary rules, their purpose would not be to serve short-term, activist aims, but to keep participants on a medium-term course of debt accumulation (or reduction) which is sustainable in terms of maintaining the cohesion of EMU. Binding guidelines would accordingly be formulated for a period of several years, though mandatory for each budget year within that period. One difficulty in using the (non-binding) authority under the 1974 Decision may have been that its premise was an ambition to pursue more activist stabilization policies than was either economically desirable or politically realistic.

The revised Treaty now submitted for ratification in the member states does appear to meet the criteria discussed in this chapter. It requests member states to avoid 'excessive government deficits' and it defines in a separate protocol the reference values for the evaluation by ECOFIN as 3 per cent of GDP for the deficit and 60 per cent of GDP for government debt. The text of the relevant Article 104C is reproduced in Appendix 1 to Chapter 13. Article 104C also lists the procedure to be followed by ECOFIN: the Commission is to prepare a report and submit it to the Economic and Financial Committee, the successor to the present Monetary Committee after the transition to the final state of EMU. The ECOFIN Council will then 'decide after an overall assessment whether an excessive deficit exists' and make recommendations to the member state concerned, at first in private, but if there is no effective follow-up, in public. If a member state persists in failing to put into practice the recommendations, the ECOFIN Council may ask for specific measures to reduce the excessive deficit. If the member state concerned still fails to comply, the ECOFIN Council may (1) require additional information to be published before any issue of bonds and securities, (2) invite the European Investment Bank to reconsider its lending policy towards the member state, (3) ask for non-interest bearing deposits, or (4) impose outright fines.

This tough gradualist procedure will no doubt bring considerable pressure to bear on a participant in EMU which persists in pursuing a divergent budgetary policy. In the light of the discussion in the present chapter the concern must be that the reference values proposed are arbitrary and so demanding that they go beyond what is required for EMU rather than that they are too loose. But arbitrariness cannot be avoided, if discussion of containment of excessive deficits is to begin. Chapter 12 returns to the application of some of the procedure already in the transition to EMU; much of the discussion in the Intergovernmental Conference centered on the suitability of the reference values as the underpinnings for a qualification system to EMU. Taken literally, they would appear to constitute a no-entry clause for some member states, an issue which is also addressed in Chapter 14.

Notes

1 For surveys on fiscal policy and EMU see Emerson *et al.* (1991), Gros (1991) and Wyplosz (1991).

2 The issues related to the transition, e.g., the idea that there should be a 'no-entry' clause in the EMU Treaty, as proposed by Giovannini and Spaventa (1991), are taken up in chapter 12.

3 See Van Rompuy, Abrahams and Heremans (1990) for a survey.

4 See, for example, Pelkmans (1991), who provides an exhaustive survey of the concept of economic union.

5 The way the Structural Funds are allocated by the Community is described in the 1990-1 Annual Economic Report of the Commission. The Commission will publish in the first half of 1992 a thorough review of the experience since the decision to enlarge regional transfers in 1988.

6 See Thygesen (1990). For a survey of macroeconomic policy-making in the Community see Mortensen (1990).

7 Delors Report para. 42, see Committee for the Study of Economic and Monetary Union (1989).

8 Some externalities remain even under flexible exchange rates: shifts in competitive conditions (if devaluations occur and are subsequently eroded) and direct demand spill-over from budgetary policy.

9 The political ones are outside the scope of this book, see also chapter 10 for an account of the politics of this aspect of the Delors Report.

10 For a thoughtful survey see Bredenkamp and Deppler (1990).

11 The remainder of this section is based, in part, on Gros (1991).

12 See Frankel and Rockett (1988) on coordination between the US and the rest of the world. Less modelling effort has gone into the intra-Community transmission of demand effects.

13 At a more political level one could argue that an EMU whose members have preached to other major industrial countries the virtue of a correct mix of monetary and fiscal policy can not leave itself with no effective means to influence that policy mix. This issue is discussed further in chapter 9.

14 Delors Report, para. 30.

15 Chapter 10 shows that the Delors Committee was aware of both points.

16 See De Grauwe (1990) for more details concerning the present fiscal position of member countries and the reasons for divergent developments.

17 We do not discuss a related argument for binding rules, namely that large budget deficits, particularly if they come on top of already large debt/income ratios, may threaten the fixity of exchange rates until the credibility of EMU has been firmly established. This is an argument for insisting on better budgetary convergence in the transitory stages, but not necessarily for binding rules once EMU has been set up.

18 For a thoughtful discussion which reaches a more agnostic conclusion, see Bredenkamp and Deepler (1990).

19 It is apparent that this mechanism can only work if the European Central Bank does not use open market operations to narrow interest-rate differentials on public debt issued by different national governments, but in fact allows risk premia to emerge reflecting the market's perception of differences in creditworthiness. See chapter 13 for more details.

20 Some research indicates, however, that the importance of these legal provisions should not be exaggerated. See for instance Von Hagen (1991), who finds little systematic relationship between actual state deficits or debts and the severity of the formal constraints.

21 The starting point for EMU resembles more that of the thirteen states which formed the United States in 1789. But, in that historical example, the new Federation took over a major share of the debt of its component states, which was to a large extent due to their part in a joint war effort.

22 In the early phases of the transition towards EMU governments that are large debtors might still have to pay a premium on outstanding debt which is not offset by faster growth in their nominal GDP, so that their debt/income ratio would rise even with a zero primary deficit.

23 For an effort along the lines developed by Blanchard (1984) see chapter 5 in Emerson *et al.* (1991). EMU resembles more that of the thirteen states which formed the United States in 1789. But, in that historical example, the new Federation took over a major share of the debt of its component states, which was a large extent due to their part in a joint war effort.

24 See for example the Annual Economic Report 1990-1 of the Commission.

25 Von Hagen (1990) seems to overstate his case by comparing (page 9) the *change* in federal income tax to the *level* of income per capita.

26 Against Belgium, on the issue of wage indexation. Article 17 of the 1974 Decision on convergence entrusts the Commission with this task, if a member state is 'pursuing economic, monetary and budgetary policies departing from the guidelines laid down by the Council or entailing risks for the community as a whole'.

27 In the United States, Congress adopted constraints on the *forecast* budget balance through the Gramm-Rudman-Hollings Act, which prescribed proportional cuts in a range of specified expenditures if the deficit forecast for the coming year exceed a prescribed downward trend. There was no subsequent sanction if the actual budget deficit was excessive. This procedure

has generated disputes about the economic assumptions underlying the budget forecasts and incentives to push some expenditures off budget.

References

Alogoskoufis, George and Frederick van der Ploeg, (1990) 'Endogenous growth and overlapping generations' Tilburg University, Center, *Discussion Paper,* 9072

Bean, Charles, Edmond Malinvaud. Peter Bernholz, Francesco Giavazzi and Charles Wyplosz, (1990) 'Policies for 1992: The Transition and After', in 'The Macroeconomics of 1992', *CEPS Paper* No. 42, Centre for European Policy Studies, Brussels.

Bishop, Graham (1990) 'Separating Fiscal from Monetary Sovereignty in EMU — A United States of Europe is not necessary', London, Salomon Brothers, November.

Bishop, Graham (1991) 'The EC's Public Debt Disease: Discipline with Credit Spreads and Cure with Price Stability', London, Salomon Brothers, May.

Bishop, Graham, Dirk Damrau and Michelle Miller, (1989) 'Market discipline can work in the EC monetary union', London, Salomon Brothers, November.

Blanchard, Olivier, Jean-Claude Chouraqui, Robert Hagemann and Nicola Sartor (1991) 'The Sustainability of Fiscal Policy: New Answers to an Old Question', *OECD Economic Studies*, No. 15, Autumn.

Bredenkamp, Hugh and Michael Deppler (1990) 'Fiscal constraints of a hard-currency regime', chapter 7 in Victor Argy and Paul De Grauwe (eds.), *Choosing an Exchange Rate Regime: The Challenge for Smaller Industrial Countries,* International Monetary Fund, MacQuarie University and Katholieke Universiteit Leuven, 35-73.

Committee for the Study of Economic and Monetary Union (1989) 'Report on Economic and Monetary Union in the European Community' (the Delors Report), Office of Publications of the European Communities, Luxembourg.

Commission of the European Communities (1990) 'Annual Economic Report', *European Economy,* 46, December.

De Grauwe, Paul (1990) 'Fiscal Discipline in Monetary Unions', Centre for European Policy Studies, Brussels, *CEPS Working Document*, 50.

Dornbusch, Rüdiger, and Mario Draghi (1990) *Public Debt Management : Theory and Evidence,* Cambridge University Press, Cambridge.

Eichengreen, Barry, (1990) 'One Money for Europe? Lessons from the US Currency Union', *Economic Policy* No. 10, April, pp. 117-87.

Emerson, Michael, Daniel Gros, Alexander Italianer, Jean Pisani-Ferry and Horst Reichenbach (1991) *One market, one money*, Oxford University Press, Oxford.

Frankel, Jeffrey and Katharine Rockett (1988) 'International macroeconomic policy coordination when policymakers do not agree on the true model', *American Economic Review*, 78, 3, June: 318-40.

Giovannini, Alberto and Luigi Spaventa (1991) 'Fiscal Rules in the European Monetary Union: A No-Entry Clause', CEPR Discussion Paper No. 516, January.

Grilli, Vittorio, Donato Masciandro and Guido Tabellini (1991) 'Political and Monetary Institutions and Public Financial Policies in Industrial Countries', *Economic Policy,* 13 October, 342-92.

Gros, Daniel (1991) 'Fiscal Issues in EMU', *Moneda y Credito,* forthcoming.

Gros, Daniel and Erik Jones (1991) 'Fiscal Shock Absorbers in the US', manuscript, Centre for European Policy Studies, Brussels, July.

Gros, Daniel and Thygesen, Niels (1992) *European Monetary Integration: From the European Monetary System to European Monetary Union*, Longman, London.

MacDougall, Sir Donald, Dieter Biche, Arthur Brown, Francesco Forte, Yves Fréville, Martin O'Donoghue and Theo Peeters (1977) 'Public Finance in European Integration', Commission of the European Communities, Brussels.

Mortensen, Jrgen (1990) 'Federalism vs. Co-ordination: Macroeconomic Policy in the European Community', Centre for European Policy Studies, *CEPS Paper,* 47.

OECD (1990) 'Annual Economic Outlook', Organization for Economic Cooperation and Development, Paris, May.

Pelkmans, Jacques (1991) 'Towards Economic Union', in *Setting EC Priorities*, Brasseys for the Centre for European Policy Studies (CEPS), November

Sachs, Jeffrey and Xavier Sala-i-Martin (1989) 'Federal Fiscal Policy and Optimum Currency Areas', Working Paper, Harvard University.

Stiglitz, Joseph and Weiss, Andrew (1981) 'Credit Rationing in Markets with Imperfect Information', *American Economic Review*, Vol. 71, No.3, June: 393 — 410.

Thygesen, Niels (1991) 'The benefits and costs of currency unification', in Horst Siebert (ed.) *The Completion of the Internal Market*, Kiel Institute of World Economics and J.C.B. Mohr, Tübingen.

Van der Ploeg, Frederic (1991) 'Macroeconomic policy cooordination during the various phases of economic and monetary union', *European Economy*, special issue, October, 136-64.

Van Rompuy, Paul, Filip Abraham and Dirk Heremans (1991) 'Economic federalism and the EMU.', *European Economy*, special issue, October, 107-35.

Von Hagen, Jürgen, (1991) 'Fiscal Arrangements in a Monetary Union: Evidence from the US', Discussion Paper # 58, Centre for Global Business, Indiana University, May.

Wyplosz, Charles (1991), 'Monetary union and fiscal policy discipline', *European Economy,* special issue, October, 165-84.

8. The Fiscal Dimension of 1992

Tony Westaway

In this chapter, the initial focus continues to be on NTBs as obstacles to the creation of a SEM. The discussion opens with a consideration of the problems posed by indirect taxes. In the second part of the chapter, the spotlight shifts to a consideration of the way fiscal factors may also distort the flow, not of goods and services, but of factors of production — specifically capital. The discussion rounds off with a brief account of fiscal measures introduced to facilitate cross-frontier business organizations.

Introduction

The role of fiscal policy

Changes to a government's fiscal policy stance are usually announced by the finance minister or chancellor of the exchequer in an annual budget, or public expenditure statement, followed by a period of parliamentary debate. In these eagerly awaited debates, the finance minister discusses a wide range of issues relating to both public expenditure and taxation. Government expenditure is devoted to the provision of a multitude of goods and services. These range from the provision of law and order, defence and roads to education and health services. The reason for intervention is usually justified by reference to some form of market failure.

The reasons for potential market failure and hence government intervention in the provision of these goods and services are however numerous. First, a government will provide goods and services for the benefit of the community that it feels would not be adequately provided if left to the free market. Clearly this is a contentious area and governments will present differing views on the amount of education or health service that should be provided by the state as opposed to the private sector. Thus the government not only has to decide on the amount of expenditure to devote to each of these areas, but it also has to decide on the most equitable method of raising the revenue to fund this expenditure.

Second, some goods have external or spillover effects. A selfish individual or producer may ignore the wider social benefits or costs incurred in the consumption or production of an item and thus the government may choose to intervene to help achieve a more socially desirable allocation of goods and services. For example, a penal tax may be imposed on goods whose consumption needs to be discouraged because their consumption harms others, such as the consumption of tobacco and alcohol, while subsidies may be given to those areas of consumption that would be under-provided by the free market, such as innoculations against contagious disease or lead-free petrol.

The second broad role of fiscal policy is to redistribute a nation's resources. This may be through a progressive tax system in which the rich contribute a greater percentage

Tony Westaway: 'The Fiscal Dimension of 1992' from *THE SINGLE EUROPEAN MARKET AND BEYOND: A STUDY OF WIDER IMPLICATIONS OF THE SINGLE EUROPEAN ACT*, edited by Dennis Swann (Routledge, 1992), pp. 81-105. Reproduced by permission of Routledge and the author.

of their income in tax than the poor, or it may be in the form of a social security expenditure designed to relieve poverty due to unemployment, old age or illness. Alternatively redistribution may be on a regional basis, with greater subsidies going to the poorer regions of a country and higher taxes being imposed on the richer regions.

Finally, fiscal policy has been used as a major instrument in controlling the macro-economy. Until recently this role would have been governed by Keynesian demand management policies, but now governments are more concerned with the supply side of the economy. Thus changes in fiscal policy are used to remove disincentives to production and employment within the economy.

The issues that arise from this multidimensional policy debate not only involve decisions about the size and distribution of public-sector expenditure but also the relative merits of alternative sources of finance. Throughout the European Community these decisions are made at both the central and local government levels. They reflect concern about issues such as the size and structure of the country's social security spending programme, the level and distribution of public sector expenditure on defence, education, roads and health, the control of pollution, scarce energy resources and smoking amongst many others.

Clearly member states will place differing emphases on both the scope and range of public expenditure in addition to the relative merits of alternative sources of revenue. In addition, public expenditure and taxation may distort the allocation of resources within the Community, intentionally or otherwise, and if one of the prime objectives of a common market is to be achieved these distortions need to be removed or at least minimized.

Market distortion and the objectives of tax harmonization

The process of removing disparities in national tax structures to the point where they no longer affect the operation of free markets and hence the allocation of resources between member states, can be referred to as tax harmonization. As has been seen, a common market is established to allow the free movement between members states not only of goods and services, but also of the factor inputs (such as labour, technology and physical capital) used to create them, together with the financial capital needed to fund economic activity. Fiscal policy should not, therefore, be designed so as distort choice between member states and hence influence this free movement of resources.

Fiscal policy is concerned with both public expenditure and taxation at both the national and local levels. This chapter will confine the discussion, in the main, to that of harmonization of taxation at the central government level and in particular with value added tax (VAT), excise duties and corporation tax. The reason for this restriction is that these are the main areas with which the EC has been concerned, and the implications of this will be discussed later in the chapter.

For the benefit of those readers who are not familiar with public finance literature it is worth clarifying some of the ways in which taxation can distort markets and hence interfere with free trade. Further examples of identified trade distortion within the Community will be discussed later in the text.

It should be said at the outset that, though some of the distortions due to tax differences are intentional, the majority result from historical accident. Simply bringing together twelve economies which have different roles for fiscal policy will inevitably result in unintentional trade distortion unless adjustments are made. Many of these tax differences will be jealously guarded and any attempt to interfere with them may be seen by some as infringements of an individual country's fiscal sovereignty, a point of which the Commission is well aware.

Taxes are usually considered as belonging to one of two categories, direct and indirect. Though it can be argued that this distinction has little meaning for economic analysis it is one that will be followed here if simply to comply with most of the public finance literature. A direct tax can be loosely defined as one which is levied directly upon the person or company on whom it ultimately falls. Examples of this type of tax include income tax, which falls on individual earnings, and corporation tax, which applies to the profits of a company.

An indirect tax, on the other hand, is not necessarily levied on the individual on whom it ultimately falls but is usually a charge incorporated in the price of a product or service. The consumer ultimately pays the tax in the form of a higher price, but the tax is actually levied on the seller of the item. Examples of indirect taxes include VAT and excise duties.

In general terms, direct taxes are usually levied on factors of production while indirect taxes are levied on consumption. Also in broad terms it is easier to alter the location of production in response to differences in tax, than to alter the location of consumption. Thus it has been argued that direct taxes are more likely to distort trade than indirect taxes;[1] there are exceptions to this generalization and that is where we shall begin.

There are examples of cross-border shopping within Europe and this may be seen as a problem in densely populated border areas. For example, lower VAT rates and excise duties in Northern Ireland have benefited shoppers from the south whilst Luxembourg, with its modest tax rates, attracts a considerable number of shoppers from its European neighbours: anyone travelling to Luxembourg may be surprised to find such a large number of petrol stations in a country with such a small population!

If an indirect tax, such as VAT, was applied on an origin basis — applied to a good at the rate applicable in the country of origin of the good — then market distortion is likely to become a more serious problem. The nature of this distortion is best explained by use of a simple, if somewhat contrived, example. Let us assume that the VAT rate on cars in country A is 25 per cent whilst in country B the rate is 10 per cent. Assume that the final manufacturing cost of a car, including an allowance for profit, is the same in both countries, say £10,000. The car from country A will sell for £12,500 (£10,000 + 25%) while that from country B will sell for £11,000 (£10,000 + 10%) in both country A and country B and thus have a clear price advantage over its competitor in both markets. This advantage is due entirely to tax differences and has nothing to do with the basic costs of manufacture, which were the same in both countries.

The European Community, however, currently utilizes a destination system for VAT. In effect this means that goods are exported free of VAT and the local VAT rate is applied to the total price of the good in the country of destination. All goods of similar type will therefore carry the same rate of tax regardless of the country of manufacture — thus both cars will sell for £12,500 in country A and for £11,000 in country B. In order for this system to work, exports are made free of tax with VAT being imposed on imports.

Even under the destination principle, there remain certain taxes which are levied on the intermediate stages of production which are not rebated on export and which will not be levied on imports. These include local business rates and taxes on fuel used to transport goods, both of which raise the costs of production.

Turning to direct taxes, one of the largest sources of tax revenue in most countries is personal income tax. Large differences in income tax rates could interfere with the free working of the labour market within the Community. Arguably if a person considers that their earnings are taxed too heavily in one country they can move to a country where the income tax situation is more favourable. However, in reality the decision to move will be influenced by a wide range of considerations of which the income tax regime is likely to play a small role. For most individuals consideration of family ties, differences in language, differences in the cost of living, especially housing, and their children's educational opportunities are likely to be more important than income tax differences. The EC has not proposed harmonization of income tax. Given the lack of international mobility of labour this will therefore leave income tax as a major independent tax policy instrument for national governments.

Corporation tax differences are, however, likely to have a greater impact. Many governments have attempted to attract productive industries to their country by, for example, offering state aid in the form of subsidies or regional incentives or by offering tax incentives such as lower rates of corporation tax. The gains from a very low rate of corporation tax may outweigh losses such as increased transport costs or labour retraining costs incurred by moving production to a new location. The decision of where to locate industry will be determined by differences in tax rates rather than differences in efficiency of production. Firms may therefore locate in high-cost but low-tax areas and in terms of economic criteria this leads to inefficient levels of production within the EEC. In addition it will encourage other countries to retaliate and lower their rates of corporation tax, a battle from which all countries will ultimately suffer.

Jurisdiction

Jurisdiction refers to the thorny question of who is entitled to collect a particular tax. Suppose a French company designs a new product in its research laboratory in Germany, manufactures it in Italy and sells it in Greece: in which country should the corporation tax on the profits of the product be paid? All four member states may claim a share of the tax on the income generated. Clearly if the tax regimes in the four countries differ then multinational companies will have plenty of scope to rearrange their accounts so as to minimize their tax liability.[2]

In theory, certain types of tax make the question of jurisdiction easier to resolve. Property tax, which forms the basis of much local government finance, is paid to the government in whose country the property is located. Indirect taxes on the other hand might be either levied at the country of supply (origin), making them production taxes, or at the country of purchase (destination), making them consumption taxes, if they are consumed in the country they are purchased. In most cases, the two places are the same but some interesting differences do arise.

Consider the case of VAT payments. The destination principle means that exports are purchased without VAT being added and VAT is applied in the country of destination. However, for individual purchases this is different. An international visitor to Scotland may buy a case of Malt Whisky, on which UK VAT and excise duty is paid. This will be refunded when the goods are exported and then local taxes are paid when the goods are imported into the country where the product is consumed, subject to the individual's duty free allowance. The treatment of services is however different. If the visitor had his or her hair cut before returning home then the service would be consumed in his or her country of residence but the VAT was paid in Scotland.

The Commission's approach to removing market distortion[3]

In providing for the establishment of a common market the 1957 Rome Treaty was concerned with removing obstacles to the free movement of goods, services and factors of production within the Community. Articles 95-9 specifically related to the taxation of products whilst Article 100 provided the legal basis for the harmonization of direct taxation. In particular, Articles 95-8 were concerned with preventing the use of taxes to discriminate between similar domestic and imported goods. For example Article 95 (1) prevents higher taxation on imported goods than similar domestic goods while Article 95(2) applies to goods in competition with each other and prohibits taxation of the sort that affords internal protection.

In its initial form Article 99 provided for the harmonization of indirect taxes in the interests of the common market. This was amended by the SEA to ensure that legislation concerning turnover taxes, excise duties and other indirect taxes were harmonized to the extent that they ensured the 'establishment and functioning of the internal market'. In other words this gave the conditions necessary to remove fiscal frontiers, which are particularly prevalent in the case of indirect taxes. Every time a product crosses a border between two countries then tax checks need to be made. Clearly this hinders the envisaged free movement of goods and services.[4]

Despite the fact that VAT had been accepted as the main turnover tax throughout the Community, there was not a common VAT base until the sixth directive on VAT was accepted by the European Council on 17 May 1977, coming into force by 1979. Similar progress on the structure of excise duties and corporation taxes still seems a very long way off.

Initially it was also assumed that rates of duty and tax would eventually be harmonized throughout the community. The Cockfield Report changed the emphasis from harmonization to approximation, recognizing that a degree of difference would not seriously affect the free movement of goods and services. These views were enshrined in the 1987 proposals for VAT reform. As December 1992 approaches the Commission has been taking an increasingly flexible approach; for excise duties it has been currently proposing a minimum rate of duty in the belief that market competition will bring the rates closer together.

The emphasis in 1991 shifted to ensuring that the principle of abolishing fiscal frontiers is not put at risk. The Cecchini Report estimated the cost of frontier formalities — physical, administrative and other barriers — to the free movement of goods across borders. The abolition of fiscal frontiers (though they must be accompanied by the removal of other barriers) is seen as a major ingredient in the completion of the internal market.

The remainder of the chapter is devoted to examining the progress made by the Commission in dealing with the problems of distortion and frontiers arising in connection with VAT, excise duties and corporation tax. But before we proceed with that discussion it is important to point out that while most harmonization activity now takes place on a majority-voting basis, following the SEA fiscal matters still require unanimity. This is bound to slow down the process of achieving agreement.

Valued added tax

Harmonization

VAT was adopted as the EEC turnover tax as long ago as 1967 following the recommendations of the 1963 Neumark committee.[5] Nevertheless, simply adopting a uniform method of taxation did not mean that potential market distortions were removed and many problems still remained. However, before considering these problems, it is necessary to ask why VAT was chosen as the main EEC turnover tax in preference to others.

Prior to the adoption of VAT, four alternative forms of taxation on the purchase of goods were in evidence. West Germany, Luxembourg and the Netherlands used a cumulative multi-stage cascade system, under which tax payments were calculated on the final price of a company's product at each stage of the production process. This price included all taxes paid by companies producing goods as part of the previous stages of the production process. In consequence if several companies are involved in producing an item then the tax payments will increase at a cumulative rate with companies further down the production process paying tax on the tax already paid by companies in the early stages of production.

Table 1 illustrates this process by reference to the tax payments of three companies, R, S and F, involved in a multi-stage production process. (Calculations are based on an assumed tax rate of 10 per cent.) The raw materials needed to make one unit of the product are produced by company R for £10 to which is added £1 in tax; it is assumed that company R does not need to buy inputs from any other company. Company S thus buys these raw materials for £11.00 and adds £9.00 in value, turning the product into its semi-finished stage. This gives a price at the end of this second stage of £20 to which is added a further 10 per cent in tax or £2.00. Company F then buys the semi-finished product for £22 and turns it into the final product by adding £8.00 in value. The price at the end of the final product stage is £30.00 to which is added £3.00 in tax to give a final selling price of £33.00 per unit of output. As can be seen from the table, this final selling price of £33.00 comprises £27 added in value during the three stages of production and £6 in tax.

If the three companies merge to form a single company M which undertakes the entire production process from start to finish, so that there is in effect a single stage of production, then the tax liability is lowered. The total value added during the production process is still £27.00 per unit to which is now added £2.70 or 10 per cent in tax. Thus the final selling price is £29.70 giving company M a clear market advantage. Clearly the multi-cascade tax system discriminates against multi-stage production processes and encourages mergers.

Table 1   Cascade tax systems.

Company/ product	Purchase price from previous stage		Value added		Price at end of stage		Tax due		Final price
	A. An example of cascade tax multi-stage production								
R Raw materials	0.00	+	10.00	=	10.00	+	1.00	=	11.00
S Semi finished	11.00	+	9.00	=	20.00	+	2.00	=	22.00
F Final product	22.00	+	8.00	=	30.00	+	3.00	=	33.00
TOTAL			27.00				6.00		33.00
	B. An example of cascade tax single-stage production								
Company/ product	Purchase price from previous stage		Value added				Tax due		Final price
M Single stage	0.00	+	27.00	=	27.00	+	2.70	=	29.70

In contrast, Belgium and Italy operated a mixed system of turnover taxes. The multi-stage or cascade system was applied down to the wholesale stage on most goods with a single tax paid at a single stage on others. France,[6] on the other hand, utilized a non-cumulative, multi-stage tax which was based on the value added at each stage of the production process. This was referred to as Tax sur la Valeur Ajoutée or VAT. The main advantage of this system of taxation was that it did not discriminate between different stages of vertical integration. As can be seen from Table 2, there is no difference in tax paid between the multi-stage and the single stage production processes. The two sets of companies are therefore able to compete equally regardless of the level of vertical integration. Thus a potential source of market distortion, prevalent in cumulative cascade systems, is overcome. Any decisions about mergers will be taken on grounds of economic efficiency rather than tax minimization.

In practice, VAT is calculated using an invoice approach rather than the value added approach shown in Table 2. Thus in the scenario quoted above, the final producer pays VAT on £27, the total invoiced value of production (including previous stages in the production process) and then reclaims VAT that has already been paid by the other manufacturers, from whom components and raw materials had been purchased. In our example company F will pay VAT of £2.70 per unit of good manufactured but reclaim the £1 paid by company R and the 90p paid by company S.

Table 2   Value added tax.

Company/ product	Purchase price from previous stage		A. An example of VAT multi-stage production				
			Value added		Tax due		Final price
R Raw materials	0.00	+	10.00	=	1.00	=	11.00
S Semi finished	11.00	+	9.00	=	0.90	=	20.90
F Final product	20.90	+	8.00	=	0.80	=	29.70
TOTAL			27.00		6.00		29.70
			B. An example of VAT single-stage production				
Company/ product	Purchase price from previous stage		Value added		Tax due		Final price
M Single stage	0.00	+	27.00	=	2.70	=	29.70

The adoption of a VAT system thus disallows one potential source of market distortion. However, it would be wrong to assume that simply adopting the same tax system throughout member states will eliminate all of the potential sources of market distortion.

The origin versus destination principle

Currently VAT is levied at the point of destination (consumption) rather than origin (production) although the Commission has made it clear that it sees this as a temporary situation and has proposed switching to the origin principle by December 1996 at the latest. This distinction between the two approaches is important when considering the problem of fiscal harmonization. The causes of potential problems are illustrated by reference to Figures 1-3.

We start by assuming that a product with similar characteristics is produced in Holland for 100 guilders and in Spain for 5,500 pesetas, which with an exchange rate of 1 guilder to 55 pesetas means that the production costs are identical. (We are ignoring transport costs in of this example.) Under the origin principle, VAT is applied at the country of origin which for standard goods, in March 1989, was 20 per cent in The Netherlands and 12 per cent in Spain.

The Dutch-produced item requires 20 per cent VAT to be added in both the home and overseas markets. Following the solid arrows in Figure 4.1 we can see that it sells on the Dutch market for 112 guilders and on the Spanish market for 6,600 pesetas. On the other hand, the Spanish-produced item has had 12 per cent VAT added and thus following the unfilled arrows sells for 120 guilders in Holland and 6,160 pesetas in Spain.

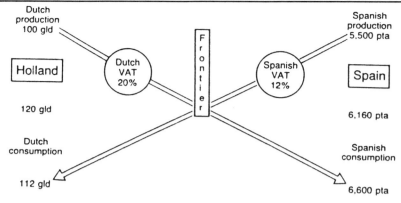

1 guilder = 55 pesetas

Figure 1   The origin principle.

This clearly gives the Spanish producer a competitive advantage in both markets which reflects tax differences rather than differences in productive efficiency. Under the origin system of VAT, international companies would choose to site their factories in those member states that imposed the lowest rate of VAT. Clearly if the rates of VAT were the same in all member states then this problem would no longer exist.

Figure 2 illustrates the destination principle of VAT which was the system of tax adopted by the EC in 1967. Under this system goods are exported tax free and VAT is paid by the importer in the country of destination when the goods cross the frontier. As can be seen the goods are now sold at the same price in both markets. However, the removal of fiscal frontiers has formed the centrepiece of the debate on taxation and the completion of the internal market.

As we have seen frontier controls are seen as a hindrance to trade: though they do not actually prevent a company from exporting, the extra paperwork they create and the costs they impose place additional burdens on exporters. The smaller the exporting company the larger the burden this is likely to cause,[7] and because of this the continued existence of frontier controls clearly gives a market advantage to large companies.[8]

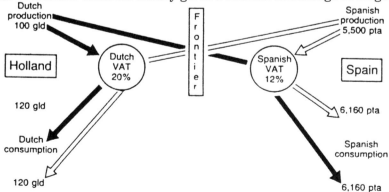

1 guilder = 55 pesetas

Figure 2   The destination principle.

What then are the alternatives once frontiers have been removed? The first is to change to an origin-based system of VAT, such that it is applied to exports at the same rate as to goods for domestic consumption. Importing producers, wholesalers and retailers then add VAT at the importing country's rate to their part of the value added.[9] This, as we have seen, requires rates of tax to be harmonized throughout the Community, if market distortion and problems of cross-border shopping are to be avoided.

However, this is not the end of the story. Changing the VAT system in this way will also affect the allocation of tax revenues within the Community. At present member states receive VAT payments on the total value of taxable imported goods but not on taxable exports. If the above alternative is chosen then this will be reversed with VAT payments being received on taxable exports but not on imports. Thus a country with a large trade surplus with the rest of the EEC, such as Germany, will gain whilst those with a trade deficit, such as the UK, will lose.

An alternative is to allow importers to reclaim the VAT paid in the exporting country and apply the importing country's rate of VAT to the total value of the good. This is in effect an alternative way of applying the destination principle and is the approach suggested in the Cockfield Report. The sale would be taxable in the hands of the vendor and the VAT incurred by the purchaser would be deductible irrespective of the member state in which it had been charged. It would then be necessary to set up a 'clearing house' system to ensure that VAT collected by the exporting member state and deducted by the importing member state was reimbursed to the latter.[10]

This system, which is illustrated in Figure 3, has attracted considerable criticism for two main reasons. First, the clearing house system was seen to be unnecessarily bureaucratic and costly. Second, some purchasers and institutions are currently exempt, or partially exempt, from VAT payments. These institutions would be required to pay VAT on their imports from other member states but would not be able to offset this against domestic VAT payments, because they have none or little by way of domestic VAT payments to set it against.

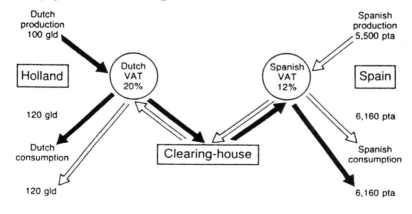

1 guilder = 55 pesetas

Figure 3   The Cockfield Report proposal.

Georges Egret, the Secretary General of the French Internal Revenue Association, suggested a solution to these problems in April 1990.[11] The proposal was for the current system to remain in operation with goods being exported free of VAT. However, rather than VAT being added at the frontier it would, after 1992, be added by the purchaser. On 8 May 1990 the European Commission announced that it found this system acceptable but only on an interim basis; it would thus be in force from the beginning of 1993 and is due to expire on 31 December 1996 at the latest.

Purchases by non-taxable institutions and exempt entities

Non-taxable institutions and exempt entities (such as banks, insurance companies and public administrations) would be allowed VAT-free purchases to an annual maximum of 35,000 ECUs per year, beyond which they will be subject to VAT as with any other company. This was the interim measure accepted by the European Commission on 8 May 1990. However, Mme Scrivener, European Commissioner with special responsibility for taxation and the customs union, made it clear that:

> the Commission found this system acceptable provided three conditions are fulfilled: a) it must be temporary, the final system being VAT payment in the country of origin of the goods; b) it must follow elimination of all border controls; c) it must include true simplification of administrative procedures for companies.[12]

Thus, before the end of 1996 the functioning of this system was to be examined and the terms of the change to a definitive system of taxation in the country of origin are to be set.

Cross-border shopping and alignment of VAT rates

A major consequence of the removal of fiscal barriers was that by January 1993 individual consumers would be free to purchase goods, for their own use and not commercial in nature, in any of the member states, provided that VAT is paid at the rate operated in the country in which the goods are purchased. This means, therefore, that limits on travellers' purchases will be eliminated and as a result cross-border shopping is likely to increase. The Commission also proposed that the ceiling on travellers' purchasing be increased from ECU 390 to ECU 800 in 1991 and further to ECU 1,600 in 1992 before being abolished altogether.

There were two important exceptions to this general rule. The first applied to purchases of new passenger vehicles which would be taxed in the country in which their license plates were registered; and the second to purchases from companies specializing in mail order sales which will be taxed in the country in which the goods arrive.

In effect, as far as individual consumers were concerned, a dual VAT system would operate after 1992. Consumers could choose whether to purchase goods in their own countries to which a domestic rate of VAT has been applied or travel to another member state and purchase the goods at a different rate of VAT with consequent market distortion. To avoid these distortionary effects, the Cockfield Report proposed that the VAT rates of the twelve member states should be brought closer together so that they were approximately equal. It was argued that experience in the USA where an absence of fiscal frontiers is combined with interstate differences in tax rates shows that complete harmonization of rates is unnecessary. Thus the Cockfield Report suggested that the target range for the standard rate of VAT should be 14-19 per cent with a norm of 16.5 per cent. (The upper limit was raised to 20 per cent in 1987.)[13] As Table 3 shows this band encompassed the standard rate for most member states.

This approach was finally accepted in December 1989 when member states agreed on guidelines concerning the narrowing of VAT tax bands; in particular, that the normal rate applicable to most goods and services would not, between the date of agreement and 1 January 1993, be reduced if it was lower than 14 per cent, increased if it was above 20 per cent or moved outside of the 14-20 per cent band if it was currently in that range.

Two subsequent refinements have occurred. First, it has been argued that there is no need to add an upper limit to the 14-20 per cent band as any state charging above 20 per cent would lose out through competition from other members. Second, on 24 June 1991, the twelve EC finance ministers reached political agreement that the normal minimum VAT rate should be raised to 15 per cent — requiring Germany, Luxembourg and Spain to increase their rates. Eleven countries accepted that the political agreement must be enshrined in a directive whilst the UK, on the grounds of sovereignty, refused to be tightly bound in this matter. In addition, the Commission proposed that member states would be free to set a reduced rate of VAT in the range 4-9 per cent which will apply to six product groups: foodstuffs (excluding alcoholic beverages); energy products for heating and lighting; water supplies; pharmaceutical products; books, newspapers and periodicals; and passenger transport.

Table 3   **VAT levels in Community member states (%) (1 March 1990).**

	Lower rates	Standard rates	Upper rates
Belgium	1 and 6	19	25 and 33
Denmark		22	
France	2.1 and 5.5	18.6	25
Germany	7	14	
Greece	3 and 6	16	36
Ireland	0 and 10	23	
Italy	4 and 9	19	38
Luxembourg	3 and 6	12	
Netherlands	6	18.5	
Portugal	0 and 8	17	30
Spain	6	12	33
United Kingdom	0	15	

Source: European Communities Commission, *Taxation In the Single Market,* Luxembourg OOPEC, 1990.

Interestingly on 24 June 1991 the Commission accepted the retention of zero-rating for a limited number of goods included in the list of products above, provided there was no risk of competition being distorted. Thus, member states would be free to set two rates of VAT with the reduced-rate band being applied to about one-third of the common VAT base.

There has however been some disenchantment with these proposals. Denmark has opposed the introduction of unlimited tax allowances for travellers. Ireland has only recently withdrawn its reservation on this issue, following an understanding that the Commission will carry out a thorough study of the budgetary implications that unlimited tax allowances would have — in particular implications that the lowering of tax bands allied to cross-border shopping would lead to a potential loss of tax revenue. Both Denmark and Ireland have had relatively high standard rates of VAT and have argued that they would face a substantial fall in tax revenues in consequence of these changes.

The EC has congratulated itself on the progress that has been made but there is still a considerable way to go before the approximation of VAT can be said to have been achieved. The major sticking point will undoubtedly be the proposed switch to the origin system of taxation and it is clear that the redistribution of tax revenue likely to follow such a switch will ensure that the debate will continue up to the 1996 deadline, and probably beyond. In addition there is continued dispute over the use of zero-rated and lower tax bands. It also seems unlikely that this will be resolved before the start of 1993 unless a compromise based on a timetable for the phasing out of these zero-rated goods is agreed upon.

Excise duties

The problem

Excise duties are, in the main, applied to three general categories of goods — tobacco, alcoholic beverages and hydrocarbon oils. However, each of these can be subdivided into a large number of excisable products — for example twenty-eight types of alcoholic beverages and seven types of mineral oil. For ease of illustration we shall concentrate on the classic five products, cigarettes, beer, wine, spirits and petrol and take a standard case to illustrate the operation of excise duties for each product group.

Traditionally excise duties have taken several forms. They may be levied as a specific tax, i.e., an amount per unit of the product, regardless of price, or as an *ad valorem* tax i.e., a tax proportional to the selling price or as a combination of the two methods. Taking the case of cigarette taxation, all member states use the latter method — a combination of the two methods with a specific excise duty being added to an *ad valorem* element which probably includes the standard VAT. However, as Table 4 shows, the balance between the two differs: specific taxes tend to be favoured in northern member states whilst *ad valorem* taxes tend to be favoured by southern member states.

A further complication arises because there are several ways of applying a specific tax. For example, some countries add a specific tax per cigarette meaning that large and small cigarettes have the same amount of tax imposed on them, while for others it is a specific tax per gram of tobacco content resulting in a higher tax on large cigarettes than on small ones. The differences do not end there. The system of enforcing and receiving payment of duties also differs between member states. Unlike VAT payments, which are made throughout the production and retailing process, excise duties are single-stage taxes. The timing of the stage at which these duties become due for payment, and hence the difference between taxed and untaxed goods, becomes important. In addition, excise duties are levied at a considerably higher rate than VAT and hence the potential gains from duty evasion or delays in tax payments are relatively high.

Table 4   **Excise duty rates.**

	Beer	Wine	Spirits	Petrol	Cigarettes
Belgium	0.13	0.33	3.76	0.25	0.15 + 66%
Denmark	0.71	1.57	10.50	0.46	1.52 + 39%
France	0.03	0.03	3.45	0.39	0.03 + 71%
Germany	0.07	0	3.52	0.24	0.52 + 44%
Greece	0.10	0	0.14	0.42	0.01 + 58%
Ireland	1.13	2.79	8.17	0.38	1.00 + 35%
Italy	0.17	0	0.69	0.53	0.03 + 69%
Luxembourg	0.06	0.13	2.53	0.20	0.03 + 64%
Netherlands	0.23	0.34	3.89	0.29	0.24 + 54%
Portugal	0.09	0	0.74	0.41	0.04 + 63%
Spain	0.03	0	0.93	0.20	0.01 + 35%
UK	0.68	1.54	7.45	0.31	0.96 + 34%
Commission proposal as at 19/12/89					
Basic	0.0935	0.0935	3.36	0.337	0.30 + 45%
Target	0.1870	0.1870	4.21	n.a.	0.43 + 54%

Source: European Communities Commission, COM (89) 525 final; COM (89) 526 final; COM (89) 527 final; S. Smith, 'Excise Duties and the Internal Market', *Journal of Common Market Studies*. vol. 27, no. 2, pp. 147 — 60, 1988.

Notes: All figures in ECUs
Beer: based on 1 litre of beer of average strength (original gravity 1050)
Wine: based on 1 litre of still wine
Spirit: based on a 0.75 litre bottle of 40% spirits
Petrol: based on 1 litre of leaded petrol. Unleaded petrol will be charged at 0.287 ECU per litre
Cigarettes: based on a packet of 20 cigarettes.

Most member states, including the Benelux countries, plus Denmark, Germany and Greece, enforce duty payment through tax stamps or 'banderoles'. This requires the physical stamping of goods on which duty has been paid: thus taxed and untaxed goods are easily distinguished. To prevent forgery these stamps are usually attached during the manufacturing stage. This has the advantage that it does not require close supervision of the production process, as untaxed goods can be easily identified at the retailing stage.

There are advantages and disadvantages for internationally traded goods in this banderole system. Exported goods do not need to bear the banderole allowing them to be easily exported duty-free. This advantage is counter-balanced by the disadvantage that, for imported goods, duty has to be paid immediately upon entry to the country. A further disadvantage of this approach is that the domestic manufacturers bear the costs of meeting the duty payments at an early stage in the manufacture and selling process with a clear incentive to minimize the time between duty payment and retail sale.[14] In addition, when the rate of duty changes there is difficulty for the authorities in ensuring that recently produced goods pay the newest rate of tax.

The UK, on the other hand, uses a system of bonded warehouses, whereby goods are stored in a bonded warehouse or other approved store without payment of duty, which is suspended until they leave the warehouse. The main disadvantage of this system is that it requires close supervision of the production process, including movement of the goods up to the point where duty is paid, with the consequent costs of administration and loss of revenue to the tax authorities. A major advantage of the system, from the manufacturers' point of view, is that payment of the duty can be delayed until the goods leave the bonded warehouse. However, goods designated for export need to be closely monitored until they leave the country and imported goods also need to enter a bonded warehouse under close control if tax evasion is to be avoided.

Progress to date

Progress in the area of excise duties was relatively slow until recent years. The initial stages were directed towards the structure rather than the rates of excise duties. However, more recently attention has been paid to the rate structure and on the 25 October 1989 the European Commission adopted the following proposal. However, to date, several questions still need to be addressed if the move towards the approximation of excise duties is to be achieved by 31 December 1992.

Under the proposal it has now been recognized that the imposition of a single rate of excise duty per product throughout all of the member states, as proposed in 1987, is unrealistic given the large differences in duties that currently exist. Thus, the new approach is to set minimum rates for all products and as an illustration, some of these are presented in Table 4. These minimum rates should be applied in all member states effective from 1 January 1993 at the latest.[15] In addition, the European Commission has also set objective or target rates to which member states are expected to converge in the medium to long run. No date has been set but the Commission's proposal envisages a revision procedure for minimum and target rates after 1992, taking into account transport, health, energy, environmental and fiscal policies. Both these rates are to be reviewed once every two years.

As can be seen from Table 4, the rates of duty are based on a variety of factors determined by the characteristics of each of the products. With regard to cigarettes, an allowance has been made for the differences in approach to the structure of taxation of this product. This is the only product for which the minimum rates are not set purely in terms of a specific duty. Thus minimum values have been set for both the specific and *ad valorem* or value added aspects of the excise duty which incidentally also includes VAT payments.

For other goods on which excise duties can be levied the situation is easier.[16] For beer the rate is per hectolitre/degree Plato and hence allowance is made for different strength beers. Translated to an average strength beer it can be seen that the rate per litre is the same as for still wine. The duty on spirits is calculated according to the pure alcohol content of the drink and thus spirits with a higher alcohol content have a higher rate of duty. Finally, because of environmental considerations there are differences in duty on unleaded and leaded petrol.

It should also be recognized that all of these products also have VAT applied to the final price, thus differences in VAT rates (with the exception of cigarettes) would further distort retail price differences. Member states have frequently argued that a low VAT rate has often been applied in combination with high excise duties and vice versa and so the Commission should consider the combined taxes rather than excise duties separately from VAT.

Clearly large differences still remain but as with VAT the Commission hopes that market forces will gradually bring rates of duty into line. Travellers' purchases are expected to be duty free and thus in the absence of approximation of rates of duty, there would be considerable scope for cross-border shopping by both traders and consumers alike.

Finally, there remains the problem of administration and control of payment of these duties, to which end the Community has proposed a system of linked warehouses. Goods would be transferred to and between warehouses without the application of excise duties, but once goods leave these warehouses then duty will be applied, and once applied, goods would be allowed to move freely within the Community. If this happens producers could be expected to choose to send their goods to the warehouse and hence pay tax in the country with the lowest duty payable, selling the goods in the country with the highest duty, a problem which is still to be resolved.

How then can the Community ensure that the duty paid is remitted to the country in which the goods are consumed, as at present? The linked bonded warehouse system could be combined with the 'banderole' system to obtain the benefits of both approaches. Goods could be tax-stamped when they reach their destination or as they leave the warehouse, if the warehouse is sited in the country of destination. Alternatively, tax could be paid when the goods leave the bonded warehouse and reclaimed or allowed against the excise duty payments due in the country of destination, if different to the country in which the warehouse is sited, so the excise duty of the country of destination is thus applied. Either way introduces administrative complications.

The use of a single stage tax such as excise duty thus highlights the problem of applying the destination principle. As can be seen applying the destination principle or a consumption-based tax requires a complicated system of rebates and administrative checks on tax payment. However, it can be argued that with a production tax (a tax at origin), administration becomes relatively easy. As with VAT, the Commission would like the Community to accept the origin principle, but the same problems arise with large revenue reallocations between member states following the change.

Corporate taxation[17]

Introduction

The European Commission has made very limited progress in the thorny area of company taxation, though recently momentum has gathered pace in this area. For example, in 18 April 1990, Mme Scrivener presented a new strategy for company taxation schemes.

Devereux and Pearson[18] have identified three possible reasons for wanting to harmonize these forms of tax. First, that the distribution of corporate tax revenues between member states is seen as 'unfair', second, that it causes administrative difficulties for both governments and business and, third, that it distorts competition within the Community.

Current corporate tax strategy may lead to multiple taxation of some company income. The profits a company is deemed to make are currently taxed in the country of production. However, if the company sends these profits to another country (say from a subsidiary to the parent) then a non-recoverable withholding tax maybe imposed. The country of residence of the parent company may then apply a further tax on these profits if the tax already applied is deemed to be too low. Finally, if the profits are distributed to shareholders, yet more tax may be levied, though this depends on the type of tax system in operation.

Thus it is with corporate taxes that the thorny question of jurisdiction becomes particularly relevant. Location of parent companies, their subsidiaries, where the products are sold and where their shareholders live will affect the amount of total tax paid, the shares of this revenue going to which country and hence the allocation of the tax burden. There is no obvious solution to who has jurisdiction or who has a just claim to a particular share of these revenues under the current system.

An equally important problem is the potential distortion of a company's decision of where to invest, produce and sell their products. A tax that does not influence this decision is referred to as a neutral tax. Economic efficiency — the condition that goods should be produced in the country most efficient at making them — requires a neutral tax system. However, the problems of applying this apparently simple objective are far from trivial as can be illustrated by use of two simple examples.

Let us assume that a multinational Belgian company is considering where to set up its new production plant, and the cost of production and the potential profits for the new product are identical in both Spain and Belgium. However, as can be seen from Table 5 corporation tax is 43 per cent in Belgium and 35 per cent in Spain. If tax was raised on a residence basis, according to the country of residence of the parent company, the company would pay a rate of 43 per cent in both countries and the question of location would not be influenced by tax structures. However, if tax were paid in the country where the goods were actually produced then the lower Spanish tax rate would make production in Spain more attractive. This is referred to as taxing at source — of production in this case. A tax that does not distort the decision of where to invest in this way is referred to as capital export neutral (CEN). Capital export neutrality will ensure that the Belgian producer will invest and hence produce in the most efficient location.

Table 5   **Company taxation.**

	Tax rate	Type of tax system	Local taxes[1]	Imputation rate[2]
Belgium	43	Imputation		33.3
Denmark	50	Imputation		20
France	42	Imputation		33.3
Germany	36/52	Imputation/ split rate	15	36
Greece	44	Imputation		44
Ireland	10 to 50[3]	Imputation		5.3
Italy	36	Imputation	16.2	36
Luxembourg	36 + 0.72[4]	Classical	6	
Netherlands	35	Classical		
Portugal	35/47	Split rate		
Spain	35	Imputation		9.1
UK	35	Imputation		25

Source: Adapted from OECD information reported to M. Devereux and M. Pearson, *Corporate Tax Harmonization and Economic Efficiency*, Institute for Fiscal Studies, Report Series no. 35, 1989 and A. Giovannini 'Capital Taxation' *Economic Policy*, October 1989.

Notes: [1] Typical rates: German and Italian are tax deductible whereas the rates given for Luxembourg are not.
[2] Percentage of gross dividend.
[3] Until 31.12.2000 for manufacturing companies only. Under bilateral treaties, other countries sometimes assume that a higher rate of tax has been paid by companies investing in Ireland. Ireland operates a top rate of 50%.
[4] 2% levy (deductible for Unemployment Fund).

The second example illustrates a further problem. Some goods such as roads, bridges and buildings can not be transported. Thus production, at least in part, takes place in the country in which the item is sold. Let us assume that Greek authorities invite tenders for the construction of a new bridge, which are then received from a Belgian and Spanish construction company. On the residence basis, if both companies are equally efficient producers, the lower rate of corporation tax in Spain will allow the Spanish construction company to tender at a lower price and make the same after tax profit as the Belgium company, even though all other costs etc are identical.

Under the residence approach to corporate taxation, these multinational construction companies will be attracted to the country with the lowest rates of tax. Musgrave[19] refers to taxes that do not distort choice as to where to invest for these reasons as capital import neutral (CIN). In this case, taxing at the source of production and sale would not distort competition and the companies from both Belgium and Spain could compete on equal terms as they will both pay the 44 per cent corporation tax rate applied in Greece.

This definition has been redefined by Devereux and Pearson to make CIN mean that all producers selling in the same market should face the same rate of tax, regardless of the country in which the good was produced. It now also includes goods produced outside of the country in which they were consumed. Thus CEN refers to the decision of where to produce and CIN to the decision of where to sell. For construction companies the country of construction, production and selling would be the same but the parent company may be based elsewhere.

In the absence of complete harmonization of fiscal tax systems, these two concepts lead to conflicts in the design of tax systems. Taxing companies on the basis of residence will guarantee CEN, thus an Italian company pays Italian tax regardless of where it invests. The achievement of CIN is more problematic but taxing companies only in the source country where the good is produced or sold, would move someway towards it.[20]

The current situation

Table 5 shows the large differences that currently exist in the rates of corporation tax paid throughout the Community. This is further complicated by the fact that some countries also impose local taxes on company income and more importantly because three different corporate tax systems operate throughout the Community.

A classical or separate tax system requires that the taxing of corporate and personal incomes are completely separated. Thus profits distributed to shareholders will first be taxed as company income and then separately as shareholders' personal income. Thus distributed profits are in effect taxed twice while profits retained by the company are only taxed once In contrast, in the split-rate system retained profits are taxed at a higher rate than distributed profits to allow for the extra tax paid on them by shareholders.

The final system is called the imputation or tax credit system and was first adopted by France in 1953, and is now used, at least partially, by nine of the twelve member states. Basically the system allows all or part of the corporation tax paid on distributed profits as a tax credit against personal income-tax liability. A major problem with the imputation system concerns the treatment of the tax credit. Should a Dutch shareholder in a British company residing in The Netherlands receive a personal tax credit against Dutch income tax when corporation tax has been paid in Britain?

Corporation tax is currently charged at a standard rate on all operations within a member state regardless of who owns the company, i.e. on a source basis. In addition, most countries also charge a withholding tax on all dividends or interest payments that are distributed to either shareholders or a parent company in another country,[21] which can distort a company's decision of where to invest and so is incompatible with CIN.

Harmonization progress to date

As mentioned earlier, progress on reforming corporation taxation to move towards a harmonized tax structure has been very limited. The Neumark Committee Report of 1963 proposed the introduction of a split rate system whilst the Van den Tempel report of 1971[22] recommended the adoption of a classical system, but this was not the end of the story. A draft directive in 1975 advocated the adoption of the imputation system following the adoption of that system by the majority of member states and the draft directive further proposed harmonization of tax rates within a 45-55 per cent band.[23]

The 1975 proposals were concerned with the system of tax and the rates but not the tax base and so a further preliminary draft proposal was made in 1988. This deals with aspects such as allowances for depreciation and the methods of calculating commercial profits. If adopted it would have allowed for little difference between corporate tax systems in member states.

However, apparently in the spirit of the new approach to Community integration, the 1975 proposal for fiscal harmonization was withdrawn on 20 April 1990. The harmonization route has thus been abandoned in preference to 'a reliance on the coordination and approximation of national policies', which is a euphemism for a market-led approach. This approach has been most closely linked with that supported by the British government and is based on the belief that after 1992, market forces will operate to bring corporate tax systems into line since otherwise high-tax countries will lose their competitive position.

The 1990 proposals include the establishment of a committee to make a report within a year with a view to answering the following questions: do the current systems result in distortions in investment decisions now and potentially post-1992?; and can market forces alone be expected to remove any perceived distortions should they be seen to exist? If not will the Community need to devise measures to remove them?

Cross-frontier business arrangements

As we indicated in chapter 1 the Community, as part of its industrial policy, has for a long time been endeavouring to create the legal and fiscal conditions to enable companies to conduct their affairs on a Community-wide basis without discrimmination or inhibition. On the legal front the Commission's approach has been to seek approval for a company law directive which would harmonize national company laws so that international mergers are possible; and for a regulation which would set up a system of European company law (hence the *Societas Europea*) alongside national company laws. Both these measures were identified in the Cockfield Report.

However, these legal measures are not of immediate relevance: what is of relevance is that the Commission has for a long period also been endeavouring to eliminate fiscal barriers which have discriminated against cross-frontier operations and these particular aims have been at the forefront of the Commission's proposals. First, companies should be able to organize themselves so that the parent might be located in one member state and the subsidiary (or subsidiaries) might be located in another (or others) without fiscal discrimination. This has not been the case since, as we have seen, subsidiaries have been required to deduct withholding tax when making payments to parents. Second, the Commission has sought to sweep away fiscal inhibitions which arise when a company in one member state acquires a company in another member state. In practice and in comparison with domestic transactions such acquisitions have been discriminated against, since the fiscal authorities have tended to demand immediate payment of capital-gains tax arising at the time of the transaction. If the tax liability was substantial it could make the cost of the amalgamation prohibitive.

Proposals to counter these problems were put forward as early as 1969, an interesting example of the degree to which the SEM had stagnated, and the Cockfield Report singled out these issues for action. They were dealt with in 1990 when the Council of Ministers adopted two directives whereby subsidiaries would no longer be required to deduct withholding tax when making payments to parents. Germany has until 1996 to comply with this directive.[24] Another directive provided that capital-gains tax arising in connection with cross-border acquisitions would no longer immediately attract capital gains in the country of the target — the tax could be deferred provided certain conditions were fulfilled.[25] In addition a Convention was also signed establishing a body to arbitrate in respect of transfer payments disputes concerning companies operating in more than one member state.[26] This had first been proposed in 1976 and was also identified as as area for action in the Cockfield Report.

Assessment

As with many areas of taxation reform, it is not possible to achieve all desirable characteristics, namely economic efficiency, administrative simplicity and political acceptability which in this case means a degree of fiscal sovereignty. Complete harmonization achieves the former but means that sovereignty has to be foregone, while a residence-based or world-wide tax system achieves sovereignty but not efficiency.

The world-wide tax system requires domestic residents to be taxed on all of their investment income irrespective of the country of origin of that income. However, the 1990 proposals removed the worst aspects of double taxation but still left the problems of disparate tax rates and so forth. It remains to be seen whether rates become more closely aligned after 1992: if, following the introduction of the Commission's proposals, distortions still exist, a range of alternative reforms which may deal with the problem have been suggested by Devereux and Pearson[27] or Giovannini.[28]

Conclusions

During the late 1980s there was a noticeable shift in emphasis in the Commission's approach to fiscal matters. The earlier approach was to attempt to push the Community towards a system of complete fiscal harmonization. The Cockfield Report changed this to fiscal approximation and then, as the actual date for completion of the internal market approached, the expediency approach has changed the emphasis yet again towards the less rigid desire to simply remove fiscal frontiers and allow market forces to force competing nations to move their fiscal systems closer together.

One could argue that any move towards harmonization of disparate, well-established and jealously guarded fiscal structures was a major achievement and thus the Commission could rightly congratulate itself on progress to date. On the other hand the Community is still a long way from achieving the fiscal neutrality that will allow the free movement of goods and services required for completion of the internal market. Even if the much simpler desire of changing indirect taxes from the destination to the origin principle is considered we can see that this is unlikely to be achieved, even by December 1996, given the large amount of revenue reallocation it is likely to cause.

Large differences still exist in the key areas (from the Commission's viewpoint) of VAT and excise duty. However, most public finance commentators argue that differences in direct tax systems are more likely to cause market distortion than indirect taxes and that this is particularly relevant for company taxation as people are less mobile than companies. As we have seen progress in this area has been poor, in part because current systems of raising corporate taxation seem outdated in the modern world of multinational companies and international mergers. It is difficult to see what can be done in this area unless a totally new approach to taxing company profits is found. More importantly the Commission appears to have almost totally ignored local taxation together with income taxation and social security contributions. In the words of the Commission itself:

> Taxation is an important and, at the same time, difficult aspect of the programme for completing the internal market: important because, without proper rules governing the tax treatment of cross-frontier transactions, tax barriers would remain in place, and difficult because any decision relating to taxation has immediate repercussions for national budgets. The unanimity required by the Council of Ministers compounds the difficulty.[29]

Recently, there have been limited signs that finance ministers are beginning to accept the need to accept fiscal changes which will enable the internal market to work more efficiently. The Commission has pointed to agreements made in 1990 concerning the tax arrangements for transnational cooperation between firms. There is still a long way to go and it is difficult to see how complete agreement on fiscal matters can be achieved while member states are allowed to retain significant amounts of fiscal sovereignty.

Notes

1   See J. Kay and M. King, *The British Tax System,* 5th edition, Oxford, Oxford University Press, 1990, for a discussion of these issues.

2   Ibid., pp. 202-7.

3   C. Lee, M. Pearson and S. Smith, *Fiscal Harmonization: an Analysis of the European Commission's Proposals,* London, Institute for Fiscal Studies, Report Series no. 28, 1988.

4   M. Bos and H. Nelson, 'Indirect Taxation and the Completion of the Internal Market of the EC', *Journal of Common Market Studies*, vol. 27, no. 1, pp. 27-44; P. Guieu and C. Bonnet, 'Completion of the Internal Market and Indirect Taxation' *Journal* of *Common Market Studies,* 25(3): 209-22.

5   'Report of the Fiscal and Financial Committee' in *Tax Harmonization in the Common Market,* Chicago, Commercial Clearing House, 1963.

6   The UK was operating a system of purchase tax at this time. This was a single stage tax normally charged at the wholesale stage. This enabled manufacturers to trade without making turnover tax payments.

7   The continued existence of twelve separate currencies also imposes additional frontier costs.

8   See C. Jenkins, 'Taxation and the Single Market', *EIU European Trends,* no. 2, pp. 79-86 who claims that surveys show that business regard frontier barriers as being of roughly equal importance with the whole range of technical barriers as an obstacle to trade.

9   A Dutch importer of components produced in Spain for 5500 Pesetas will buy them for 6160 Pesetas (5500 + 12 per cent) or 112 Guilders. The importer turns the components into a fully manufactured product which adds an extra 200 Guilders in value to the product. To this is added a further 40 Guilders in Dutch VAT (or 20 per cent on the value added by the Dutch importer). Thus the Spanish government receives 660 Pesetas and the Dutch government 40 Guilders in VAT payments.

10 European Communities Commission, *Completing the Internal Market,* COM (85) 310 final, 14 June 1985, p. 43.

11 This solution was presented to the European League for Economic Cooperation at a symposium in Brussels on April 21 1990.

12 Agence Europe, *Europe,* 9 May 1990.

13 European Communities Commission, COM (87) 320 final, 21 August 1987.

14 See S. Smith, 'Excise Duties and the Internal Market', *Journal of Common Market Studies,* 27(2): 147-60 who refers to these as compression costs i.e. the costs of compressing the post-duty stages of the production and selling chain.

15 European Communities Commission, *Amended Proposal for a Council Directive on the approximation of taxes on cigarettes. Amended Proposal for a Council Directive on the approximation of taxes on manufactured tobacco other than cigarettes,* COM (89) 525 final, 19 December 1989; *Amended Proposal for a Council Directive on the approximation of the rates of excise duty on mineral oils,* COM (89) 526 final, 19 December 1989; *Amended Proposal for a Council Directive on the approximation of the rates of excise duty on alcoholic beverages and on the alcohol contained in other products,* COM (89) 527 final, 19 December 1989.

16 As far as other goods are concerned, (e.g. playing cards, light bulbs, bananas, coffee, tea, etc.) member states will be allowed to retain the possibility of keeping or introducing excise duties on those products, notably for environmental purposes. However, the overriding aim is to ensure the free movement of goods and services and thus member states are expected to abolish all excise duties that do not give rise to border controls (except of course for the three product groups discussed in the text), see European Communities Commission, COM (90) 430 final, 26 September 1990.

17 See, M. Devereux and M. Pearson, *Corporate Tax Harmonization and Economic Efficiency,* Institute for Fiscal Studies, Report Series no. 35, 1989; M. Devereux and M. Pearson, 'Harmonizing Corporate Taxes in Europe' *Fiscal Studies,* vol. 11, no. 1, February 1990, pp. 21-35; A. Giovannini, 'Capital Taxation', *Economic Policy,* October 1989, pp. 346-86.

18 Ibid.

19   P. B. Musgrave, 'Interjurisdictional coordination of taxes on capital income', in S. Cnossen (ed.), *Tax Coordination in the European Community,* London, Kluwer, 1987.

20   See Giovannini op. cit.

21   Differences in rates are explained in Devereux and Pearson (1989), op. cit.

22   European Communities Commission, *Corporation Tax and Individual Income Tax in the European Communities,* Brussels, OOPEC, 1971.

23   European Communities Commission, COM (75), 392 final, 23 July 1975.

24   *Official Journal of the European Communities*, L 225, 20 August 1990. (The 1990 guidelines also require all firms engaged in cross-frontier activities to take account of foreign profits or losses.)

25   Ibid.

26   Ibid.

27   Devereux and M. Pearson, (1989, 1990) op. cit.

28   Giovannini, op. cit.

29   European Communities Commission, *Taxation in the Single Market,* Luxembourg, OOPEC, 1990.

Part III

Redistributive Policy Issues

9. The European Community between Social Policy and Social Regulation

Giandomenico Majone

1. The many dimensions of Europe's 'social dimension'

Community policy-makers, as well as many scholars, speak of the 'social dimension' of European integration as if the expression were sufficiently precise to be operationally or analytically useful. In fact, the expression is ambiguous since it encompasses a number of distinct and partly conflicting dimensions. For this reason opinions about the present state and future prospects of social Europe range from cautious optimism to outright pessimism.

There is considerable ambiguity about the meaning of a European social policy in the Treaty of Rome itself. The section on social policy — Title III of Part Three of the Treaty — enumerates a number of 'social fields' (employment; labour law and working conditions; vocational training; social security; occupational health and safety; collective bargaining and right of association) where Member States should co-operate closely (Art. 118, EEC). In the following Article, Member States are urged to 'maintain the application of the principle that men and women should receive equal pay for equal work'. The same Title III also establishes the European Social Fund with the goal of improving employment opportunities and facilitating the geographical and occupational mobility of workers.

What is arguably the most significant social policy provision in the Treaty of Rome — the social security regime for migrant workers — appears not in the section on social policy but in that on the free movement of persons, services and capital (Title III of Part Two, Art. 51, EEC). Finally, one of the objectives of the Common Agricultural Policy is, according to Art.39(b) of the Treaty, 'to ensure a fair standard of living for the agricultural community, in particular by increasing the individual earnings of persons engaged in agriculture'.

Thus, to the framers of the Treaty 'social policy' included not only social security and interpersonal distribution of income, at least for certain groups of workers, but also inter-regional redistribution, elements of industrial and labour market policy (vocational training, measures to improve labour mobility) and social regulation (primarily occupational health and safety and equal treatment for men and women).

However, the enumeration of matters relating to the social field in Art. 118, and the limited role given to the EC Commission in Title III — to promote co-ordination of national policies, to make studies, deliver opinions and arrange consultations — indicate that the social policy domain, with the exceptions noted above, was originally considered to be outside the supranational competence of the institutions of the

Giandomenico Majone: 'The European Community between Social Policy and Social Regulation'. *JOURNAL OF COMMON MARKET STUDIES*, (June 1993), Vol. 31, No. 2, pp. 153-170. © Basil Blackwell Limited 1993.

Community (Vogel-Polski and Vogel, 1991). In fact, Commission activity in the area of social policy and social regulation was quite modest between 1958 and the end of the 1970s, with one notable exception: environmental policy. The terms 'environment' or 'environmental protection' do not even appear in the Treaty of Rome. Despite the lack of an explicitly legal basis, a Community environmental policy has been growing vigorously, even if not harmoniously or systematically, since 1967. The significance of this development will become clear as we proceed with our argument.

The Single European Act (SEA) assigns a number of new competences to the Community in the social field. The main lines of development of Community activities in this field are beginning to emerge clearly: they are regional development (new Title V, Economic and Social Cohesion), and social regulation (Art. 100A, Art. 118A, and the new Title VII, Environment). As noted above, before this social policy belonged to the competence of the Member States, with the Commission's power of initiative essentially limited to promoting collaboration among those Member States. In particular, Art. 118 of the Treaty of Rome gave the Community no power to regulate in the field of occupational health and safety. Hence the first directives in this area had to be based on Art. 100 (which deals with the approximation of laws directly affecting the functioning of the common market), and thus needed unanimity in the Council of Ministers. Under the new Art. 118A, directives in the field of occupational health and safety can be adopted by the Council by qualified majority, and with no proof needed that they are essential for the completion of the internal market.

Another innovation introduced by Art. 118A is the concept of the 'working environment', which makes possible regulatory intervention beyond the traditional limits of health and safety in the workplace. Under the wider interpretation favoured by the European Parliament, the objective of improving the working environment would include all conditions which may affect the health and safety of workers: organization of the labour market, length of work, its organization and nature, as well as physical and psychological stress. Although such a broad interpretation is opposed by both the Council and the Commission, some recent directives (to be discussed in more detail in Section 4) go beyond existing regulations in most Member States in taking into consideration ergonomic and other 'soft' factors, within the spirit of Art. 118A.

To complete this picture of significant progress in social regulation at Community level, we should also mention Art. 110A(3) which states that the Commission will start from a high level of protection in matters relating to health, safety, and environmental and consumer protection. This implies that the reference to minimum requirements in Art. 118A ('the Council ... shall adopt, by means of directives, minimum requirements for gradual implementation, having regard to the conditions and technical rules obtaining in each of the Member States') does not mean that Community health and safety standards should reflect the lowest level prevailing in the Member States. Rather, Community standards represent a lower threshold for national regulators who are free to maintain or adopt standards incorporating higher levels of safety.

The increasing importance of social regulation is also revealed by the action programme implementing the Community Social Charter adopted by the Member States, with the exception of the UK, on 9 December 1989. Of the 20 directives/regulations listed in the programme, 10 are in the area of occupational health and safety, 3 deal with improvements in living and working conditions, 3 deal with equal treatment for men and women, disabled persons, and protection of children (COM (89) 568 final).

The Treaty of Maastricht, if ratified, will confirm that trend. It contains a new section on consumer protection (Title XVIII); it introduces significant innovations in the area of occupational health and safety; it introduces qualified majority voting for most environmental protection measures. It even adds transport safety to the regulatory tasks of the Community (Art. 75, 1 (C)). But the Treaty is silent on most areas of traditional social policy.

These developments show that EC policies in the social field are evolving along quite different lines from those followed by the Member States. National historical traditions have created a dense web of welfare institutions covering most citizens 'from the cradle to the grave', while the Community remains, and will very possibly remain, a 'welfare laggard'. In the field of social regulation, however, the progress has been so remarkable that some recent EC directives exceed the most advanced national measures in the level of protection they afford. The aim of this article is to clarify the reasons for these divergent patterns of policy development, thus providing a more accurate picture of the social Europe of the future.

2. What makes social regulation different

Since the passing of the SEA, an increasing number of EC directives dealing with quality-of-life issues no longer need to be justified by reference to the completion of the internal market. In this sense, social regulation has succeeded in acquiring a measure of autonomy with respect to other EC policies. But even if they no longer have to be justified in functional terms, measures proposed by the Commission in the social field must be compatible with the 'economic constitution' of the Community, that is, with the principles of a liberal economic order. This requirement creates an ideological climate quite unlike that which made possible the development of the welfare state in the Member States.

At least until the late 1970s, few students and practitioners of social policy in Europe bothered to inquire whether the measures they advocated were in fact compatible with the logic of a competitive market economy. The English sociologist, T.H. Marshall, expressed widespread and long-held views, when he wrote that 'social policy uses political power to supersede, supplement or modify operations of the economic system in order to achieve results which the economic system would not achieve on its own, and ... in doing so it is guided by values other than those determined by open market forces' (Marshall, 1975, p. 15).

Community social policy could not be justified in such terms. The economic liberalism that pervades the founding Treaty and its subsequent revisions give priority to the allocation function of public policy over distributional objectives. Hence the best rationale for social initiatives at Community level is one which stresses the efficiency-improving aspects of the proposed measures. Welfare economics provides a theoretical foundation for such justifications. A fundamental theorem of welfare economics states that, under certain conditions, competitive markets lead to a

Pareto-optimal allocation of resources, i.e. to a situation where there is no rearrangement of resources (no possible change in production and consumption) such that someone can be made better off without, at the same time, making someone else worse off. Theoretical research in economics during the past few decades has identified six important conditions under which the market is not Pareto-efficient (Stiglitz, 1988). These are referred to as 'market failures'. They provide a set of rationales for government interventions acceptable, in principle, even to the advocates of a liberal economic order. They are:

1. Failure of competition;
2. Public goods;
3. Externalities;
4. Incomplete markets;
5. Information failures;
6. Unemployment, inflation and disequilibrium.

Two further rationales for government intervention not related to market failure are:

7. Redistribution;
8. Merit goods.

These eight reasons fall into three groups which correspond to the three fiscal functions of government in the Musgrave sense: the allocation function (1-5), the stabilization function (6) and the distribution function (7 and 8). Thus an analytic distinction between social regulation and social policy may be drawn on the basis of the rationales for government intervention. In the perspective of welfare economics, the purpose of social regulation (health and safety, environment, consumer protection) is to solve problems created by specific types of market failure — especially public goods, negative externalities and information failures. Air and water pollution are prime examples of externalities, while a number of regulatory activities in the fields of safety and consumer protection are motivated by imperfect information and the belief that the market, by itself, will supply too little information. Examples include regulations requiring lenders to inform borrowers of the true rate of interest on their loans, regulations concerning labelling of food or medicinal products, disclosure of contents, etc. To the extent that such regulations succeed in correcting the market failure they address, they not only increase consumer welfare but, as a consequence, also improve market efficiency.

If there are no market failures the economy is Pareto-efficient, and there is no economic justification for government intervention. But the fact that the economy is Pareto-efficient says nothing about the distribution of income. A very unequal distribution of income may be unacceptable to a majority of citizens, and this will legitimize government intervention on political and moral grounds, even at some loss in economic efficiency.

The second argument for government intervention in a Pareto-efficient economy arises from concern that individuals may not act in their own best interest. Goods that the government compels individuals to consume, like elementary education and low-cost housing for the poor (instead of giving cash grants), are called *merit goods*. Of course, the paternalistic argument is plausible only if one assumes that government knows what is in the best interest of individuals better than they themselves do. It is important to note that the paternalistic argument for government activities is quite distinct from the externalities argument (Stiglitz, 1988, p. 81). Smoking in public places imposes a cost on non-smokers, and hence a ban can be justified by an externalities argument. Those who take a paternalistic view might argue that individuals should not be allowed to smoke even in the privacy of their own homes and even if a tax is levied which makes the smokers take account of the external costs they impose on others.

While 'social policy' is not a technical term with exact and uniform meaning, there is general agreement that its central core consists of social insurance, public assistance, health and welfare services, and housing policy. Titmuss has identified three main models of social policy: the *residual welfare model* — social welfare institutions come into play only when an individual's needs are not adequately met by the private market and the family; the *industrial achievement-performance model* — social needs should be met on the basis of merit, work performance and productivity; and the *institutional redistributive model* — social policy should provide universalistic services outside the market on the principle of need (Titmuss, 1974, pp. 30-1).

It should be clear from this discussion that all three models of social policy, especially the third one, are quite different from social regulation both in the range of government activities they include and in their underlying rationale: public goods, negative externalities and information failure in one case, redistribution and merit goods in the other. Of course, the distinction is not absolute. Thus, merit goods play a limited role also in social regulation, e.g. protective equipment for workers or seat-belts for drivers. Even in those cases, however, the justifications tend to be different. For example, it is argued that, given incomplete consumer information, temporarily imposed consumer choice may be desirable as part of a learning process, so as to permit more intelligent free choice thereafter.

Analytically distinct, social policy and social regulation are historically and institutionally related; they belong to the same 'policy area' — a policy area being a set of policies that are so interconnected that it is impossible to make useful descriptive or analytic statements about one of the policies without taking the other elements of the set into consideration (Majone, 1989a, pp. 158-61). The most interesting aspect of a policy area is how its internal structure changes in time. As the number and importance of some elements grow relative to the size of the area (which is determined by the amount of financial and political resources devoted to it), individual policies increasingly compete with each other for public support. Some policies may become so important that they form a distinct sub-area within the original area. This is how social regulation has evolved within the social-policy area — a development most students of social policy have failed to notice because of their fixation on particular programmes and institutional arrangements. In thinking about the future shape of a European 'social state', it is important to pay attention to the dynamics of the entire social-policy area. Nowadays, quality of life depends at least as much on environmental and consumer protection as on traditional instruments of social policy (Kaufmann, 1985).

3. The infeasibility of a European welfare state

The idea of a European welfare state somehow emerging as a 'transnational synthesis' (Offe, 1990, p. 8) of national welfare systems has been discussed repeatedly in recent years. The advocates of this idea are generally motivated by an historical analogy, but particularly by concerns about the future of social entitlements in an integrated European market.

The analogy is with the integrative role of social policy in the formation of the nation-state in nineteenth-century Europe. Historically, social policy has made an essential contribution to the process of nation-building by bridging the gap between state and society. National insurance, social security, public education, socialized medicine were, and to a large extent remain, powerful symbols of national solidarity. It is argued that a supranational welfare state would provide an equally strong demonstration of Europe-wide solidarity (Streeck, 1990; Offe, 1990; Leibfried, 1991; Leibfried and Pierson, forthcoming).

However, the very success of the national welfare state sets limits to an expanded social policy competence of the Community. Indeed, there is a striking difference between the scale and scope of national policies and the modest role of (traditional) social policy in the process of European integration. It is also possible that the development of welfare-state institutions at Community level, instead of generating a sense of supranational solidarity would reinforce popular feelings against centralization, bureaucratization and technocratic management. Finally, it should be remembered that, in Germany and elsewhere, acceptance of the social state by entrepreneurs was bought with the promise of protection against foreign competition by tariffs and other means (De Swaan, 1988). Such a bargain would hardly be possible under present circumstances.

If the historical analogy is dubious, how well founded are the fears that competition among different national welfare regimes in an integrated market would lead to regime shopping, social dumping and deregulation? To answer such a question one must rely on indirect empirical evidence. The level and direction of foreign investments in developing countries, for example, seem to indicate that firms do not invest in low social wage countries unless other factors like infrastructure and worker productivity justify such investments (Knödgen, 1979). High social wage countries like Germany continue to attract foreign investments precisely because of the advantages they offer in terms of superior infrastructure and high worker productivity. In fact, the ambiguous social consequences of integration 'are revealed by the fact that northern Europe's concerns about "sunbelt effects" are mirrored by southern Europe's concerns about "agglomeration effects" in which investment would flow towards the superior infrastructures and high-skilled workforces of Europe's most developed regions' (Leibfried and Pierson, forthcoming, p. 26).

Even in the United States, well-developed welfare regimes, like those of Wisconsin and California, coexist with more primitive ones. For example, California provided welfare recipients in 1990 with benefits nearly six times larger than those provided by Alabama. The maximum welfare benefit paid to a California family of three was $694 a month, compared with $118 paid to a similar family in Alabama (Peterson and Rom, 1990, p. 7). As these authors point out, these policy differences are not just the peculiarities of a few states, nor are they gradually disappearing. Instead, the statistics show that benefits varied as much in 1990 as they did in 1940. Such disparities give rise to the phenomenon of 'welfare magnets' — states with comparatively high benefits that attract the poor. However, because of linguistic and cultural barriers, and an increasing standard of living even in the poorer regions of the Community, this is not likely to become a problem in Europe, even after the completion of the internal market. If one also keeps in mind the relatively high level of Community standards of health and safety, it appears that fears of an erosion of the national welfare state *as a consequence of European integration* are exaggerated. If there is a crisis of the welfare state — a question about which opinions widely diverge — this is because of factors which have nothing to do with the process of integration: demographic trends, the mounting costs of health care, the world crisis in social security, tax-payers' revolts, excessive bureaucratization, and so on.

It is fortunate that the normative case for a European welfare state is not compelling, for the practical prospects are extremely poor. To begin with the most obvious difficulty, the Community does not have, and will not have in the foreseeable future, anything approaching the financial resources required by modern welfare states. The EC budget, even after approval of the 'Delors II package', amounts to less than 1.3 per cent of the total GDP of the Member States and to less than 4 per cent of the central government spending of these countries (average government spending in OECD countries is 40 per cent of GDP). The Common Agricultural Policy and a handful of redistributive programmes absorb over 80 per cent of the budget; what remains is clearly insufficient to support a Community-wide social policy, even on a modest scale. It should be noted, however, that such limited resources are sufficient to set up ambitious programmes in social (and economic) regulation. In fact, an important characteristic of regulatory policy-making is the limited influence of budgetary limitations on the activities of regulators. The size of non-regulatory, direct-expenditure programmes is constrained by budgetary appropriations and, ultimately, by the size of government tax revenues. In contrast, the costs of most regulatory programmes are borne directly by the firms and individuals who have to comply with them. Compared to these costs, the resources needed to produce the regulations are trivial. This general feature of regulatory policy-making is even more pronounced in the case of the Community, since not only the economic, but also the political and administrative costs of enforcing EC regulations are borne by Member States (Majone, 1989b, 1991).

A second problem is the variety of welfare-state forms existing in Europe. At least four main types have been identified: a Scandinavian model, an Anglo-Saxon model, the model of the 'Bismarck counties', and the welfare systems of the countries of the southern rim of the Community (Leibfried, 1991; for another typology see Esping-Andersen,1990). Each of these models and their numerous variants are rooted in peculiar historical and political traditions, and are deeply embedded in different socio-economic contexts. Any attempt to harmonize such varied systems is bound to fail, as EC policy-makers clearly understand. Title XV of the Treaty of Maastricht explicitly excludes any harmonization of the laws and regulations of the Member States in the field of health policy. The 1989 Action Programme implementing the Community Social Charter (COM (89) 568 final) has this to say on social security:

> The social security schemes vary greatly in nature from one Member State of the Community to another. They reflect the history, traditions and social and cultural practices proper to each Member State, which cannot be called into question. There can therefore be no question of harmonizing the systems existing in these fields.

For the same reasons, a well-known scholar has suggested that, instead of aiming at supranationalism in the field of social policy, it would be better for the members of the EC to work within the framework offered by the Social Charter of the Council of Europe. A more flexible and less constraining approach based on multilateral agreements would provide an opportunity to learn from the best national experiences and thus stimulate changes in the national legislation (Kaufmann, 1986).

It could be argued that if a fully-fledged European welfare state is, at present, politically unfeasible, it should at least be possible to develop certain of its elements. At a later stage these elements could be fitted together to achieve a comprehensive regime. Thus, the Common Agricultural Policy effects a considerable transfer of money from consumers and taxpayers to farmers, and in this sense it might be considered part of a 'welfare state for farmers' (Leibfried and Pierson, forthcoming). However, the CAP represents not only an inefficient, but also a perverse type of social policy since it favours the well-to-do farmers of northern and central Europe rather than the poor hill farmers of the south. Only if the current system of price support is transformed to a direct income grant, will agricultural policy become a true social policy, though limited to a particular occupational group.

Another potential candidate is the social security regime for migrant workers. An interesting proposal in this area has been made by Pieters (1991). The proposal attempts to go beyond mere co-ordination by creating a European Social Security System (ESSS) for migrant workers. The system would be optional: migrant workers could choose between the present framework of co-ordination and the possibility of an automatic transfer from the national system to ESSS. This is an imaginative application of Article 51 EEC, but it is doubtful that the system envisaged would represent, if implemented, a first step in the direction of a comprehensive European welfare state. The historical development of the Community has shown again and again the limits of such functionalist logic.

Even if Member States were to endorse the plan, they would most probably oppose any extension beyond the case of migrant workers. In this instance, too, one should be sceptical of the analogy with the continuous expansion of national social security systems to cover ever broader groups of the population. Given the progressive loss of control over economic policy, social policy is, with foreign policy, one of the few remaining bulwarks of national sovereignty, and for this reason alone national governments will do their best to protect it.

Regional policy remains to be considered. Demands for regional redistribution within the EC have become pressing in recent years (Marks, 1992; Armstrong, 1989; Wallace, 1983), leading to a doubling in the expenditure of the structural funds — European Social Fund and the European Fund for Regional Development — by 1992. This important growth in resources allocated to the poorer areas of the Community shows that regional disparities are increasingly seen as a serious barrier to further integration. Also, the recent reforms in structural policy have created new possibilities for EC decision-makers to deal directly with political actors in individual regions.

Proponents of a 'Europe of the regions' are eager to exploit these possibilities to implement their vision of a new European order in which increasing centralization of decision-making in Brussels is counterbalanced by the emergence of powerful regional institutions directly linked to the centre (Marks, 1992; Majone, 1990).

Despite these interesting political perspectives, regional redistribution must be considered a rather inefficient instrument of social policy. In their enthusiasm for 'social cohesion', EC policy-makers often seem to forget that there is an important distinction between reducing inequality among individuals and reducing disparities across regions. The problems of targeting regions to achieve a better individual state of distribution are well known (Musgrave and Musgrave, 1973). Since most regions contain a mix of poor and rich individuals, a programme aimed at redistributing resources to a region whose average income is low may simply result in a lowering of the tax rate. The main beneficiaries of the programme will thus be rich individuals within poor regions — a phenomenon well known in the Italian Mezzogiorno — and which may be replicated in other regions of the Community as a result of the increases in the regional funds.

On the other hand, it is politically difficult to aim redistribution directly at individuals in a federal or quasi-federal system. Even in the United States, where the federal government pays three-quarters of the cost of welfare assistance, the states set the benefit levels. States differ in their assessment of what a family needs to achieve a reasonable standard of living, and in the percentage of that standard they are willing to pay to help that family meet its needs. States also differ in the requirements an applicant must satisfy in order to be eligible for welfare assistance. It was already mentioned that, as a consequence of these differences, the level of welfare assistance among the American states varies widely, more so than interstate disparities in wage rates or cost of living. Similarly in Europe, the governments of the countries of the southern periphery, particularly Spain, are at present advocating non-individualized transfers of Community funds.

In sum, it is difficult to see how a coherent and effective European social policy could emerge from such disparate elements as benefits for farmers, a social security regime for migrant workers, and some regional redistribution. The social dimension of European integration must mean something else.

4. The widening and deepening of social regulation

As we have seen, each successive revision of the Treaty of Rome has expanded and strengthened the competences of the Community in social regulation. The SEA provided an explicitly legal basis for environmental protection, and established the principle that environmental protection requirements shall be a component of the Community's other policies (Art. 130r(2)). It also introduced the principle of qualified majority voting for occupational health and safety, and the notion of 'working environment' which opens up the possibility of regulatory intervention in areas such as human-factor engineering (ergonomics), traditionally outside health and safety regulation. Finally, Art. 100A(3) of the SEA urges the Commission to take a high level of protection as the basis for its proposals relating to health, safety, environmental protection and consumer protection. The Treaty of Maastricht, if ratified, will continue this development by establishing consumer protection as a Community policy, defining a role for the Community in public health, especially in research and prevention (Title XV), and introducing qualified majority voting for most environmental legislation.

Even more indicative of the continuous growth of Community regulation is the fact that policies were developed before the existence of a clear legal basis. Thus, three Environment Action Programmes were approved before the SEA was passed. If it is true that the first Action Programme (1973-6) lacked definite proposals, concentrating instead on general principles, subsequent documents became increasingly specific. The second programme (1977-81) indicated four main areas of intervention, while the third (1982-6) stressed the importance of environmental impact assessments and of economic instruments for implementation of the 'polluter pays' principle. Concrete actions followed. The number of environmental directives/decisions grew from 10 in 1975, to 13 in 1980, 20 in 1984, 24 in 1985, and 17 in the six months immediately preceding the passage of the SEA.

Quantitative growth has been even more impressive in other areas of social regulation. For example, by the end of 1989 the Council had approved 215 directives concerning the quality, safety and packaging of goods, and more than 100 directives adopting technical standards. Scores of directives regulating the use of food additives, the naming and composition of food products, and the composition of materials and products likely to come into contact with foodstuffs, were introduced in the same period.

More important than this quantitative expansion of Community regulation, however, has been its qualitative deepening. It is not possible to discuss here the advances made on so many fronts since the SEA, but a few examples will give an idea of the recent qualitative changes in EC regulatory policy-making.

1. Measures concerning health, safety, environmental protection and consumer protection no longer have to be justified exclusively in terms of the free movement of goods and the completion of the internal market. Social regulation is still far from possessing the same political and institutional significance as competition policy, for example, but it no longer occupies a peripheral position in European policy-making.

2. Less than 10 years ago, two distinguished scholars described EC environmental law as 'no more than a kind of regulatory patchwork' (Rehbinder and Stewart, 1985, p. 203). To some extent this is still true, but in all areas one can see increasing efforts to produce comprehensive and coherent regulations. Notable recent examples are the new Directive on General Product Safety (92/59/EEC), the Safety and Health at Work Directive (89/391/EEC) and the Machinery Directive (89/392/EEC). (See also point 5 for more discussion of the last two directives.)

3. There are signs of a new willingness on the part of Community institutions and the Member States to address the issue of implementation (House of Lords Select Committee, 1992). This issue, which is especially important for social regulation, was given a high political profile for the first time by the European Council at its meeting in Dublin in June 1990. The Council, realizing that the credibility of Community policy-making was at stake, asked for periodic evaluations of existing directives to ensure that they are adapted to scientific and technical progress, and to resolve persistent implementation problems.

    In October 1991 the Council of Environmental Ministers held an informal meeting on implementation, as a result of which the Commission was instructed to submit proposals on the future development of policy on compliance and enforcement. At the Maastricht Summit the Member States again stressed the need for Community legislation to be accurately transposed into national law and effectively applied, while the Treaty on European Union (Maastricht Treaty) contains new powers for the European Court of Justice under which it may fine Member States who fail to comply with the judgments of the Court.

4. Concerns about implementation and growing realization that 'science and technology are advancing at such a rate that the Commission, with its current resources, cannot possibly keep up with collecting and objectively analysing all the new data available ... in order to identify new dangers and then to decide whether new proposals are required' (COM (90) 564 final, 4), have revived interest in European regulatory agencies and inspectorates. A European Environmental Agency was established by Council Regulation No. 1210/90 of 7 May 1990. A proposal for the establishment of a European Agency for Evaluation of Medicinal Products was submitted by the Commission on 14 November 1990 (COM (90) 283 final), and amended on 12 November 1991 (COM (91) 382 final). The proposal has not yet been accepted by the Council. Also under discussion is another proposal made by the Commission on 25 September 1991 for a European Agency for Safety and Health at Work (COM (90) 564 final).

    The creation of European agencies faces not only legal problems concerning the separation of powers and the delegation of legislative powers in the Community (Lenaerts, 1992) but also the opposition of some Member States. This explains why the tasks of the European Environmental Agency — the only one to be formally approved by the Council so far — are essentially limited to research and data collection. However, knowledgeable observers inside and outside Community institutions believe this to be only a first step in the direction of a fully-fledged regulatory agency. Suggestions have already been made that the agency could monitor compliance and the effectiveness of environmental regulations. In time, the agency could also examine the extent to which directives have in fact resulted in substantive environmental improvements (House of Lords Select Committee, 1992, p. 19).

5. Perhaps the most surprising qualitative change — surprising because it so clearly contradicts the received view of EC policy-making — is the innovative character of some recent legislation. It used to be said that EC regulations, in order to be accepted by the Member States, had to represent a kind of lowest common denominator solution. The fact that national interests are strongly represented at each stage of Community policy-making seemed to preclude the possibility of innovation, while giving a bargaining advantage to those Member States which oppose high levels of protection (Dehousse, 1992). At best, the Community could hope 'to generalize and diffuse solutions adopted in one or more Member States by introducing them throughout the Community. The solutions of these Member States normally set the framework for the Community solution' (Rehbinder and Stewart, 1985, p. 213).

There were in fact exceptions even prior to the SEA. By admission of these same authors, some earlier environmental directives represented significant policy innovations. Thus the PCB Directive (76/769/EEC) 'had no parallel in existing Member State regulations', while the Directive on sulphur dioxide limit values (80/779/EEC) established, on a Community-wide basis, ambient air quality standards, which most Member States did not previously employ as a control strategy (*ibid.*, p. 214).

However, the most striking examples of regulatory innovation were made possible by the SEA, in particular by the introduction of qualified majority voting, not only for internal market legislation, but also for key areas of social regulation. Leaving aside cases of economic regulation, I shall briefly return to two directives mentioned above (see point 2). In many of its provisions, the framework Directive 89/391 on Health and Safety at Work goes beyond the regulatory philosophy and practice even of advanced Member States like Germany (Feldhoff,1992). Only a careful reading of the full text can convey an adequate impression of the many elements of novelty introduced by the directive. By way of example, I shall mention only some of the general obligations imposed on employers by Art. 6:

- adapting the work to the individual, especially as regards the design of workplaces, the choice of work equipment and the choice of working and production methods, with a view in particular to alleviating monotonous work and work at a predetermined work rate and to reduce their effect on health (Art.6(2)(d));

- developing a coherent overall prevention policy which covers technology, organization of work, working conditions, social relationships and the influence of factors related to the working environment (Art.6(2)(g));

- giving collective protective measures priority over individual protective measures (Art.6(2)(h));

- giving appropriate instructions to workers (Art.6(2)(i)).

Other notable features of the directive are its scope (it applies to all sectors of activity, both public and private, including service, educational, cultural and leisure activities), its requirements concerning worker information, and the emphasis on participation and training of workers.

Equally innovative are the Machinery Directive (89/392/EEC) and, in a more limited sphere, Directive 90/270 on health and safety for work with display screen equipment. Both directives rely on the concept of 'working environment', and consider psychological factors like stress and fatigue important elements to be considered in a modern regulatory approach. It is difficult to find equally advanced principles in the legislation of any major industrialized country, inside or outside the EC. In order to explain such policy outputs we need new, more analytical theories of the policy process in the Community. The new theories must include detailed models of the Commission as an actor enjoying more autonomy and discretion than has been assumed so far.

5. Conclusion: which social policy for the EC?

The 'big trade-off' between economic efficiency and a more equal distribution of income and wealth has confronted every democracy since the dawn of industrialization. Today's social policies are the outcome of the struggles of the past over the division of the domestic product. Because those struggles have taken different forms in different countries, social policies differ widely even when they appear to use the same instruments and institutional arrangements. Moreover, the delicate value judgements about the appropriate balance of efficiency and equity, which social policies express, can only be made legitimately and efficiently within homogeneous communities. It is difficult to see how socially acceptable levels of income redistribution and of provision of merit goods can be determined centrally in a community of nations where stages of economic development and political and legal traditions are still so different. At the same time, because historical and linguistic barriers reduce the mobility of European society, the case for centralizing income redistribution is less compelling in the EC than in the nation-state or in a mature federal system like the United States. Finally, recall that regional redistribution tends to be inefficient because of the difficulty of targeting for redistribution communities containing a mix of rich and poor people. If our concern is with inequality among individuals, redistribution should be aimed at individuals, not regions. But this is precisely what Member States do not want the Community to do; as we saw in Section 3, the governments of the poorer countries insist on non-individualized transfers of Community funds.

For these and other reasons discussed in the preceding pages, a European welfare state seems politically unfeasible and, at the present level of political development of Community institutions, perhaps even undesirable. Some will see in this conclusion another reason for castigating the insufficient democratic legitimation of the Community. I submit that this view is shaped by a somewhat dated model of state-society relations. Even in national societies, traditional cleavages along class, party or religious lines are becoming less significant than new 'transversal' divisions over cultural diversity, citizen participation, the environment, the risks of modern technology, and other quality-of-life issues.

It is a fact of great significance that for many of these issues the national dimension is essentially irrelevant: solutions must be found either at a local or at a supranational, even global, level. There is, in other words, a natural division of labour between local, national, Community and international institutions. The nature of the problem, rather than ideological preconceptions or historical analogies, should determine the level at which solutions are to be sought.

It is certainly true that the creation of a 'common market' is not a goal capable of eliciting the loyalty and attachment of the people of Europe to their supranational institutions. A social dimension is also needed, but one must be clear about the meaning of this ambiguous expression. As I have tried to show, the European Community, rather than undermining the achievements of the welfare state, is in fact addressing many quality-of-life issues which traditional social policies have neglected — consumer protection and equal treatment for men and women, for example. The evidence I have presented strongly suggests that the 'Social Europe' of the future — the outlines of which are beginning to emerge clearly from the jurisprudence of the Court of Justice, from the Single European Act and from the Treaty of Maastricht, as well as from the pattern of Community policy-making — will be, not a supranational welfare state, but an increasingly rich space of social-regulatory policies and institutions.

References

Armstrong, H. (1989) 'Community Regional Policy'. In Lodge, J. (ed.), *The European Community and the Challenge of the Future* (New York: St. Martin's Press) pp. 167-85.

Commission of the European Communities (1989) *Action Programme Relating to the Implementation of the Community Charter of Basic Social Rights for Workers*. COM(89) 568 final.

Commission of the European Communities (1990) *Proposal for a Council Regulation (EEC) Laying Down Community Procedures for the Authorization and Supervision of Medicinal Products for Human and Veterinary Use and Establishing a European Agency for the Evaluation of Medicinal Products*. COM(90) 283 final.

Commission of the European Communities (1991) *Proposal for a Council Regulation (EEC) Establishing a European Agency for Safety and Health at Work*. COM(90) 564 final, amended COM(91) 362 final.

Dehousse, R. (1992) 'Integration v. Regulation? On the Dynamics of Regulation in the European Community'. *Journal of Common Market Studies*, Vol. 30, No. 4, pp. 383-401.

De Swaan, A. (1988) *In Care of the State* (Cambridge: Polity).

Esping-Andersen, G. (1990) *The Three Worlds of Welfare Capitalism* (Cambridge: Polity).

Feldhoff, K. (1992) 'Grundzüge des Europäischen Arbeitsumweltrechts'. Mimeo (Bochum: Ruhr Universität).

House of Lords, Select Committee on the European Communities (1992) *Implementation and Enforcement of Environmental Legislation* (London: HMSO).

Kaufmann, F. (1985) 'Major Problems and Dimensions of the Welfare State'. In Eisenstadt, S.N. and Ahimeir, O. (ed.), *The Welfare State and its Aftermath* (London: Croom Helm) pp. 44-56.

Kaufmann, F. (1986) 'Nationale Traditionen der Sozialpolitik und Europäische Integration'. In Albertin, L. (ed.), *Probleme und Perspektiven Europäischer Einigung,* (Düsseldorf: Landeszentrale für politische Bildung Nordrhein-Westfalen) pp. 69-82 .

Knödgen, G. (1979) 'Environment and Industrial Siting'. *Zeitschrift für Umweltpolitk,* Vol. 2, pp. 403-18.

Leibfried, S. (1991) 'Europe's Would-Be Social State'. Mimeo (Bremen: Centre for Social Policy Research).

Leibfried, S. and Pierson, P. (forthcoming) 'Prospects for Social Europe'. *Politics and Society.*

Lenaerts, K. (1992) 'Regulating the Regulatory Process: Delegation of Powers in the European Community'. Mimeo.

Majone, G. (1989a) *Evidence, Argument and Persuasion in the Policy Process* (New Haven, Conn.: Yale University Press).

Majone, G. (1989b) 'Regulating Europe: Problems and Prospects'. In Ellwein. Th. *et al. (ed .), Jahrbuch zur Staats-und Verwaltungswissenschaft,* Band 3/1989 (Baden-Baden: Nomos) pp. 159-78.

Majone, G. (1990) 'Preservation of Cultural Diversity in a Federal System: The Role of the Regions'. In Tushnet, M. (ed.), *Comparative Constitutional Federalism* (Westport, Conn.: Greenwood Press) pp. 67-76.

Majone, G. (1991) 'Cross-National Sources of Regulatory Policymaking in Europe and the United States'. *Journal of Public Policy,* Vol. 11, No. 1, pp. 79-106.

Marks, G. (1992) 'Structural Policy in the European Community'. In Sbragia, A. (ed.) *Europolitics* (Washington, D.C.: Brookings) pp. 191-224.

Marshall, T.H. (1975) *Social Policy* (London: Hutchinson).

Musgrave, A. and Musgrave, P.B. (1973) *Public Finance in Theory and Practice* (New York: McGraw-Hill).

Offe, C. (1990) 'Europäische Dimensionen der Sozial Politik'. Mimeo (Bremen: Centre for Social Policy Research).

Peterson, P.E. and Rom, M.C. (1990) *Welfare Magnets* (Washington, D.C.: Brookings).

Pieters, D. (1991) 'Europäisches und nationales Recht der Sozialen Sicherheit-Zukunftsperspektiven'. *Zeitschrift für ausländisches und internationales Arbeits-und Sozialrecht,* pp. 72-94.

Rehbinder, E. and Stewart, R. (1985) *Environmental Protection Policy* (Berlin and New York: De Gruyter).

Stiglitz, J.E. (1988) *Economics of the Public Sector,* 2nd ed. (New York: Norton).

Streeck, W. (1990) 'La dimensione sociale del mercato unico europeo'. *Stato e Mercato,* No. 28, pp. 29-68.

Titmuss, R.M. (1974) *Social Policy (London:* Allen & Unwin).

Vogel-Polski, E. and Vogel, J. (1991) *L'Europe sociale 1993: illusion, alibi ou réalité* (Bruxelles: Editions de l'Université de Bruxelles).

Wallace, H. (1983) 'Distributional Politics: Dividing Up the Community Cake'. In Wallace, H., Wallace, W. and Webb, C. (ed.), *Policy-Making in the European Community,* 2nd ed. (Chichester: Wiley) pp. 81-113.

10.   A Social Charter for a European Social Market?

Mark Wise and Richard Gibb

The European Commission, backed by a majority in the European Parliament, was determined that the move towards an integrated EC 'economic space' should be matched by the development of a corresponding 'social space' based on fundamental employment rights applicable throughout the single market. It was

> convinced that 1992 will be a success only if both sides of industry are involved in it. A social consensus is an essential factor in maintaining sustained economic growth. Europe cannot be built against the opinions of the employers or of the workers or of the general public, and efforts must be made, as the Commission has been stressing since 1985, to prevent distortions of competition from leading to forms of social dumping. (Commission 1989a:1)

The term 'social dumping' entered the '1992' debate to articulate fears that economic liberalization in the single market could be used to weaken social protection of workers competing for jobs in a more 'laissez-faire' international environment. There was a strong feeling in labour circles, forcibly expressed by the European Trade Union Confederation (ETUC), that Community action would be necessary to prevent companies playing one group of national workers off against another in an effort to minimize costs and remain competitive. The potential ability of companies, freed from national shackles on capital investment movements in a genuine common market, to force workers to accept reduced pay and conditions is considerable. Unions and political leaders in richer states like West Germany and Denmark where high wages, wide social security provisions, good working conditions and relatively heavy taxation prevail, suspect that investment — and jobs — could drift away from them towards countries where income expectations are lower, social provisions far less protective and environmental legislation less restrictive. In effect, ruthless competition in an unregulated market might lead to 'social dumping', a rather imprecise, but increasingly used concept to describe the potentially adverse effects outlined above (Boyer 1988).

During the 1980s the social dumping thesis gained ground for several reasons. First, the entry of Greece, Spain and Portugal into the EC widened the gap in social standards enormously, thus increasing the possibilities of trade, price and wage wars (see Tables 1 - 5 and Fig 1- 2). Secondly, the internationalization of business, with multinational companies devising trade and investment strategies which straddled national boundaries, made the potential for social dumping practices ever more actual (Wadley 1986). Thirdly, the successful promotion of the single European market project drew consideration of such social matters out of esoteric conferences into more open public

Mark Wise and Richard Gibb: 'A Social Charter for a European Social Market?' in *SINGLE MARKET TO SOCIAL EUROPE: THE EUROPEAN COMMUNITY IN THE 1990s* (Longman Scientific and Technical, 1993). pp. 152-199.

debate as people began to assess the costs and benefits of '1992' to them. The creation of some Community-wide social rights began to look less like the product of meddling 'Eurocratic' minds divorced from reality, but something of tangible benefit to workers in all Member States (Willis 1989). Supporters of this thesis had varying ideas on who would be the losers. Some feared that the wealthier countries would lose jobs and see their standards undermined, whilst others feared that poorer regions would never be able to raise their standards as they fought to compete with more powerful areas by constantly cutting prices and wages. Another tendency was to worry that the whole Community could suffer from unregulated competition. Peripheral countries might start the process of price-wage reduction to increase their exports or reduce import penetration of their previously protected home market. This in turn could provoke a retaliatory lowering of prices and incomes in the core states which might destabilize the Community's economy as a whole in a deflationary spiral. Profit margins would be reduced along with purchasing power, tax yields would decrease, investment in new products and technology could dry up as managers and governments became obsessed with cost-cutting to maintain short-term advantage in a shrinking, but increasingly competitive market (Teague 1989: 77-80).

Table 1   Expenditure on social protection in EC member states as a percentage of national GDP, 1984.

Netherlands	33.2%
Denmark	30.5%
Belgium	30.2%
W. Germany	29.4%
France	28.0%
Luxembourg	27.0%
UK	23.9%
Ireland	23.0%
Italy	22.4%
Spain	17.0%
Portugal	15.7%
Greece	n.a.

Source: Eurostat 1989

Table 2 **Comparative industrial labour costs per hour in EC member states, 1984.**

	PPS	**ECU**
Belgium	16.04	13.09
W. Germany	14.52	14.14
Netherlands	14.47	13.59
France	13.40	12.17
Luxembourg	13.24	10.96
Italy	13.24	10.39
Ireland	10.67	8.79
UK	10.12	8.84
Denmark	9.26	11.90

Table 3 **Average hourly gross earnings for manual industrial workers in EC member states, 1986 (current PPS).**

	PPS (Purchasing Power Standard)
Denmark	9.18
Luxembourg	9.03
Netherlands	8.54
W. Germany	8.48
UK	8.40
Belgium	8.17
Ireland	7.58
Italy	7.28 (est)
France	6.46
Spain	6.42 (est)
Greece	5.01
Portugal	3.55

Source: Eurostat 1989

Table 4   **Structure of labour costs in EC member states 1984 (% of total cost).**

	Direct costs (%)		Indirect costs %	
	Basic salary	Other payments	Social security contributions	Other costs (eg. training)
France	52.6	16.1	27.7	3.6
Italy	54.2	19.4	26.4	6.9
Netherlands	55.8	17.3	24.1	2.8
Belgium	54.9	20.3	23.7	1.1
W. Germany	56.0	20.7	21.0	2.3
Portugal	58.6	16.5	18.0	6.9
Greece	61.0	20.0	18.0	1.0
Luxembourg	69.0	14.8	14.8	1.4
UK	71.3	11.8	14.4	2.5
Ireland (1981)	73.7	10.4	12.9	3.0
Denmark	83.6	8.8	5.7	1.8
Spain	n.a.			

Source: Eurostat 1989

Table 5   **Unemployment rates in EC member states (1983-87).**

	1983	1984	1985	1986	1987	1988-7 average
Spain	17.8	20.6	21.9	21.2	20.6	20.4
Ireland	15.2	17.0	18.5	18.3	18.0	17.4
Belgium	12.6	12.6	11.7	11.8	11.6	12.1
UK	11.2	11.4	11.5	11.5	10.6	11.2
Netherlands	12.5	12.5	10.5	10.2	10.0	11.1
Italy	9.0	9.5	9.4	10.6	11.0	9.9
France	8.2	9.8	10.3	10.4	10.6	9.9
Greece	9.0	9.3	8.7	8.2	7.9	8.6
Portugal	7.7	8.4	8.5	8.2	6.8	7.9
Denmark	9.5	9.2	7.6	5.8	5.9	7.6
W. Germany	6.9	7.1	7.3	6.5	6.4	6.8
Luxembourg	3.6	3.0	3.0	2.6	2.7	3.0
EC12	10.0	10.8	10.9	10.8	10.6	10.6

Source: Eurostat 1989.

In addition to the potential costs of ruthless price competition, adherents of the 'social dumping' thesis felt that an excessively deregulated 'Europe without frontiers' might lead to large companies devising strategies which intensified the geographical division of the Community's labour market into two distinct spheres (Gibb, Treadgold 1989:

75-82; Lipietz 1988). In the core areas of the internal market, companies could intensify the location of more sophisticated, high-salaried production tasks, whereas the poorer peripheries would continue to accumulate labour-intensive, lowly-skilled and poorly-paid jobs. Such an economic division could lead to serious political divisions in the Community which might ultimately threaten the effort to build political and economic union among its Member States.

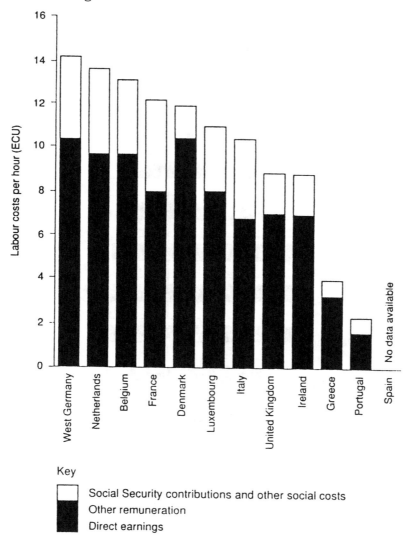

Figure 1 **Structure of industrial labour costs in EC countries, 1984.**
(*Source*: Commission, 1988h; Eurostat, 1990b).

247

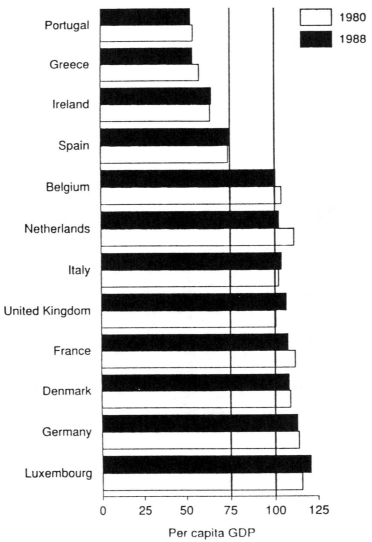

Figure 2   **Gap between EC countries in terms of GDP per capita, 1980-8**
(*Source*: Eurostat, 1975-90).

The Social Charter

A conviction that fears of social dumping in the single market were not unfounded led the Commission to formulate the *Community Charter of the Fundamental Social Rights of Workers* which was accepted by all Member States except Britain in December 1989. The relationship of this so-called 'Social Charter' to the '1992' project was explicitly recognized by Mrs Vasso Papandreou, EC Commissioner for Social Affairs and Employment:

> efforts towards completing the internal market in 1992 have highlighted the importance of this social dimension. It is not simply a question of ensuring freedom of movement for persons, together with goods, services and capital. It also contributes to improving the well-being of Community citizens and in the first place workers. The construction of a dynamic and strong Europe depends on the recognition of a foundation of social rights. A political signal given at the highest level was crucial.
> (Commission 1990a: 5)

Mrs Papandreou insisted that this initiative did not mean that 'we want to impose a uniform order in the EC'. On the contrary the Commission was 'aware that there are different attitudes, different historical developments, different cultures, different conditions ...(and)...we don't want to over-regulate from Brussels' (Commission 1989b:2). She stressed that the principle of 'subsidiarity' should apply in the social field so that what can best be done at local level should be done at local level, what can best be done at national level should be done at that level, and then only those things best done at European level should involve Community action. Thus, there was no reason why many of the Charter's, aims could not be achieved by action at national, regional or local levels. However, to win widespread support for the single market it was essential that the Community's leaders — that is the governmental heads of Member States — give a very visible 'political signal' to ordinary people that they were not only concerned to construct a 'businessman's Europe'; hence the importance of getting the European Council to accept the much publicized 'Social Charter' in December 1989.

This Charter had no legally binding consequences, but was a 'solemn declaration' laying a foundation upon which a programme of Community legislation could be built. In the words of Jacques Delors, the President of the European Commission:

> It is a solemn declaration and lays down the broad principles underlying our European model of labour law and, more generally, the place of work in our societies. It incorporates a foundation of social rights which are guaranteed and implemented, in some cases at the level of the Member States or at Community level depending on the field of competence. But it cannot be put into practice without the active participation of the two sides of industry. (Commission 1990c 3)

So the Social Charter was not a rigid legal prescription to be applied in some homogenizing manner across a diverse Community, but an attempt to win mass allegiance for the ideal of European integration by defining some basic minimum rights in the world of work including:

> freedom of movement of EC citizens within the Community;
> equitable wages sufficient to enable a decent standard of living;
> rights for part-time and temporary workers;
> improved living and working conditions involving the progressive Community-wide harmonization of holiday periods and so on;

> adequate social protection for both those in and out of work;
> freedom of association and collective bargaining;
> the right to vocational training;
> equal treatment for men and women;
> adequate participation of employees in the affairs of the companies that employ them;
> satisfactory health and safety at work;
> protection of children and adolescents at work;
> proper retirement pensions;
> the integration of disabled persons into the world of work.

Many states — notably West Germany with its 'social market' model — already had legislation which met, or exceeded, most of the requirements of the Social Charter. The aim of the Charter was not to undermine such Member State legislation nor to harmonize all national social policies. Rather it sought to lay down some 'fundamental social rights' which would establish basic minimum conditions (which individual countries could exceed if they so desired) and encourage movement towards 'best practice' in the Community. Thus, where necessary, the Commission would propose common legislation to ensure that no group of workers in any EC country be left far less protected than their counterparts elsewhere in the Common Market. In this way 'fair' as well as 'free' competition would be achieved in the single market.

The Commission also saw social policy as contributing to, rather than hampering, economic efficiency. It argued that social consensus, along with market competition, was a vital ingredient of sustained economic growth and job creation. Obviously, this approach clashed with the basic tenets of right-wing economists who blamed the relative economic stagnation of EC countries during the 1970s and 1980s on the systems of social protection and labour organization associated with the growth of post-war 'welfare states' (Commission 1988 c: 57). The EC's declining proportionate share of international markets, its relative slowness in adjusting to new technologies, and its rapidly growing unemployment problem (see Wise and Gibb 1993: 49-67 and 126-151) were attributed, at least in part, to its extensive social welfare provisions which not only led to high labour costs and reduced competitiveness, but encouraged resistance to change in a world where the ability to adapt rapidly was a key to economic success. Whilst recognizing some elements of truth in these arguments (hence its proposals for greater competition in a single market), the Commission insisted that social policy and 'workers rights' could be used to combat 'Eurosclerosis' rather than aggravate it. In the most general sense, this argument maintains that a contented labour force, given a clear sense of participation in its company, is more likely to generate long-term economic efficiency than one which feels alienated from its employers and prone to disruptive industrial actions. More specifically a 'productive social policy' of the sort envisaged by the authors of the Social Charter could point to things like investment in training and improved working conditions as elements of social policy leading directly to increased economic efficiency. Clearly, the Commission was determined to build a social dimension which not only had a 'moral' foundation based on notions of equity (however difficult to define in precise terms), but which was also rooted in the belief that social policy and economic policy were not in some sort of inevitable conflict or 'zero-sum' game where one could only win at the expense of the other.

Reactions to the Social Charter

In adopting this strategy the Commission enjoyed the broad support of most Member State governments and the European Parliament. The general consensus was that European economic and political unity could not be based simply on laissez-faire competition within a common market. Unbridled competitive forces could engender serious social conflicts and lead employers, employees and the general public to reject the larger objective of European union. Free competition, whilst desirable, had to take place within a market where there were rules to ensure 'fair play' and mitigate social tensions which could create political instability. Thus, in 1988 the socialist French Prime Minister, M. Rocard, confirmed his government's commitment 'to the principles of the free market, tempered by the claims of social justice' (Rocard 1988). Such sentiments are to be expected from a socialist leader but it is important to note that the majority of Member State governments, whatever their political leanings, supported the general contention that the single market should be a single social market. For example, the 'right-wing' conservative government of Germany under Chancellor Kohl accepted the Social Charter like the 'left-wing' socialist government of France under President Mitterrand. Whatever their precise appreciation of the questions involved — and this clearly does vary — they shared a basic 'social market' philosophy common in continental Europe. When the Commission talked of defending and developing a 'European social model' — distinct from those found in the USA, Japan and the communist world — integrating elements of free-market capitalism and welfare-state principles most national governments could respond positively to the general idea, whatever their reservations on particular points. Similarly, when the Greek President of the European Council, addressing the European Parliament in 1988, stressed the need to match the '1992' single economic area with a 'single social area', he struck a responsive chord amongst the majority of MEPs (Commission 1988b: 169). In fact, the European Parliament, with Socialists forming its dominant group in the late 1980s and early 1990s, had espoused the social Europe concept with enthusiasm and was constantly chastizing the Commission, and, more particularly, the Council, for the delay in turning the many EC social policy proposals into legislative action!

British reluctance to accept the Social Charter

However, this general consensus in favour of social Europe amongst the leaders of Community states did not include the British Conservative government of the 1980s and early 1990s. It felt very uncomfortable with what it was apt to dismiss, sometimes with good cause, as vague 'rhetoric'. Moreover, it was more prone to look towards the USA (and in some ways Japan) for 'social models' able to generate economic success. That is why the UK government, unlike all its partners, refused to accept the Social Charter in December 1989, seeing it as a way in which 'bureaucratic, socialist' practices would be reintroduced into Britain by the 'back door of Brussels' (Thatcher 1988). Mrs Thatcher's Conservative government had spent a decade reducing what it saw as excessive trade-union power and government intervention in the economy; it feared that the Social Charter might reverse this process of economic liberalization and deregulation. It felt that employers would become more reluctant to take on workers if they feared a burden of strict legislation on equitable wages, working hours, benefit contributions and so on. Thus, it was argued, the social objective of greater employment would be jeopardized by misguided social policies. Typical British 'Euro-scare' stories were conjured up to reinforce such fears; for example, statements that baby-sitters would require formal contracts of employment whilst boys and girls would be prevented from delivering newspapers were widely circulated in the media!

So, wedded to a strong 'free-market' ideology, the 'Thatcherites' in Britain's Conservative Party rejected the assumptions of the social dumping school. Firm believers in the benefits of market liberalization, deregulation and open competition, they mounted a battery of counter-arguments. What was wrong, they insisted, with investment shifting from high-wage, high-cost economies to those with lower standards? Was there any more efficient way of generating growth and employment on Europe's poorer peripheries? Surely, this was a better way to transfer resources from richer to poorer areas than cumbersome, bureaucratic, interventionist regional policies? Such policies had remarkably little effect on the basic geographical pattern of socio-economic disparities in post-war Europe and cast serious doubts on the efficacy of government intervention in shaping socio-economic outcomes (Wise, Chalkley 1990). Rather than entangle employers and employees in common European legislation, let them compete in social as well as economic terms; if Spanish car workers were prepared to work longer hours for less pay and shorter holidays than their German counterparts in order to attract investment from Volkswagen, why put obstacles in their way?

In the run up to the adoption of the Social Charter this ideological clash between a social protectionist approach and a belief in the virtues of labour market deregulation became increasingly open. The British government, under the dominant leadership of Mrs Thatcher, strongly opposed a series of socially protective proposals from the Commission. While other Member States were prepared to accept the general thrust of these proposals, albeit with modifications, the British adopted an uncompromising stance. Very different ideas on job creation and social justice lay at the heart of this debate. For the UK government, increased employment depended on freeing the labour market from all the rigidities which successive waves of social legislation had built into it, notably in the post-war 'welfare states'. Employers would not employ if discouraged by a deterrent mass of legislation on pay, dismissals, hours of work and so on. During the 'Thatcher era' of the 1980s, such a policy had been vigorously pursued in Britain. The Commission, along with other Member States, agreed that greater flexibility was required in labour markets, but were not prepared to seek this at the expense of rights for workers. Indeed, it hoped to win flexibility by providing employees with sufficient social protection against the fears associated with job loss (Commission 1987).

The opposition of the British government to these social-market initiatives was stiff; even the most unbinding of 'recommendations' were resisted. For example, its attitude to the proposed 'Recommendation on the Reduction of Working Time' can be cited. This recommendation, which had no binding legal force, was put forward in the early 1980s in response to growing unemployment and the perceived need for more work-sharing. However, the UK government, firmly opposed this limited initiative on the grounds that it would be the 'thin end of the wedge' leading to ever more bureaucratic, socialist interference with British labour market procedures (Welsh 1987).

But not simply 'Britain versus the rest' on Social Europe

The British government's refusal to sign the Social Charter and its clear ideological opposition to many of the EC's social policy initiatives often made it seem yet another simple case of Britain fighting a lone 'anti-European' battle. In reality the picture was more complicated. Diverse countries and interest groups in an intricate interrelated network of Community and national institutions sought to impose their views on the many and complicated social issues involved. Just as British governmental opposition to the Social Charter did not represent the views of all in Britain, so the general accord expressed by other national governments did not signify complete unanimity on these social issues elsewhere. In fact there was a fairly widespread feeling that many governments found it convenient to hide behind Britain's (and more especially Mrs Thatcher's) skirt on these questions (Le Monde 1991: 73-8). How convenient to court political favour by making grand declarations of generous social intent in the sure knowledge that the UK government could be counted on to block concrete and potentially costly proposals! A closer look at some of the real complexity which lay behind an excessively simplistic 'Britain versus the Rest' scenario illustrates again the enormous difficulties of translating general social Europe ideals into concrete realities in the developing single market.

The Social Charter and the Left in Britain

The hostile reaction towards the Social Charter emanating from Britain's government and business circles — but not its Trade Unions — was a variation on an old theme. Debates about the European Community in Britain have traditionally been couched in essentially economic terms with a reluctance to get drawn into wider forms of social and political union. Back in the 1950s and 1960s there were innumerable analyses of the potential economic costs and benefits of UK membership. Efforts were made to draw up some kind of gigantic financial balance sheet to help decide whether entry into the Community would make Britain richer or poorer. Issues like the price of food and the business gains to be made from access to a larger market dominated discussion at all levels of society. The widespread use of the term 'Common Market', or insistence on saying European Economic Community, betrayed this propensity to perceive the EC in uni-dimensional economic terms. The '1992' project reinforced this tendency by emphasizing the creation of a single European market, the business opportunities therein and the economic growth it is expected to generate. Only the Liberals and their successors in the Liberal Democratic Party have long felt comfortable with the wider aspirations of the drive towards European unity and the broadly social-market philosophy which was a major guiding force.

However, the Social Charter highlighted a significant change in some British attitudes to the Community. The Labour Party and trade unions in the UK had often been at the forefront of opposition to EC membership from the early 1960s to the late 1980s. But in September 1988, Jacques Delors, President of the European Commission and a prominent member of the French Socialist Party with lengthy ministerial experience, made an address at the annual conference of Britain's Trades Union Congress in Bournemouth (Delors 1988). This event symbolized a sea change in how the majority on the left of UK politics viewed the European Community. Hitherto, perceptions of it being a rich man's capitalist club notorious for such things as 'feather-bedding farmers' at the expense of the poor British consumer and draining investment from Britain's remoter regions into the Common Market's core areas dominated British left-wing attitudes to European integration. However, a shift was taking place towards acceptance that there were social aspirations associated with the moves towards European unity which could help workers within the UK.

Several factors lay behind this change. Many Labour MEPs departed for the European Parliament implacably hostile to the Community, but cooperation with socialist colleagues from other Member States clearly had a 'Europeanizing' effect as the potential benefits of combined European action in the social field became apparent to them. Furthermore, a succession of Conservative electoral victories in the UK from 1979 onwards had been associated with a marked decline in the influence wielded by organized labour in British society. Contact with counterparts from Member States where such things as employee participation in the management of companies was legally ingrained led some to see Community legislation as a means of checking further erosion of trade union and worker rights within the UK. Awareness of the growing inadequacy of national action alone to counter the power of transnational businesses, ever more able to shift investment capital from one country to another in search of labour, also played a role in the change of European mood on the left of British politics. These forces eventually led the Labour Party to abandon its pledge to withdraw from the Community and begin to champion European social causes resisted by the Conservative government. A speech in September 1988 by Mr Kinnock, leader of the Labour Party, to the Socialist Group of the European Parliament clearly marked this strategic change. Echoing sentiments long held by continental colleagues he challenged the view that the single market 'will exclusively and inevitably be an open space for the operation of New Right economics'; he continued:

> Every one of our (socialist) movements in every one of our countries has, by a variety of means... made constant efforts to civilize the operation of markets and make economic activity compatible with human security. In some respects, the relative comfort and safety of modern life is due to the success achieved by socialists and others who realize that life is too important to be left to the dictates of demand and supply. That is the spirit in which we must approach the new scale of market operation. (Kinnock 1988)

Thus, the artificial separation of 'economic', 'social' and 'political' aspects in the process of European integration was slowly beginning to break down in more and more British minds. This conversion to a fuller concept of the 'European idea' was sometimes admitted with extraordinary candour; for example, the Labour MP Bryan Sedgemoor, on the left of the party and erstwhile opponent of the EC, argued to the House of Commons in June 1990 that 'it is time that left-wing members regarded the European Community as a stunning opportunity' (Economist 1990a). Obviously, not all of Mr

Sedgemore's party colleagues, including stalwarts like Tony Benn, shared this enthusiasm. Nevertheless, the statement did reflect a fundamental shift in overall Labour Party thinking. Long-time Labour pro-Europeans were astonished by the change of mood; one of them, Giles Radice, described it as '... one of the most astonishing transformations in British political history...'(Economist 1990a). Liberal Democrats and pro-European Conservatives such as Edward Heath were no longer so isolated as a more comprehensive vision of the Community spread across more of the British political spectrum.

Attitudes of the EC's 'Social Partners' to Social Europe

In explaining the UK government's opposition to the Social Charter (see above), the broad ideological clash confronting those who thought that social interventionism in the economy was essential to promote justice and political-economic harmony with those who believed that it introduced burdens which stifled the economy and, ultimately, social welfare has already been highlighted. Our discussion of attitudes towards the Social Charter on the British Left, not to mention the social-market devotees in Britain's pro-European Centre parties, has already indicated that the broad dividing line between these two camps did not extend neatly down the English Channel. The same big debate, and elaborations of it, ignored national boundaries and can be found to a greater or lesser extent in all Community countries.

For example, major elements of the debate opposing the UK government to the Commission and others (see above) were ritually played out in discussions between what are known as the EC's 'social partners'. Just as employers and employees organize themselves into distinct bodies like the British CBI and TUC at national level, so equivalent EC organizations exist. The main employers' body is the Union of Industries of the European Community (UNICE after its French initials) set up in 1957 before any other at the very onset of the the EEC (those on the Left would think it significant the capital interests were immediately organized to play a Common Market game which suited them!). Its principal task is to seek to influence Community policy-making and inform national members of relevant EC developments. The European Trade Union Congress (ETUC) is the trade union equivalent of UNICE. It was not formed until 1973 (again it is interesting to note the way in which 'labour' followed 'capital' in the usual reactive fashion of 'social' actions responding to those of an 'economic' nature). This body brought together all the socialist and social-democratic trade unions in the EC, with its main members being the German DGB, the French CFDT and the British TUC. However, several major unions remained outside the ETUC, most notably the communist organizations like the CGT in France, the CGIL in Italy and the Spanish Workers Commissions. Despite this fragmentation of the labour response to the EC, those bodies which do belong to ETUC have gradually become more integrated and ready to accept Community action as an awareness has grown that national unions need to cooperate across state borders to defend their interests in a business environment increasingly shaped by multinational companies. The importance of public enterprises has also been recognized by the Community institutions in conferring the status of 'social partner' on the European Committee for Public Enterprises (CEEP) as well. Inside the machinery of Community policy-making these three major social partners — the UNICE, the ETUC and the CEEP — enjoy equal status. In effect, this means that they are represented on the multiplicity of advisory committees which link national governments, interest groups, specialist agencies and others into the overall Community system of government. For example, they will inevitably participate in the deliberations of the Economic and Social Committee as well as more specialist bodies like the Standing Committee on Employment. Moreover, they will also be found on the governing boards of bodies like the European Centre for Vocational Training or the European Foundation for the Improvement of Living and Working Conditions (see Wise and Gibb, 1993: 126-151).

Most importantly, these major representatives of capital, labour and the public sector meet regularly in the so-called 'Val Duchesse talks' where they set up working parties to examine a whole range of socio-economic issues (see Wise and Gibb, 1993: 126-151). When confronted with the Commission's efforts to promote a 'European social space', the reactions of these social partners mirror the disputes that have taken place between the UK and those who are pressing to strengthen Commmunity social policy. Thus, the business leaders of the whole Community list a number of priorities in UNICE's 'Agenda for Europe' which would not offend the thrust of British Conservative Party policy in recent years (Brewster, Teague 1989: 126). First, they echo the UK government's demand for a genuine internal EC market: in the words of their secretary-general they want

> a strong and coherent Community, with its energies directed towards enterprise and innovation and enjoying healthy economic growth upon which depend employment, living standards, working conditions and social security. (Le Monde 1991: 74)

But in line again with British governmental thinking in the 1980s they firmly resist the Commission's drive to build social policies to complement it. Instead they urge the creation of a more favourable climate for enterprise, a reduced burden of 'social' legislation on employers, a general 'rolling back' of state intervention to liberate entrepreneurial energies and so on. Finding the term 'social dumping' devoid of meaning, they rejected most proposals to harmonize or coordinate social policies across the Community (except in certain very limited fields like occupational health and safety); again the words of its Secretary-General would not sound out of place in the mouth of a British Conservative politician:

> let the accent be on dialogue and adaptability. Centralization, harmonization and European legislation in the social field would create new rigidities and further reduce our ability to compete and pay for the society we want. (quoted in Brewster, Teague 1989: 127)

Predictably, the response of the ETUC to the '1992' and social Europe programmes in the Val Duchesse talks and other Community bodies is very different. Whilst accepting the single market objective, albeit with more reservations than UNICE, it argues that a European social dimension is essential for all the reasons that have already been rehearsed above. Thus, whilst many employers across Europe wanted local wage settlements, the ETUC pressed for collective bargaining at a European level if necessary. Whilst European company leaders sought to reduce the constraints of social legislation, European union leaders advocated a growth of Community-wide regulation to protect workers in the new, competitive single market. The Social Charter was very much a reflection of ETUC aspirations.

So the enduring confrontation between UNICE and ETUC over the Community's economic and social dimensions in the Val Duchesse context was very similar to the battle that the UK government had with the Community on the same issues, but it reveals that the real argument behind some very generalized public rhetoric was by no means a simple nationalistic one of 'Britain versus the Rest'. In the more concealed and serious debate in the many corridors of Community power, the evidence up to the present suggests that employers have been more successful than trades unionists in defending their interests in the Community's decision-making system. Thus the programme to create a single market has surged ahead on the basis of concrete EC law, whilst the proposals to build a social Europe have dragged behind and encounter the utmost difficulty in being translated into legislative action. There is nothing new about this as a brief examination of the fate of the Commission's so-called 'Vredeling Directive' illustrates.

This proposed Directive, which first appeared in formal draft form in 1980, was designed to guarantee a basic right for employees to be informed and consulted about company policy which might affect their working lives (see Wise and Gibb, 1993; 126-151). As such it fell into a long-established effort by the Commission to develop a 'European social model' managing economic activity. The employers in UNICE were extremely hostile to the proposal, whereas the ETUC was emphatic in its support (Brewster, Teague 1989:133-7). The latter argued that Community legislation was urgently required, given the scale of industrial restructuring that was being effected by multinationals across Europe and often entailing dramatic job losses (see Wise and Gibb, 1993: 200-238). However, the ability of ETUC to mobilize support for its case was far outweighed by the forces which UNICE was able to muster. National employers' organizations like the CBI employed all their lobbying skills to block the Directive; even the German employers' federation, used to worker consultation procedures, rejected the Directive. Furthermore, the leaders of American and Japanese multinationals, which would be much affected by Vredeling's proposal, mounted an enormous campaign to stop it. For example, the Commission was directly threatened with a reduction of US and Japanese investment in the EC if this proposal became law. Similar pressure was applied to all the other public and private pressure points in the Community system of decision. Despite its best efforts, the ETUC could not marshall its members so effectively, nor did it enjoy the same financial resources. Thus when the issue was debated in the European Parliament, a journalist was able to describe the following scene:

> On Tuesday taxis swept up to the Parliament building bearing the most formidable galaxy of professional lobbyists Strasbourg has seen... (whereas)... the union lobby consisted of a couple of pleasant individuals from the European TUC handing out leaflets. (quoted in Brewster, Teague 1989:136).

As a result of all this pressure, an important element of the attempt to construct a European social space to match its fast-integrating economic space was indefinitely shelved. Those wanting to enlarge the EC's social dimension will have to find ways of becoming as effective in Community politics as those moulding its economic shape.

Attitudes to Social Europe in the European Parliament

One body which has increasingly been looked to in order to find ways of strengthening the EC's social dimension is the European Parliament, long the 'poor relation' of the Council-Commission-Parliament institutional trio at the head of the Community's political system. A survey of Parliamentary attitudes to EC social policy initiatives provides further elaboration of how the single market-social Europe issue is seen across the Community. Whatever the real limitations of this democratically-elected forum, its public debates clearly reveal the divergences and convergences of interest which are also played out in the more confidential confines of the Commission and Council as well as the Community's intricate network of committees meshing national and sectional bodies into the EC system.

The EP is widely regarded as a 'talking shop' with little power to influence the critical policy-making dialogue between the Commission and the Community's final decision-making body, the Council of Ministers. However, whatever its relative marginality to the key centres of EC power, its ability to mould Community policy has been steadily growing (Wise and Gibb, 1993: 1-48) and is far from negligible; about 50 per cent of its amendments to policy proposals now find their way into the finally adopted Community law and this proportion is likely to increase (Lodge 1989a: 58-83; Pinder 1991: 34-9).

Those wanting a strong Community social policy have often criticized the Parliament's past performance (Le Monde 1991: 75) and lamented its failure or reluctance to provide effective support for the various social Europe initiatives during the 1970s and 1980s (see Wise and Gibb, 1993: 126-151 and discussion of the Vredeling Directive, above). However, the much publicized '1992' programme to create a single market sparked off a major movement in the EP to reinvigorate the idea of a complementary EC social space. The Socialists, who already formed the largest EP grouping, led this revolt against what they saw as the unbalanced 'Thatcherite' liberalism underpinning the single market initiative, but MEPs from other parties (for example those of a Christian-Democratic tradition) also supported this effort to balance 'economic' and 'social' aspects of EC policy. This pressure helped lead to the Commission's proposal for a Community Charter of the Fundamental Social Rights of Workers (the so-called Social Charter) even though the Parliament was largely ignored during its final formulation in 1989. However, it was consulted on the Commission's action plan to draw up specific proposals to put the Social Charter into effect. In due course the EP's Committee on Social Affairs, Employment and the Working Environment produced the so called van Velzen report on this action plan (European Parliament 1990a). This report, which was eventually adopted by a majority vote in the Parliament, represented an enthusiastic endorsement of the most comprehensive kind of social Europe concept. Typical of its numerous demands was one which wanted the Commission to propose, by the end of 1990, a Directive 'on the reduction of working hours with a view to a 35 hour week'.

Furthermore, it demanded that the fate of this Directive should be decided by the Council on the basis of qualified majority voting (Article 118a of the EEC Treaty amended by the SEA) so that a small minority of Member States opposed to such measures could not block a measure acceptable to most countries (the UK Conservative government was clearly uppermost in many minds on this point). Amongst the mass of demands there were many others destined to provoke criticism that the social engineering aspects of the report reflected obsolete utopian ways of thought; for example, the call 'to ensure that at least half those receiving aid from the European Social Fund are women' might be motivated by the best of intentions, but the bureaucratic costs of trying to implement what some would reject as a sexist measure would doubtless be high and of dubious efficacy.

The plenary session debates in the European Parliament obviously reflected the usual ideological divisions on the issue with those on the Left making pleas to implement the Social Charter with the same sense of urgency being applied to the single market programme; as the words of Mr McMahon illustrate, none were more passionate than Labour MEPs from-supposedly isolated Britain:

> The social dimension is important. It is particularly important for those who come from the United Kingdom where trade union rights are being denied, where workers are being sacked in the North Sea (sic) because they are fighting for safety and trade union organization. In the city of London people are sleeping in cardboard boxes because of the social policies of the (UK) government supported by Lord O'Hagan and his friends.... When we see what has happened in the United Kingdom in the last eleven years, my God how we need a social dimension! We need Europe to come like the cavalry to the rescue. (European Parliament 1990c: 222)

Although Lord O'Hagan, a British Conservative MEP, was personally attacked in McMahon's speech, he actually exemplifies the point that many towards the Right in the EP did not reject the social Europe concept with the vehemence of many of their national counterparts; he declared:

> I am strongly in favour of the single market but a single social market. You cannot have a single social market without legislation to help workers and to help citizens. (European Parliament 1990c: 32)

His major criticism of the approach adopted by the Socialist group in the Parliament — shared by others on the moderate Right — was that its proposals were too many and often too impracticable to have any hope of success. Rather than drawing up vast plans of action with little sense of priority a more methodical pursuit of a limited number of precise pieces of legislation appropriate for the European level 'would actually affect and alter the lives of our citizens'; thus:

> This Parliament is not adapting to the modern requirements of what we are meant to be doing in the new emerging European Community where we have to have a social market to make 1992 work. (European Parliament 1990c: 221)

Others towards the Right shared similar views. Thus Mr Suarez Gonzalez, a Christian-Democrat MEP from Spain noted

> the curious spectacle of how dissatisfied the liberals (ie, non-socialists) feel with what the Commission is doing on social issues. I am not referring to the position of the more ideologically interventionist, more equalizing, more progressive sectors — if I may use these terms — but to liberal thinking in today's Europe. There is unanimity in the Parliament that the Commission really must stop fussing about empty terminology and get down to harmonizing social legislation....The workers of Europe are not going to believe it is so difficult to make the effort over social harmonization when they see even the width of lawnmower wheels being harmonized. (European Parliament 1990b: 185)

Of course behind the assumed 'unanimity' referred to in the above extract there were sharp divergences of opinion behind the general feeling that some sort of EC social policy was required. Indeed speeches that would have been warmly endorsed by British Conservative ministers were made by MEPs from a number of Community countries. For example, M. Le Chevallier from France criticized the drawing up of lengthy catalogues of social proposals which allowed the Parliament 'to indulge its demagogic fanaticism' and which took 'no account...of the state of social legislation in the different Member States, which prevents harmonization aligned with the highest standards if the social budgets of some Member States are not to explode' (European Parliament 1990b: 87). Others expressed reservations which were akin to those emanating from the UK government and employers' organizations like UNICE. Mr Nielson of Denmark stressed that it was 'crucial' to 'respect the different approaches and traditions in the Member States'; thus for example:

> Wages and working hours are some of the matters upon which...the Community has no powers to take decisions. In some countries they are settled by legislation. In Denmark we have a long-standing tradition by which the two sides of industry negotiate agreements on them. It is important to uphold this principle, because the agreements impose a system of joint responsibility....The Community cannot and must not take over this role. We must respect different traditions and hold back from any action to centralize and bureaucratize the decision-making process. We must have flexibility. It is essential to avoid decisions on matters of detail within the Community framework. (European Parliament 1990c: 36)

Whilst some Danish MEPs were worried that the consequences of the Social Charter would disrupt their national system of labour relations and threaten their ability to compete (talk of an imposed 35-hour week horrified them as much as conservatives and liberals in other Member States), others were worried that harmonized Community social policy might undermine their 'Nordic model' of social welfare. Mr Sandbaek of the EP's 'Rainbow' group was very emphatic on this point. After explaining the distinctiveness of Denmark's social security system based on high taxation financing generous benefits 'not tied to employment record', he insisted:

We will not in any circumstances accept a situation in which rights and entitlements under Danish agreements can be set aside by an EC Court in Luxembourg. If there are to be common rules, it must be clearly and unequivocally stated that they are minimum rules, under which all countries are free to go further in the direction of social protection. We will never approve a procedure under which EC Directives can invalidate our own standards. (European Parliament 1990c: 30)

Then, in a direct reference to the drive to eliminate national barriers in the single market, he stated

The most immediate threat to the Nordic model, however, is the planned abolition of the frontier between Denmark and West Germany, which will make it impossible to collect the higher taxes and duties needed to fund our system of social provision. We therefore want the frontier to be maintained. (European Parliament 1990c: 30)

This belief that harmonization of social security at EC level was not essential in the single market was supported by a Danish academic analysis which concluded:

Neither the analysis of the principle of subsidiarity, nor the analysis of the 'social dumping' argument call for extended social security decision-making at Community level. The extent to which an ex-ante harmonization of social security is required for the effective operation of a single market seems to be smaller than is often thought. (Petersen 1991: 513)

Whilst many Danes, and others in wealthy northern countries, feared that the Community might dilute their social security systems, MEPs from southern Europe saw social Europe as another means to transfer resources to the EC's peripheries in order to improve living conditions. Thus, Mr Ephremidis, a Greek from the Left Unity group, spoke of the urgency of implementing a social programme to match the single market and so avoid political disruption; failure to do so would place 'a time-bomb.. underneath this union which will explode, in the form of social upheaval'; he continued:

I wish to refer to a specific example of what is happening in my country: for three months the government has been butchering social security rights, the right to a decent wage for workers, and is even blocking their demands and their industrial action by resorting to the courts, labelling them untimely, illegal and so forth. (European Parliament 1990c: 37)

Irish voices from the Community's northwestern periphery echoed the sentiments of their southern brethren at the bottom end of the EC's socio-economic welfare ladder. Mr de Rossa of the EP's Left Unity group was one of many who accused their national governments of mouthing soothing sentiments on social Europe to soften the harder edges of the single market programme, whilst in reality they were happy to hide behind the UK government's outspoken opposition to it; thus:

Few issues have generated as much hypocrisy as this one has. From the outset it has been used as a placebo to placate workers and their representatives and lead them to believe that they were not being left behind in the drive towards the single market.

The final version of the (Social) Action Programme was a pale shadow of what it could have been. What was worthwhile of what remained was optional and unlikely to be implemented. And even at that, the timetable was too vague and constantly edged off the agenda by commercial aspects of the single market project....

It is clear from their own briefing document that the strategy of the Irish Government was to dilute and stall on the Social Charter Action Programme behind the scenes but not to take 'too prominent a defensive posture' in public lest they be accused of 'reneging on the agreement' and of 'sharing the ideological position of the UK'. (European Parliament 1990c: 223-4)

Mr de Rossa was in no doubt about what needed to be done to turn social Europe rhetoric into some form of reality:

Irish and European trade unions need to get their acts together to counter the more successful efforts of employer organizations to dilute and delay the Action Programme on the Social Charter....It is time that the Left majority in this Parliament who (sic) genuinely supports a worthwhile Social Charter decided to withdraw support for other aspects of the legislative programme until firm guarantees are given on the content and implementation of the Action Programme. The Trade Union movement needs to raise the level of awareness of employees concerning the impact of an internal market without a social dimension on their job security and working conditions. Only when industrial policy and social policy is as much an election issue as the common agricultural policy will governments and the Council take it seriously. (European Parliament 1990c: 223)

Thus, debates in the European Parliament reflected a range of diverging and converging interests over the Community's social dimension which tended to be hidden by the UK government's much publicized refusal to sign the Social Charter accepted by all the other Member States. However, the majority of MEPs expressed dismay, even anger, that the Commission's Action Programme, designed to give precise substance to the Charter's general aims, was meeting such resistance in the Council of Ministers. There was also harsh criticism of a Commission that was seen as being far too weak in pressing for its objectives. The Parliament's Report on the Commission's Social Action Programme (European Parliament 1990a) deliberately outlined 'almost 100 concrete proposals' thought necessary to supplement the Commission's proposals and produce a 'worthy counterpart to the (1992) White Paper' (European Parliament 1990c: 26). It also wanted such a programme to be decided in the Council of Ministers by an extended use of the qualified majority voting procedure (as for the single market programme) rather than allow individual Member States to block progress by insistence on unanimity: in other words, the procedures laid down in Articles 100A and 118A of the SEA. MEPs were perfectly aware that the Council's readiness to adopt majority voting for single market measures (although key areas like taxation and monetary union were exempt from this procedure) was not matched when it came to social policy proposals.

The greater reticence of Member States to concede national sovereignty in the social as opposed to the economic dimension of EC policy was noted elsewhere by the EP. The rapporteur of an EP Committee report on the social action programme noted the enthusiasm with which national governments supported the EC's 'subsidiarity' principle (ie., devolving government functions to the lowest appropriate level) when it came to social policy, but their lack of interest in it when economic matters were at stake:

> There is incidently something strange about the concept of subsidiarity, for the emotion with which it is referred to in discussions about the social dimension is in stark contrast with the lack thereof in discussions about economic and monetary subjects. As though the orientation of the economy might not be extremely decisive for the culture of a Member State. (European Parliament 1990c: 26)

Mr van Velzen detected the same inequality of approach concerning competition policy. He criticized what he saw as a tendency of the Commission and Council to apply EC competition laws in a purely 'economic' context without reference to social policy. This was unfortunate because:

> In my view, competition ought to be fair and in no way should social policy be used as an instrument for acquiring a stronger competitive position. At the present time major differences in social policies very often obscure the competition situation. I would therefore urge those people who find the concept of competition important to view it in relationship to sound instruments in social policy. (European Parliament 1990c: 26)

However, despite this majority Parliamentary pressure to promote the social Europe concept, the implementation of the single market project sped ahead at a far greater pace. In late 1991 the Commission was able to report that of the 282 measures in the single market programme well over 200 had been adopted by the Council, using qualified majority voting to get quick decisions, and that 168 were in force. This was five years after the 1985 White Paper, three years after the entry into force of the SEA and one year ahead of the '1992' deadline. In stark contrast, the Community's social action programme flowing out of the SEA and the Social Charter was limping along extremely slowly. By mid-1991 the Commission had drawn up a mere 18 concrete proposals out of the 48 envisaged in the social action programme (Commission 1991a). These measures encountered stiff resistance in the Council of Ministers, particularly from the UK. This resistance focused on both the substance of the proposals (see above) and the means of deciding upon them. Whilst some were prepared to accept that qualified majority voting should be the norm in the social policy area (as for much of the single market), others, led pugnaciously by the British government, were insisting on unanimous agreement in the Council before social measures could be passed. Thus, as the end of 1991 approached, there was virtually nothing of substance related to the Social Charter converted into concrete EC legislation (Economist 1991: 80). The contrast between a 'fast track' approach to the single market and a 'reluctant crawl' towards social Europe could not have been sharper.

Broad principles and specific provisions in EC social policy

We have seen that divergences over the Community social policy cannot be oversimplified into a question of 'Britain versus the Rest'. However, it is a fact that the British Conservative government of the 1980s and early 1990s led the campaign against what some saw as the excessive centralization of social policies at European level. Its particularly strong stance in this regard was highlighted by its solitary refusal to sign the Social Charter. Whatever the detailed substance of each debate about a proposed EC social measure the British style stood out in clear ideological opposition. This distinctive British governmental approach to EC social policy — and other Community matters — could also be detected in another significant way. Whereas most Member States were happy to sketch out broad visions and then get down to the somewhat messier, conflict-ridden process of working towards them, the British tended to be dismissive of such grand general schemes. For example, Mrs Thatcher — then Prime Minister — had her continental counterparts reaching for their advanced English dictionaries when she described their plans to move towards a single currency as belonging to the realm of 'cloud-cuckoo-land' (Economist 1990b: 57). Her reaction was true to a long-standing British tradition (deeply ingrained in both major parties) of discomfort in face of the big 'European idea'; hence the failure to join the various European Communities in 1950 and 1957, the refusal to join the European Monetary System fully in 1979 and, of course, the rejection of the Social Charter in 1989.

Those states signing the Social Charter were more ready than Britain to set grand general objectives and then negotiate specific policy details afterwards. They were happy to accept the broad principles within it before dealing with the concrete proposals of the Commission's Social Action Programme that was to follow. Commitment to a broad ideal did not prevent them bargaining hard over the precise shape of particular policies and attempting to employ the Community principle of 'subsidiarity' to their own national advantage. This latter principle, much promulgated by the Commission, states that the Community only seeks to take common action when set objectives (in this case those of the Charter) can be reached more effectively at European rather than national, regional or local level. Of course, there will always be argument about what is the most 'effective level' for action; but most accept this as the normal democratic process to be pursued within the Social Charter's broad guidelines. Nobody expected that this process would be easy, given the enormous diversity of national, regional and sectoral traditions within Europe's would-be 'social space'. Even the notion of 'subsidiarity', seen as a way of recognizing the varied socio-economic geography of the Community and refuting the charge of excessive centralization, is challenged by those who preferred the concept of 'complementarity'. This latter idea envisages cooperation between different levels of government in the pursuit of social aims, rather than a neat division of labour between them.

Harmonization or mutual recognition in the field of social policy?

More fundamentally, there was also the question of whether EC social policy should be based on the principle of 'harmonization' rather than that of 'mutual recognition'. Traditionally, the Commission's approach to such issues had been to seek a harmony of national practices. However, this tactic had yielded few results in the social field, or indeed any other, as proposals proved unable to make headway against a diversity of national practices and interests. So the Commission had switched progressively to the idea of mutual recognition of national systems, subject to a minimum standard acceptable across the Community. This strategy, adopted in the drive to create a single market (see Wise and Gibb, 1993: 68-103) could also be applied in the effort to create a European 'social space'. In 1986, the Belgian presidency of the Council of Ministers put forward the idea of building up a 'minimum body of Community social provisions' to prevent such things as 'social dumping' in the single market (Commission 1988c: 61-2). This would involve agreement on a package of basic social rights which national systems would eventually have to accept, but not try to enforce complete harmonization across the very varied economic and social circumstances. This was increasingly seen as undesirable as well as impossible in such a diverse Community.

One such 'basic right' would require formal procedures to ensure that employees are consulted about the affairs of the company in which they work. This obligation could be met and elaborated upon in a variety of ways depending on national, regional, local or sectoral conditions. In other words, the Commission 'argues in favour of developing the social dialogue to allow better management of the diversity and flexibility of situations' (Commission 1988d: 8). So, following agreement on such fundamental principles, Member States could mutually recognize their different practices, and workers moving from country to country would have to accept them. Of course, even agreement on such principles is not easy; in 1989, Britain refused to accept those incorporated in the Social Charter despite their general character. But the other Member States were able to accept its broad guidelines more easily, expecting that they could then negotiate within them to produce a complex blend of Community harmonization and national mutual recognition of social policies operating at different levels. Indeed, the Commission set up a steering group of the so-called 'social partners' (ETUC, UNICE and CEEP — see above) in 1989 and invited them to formulate some proposals on employee participation in company affairs (Le Monde 1991: 74). Following the almost symbolic 'top down' gesture of the Social Charter, the Commission was trying to trigger off a 'bottom up' process whereby those directly concerned devise acceptable forms of workers' consultation in companies which could then form the basis of EC legislation.

Implementation of the Social Charter

The Charter was not a detailed set of European regulations that were to be imposed on the Member States by 'Eurocrats in Brussels'. Indeed, the Charter itself stated that:

> It is more particularly the responsibility of the Member States, in
> accordance with national practices, notably through legislative measures
> or collective agreements, to guarantee the fundamental social rights in this

> Charter and to implement the social measures indispensable to the smooth operation of the internal market as part of the strategy of economic and social cohesion. (Commission 1990a: 20)

In language which clearly indicated the will not to relinquish all control of social policy to Community institutions, the Charter also requires that the Commission

> submit as soon as possible initiatives which fall within its powers...with a view to the adoption...as and when the internal market is completed...of those (social) rights which come within the Community's area of competence. (Commission 1990a: 20)

Thus, within this restraining framework, which once again explicitly linked progress on creation of a European social space to success in completing the single market, the Commission began the process of drawing up concrete proposals to give effect to the Charter. This process is a dynamic one that still has far to go, but a selective indication of what is to come can be given under the main headings of the Charter (Commission 1990d).

1. Freedom of movement

In order to guarantee every worker the right to freedom of movement throughout the Community, the Commission would continue its efforts to eliminate obstacles arising from such things as non-recognition of qualifications and inability to avail themselves of social security benefits when they move from one country to another.

2. Employment and remuneration

To ensure, amongst other things, that workers, 'in accordance with arrangements applying in each country', receive 'a wage sufficient to enable them to have a decent standard of living', the Commission will propose a Directive setting minimum requirements for part-time working, fixed-term working, casual work, etc.

3. Improvement of living and working conditions

In order that 'the conditions of employment of every worker of the European Community shall be stipulated in laws, a collective agreement or a contract of employment', the Commission would propose a Directive to require written proof of an employment contract. Part of such a contract would give the 'right to a weekly rest period and to annual paid leave, the duration of which must be progressively harmonized in accordance with national practices'.

4. Social protection

To ensure that 'every worker shall have the right to adequate social protection...and enjoy an adequate level of social security benefits', the Commission would make a 'Recommendation on convergence of Member States' objectives in regard to social protection'.

5. *Freedom of association and collective bargaining*

To protect the rights of employers and workers 'to constitute professional organizations or trade unions of their choice for the defence of their economic and social interests', as well as 'the right to strike, subject to the obligations arising under national regulations', the Commission would insist on developing 'the dialogue between both sides of industry at European level' and produce 'a communication on their role in collective bargaining, including collective agreements at European level'.

6. *Vocational training*

The Commission would, amongst other things, propose measures to meet a basic requirement of the Charter that 'every worker of the European Community ...have access to vocational training...throughout his working life'.

7. *Equal treatment for men and women*

To assure 'equal treatment' and develop 'equal opportunities' for both sexes, as well as enabling them 'to reconcile their occupational and family obligations', the Commission would prepare a third action programme on equal opportunities for women, make recommendations on the protection of working women during pregnancy, maternity leave, child care and so on before drawing up relevant legislative proposals.

8. *Information, consultation and participation of workers*

To achieve the Charter's requirement that 'information, consultation and participation of workers must be developed along appropriate lines', the Commission would draw up proposals relating especially to workers in undertakings of European or transnational scale as well as proposals on equity sharing and financial participation by employees.

9. *Health protection and safety at the workplace*

To ensure that 'every worker must enjoy satisfactory health and safety conditions in his working environment, the Commission would propose minimum health and safety requirements in a range of sectors so as to achieve further harmonization of conditions in this area while maintaining the improvements made'.

10. *Protection of children and adolescents*

In order to achieve the Charter's aim of ensuring that young people are not used as cheap labour to the detriment of their education and training, the Commission, 'without prejudice to rules as may be more favourable to young people...(and)...subject to derogations limited to certain light work', would propose a Directive 'approximating the laws of the Member States on the protection of young people in regard to employment' which insisted, amongst other things, that 'the minimum employment age must not be lower than the minimum school-leaving age and, in any case, not lower than 15 years'.

11. *Elderly persons*

To ensure that every retired worker must have sufficient resources to afford 'him or her a decent standard of living' as well as 'medical and social assistance specifically suited to his or her needs', the Commission would propose an action programme to support pilot projects, exchanges of information, etc., and highlight the problems involved by organizing a 'Year of the Elderly' in 1993.

12. Disabled persons

To attain the Charter's objective of entitling 'all disabled persons . . . to additional concrete measures aimed at improving their social and professional integration', the Commission would prepare a third Community action programme on integration and equality of opportunity for the disabled, including a Directive to promote better travel possibilities for workers with disabilities hindering their mobility.

This selective outline of the Commission's strategy to implement the Charter highlights some crucial points. First, there was no intention of trying to centralize all aspects of social policy at Community level; there were numerous references to the need to respect national practices and so on. Secondly, much of the action envisaged at EC level was designed to encourage rather than compel movement towards more coordinated policies. Hence, the plans to have a 'Year of the Elderly', to set up a 'European agency' to provide scientific and technical support in the fields of safety, hygiene and health at work, to establish an 'employment observatory' for the Community to forecast trends in labour supply and demand with a view towards marrying workers and jobs more effectively across the single market, and so on. Thirdly, where the Commission did believe that Community law was required, it usually formulated its legislative proposals in the form of a Directive rather than a more rigid Regulation. Whereas EC Regulations are directly enforceable laws, identically formulated and applicable throughout all the Member States without the need for any intervening national laws, Directives are more flexible and allow account to be taken of different national traditions and varied socio-economic conditions. Although they are also legally binding, they lay down the intended results of EC legislation, leaving it to individual Member State governments to produce the precise national laws by which these aims will be achieved. Thus, a Directive may lay down minimum health and safety standards to be attained in workplaces throughout the Community, but allow each individual state government to devise the most appropriate local means of achieving the common end. It is important to grasp this element of spatial flexibility in the Community's legal structure, which helps mitigate criticisms of a monolithic centralist mentality in Brussels insensitive to geographical variety. Other elements of the Commission's action plan to implement the Social Charter were based on Recommendations and Opinions, for example in the fields of child care and the progress of countries towards ensuring an 'equitable wage'. These Community instruments are not legally binding, but are designed to put political pressure on governments to move towards Community objectives.

Thus, implementation of the Charter is not going to be some simple process of 'imposing' social policy on Member States from an all-powerful Community bureaucracy in Brussels. Obviously, the process of putting it into effect is going to be long and hard with many opposing viewpoints emanating from different groups in all Member States. Furthermore, there is no guarantee that its objectives will be achieved. It was not long before this became apparent.

Proposals for part-time and temporary workers

In the summer of 1990 the Commission presented three draft Directives to eliminate 'distortions of competition' within the Community arising from the different entitlements of part-time and temporary workers in different countries (Local Government 1990a). The basic principle underlying the Commission's proposals was that there should be a Community framework ensuring a minimum of consistency between the various forms of open-ended contracts in the different Member States. This meant: first, employers should have to bear the same types of costs (obviously the actual sums would differ from country to country) when they employ part-time and temporary workers; secondly, that there should be movement towards the best practice in Europe rather than a reduction in standards. The aim was to prevent employers in one country from undercutting prices and tenders of employers in another country by treating this particular group of workers markedly less well than elsewhere in the Common Market. To this end, the draft proposals required:

> the elimination of provisions leading to unfair competition (differences in social protection of part-time workers, paid leave, etc.);
> that workers in part-time and temporary employment should have the same access to vocational training, social services and so on as those enjoyed by full-time workers employed for an indefinite duration;
> that such workers should also be taken into account in the setting up of workers' representative bodies;
> that any clauses preventing the conclusion of a contract of employment for temporary work should be made null and void;
> that such workers enjoy the same health and safety conditions as other workers and not normally used for work requiring special medical provision.

Apart from the health and safety proposals, these provisions would also apply to seasonal workers, but not to those who worked for less than eight hours a week (those employing children to deliver newspapers in Britain could relax!).

The response of the UK government to these proposals was predictably hostile, given its ideological commitment to reducing governmental intervention in workplace activities (see above). It argued that by increasing employers' costs as well as the administrative burdens of 'needless regulations', the number of part-time and temporary staff in the UK would be reduced along with labour market flexibility. In a memorandum to this effect, the Department of Employment also maintained that the proposal would thus discriminate against women and the disabled who form a large part of the part-time/temporary workforce; a pointed riposte to the claim that such measures were designed to protect such exposed sections of the workforce (Local Government 1990a). The British government also challenged the legal basis of the Commission's claim that such measures should be adopted by qualified majority vote in the Council of Ministers (Article 21 of the SEA: see above). In its view, issues relating to the rights and interests of employees should be subjected to unanimous voting in the Council.

As these proposals were put forward in 1990 there were more than 14 million part-time and some 10 million temporary employees in the Community, making up nearly a quarter of the employed population (ie, excluding employers, self-employed and family workers). Britain had the third largest proportion — 29 per cent — of its workforce in this category and they had a relatively poor deal in comparison with 'best practice' in the Community. For example, if applied in the UK, the proposals would require a reduction in the qualification period for entitlement to employment protection rights. Furthermore, all workers working more than eight hours per week would be brought into the National Insurance system however little they earned. In addition, there would have to be equal rights of access to non-wage benefits at work such as training.

Although, the British government and many employers resisted these proposals, the Trades Union Congress (TUC) supported them. In its view it was not simply a matter of granting basic rights, but encouraging the development of a skilled workforce. It argued that the crisis in the British labour market related to lack of skills and low productivity. Any move towards mitigating a two-tier labour market by establishing equal rights of training and employment conditions was to be welcomed. There were plenty of sources of cheap labour and goods outside of the Community, including in Eastern Europe; why encourage the growth of industries based on cheap labour within the single market? This approach was in tune with those prevalent in the Commission and most Member State governments felt that the future of the EC lay in developing highly-skilled, highly-productive and highly-paid workforces, although there were obviously divergences of view to be found right across the Community.

Proposals on working time

Similar arguments met other proposals flowing out of the Commission's Action Programme to implement the Social Charter. For example, in July 1990 the Commission presented a draft Directive on working time which aimed to provide workers with a basic 'safety net' for daily and weekly periods of leave (Local Government 1990b: 11). In summary, the proposals required a minimum daily rest period of 11 out of 24 hours; a least one rest day a week; night workers should not work more than 8 hours in 24 and be forbidden overtime. Certain exceptions would be allowed, mainly in seasonal work, provided that compensatory leave was granted within reference periods of less than 6 months. Other exemptions would include farmers, some long-haul transport workers and those in sections of the oil industry.

Despite the far from radical character of these proposals, with flexibility built in to take account of special cases, the British government once again led the the attack on them by arguing that they would be too rigid and add to costs. Unlike other Member States, the UK had no statutory regulations on working times, believing that these were matters best left for negotiations between employers and employees (Table 6). The fact that the UK had the highest proportion of night and shift workers in the Community and would find itself under pressure to make legal changes intensified the government's resistance. The Commission pointed out that no amendments to national legislation would be required as long as local collective bargaining agreements upheld the Directive's provisions, but the familiar criticisms of costly centralized bureaucracy persisted in British governmental and business circles, highlighting an opposition which was not entirely restricted to Britain.

Table 6.   **Statutory regulation of working time in EC states 1991.**

Country	Working Week	Overtime	Nightwork
Belgium	40 hours	65 hours per 3 months	20.00-06.00
Denmark	no legislation	governed by collective agreement	no legislation
Germany	48 hours	2 hours/day for up to 30 days/year	20.00-06.00
Greece	5-day week 40 hours in private ind.	3 hours/day 18 hrs/week 150hrs/year	22.00-07.00
Spain	40 hours	80 hours/year	22.00-06.00
France	39 hours	9 hrs/week 130 hrs/year	22.00-06.00
Ireland	48 hours	2 hours/day 12 hrs/week 240 hrs/year	no legislation
Italy	48 hours	no legislation	24.00-06.00
Luxembourg	40 hours	2 hours/day	No general legislation nursing mothers & pregnant women 22.00-06.00
Netherlands	48 hours	0.5 to 3.5 hours/days	20.00-07.00
Portugal	48 hours	2 hours/day 160hrs/year	20.00-07.00
UK	no legislation	no legislation	no legislation

Source: Commission 1991b.

On the other hand, the European Trade Union Confederation (ETUC), reflecting views also prevalent amongst representatives of labour in the UK, strongly criticized the Commission's proposals as an 'empty shell' (Local Government International Bureau 1990b: 11). It felt that the Commission was too concerned to avoid confrontation with the British government by setting unambitious objectives and being excessively flexible about the need for legislative changes. Thus, it was trying to persuade the European Parliament to amend the Commission's proposals by introducing more restrictive rules such as a maximum working day of 8 hours within a maximum working week of 40 hours. In all Member States except Britain, limits were already set at this level or were even stricter, so the Commission's proposals did little to move towards 'best practice'. The ETUC was also concerned by the large number of exceptions in the draft Directive, feeling that they should be negotiated between the relevant management and union representatives rather than defined by an EC law.

Proposals on pregnant workers and maternity leave

Predictably, in the autumn of 1990, a proposed Directive to protect pregnant women at work and those who had recently given birth again provoked the usual hostile response from the British government (Commission 1990e; Local Government 1990c:10). This measure was designed to entitle pregnant workers to at least 14 weeks of leave on full pay with no loss of pay or promotion prospects. Employers would have to find alternatives to night work for such women, who would also be exempt from work in the fortnight before birth. If employers decided to extend night work beyond the minimum of 14 weeks, they would have to pay 80 per cent of the full wages. Amongst other things, these proposals would entail a substantial increase in entitlement to paid leave in Britain. Under UK law pregnant workers were entitled to only 6 weeks of maternity leave on 90 per cent of full pay, a further 12 weeks on an agreed reduced sum and, subject to the approval of the employer, a further 22 weeks without remuneration. In relation to existing UK practice, the draft Directive would also greatly relax the conditions relating to unfair dismissal due to pregnancy. Thus, the Conservative government condemned the proposal on the grounds that it would increase costs and discourage employers from taking on young women staff. In its view, far from improving female rights, it would reduce employment and consequently discriminate against women! The Labour opposition, in contrast, deplored what it saw as yet another isolated and backward British stand on such matters.

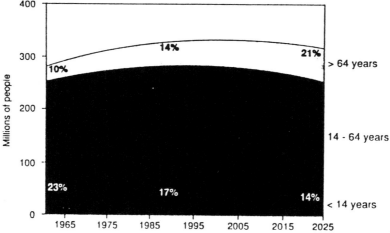

Figure 3   **Evolution of the EC's demographic structure, 1961-2025**
(*Source*: Commission, 1988f).

The Commission, as usual, tried to strengthen the moral basis of its social proposals by appeals to economic logic as well. It pointed out that only 1 per cent of the 52 million female workers in the Community were pregnant at any one time, so costs would not be raised unduly. Furthermore, it related the initiative to falling birth rates and shortages of skilled labour in the EC (Fig 3 and 4). Most Member States had fertility rates below replacement level and some were heading rapidly towards absolute population decline; for example, the population in former West Germany was expected to shrink from 61 million to 47 million by 2030, a drop of nearly a quarter (Financial Times 1990). Similar trends were discernable elsewhere, even in the 'Catholic' southern Mediterranean countries such as Italy and Spain. Such major demographic changes made it imperative to encourage women, especially those with skills, both to stay in the workforce and have children; hence the draft Directive. Social policy was thus presented as an economic investment as well as a moral imperative in the single market.

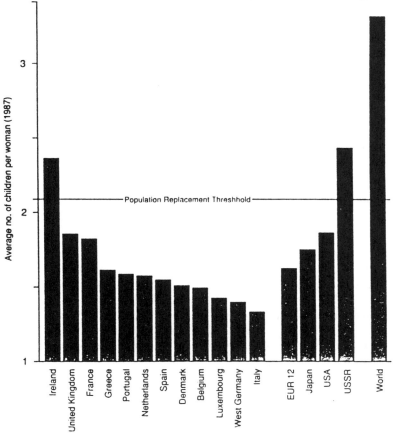

Figure 4 **Average number of children per woman in EC and elsewhere, 1987** (*Source*: Commission, 1990b).

Eventually in November 1991 a somewhat diluted Directive on pregnant women was finally adopted in the Council despite strenuous opposition from Britain and reservations felt in other countries. The UK government abstained in the qualified majority vote on the question, still opposed in principle to Community encroachment on such social matters, but unable to apply a veto. Thinking that such matters should be decided by unanimity, British ministers were considering a challenge to the legality of the Council's decision in the European Court. However, their resolution to do so was being weakened by the prospect of potentially hostile public opinion. A UK general election was due to take place in the six months following this decision on maternity rights and Conservative MPs were reportedly worried that votes could be lost if their government was seen to be opposing an improvement in working women's rights (Guardian Weekly 1991a:3). Despite the talk of democratic deficits in the Community system, public opinion clearly does impinge on EC policy-making in a variety of ways.

In conclusion: single markets, social charters and politics

The Social Charter was a clear 'political signal' from the highest Community level that a 'European social area' should be strengthened to counterbalance the fast-integrating 'economic area' of the single market. Whatever the particular national differences of interest and emphasis, the majority consensus throughout the EC favoured this approach. But in Britain, its adoption by the other eleven Member States without the accord of the UK government highlighted major ideological clashes about the future character of the European Community. On one side, many British Conservatives saw the Charter as part of an attempt to reintroduce bureaucratic socialism into Britain via the 'backdoor of Brussels'. In her 'Bruges speech' of September 1988, when the Commission was drawing up its Charter proposals, Mrs Thatcher, then Prime Minister, emphasized her determination to protect the achievements of the 'Thatcherite revolution':

> we have not successfully rolled back the frontiers of the State in Britain, only to see them re-imposed at a European level, with a European Superstate exercising a new dominance. (Thatcher 1988: 4)

Such sentiments flowed out of a tradition which saw the 'free enterprise' economic elements of the '1992' project as an adequate basis upon which to build European unity; talk of developing a European 'social space' ignored 'the lesson of the economic history of Europe in the 1970s and 1980s'. For Mrs Thatcher this lesson was that a 'state-controlled economy is a recipe for low growth...(whereas)... free enterprise within a framework of law brings better results'. The framework of law she had in mind would rid the market place of barriers hindering open competition rather than build up a European edifice of workers' rights:

> our aim should not be more and detailed regulation from the centre.. .(but).
> . .to deregulate and remove constraints on trade. (Thatcher 1988: 6)

Mrs Thatcher's reading of the SEA had clearly focused on its requirement for a single internal market and ignored, or underestimated, the sections on 'social and economic cohesion'. However, opponents of her government's approach to the EC were reading developments differently. The Labour Party's traditional hostility to the Community was changing to enthusiasm as the Commission strove to give renewed substance to the stagnating 'social dimension' of European integration. In the words of Mr Kinnock, unrestrained 'market power' would have detrimental consequences for 'civil rights and environmental conditions, individual opportunities and collective provisions' (Kinnock 1988: 3). In signing the Social Charter, eleven Member State governments — of various political colours — had indicated their broad agreement with this view despite their particular differences over detail and precise implementation of general objectives.

Observers of this debate, aware of Europe's complexity and the subtlety of Community processes, can easily conclude that both sides overstated their case. The Thatcherite spectre of an all-powerful, corporatist European 'superstate' ready to 'extinguish democracy', made far too light of the power wielded by national governments within the Community's supranational institutions (Wise and Gibb, 1993: pp. 1-48). For example, the Commission had been trying to promote forms of worker participation throughout the Community since the 'Vredeling' Fifth Directive had been proposed in 1972 (see Wise and Gibb, 1993: 126-151). However, although most Member States required formal employee involvement in company affairs, countries such as Britain had successfully blocked even the most general type of EC regulation in this area. Similarly, the broad and legally unbinding provisions of the Social Charter gave enormous scope to member governments to resist, amend and find very flexible solutions adapted to national, regional and local conditions. Many years of complex negotiations involving numerous institutions and interest groups at both European and national level are clearly in store before strong social policy linkages cross the frontiers of the Common Market. Thus, while some on the Right of British politics gird themselves to fight the paper dragons of a would-be socialist superstate, some on the Left are in danger of lurching from simplistic opposition to a 'rich-man's club' to naive enthusiasm for a vision of social Europe where an equitable balance of power between employers and employees in an increasingly European and international economy will apparently deliver 'productive and socially just solutions' (Kinnock 1988: 6).

In truth, the balance between 'economic' and 'social' policy in the future European Community will depend, as always, on the political balance of forces within its intricate interlocking network of European, national and, in some cases, regional institutions. This obvious fact can be too easily overlooked in European debates dominated by crude '1992' deadlines and simplistic visions of a 'Europe without frontiers'. The precise policies that emerge from the general guidelines of the Social Charter will be shaped by a very pluralistic process involving the various EC institutions, some regional bodies, big business, representatives of organized labour and, above all, 12 or more national governments operating together in the Council of Ministers. In the past, the balance of these forces has produced a European Community which has emphasized economic integration based on free-market competition. But the socially protective aspects of the CAP, maintained as a result of the political pressure farmers have been able wield, are clear evidence that there are no inevitable outcomes to the interplay of economic and social forces in the Community. The following chapter on a long-established social aspect of EC activities — regional policy — provides further insights into the importance of analysing the inter-relationships between the Community's economic, social and political dimensions.

Bibliography

Boyer R (1988) *In Search of Labour Market Flexibility: European Economies in Transition.* Oxford, Clarendon Press

Brewster C, Teague P (1989) *European Community Social Policy: its impact on the UK.* London, Institute of Personnel Management

Commission of the EC (1987), *Internal and external adaption of firms in relation to employment* COM (87) final 229, Brussels.

Commission of the EC (1988a) 'Social Policy of the European Community: looking ahead to 1992'. *European File* 13/88. Luxembourg, Office for Official Publications of the EC.

Commission of the EC (1988b) *Bulletin of the European Communities* No. 7/8. Luxembourg, Office for Official Publications of the EC.

Commission of the EC (1988c) 'The social aspects of the internal market'. *Social Europe* 1, Supplement 7/88, D-G for Employment, Social Affairs and Education. Luxembourg, Office for Official Publications of the EC

Commission of the EC (1988d) 'La dimension sociale du marché intérieur'. *Europe Sociale* Numéro spéciale. Luxembourg, Office for Official Publications of the EC

Commission of the EC (1989a) *Background Report.* ISEC/B25/89, 11.10.89, London

Commission of the EC, (1989b) *Background Report.* Speech by Mrs V. Papandreou, ISEC/B30/89, 11.12.89, London

Commission of the EC (1989c) *ERDF: Thirteenth Annual Report(1988).* COM (88) 728 final, 10/1/89, Brussels

Commission of the EC (1990a) *Community Charter of the Fundamental Social Rights of Workers.* Luxembourg, Office for Official Publications of the EC

Commission of the EC (1990b) 'The new structural policies of the European Community'. *European File.* 7-8/90, Luxembourg, Office for the Official Publications of the EC

Commission of the EC (1990c), Jacques Delors introduction to the *Community Charter of the Fundamental Social Rights of Workers.* Luxembourg, Office for Official Publications of the EC

Commission of the EC (1990d) 'The Community Charter of Fundamental Social Rights for Workers'. *European File,* 6/90. Luxembourg, Office for Official Publications of the EC.

Commission of the EC (1990e) *Background Report.* ISEC/B25/90, 5.10.1990, London referring to Commission of the EC (1990) COM (90) 406 final, Brussels

Commission of the EC (1991a) *Background Report.* ISEC/B15/91 28.5.91

Commission of the EC (1991b) *Background Report.* ISEC/B20 22.7.91, London

Delors J (1988) *Europe 1992: the social dimension.* Address to the TUC Congress, Bournemouth 8 September 1988. Brussels,Commission of the EC

Economist (1990a) 'The tale of two parties'. *The Economist,* 23 June, London.

Economist (1990b) 'Its cold in cloud-cuckoo-land'. *The Economist,* 10 November, London.

Economist (1991) 'Never on a Sunday'. *The Economist,* 19 October, London.

European Parliament (1990a) 'Report of the Committee on Social Affairs, Employment and the Working Environment on the ...action programme relating to the implementation of the Community Charter of fundamental social rights for workers'. *Session Documents,* Series A, Document A 3-0175/90

European Parliament (1990b) 'Debates of the European Parliament'. *Official Journal of the EC* No 3-386, 12-16.2.90

European Parliament (1990c) 'Debates of the European Parliament'. *Official Journal of the EC* No 3-393, 10-14.9.90

Eurostat (1975-90) Annual editions of *Basic Statistics of the Community*. Statistical Office of the EC. Luxembourg, Office for Official Publications of the EC

Eurostat (1989) *Basic Statistics of the Community*. Statistical Office of the EC. Luxembourg, Office for Official Publications of the EC

Financial Times (1990) 29 November, London

Gibb R A, Treadgold A (1989) 'Completing the internal market: implications for the regions'. *Area* 21 (1): 75 82

Guardian Weekly (1991a) 17 November

Kinnock N. (1988) *Speech by the Leader of the Labour Party to the Socialist Group of the European Parliament*. Glasgow, mimeo

Lipietz A (1988) 'L Europe: dernier recours pour une relance mondiale. *Le Monde Diplomatique* May

Local Government International Bureau (1990a) *European Information Service* 115, 5.11.90, referring to Commission of the EC, COM(90) 228 final, 13.6.90, Brussels

Local Government International Bureau (1990b) *European Information Service* 113, 20.8.90

Local Government International Bureau (1990c) *European Information Service* 114, 1.10.90

Lodge, J (1989a) 'The European Parliament — from assembly to co-legislature'. In: Lodge, J (ed) *The European Community and the Challenge of the Future*. London, Pinter Publishers

Le Monde (1991) 'Europe: l'engrenage du marché unique'. *Dossiers et Documents*. avril 1991 73-8

Petersen J H (1991) 'Harmonization of Social Security in the EC revisited'. *Journal of Common Market Studies* XXIX (4): 505-26

Pinder J 1991 *European Community: the building of a union*. Oxford, Oxford University Press

Rocard M (1988) *Financial Times* 24 October, London

Teague P (1989) *The European Community: the social dimension*, London, Kogan Page.

Thatcher M (1988) *Britain and Europe*. Text of the Prime Minister's speech at Bruges on 20 September 1988, Conservative Political Centre, London

Wadley D (1986) *Restructing the regions*, OECD. Paris.

Welsh M (1987) *Labour market policy in the European Community: the British presidency of 1986*. Discussion Paper No.4, London, Royal Institute of International Affairs

Wise M, Chalkley B (1990) 'Unemployment: regional policy defeated?' In: Pinder D (ed.) *Challenge and Change in Western Europe*, London, Belhaven Press: pp. 179-94

Wise, M and Gibb, R (1993) *Single Market to Social Europe,* Harlow, Longman Scientific and Technical

11.   Community Regional Policy

Harvey Armstrong

Introduction

Member states are anxious to strengthen the unity of their economies and to ensure their harmonious development by reducing the differences existing between the various regions and by mitigating the backwardness of the less favoured regions. [Preamble, Treaty of Rome, 1958]

In order to promote its overall harmonious development, the Community shall develop and pursue its actions leading to the strengthening of its economic and social cohesion. In particular, the Community shall aim at reducing disparities between the various regions and the backwardness of the least favoured regions. [Article 130A, Single European Act, 1986]

Despite thirty years of unqualified commitment to the cause of regional policy within the EC, regional disparities survive and pose a stumbling block to the full integration of the economies of the member states. It must be noted, however, that for much of the EC's history regional policy (as distinct from the individual regional policies of the member states) has been very weak. The EC's own onslaught on regional problems really only dates from the establishment of the European Regional Development Fund (ERDF) in 1975. The period since 1975 has witnessed a flowering of EC regional policy initiatives. The ERDF underwent major reform in 1979, and again in 1984. These reforms have been accompanied by a succession of other regional policy initiatives.

This chapter assesses the EC's regional policy, the ERDF, the extent of regional disparities within the EC and reviews briefly arguments used to justify an EC regional policy. It assesses the various initiatives designed to improve the coordination of the regional policy effort and briefly reviews the role of the European Investment Bank (EIB), the European Social Fund (ESF), the European Coal and Steel Community (ECSC) and the European Agricultural Guidance and Guarantee Fund (EAGGF) in helping to reduce regional disparities. An agenda for reforms to EC regional policy in the 1990s is presented.

Regional problems in the EC

The EC is one of the world's great economic powers, has 7 per cent of the world's population — a market of 320 million people. Such a vast economic entity is inevitably a diverse one. Not surprisingly, great differences exist from region to region in prosperity and job opportunities.

There is no single universally accepted method of measuring the economic well-being of a region. A variety of measures (or indicators) of a region's economic welfare exists.

Harvey Armstrong: 'Community Regional Policy', in *THE EUROPEAN COMMUNITY AND THE CHALLENGE OF THE FUTURE* (1989), edited by Juliet Lodge, pp. 167-185. Reproduced by permission of Pinter Publishers Ltd, London. All rights reserved.

Measures of per capita income (or output) are very popular and suffer fewer of the drawbacks of traditional indicators such as rates of unemployment. It is possible for example, to measure the Gross Domestic Product (GDP) of a region in much the same way as is done for national economies. Figure 1 shows GDP per capita in the EC regions in 1985. This map highlights a number of key features of the regional problem in the EC. Apart from one or two exceptional areas (for example the Aberdeen region of Scotland which has benefited from North Sea oil exploitation), the EC's depressed regions are on the periphery and the highest per capita income levels are mainly in the centre. The 'centre-periphery' nature of regional disparities within the EC is a long-standing one (COM(73)550; Armstrong, 1978). Fundamental economic processes systematically favour the centre. Severe regional problems exist in the depressed Mediterranean periphery. Many of these southern disadvantaged regions suffer particularly deep-seated problems and have levels of deprivation rarely seen in the more northerly member states. The 'depressed south' is now the most important regional problem confronting the EC, and its greatest challenge.

Another very popular indicator of economic disadvantage is regional unemployment rates that are very difficult to compare. Each country has its own definition of unemployment and different criteria for claiming unemployment benefit. Unemployment rates confirm the broad 'centre-periphery' pattern of regional disparities. They do, however, pick out pockets of economic disadvantage in more central areas which GDP per capita figures do not. There is high unemployment in parts of Belgium, and in northern France in areas formerly dependent on coal mining and heavy industry. By contrast, large areas of Greece and Portugal which are low-income regions appear to have low unemployment rates. This apparent paradox is easily explained. In Greece and Portugal, unlike the Belgium and French coalfield areas, the problem is not one of industrial decline but rather of rural underdevelopment, with large numbers of people continuing to work in an impoverished agricultural industry. In rural agricultural areas the problem is largely one of low incomes and under-employment. People are rarely completely unemployed. As a result, unemployment rates understate the true scale of the problem.

The apparent anomalies revealed from the study of the unemployment rates hint at the extraordinary diversity of types of regional problem faced by the EC. Indeed, the EC Commission identifies several main types of disadvantaged region in the EC:

(i) *Underdeveloped regions*. These regions have simply never enjoyed the benefits of industrial and economic progress and are particularly prevalent in the EC's Mediterranean areas. The preponderance of agriculture, often of a very inefficient kind, the exceptionally low incomes, and the lack of basic infrastructure, such as good roads and telecommunications, makes these regions especially difficult cases.

(ii) *Declining industrial regions*. These regions have often been prosperous in the past but have now declined because of the loss of competitiveness of industries on which they were once dependent. Most of the depressed north and west of the UK is dominated by regions of this kind.

(iii) *Peripheral regions*. The development of a single EC market for goods and services poses particularly severe problems for geographically isolated areas (for example island communities such as Sicily or Ireland) and for the mainland's periphery. Such regions face long-term problems related to lack of easy access to the markets of the EC.

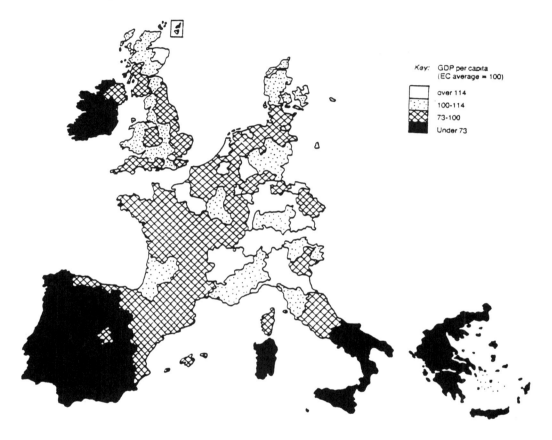

Figure 1   Regional gross domestic product per capita in the EC, 1985.
Source: Commission of the European Communities, *The Regions of the Enlarged Community: Third Periodic Report on the Social and Economic Situation and Development of the Regions of the Community*, Brussels, 1987.

(iv) *Border regions*. The creation of a common market poses particular problems for regions along the frontiers of member states. Areas close to national frontiers often develop distinctive types of industry which exploit legal barriers to trade between countries or which take advantage of the need to off-load and on-load freight (for example at Channel crossings). A distinction is often drawn between *internal* border regions (that is borders between pairs of member states) which face adjustment problems as frontier regulations are swept away; and *external* border regions whose traditional trade patterns with non-EC neighbours may be disrupted by the Common External Tariff and other external trade barriers.

(v) *Urban problem areas*. The big cities of the EC face congestion, pollution, crime and social deprivation notably in the inner city areas of large metropolitan agglomerations.

There can be no doubt that the extent of the regional problems facing the EC is cause for great concern. Regional disparities are enormous by any standard. GDP per capita disparities in the EC are some two times and unemployment disparities three times as high as in the US. Moreover, things have worsened considerably in recent years. The entry of Greece, Spain and Portugal significantly widened the existing disparities. The rapid growth and gradually narrowing regional differences so characteristic of the EC of the 1960s and early 1970s has been replaced by much slower rates of growth and higher unemployment in the late 1970s and early 1980s. The harsher economic conditions of the 1970s and 1980s have resulted in a reversal of convergence trends in the EC. The challenge facing EC regional policy is immense.

The case for EC regional policy

The need for government to act to try to reduce regional disparities has long been recognized in Europe. All the EC's principal member states have their own well-established regional policies. In the UK, for example, regional policy has existed continuously since 1928 (Armstrong, 1988; Armstrong and Taylor, 1988). By contrast, the existence of a separate, EC regional policy is a very recent phenomenon. The ERDF was only established in 1975. The arguments for and against a distinctively EC-level regional policy are complex and controversial. At one extreme are those who would like to see members states' regional policies ended and replaced by a single comprehensive EC regional policy. At the other extreme are those who feel that the member states are the ones most qualified to administer regional policies and that EC involvement is at best unnecessary bureaucracy, and at worst interference with the effective operation of member states' own regional policies.

Four main arguments support a separate EC regional policy. First, the EC can improve the efficiency of regional policy by ensuring that regional policy spending is *concentrated* where it is most needed — that is in the most severely disadvantaged regions. At present, some member states are virtually depressed regions in their own right (Portugal, Greece, Republic of Ireland). Others, like Spain and the UK have many depressed areas within their borders whereas countries such as Germany, France and the Netherlands have few major problem areas. With the problem regions so heavily concentrated in certain member states, it is impossible for member states left to their own devices to target the most financial help on the most severely disadvantaged areas. Poorer member states simply cannot afford to pay the bill. There is a clear role for the EC here: a fund like the ERDF can be used to channel resources into the most severely depressed areas.

The second argument for a separate EC regional policy concerns *coordination*. Twelve states each trying to solve their own regional problems produce chaos. Many regional agencies and governments actively promote industrial development and so too do many local authorities. With so many different participants great inefficiency can occur. Many member states, for example, have used their regional financial incentives to 'bid' aggressively for investment projects seeking a location within the EC. Many Japanese and US companies are wooed by the member states. Such 'competitive bidding' is very costly and inefficient. The EC has launched a whole series of regional policy initiatives to try to improve coordination. Coordination is also necessary amongst the different policies of each government. It is known, for example, that the CAP has tended in the past to favour farmers in the EC's more prosperous northern agricultural areas rather than in the chronically depressed Mediterranean. There is clearly a case for the EC to ensure that the regional effects of *all* of its own policies are carefully monitored and where possible redesigned to bring more help to the depressed areas.

The third broad argument concerns 'common interest'. Each EC member has a vested interest in what goes on in fellow member states. Depressed regions benefit no one. All benefit from all the labour in the EC being fully occupied and producing goods and services. High unemployment in certain areas is also very inequitable. There is considerable evidence that Europeans do feel that such inequities should be eliminated. An EC regional policy would therefore benefit all.

The fourth and final argument in support of an EC regional policy is a dynamic one. Regional disparities may be a severe barrier to further integration. The EC advances by way of the mutual consent of its members. Where large areas remain underdeveloped it is difficult to obtain the consent to move further along the road to economic and monetary union. The EC can only advance if everyone feels they are benefiting. In such circumstances a strong EC regional policy is essential.

Taken together, the various arguments in favour of a separate EC regional policy represent a powerful case. It should be noted, however, that there is no suggestion that the members' own regional policies should be abolished. The local knowledge and long experience of member states and local authorities are of great value. The EC must therefore seek to work with national and local governments to solve regional problems.

The ERDF

The ERDF was established in 1975. Prior to this EC regional policy was rudimentary: limited help was given by way of funds and programmes whose main functions were not regional policy. The ECSC and EAGGF gave some financial assistance to depressed areas simply because of the kinds of industries in which they were involved. The EIB provided loans to depressed areas. There was, however, little in the way of a systematic EC regional policy. Depressed regions were forced to rely almost entirely upon their own national governments for help. These disparate member state regional policies were themselves perspectives subject to a number of fairly ineffective EC competition policy regulations designed to try to prevent member state regional inducements being misused in ways which would undermine free trade and free competition. The ERDF's creation was a major turning point. The UK played an important role in the setting up of the new ERDF. The long experience of the UK in regional policy provision was of great value in the design of the ERDF. Since 1975 EC regional policy has steadily grown in stature. The EC has proved an innovator in its regional policy. Many new initiatives have been introduced in the years since 1975. Today's EC regional policy can be divided into three main constituent parts. First, there is the ERDF itself: the principal financial instrument of EC regional policy. Second, there are numerous EC initiatives to improve EC *coordination* of member states' regional policies, with those of regional and local authorities. Finally, a number of other EC funds and institutions operate with a deliberate regional bias.

The ERDF prior to 1984

Since 1975 the ERDF has undergone two major reforms — in 1979 and 1984 (Commission, 1981a, OJL 169 28/6/84). The history of the ERDF is largely one of a struggle to throw off the many restrictions imposed by the Council of Ministers in the original 1975 Fund Regulation. Most of the restrictions on the ERDF's field of action remained immediately prior to the major 1984 reforms. Table 1 compares the ERDF prior to the 1984 reforms with that set up afterwards. Before the 1984 reforms, the ERDF was divided into two parts: a quota and a non-quota section. The quota section took 95 per cent of ERDF allocations; the non-quota section was restricted to a maximum of 5 per cent of ERDF allocations.

Quota section assistance was hedged around with restrictions which limited severely the EC's discretion to decide exactly how its own fund's money should be spent. Only grants and interest rebates could be given. This represented a very limited range of types of assistance. On the other hand, quite a wide range of industrial investment projects (including craft and service industries such as tourism) and infrastructure projects were eligible for assistance. Quota section assistance was, however, restricted to those assisted areas designated by the member states for their own regional policies. The EC itself could not, therefore, decide where ERDF money was to be spent. The result was an extraordinary 'patchwork' of areas eligible for ERDF quota section assistance. Each member state had, of course, its own ideas on which areas were in need of help.

To make matters worse, the EC did not (and still does not) have the manpower to administer locally ERDF quota section applications. Applications were channelled through members' ministries such as the UK Department of Industry. This gave them a strangle-hold on the flow of applications and hence a considerable degree of control over who got ERDF assistance. A further limit on the EC's freedom of action before 1984 was the quota system itself. The predominant quota section was so-named because each member state was guaranteed a fixed annual share (or quota) of ERDF allocations. In 1984, these quotas were: UK, 23.8 per cent; Belgium, 1.11 per cent; Denmark, 1.06 per cent; France, 13.64 per cent; Republic of Ireland, 5.94 per cent; Italy, 35.49 per cent; Luxembourg, 0.07 per cent; Netherlands, 1.24 per cent; Germany, 4.65 per cent; and Greece, 13.0 per cent. Finally, the quota section before 1984 was subject to a Fund Regulation which contained numerous restrictions on the precise terms and conditions under which an ERDF grant could be given (for example rates of assistance, 'ceilings' on funds offered, types of eligible project etc). Moreover, assistance could only be given on a project-by-project basis, greatly hampering EC attempts to put together carefully planned and closely coordinated programmes of regional assistance.

Table 1   **1984 reforms to the ERDF.**

	Before 1984	After 1984
Expenditure	Determined annually as part of the EC budget decision	No change.
Project-by-project assistance	*'Quota' section* Assistance given on a project-by-project basis as a means of supporting the regional policies of the individual member states; this quota-section assistance formed a fixed 95% of all ERDF allocations: it derived its name from the fact that each member state was guaranteed a predetermined share (or 'quota') of this type of assistance. UK quota for 1984 was 23.8%.	*Project assistance* The previous distinction between 'quota' and 'nonquota' section is abolished; in place of a predetermined quota the United Kingdom was guaranteed a share of ERDF allocations between 1984 and 1987 of between 21.42% and 28.56% (the so-called 'indicative range'); the project-by-project assistance so characteristic of the quota section is retained as a separate category of ERDF aid-project assistance.
	(a) *Type of assistance offered* Principally investment grants given as a percentage of eligible capital expenditure; also interest rebates on other EC loans.	(a) *Type of assistance offered* Principally investment grants; also interest rebates - especially on loans made to small- and medium-sized enterprises.
	(b) *Eligible activities* Eligible projects must exceed 50,000 European units of account (Eua): must also be benefitting from member state aid; and, in the case of assistance to industrial projects must create or maintain jobs. Projects must be justifiable as part of the member state's regional development programme.	(b) *Eligible activities* As before.
	(c) *Eligible areas* The assisted areas are designated by member states for their own regional policies	(c) *Eligible areas* As before; exceptionally, a small part of the ERDF resources may be allocated to infrastructure projects outside of the member states' Assisted Areas where the project is 'an essential complement to the infrastructure of an assisted area' (CEC, 1984).
	(d) *Eligible industries* Industrial, handicraft, and service industries (that is those services concerned with tourism or which have a choice of location); infrastructure *projects* also eligible.	(d) *Eligible industries* As before.

Table 1   1984 reforms to the ERDF (Continued).

	Before 1984	After 1984
	(e) *Rates of grants* Industry, craft, services 20% of the investment cost (up to a maximum of 50% of aid given by member states to the same project); cost-per-job ceilings of 100,000 Eua per job created or 50,000 Eua per job maintained; aid may exceed 20% for handicraft and service projects (up to 50% of member state aid and with a 100,000 Eua cost-per-job ceiling); infrastructure-10%-30% of the expenditure incurred by member states (up to 40% in the case of projects of particular importance for the regions).	(e) *Rates of grant* Industry, craft, services 50% of aid granted by member states to the project; infrastructure-30-50% of the expenditure being met by the member states' public authorities (55% for projects of particular importance).
Programme assistance	*'Nonquota' section* 5% of ERDF allocations; assistance offered not to individual projects but through programme contacts; these are multiannual programmes of assistance, agreed jointly by the EC and member states involved, to tackle specific Community regional problems (for example to counter adverse effects of other EC policies); three programmes initially agreed for the United Kingdom — Ulster-Eire border regions, shipbuilding areas, and textile areas. Each programme encompasses many projects and coordinates EC, national, regional, and local aid; not limited to member states' Assisted Areas and a flexible range of types of assistance permitted (not limited to investment grants and interest rebates).	Quota and nonquota sections abolished; the programme contract approach is, however, retained and greatly expanded; programmes are expected to increase to 20% of all ERDF operation within three years (at expense of project assistance). Two distinct types of programmes: (1) Community programmes: agreed with the member state but initiated by the EC and intended to 'directly serve Community objectives' to be given priority over other types of programme; normally will encompass more than one member state; aimed at new activities and not simply the reorganization of declining industries such as steel or textiles; above all, aid is given much more flexibly under programmes than project-by-project assistance. (2) National programme of Community interest: initiated by the member state to which they are confined, but jointly agreed with the EC; up to 50% of member state aid (55% in exceptional cases).

Table 1   1984 reforms to the ERDF (Continued).

	Before 1984	After 1984
Other provision	(a) *Indigenous development* Nonquota section used to pioneer more flexible types of assistance for small firms (see 'after 1984' reforms).	(a) *Indigenous development* Special provision is made for measures designed to exploit the indigenous development of regions especially for small firms which involve assistance of up to 55% of aid given by the member state, and a variety of types of assistance (for example, assistance in obtaining consultancy advice, aid for local research organisations, aid for tourist promotion etc).
	(b)*Integrated development operations* ERDF resources devoted to pioneering integrated operations in Belfast and Naples; these are closely coordinated schemes (EC, national, regional, and local agencies involved) to tackle the problems of specific small areas; coordinated and flexible assistance.	(b) *Integrated development operations* To be continued and expanded.
	(c) *Studies* The ERDF also funds studies on regional policies and problems.	(c) *Studies* As before.
Coordination initiatives	A variety of initiatives exist to try to coordinate EC, member state, and, to a lesser extent, regional and local involvement in regional policy, these include the regional development programmes of member states; the periodic report on regional problems in the EC; the Commission's regular guidelines and priorities for regional policy; the regional impact assessment procedure; annual reports from member states to the EC and the use of programme contracts and integrated operations.	All previous initiatives retained and strengthened, especially substantial strengthening of programme contracts and integrated operations.

Source: Armstrong, 1986

The small non-quota section of the pre-1984 ERDF was much less hampered by regulations and restrictions and proved to be an important break-through when it was introduced in 1979. The EC had much greater freedom of action with non-quota section assistance. For example, non-quota assistance could, if necessary, be spent partly or wholly outside member state assisted areas. Moreover, fewer restrictions were placed on the types of help which could be given and on the terms of the assistance. The EC, slowly at first after 1979 and then with gathering momentum, began to put the non-quota section finance to use in a radical new manner. The concept of a *programme contract* was developed with finance from the small non-quota section. A programme contract is a coordinated 'package' of initiatives, jointly agreed between the EC and member states, and specifically designed to alleviate a clearly identified regional problem. The programmes are designed to run for several years (and, indeed, have been frequently re-financed with new tranches of assistance). They draw together many different projects and initiatives.

The early programmes set up between 1979 and 1984 tended to concentrate on areas heavily affected by the run-down and restructuring of particular industries, especially those industries where the EC was encouraging a radical restructuring. By 1984 the UK was (together with other member states) benefiting from five programmes (or 'specific Community measures' as they had by then come to be known):

1. Steel areas programme;
2. Shipbuilding areas programme;
3. Border areas programme (along the Northern Ireland border);
4. Textile areas programme;
5. Fisheries programme.

All but one (the Border areas programme) were designed to encourage new types of industry in areas affected by the run-down of a local staple industry. These 'specific Community measures' continue to be financed. By 1991 it is estimated that the UK will have received about £180 million from these five programmes (ERDF: Twelfth Annual Report). The early 1979-84 experimental programmes proved a successful 'model' for the many new types of programmes now being introduced in the EC. In addition to programme financing, by 1984 initiatives had been introduced which greatly improved the EC's role in the coordination of regional policy. A comprehensive system for monitoring and analysing states' regional policies had been introduced in 1979. Member states were required to plan their regional policy efforts and to coordinate with other member states (see below).

The 1984 reforms of the ERDF

The 1984 reforms of EC regional policy proved to be the most important since the ERDF was set up in 1975. Full details of the 1984 reforms are set out in Table 1. Two 1984 reforms have significantly strengthened the degree to which the EC itself actually takes decisions concerning the ERDF and have weakened the power of the member states.

The quota/non-quota distinction was abolished in 1984. Quota section assistance continues in the form of Project Assistance and non-quota assistance as Programme Assistance. Radical changes have been made in the operation of these two sections. Project Assistance (that is project-by-project help in the form of grants and interest rebates) while the dominant part of the ERDF is being systematically cut. Project Assistance was cut from 95 per cent to 80 per cent within three years of the 1984 reforms and is being further reduced. Programme assistance (programme contracts of the type pioneered between 1979 and 1984) is being rapidly expanded. Since programme contract assistance is more flexible and more at the discretion of the EC, the expansion of Programme Assistance greatly strengthens EC control of the ERDF.

The 1984 reforms weakened member state influence over ERDF decisions in other ways. Before 1984, Project Assistance was allocated to member states on the basis of pre-determined shares or 'quotas'. This is now no longer the case. Rigid quotas have been replaced by a system of 'indicative ranges' for Project Assistance. For example, before 1984 the UK was guaranteed 23.8 per cent of quota section assistance. Immediately after the 1984 reforms this was changed to an 'indicative range' of between 21.42 per cent and 28.56 per cent. The introduction of 'indicative ranges' gives the EC a greater say in where ERDF money is spent. The UK is guaranteed a minimum amount (21.42 per cent between 1984 and 1987), but if it wants more must persuade the EC to agree to assist more of the project applications sent to Brussels. The 'indicative ranges' have, of course, been altered with the entry of Spain and Portugal. On entry, Spain was given an 'indicative range' of 17.97-23.93 per cent while Portugal's was 10.66-14.20 per cent. Naturally, the United Kingdom's 'indicative range' has had to be cut — to between 14.50 per cent and 19.31 per cent.

In addition to relaxing quotas, the 1984 reforms relaxed some of the many detailed restrictions on the way in which Project Assistance can be given. Of even greater importance are the changes to the non-quota section (i.e. 'Programme Assistance'). Programme Assistance has been substantially reformed. An attempt was made to move programme contracts away from being sector-specific (i.e. steel, shipbuilding, textiles and fisheries areas programmes) and into more varied types of programme contracts. The 1984 reforms defined two distinct types of programme:

(a) *Community Programmes* are jointly agreed by the EC and member states but initiated by the EC. These EC-wide programmes are meant to 'directly serve Community objectives' (OJ LI69 28/6/84).

(b) *National Programmes of Community Interest (NPCI)* are initiated within a member state and EC approval is sought. Normally they are specific to a single member state.

The ability to initiate Community Programmes, and the need to be actively involved in National Programmes, has increased EC influence in the ERDF. Moreover, priority is given to Community Programmes over National Programmes. It was envisaged that Community Programmes would gradually grow until they dominated the Programme Assistance section of the ERDF.

The impetus given to regional policy based on coordinated programmes of help by the 1984 reforms was strengthened by two further changes introduced by the 1984 Fund Regulation. First, the go-ahead was given for a rapid expansion of *Integrated Development Operations* (IDOs). Between 1979 and 1984 the EC had experimented with two IDOs, one in Belfast, the other in Naples. IDOs are designed to redevelop and revitalize severely deprived inner-city areas. As well as ERDF, the IDOs draw upon other EC finance, and assistance from national and local governments in the cities concerned. Second, the 1984 reforms gave the go-ahead for more transfrontier programmes designed to tackle regional problems which straddle national frontiers.

Finally, the 1984 reforms signalled a major change in the direction of EC regional policy. For a number of years it had become increasingly obvious that the traditional approach of encouraging large manufacturing plants to move from prosperous to depressed areas was not working: regions need to be helped to grow 'from within'. Stimulating indigenous development means helping small firms and service industries as well as manufacturing. Small firms have special needs. Simple cash grants for investment in plant and machinery are not enough. Small firms need advice. They need to hire consultants. They need help with research and development, and they need to share common services such as accountants and lawyers. The 1984 reforms included special types of assistance to help to stimulate indigenous development of depressed regions. Such measures attract higher rates of ERDF assistance.

The ERDF: the way forward

The ERDF can claim a considerable degree of success. Despite compromises between the EC and member states which have been an inevitable feature of successive Fund Regulations, much good work has been done. The ERDF has ensured that the greatest volume of assistance has gone to the most depressed regions. Southern Italy, the Republic of Ireland, Northern Ireland and the north of Britain have been the principal beneficiaries. Greece has also had considerable assistance. Spain and Portugal have, as yet, received only small sums from the ERDF despite their serious regional problems but will get much more help in future. ERDF expenditures in the UK have grown steadily to over £2.7 billion since 1975, both in nominal and real terms. This is in marked contrast to the real values of expenditures by the Department of Industry on government regional policy initiatives. The ability of the ERDF to continue to increase its expenditures in real terms over a prolonged period when the UK government has been cutting back on its own regional policy budget is very impressive.

Despite its many successes a number of serious criticisms can be levelled against the ERDF that point the way forward for future reform.

The size of the ERDF budget. Despite what appears superficially to be large sums of money, the ERDF is wholly inadequate for the task it confronts. In 1987 the ERDF was allocated 3.3 billion ECUs (1 ECU = £0.697 in September 1988), some 8 per cent of the EC budget. This is an improvement on the 1970s but the budget now has to serve twelve states. ERDF spending continues to be dwarfed by the Twelve's regional policy spending. Yet even the combined activities of both the EC and the states have failed to prevent a serious widening of regional disparities in the EC.

Table 2   Allocations from the ERDF to UK regions, 1979-87.

£ million
Project assistance

Region	Industry	Infrastructure	Studies	National Programmes of Community Interest	Total
North	84.68	309.96	0.53	14.82	410.00
Yorkshire/Humberside	23.28	204.92	0.42	0.00	228.62
East Midlands	7.58	32.19	0.55	0.00	40.32
South-west	8.35	121.04	0.24	0.00	129.64
West Midlands	6.10	156.52	0.10	14.82	177.54
North-west	53.13	251.79	0.46	61.47	366.85
Wales	77.79	329.65	0.85	9.83	418.12
Scotland	151.33	447.92	0.95	54.37	654.58
Northern Ireland	94.54	190.47	0.80	0.87	286.67
Multi-regional	60.00	14.25	1.06	2.65	77.96
Total United Kingdom	566.78	2,058.71	5.96	158.83	2,790.28

Notes: 1. 'Multi-regional' assistance is assistance which encompasses more than one region simultaneously.
2. Figures are not shown for Community Programmes. Being definitive, such programmes encompass the whole EC and the UK share of such aid is not known in advance of the money being spent.

Source: Commission of the European Communities, *Press Release* ISEC/3/88, 27 January, 1988.

In February 1988 the Council of Ministers announced that the 'structural funds' (the ERDF, the European Social Fund and the Guidance Section of the European Agricultural Guidance and Guarantee Fund) would be doubled in size between 1987 and 1993 (OJC245, 12/9/87). This a is a radical decision. It gives little in the way of grounds for optimism, however. Enlargement has greatly increased the number of regions in need of urgent help. Much of the new money is earmarked for regions which are particularly severely depressed (that is with a GDP per capita of less than 75 per cent of the EC average), most of which are in the south of the EC. In the UK, for example, only Northern Ireland falls into this category. Of course, the UK may benefit more even though it obtains a small share of future allocations, since the Fund itself is to be doubled. The full effects of enlargement on the United Kingdom allocation have yet to be felt. In addition, the SEA envisages 1992 as marking much greater internal integration of the EC economies. Further economic integration will inevitably widen regional disparities. The accessible central regions will become even more attractive locations for industry. Improved integration will increase the size of the task which confronts the ERDF. This, in turn, places greater burdens on the enlarged ERDF.

The CAP is the root cause of the inadequate size of the ERDF. It absorbs over 60 per cent of the EC budget — and cost over-runs are endemic. A properly funded ERDF must await effective measures to control CAP spending.

Additionality as a concept. The problem of the ERDF's small size is compounded by the tendency of some member states to substitute ERDF spending for spending under their own regional policies. The EC, not unnaturally, is keen to see its spending being used in an 'additional' manner, and not for member states simply to view it as a convenient means of financing their own budgets. Vigorous EC attempts to persuade states to use ERDF aid in a truly 'additional' manner have, unfortunately, in many cases been met simply by deception. It is impossible to estimate how much ERDF money represents a genuine increase in regional policy spending. Considerable substitution has clearly occurred and directly undermines the ERDF's effectiveness.

The predominance of assistance to infrastructure projects. Between 1975 and 1987 (tenth allocation) some 84.3 per cent of all Project Assistance went on infrastructure projects (and Project Assistance comprised 96.3 per cent of all assistance, with programmes accounting for only 3.7 per cent). The predominance of infrastructure assistance, and the paucity of help for industrial projects is a source of serious concern. (Even in the UK, a country with a long history of giving grants to industrial projects, infrastructure projects took 73 per cent of all ERDF Project Assistance between 1975 and 1987.) The reasons for the high proportion of ERDF help going to infrastructure projects lie partly in the fact that infrastructure grants are easier to apply for and obtain, and partly because of the severe recession of the early 1980s which choked off industrial investment (and therefore the flow of applications to the ERDF). A better balance of infrastructure and industrial assistance is clearly needed.

The slow development of Programme Assistance. The painfully slow development of programmes is beginning to speed up dramatically. Not until October 1986 were the first two Community Programmes approved, and the money is only now beginning to flow freely. The first two Community Programmes were the STAR programme, designed to improve access to modern telecommunications for depressed regions; and the VALOREN programme, designed to tap local energy supplies and improve the efficiency of energy use in the depressed regions. Progress on other Community Programmes has, however, been slow.

National Programmes of Community Interest (NPCI) were also rather slow off the mark. A wave of NPCIs is now being introduced in all member states. The early UK NPCIs (such as the Tees Corridor and the Mersey Basin programmes) are now being joined by many more, for example NFCs in Birmingham and West Lothian were approved in 1988. Interest in devising new programmes in the UK is now intense. The EC approved fourteen NPCIs in 1986 and twenty-seven in 1987. Genuine Community Programmes (as distinct from NPCIs) are still thin on the ground. Particular attention needs to be directed at proposals for stimulating the indigenous potential of depressed regions where small firms are the main target. In 1987 there were still only eighteen such 'indigenous development' measures approved by the ERDF.

The balance of power between the EC and member states. The 1984 reforms have strengthened the EC's hand in the ERDF at member states' expense. This is a good development. In the past member states tended to dominate ERDF decisions through their control of applications for Project Assistance and by way of the tight constraints built into the Fund Regulation. A worrying feature of the existing ERDF is that no attempt has ever been made to spell out precisely what the balance of powers between the EC and member states should be. The ERDF has simply moved from one compromise to another. The programme approach to regional policy means that the EC and member states must work together (Croxford, 1987). Both have a role to play in regional policy. What is missing at present is a clear statement of 'who should do what' (Armstrong, 1985, 1986). Too much state control of the ERDF is a bad thing; no member state regional policies whatsoever would be even worse. The balance must be carefully calculated and rigorously adhered to.

The paucity of formal evaluation of ERDF activities. Evaluating the effectiveness of ERDF assistance has proved extremely difficult not least because to evaluate its effects one must calculate what would have happened had there been no help. This is a difficult concept to quantify. To make matters worse, ERDF help is always given in conjunction with help from other sources (for example from the member state). Disentangling the effects of ERDF help from that of other organizations is an extraordinarily difficult task. Great efforts are now being made to devise methods to evaluate formally ERDF assistance. They must be given priority. No policy can ever be made effective unless it is properly monitored and evaluated.

Coordination of regional policy

The EC is uniquely placed to help to improve the coordination of regional policy in the EC. A number of different types of coordination are now being developed.

Coordination between EC and member states' regional policies

The most important task facing EC regional policy in the 1990s is the need to improve the coordination of member states' regional policies one with another and jointly with the EC itself. To this end the EC has introduced three main initiatives.

Competition policy regulations. The EC uses its competition policy regulations to try to control and coordinate member state regional policies. A system of ceilings has been established which places limits on the total amount of financial help which can be offered to a project by governments (Deacon, 1982). These ceilings are highest in depressed regions and lowest in prosperous regions. In addition, competition policy regulations are used to try to prevent member states from using 'opaque' financial incentives (that is incentives whose true value is hard to ascertain), and to limit the use of continuing subsidies (for example labour subsidies paid week-in, week-out). EC competition policy regulations have not been very successful as a coordinating mechanism. They face enforcement problems. More importantly, they are restrictions and as such tend to impede states' room for manoeuvre.

Monitoring and analysis. In 1979 a comprehensive system for monitoring and analysing member states' and EC regional problems and policies was introduced. Member states are required to produce regular annual reports and information statements on regional policy activities. In addition, each member state must produce and regularly update a Regional Development Programme setting out regional policy plans. The EC produces major biennial periodic reports on regional problems in the EC that form the basis of sets of Commission regional policy guidelines and priorities to guide the EC and member states in their regional policy decisions. The EC's Regional Policy Committee also analyses regional issues and advises the Commission.

Community and national programmes of the ERDF. These, as we have seen, bring the EC and member states together in jointly mounted attacks on specific regional problems. Integrated Development Operations perform a similar function in the urban areas.

All three initiatives are welcome. There is scope for tightening the competition policy regulations further, particularly by bringing into the regulations more member state industry policy subsidies (that is, subsidies offered everywhere in a member state and therefore, by definition, not part of regional policy). Great caution must, however, be exercised. The regulations must not be allowed to develop in ways which hamper states' regional policies for it is the member states and not the EC which continue to provide most help for the depressed regions.

The comprehensive monitoring and analysis system is also very welcome. One can question, however, how effective the Commission's guidelines have been in influencing the ERDF's activities and those of the member states. Many member state Regional Development Programmes also seem to carry too little weight in the decision-making process. It is the ERDF's own programme contracts which, paradoxically, offer the greatest immediate opportunities for improved EC-member state coordination. Programmes are, by definition, joint ventures between the EC and member states. They literally force the two sides to work together. This is fine at the level of an individual programme — in the fine details of its implementation and in decisions on who is helped and how the help is given. But who is to coordinate the programmes? Only time will tell whether the EC can ensure that programmes are accepted or rejected in a logical and consistent manner and in a way which ensures that those that are accepted genuinely complement the regional policy activities of the member states. Moreover, there is little sign as yet of member states such as the UK taking similar steps to coordinate national regional policy activities with the ERDF. UK regional assistance continues to be given on a project-by-project basis and with precious little reference to EC activities in Britain.

Coordination between the ERDF and other EC policies

The EC has made a serious attempt to improve coordination between the ERDF and other EC policies. All major EC policies have their own distinctive geographical pattern of effects. This has long been known. Indeed, some EC funds and institutions have played a major role in helping the depressed regions. Since 1952 the ECSC has been helping the coal and steel industry and the mostly very depressed areas dependent on it. As well as financial help the ECSC subsidizes the retraining and resettlement of redundant coal and steel workers, and gives 'conversion' loans to new companies (in any industry) setting up in coal and steel areas. In 1987, 238 million ECUs of 'conversion' loans were made in the EC, of which 9.2 million were in the UK.

The European Investment Bank gives loans and loan guarantees (often on very favourable terms) in many depressed areas of the EC. The EIB operates with a strong and deliberate regional bias. In 1987 no less than 58 per cent of the 7,450.4 million ECUs loaned by the EIB in the EC were for regional development purposes. The European Social Fund (ESF) also operates with a deliberate regional bias, helping to finance training, retraining, resettlement and other schemes to help many different groups of people. In 1987 44 per cent of the 3.15 billion ECUs allocated from the ESF was spent in the most depressed regions. The UK took 19 per cent of ESF allocations in 1987. The EAGGF's Guidance Section also helps depressed regions. Farmers receive financial assistance in many ways: for farm investment projects, land consolidation, early retirement, environmentally sound production methods etc., amounting to 917 million ECUs in 1987. It should be noted, however, that the EAGGF Guidance Section is dwarfed by the farm price support system which swallowed a massive 22,988.5 million ECUs in 1987. Unfortunately, the price guarantee section of EAGGF tends to help farmers in the richer north of the EC much more than poorer farmers in the south and in hill farm areas (for example, Scotland).

The four funds and institutions discussed above (ECSC, EIB, ESF and EAGGF Guidance Section) have been the subject of a series of reforms designed to improve their contribution to the depressed regions even further. A recent Commission proposal (OJC 245, 12/9/87) to reform the structural funds (ESF, ERDF, and EAGGF Guidance Section) has now been accepted. As well as doubling in size by 1993, they are to be more closely coordinated and their regional bias is to be sharpened with more money being directed at the worst affected regions.

The success achieved in coordinating the ERDF with the ESF, EAGGF Guidance Section, the EIB and the ECSC should not obscure the real failures of the EC coordination effort. Foremost among these is the CAP: EC price support policy is distinctly anti-regional. It tends to help the farmers in the richest areas. The EC has, as yet, been unable to rectify this anomaly. The huge size of the amount spent makes this a truly alarming failure of coordination. The EC has a well-established system of *Regional Impact Assessment* (RIA) designed to discover the geographical pattern of effects of major EC policies (Regional Policy Series, 28-29), but as the CAP shows, it is one thing to identify a need for coordination with the ERDF; it is something else to achieve it.

Conclusion

Much has been achieved by EC regional policy in the years since the ERDF was established in 1975. Much remains to be done in the 1990s. The next decade will witness new and severe demands on EC regional policy. Turkey has applied for EC membership and Morocco waits in the wings. The entry of these two extremely disadvantaged

Mediterranean countries would exacerbate the ERDF's problems. There is a demanding EC regional policy agenda for the 1990s. Six steps in particular are urgently needed:

(a) The ERDF must be greatly increased. Doubling the fund by 1993 will not be sufficient to allow the ERDF to begin reducing regional disparities. Without more the disparities will widen.

(b) The extra finance should be at the expense of the agricultural price guarantee policy, itself profoundly anti-regional.

(c) The EC urgently requires greater powers to try to force member states to use ERDF money in a truly 'additional' manner.

(d) There is a need to reduce the amount of money the ERDF gives to infrastructure projects and, instead, direct more to industrial projects and to small firms.

(e) The EC has been only partially successful in coordinating the ERDF and member states' regional policies. Simply relying on the new generation of programme assistance schemes will not be sufficient in itself to achieve the required extra coordination.

(f) Improved evaluation of the effectiveness of ERDF operations is needed.

Finally, for too long EC regional policy has been viewed as something separate from EC industrial policy as a whole. With the EC now finally beginning to assemble an active industry policy it is essential that regional policy be seen as an integral part of industry policy. Ideally, the two would be part of a single policy. The essence of regional problems is industrial change. In responding to the challenge of industrial change at EC level the Community must simultaneously mount attacks on the geographical problem areas which emerge as industrial change occurs.

References

Armstrong, H.W. (1978) 'Community regional policy: a survey and critique', *Regional Studies,* 12(5), 511-28.

— (1985) 'The reform of the European Community regional policy', *Journal of Common Market Studies,* XXIII, (4), 319-43.

— (1986) 'The division of regional industrial policy powers in Britain: some implications of the 1984 policy reforms', *Environment and Planning: C Government and Policy,* 4, 325-42.

— (1988) 'Regional problems and policies', in B.F. Duckham *et al.* (eds), *The British Economy Since 1945,* Oxford University Press.

— and Taylor, J . (1985) *Regional Economics and Policy,* Philip Allan Ltd.

— and Taylor, J. (1988) *Regional Policy: The Way Forward* (Revised Version), London, The Employment Institute.

Commission of the European Communities (1973a) 'Proposals for a Community regional policy', *Official Journal,* OJ C86 of 16/10/1973 and OJ C 106 of 6/12/1973.

— (1973b) *Report on Regional Problems in the Enlarged Community,* COM (73)550 final, Brussels.

— (1975) 'Regulations establishing a Community regional policy', *Official Journal*, OJ L73 of 21/3/1975.

— (1981a) 'Principal regulations and decisions of the Council of the European Communities on regional policy', *Office for Official Publications of the European Communities*, Luxembourg.

—(1981b) *Study of the Regional Impact of the Common Agricultural Policy*, Regional Policy Series 21, Brussels.

— (1983) *Study of the Regional Impact of the Community's External Trade Policy*, Regional Policy Series 22, Brussels.

— (1984) 'Council regulation (EEC) No. 1787/84 of 19 June 1984 on the European Regional Development Fund', *Official Journal*, OJ L169 of 28/6/1984.

— (1985) *The Effects of New Information Technology on the Less Favoured Regions of the Community*, Regional Policy Series 23, Brussels.

— (1987a) *The Regions of the Enlarged Community*, Third Periodic Report on the Social and Economic Situation and Development of the Regions of the Community: summary and conclusions, Luxembourg.

— (1987b) 'Proposal for a Council Regulation on the tasks of the structural funds and their effectiveness and on coordination of their activities between themselves and with the operations of the European Investment Bank and the other financial instruments', *Official Journal*, OJ C245 of 12/9/1987.

— (1988) *European Regional Development Fund: Twelfth Annual Report (1986)*, Luxembourg.

Croxford, G.J., Wise, M. and Chalkley, B.S. (1987), 'The reform of the European Regional Development Fund: a preliminary assessment', *Journal of Common Market Studies*, XXV (1), 25-38.

Deacon, D. (1982) 'Competition policy in the Common Market: its links with regional policy', *Regional Studies*, 16(1) 53-63.

Hansen, N.M. (1977) 'Border regions: a critique of spatial theory and a European case study', *Annals of Regional Science*, XI, (1), 1-14.

Keeble, D., Owens, P.L. and Thompson, C. (1982) 'Regional accessibility and economic potential in the European Community', *Regional Studies*, 16(6), 419-31.

McCrone, G. (1971) 'Regional policy in the European Community', in G.R. Denton (ed.), *Economic Integration in Europe*, London, Weidenfeld and Nicolson.

12. The Continental Meso: Regions in the European Community

Michael Keating

Europeanism and regionalism

European integration and regional devolution have presented twin challenges to the Western European nation state. At first sight these may appear contradictory forces, the one aiming at larger-scale government and centralization, the other at disaggregation. In practice, their relationship is more complex, at times conflicting, at others linked in efforts to circumvent the nation state. Indeed, each itself is composed of a complex of strands.

European integration was based on an economic logic, a political logic and a theory linking the two. Economically, integration was justified in terms of free trade theory and comparative advantage, the assumed economies of large-scale operation and the need for Europe to compete in a world of large trading blocks. Politically, the first imperative was to prevent war and secure the conditions of Franco-German *rapprochement;* to secure the position of small nations in the new world order; and to overcome the legacy of nationalism. Idealists dreamed of a united states of Europe organized on federal lines. The theory linking economic and political logic was that of functionalism, the idea that increasing exchange in the economic and social spheres would be mutually reinforcing so that functional cross-linkages would lead to a decrease in national identity and the forging of a new European identity as the underpinning of new political institutions.

Regionalism was a response both to the needs of national states and to external pressures upon them (Keating, 1988). Unitary states committed to indicative planning came to realize the need for a spatial articulation of this in the form of regional policies and plans. They also accepted to a greater or lesser degree the need to promote dialogue at the intermediate level and gain the collaboration of local governments, with their land-use and service responsibilities, and of regional economic elites in the promotion of development strategies; hence the establishment of consultative regional planning mechanisms in a number of European countries in the 1960s. These themselves became an object of political contestation and in Italy and, later, France grew into an elected tier of government. In Spain, the paranoia of the Franco regime about regionalism prevented even modest steps towards regional planning, while in Britain regionalists failed in their efforts to follow the Italian and French path.

Regionalism was also promoted in Europe as a response to reassertions of cultural and historical identity. The Belgian state has progressively decentralized to become a federal system, while in Spain recognition of the demands of Catalonia and the Basque

Michael Keating: 'The Continental Meso: Regions in the European Community'; in *THE RISE OF MESO GOVERNMENT IN EUROPE* (1993), edited by L J Sharpe, pp. 296-311. Reprinted by permission of Sage Publications Ltd.

Country was a priority after the end of the Franco regime. In Britain, increasing pressures from Scottish and Welsh nationalism led to the abortive devolution proposals of 1975-9. Regionalism has also been a response to pressure for democratization, most notably in Spain but also in previously centralized democracies where the legitimacy of pluralism and diversity is now recognized. Germany is a case apart, because of its history as well as its status as the only federation within the European Community. There federalism represented a reassertion of old traditions as well as a measure pursued at the insistence of the Allies to prevent the resurgence of centralized dictatorship. Germany's cultural homogeneity, the absence of separatist movements and the practice of co-operative federalism have made decentralization here a means of strengthening the state rather than a threat to its integrity.

The development of the Community itself has affected the development of regionalism, first through the effects of economic integration. The progressive opening of the European market carries the danger of a homogenization of space, as historic territories are forced into the same relationship with the global market. Indeed, some critics see European integration as the latest phase in a process by which states, in the service of capitalist industrialism, have eroded traditional societies and cultures and broken down self-reliant communities.

In the peripheral regions of Europe, there are fears that the integrated market will accentuate the advantages of the 'golden triangle', the central part of the Community, and increase the existing economic disparities. These are already large, with a GDP per head ratio of 2.1:1 between Denmark and Portugal, compared with a maximum of 1.5:1 among American states (Andre et al., 1989). Peripheral regions with low output and unfavourable economic structures are in need of substantial long-term development assistance (Keeble et al., 1988). In some regions dependence on a single industry has meant vulnerability to Community-inspired rationalization. The free market is one of the bases of the Community, and national and regional protectionism, together with subsidies, are in principle outlawed. Yet the impact of the Community's own Common Agricultural Policy has served to increase regional disparities (Strijker and de Veer, 1988) while deregulation of transport and telecommunications, by eliminating cross-subsidization, may damage remote peripheries (Fullarton and Gillespie, 1988). Concerns about the spatial impact of economic integration together with the weakening of national regional policies have sparked off a series of territorially based oppositions to European integration (Lankowsky, 1993), focused on the extension of the global market and the centralization of political power in Brussels. National governments and existing territorial elites, which were able to handle previous manifestations of regional discontent through protectionism, selective subsidy, marginal redistribution and various types of pork-barrel, find themselves unable now to respond because of Community restrictions. So crises in steel, viticulture, textiles or fishing take on both regional and Community dimensions and, while sometimes allowing national governments to deflect local anger, create a source of opposition to European integration.

Political dynamics

The development of the European Community and of regionalism creates the possibility of a new political dynamic around the triangular relationship of Europe-state-region. Such a dynamic can indeed be observed but it has taken a long time to develop and varies in importance across the Community. For the first thirty years of the Community's existence, nation states showed a remarkable resiliency and an ability to use both European integration and regionalism to strengthen rather than weaken their authority. European integration was reduced to a neo-functionalist logic, based on elite collaboration focused on the Council of Ministers. The supranational elements of the Community were downgraded in favour of intergovernmental bargaining. A doctrine of the Community as 'foreign affairs' was adopted which gave national governments wide powers to enforce Community policy even in areas formally devolved to sub-national levels. It is striking, indeed, that states have largely avoided changing their constitutions to recognize the permanence of the Community. Even where states have undertaken constitutional revisions or changes in the structure of territorial government, they have not taken the opportunity formally to incorporate the European dimension. This is true, notably, of Spain, Italy, France and Belgium. The response to the pressures of peripheral nationalism, too, was framed in a way calculated to strengthen the central state, by defusing separatism while treating autonomy as exceptional, confining it to specific regions and so warding off pressures to federalize the state. This was the Italian strategy after the war, when the special status regions were established, and the British response to Scotland and Wales in the 1970s. In Spain, there were attempts to confine regional autonomy to the 'historic nationalities' in Catalonia, Galicia and the Basque Country, while France conceded special status to Corsica. When deployed more generally, regionalism was, as far as possible, treated as an administrative matter. Even where, as in Italy and France, the state conceded elected regional governments, devolution took a functional form with regions tied in closely to national programmes and political autonomy de-emphasized. At the same time, the European and regional levels were convenient places to off-load policies considered too expensive or politically onerous for national governments, like agricultural support and retrenchment or the adjustment of regions to structural economic change. The example most pertinent to our theme is the development of the common regional policy.

Community regional policies

The Commission like other exponents of European unity has believed that a vigorous anti-disparity policy is an essential concomitant to the building of Europe. Such a policy can speed the process of restructuring while enhancing the legitimacy of the EC in the regions where support is most problematic. The Treaty of Rome established the European Social Fund (ESF) in order to deal with the employment consequences of industrial change, notably through training. In 1972, it was reformed to tie in more closely with the needs of sectoral and industrial restructuring, with priority regions receiving at least 50 per cent (but in the event about 80 per cent) of the funds. The European Regional Development Fund (ERDF) was established in 1975 partly as compensation to Britain which, following its accession in 1973, stood to lose heavily through other Community mechanisms. In principle, it was a centrally administered fund to award grants to public or private organizations in depressed or underdeveloped regions for industrial infrastructure investment.

In practice the structural funds, and in particular the ERDF, were caught up in intergovernmental conflict over control and power. Despite repeated attempts by the Commission to turn it into the instrument of a genuine regional policy (Mawson *et al.*, 1985), all national governments applied the 'non-additionality' rule under which EC contributions were regarded as reimbursement for national spending on the projects in question. National quotas for ERDF funds, although progressively relaxed, supported this interpretation. The result was that the political presentation of Community regional policies bore very little relation to the reality, producing an extraordinary world of make-believe. In Britain, for example, all ERDF moneys were regarded as compensation for spending items already planned and in many cases completed, yet the need to sustain support for EC membership in the periphery, where it was consistently weak, dictated that Europe should receive credit. So the Scottish Office would proudly announce that such-and-such a firm had just been granted an ERDF award as evidence of the benefits of Community membership for Scotland, though the award in question had long been paid and spent under *national* regional policy, the ERDF money going to repay the Treasury. In the case of awards to local governments, European spending had to be accommodated within existing capital expenditure limits, though there was a small saving on loan charges. The most dishonest treatment of all was given to the 'rebates' received in the early 1980s on Britain's budget contributions. Although it was stipulated that these should go to investment projects in the regions, all the money was retained in the Treasury in London and signs placed on existing central government projects such as the A9 road and the Kessock Bridge announcing that these were the recipients of the funds. Press releases made the same claims. In France, by contrast, support for the Community was not a problem and the central government was able to corner structural fund moneys for its own purposes while giving no publicity to their existence (Mény, 1985).

The Commission has consistently tried to regain control over the structural funds and to make them the instruments of a genuine regional policy. In this it has had the support of regional governments and interest groups. The sheer administrative complexity of the matter and the relatively small size of the Commission bureaucracy, however, have ruled out direct administration. Instead, the Commission has tried to move towards a programmatic approach based on regional development plans which it will finance according to Community priorities. A 1984 reform relaxed the system of national quotas by expressing them as a range rather than a fixed amount. Member states would have to produce worthy projects to obtain the maximum. Projects themselves would have to form part of regional development programmes, some of which would be recognized as of special Community interest (Mawson *et al.*, 1985). This did have one effect, in that the requirements for ERDF claims were the main reason why the British government retained a system of regional development grants in the mid-1980s. Development programmes for Britain, however, retained their fairy-tale character. At one stage, the British government submitted the entire capital programme of the Scottish Office as a 'regional development programme'. Other programmes were hastily assembled clippings of existing documents.

The Commission also sought to control its development funds through a series of 'integrated' operations, including the Integrated Development Operations (IDOs) for Belfast and Naples and smaller-scale efforts for other cities. Given the limits on the structural funds and national additionality rules, these have generated a great deal more publicity than hard cash. A consultants' report for Glasgow admitted that there is 'no new EC budget specifically for an IDO: benefits lie in increasing the effectiveness of existing funds, in increased priority accorded to applications and higher rates of grant, and in the unquantifiable gains following from a closer relationship with the Community' (Roger Tym, 1984). This did not stop them talking of a £500 million 'forward programme' for five years, a figure derived from thin air and largely by assembling various elements of expenditure which would occur in any case. Not surprisingly, this figure gained the headlines and has surfaced again since. There have also been Integrated Mediterranean Programmes which have permitted some flexibility in the use of funds.

The accession of Greece, Spain and Portugal greatly widened the extent of regional disparities in the Community and the commitment to the internal market by the end of 1992 posed new fears for the fate of the peripheral regions and the prospects of opposition from them. As part of the commitment to the internal market, therefore, a doubling of the size of the structural funds was agreed upon and a new regulation devised for their administration. Again, the Commission's aim has been to make the funds a genuine instrument of Community policy, to target them effectively and to involve regional interests themselves in their disbursal. The new ERDF regulation limits support to regions designated according to Community-wide criteria. This has required the elaboration of the Community's own data base and comparative indices of economic problems. The Community distinguishes three levels of territory or NUTS ('nomenclature of territorial units for statistics'). Luxembourg, Denmark and Ireland are themselves regarded as level 1 and 2 units. Elsewhere, units are formed from regional and local government divisions and their groupings. The divisions are given in Table 1.

Regional problems are now measured by a 'synthetic index' including GDP per head of population and per person employed, unemployment and the jobs required for anticipated population expansion. The new regional development fund regulation is based on this and emphasizes the needs of local enterprise and partnership. Global grants will be made on the basis of development plans to regionally based managing organizations designated by agreement between the member state and the Commission. These will have to be based in the regions concerned, to have a public mission and to involve local social and economic actors. Early evidence indicates that traditionally centralized states such as Britain, France, Spain and Italy have continued to administer those funds in a centralized manner. Decentralized states such as Germany and Belgium have given a larger role to sub-national authorities, National quotas are still informally recognized.

Table 1   Nomenclature of territorial units for statistics (NUTS).

	NUTS 1	NUTS 2	NUTS 3
Belgium	Regions	Provinces	*Arrondissements*
Denmark	—	—	*Amter*
Fed. Rep. Germany	*Länder*	*Regierungsbezirke*	*Kreise*
Greece	NUTS 2 groupings	Development regions	*Nomoi*
Spain	NUTS 2 groupings	Autonomous Communities	Provinces
France	ZEAT (*Zones étendus d'aménagement du territoire*)	Regions	*Départements*
Ireland	—	—	Planning regions
Italy	NUTS 2 groupings	Regions	Provinces
Luxembourg	—	—	—
Netherlands	*Landsdelen*	Provinces	COROP-*regios*
Portugal	NUTS 2 groupings	NUTS 3 groupings	Groupings of *concelhos*
UK	Standard regions	NUTS 3 groupings	Counties, Scottish regions

Source: Commission of the European Communities, 1987.

The new system shifts resources into the less developed areas of Southern Europe and Ireland. Small amounts of funding were retained for declining industrial regions, to keep the northern countries on side. Regional funds remain small in relation to the overall Community budget. In 1988, structural funds comprised 16.9 per cent of the budget, of which 8 per cent was for the ERDF. By 1992, structural funds accounted for 25.4 per cent of the budget . Poorer countries, led by Spain, have bargained progress towards political and monetary union against increases in structural fund support but still tried to maintain control of the funds at national level. So, instead of a large expansion of regional aid, the Maastricht summit produced a new inter-state cohesion fund. While Commission officials calculated that achieving regional convergence would require a tripling of the main regional expenditure by 2010, Germany was complaining at the size of the existing bill.

Institutional linkages

Regions and regional policy have thus become an object of contestation among regional, national and European elites. Despite the tendency of national states to defend their autonomy in the face of European and sub-national challenges, there has been a gradual process of change. The Community and, in some states, regions have strengthened their power and new patterns of institutional linkages have emerged tying Europe to the regions. It is too simple to see this purely in terms of 'direct access' to Brussels by regions. Preponderant power remains in the hands of national governments acting through the Council of Ministers and European Council and there is no question of circumventing on these major policy issues. There is a common interest on the part of the Regional Policy Directorate of the Commission and regions in promoting contact and exchange to improve their information flow and encourage the emergence of a more European framework for discussion. The Competition Directorate, on the other hand, has opposed moves towards a stronger industrial or regional policy. The European Parliament, also seeking to expand its influence against national governments and the Commission, is a natural ally of the regions and has pressed both the Commission and the Council of Ministers to give more recognition to regional governments in the policy process. Given the varying national traditions and constitutional arrangements in the twelve countries, a variety of patterns has emerged.

In a complex intergovernmental network such as the triangular relationships emerging in the European Community, regions require both a degree of local autonomy and access to and influence over levels. Autonomy permits an area of independent action in response to regional demands as well as supporting a politics in which these can be formulated. Yet autonomy itself does not provide influence at the higher levels to which power has retreated. Indeed, it may diminish it as regional elites are politically isolated and contained. Systems in which devolution of power is organized strictly on functional lines may similarly serve to contain regional governments while not preventing national governments, under the foreign affairs doctrine, from using the Community as a pretext to encroach on regional matters.

Access and influence without autonomy are represented in the United Kingdom. There are no autonomous governments for the peripheral nations of Scotland and Wales. Instead, these are governed by territorially differentiated departments of the national administration which have the additional responsibility of acting as lobbyists for Scottish and Welsh interests in London (Midwinter, Keating and Mitchell, 1991). As part of the national administration, they are able to influence the British negotiating position in the Community. On matters affecting Scotland, for example, there will be a Scottish minister in the British negotiating team and occasionally, notably for fisheries matters, the Scottish minister will take the lead. In turn, the Scottish Office tries to ensure that the Scottish interests concerned are behind it. While this style of insider influence has proved quite effective on some issues, however, its weight should not be exaggerated. The influence of the Scottish Office in British government has been declining in recent years and since 1979 its ministers have become less and less representative of Scottish opinion. There is also a constant suspicion that, where trade-offs have to be made among policies, the Scots and Welsh are liable to lose out. In France, the tradition of accumulation of mandates provides another form of intergovernmental influence within a unitary state. There is a degree of territorial autonomy but the powers and resources of the regions are restricted and, despite the reforms of the 1980s, there is relatively little functional differentiation between them and central government. The very centralization of the French state, however, has generated its own forms of territorial power. Mayors of large cities and presidents of departmental and regional councils will sit in the national and European parliaments and, in some cases, be ministers in the national government. This provides a territorial input to national policy-making, including policy-making on European matters. The design and implementation of many development initiatives, too, require a complex negotiation with territorially based elites.

Autonomy without access is illustrated in the Italian and Spanish cases. In Spain, as Cuchillo notes, there is no formal mechanism for involving the regions in Community matters and the state has jealously guarded its prerogatives. Similarly in Italy, the centre has retained control of Community matters even where these involve matters of regional jurisdiction. On the other hand, the institution of the State-Regions Conference indicates that Italy may be moving in the direction of co-operative federalism, with formal functional division becoming less important and intergovernmental exchange taking place over a broad range of issues. In both Spain and Italy, regional governments have complained about being forced to implement Community directives in devolved areas but have reluctantly complied.

The combination of autonomy and influence is best represented in the German system of co-operative federalism. This provides for *Länder* influence in national policy and thence Community policy through the Bundesrat and other devices. The *Länder* are able to participate in the German delegation in various community forums. This includes representation on EC committees and the team backing the representative to the Council of Ministers. In addition, the *Länderbeobachter*, a civil servant appointed by the *Länder* collectively, is responsible for collecting information about Community matters and can attend the Council of Ministers as a non-speaking member of the German delegation, can join the preparatory meetings for the Council held in the Ministry of Economic Affairs and receives the orders of the German delegation to the Committee of Parliament of Permanent Representatives (Gerstenlauer, 1985). After the passage of the Single European Act, the role of the Bundesrat in EC affairs was further strengthened. Given the German tradition of co-operative federalism and consensus politics, this permits a considerable degree of influence to be be exercised.

While co-operative federalism allows for a regional input into Community policy it tends to be marked, in Germany as in other federations, by executive dominance. There is therefore a danger that its spread might exacerbate the 'democratic deficit' of the developing Community and increase tensions unless the Parliament strengthens its capacity for territorial representation. Systems of election to the European Parliament continue to differ among member states and not all have a territorial basis. Denmark, Greece, Luxembourg and the Netherlands have national list systems. France also has a national list system of election but the parties make sure that their lists have a balanced regional representation to the extent of including the territorial designation of each candidate in the publicity. Elsewhere, candidates are elected on constituency and regional bases and have explicit territorial mandates. The Parliament, struggling to assert itself against the Commission and national governments and parliaments, has on occasion shown itself sympathetic to the similar plight of regional governments. This attitude may also owe something to the influence within the Parliament of regional and local *notables* and especially those French *notables* who continue to hold local office. Several prominent French politicians, forced by the law on accumulation of mandates to surrender an elective office, have given up their national parliamentary mandate, choosing to retain their local and European ones. In 1988, having succeeded in persuading the Commission to establish a Consultative Council of Regional Authorities, the Parliament pleaded for a charter of regionalization for member states, providing for democratic election, adequate powers and finance, autonomy and the participation of regions in defining the negotiating positions of member states in Community institutions (Chauvet, 1989). Of course, this remains a non-binding recommendation adopted neither by the Commission nor by the member governments.

Several regions and local governments have sought direct links with the Community by opening offices in Brussels. Although there has been some opposition from national governments, this practice has spread and now includes all ten West German *Länder* and West Berlin (in nine offices), four Spanish regions (each with its own office), six French regions and two departments (in four offices) and four British local authorities (each with its own office) (Serignan, 1989). The main value of such offices is the ability to monitor developments in the Commission so as to be ready to put pressure on national governments to respond and to inform regions about the availability of various Community funds. In addition, there has been a sharp increase in the number of visits to Brussels by regional and local delegations, for information and to try to expedite specific dossiers. There is, however, no question of individual regions negotiating directly with the Community or acting in opposition to their national governments. Commission officials welcome visits but point out that under the rules and procedures they are powerless to provide extra funds to individual regions.

More important politically are the various regional lobby and consultative groups. The Commission is traditionally more receptive to transnational interest groups and there are several organizations which aspire to this role. The International Union of Local Authorities and the Council of Communes and Regions of Europe are both wider in scope than the Community and have been closely associated with the Council of Europe, which they persuaded to establish a Permanent Conference of Local and Regional Authorities in 1957. In 1986, they opened a joint office to deal with the EC (Chauvet, 1989). In 1985 the Council (later Assembly) of European Regions was launched with 107 members including eleven Swiss cantons and Austrian *Länder*. The establishment of formal rights of consultation with the Community owed a great deal to the pressure of the European Parliament, which, in the course of the reforms of the Community regional fund, stressed the need for greater involvement of regions themselves. In 1988, the Commission finally established a Consultative Council of Regional and Local Authorities with consultative rights over the formulation and implementation of regional policies as well as the regional implications of other Community policies. Its forty-two members are appointed by the Commission on the joint nomination of the Assembly of European Regions, the International Union of Local Authorities and the Council of Regions and Communes of Europe (Chauvet, 1989). The Maastricht treaty provided for a stronger, but still consultative, council of regions.

Other regional organizations seeking to influence policy-making in Brussels are the Conference of Peripheral Maritime Regions, the Association of European Frontier Regions, the Working Group of Traditional Industrial Regions and three Alpine groups. In addition, the development of the Community has encouraged the formation of a number of transnational frontier organizations.

There is thus a great deal of activity in the region-Europe link. The difficulty lies in picking out the significant dialogue amid the surrounding noise. The Commission encourages lobbying by non-national groups as a source of information and a strengthening of the *communautaire* spirit. Sometimes this has aroused national jealousies, as in the ease of the French Economic and Social Council which complained about the establishment of the Consultative Council of Regional and Local Authorities which merely created expectations and encouraged demands among which the national government would have to choose (Conseil Economique et Social, 1989). Yet the Commission has a fairly small bureaucracy and could not sustain continuous direct links with all regional authorities. One reason why national governments themselves have consolidated local governments is the difficulty of control in an excessively complex system. Nor is the Commission in a position to monitor the detailed administration of its own policies. While it can and does use regional governments as a resource, its main links are necessarily with member states. In those cases where regions have established links with Brussels, as in the German instance, these are not a means of bypassing national governments, which remain the key actors in policy-making, but a device to reinforce national-level lobbying (Anderson, 1990).

Beyond 1992

The programme to complete the internal market by the end of 1992 and proposals for monetary and political union will have major implications for the position of regions within the Community. The internal market and monetary union will tend to increase territorial disparities while reducing national governments' ability to protect vulnerable sectors and regions. A 1990 report for the Commission warns that the old industrial regions of northern Britain, north-west France and the Basque Country could suffer severely (Observer, 14.1.90). This in turn is likely to spawn coalitions of regional defence such as were seen in several European countries in the 1970s. The expansion of the regional development funds will provide help in economic restructuring but, if the experience of national regional policies is a precedent, may raise expectations by more than the capacity to satisfy them. The opening of the European market, together with the strengthening of decentralist trends in politics, is also increasing territorial competition for mobile investment on a European scale, to the advantage of the regions best equipped to receive it. National governments are less and less able to control this. Nor would they wish to do so, since attempts at diversionary policy are likely to drive investment to other states. As the spatial economy restructures, large costs are imposed on communities in terms of job losses, migration and social stress. Indeed, it is at the local and regional level that the conflict between the economic conception of Europe based on market liberalism and the social conception based on solidarity and welfare is most acutely felt.

Regions differ markedly in the extent to which they are able to compete in this new environment and to manage the social consequences of change, in terms both of their natural endowments and their institutional structures. In Germany, there is a well-established regional level which is linked closely to national politics and which has been increasingly active in economic development including infrastructure planning, research and development and technology transfer (Esser, 1989). Germany and

Belgium, indeed, are the only member states to have a level of government corresponding to the Community NUTS 1 level. In France, Italy and Spain, regional governments are less well endowed but there is evidence that some regional governments are learning more about mounting effective development policies. In France regions remain too small and arbitrarily drawn for the purposes of European competition, and decentralization has sparked off a great deal of competition among cities and departments within regions for mobile investment, to the detriment of the region as a whole. Since 1988, there have been moves to rationalize the spatial development effort through strengthened national urban policies and a relaunching of regional planning contracts, but radical proposals for redrawing regional boundaries are likely to meet the fate of earlier attempts to consolidate local government. In Britain, the absence of regional government was identified by the Commission report as a hindrance to progress. The pre-elected Conservative Government remains opposed to regional devolution.

Integration also carried implications for the character of politics within specific territories. In parts of Southern Europe, where class and territorial opposition to the internal market coincide, new movements of social protest can be anticipated, focused on the Community, as happened in the original Mediterranean members in the 1970s. Similar developments may occur in declining industrial areas of Northern Europe, though their target may depend on the content of national and Community policy. In Scotland where class and territorial oppositions combined to produce widespread rejection of the Community in the 1970s, matters changed as both Labour and nationalists saw Europe as a way of circumventing the centralist and market-oriented policies of the Thatcher government. The support of territorially based labour movements for the European project will hinge on the importance given to the social dimension.

Political integration has more radical implications for the territorial configuration of European states. A politically unified Europe, transcending the limitations of existing states, provides a new context in which problems insoluble in the national context may find solutions. German unification is the most prominent example but it also applies to other territorial issues. Some observers have hoped that the growing irrelevance of national borders might solve the Irish question, though the basis of that conflict in community struggles within Northern Ireland makes this unlikely. European unity has, however, given a new meaning to peripheral nationalist movements, which by campaigning for independence within Europe can discard the separatist label and, indeed, appear more cosmopolitan than their opponents within the existing states. Community membership has supplied a political and economic support system for small states since 1958 and may do so for more. The Scottish National Party has now adopted a policy of independence in Europe, reminiscent of an earlier phase when late-nineteenth-century nationalists called for independence within the Empire. Basque nationalists stress a similar message. In Catalonia attitudes are more ambiguous. Nationalism there has historically been caught between regional assertiveness and a continued commitment to the Spanish state. The dominant Convergència i Unió (CiU) continues this theme, seeing the Community as a way of reconciling its European and Spanish missions. It is in Belgium that this process has gone furthest. The existence of the Community has allowed the dismantling of large parts of the central state itself in favour of the regions and autonomous communities. The constitutional provision allowing the latter to make international agreements in cultural matters has given them some independent scope in the Community. In other fields, the absence of national ministries has meant that regional representatives are the only Belgian presence in the Council of Ministers and meetings of officials.

There is a certain logic to these developments. In Scotland, Catalonia, the Basque Country and other peripheries, membership of the 'national state' has always been somewhat contingent. In the absence of the deep-seated and exclusive national loyalty which French governments were able, with some success, to impose, Scots, Catalans and Basques preserved dual loyalties, favouring inclusion in the wider state when it coincided with class or other interests and was not unduly oppressive. The state also provided physical protection and economic support through trade policies, tariffs and subsidies. With military tensions relaxed in Europe and control over the key economic decisions moving to the Community level, this function is less important.

The more critical problem concerns the practicalities of the demand for independence within Europe. There is at present no provision for territories to secede from national states and rejoin the Community as independent members. It is difficult to envisage the Community refusing membership to a Scotland which had gained independence with the consent of the United Kingdom Parliament, since refusal would amount to expulsion; but the governments of Spain, France, Belgium and Italy would hardly welcome the precedent. The vision of all nation states breaking up into a 'Europe of the regions' remains strictly Utopian. Instead, there is likely to be increasing institutional differentiation within a wider European state order which itself is in rapid evolution. Some states will remain united and homogeneous. Others may tolerate degrees of autonomy coming close to separatism. Others may succeed in rationalizing their internal structures and stabilizing the relationship between state and region with the broader Community. It is very possible that the Community itself will divide into a core of integrated members and an outer circle of more loosely associated states. The opening of the Community to Eastern Europe will create yet further patterns. The future of the European state order is an issue too broad for this chapter, but what seems certain is that the clarity and logic of the nineteenth-century nation-state ideal or even the Community of nation states will give way to a new, and also older, picture of territorial differentiation and complexity.

Further readings and references

Anderson, J. (1990) 'Skeptical reflections of a "Europe of the regions" : Britain, West Germany and the European Regional Development Fund'. Paper to the American Political Science Association annual meeting, San Francisco.

André, C, Drevet, J -F and Landaburu, E (1989) 'Regional consequences of the internal market'. *Contemporary European Affairs*, 1 (1-2) 205-14.

Chauvet, J.-P. (1989) 'Participation des collectivités territoriales aux décisions européenes. Le rôle des lobbies locaux et régionaux', *Après- demain,* 314 -15: 9-12.

Commission of the European Communities (1987) *The Regions of the European Community: Third Periodic Report on the Social Situation and Development of the Regions of the European Community*. Luxembourg.

Conseil Economique et Social (1989) Report on meeting of 25 and 26 April 1989, *Journal officiel de la république française*, 12, 26 May.

Esser, J. (1989) 'Does industrial policy matter? *Land* governments in research and technology policy in Germany', in C. Crouch and D. Marquand (eds). *The New Centralism*. Oxford: Blackwell.

Fullarton, B. and Gillespie, A. (1988) 'Transport and telecommunications', in W. Molle and R. Cappelin(eds), *Regional Impact of Community Policies in Europe,* Aldershot: Gower.

Gerstenlauer, H-G. (1985) 'German *Länder* in the European Community', in M. Keating and B. Jones (eds), *Regions in the European Community*. Oxford: Clarendon.

Keating, M. (1988) *State and Regional Nationalism: Territorial Politics and the European State*. Hemel Hempstead: Harvester Wheatsheaf.

Keeble, D., Offord, J. and Walker, S. (1988) *Peripheral Regions in a Community of Twelve Member States*. Luxembourg: Commission of the European Communities.

Lankowsky, C (ed.) (1993) *Europe's Emerging Identity: Regional Integration vs Opposition Movements in the European Community*. Boulder, CO: Lynne Rienner.

Mawson, J., Martins, M.R. and Gibney, J. (1985) 'The development of the European Community regional policy', in M. Keating and B. Jones (eds), *Regions in the European Community*. Oxford: Clarendon.

Mény, Y. (1985) 'French regions in the European Community', M Keating and B. Jones (eds), *Regions in the European Community*. Oxford: Clarendon.

Midwinter, A., Keating, M. and Mitchell, J. (1991) *Politics and Public Policy in Scotland*. London: Macmillan

Molle, W. and Cappelin, R. (1988) 'The co-ordination problem in theory and policy', in W. Molle and R. Cappelin (eds), *Regional Impact of Community Policies in Europe*. Aldershot: Gower.

Roger Tym (1984) *Integrated Development Operation for Strathclyde. Final Report. Preparatory Study*. London: Roger Tym & Partners.

Serignan, M. (1989) 'L'Evolution des relations entre la CEE et les collectivités territoriales' *Après-demain,* 314-15: 4-7

Strijker, D. and de Veer, J. (1988) 'Agriculture', in W. Molle and R. Cappelin (eds), *Regional Impact of Community Policies in Europe*. Aldershot: Gower.

Part IV

External Trade Relations

13. The EC, the USA and Japan: The Trilateral Relationship in World Context

Peter Holmes and Alasdair Smith

Introduction

In this chapter we address the central issue of Europe's economic relations, past and future, with the rest of the world: we concentrate on the trilateral relationship between the EC, the USA and Japan. The formerly communist countries of Eastern and Central Europe (including the 'independent states' which have replaced the old Soviet Union) play a small role in world trade, partly because of their low income levels, partly because the economic system under which they operated until a few years ago discouraged international trade (see Dyker, 1991: 101-116). EFTA is small by comparison with the EC, and its trade patterns are in any case very similar to those of the Community. From 1 January 1993, furthermore, the EC and EFTA will be linked together in the 'European Economic Area' (EEA), which formalises and extends the *de facto* free trade regime that has governed trade between the two areas for many years. In using the EC as a proxy for Europe, then, we make a useful and reasonable simplification. The grounds for focusing on the relationships of the EC with the two other industrial giants are obvious: those relationships account for the bulk of the Community's extra-European trade, just as the three sides of the triangle account for the bulk of total world trade. EC trade with the developing world is quantitatively on a fairly small scale. But it is immensely important for a number of reasons, and is treated separately by Christopher Stevens in Dyker (1992: 211-229).

The basic facts of Europe's present position in world trade are set out in Tables 1-3.

Trade between developed countries is largely *intra-industry trade*, in which fairly similar goods are exchanged — a given country exporting cars, electrical appliances and metal products to its partners, and importing cars, electrical appliances and metal products from its partners. By contrast, most trade between developed and developing countries can be explained in terms of differences in factor endowments or conditions of production: labour-rich, low-technology countries trading labour-intensive, low-technology products like clothing and toys for capital-intensive or skill-intensive, higher-technology products like computers and cars from skill-rich and capital-rich advanced countries. It is one of the key features of the trade relationship between Japan and the rest of the industrial world that it involves inter-industry as well as intra-industry trade, and this sheds a lot of light on the tensions that affect that relationship.

Peter Holmes and Alasdair Smith: 'The EC, the USA and Japan: the trilateral relationship in world context', in *THE EUROPEAN ECONOMY*, edited by David Dyker (Longman, 1992). pp. 185-210.

Table 1 **European Communities (EC6, EC12) third country exports by product group, 1968-88 (per cent).**

	1968		1978		1988	
	EC6	EC12	EC6	EC12	EC6	EC12
Chemicals	12.1	11.1	12.1	11.4	13.4	13.6
Other non-electric machinery	15.2	14.4	15.9	15.7	13.7	13.6
Other consumer goods	7.4	7.7	8.1	8.5	10.3	11.2
Automotive products	11.4	11.6	11.0	9.5	12.8	9.3
Other semi-manufacturers	8.7	9.3	9.4	11.0	9.4	9.3
Food	7.4	8.6	7.0	7.6	7.3	7.3
Office machinery and telecommunications	4.5	4.3	4.1	3.8	5.4	5.3
Other transport equipment	3.7	4.5	3.8	4.6	3.6	5.2
Electric machinery and apparatus	4.7	4.6	5.1	4.8	4.7	4.4
Iron and steel	7.3	6.4	7.0	6.7	4.4	4.3
Textiles	5.1	5.2	3.5	3.3	3.6	3.0
Fuels	3.7	2.8	4.2	4.0	1.9	2.8
Residual	0.9	1.2	1.7	2.0	2.3	2.6
Clothing	1.7	1.9	1.5	1.6	2.1	2.2
Power generating machinery	0.6	0.7	2.0	2.3	1.4	2.1
Non-ferrous metals	2.6	2.8	1.6	1.5	1.7	1.6
Raw materials	2.2	2.2	1.4	1.2	1.5	1.5
Ores and minerals	0.8	0.7	0.6	0.5	0.5	0.7
Total merchandise exports	100	100	100	100	100	100

Source: GATT 1991 from UNSO, Comtrade database.

Symmetry and asymmetry in the trilateral relationship

Trade between the USA and Japan was notoriously imbalanced throughout the 1980s, with the United States frequently reporting trade deficits in excess of $100 billion, of which over half found a counterpart in the Japanese trade surplus with the United States. At times Japanese imports were about half Japanese exports, and vice versa for the USA. Meanwhile the EC as a whole had a current account surplus of just under 1 per cent of GNP from 1983 to 1990. The overall EC surplus was, of course, composed of a series of sub-totals, with Germany running a consistent surplus while other EC states had deficits totalling less than the German surplus. The EC has, certainly, run a trade deficit with Japan, but the nature of the deficit is quite different from that of the corresponding American one. These deficits have been a fruitful source of controversy and misunderstanding, so it is worth pausing to clarify some important points of principle.

Table 2   **European Communities (EC6, EC12) third country imports by product group, 1969-88 (per cent).**

	1968		1978		1988	
	EC6	EC12	EC6	EC12	EC6	EC12
Fuels	18.0	17.9	26.5	28.1	12.2	12.8
Office machinery and telecommunications	2.7	2.5	4.5	4.4	10.3	11.4
Food	21.6	22.6	15.8	15.6	11.0	10.0
Other consumer goods	3.4	3.3	5.7	5.5	8.9	9.2
Other semi-manufacturers	6.1	6.8	6.9	7.8	8.1	7.9
Chemicals	5.2	4.7	5.9	4.9	8.1	6.6
Raw materials	11.6	12.4	6.0	6.8	5.0	5.6
Other non-electric machinery	4.9	4.1	4.3	3.9	5.5	5.4
Automotive products	1.7	1.0	3.0	2.2	5.4	4.5
Clothing	1.0	1.0	3.0	2.6	4.6	4.3
Residual	1.6	1.2	2.4	2.1	3.5	3.9
Electric machinery and apparatus	1.9	1.7	1.9	1.6	3.2	3.2
Other transport equipment	2.6	3.3	2.3	3.3	2.3	3.2
Non-ferrous metals	7.1	7.3	2.8	2.7	2.9	2.9
Ores and minerals	6.6	6.1	3.5	3.5	2.6	2.8
Textiles	1.9	2.0	2.5	2.2	2.7	2.6
Iron and steel	1.9	1.9	2.2	1.9	2.4	2.1
Power generating machinery	0.2	0.2	0.8	0.9	1.3	1.6
Total merchandise imports	100	100	100	100	100	100

Source: GATT 1991 from UNSO, Comtrade database.

A trade deficit represents an excess of consumption and investment over production, or, to put it another way, an excess of investment over saving; a trade surplus represents precisely the reverse. It is possible on this basis to interpret the US deficit with Japan as the natural outcome of interaction between a low-saving economy and a high-saving one, between a country that wants to spend a lot of money on defence without raising taxes and one that does not want to spend much money on defence at all. The Japanese sell cars to the United States and invest the dollars thus earned in US government bonds. To describe this as a 'natural' outcome of differences in saving behaviour is not to imply that there are no grounds for concern. On the contrary, such a process implies a sustained growth of US debt to Japan, and ultimately a major readjustment or even financial crisis if the Japanese ever decide that they do not want to hold any more American assets. But to see the deficit, as do many American observers and especially many American politicians, simply as the result of 'unfair' Japanese practices or of American uncompetitiveness, is at best to miss a central *macroeconomic* point. We return to this issue later.

Table 3   **Leading partners in European Communities (EC12) merchandise trade, 1981-8 (million ECU and per cent).**

Countries	Exports				Countries	Imports			
	Million ECU	Share in total exports	Compound annual growth rate			Million ECU	Share in total imports	Compound annual growth rate	
	1988	1988	81-8	85-8		1988	1988	81-8	85-8
United States	71,795	19.8	9.3	-5.7	United States	68,319	17.6	3.2	-0.3
Switzerland	35,872	9.9	7.1	7.1	Japan	41,565	10.7	13.4	13.3
Austria	22,510	6.2	9.7	7.6	Switzerland	29,428	7.6	8.2	7.5
Sweden	21,120	5.8	7.8	0.5	Sweden	21,943	5.7	8.0	3.8
Japan	17,016	4.7	16.3	17.6	Austria	16,869	4.4	11.8	9.5
Canada	10,122	2.8	11.8	0.7	Soviet Union	12,988	3.4	-1.2	-14.4
Soviet Union	10,113	2.8	2.9	-6.8	South Africa	12,533	3.2	8.0	9.8
Norway	8,510	2.3	4.7	-3.9	Norway	12,498	3.2	2.6	-11.0
Finland	7,762	2.1	9.8	6.3	Brazil	9,329	2.4	7.2	-3.8
Saudi Arabia	7,571	2.1	-5.1	-11.7	Finland	8,993	2.3	8.3	5.9
Hong Kong	6,766	1.9	14.3	14.1	Canada	8,407	2.2	2.8	3.6
Australia	6,365	1.8	6.7	-4.0	Taiwan	8,064	2.1	17.2	26.4
South Africa	6,358	1.8	-1.5	3.8	Korea, Rep. of	7,233	1.9	17.0	29.2
China	5,801	1.6	16.7	-6.9	China	7,004	1.8	16.6	21.2
Yugoslavia	5,713	1.6	3.7	-1.1	Hong Kong	6,316	1.6	6.8	9.4
India	5,637	1.6	7.2	-0.7	Yugoslavia	5,891	1.5	14.9	7.0
Turkey	5,225	1.4	12.5	-1.1	Saudi Arabia	5,470	1.4	-24.9	-14.0
Israel	4,712	1.3	11.2	6.3	Libya	5,223	1.3	-6.4	-24.1
Taiwan	4,459	1.2	21.6	24.9	Australia	4,884	1.3	8.4	-0.5
Korea, Rep. of	4,391	1.2	21.0	16.7	Algeria	4,863	1.3	-4.1	-25.2
Singapore	4,066	1.1	9.8	2.2	Turkey	4,346	1.1	17.1	10.4
Algeria	3,703	1.0	-6.9	-20.5	Poland	3,360	0.9	6.8	-2.0
Egypt	3,675	1.0	-3.1	-17.4	India	3,256	0.8	7.7	2.9
Brazil	3,121	0.9	2.3	5.2	Iran	3,106	0.8	-3.3	-22.7
Iran	2,872	0.8	-6.3	-18.7	Singapore	2,993	0.8	12.1	12.3

Table 3 (Continued)   **Leading partners in European Communities (EC12) merchandise trade, 1981-8 (million ECU and per cent).**

Countries	Exports				Countries	Imports			
	Million ECU	Share in total exports	Compound annual growth rate			Million ECU	Share in total imports	Compound annual growth rate	
	1988	1988	81-8	85-8		1988	1988	81-8	85-8
Poland	2,756	0.8	2.4	0.3	Thailand	2,966	0.8	10.2	9.1
Libya	2,716	0.7	-15.0	-9.5	Israel	2,885	0.7	7.0	1.7
Morocco	2,609	0.7	3.5	-0.8	Nigeria	2,876	0.7	-10.1	-36.8
Iraq	2,420	0.7	-14.7	-17.6	Iraq	2,786	0.7	-4.3	-26.5
Venezuela	2,403	0.7	0.9	1.6	Malaysia	2,687	0.7	5.1	-1.5
Hungary	2,354	0.6	2.4	-1.8	Argentina	2,623	0.7	3.4	-7.2
Mexico	2,296	0.6	-6.5	-6.5	Mexico	2,456	0.6	-6.1	-21.8
United Arab Emirates	2,288	0.6	-2.6	-11.1	Morocco	2,271	0.6	7.2	2.1
Czechoslovakia	2,170	0.6	6.2	3.3	Romania	2,234	0.6	1.9	-8.4
Nigeria	2,165	0.6	-17.4	-21.5	Czechoslovakia	2,211	0.6	4.7	-0.9
Thailand	2,071	0.6	12.2	8.2	Chile	2,183	0.6	7.7	7.6
Tunisia	2,003	0.6	-0.2	-4.5	Hungary	2,158	0.6	5.5	2.3
Indonesia	1,934	0.5	-1.2	-5.2	Indonesia	2,134	0.6	8.3	3.3
Pakistan	1,605	0.4	5.9	-1.1	Kuwait	2,099	0.5	-6.1	-24.3
Kuwait	1,394	0.4	-5.8	-18.6	Egypt	1,641	0.4	-9.8	-26.6
Total of the above	318,439	87.8	5.1	-1.3	Total of the above	351,091	90.6	3.4	-0.9
Total trade	362,788	100.0	4.6	-1.4	Total trade	387,519	100.0	2.9	-1.6

Source: GATT 1991 from Eurostat, External Trade Statistical Yearbook, 1989.

The European deficit with Japan is different because it is not an element within a greater deficit. Rather it is a specific deficit matched (in fact more than matched) by a trade surplus with the rest of the world (including a substantial one with the United States). The 'natural' explanation for this pattern would be that Japan is a resource-poor country which has to import natural resources, especially energy from the Middle East, and has to pay for these imports through exports to the EC (and the USA). European politicians and observers are, however, as reluctant as their American counterparts to accept 'natural' explanations of Japanese success in exporting manufactures, and are subjecting the Japanese phenomenon to ever closer scrutiny.

The real problem which both the USA and the EC face is that Japanese imports, whether they contribute to overall balance of payments problems or not, are concentrated in particular sectors, namely cars and electronics. This brings us back to one of our earlier points. In contrast to the general pattern of trade between advanced economies, Japanese-EC/US trade is to a great extent based on inter-industry rather than intra-industry trade. Competitive pressures in intra-industry trade can be handled by a given enterprise through a relatively painless process of seeking a new niche in the same market. Japanese competition, by contrast, seems to require an all or nothing response, and to threaten the extinction of whole industries and therefore whole lines of technological development (see Dyker, 1992: 233-323). The OECD forecasts that the macroeconomic imbalances will shrink sharply in the 1990s, but that the problem of industrial mix will remain.

Finally in this introductory section, it is increasingly inappropriate to think about world economic relations in terms of trade alone. Investment flows are becoming an increasingly important dimension of the world economy. Investment is harder to trace than trade, so we have a less reliable picture of world investment flows than of flows of imports and exports; but in general terms the pattern of world investment is similar to that of trade, with the biggest flows being among the developed countries rather than from the developed to the developing. Inevitably, given the overall balance of payments trends we have just noted, the outward flow of Japanese investment has been among the most marked, and most controversial, of the features of the 'globalisation of business'.

It is these issues that set the agenda for the succeeding sections of this chapter. First, we look at the institutional context of EC trade policy and assess the real level of protection that policy has afforded. Then we look at the question of how 'common' the policy has in fact been and how it has related to competition policy, devoting a special section to the Common Agricultural Policy. The next two sections come back round to the crucial trilateral issues outlined above, by focusing on two key manufacturing sectors — electronics and cars. In shifting the perspective towards the future we look first at the concept of 'strategic trade policy' and then at the special issues raised by the reform process in Eastern Europe. We end by posing two fundamental and interrelated questions. Will '1992' bring the European Community closer to the rest of the world? And what is the future position of Europe in the international division of labour?

The framework of trade policy

The EC is part of the GATT system. Though it is the member states, not the EC itself, that are the signatories of GATT, the Community (in the future the Union) negotiates as a single entity. The original Rome Treaty specified under Article 113 that by 1969 there should be a true common commercial policy with all trade barriers against third countries unified, while Article 115 provided an escape clause in allowing for the survival of national trade policies as long as the common policy stayed on the drawing-board. In the event, the member states achieved the goal of a common tariff regime, but failed to unify other policies affecting trade, such as technical barriers, administrative restrictions and 'voluntary export restraints'. In 1982 the Commission produced a list of national trade policy measures which it recognised as formal derogations from the common commercial policy. The Commission chose to ignore many other measures in the hope that the reality of a single market would eventually lead to their abandonment.

Common tariff or no, tariff barriers are in practice of very limited significance. As much as 29 per cent of EC imports bear a tariff of 5 per cent or under, and 90 per cent pay under 15 per cent (GATT 1991: 263). What is perhaps more important than the height of tariffs is the fact that they are 'bound' under GATT rules. All GATT members are bound not to raise tariffs on industrial products, and indeed are committed to a series of 'rounds' of tariff cuts.

One of the unspoken aims of the '1992' Plan was to *force* the member states to accept the logic of having a single regime *vis-à-vis* the outside world, and it will in a sense be possible from 1993 to treat the EC as a single trading body. The GATT secretariat has already, in its series of reviews of trade policy by signatories, published a single report on the trade policy of 'the European Communities'. The EC has just joined its first international organisation (the UN Food and Agriculture Organisation) as one entity. But member states are still jealous of their trade policy powers. A complex legal debate is going on about whether the European Commission is authorised to negotiate and the Council of Ministers to agree trade accords on behalf of individual member states, or whether the whole EC can only be bound if each individual state signs given agreements (see Victor 1990). The EC Commission tends to argue that where there is Community competence only Community organs can act. Some member states insist that unless the EC Treaties specifically provide for Community agencies to act, member states must endorse any collective action. This is a minor technicality when all member states are agreed, but there is more than symbolism at issue when, by insisting on the need to sign separately, member states are reaffirming their ultimate right to act independently (see Dyker, 1992: 51-69 and 71-87). The Uruguay Round of GATT negotiations appears to have led to more formal collective action by the EC-12 than previous rounds, in that the EC Commission is authorised to be the spokesman for the twelve member states. But the pattern of that authorisation makes for a certain rigidity. The EC's negotiators come to the conference table with a negotiating position that has already been hammered out in intra-EC deliberations, and this may make it difficult for them to make concessions. The point has come out with particular clarity in relation to negotiations on agriculture, where the inflexibility of the EC's position is surely linked to the lack of an intra-EC consensus on the right direction to go in. (Contrast this to the position of the US administration, which is given 'fast track' negotiating authority by Congress to get the best deal it can, and then submit it for ratification or rejection as a package.) Thus a final agreement (uncertain at time of writing) will have to have the support of all EC member states. Draft agreements drawn up by the GATT secretariat have provided for a compromise on the legal issue of who should sign, by allowing both the European Communities and all the member states to sign.

The member states of the EC are obliged under EC law to remove all mutual trade barriers. The EC itself bears the GATT obligation to offer 'most favoured nation' (MFN) treatment to all the other signatories of GATT, ie to eschew any kind of discrimination that might lead to suspicion of the formation of trade blocs. In fact it does not do so. The

EC is embedded in a web of preferential trade agreements which exploit various exception clauses in the GATT text to offer lower tariffs to its immediate neighbours, and to certain less developed countries with which it wants good diplomatic relations.

Exception clauses or not, doubts have been raised as to the compatibility with GATT of the EC's modes of circumvention of the MFN rules. Even the links with the EFTA zone left a GATT panel 'unable to reach a conclusion' on the question of compatibility with the General Agreement (GATT 1990: 62). However, the EC has, by and large, respected 'tariff binding' — the other pillar of GATT. We argue elsewhere (see Dyker, 1992: 51-69) that the crucial achievement of the EC on the internal plane was the solidity of the pledge that trade barriers inside the EC would never be increased. Forcing them down to zero was a way of signalling this intent with the maximum clarity. The GATT system has set itself the more modest aim of binding tariffs; that is, ensuring that they could only go down, never up. Like other trading powers, the EC has basically stuck to this bargain. Thus tariffs are not an instrument that European politicians can use at their discretion to favour selected interest groups. Both importers and home producers know that the current level of tariff is a ceiling offering the carrot of free market access to those producers who can be competitive at the given rates and the stick of free competition from outside to those who cannot (see OECD 1987). Agriculture apart (see Dyker, 1992: 325-347), this principle holds pretty well. But it leaves quite a lot of room for discretion on matters other than the basic tariff rates. Indeed just as the removal of tariffs caused the relative, sometimes even absolute, prominence of non-tariff barriers to rise *within* the EC, as governments intent on pursuing their own trade policy *vis-à-vis* the non-EC world found it necessary to erect barriers against the 'deflection' of non-EC goods entering the Community through other member countries with different trade policies, so the GATT rules on tariff binding have induced an exploration at the Community's interface with the rest of the world of grey area measures that do not violate GATT openly.

The Rome Treaty laid down that EC commercial policy was to be agreed by Qualified Majority Voting in the Council of Ministers — on proposals from the EC Commission — and then implemented by the Commission. A complex of committees was set up to oversee the activities of the Commission in this connection. There is considerable controversy over the way the Commission uses the powers that have been delegated to it by the Council of Ministers. Some British observers claim that the Commission has resorted to something akin to cunning to get its own way in the face of potential resistance from the Council of Ministers. It must be said, however, that on the whole the Commission has to act within guidelines set by ministers. To the extent that it has room for manoeuvre, it uses it not to thwart any collective vision, but rather to exploit differences between member states and to choose which one of a number of possible compromises should prevail. As we shall see below, there is considerable debate about anti-dumping actions by the Commission, an area where it enjoys delegated executive power, but it seems that even here there is no general dissatisfaction in the Council of Ministers with the way the Commission is exercising its powers. If there were, the Council would, of course, have the power to instruct the Commission to alter its policy.

One of the most sensitive implications of the '1992' Plan is that all goods from third countries will have to be permitted to circulate freely and on equal terms inside the EC, wherever they enter, as Articles 9 and 10 of the Rome Treaty actually lay down; only then will we be able to talk of a truly single market. That means in effect that member countries will no longer be able to maintain national policies sanctioned under Article 115. We can assume, therefore, that from 1993 there will indeed be a common external trade regime. A *second layer of discrimination* exists, however, and the treatment of external imports will continue to differ according to where they come from, even after 31 December 1992.

There is a complex hierarchy of preferential trade agreements affecting less developed countries (see Christopher Stevens in Dyker, 1992: 211-229). As far as advanced industrial countries are concerned, we can distinguish between intra-European relations and relations with Japan and the USA. As we saw earlier, the EC plus EFTA is effectively a free trade zone; it is also understood that formal non-tariff barriers are not applied between the EC and EFTA, though the EEA agreement does allow the invocation of emergency safeguard measures (see pp. 194-5). In contrast, goods imported from Japan and the USA are subject to the full Common External Tariff and any other measures of trade policy the EC cares to impose.

The actual level of protection

It is a paradox of the present trade policy debate that where special measures such as VERs or anti-dumping duties are not applied, EC trade policy is actually very liberal. Even for Japan and the USA, which do not benefit from any trade concessions beyond the standard GATT obligations, the operational rates of tariff are low. GATT estimated the simple average rate of tariff on industrial products at 6.4 per cent in 1988. There is relatively little deviation around this average. Even for sensitive sectors tariffs are modest: cars bear an average tariff rate of 10 per cent (though some vehicles bear 22 per cent), and textiles and clothing tariffs go from 0 per cent to 17 per cent. Photographic and optical goods carry an average of about 7 per cent. These figures reinforce the view that tariff barriers and their removal are not the most significant element in world trade today.

The standard deviation in 1988 across all EC industrial tariffs was 2.6 per cent. This is important, as it is the differences between tariff rates that determine how much the protective system is altering the direction of economic activity. If some industries have heavy protection and others little, there is an incentive for resources to move into or stay in some sectors rather than others. If, by contrast, all industrial goods were protected equally, then no one industry would benefit relative to others. There are, indeed, some trade restrictions which affect individual sectors very strongly, and without which it is hard to imagine investment taking place within the EC in these sectors, but such measures are usually other than the conventional tariff which figures in the trade textbooks. Non-tariff barriers apart, the most important forms of 'extraordinary' protection are 'safeguard' and 'anti-dumping' tariffs.

Broadly speaking the USA is not subject to trade restrictions other than the regular tariffs in relation to its exports to the EC. The exceptions, and the main bones of contention on trade between the EC and the USA, concern agricultural products and a very limited number of high-tech products. Japanese imports into the EC are in principle treated on the same basis as imports from the USA. The rapid rise of EC imports from Japan in certain very sensitive areas, however, combined with the recession conditions of the 1980s, has led to considerable pressure on the Japanese to 'moderate' their exports to the EC. So far these measures have been negotiated, sometimes tacitly, between the Japanese and individual member states. From 1993 this will no longer be feasible. We take up this point again on pp. 329-334.

Obstacles to a common policy

Let us return to the issue of 'trade deflection' and Article 115. Where a member state has a national barrier to external imports recognised under EC law, and if trade deflection via member states that do not have such barriers is causing 'disruption', the member state in question may at present apply to the EC Commission for permission to impose controls on extra-EC imports as they come in across the intra-EC border. Italy, for example, has exercised the right to stop Japanese cars coming in via France. The most striking use of Article 115 has been in relation to imports of textiles and clothing from less developed and industrialising countries over a period of some thirty years (see Christopher Stevens in Dyker, 1992: pp. 211-229). Under the rubric of 'Multifibre Arrangements' (MFAs) lasting four to five years each, the main exporting and importing countries sign a series of bilateral voluntary export restraint agreements. These are totally against the principles of GATT, and in order to preserve a facade of legality a special set of exceptional rules have been laid down to govern the quotas.

The cost to consumers in the developed countries is high. The World Bank (1987: 152) cites estimates ranging from $1.4 billion to $6.6 billion for the cost to EC consumers of having to buy textiles and clothing from more expensive sources. Nor is there any evidence that this kind of protection saves jobs. The OECD (1985) notes that in textiles and clothing, as well as in the highly protected iron and steel sector, job losses have continued unabated despite protection. This is partly because restricting imports to keep up prices not only permits the survival of old-fashioned, inefficient firms, but also facilitates the entry of new, more efficient domestic firms. This new entry ultimately drives out the weaklings just as surely as import competition. Peter Holmes (in Dyker, 1992: 51-69, on the integration process) discusses the phenomenon of trade diversion. In the context of the MFA what this means is that inefficient clothing firms in the North of England cannot be protected as long as the UK is part of a customs union, since Italian firms can replace imports from outside the EC. In fact, this is not as high a 'cost' as it seems. The pressure of competition from Italian firms forces UK clothing firms to become more efficient. On the other hand, the higher prices permitted by protection may promote new investment even from local sources, and so induce excess capacity. (The problem is, of course, further intensified when foreign investors from the extra-EC exporting countries can set up plants behind the protective walls too.)

Producers are not easily convinced of the proposition that cutting out one source of competition may simply lead to its replacement by another, so they often plead for the use of intra-EC border measures to segregate national markets against third country competition. The Single European Act did not, in fact, repeal Article 115, and the original White Paper (EC Commission 1985) on the Single Market posited only that Article 115 should not be implementable by the use of intra-EC border controls. Yet the logic of the '1992' Programme is surely its total abolition. What is in practice happening is that the EC Commission is steadily proceeding with its aim of phasing out the use of Article 115 and thus creating a truly common commercial policy. The matter is so sensitive that the Commission is endeavouring to convince the member states of the necessity of *simultaneously* implementing a common external policy and putting an end to the use of Article 115. The directorates of the Commission were at time of writing working on the assumption that the EC will in the future have a totally unified approach to textiles and clothing, with global quotas for products between individual exporters and the entire EC, and with no use of Article 115. However, it is being hinted to exporters that they should not increase their sales to the previously most restricted markets too fast.

The essence of the debate that is going on at the moment is whether the new measures aimed at fashioning a common commercial policy will mark steps towards protectionism or away from it. The external relations directorate of the Commission, in association with the industrial policy divisions, is seeking to 'reassure' business that moving from national to Community policies will not leave them totally at the mercy of Japanese or Korean imports. The reasoning here is entirely political rather than economic, but the economic implications are disturbing. Many writers (eg Hindley 1988) are very concerned about the way that the EC Commission is increasingly invoking anti-dumping duties in areas where national measures were previously in force. Anti-dumping duties were originally developed at the turn of the century to guard against 'predatory pricing', whereby a potential monopolist could undercut newer smaller rivals in order to corner a market. It is widely agreed (Ordover and Saloner 1989) that a special set of rules that go beyond normal anti-trust regulations may be needed for imports. The reason is that it is very expensive for a big firm to engage in predatory price cutting against a small rival, if it is operating in a single geographical territory. The small firm can retaliate against the big firm's home sales base, and the big firm cannot easily confine its price discounts to customers who might be thinking of switching to the new firm. In contrast, where the 'attacking' firm is in a separate country and its home market is protected by tariffs, it is possible to cut prices selectively without suffering either retaliation or loss of home base sales. Thus predatory dumping to capture a world market, and certain other forms of related 'unfair trade practice' often relating to subsidies, are indeed real possibilities (see pp. 334-335 on strategic trade policy). However, most analysts (eg Stegemann 1991) have concluded that there has been widespread abuse of the anti-dumping rules.

GATT permits two forms of contingency measure. Article XIX allows countries suffering a sudden and unforeseen 'surge' of imports to take emergency safeguard measures. But the conditions for doing this are rightly circumscribed, and 'compensation' may have to be offered to injured parties. This puts the country using Article XIX measures in the dock as a violator of GATT, so countries prefer to use Article VI, which permits the use of anti-dumping duties where an exporter is gaining in market share 'unfairly', by selling below his normal price on the home market. The EC Council of Ministers has laid down very complex regulations governing the way the Commission imposes anti-dumping duties. First, sales below 'normal' price must be proved, and then injury must be proved. Even then, the 'Community interest' has to be considered before duties are actually imposed. Considerable discretion exists at each step in the calculation. Critics argue (eg Schuknecht 1991) that it is always exercised in a protectionist way. For example, comparing export prices with 'normal' home prices involves an averaging process. Any home sales below full cost will be treated as abnormal and excluded from the calculation, while any export prices above normal price will be excluded because 'negative dumping' is impossible. The calculation of injury is always dependent on data supplied by the injured party, and the Commission uses informal judgement rather than independent analysis to decided whether loss of intra-EC market share is due to 'unfair' competition. The analysis of Community interest is based on the proposition that the best interests of users and consumers alike are served by the existence of a 'viable community industry', an argument that is, to say the least, controversial.

The Commission has been extremely active in using anti-dumping procedures, particularly in the electronics field on (see pp. 329-330 in this chapter and Dyker, 1992: 273-297) and especially against Japan, the NICs and Eastern Europe. Member states have in the past been prepared to use voluntary export restraints as a way of extending the range of restriction on imports from Japan and Korea beyond the coverage of the MFA. However, these risk violating GATT and represent a violation of the Rome Treaty's competition rules as well. The practice has developed among well-organised industries, faced with strong import competition, of seeking government approval for 'industry-to-industry' agreements to limit sales. 'Approval' means that the government may tacitly threaten use of Article XIX measures against the foreign industry, or may just turn a blind eye. Under Japanese law, the Fair Trade Commission can permit limitations on exports if there would otherwise be a threat of trade policy intervention (see GATT 1990). For example the Japanese have agreed with the British car industry to take no more than 11 per cent of the UK market (see Dyker, 1992: 200-203 and 255-271). Where agreements like this are made between governments, GATT rules are violated, but the only people who can complain are the other governments — who are not, of course, going to. Where firms or trade associations meet to do deals restricting sales or raising prices, they are in fact forming a cartel. A series of decisions and court cases under Article 85 of the Rome Treaty (see Bourgeois 1989) has made it very clear that such practices are illegal. (The first such case arose when French and Japanese ball-bearing manufacturers agreed to share the French market.)

Anti-dumping actions and VERs carry an importance that goes far beyond their immediate impact. They create disincentives to investment in export success, since they imply that export success may be stymied by European trade barriers; and they create uncertainty for exporters, as they are applied with a high degree of discretion. Outright cartelisation apart, both anti-dumping measures and voluntary export restrictions are likely to have significantly anti-competitive effects. As Patrick Messerlin (1990) has argued, if a price-cutting firm is threatened with anti-dumping action by its less aggressive rivals, there is a clear incentive for all the firms to get together to agree prices that are mutually satisfactory, if less satisfactory for consumers. Export restraints have two kinds of anti-competitive effect: by limiting sales from restrained firms, they reduce the competitive pressure on other firms; and by requiring market-sharing arrangements to be set up by the exporting firms, they make entry of new firms in the exporting country more difficult.

Restrictions on direct imports do, of course, have the perverse effect of attracting inward investment that neutralises the protection. There is, certainly, some disagreement as to how far Japanese inward investments are stimulated by actual or threatened, EC protectionism. Thomsen and Nicolaides (1990) argue that globalisation of production is a natural process involving all firms — including the Japanese (see Dyker, 1992: 233-253). But other writers (eg Belderbos 1991) suggest that EC trade policy *has* been an important factor. In the 1960s many governments were willing to restrict inward investment as well as trade, but considerations of employment and technological conditions make this unrealistic today. Globalisation, whatever its roots, creates a whole new complex of interrelated trade and competition issues, which we treat in the next section.

Trade policy and competition

In an increasingly globalised market it becomes more and more difficult to sustain the view that competition from non-EC-owned firms or non-EC-located production should be regulated differently from wholly indigenous production. The US writer Robert Reich (1990) asks 'Who is "us"?' An increasing proportion of EC-based production is by foreign-owned firms, while EC-owned firms produce more and more abroad. An integrated world market probably brings more technology transfer. And if there are problems of global unfair competition they can be dealt with only by world-wide antitrust agreements (see Hansen 1991). The internationalisation of business may, in fact, have a major impact on the way the business world on balance views the benefits of protection. Schuknecht (forthcoming) interprets the commitment to an open trade policy within the EC as essentially a triumph of political and economic interests with an export orientation over those more interested in protection against imports. Milner (1988) has shown that multinational firms may well lobby for free trade rather than protection. However, some of the same incentives to take the edge of competition that exist in an national oligopoly situation also exist on a global scale. The European Community, in its most recent statement of principles on industrial and trade policy (EC Commission 1990), has argued that free external competition is an necessary counterpart of a free internal market. However, there are important and difficult issues to face in certain sectors where economies of scale are so large that there may be room only for a very small number of firms in the EC. Merger policy must take trade and technology issues into account. On the whole it seems sensible to argue that we can be more lax about permitting mergers the more open the EC market is. But there does come a point where we must start worrying about global oligopolies, which may form 'strategic alliances', sometimes ostensibly to imitate Japanese *keiretsu* (interlinked) firms. The head of the German Federal cartel office, W. Kartte, has warned that "strategic alliances" are often tantamount to private market orders, which necessarily lead to distortions of the world economy' (Hansen 1991: 215; see also Holmes 1991). We do therefore need to be vigilant about unfair competition, but not in an oversimplified way that sees all external competition as harmful.

The Common Agricultural Policy

It is certainly the trade effects of the Common Agricultural Policy that have contributed most to the Community's protectionist image. It is fair to add, however, that the Community inherited national traditions of protecting agriculture, traditions found in other developed countries in equal measure, and simply merged them into the CAP.

The CAP attracts particular attention, first because the sheer size of the Community's agricultural trade gives it a major influence on world markets. As the Community limits imports, for example, by imposing levies to bring import prices up to levels at which European farmers can compete, the effect is to depress prices on world markets. Anderson and Tyers (1986) found that the effects of the EC's farm policies on world markets were much bigger in every sector that they studied than the effects of other countries' policies, with the single exception of the rice market, where Japanese import restrictions have indeed a greater impact than the CAP. It is also worth noting that the effects of the CAP are not just on the level of world prices, but also on their variability: guaranteed prices insulate European farmers and consumers from the low prices that obtain in years of plenty, so ensuring that the European market plays no part in absorbing the plenty and implying a bigger price reduction in the rest of the world.

The second feature of the CAP that has brought it into the international spotlight is its 'success' in generating European self-sufficiency through high farm prices. In the early 1960s the Community covered around 90 per cent of its agricultural consumption with own production; by the mid-1980s, according to Anderson and Tyers (1986), it was producing around 105 per cent of its consumption. Keeping up the price of an imported good requires an import tax, whose impact on the level of consumer prices may not be visible to the average citizen, and which contributes positively to budget revenue. Keeping up the price of an exported good requires budgetary expenditure to cover buying the product at the high European price and selling it at the lower world price. As the costs of the CAP have started to appear on the EC budget as well as on consumer budgets, the Community has become more concerned to contain those costs. More important in the present context, as the CAP has constrained the EC to offload its surpluses on to world markets, the costs to farmers outside the Community have become more apparent — and the United States in particular, has become more militant in its demands for CAP reform.

Although the CAP has ill effects on developing countries, especially in relation to the sugar market (sugar is an unusual product in that it is produced in two quite different ways in temperate and tropical climates), it is other developed countries that (together with European consumers) incur the greatest costs. The CAP has its biggest impact on temperate products, such as beef, lamb, dairy products, sugar beet and grains; it is the interests of exporters of these products in Australia, New Zealand and North America which are most affected.

The extent of the problem that the CAP creates for the world trading system is clearly indicated by the obstacles that it placed in the way of the Uruguay Round of trade negotiations in the period from 1986 to 1992. The Community has been faced with determined pressure from the United States, not itself particularly committed to freer agricultural trade as such but concerned about the increasing competition it faces on world markets from the EC's surpluses, and from the Cairns group of countries, including Australia, whose clear interest as temperate zone agricultural exporters is in freer trade. It continues to defend a policy that imposes great costs on European consumers, increasing costs on the Community budget, and has threatened to scupper a set of trade negotiations in the success of which the Community has a vital interest. Faced with all of these considerations, the EC has been reluctant, to the point of intransigence, to embrace the case for reform. What clearer message do we need about the power of the agricultural lobbies?

Electronics

Many of the points that arose in the discussion of commercial policy can be illustrated by the experience of the electronics industry. The most striking development in this sector is the rise of Japanese firms over the last ten to twenty years. They have moved from being major producers of consumer electronics products in the 1970s to the position of dominant producers in this area and in certain components fields (see Dyker, 1992: 273-297).

EC industry has lobbied intensely for support in this connection. Since the early 1980s the EC has put in place a series of programmes for intra-EC industrial collaboration, but these initiatives have merely served to confirm that here more than anywhere, in the context of a rapidly evolving structure in the industry, trade, competition and technology policy must be integrated.

The Commission has responded to lobbying by embarking on a series of anti-dumping actions in virtually all the areas where Asian producers have been successful — colour TVs, CD players, audio tapes, VCRs. There are strong grounds for querying whether that this kind of protection can work (see Cawson and Holmes 1991). The most obvious one is that since the late 1980s Japanese, Taiwanese and Korean firms (and even one Chinese TV firm) have been investing heavily inside the EC to take advantage of the artificially high prices produced by the anti-dumping duties. The cost to consumers has been considerable, but the gain to EC-owned firms has been minimal. Indeed the latter have almost certainly lost something from the false sense of security arising from the notion that they could afford to delay entry into new product lines. Technological protection through ingenious technical standards does not work either. The new MAC TV standard, for example, is unlikely to be of great benefit for EC industry. Even if it proves to be exactly what EC consumers want, there is no way of ensuring that Asian firms do not simply invest first. If they do, there is no legal way to prevent these firms having access to the entire EC (plus EFTA) market. The EC Commission has tried to impose 'local content requirements' in some cases. This means that electronic products made in foreign-owned factories using imported components may find import restrictions that apply to the relevant finished product being imposed on them as they emerge from the factory. But an EC regulation covering the levying of anti-dumping duties on so-called screwdriver plants making electronics goods has been condemned by GATT. The EC Commission has stated that it will keep this regulation on its books until a new GATT anti-dumping code is agreed, but observers agree that the regulation cannot be used in practice (see EC Commission 1991b: 23).

There is considerable evidence (see Porter 1990, for example) that the success of Japanese consumer electronics may depend as much on fierce internal competition as on any exclusion of foreign firms or 'unfair' trading practice. EC commentators (see EC Commission 1991a) may have more grounds for concern in relation to the electronic components industry. Plausible complaints of dumping have been made with respect to semi-conductors. The Japanese stand accused by the USA and the EC of subsidising production of DRAM memory chips, and thus collectively gaining a near monopoly. This probably represents the most acute challenge there has been to the principle of free trade. Here is a sector where most commentators (see Flamm 1990) accept that Japanese success has been significantly affected by government policies. European firms were never very significant in the sector, but the 1980s saw a retreat by US firms from the memory market, with a 90 per cent share going to Japanese firms according to the EC Commission (1991a). It is no less worrying that in the even more strategic sector of microprocessors two US firms, Intel and Motorola, hold 85 per cent of the world market. It is frankly not at all clear what trade policy can do about this. Selective public procurement led in the past to the promotion of 'national champions' which tended to develop the mentality of defence contractors. There may be a theoretical case for strategic trade policies in such cases (see pp. 334-335). But where the leading EC-based electronics firms are Japanese, there may be more of a case for focusing on the articulation of a binding international code on monopoly and restrictive oligopolistic practices.

Another sector where this kind of problem is likely to arise acutely is telecommunications, where once again globalisation of business means that trade, telecommunications and technology policy issues meet. In the past telecommunications equipment was supplied by 'clubs' of producers to state telecommunications monopolies which could pass on high prices and low quality to captive customers. For better or worse, the utilities are now privatised and on the lookout for the cheapest equipment available. The high R&D costs of telecoms equipment mean that in this industry there is always a temptation to subsidise in order to ensure that exports are offered at (low) marginal cost. The liberalisation and privatisation of intra-EC public procurement raises the question of what will happen if the cheapest supplier is not from another EC state but from the USA or Japan, where huge economies of scale do, indeed, permit sales abroad at lower prices. As with semi-conductors, there is a genuine possibility of unfair competition, and plenty of scope for the interests of users and producers to clash.

In all these policy areas relating to electronics the member states of the EC have pursued rather divergent policies in the past. It is a major challenge to produce a common set of policies that are coherent on all the dimensions involved:

1   across the twelve member states

2   between trade, competition and technology fields

3   across the different elements of the industry (protecting chips production, for example, hurts computer firms).

It would be difficult to overstress the size of the task ahead here.

Cars

The European automotive industry provides a fascinating case-study of European Community trade policy-making. The elimination of non-tariff barriers, as part of the '1992' process, has major implications for external trade policy where different countries have had different external policies. As a result, the Community's institutions face major political and economic difficulties as they confront the implications of the single market programme for the vehicle market.

The car market in Europe shows strong patterns of national preference: the two French producer groups, which have 23 per cent of the EC market, take 60 per cent of the French market and 34 per cent of the Spanish market; Fiat has over 50 per cent of the Italian market, while the UK market is dominated by the US multinationals. The asymmetric pattern of market shares means that some producers are dependent on a limited number of national markets for most of their sales: Fiat makes two-thirds of its Western European car sales in Italy alone, while the two French groups are very dependent on the French and Spanish markets.

Further, a number of EC markets have been subject to restrictions on imports of Japanese cars. In 1977 the Japanese producers agreed a voluntary export restriction with the UK industry, with the connivance and encouragement of the UK government, under which they committed themselves to hold their imports to a share of 11 per cent of the UK market. In France, the Japanese import share is fixed at 3 per cent, by an agreement between the French government and the Japanese producers; while in Italy, Spain and Portugal, Japanese car imports are held to even lower levels through quotas. In the Italian case, a bilateral quota of just 3,000 vehicles was agreed with the Japanese as early as the early 1960s. By contrast, the Japanese market share in the essentially unrestricted German market was 16 per cent in 1990, and averaged 24 per cent in the EC countries other than those specified above in the same year.

Restrictions on imports inevitably impose costs on consumers, because they raise prices. In this case, European producers' market shares are increased, and the combined effect of higher prices and larger shares clearly benefits these producers. Since, however, the principal effect on prices is to raise the prices of Japanese cars, there are benefits to Japanese producers too, to set against their loss of market share. Import restrictions also have subtler effects on the nature of competition in the car market. When Japanese firms face import restrictions, European firms know that an important group of their competitors face limitations on their ability to compete. European firms can therefore set prices that much higher than if they had to worry about their Japanese competitors cutting prices to increase sales. Also, the fact that many of the import restrictions are administered by the Japanese industry acts as a barrier to the entry of new Japanese firms. Thus quantitative restriction on imports is inherently anti-competitive in its implications.

Technically speaking, the planned abolition, after '1992', of Article 115 has limited application to the car market, since the French and UK restrictions on Japanese imports are 'grey area' measures; that is to say, they are not trade restrictions officially recognised by the European Commission as derogations. Their existence has therefore not been dependent on Article 115 support. Nevertheless, national restrictions on Japanese car imports have to be supported by mechanisms which have the same effect as Article 115 border restrictions. A French car-buyer who attempts to circumvent the restrictions on Japanese car imports by buying a car in Germany, for example, will encounter considerable bureaucratic obstacles to registering the car in France. If, however, '1992' abolishes this particular kind of bureaucratic non-tariff barrier to intra-EC trade, by introducing a single European 'type-approval' certificate, for example, then the national restrictions on Japanese car imports will become unsustainable. In the above case, the French restriction on Japanese imports would become ineffective and irrelevant.

The opening up of the French, Spanish and Italian markets to unrestricted Japanese imports would clearly cause great problems for European car-makers, especially for the French and Italian producers who have large shares in these markets. There has been pressure, therefore, on the EC not just to let '1992' destroy national restrictions, but rather to replace them with an EC-wide restriction on Japanese imports.

To add to the difficulties about arriving at a European policy on car imports from Japan, the role of the Japanese firms within the European market is rapidly changing as 'transplant' operations are established. Nissan's plant in England has been functioning since 1988. Toyota and Honda are due to open plants in England in 1992; there are significant Japanese investments in other EC countries, including Spain. The European Commission estimates that the capacity of these transplants will be around 1.2 million cars by the end of 1999, while the UK government is reported to estimate a figure of 2 million (EC vehicle sales . . . 1991). Clearly, if cars produced in Europe by Japanese firms are treated as EC-produced cars — and legally they are entitled to such treatment under Articles 9 and 10 of the Treaty of Rome — then the Japanese transplant operations can ultimately get around any European import restrictions.

In the face of all of these difficulties, it is perhaps unsurprising that it took two years of difficult negotiations within the Community, and then between the Community and the Japanese, to arrive at a post-1992 policy. Agreement with the Japanese was reached at the end of July 1991 (Japan, EC . . . 1991). The agreement has four main components:

1   Intra-EC trade will be liberalised by the adoption of an EC-type approval scheme by 1 January 1993, and all national import restrictions will be abolished by the same date.

2   Imports of cars from Japan will be unrestricted after 31 December 1999, and in the intervening period will be limited to the level of 1.23 million (approximately the current level of imports).

3   Cars produced in Japanese-owned plants in the EC will have unrestricted access to the EC market.

4   There is an understanding about the levels of Japanese imports into France, Italy, Spain, Portugal and the UK from which it can be inferred that a deliberate attempt

will be made by Japanese firms to reduce adjustment pressures in the markets from which national import restrictions have been removed.

On the face of it, this agreement provides a nice compromise between the competing pressures on the Community — on the one hand to fulfil its promises about '1992', and on the other to safeguard the interests of a key industry. It seems to imply a considerable liberalisation of the market, since the combined effect of imports and transplants should be to double the Japanese share of the EC market in the medium term, and since full liberalisation is promised for the year 2000. There are some unresolved difficulties, however.

Let us begin with the proposed provision for 'restraint' in the five currently restricted markets. If the announced levels of expected imports into these markets are purely forecasts, then it is not clear that they have much real meaning. Assuming that Japanese firms avoid deliberate attempts to exceed the forecast levels of sales, are there going to be measures to discourage French car-buyers, for example, from buying cars in Germany? If so, then we shall effectively be keeping some kind of market-segmenting non-tariff barriers to intra-EC trade, and not fulfilling the promise of 1992 until 2000. The apparent willingness, explicit in the case of the French, to postpone '1992' at least until 1999 is a measure of the perceived importance of the sector under review.

Even more important is the problem raised by the transplants: the European Commission stipulated the import limit of 1.23 million in the expectation that transplant output would reach 1.2 million by the end of 1999. What has been agreed is that transplant output will be treated, in accordance with Article 9 of the Treaty of Rome, as EC goods entitled to free circulation within the Community. However, there is no agreement on what should be done if the estimated transplant output of 1.2 million turns out to be inaccurate (A car sales . . . 1991). In the light of the possibility that the actual level of transplant output might be as high as 2 million, this could be a critical issue.

If transplant output rises faster than the EC expects, then either it will have to accept a still larger Japanese share of the EC market, or it will have to seek to persuade the Japanese to reduce their imports below the agreed level of 1.23 million. The first alternative would be politically and economically uncomfortable, and would make the import restriction irrelevant; while the second would imply that the EC-produced cars are in fact included in an overall sales restriction on Japanese cars, which would imply in turn a very significant departure from a central principle of the Community, namely the free circulation of goods.

A further, possibly minor but none the less interesting, twist is introduced by the existence of Japanese-owned transplants in the United States. Several Japanese producers are now producing in the USA on a very large scale. Honda cars are exported from the USA to Japan, and Honda has repeatedly announced its intention of exporting US-built cars to the EC. There can be no question of the imposition of a restriction on such imports. US-made Hondas are American cars, not Japanese cars, so far as the normal rules of international trade are concerned. The US government would object strongly and successfully to any attempt to impose restraints, direct or indirect, on their export to Europe. Nevertheless, imports from the United States could be influenced by the existence of the import restriction on Japanese-made cars. If the Japanese firms believe that rapid growth of sales from North America will lead to tighter 'monitoring' of imports from Japan, then that belief could itself lead to sales restraint without the need for any explicit statement by the Community.

This leads to the disturbing conclusion that voluntary export restrictions always partake of the character of government-encouraged market-sharing arrangements, whatever their form, whatever the level at which they are imposed. As the European Commission seeks to 'monitor' the sales of 'Japanese' cars in the Community, it has to take account of transplant output if the monitoring is to be effective. The device of 'forecasting' transplant output before arriving at the guidelines for direct imports from Japan helps to make it appear as if transplant output is not subject to any restriction; but in reality Japanese producers are likely to expect that attempts will be made to cut back on their import quotas if their transplant output rises by more than expected. Thus Nissan, Honda, Toyota and all other Japanese producers will receive signals as to what are their respective 'acceptable' shares of the European market. Such market-sharing removes any incentive for them to compete with each other, reduces the competitive pressure on non-Japanese firms, and makes it harder for new entrants to the market. All of these effects run counter to the provisions of Article 85 of the Treaty of Rome.

The ultimate objective of European policy towards the car industry should be to help European producers become more competitive. Comparative studies of car plants in Japan, the USA and Europe have exposed the vast productivity gap between European producers and their competitors. According to Jones *et al* 1990 (see also Dyker, 1992: 255-271), European plants seem to require on average twice the labour input per car that Japanese plants need. In addition, European producers lag far behind Japanese in reliability and consumer satisfaction. Protection has not so far been effective in raising European competitiveness, and this makes it difficult to believe that another seven or eight years of protection will do any better. It is much more plausible to argue that open competition with the Japanese is the incentive that the industry needs to improve its performance. There is evidence from the United States to back up this view: American producers have narrowed the productivity gap with the Japanese as their market has become more and more exposed to Japanese competition. It is high time European producers were subjected to the same discipline.

Strategic trade issues

Much of European trade policy seems concerned with keeping European industry competitive with the Japanese and the Americans, in areas such as consumer electronics, aircraft, cars and computers. Governments often seem to take it as self-evident that special efforts should be made to attain or maintain competitiveness in such sectors. Can this attitude be justified? Or would we do better simply to let the free market determine where we fit in to the world division of labour?

The simplest justification for active trade policy is based on the proposition that the countries and regions which specialise in the production of such high-tech products are better off than those that produce more traditional products. Thus California is richer than Pennsylvania, Japan than China. But this simplistic argument begs the question of what is cause and what effect. Highly skilled and highly educated labour certainly commands much higher rewards in the world market than unskilled and uneducated labour, and is certainly used in high-technology industries. It is equally clear, however, that the artificial fostering of high-technology development is unlikely in itself to create a self-sustaining high-wage economy.

But that is not the end of the story. Paul Krugman (1991) draws our attention to the fact that highly skilled American labour concentrates in California, and on the northeastern seaboard, even though the American education system is of reasonably uniform quality throughout the country and labour is both free to move and, by European standards, remarkably willing to move across all parts of the country. The concentration of the American microelectronics industry in one particular part of California and one particular part of Massachusetts is strongly suggestive that there are gains to producers from proximity to other producers in the same or related lines of business. Belief in such 'positive externalities' provides one justification for seeking to promote or protect particular activities.

A rather different argument in favour of interventionist policy was presented by Brander and Spencer (1985), who proposed a model in which government assistance to its national champion firm could persuade the champion's rivals to sell less aggressively and thus let the national champion have a disproportionate share of a supposedly profitable market. The simplest illustration of this argument is provided by a story about the aircraft market. Suppose some sector of the market is marginally unprofitable if two producers enter, but very profitable for a single producer. Only one will enter, but which one? A government subsidy to one firm, just large enough so that it is marginally profitable for the firm to enter even in the presence of a rival, will ensure that that firm does, indeed, enter. But then the unsubsidised rival will not, and at a small cost the government has ensured that its champion grabs the profits!

Many observers see in the success of Japanese industrial policy evidence in support of the idea that there are strategic sectors which policy intervention can promote in the national interest. The problem is not so much in accepting that intervention in Japan (and in Korea and Taiwan, also) has been remarkably successful, as in identifying what it is about East Asian industrial policies that has made them so much more successful than industrial interventionism in South Asia or South America. There may well be lessons to be learned by Europe, but it is unfortunately not quite obvious what the lessons are.

The structural impediments initiative

As we saw earlier, both the United States and the European Community are very concerned about competition from Japan, especially in areas such as cars and electronics. There is a strong feeling that Japanese success is the result of 'unfair' features of Japanese policy or of the Japanese economy. Much attention focuses on Japanese trade policy — the presumption being that the present success of the Japanese car industry is the result of past protection. Industrial policy is also seen as playing a role, with the government cooperating with industry in choosing sectors on which to 'target' export efforts. Finally, there are features of the Japanese economy that are not directly related to government policy, such as the high savings rate and the work ethic.

Traditionally, governments have negotiated about each other's trade policies, exchanging 'concessions' in the form of trade barrier reductions. In recent years, the United States has, under the rubric of the 'Structural Impediments Initiative', sought to broaden the agenda of trade negotiations with Japan to encompass a number of aspects of the Japanese economy which are seen as contributing to its 'excessive' trade surplus. While the EC has not been as active as the USA in pursuing this line of action, it has certainly shared the concerns of the USA.

There are considerable difficulties in deciding what are appropriate issues for intergovernmental negotiation. If governments are to negotiate on tariffs and non-tariff barriers which directly affect trade flows, it is hard to argue that industrial or agricultural subsidies which have a strong impact on trade flows should not also be included in the agenda. But there are a number of dimensions to the structural impediments debate which go far beyond the realm of price distortions, however induced, and which introduce some very tricky issues into the discourse. The Japanese market may be hard for Western firms to penetrate because the Japanese language is difficult to learn. But that seems best treated as a fact of life rather than as an unfair Japanese practice requiring a compensating concession from the Japanese. If the Japanese work longer hours than Europeans, is that fair or unfair competition? It is generally accepted that competition from low-wage countries is not unfair; for lower wages may be the only way that these countries can compensate for their relative disadvantages in technology, and/or in capital. But if it is 'fair' to compete by offering lower wage rates, is it equally fair to compete by offering longer working hours, or by accepting unsafer working conditions or a higher degree of environmental pollution? If the structure of Japanese retail trade makes it harder for foreign producers to gain market access, is that a 'natural' feature of the trading world, or an artificial and unfair barrier?

Clearly the wider the agenda for negotiation, the greater the scope for increased friction and tension. The underlying issue is the extent to which the Japanese trade surplus is the natural consequence of a high Japanese rate of saving, or the natural consequence of Japanese efficiency in the manufacturing of products such as cars and CD players, or the 'unnatural' result of unfair policies targeted on particular sectors. Whatever justification can in principle be offered for the Structural Impediments Initiative, its existence is eloquent testimony to the strains imposed on the world trading system by the asymmetries in the trilateral relationship between Europe, Japan and the United States.

The implications of economic reform in Eastern Europe for future trade trends

The evolving pattern of intra-European trade will clearly be an important influence on trade relations between Europe as a whole and the rest of the world. At the same time, the path of economic change in Central and Eastern Europe is unpredictable. Therefore the effects on international trade of that process of change are equally unpredictable.

But the question is so important that is worth having a go. Preliminary answers have been offered by CEPR (1990), Collins and Rodrik (1991) and Hamilton and Winters (1992).

Whether we look at historical patterns of trade, or try to infer from the trade patterns of comparable market economies, the indications are that the countries of Eastern and Central Europe will see dramatic changes in the volume of their trade with the 'West' — the United States and Japan as well as Western Europe. But what structural trends will emerge as this trade expands?

The simplest observations to be made relate to natural resources. Several of the successor states to the Soviet Union are rich in energy, and should increase their energy exports *if* economic reform succeeds in improving the technical efficiency of the energy sector. Most of the countries in the region are well endowed with agricultural resources, though backward in agricultural performance. Agriculture, is, of course, the area in which the most dramatic responses to domestic economic liberalisation may be expected. Here again, then, substantial increases in exports could, *ceteris paribus*, be expected.

More subtle changes might be anticipated in the pattern of manufacturing output and exports. Comparative advantage in industrial products is much influenced by endowments in factors of production. Eastern and Central Europe are certainly short of modern capital, but there is impressive evidence that they are relatively well endowed with well-educated labour. Hamilton and Winters unearth evidence to suggest that the Hungarian education system could be one of the best in the world! In the recent past, much of this educated labour may have been wasted in military and other socially unproductive employments, and there is undoubtedly a desperate shortage of basic commercial skills (in marketing, accountancy, banking, for example). None the less, the labour endowments of Poland, Hungary and Czechoslovakia, and maybe also those of Russia, the Baltic states, Byelorussia and Ukraine, do not suggest that these are countries that will slot into the international division of labour on the same rung as Singapore and Indonesia, or even Greece and Portugal, but rather at the level of Spain, Italy and Ireland, as producers of a wide range of industrial products including some involving quite high technology, and as the hosts of substantial volumes of foreign direct investment.

The path to this happy state will not, however, be a smooth one. From the standpoint of the individual economies of Eastern and East-Central Europe, it is clear from the relevant chapters of *The National Economies of Europe* that restructuring policies, with all their undoubted successes, have still not provided a reliable key to 'unlock' comparative advantage. On the international side, too, there are still plenty of obstacles. The European Community has the central role of overseeing and facilitating the re-entry into the world economy of the Eastern and Central Europeans. The first major step was taken in December 1991, with the signing of association agreements between the Community on the one hand and Poland, Hungary and Czechoslovakia on the other. These agreements represented a major advance, not least because they seemed to hold out the promise of eventual membership of the Community. But, as ever, the Community is mindful of its own short-term interests as well as its historic mission:

the reforming economies continue to face the threat of anti-dumping actions and pressures not to allow too rapid export growth in 'sensitive' product areas, such as steel, textiles, footwear and agricultural products — notwithstanding the fact that such products may offer the best prospects to the Eastern and Central European economies in the short to medium run.

Will 1992 make the EC more protectionist?

The attention of the European Community is now centred on progress towards political and monetary union. But these two developments flow from the '1992' Programme, and it is from the '1992' Programme that we shall learn whether the Community is to be a fortress or a member of a more open world order. Mrs Margaret Thatcher argued in late 1991 that the more integrated the Community becomes, the less open it becomes to the rest of the world. Is this a fair judgement?

The Common Agricultural Policy lies at the root of most of the fears of the rest of the world. As we have seen, the CAP is harmful to European consumers as well as non-EC farmers, and it is not particularly beneficial for many EC farmers. In spite of its economic and budgetary costs, the CAP has proved remarkably resilient, and remains the major obstacle to the completion of the Uruguay Round of trade negotiations. Not only does the EC start off from a point that is unacceptable to its trading partners, but it shows little inclination to move from that point. And this is a *Common* Agricultural Policy — the first genuinely EC-wide economic policy. It is dangerous, however, to assume that a bad EC policy is the result of the process of European integration. Many non-EC countries in Europe, eg Austria, Switzerland and Norway, have agricultural policies that are more irrational and costly than the CAP, so it is not obvious that the CAP is worse than the policies that a non-integrated Western Europe would have adopted.

In Christopher Steven's chapter (Dyker, 1992: 211-229), on European relations with the Third World, we see that the EC's position in this area is certainly ambiguous. The Community is generous so long as its own sensitive interests are not threatened, and this sense of conditional generosity is strengthened as we move down the hierarchy of preferences to those trading partners in Asia that have been most consistently subjected to anti-dumping measures and VERs. The EC has been strongly criticised for its misuse of such measures, but again it is not clear that these policies are the result of European integration, or that they will get any worse as integration proceeds.

If we want to obtain a clear perspective on the likely impact of European integration on the world trading system, we need to look more closely at what the '1992' process really means. The essential objective is increased international competition *within* the EC. The emphasis on mutual recognition of standards as the principal means of removing border barriers has in itself a strongly deregulatory effect, as the least demanding national standard will tend to become the European standard. One result will obviously be to open the EC market to non-EC producers. As the German market is opened to French beer, it is opened also to American beer (because the French market is already open to American beer). When European car manufacturers are required to obtain only one set of certification to give their products access to the whole EC market, so Japanese manufacturers will enjoy the same benefit.

At the same time there will be trade diversion, as barriers are reduced in a way that favours intra-EC trade against extra-EC trade. More important, as European producers face the rigours of increased intra-EC competition, they may lobby for increased barriers to extra-EC competition.

The European car market (which we discussed above) provides a nice illustration of the difficulties for the Community. Proponents of open and competitive markets will not applaud the agreement between the EC and the Japanese; but we should observe that national trade restrictions have been replaced by an EC-wide restriction whose effect is not more restrictive than the national restrictions, and which we are promised is to end in 1999; while the effect of Japanese foreign direct investment will be further to weaken the efficacy of protectionist measures. This important example suggests that it is still too early to say whether the '1992' Programme is going to restrict access to EC markets for the rest of the world. The fact is that there are strong forces pulling in both directions.

The future of Europe in the international division of labour

Europe faces an intensification of international competition from a number of different directions. Within the developed world, the United States may be a faltering rival, but Japanese competition becomes more and more formidable. The newly industrialising countries, such as Korea and Taiwan, continue to display rapid export growth, and their success has encouraged other Third World countries to follow the path of export-led growth. The future role of China in the world economy is somewhat dependent on political developments; but in any event, it seems that Europe faces increasing competition in labour-intensive and medium-technology products from that part of the Third World that properly earns the title developing. Some of the competition will come from the Mediterranean periphery — the Maghreb, Israel, Egypt and Turkey.

The kinds of international competition that Europe will face in the future pose considerable policy challenges. The pressure of competition from lower-wage developing countries, and the consequent need for Europe to move up the technological spectrum, will have effects on the distribution of income both between individuals and between regions. The income differential between the more skilled and the less skilled is likely to widen, as the less skilled are subject to stronger competitive pressure on world markets. Those regions, many of them on the European periphery, whose industrial structure is less advanced, may similarly find that international competition widens the gap between them and the more prosperous regions in the core.

Global competition is evident not only in markets for goods, but also in international flows of labour and investment. European firms may come off worst in competition with the Japanese, but those parts of the European economy that succeed in attracting investment by Japanese multinationals will likely do well. The direct competitive pressure on less skilled European workers comes not from the products of Third World workers, but from immigration, and there is a link between the two pressures. Increased protection of European goods markets against the products of the developing world may help to maintain the wage rate of less skilled European workers; but it simultaneously increases the incentive to immigrate into Europe. The development of policy toward migration is one of the major challenges that Europe now faces, to match the challenge of policy-making on capital from outside Europe, as the notion of globalisation develops ever newer layers of meaning.

References

'A car sales accord light on consensus' (1991) *Financial Times* 23 September: 4.

Anderson K, Tyers R (1986) 'Agricultural policies of industrial countries and their effect on traditional food exporters'. *Economic Record* 62(3): 385-99.

Belderbos R (1991) 'On the advance of Japanese electronics multinationals in the EC'. Paper presented at INSEAD Conference, Fontainebleau. October.

Bourgeois J (1989) 'Anti-trust and trade policy: a peaceful co-existence?' *International Business Lawyer* 17(3): 115-21.

Brander J A, Spencer B J (1985) 'Export subsidies and international market share rivalry'. *Journal of International Economics* 18(1/2): 83-100.

Cawson A, Holmes P (1991) 'The new consumer electronics'. In Freeman C, Sharp M, Walker W (eds) *Technology and the Future of Europe: Global Competition and the Environment.* Pinter.

Cawson A, Morgan K, Holmes P, Stevens A, Webber D (1990) *Hostile Brothers: Competition and Closure in the European Electronics Industry.* OUP.

CEPR (1990) *Monitoring European Integration: The Impact of Eastern Europe.* A CEPR annual report. Centre for Economic Policy Research

Collins S M, Rodrik D (1991) *Eastern Europe and the Soviet Union in the World Economy.* Institute for International Economics, Washington DC.

Dyker, D. (ed) (1992) *The European Economy.* Longman, London.

EC Commission (1985) *Completing the Internal Market.* White Paper from the EC Commission to the European Council, Luxembourg, June

EC Commission (1990) *Industrial Policy in an Open and Competitive Environment.* Brussels

EC Commission (1991a) *The European Electronics and Information Technology Industry: State of Play, Issues at Stake and Proposals for Action.* Brussels

EC Commission (1991b) *Ninth Annual Report on Anti-Subsidy and Anti-Dumping Activities.* Brussels, May

'EC vehicle sales accord with Japan to include light trucks' (1991) *Financial Times* 5 August: 4

Flamm K (1990) 'Semiconductors'. In Hufbauer G C *Europe 1992: An American Perspective.* Brookings Institute, Washington DC

GATT (1990) *Trade Policy Review of Japan.* Geneva

GATT (1991) *Trade Policy Review of the EC.* Geneva

Hamilton C, Winters L A (1992) 'Opening up international trade in Eastern Europe'. *Economic Policy* 14, April.

Hansen K (ed) (1991) *International Instruments to Control Restraints of Competition after 1992.* Proceedings of the 1990 Berlin International Cartel Conference. Bundeskartellamt, Berlin

Hindley B (1988) 'Dumping and the Far East trade of the EC'. *World Economy* 11(4): 445-64

Hine R C (1985) *The Political Economy of EC Trade Policy*. Wheatsheaf

Holmes P (1991) *Trade and Competition Policy: The Consumer Interest*. National Consumer Council. Working Paper 5. London, April.

'Japan, EC agree on car imports' (1991) *Financial Times* 1 August: 6

Julius D (1990) *Global Companies and Public Policy*. RIIA/F. Pinter

Krugman P R (1991) *Geography and Trade*. MIT Press, Cambridge, Mass.

Messerlin P (1990) 'Anti-dumping regulations or pro-cartel law? The EC chemical cases'. *PRE Working Paper Series* no 397. World Bank, Washington. DC

Milner H (1988) *Resisting Protectionism, Global Industries and the Politics of International Trade*. Princeton University Press.

O'Clearacain S (1990) 'Europe 1992 and gaps in the EC's Common Commercial Policy'. *Journal of Common Market Studies* 28(3): 202-17

OECD (1985) *The Costs and Benefits of Protection*. Paris.

OECD (1987) *Structural Adjustment and Economic Performance*. Paris.

Ordover J, Saloner S (1989) 'Anti-trust and predation'. In Schmalensee R, Willig R (eds) *Handbook of Industrial Organisation* (Vol 1). North Holland Publishing House

Porter M (1990) *The Competitive Advantage of Nations*. Macmillan

Reich R (1990) "Who is 'us' "? *Harvard Business Review,* April

Schuknecht L (1991) 'Dumping and anti-dumping in EC-CMEA trade'. *Working Paper Series II* no 140. University of Konstanz

Schuknecht L (forthcoming) *The Political Economy of EC Trade Policy*. University of Konstanz

Stegemann K (1991) 'The international regulation of dumping'. *World Economy* 14(4): 375-406

Thomsen S, Nicolaides P (1990) *Foreign Direct Investment: 1992 and Global Markets*. RIIA

Victor J-L (1990) *The EC Legal Order*. European Perspectives Series. Commission of the European Communities, Luxembourg

Womack J P, Jones D T, Roos D (1990) *The Machine that Changed the World,* Rawson Associates/Macmillan, New York

World Bank (1987) *World Development Report 1987*. OUP

14.   The EC and the Third World

Christopher Stevens

Introduction

As the 'Third World' has become increasingly differentiated as a grouping, so has Europe's relationship with its constituent parts. But there has been a lag, especially in respect to political relations. Consequently, formal policy has diverged increasingly from effective practice. A sharp reorientation is likely to occur in the former as Europe adjusts to the changes required by the completion of the single European market, by the possible move towards greater monetary and political union, by the extension of the 'European space' to include Eastern and Northern Europe, and by the GATT Uruguay Round of trade liberalisation.

There will be winners and losers in the Third World as a result of these changes. The losers are likely to include many of the poorest countries. The main imponderable is the future impact of 'new issues' such as migration, the environment and public health. There is increased awareness that phenomena which originate in developing countries may adversely affect EC welfare. These may require Europe to take a greater interest in the Third World than short-term economic and strategic considerations alone would counsel.

The foundations of EC — Third World relations

Europe and the Third World affect each other in a host of ways, not all of them economic. Many facets of the relationship are still organised primarily on a bilateral, national basis, eg., France and Senegal, Britain and India, Germany and Singapore. Purely for reasons of practicality, this chapter focuses largely on the Community-level dimension of the relationship.

Development aid is only one vehicle for Europe's economic influence on the Third World, and not necessarily the most important. European policies on trade, agriculture, industrial subsidies and exchange rates, for example, can all have a much larger impact. The range of such policies is limited by the characteristic of the European Community (as opposed to its member states) that it does not possess the full array of attributes of a nation-state. It cannot conduct a normal foreign or defence policy; even its responsibilities on debt are limited. Among this limited range of policy instruments there are three principal foundations for Community-level policies affecting the Third World. They are the common commercial policy, the Common Agricultural Policy (CAP), and the partially common aid policy.

Christopher Stevens: 'The EC and the Third World', in *THE EUROPEAN ECONOMY*, edited by David Dyker (Longman, 1992). pp. 211-229.

Trade policy

The existence of the common external tariff (CET) means that the foundations of Europe's foreign trade regime must be established at Community level. The member states adopt a common position at meetings of the GATT and UNCTAD, and have negotiated at EC level a host of bilateral and multilateral trade agreements with the Third World states.

The CET's purity is reduced in practice inasmuch as member states adopt, to a greater or lesser extent, national policies that influence trade flows. Most important are the growing number of non-tariff barriers (NTBs) to imports. Whereas EC institutions have an unambiguous responsibility for setting tariff policy, their position on NTBs has been less secure (although this will change as part of '1992'). Individual member states have negotiated bilaterally numerous so-called voluntary export restraints (VERs) with developing countries. In addition, there are many national quotas within Community NTBs which restrict the volume of imports that have access to the national markets of particular member states.

The precise number of effective national NTBs is unknown: some are secret, some are not enforced, and some are made on an industry-industry basis and fall outside government scrutiny. But an indication of their extent may be gauged by analysing member states' recourse to Article 115 of the Treaty of Rome. This article, which permits a member to restrict imports from its neighbours of goods originating outside the Community, is a legal linchpin of the national NTB system. Clearly, a French NTB on, say, Taiwanese footwear, would be unsustainable if exporters could evade the restrictions by routing goods indirectly via Germany. During 1988 and the first seven months of 1989, there were sixteen cases of LDC exports being excluded from an EC national market through the use of Article 115, and a similar number of cases in which there was surveillance of imports (Davenport and Page 1991: 43). The import exclusions were imposed in the French, Italian and Spanish markets; the LDCs affected were Brazil, China, Hong Kong, Singapore and Taiwan; and the products involved were footwear, umbrellas, toys, car radios, televisions, silk, handtools, sewing machines, slide fasteners, videos, imitation jewellery and cars.

The Common Agricultural Policy

The CAP is particularly important because of the dominance of agriculture in many developing countries. The transformation of the EC from a major importer of agricultural products to a net exporter of an increasing number of commodities has had profound and complex effects on the Third World. The precise nature of the impact is not easy to identify since it depends upon the commodity composition of each country's imports and exports and also on the time period selected. In broad terms, the impact depends on a given LDC's balance of agricultural trade. The short-term effect on net agricultural exporting states in the Third World has tended to be negative (because the CAP has increased world supply and hence reduced prices), while the impact on food importing states has been positive (for precisely the same reasons). In addition, world price instability for agricultural products may have intensified to the detriment of both agricultural exporters and importers. In the longer term, even food importing LDCs *may* have suffered — for two reasons. First, if low world prices for temperate agricultural products are of a temporary nature, but have encouraged the neglect of an LDC's domestic agriculture, the long-term effect could be to increase the burden of food imports rather than the reverse. Second, if the general equilibrium effects of the CAP have reduced non-agricultural production in Europe, the terms of trade gain of LDC food importers from low world food prices may be offset by the loss incurred on account of higher non-agricultural import prices.

Despite this negative overall verdict, there are some positive aspects of the CAP for some LDCs, at least from a static viewpoint. In addition to the terms of trade effect of food-importing states, a small number of privileged LDCs receive artificially high prices for at least part of their exports because of the CAP. These gains are concentrated on some of the signatories of the Lomé Conventions, together with the non-EC Mediterranean states. Other LDCs have also benefited where the price distortions of the CAP have created a demand for commodities which would not otherwise exist, as in the case of European demand for Thai manioc as an animal feed.

Aid programmes

Unlike trade and agriculture, aid policy is only partially common. There are three main strings to Europe's aid bow: multi-annual Community-level programmes, annual EC programmes, and member state national programmes.

Only a small part of the aid provided by the EC member states is channelled through Community institutions. The greater part is disbursed either through the bilateral programmes of each member state or through other intermediaries, such as the multilateral institutions. The four main contributors to the EC aid budget are Germany, France, UK and Italy which, between them, account for some four-fifths of the total (Table 1). The proportion of aid which is channelled through the Community institutions varies widely between the member states. Of the larger EC states, the UK has the highest proportion of its aid going through the EC (at 19 per cent) and France the smallest (at 8 per cent).

The most important element of the Community-level aid programme is the European Development Fund (EDF), which finances the aid provisions of the Lomé Convention. But there are other elements of Community-level aid as well. There are financial protocols to the commercial agreements that the EC has with many of the states of the Mediterranean. Then there is an annually agreed 'non-associates aid programme', which provides financial assistance out of the EC budget in equal proportions to Asia and Latin America. And of particular importance is the food aid programme: cereals food aid is provided from both a Community and a number of bilateral programmes, while dairy product food aid is wholly a Community-level affair. In 1989 some 50 per cent of Community-level aid disbursements took the form of funds from the EDF, and a significant part of the remainder that of food aid (although there are question marks over the appropriate valuation for some of the EC food aid commodities, notably dairy products).

Table 1   **Sources of EC aid,* 1989.**

Member state	Contribution to EC aid	Total aid	Contribution to EC aid as % of total aid	Share of total EC aid (%)
Belgium	111	703	16	4
Denmark	62	937	7	2
France	628	7,450	8	24
Germany	735	4,949	15	28
Ireland	20	49	41	1
Italy	407	3,613	11	16
Netherlands	173	2,094	8	7
United Kingdom	499	2,587	19	19

Notes:
* Oda net disbursements, $ million
Columns may not add up due to rounding
This table includes only those EC states that are members of the OECD DAC (Development Assistance Committee). It excludes, therefore, Greece, Luxembourg, Portugal and Spain. Expect in the case of Spain, these are relatively small donors; their 1988 oda was equivalent to under 2% of total disbursement by the other member states.

Source: © OECD, 1990, *OECD Development Cooperation*. Reproduced by permission of the OECD

Some of the bilateral aid programmes tend to reinforce the geographical and political bias of Community efforts, but with some member states the reverse is true. EC aid has tended to focus on sub-Saharan Africa, and, to a lesser extent, the Mediterranean (Middle East and North Africa) (Table 2). The share of aid directed towards sub-Saharan Africa has grown slightly over the past fifteen years, while that going to the Mediterranean has declined slightly. Between them, however, these two regions account for around 70 per cent of the total. The principal differences in current geographical orientation between the EC and the bilateral programmes of the large member states are as follows. France, perhaps surprisingly, has a less dramatic concentration on sub-Saharan Africa, even though this remains the most important region for France, and provides a higher proportion of aid than the EC as a whole to Asia and Latin America and the Caribbean. In the case of Germany, the focus on sub-Saharan Africa is much less marked, while a relatively higher proportion of aid is directed to South Asia, Other Asia and the Mediterranean. The most important distinguishing feature with the UK is that its aid programme gives more prominence to South Asia than does that of the EC as a whole.

The 'pyramid of privilege'

On the basis of these three policy instruments the Commission has fashioned a complex set of agreements through which it has conducted a quasi-foreign policy *vis-à-vis* the Third World (Table 3). Because of the nature of the instruments, that policy has a high economic content.

Table 2 **Geographical distribution of EC aid (percentage of gross disbursements).**

Countries	Sub-Saharan Africa			South Asia			Other Asia & Oceania			Middle East & North Africa*			Latin America & Caribbean		
	75/76	80/81	88-89	75/76	80/81	88/89	75/76	80/81	88/89	75/76	80/81	88/89	75/76	80/81	88/89
Belgium	66.6	66.0	76.5	5.8	5.0	2.0	8.9	11.9	8.3	12.5	12.2	5.6	6.2	4.9	7.6
Denmark	52.7	51.6	65.4	17.9	31.2	22.1	16.4	8.9	6.0	9.8	6.2	5.0	3.3	2.1	2.9
France	46.5	48.0	52.6	4.2	2.8	3.2	11.1	12.9	15.9	14.6	12.5	9.1	23.6	23.8	19.2
Germany	20.8	29.5	28.5	27.2	20.6	16.0	9.2	9.4	13.7	30.4	28.8	29.0	12.5	11.7	12.7
Ireland	79.8	96.7	95.8	12.5	1.0	3.1	—	0.6	0.3	2.9	0.3	0.3	4.8	1.3	0.5
Italy	24.3	56.1	58.9	18.2	1.7	6.1	6.8	6.6	6.8	45.6	28.1	11.7	5.1	7.5	16.6
Netherlands	19.7	31.2	36.6	24.2	24.9	19.2	14.9	10.6	18.5	4.3	5.4	5.3	36.9	27.9	20.4
United Kingdom	28.4	37.0	52.6	41.0	40.0	25.6	11.6	8.5	10.0	6.5	8.3	4.9	12.5	6.2	6.8
EC	59.6	60.3	63.2	20.8	16.9	10.4	1.9	4.9	6.7	12.4	11.8	8.2	5.4	6.0	11.6

Notes:
* Includes small amounts to southern France
Percentages in lines add up to 100% for regional distribution in each two-year period for each individual country/institution.

Source: © OECD, 1990, *OECD Development Cooperation*. Reproduced by permission of the OECD

Although the Lomé Convention is the EC's most prominent regional preferential arrangement, it is not the only such European accord: nor is it the only North-South package of its kind. The EC has a predisposition to favour formal trade and cooperation agreements, partly because it establishes the legitimacy of Community as opposed to national action. The result has been a series of 'framework agreements' with different parts of the Third World. The Lomé Convention has also spawned imitative action by other countries. In addition to the USA's Caribbean Basin Initiative, the Nordic initiative for a mini-NIEO (New International Economic Order) can also be seen as an attempt to emulate, and improve upon, the regional package approach of Lomé.

The EC's bilateral and multilateral agreements have been described as a 'pyramid of privilege', by virtue of the fact that those at the top provide more favourable treatment than those at the base. The countries at the top have preferences not only over some developed countries, but also over other LDC members of the pyramid. It is therefore a shifting pyramid, since improvements in the terms for states lower down the hierarchy can cut the value of concessions made to those higher up.

Preference agreements can be grouped into three broad categories.

1   At the apex of the pyramid sits the Lomé Convention. Under it the sixty-nine African, Caribbean and Pacific (ACP) states benefit from the most liberal set of non-reciprocal trade preferences that the EC has offered to any group of states. They also receive more EC-level aid than do other LDCs in both absolute and per capita terms. The practical effects of these liberal trade preferences have been limited, however, by the fact that many of them apply to products that the ACP have a very limited capacity to produce (see below).

Table 3   Major EC trade arrangements with the developing countries.

Country	Trade agreement
African, Caribbean and Pacific countries	Lomé Convention
Least developed countries	Nine non-Lomé signatories in this category receive special concessions
Northern Mediterranean	
Cyprus, Malta, Turkey, Yugoslavia	Association agreements, trade and co-operation agreements
Southern Mediterranean	
Maghreb countries (Algeria, Morocco, Tunisia), Egypt, Jordan, Lebanon, Syria	Preferential trade and co-operation agreements involving free access for industrial exports, specific concessions for some agricultural output, and financial aid and co-operation agreements
Asia	
India, Pakistan, Sri Lanka, China	Non-preferential commercial co-operation agreements with each country
Association of South-East Asian Nations (Indonesia, Malaysia, Philippines, Singapore, Thailand)	Regional framework agreement
Latin America	
Argentina, Brazil, Mexico, Uruguay, Andean Pact countries	Non-preferential economic and trade co-operation agreements with each country
Central America	Regional framework agreement
Near East	
Gulf States (Saudi Arabia, United Arab Emirates, Kuwait, Oman, Qatar, Bahrain)	Gulf Co-operation Agreement
Yemen	Non-preferential agreement covering trade and economic co-operation

Note: Non-preferential agreements involve no preferences in addition to those available via the Generalised System of Preferences

Source: McAleese 1989

2   In the middle of the pyramid are the Mediterranean states, which are accorded trade preferences that are nominally less favourable than those of the ACP but may in practice be the most valuable. The main limitations on these agreements (all of which are bilateral and differ from each other in their details) is that they limit diversification into 'sensitive' product areas, while allowing the states to continue with traditional exports, albeit often under the constraint of quotas.

3   The broad base of the pyramid includes all the remaining LDCs (ASEAN, Latin America, South Asia, etc.). Despite a number of impressive-sounding 'framework agreements', these countries trade only on terms of the Generalised System of Preferences (GSP), and receive Community aid only from the relatively small annual 'non-associates' aid budget and the food aid programme. The GSP is the lowest common denominator of the EC's trade preferences. It covers most industrial and a few agricultural products and offers tariffs that are generally lower than MFN levels. However, the preference margins are usually lower than those available to the ACP and Mediterranean states through their association agreements with the EC, and are often limited by quotas for sensitive items.

The pattern of trade

Since the mid-1960s the Third World has become relatively less important overall for Europe in terms of trade, finance and military strategy. The share of all third parties in total EC imports and exports has fallen since 1960 as the creation of the Common Market has encouraged members to trade with each other (Figures 1 and 2). While non-EC developed countries (DCs) were more severely affected by this decline than were LDCs in the period 1960-75, the reverse has been true since then. The LDC share of total EC imports has fallen continuously in the post-Oil Shock period (from 23 per cent in 1975 to only 13 per cent by 1988), while the DC share has stabilised (and was, indeed, slightly higher in 1988, at 26 per cent, than its 1975 level of 23 per cent). In the case of EC exports, the DC share has tended to hold up better than that of the LDCs throughout the period, although, once again, the differentially poor LDC performance was more marked during the second sub-period.

The extent of the decline and the reasons for it have varied between LDC regions. The principal constraint on further deepening of relations with East and South-East Asia is not a lack of European interest, but a lack of European competitiveness *vis-à-vis* Japan and USA. In the case of links with the ACP, there has been a substantial decline in relative importance, first in economic and now, increasingly, in political terms, largely as a result of European withdrawal. By contrast, relations with the Mediterranean and Middle East have remained strong, reflecting substantial European economic and political interests in the region. South Asia and Latin America have retained fairly close links with some member states, but have remained on the periphery for the Community as a whole.

The sharpest fall in trade share has been experienced by the ACP. Their share of EC imports outside the Community fell from 10 per cent in 1960 to 4 per cent by 1988 (Figure 3), and a similar picture applies to EC exports (Figure 4). The share of Latin America in both imports and exports also fell sharply, while that of the Mediterranean and ASEAN held broadly stable. The only states to have experienced a steady rise in trade share are the East Asian newly industrialising countries (NICs) — Korea, Taiwan and Hong Kong. Their share of extra-EC imports rose from 1 per cent in 1970 to 6 per cent in 1988, while for exports the rise was somewhat slower — from 1 per cent to 4 per cent.

These changes are related to the commodity composition of trade (Figure 5). Over the period as a whole there has been a change in the relative importance of the various sources of European growth, with non-traded services and intra-developed country trade increasing in relative significance. The distortions caused by the CAP have simply accentuated a trend away from the traditional colonial trade pattern of importing raw materials from the South and exporting manufactures to it. In its place, a trade has developed with parts of the South that emphasises a two-way flow of manufactures and services. The leaders of the new pattern of trade have been, on the European side, the states with relatively weak colonial ties (notably Germany) and, in the South, the countries of East and South-East Asia. By contrast, formal development policy has been fashioned largely by the major ex-colonial states (France and UK), and has focused on their erstwhile colonies.

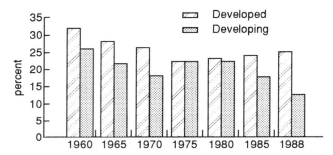

Figure 1   **EC imports from developed and developing countries as a share of total imports (intra and extra) 1960-88.**
Source: Eurostat

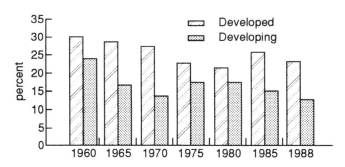

Figure 2   **EC exports to developed and devloping countries as a share of total exports (intra and extra) 1960-88.**
Source: Eurostat

350

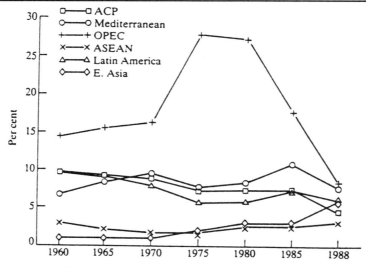

Note: E. Asia = Korea, Taiwan, Hong Kong

Figure 3 **EC imports from developing countries by region as a share of extra-EC imports, 1960-88.**
Source: Eurostat

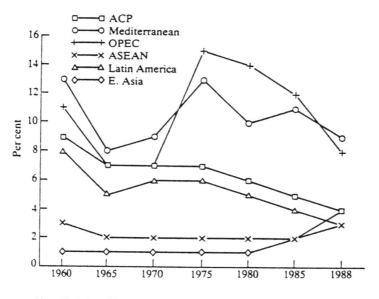

Note: E. Asia = Korea, Taiwan, Hong Kong

Figure 4 **EC imports from developing countries by region as a share of extra-EC exports, 1960-88.**
Source: Eurostat

351

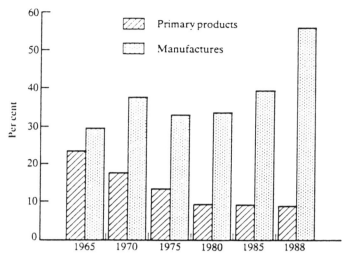

Note: Primary = SITC 0 + 1; Manufactures = SITC 6 + 7 + 8

Figure 5   Share of primary products and manufactures in extra-EC imports, 1965-88.
Source: Eurostat

Have trade preferences worked?

One striking feature of this differential performance is that it is the inverse of the pattern created by formal relationships. At both Community and member state level, sub-Saharan Africa and, to a lesser extent, the Caribbean have been given pride of place in formal policy. Yet during the period from 1975 to 1987 the ACP's share of EC imports from developing countries (LDCs) fell by one-quarter, from 20.5 to 15.1 per cent. East and South-East Asia, by contrast, have been relatively neglected in Community-level policy and at best ambiguously favoured by member states. Only in respect to the Mediterranean and Latin America have pronouncements and practice been broadly consistent: close with the former and distant with the latter.

So incongruous has been the ACP's position as most preferred and yet least successful trading partners with the EC that commentators have begun to question the efficacy of the EC's extensive preference system and, moreover, to assert that since the ACP have gained little from preferences their potential losses from liberalisation will be correspondingly modest (see eg., Brown 1988; Davenport 1988).

However, it is too easy to write off the Lomé trade preferences as valueless; much more cautious conclusions are in order. The ACP's poor overall performance reflects two factors: first, the Lomé Convention provides the ACP with either zero or very limited preference over their major competitors for the greater part (by value) of their exports. Second, ACP exports are more heavily concentrated than are those of other LDCs on commodities for which world demand is growing slowly.

The implication is that while Lomé has been by definition low-powered, ACP trade performance would have been even worse without the Convention. As explained below, there have, indeed, been some positive trade effects of Lomé for the ACP.

The extent of preferences

Despite the apparent liberality of the EC's preferential trade arrangements, it is by no means clear that LDCs are always the beneficiaries of positive discrimination by the EC. In respect to tariffs, for example, the actual rates applying to LDC exports may be higher than those that apply to DC exports. LDCs appear to face lower tariff barriers in the EC market than do DCs only if the analysis is limited to formal tariff rates. In 1983, for example, the average MFN rate applied to total EC imports from DCs was 7.2 per cent; this was much higher than the average GSP rate applied to imports from LDCs. But the average tariff rate *actually imposed* by the EC was lower on imports from DCs than from LDCs (at 4.7 per cent as against 5.3 per cent) (Sampson 1989). There are two reasons for this. First the DCs benefit from a number of EC trade preferences and so do not usually trade on MFN terms. Second, LDC exports to the EC tend to include a higher proportion of 'sensitive' goods than do DC exports.

In the case of NTBs, too, the commodity basket of exports may result in discrimination against LDCs. In 1983, for example, 25 per cent of the EC's imports from LDCs faced NTBs compared with only 19 per cent of its imports from DCs. The impact of NTBs can be especially severe on some of the poorest LDCs: EC imports from India, for example, face significantly more NTBs than do imports from the NICs (Sapir and Stevens 1987: Table 1).

In the case of the Lomé preferences, ACP exports to the EC fall into three broad groups. The largest group is of commodities that enter the Community market duty-free, but would do so even without the Lomé Convention. Hence in this case Lomé provides no preferences *vis-à-vis* exports of the ACP's principal competitors. The second group, accounting for a large part of the remainder, are products which enter duty-free under Lomé but do not do so under the GSP or MFN provisions, and do not compete directly with European production. Hence the ACP states here receive a tariff preference over other third-party exporters to the EC. But the level of GSP or MFN tariffs, and hence the ACP margin of preference, is very low in many cases. In 1987 five commodities accounted for 63 per cent of the total value of ACP exports to the EC. They were crude petroleum, coffee, cocoa, copper and rough wood; the relevant ECMFN tariff rates were 0, 5, 3, 0 and 0 per cent respectively. Moreover, there are no major non-tariff restrictions at either national or Community level on imports into the EC of most traditional ACP exports. Hence, the Lomé regime is unlikely to have significant dynamic effects on ACP exports of these commodities.

The third category is the smallest in terms of ACP export value but is potentially the most significant. It consists of goods that are also produced within Europe and that benefit from substantial EC protection. Preferences on such goods are particularly valuable for three reasons. First, they may facilitate export diversification. Second, ACP exporters, like European producers, are protected against competitive imports from other third-party suppliers. And, not least, ACP export earnings are supplemented by the artificially high prices in the European market brought about by the restriction of supply.

Most notable in this category are products that fall within the CAP, plus clothing and textiles lines that are controlled by the Multifibre Arrangement (MFA), effectively a Community-sponsored VER. In the case of temperate agricultural products, the ACP benefit from a number of openings to the European market, although these are usually restricted by quotas, calendars (that limit preferential access to certain periods of the year) or both. In the case of clothing the ACP are not subject to the MFA, though there have been a number of instances of VER and anti-dumping actions.

The range of CAP products on which the ACP benefit include sugar, rice, beef and horticultural products. Although the mechanisms employed vary between these products, the fundamental nature of the benefit is the same in each case. Because the CAP restricts supply on to the EC market, prices prevailing in Europe are artificially high. The ACP gain at least part of this economic rent for at least part of their exports. The reason for the 'at least part' caveat is that in some cases the EC treasury obtains part of the economic rent through the application of import tariffs, and because ACP access to the EC market is normally limited to a fixed quota which may be less than total exports. If a country is able to sell only a part of its total exports to the EC the effects of high European prices may have to be offset against 'abnormally' low returns in other markets. This would happen if, for example, the CAP pushed world market prices down below what they would otherwise be. Hence the critical factors in determining whether, in the short term, the export revenue of LDC preference holders is higher or lower as a result of the CAP are: the proportion of exports that gain access to the EC market, the level of economic rent received by the exporter, and the price-depressing effects of the CAP in other markets.

Let us now look at the main relevant product categories in turn.

Sugar

The EC-ACP Sugar Protocol is attached to the Lomé Conventions, although it is not part of them. The principal reason for this distinction is that it is of 'unlimited duration', and therefore not subject to periodic renegotiation.

The Protocol provides sixteen ACP states, plus India, with a global quota of 1.3 million tonnes of sugar (white sugar equivalent) for which the EC guarantees to pay similar prices to those offered to European sugar beet producers. These prices are normally well above world levels. The Protocol, which represents a major breach in the CAP system of protection, was negotiated as part of Britain's accession to the Community. The imports are consumed almost exclusively in the UK market.

The share of sugar exports covered by the Protocol varies between the ACP beneficiaries. But all in all, with a possible exception in the case of Zimbabwe, the financial gain of high prices on the EC quota has almost certainly exceeded the financial loss due to the CAP-induced depression of world market prices.

Rice

Most rice imports face a levy calculated to bring the price up to domestic Community levels. But for the ACP 50 per cent of the levy is replaced by an equivalent tax in the exporting state. The preference is volume-constrained. Under Lomé I (1975-80) and Lomé II (1980-5), the EC was entitled to suspend the preference if total imports from the ACP exceeded the average of the previous three years plus 5 per cent. For Lomé III (1985-90) this threshold was replaced by a fixed quota that was significantly in excess of actual flows during Lomé II. For long-grained husked rice it was set at 122,000 tonnes annually, compared with average annual imports 1982-6 of 95,673 tonnes. However, ACP exports increased rapidly during Lomé III, so that the quota became a binding constraint. For Lomé IV (1990-2000) the quota has been increased to 125,000 tonnes of husked rice equivalent, plus 20,000 tonnes of broken rice.

Beef

Five African states (Botswana, Kenya, Madagascar, Swaziland and Zimbabwe) have a special regime for the export of beef to the EC. They benefit from a 90 per cent reduction in the variable import levy for a quota of beef. The total quota under Lomé IV is 39,100 tonnes annually, but it is subdivided into national quotas with discretionary provisions for a surplus on one state's quota to be transferred to another.

Horticulture

The CAP regime for horticultural products is complex. The basic rule is that the system for supporting European farmers is relatively lightly structured, without the mandatory intervention buying and variable import levies characterising the cereals and meat regimes. For the fresh products of most interest to LDCs the normal regime applying to imports is that the EC levies an *ad valorem* tariff and also establishes a 'reference price'. Countries exporting to the EC are obliged to sell their goods at a 'minimum import price' equal to the reference price plus the tariffs. Failure to comply results in a countervailing levy being imposed to bring the cost of imports up to the required level. Hence it is possible to export fresh fruit and vegetables to the EC, but only if the landed price exceeds the level at which domestic produce is sold.

For the ACP, and some other third-party suppliers (primarily states in the Mediterranean), concessions take the form of full or partial rebates of the *ad valorem* tariff. But there are two provisos. The first is that LDC preference holders must still respect minimum import prices. In other words, they are barred from undercutting domestic European producers, but retain a larger share of the proceeds from any exports they do make, which helps them to compete with other third-party suppliers that have to pay the full tariff.

The second proviso is that these concessions are limited for some products to a fixed quota or specific period of the year (calendar) or both. Such quotas may be very small, eg the quota under Lomé IV for small winter cucumber is 100 tonnes for the whole of the ACP group! Moreover, it does not follow simply from the existence of a preference on paper that all (or any) ACP states can actually exploit that preference within the seasonal restriction imposed. There have been cases in the Mediterranean where the

EC has granted a calendar-restricted preference for a product which, for climatic reasons, the 'beneficiary' cannot harvest at that time of the year!

The extent of diversification

The need for the ACP to diversify into new products is particularly pressing, since the central ACP export problem is one of over-reliance on goods facing slow-growing markets. Contrary to the conventional wisdom, the ACP have not performed less satisfactorily than other LDCs on their exports of those tropical products on which they receive modest preferences (Davenport and Stevens 1990). Rather, the problem is that their exports are more heavily concentrated than are those of other LDCs on a product range for which world demand is growing only slowly. The ACP have simply been less successful at diversifying into products with a better market outlook than have other LDCs.

The evidence of the 1980s is that a number of ACP states have begun to break out of this unsatisfactory export product range, and while the EC's trade preferences for the ACP have not had a major effect on trade patterns, there may have been some impact on the margins. They have not prevented the emergence of a trend towards the sidelining of the ACP in EC trade, but there are reasons to believe that this trend would have been more severe in the absence of the Convention.

The number of states within the ACP group that have achieved significant diversification is still a minority, but it is not an insignificant one. The success of Mauritius in developing its clothing exports is well known, but it is by no means unique. In Kenya, for example, horticultural exports have developed very rapidly since the mid-1980s and are now the country's third largest merchandise export to the EC. Some twenty-eight ACP states have emerged as significant exporters of non-traditional products, and, although many still export only a small number of items, one-third export six or more, and five more than fifteen (McQueen and Stevens 1989). Moreover, diversification is not limited to the more advanced African states, such as Kenya, Mauritius, Zimbabwe and Côte d'Ivoire. It also extends to poorer countries at lower levels of economic development, such as Ethiopia, Sudan and Ghana. By 1987 such non-traditional exports accounted for about 8 per cent of total ACP non-fuel exports to the EC, and were also prominent in exports to major non-EC markets, most notably the USA.

The impact of Lomé preferences

How far can the growth of non-traditional exports be attributed to the Lomé preferences? To try to answer the question, studies have been carried out in a selected group of states, the results of which are reported in three working papers: on Jamaica, Kenya and Ethiopia; on Zimbabwe; and on Mauritius (Stevens 1990; Riddell 1990; McQueen 1990). Between them, these five states illustrate the differential importance of the various Lomé trade preferences in relation both to each other, and to those offered by the ACP's other trading partners. They show also the interaction of demand-side constraints (such as the rules of origin) and those on the supply side (notably unsupportive government policies), and the scope for aid to ease the bottlenecks that limit further diversification.

In none of these particular cases do the non-traditional exports 'solve' the problem of stagnant demand for traditional exports. The new markets into which the countries in question have diversified are highly competitive; diversification is a continuing exercise, not a once-for-all shift. But the studies confirm that the ACP are not somehow incapable of diversification. Furthermore, they provide some evidence that the Lomé preferences have made a contribution to diversification.

It has not been possible to draw an unambiguous causal link between the Lomé Convention and the development of non-traditional exports. A host of factors is at work to explain both the success in exporting *these* new products and the failure to export *others* for which Lomé preferences are also substantial. Government policy in the exporting state is clearly a critical factor. In the cases of both Jamaica and Kenya, for example, the move into non-traditional exports has been very recent, partly because of the unsupportive nature of government policies in the earlier period. None the less, there is some degree of circumstantial evidence to suggest that a link exists.

There is also evidence that imperfections in the Convention are a constraint on more rapid diversification. The rules of origin have been a clear impediment, and the quotas that apply to many of the CAP concessions may become a binding constraint in the future. Significantly, EC imports of manufactures from the ACP have risen much more slowly than those of the USA. Although the EC remains the ACP's principal trade partner, it is fast losing this position. ACP exports of clothing to the USA, for example, now exceed sales to the EC. And the ACP export to the USA some manufactured goods, such as electrical machinery, which do not figure in their trade with Europe.

The growth in exports to the USA can be explained partly in terms of buoyant American demand, but there is also an element of EC protectionism in the story. Jamaican exports of clothing, for example, increased by an annual average of 81 per cent (in US dollar value terms) between 1983 and 1988. But almost all of this increase was accounted for by exports to the USA, with nascent exports to the EC emerging only at the end of the period. The dominance of the USA reflects in part the fact that it is very close geographically to Jamaica and has been able to absorb almost everything that Jamaica is capable of producing. However, US trade preferences are superior to those of the EC in a number of respects. In particular, US legislation allows Jamaica to produce woven clothing from Far Eastern material: the Lomé Convention specifically prohibits this. Hence, while Jamaica is able to export both woven clothing (eg shirts) and knitted goods (eg pullovers and T-shirts) to the USA, it is able to export only the latter to the EC.

Emerging trends

A tension has developed between the focus of formal policy towards the South and the focus of the EC's immediate economic interests. In addition to the changes in the pattern of trade already noted, the disparity between formal policy and effective interests has been reinforced by three factors. Firstly, the lack of strong formal links with newly industrialising countries reflects the fact that the EC has very little to offer in terms of non-commercial inducements. The policy instruments available to the EC are designed primarily to assist poor, not-very-competitive states; they are not well suited to the task of reinforcing relations with highly competitive, middle-income states. Attempts to implement more appropriate policies have hit two hurdles: most would be dependent upon private rather than public sector action; and those that are in the public domain (eg on trade policy) often face strong opposing lobbies.

Second, the panoply of Community and member state policies that have fostered relations with Africa may be regarded as a psychological device to ease the process of decolonisation and disengagement for the Europeans. As with the Commonwealth, so francophony and the Lomé Conventions created the appearance that the break between metropole and colony following decolonisation was less than total. This was comforting not only to the Europeans but also to the europhile elites in the new states. As time has passed, however, the European need for such psychological support has diminished.

A third, related, point is that post-colonial agreements gave the appearance and, to some extent, the reality of safeguarding traditional markets for both sides. On the European side, however, this was of interest primarily to France and UK as the most recent colonial powers. These states have become relatively less powerful influences on Euro-South policy and, in addition, have begun to regard traditional commercial links with Africa as an irrelevance or, worse, a distraction.

As formal policy and effective practice have thus diverged, the framework of policies established after independence has come to look increasingly like a hollow shell. The tension has been partially defused up to now by the retention on the part of each EC member state of control over many of the most potent commercial policy instruments. Export credits, investment promotion, debt rescheduling, remain member state responsibilities. Germany, for example, may be inclined to use these to promote its interests in South-East Asia regardless of the Community focus on the ACP. Indeed, it may prefer the Community to concentrate on the ACP so as not to queer its pitch in Asia. But as powers are transferred increasingly from national to Community level, this capacity to run an independent shadow policy withers; the emphasis within Community-level policy acquires a direct importance for national interests.

Recent developments have thus begun to fracture the shell, a process which is likely to intensify in the medium term. The principal agent of change is *trade liberalisation,* externally within the GATT Uruguay Round and internally with the completion of the Single European Market.

The effects of external trade liberalisation

Trade preferences bulk large in Euro-South relations because they are for the south the most tangible of the limited number of instruments available to the Commission. Their value to the beneficiary is related inversely to the level of protectionism (at least if the matter is viewed in a strictly short-term, static perspective). If the level of protection is high, the competitive advantage afforded by preferences may be substantial. By the same token, if the level of protection is low, the opposite is true. Which way is the trend likely to go in the short- to medium-term future? Despite the set-backs on GATT, there is surely a reasonable chance that the 1990s will be a decade of liberalisation.

As a result, the whole edifice built up over the years by the EC is likely to subside gently as its foundations are weakened by liberalisation. Since this is happening at a time when the pace of European integration is quickening, we may expect that a new edifice will be thrown up to replace the old. The Community institutions will acquire a wider range of powers. Among them, no doubt, will be instruments that are of value to the South, and that may be used to construct a new relationship.

The effects of 1992

Why should the new ways not be just as favourable as the old were to the states at the apex of the pyramid of privilege? The answer is that to an extent they may, but that full replacement of old by new is unlikely, for two reasons. The first is that current EC policy reflects the interests of the past; the new policies and practice are more likely to reflect current interests in which the ACP are, at best, less prominent. The second is that parts of the ACP appear to be ill prepared to take advantage of Europe's new methods and instruments.

The impact of 1992 on LDCs may be profound, simply because it brings into play a host of other issues on which an EC decision will be required as circumstances change. It is these *consequential* decisions that may have the most potent effects on Euro-South relations. The removal of border controls as part of '1992', for example, will remove the power of member states to limit imports from their neighbours and, accordingly, their opportunity to police any national NTBs that may be in place. The countries that make most use of national NTBs are France, Ireland and Italy. Those with the fewest restrictions over and above Community-level quotas are Germany and Denmark. Hence, states that export primarily to France, Ireland and Italy have more reason to be worried about possible increased competition from the NICs and other third-party exporters than do countries exporting primarily to Germany/Denmark or having a broad geographical spread. In fact, France tends to be the largest market for the manufactured exports of both the ACP and the Mediterranean.

The impact of the changes in Eastern Europe

A further source of shock to the shell of formal Euro-South relations stems from the EC's need to redefine its policies towards its Eastern neighbours. While it is far too early to judge the speed and success of Eastern Europe's conversion to a free market economy (see Chapters 9. 10, 11 and 12 in *The National Economies of Europe),* it is possible to identify in broad terms the potential consequences for third parties. In the short to medium term, a successful shift to a free market economy in Eastern Europe is likely to be accompanied by increased demand for external capital, and increased supply of exports of basic manufactures and temperate agricultural products. Failure to make the required adjustment successfully, in contrast, could result in an increase in outward migration.

In either case, the tendency would be to increase competition for some LDCs. Eastern Europe could be competitive with the Mediterranean in particular as a host for foreign direct investment and a borrower of commercial and semi-commercial funds; as a supplier of manufactured exports to the Community and as a source of migrant workers.

By contrast. the ACP would benefit if rising incomes in Eastern Europe result in an increase in world demand for tropical products. Eastern Europe is one of the few areas of the world in which substantial increases in per capita consumption of tropical products could occur in the medium term.

The degree of competition will be greater if, as seems likely, the EC accords preferential treatment to East European countries. Until the revolution in Eastern Europe the region ranked at the bottom of the EC's hierarchy of trade preferences — the 'pyramid of privilege'. Poland, Romania. Czechoslovakia, Hungary and Yugoslavia were, of course, members of GATT, but only Romania and Yugoslavia benefited from the EC's GSP, and all East European countries faced significant non-tariff barriers to the EC market. In the late 1980s negotiations took place on improving the terms of access. Following the revolutions, the pace of transformation has accelerated. For Hungary and Poland, quantitative restrictions on EC imports of industrial products (except textiles and Coal and Steel Community products) were reduced or abolished from 1 January 1990, and the countries integrated into the GSP. By the middle of 1990 similar agreements had been reached with Czechoslovakia and Bulgaria. However, Eastern Europe's more ambitious hopes of an extensive liberalisation of access on products of key importance are making slow progress. In December 1991 the EC agreed with Poland, Czechoslovakia and Hungary a ten-year transition to mutual free trade, with asymmetrically large tariff cuts on imports into the EC during the first five years. But the deal excluded agriculture, steel and textiles, which are the sectors of most importance to Eastern Europe, and the EC approach to Eastern Europe remains cautious, if not illiberal. None the less, the EC cannot avoid taking an increased interest in the East. For all regions of the South, the most potent effect of the East European revolution may be its influence on EC perceptions. It has reinforced the loss of European interest in the South on both political and economic grounds.

The future

Although GATT, 1992 and Eastern Europe are likely to reinforce the trends of the 1960s, 1970s and 1980s, there are also some 'jokers in the pack' which may result in new relationships. Most potently, European interest may be sustained by concern that LDC actions could have undesirable consequences. The two instances that have received most attention concern migration and the environment.

The differential rates of economic and population growth in the EC and the non-EC Mediterranean region have already given rise to substantial inward migration into the Community, and the trend is likely to intensify sharply. This new wave of immigration differs from past flows in two respects, both of which have political implications: the proportion of political as opposed to economic refugees rose strongly during the 1980s to 70 per cent: and two-thirds of immigrants are Muslim.

There is increased awareness that what happens in LDCs may adversely affect EC welfare. Global warming as a result of forest burning, AIDS and drugs are simply the most publicised instances of the ways in which modern technology and more intense global communications have linked North and South on new dimensions.

These new issues present EC policy-makers with a critical problem. They can, to put it crudely, attempt to influence behaviour in the South by 'bribes' or 'threats', but neither is entirely satisfactory. Bribes, in the form of assistance to help an LDC cope with a specific problem (or grow faster to reduce migration) need to be much larger than is likely to be politically acceptable if they are to be effective. Threats, in the form of leverage applied to existing flows, may cause LDC governments to change officially stated policy, but are rarely effective in altering practice on the ground.

If existing instruments are unsuitable for the task, Europe may seek new ones; or it may be forced to tolerate a higher degree of Third World influence on its domestic affairs than it would wish. In either case, the course of Euro-South relations in future may not flow as rapidly towards disengagement as past trends would suggest.

References

Brown D K (1988) 'Trade preferences for developing countries: a survey of results'. *Journal of Development Studies* 24(3)

Davenport M (1988) 'European Community trade barriers to tropical agricultural products.' Overseas Development Institute. *Working Paper* 27

Davenport M, Stevens C (1990) 'The outlook for tropical products'. In Stevens C, Faber D (eds) *The Uruguay Round and Europe 1992: Implications for ACP/EC Cooperation.* European Centre for Development Policy Management. Maastricht

Davenport M, Page S (1991) *Europe: 1992 and the Developing World.* Overseas Development Institute

McAleese D (1989) 'External trade policy of the EC'. Paper presented to the Senior Policy Seminar of the World Bank and HEDCO *Africa and Europe after 1992* Dublin Nov. 27-30

McQueen M (1990) 'ACP export diversification: the case of Mauritius'. Overseas Development Institute, *Working Paper* 41

McQueen M, Stevens C (1989) 'Trade preferences and Lomé IV: Non-traditional ACP exports to the EC'. *Development Policy Review* 7: 239-60

Riddell R (1990) 'ACP export diversification: the case of Zimbabwe'. Overseas Development Institute. *Working Paper* 38

Sampson G P (1989) 'Trade expansion through the Generalised System of Preferences'. In Kiljunen K (ed) *Mini-NIEO: the Potential of Regional North-South Cooperation.* Institute of Development Studies, Helsinki

Sapir A, Stevens C (1987) 'India's exports of manufactures to the European Community: recent performance and constraints'. *Development Policy Review* 5: 379-98

Stevens C (1990) 'ACP export diversification: Jamaica, Kenya and Ethiopia'. Overseas Development Institute. *Working Paper* 40

15. Fuelling a New Engine of Growth or Separating Europe from Non-Europe?

Rolf J. Langhammer

1. Europe 1992 and changes in the international trading system: problems of simultaneity

Non-EC Member States in general and developing countries in particular have frequently raised concerns about the completion of the Internal Market. Studies stressing its positive effects on growth, structural change and import demand failed widely to dissipate the argument that the Community would be tempted to shift parts of the burden from internal adjustment to third countries. Basically, this argument extrapolates past experience with EC protectionism and receives further support from uncertainty about the stage of integration after 1992. In particular, what matters is that:

1. The Cecchini Report (1988) as well as the empirical studies presented in the so-called Emerson Report (CEC, 1988) focused on the internal effects and visibly neglected the external ones;

2. The common trade policy of the EC can be subsumed under those policies with the largest amount of instability, non-transparency, and conceptual deficiencies (Pelkmans, 1986, p.69);

3. Differences in the protection level between individual Member States are still sizeable and compromises towards a common protection level are highly disputed in some sectors;

4. The effects of liberalizing factor movements and trade in services escape much more from forecasts than did merchandise trade effects some 20 years ago when the impact of the customs union was estimated (trade creation and trade diversion).

Finally and most importantly, uncertainty is enhanced by the fact that parallel to 'operation 1992', four changes in the international trading environment will occur which determine the absolute level of market accessibility for third countries. In principle, they are independent from the completion of the Single Market but have often been evaluated as an integral part of the integration process.

The changes will arise from (1) the completion of the GATT Uruguay Round scheduled for the end of 1990; (2) the reform of the Generalized System of Preferences (GSP) after 1990; (3) the principles of trade in textiles and clothing after the expiration of MFA IV in 1991; and (4) the new Lomé Convention to be negotiated in 1990.

Rolf J. Langhammer: 'Fuelling a New Engine of Growth or Separating Europe from Non-Europe? *JOURNAL OF COMMON MARKET STUDIES* (December 1990), Vol XXIX, No 2, pp. 133-155. Reprinted by permission of Basil Blackwell Ltd.

Whereas each of these events will have a direct impact on prices and conditions of market entry of extra-EC imports, operation 1992 influences changes in internal prices. Altogether, the five events determine the critical parameter of competitiveness, that is the changes in relative prices between imports and domestic substitutes. Countervailing effects are possible and the net outcome is highly speculative, especially if the Community should try to link some events in a package approach.

As a result, the following discussion is scenario-oriented and not a forecast. Forecasts are not possible given the fact that the core of the Internal Market approach will be liberalization of services where very little information is available on the initial amount and structure of intra-and extra-EC trade in services (Langhammer, 1990; Nicolaides, 1990).

2. Growth effects of the Internal Market

The removal of all physical barriers to intra-EC trade in goods and services, as well as the scale effects of a large single market constitute the basis of single market-induced additional growth. Estimates range between 4.5 per cent over a 5-year period (CEC, 1988, Part A) under optimistic assumptions and only 2.3 per cent over the same period (Bakhoven, 1990). Both have in common that they fail to consider the dynamic effects of structural change after 1992 but instead focus on cost reductions (process innovations). A 1 per cent additional growth per year can be assumed as a reasonable yardstick and serves as a reference measure for estimates of import demand elasticities.

'Normal pattern' estimates arrive at similar results. They measure the relation between sectoral value-added as a dependent variable and per capita income and population as independent variables in a cross-country regression. The difference between the sum of estimated individual EC Member States figures of value-added on the one hand, and the theoretical value for the Community as a single entity on the other hand, is taken as a proxy for scale-induced additional growth. Using a sample of 61 OECD and middle-income developing countries, this relationship can be described as follows:

$$\log V = -1.146 + 1.033 \log y + 1.178 \log P \qquad R^2 = 0.95 \quad F = 663.18$$

$$(-6.479) \quad (20.500) \qquad (27.571)$$

where V is gross manufacturing value-added, y is per capita income and P is population (t-statistics in brackets). Data refer to and are expressed in prices of 1986 (World Development Report, 1988). Inserting individual EC Member State data and summing them up yields US$552 billion in 1986, compared to an individual figure for the Community as an entity of US$910 billion. The difference amounts to 11 per cent of the 1986 GDP of EC-12. Alternatively this would be equivalent to 1.4 per cent of the accumulated GDP of EC-12 in the period 1986-92 (based on the assumption of average annual growth rates of GDP of 2.0 per cent).

3. Single market-induced growth and EC import demand for manufactures from developing countries

Additional economic growth due to the completion of the Internal Market is expected to fuel import demand. Yet, an empirical assessment of this demand effect has to take into account that demand elasticities differ significantly by products and suppliers.

As far as products are concerned, the Lewis-Riedel controversy on the relation between economic growth in developed economies and developing countries' exports has exposed this relation to be rather unstable, even if it is confined to a relatively homogeneous bundle of products like commodities (Lewis, 1980; Riedel, 1984). Differences in elasticities as well as elasticities themselves increase with rising disaggregation. 'Iron' relationships, such as that between the growth in industrial production in developed economies and growth of world commodity trade measured by Lewis for the period 1873-1913 and 1953-73, vanish if the product sample is widened from few tropical agricultural products to total export supply of developing countries including manufactures.

Furthermore, elasticities estimated for all developing countries differ from those measured for individual countries and subregions as a result of differences in economic policies pursued by the countries (see also on this issue Matthews and McAleese, 1990; Davenport, 1990). Artificial market segmentation such as preferences may cause a further spread in demand elasticities. With respect to developing countries, there is reason to assume that export demand elasticities estimated for developing countries are higher than those assessed for all extra- EC suppliers. This hypothesis is based on the observation that during the seventies and eighties, developing countries in general and some countries in particular (e.g. South Korea), succeeded in raising their share in apparent consumption of all OECD countries (OECD, 1986). This holds true for those countries in particular which achieved rising shares of non-traditional products in their export supply.

In the following, an EC and US import demand function is estimated for manufactures exported by developing countries. The latter function serves as a yardstick for elasticities existing in a large internal market comparable to the one now formed by the Community.

Table 1 displays the estimated function.[1] Problems of positive autocorrelation emerge in the EC case as can be derived from rho-values. This may be due to the fact that there is no EC price index available and that West German price indices are comparatively poor proxies. Thus, in the EC, function price elasticities do not have the theoretical expected signs ($a_2 < O$ and $a_3 > O$).

Table 1   Import Demand of the European Community and the US for Manufactures from Developing Countries, 1970-86.

$\ln M_r = a_0 + a_1 \ln Y_r + a_2 \ln (P_m/P) + a_3 \ln (P_d/P)$

	a_1	a_2	a_3	R^{-2}	D.W.	Rho
EC	5.49 (4.40)*	1.66 (0.53)	-2.36 (-0.69)	0.979	1.53	0.81
US	4.98 (11.83)*	-0.96 (-2.22)*	0.53 (0.88)	0.969	1.72	0.17

Sources: © OECD, 1995, OECD, *National Accounts, Vol 1. 1966-1993.* Reproduced by permission of the OECD; UN, *Monthly Bulletin of Statistics*, current issues; IMF, *International Financial Statistics 1988 Yearbook*; US Department of Commerce, *Survey of Current Business*, current issues; Bundesbank, Fachserie 17, Reihe 8, *Preise und Preisindizes für die Einund Ausfuhr*, October 1988; own calculations.

Regression equations were estimated by applying the CORC procedure (t-statistics in brackets).

* = statistically significant at the 5 per cent level
M_r = manufactured imports in US$ million deflated with the West German import price index for finished goods (1980 = 100) as a proxy for an EC price index, and with the implicit deflator for US consumer goods imports (1972 = 100), respectively
Y_r = GDP of EC-10 and of the US in prices and exchange rates of 1980 in US$ billion
P_m = For the EC: West German import price index for finished goods (1980 = 100); for the US: implicit deflator for US consumer goods imports (1972 = 100)
P = GDP deflator for West Germany and the US respectively (1980 = 100)
P_d = Index of domestic producer prices for manufactures in West Germany and the US (1980 = 100) Durban-Watson statistics refer to regression residuals after applying the CORC procedure.

What matters for the assessment of growth effects on import demand are the income elasticities. The estimates yield that they do not differ significantly between the EC and the US, and that they are in the range of 5-5.5, with the higher value attributed to the EC. To apply this estimate would mean that — under the assumption of 1 per cent additional growth in the EC — real manufactured imports would rise by 5.5 per cent annually, that is by US$2 billion in current 1986-7 prices or — in terms of world manufactured exports of developing countries in 1986 — by slightly more than 1 per cent. This growth effect has to be confronted with estimates on the static trade effects due to a 'once-and-for-all' change in relative prices between domestic supply and imports. The Emerson Report (CEC, 1988, pp. 180-2) estimates that there will be a fall in relative prices as a result of the removal of internal trade barriers, and that this fall will lead to a purely static trade diversion effect in the range of 10 per cent of the initial level (extra-EC imports 1985) for all products and cumulated over two stages. In relation to the amount of EC manufactured imports from developing countries in 1985 and compared to the growth-induced additional import demand, the 'once-and-for-all' reduction of imports from developing countries would amount to approximately US$2.3 billion, that is slightly more than the value of additional import demand for *one* year estimated above. Thus, over a period of five years, additional import demand is expected to exceed the trade diversion effect by more than four times. It should be stressed that this estimate is based on *status quo* assumptions and that the Emerson Report does not make explicit the assumption underlying its estimate of trade diversion. It extrapolates favourable export trends from the past and will have to be revised should the import propensity decrease after the completion of the Internal Market.[2]

Thus, the questions arise whether import demand rises under constant import propensity because of fuelled growth, whether it rises because of an ascending import propensity, or whether there is an effect of declining import propensity offsetting the growth-induced additional import demand. To answer these questions, scenarios on likely changes in the production structure of the Community after 1992 are required. The following scenarios can be sketched:

1. The sector which receives the largest benefits from intra-EC liberalization is the service sector. This sector will expand much more than predicted by a long-term trend (based on a 3-sector hypothesis). The US, which has already liberalized its service markets and where private services have expanded more rapidly than in the EC, may serve as a reference for the extent of the expansion. However, input-output analyses show that the import propensity of final demand for services is generally lower than the import propensity of final demand for commodities and manufactures. If this does not change, the import propensity could decline.

2. There is a countervailing effect in the sense that the income elasticity of demand for some consumer services (tourism, passenger transport, non-commercial insurances, banking) is higher than for manufacturers and tends to increase with rising income. Some more advanced developing countries which have already proved to be competitive in supplying services to EC consumers in aviation, maritime shipping and travel could draw benefits from rising incomes and high elasticities of income demand. For these countries, import market penetration could be accelerated.

3. The completion of the Internal Market involves an over-proportionately strong integration of those two new Member States of the EC which have the strongest similarities in relative resource endowment with developing countries. Spain and Portugal will have to pass through the three stages of integration (free trade area, customs union, common market) much more rapidly than the old members. Increasing risk capital flows into the applicant countries reflect the progress of integration of the two countries into the core Community, and they contribute to the establishment of new production capacities replacing imports of the old members from non-member countries (trade diversion). Furthermore, Spanish and Portuguese currencies may appreciate in real terms because of the capital inflows, thereby improving the competitive position of developing countries' suppliers on home and international markets *vis-à-vis* the applicant countries. As new members of the European Monetary System (EMS), Spain and — probably soon — Portugal, will not be able to realign their exchange rates autonomously. Claims for protection against developing countries are then likely to become stronger, and that would mean that part of the adjustment burden faced by the applicant countries will be shifted to developing countries. Here, 'fortress Europe' perceptions can be materialized and so can fears of declining (extra-EC) import propensities, at least in some industries.

367

4. The Internal Market increasingly attracts the inflow of foreign risk capital which otherwise would have been exported to developing countries. Such declining relative attractiveness of non-Member States as hosts may impede the technology transfer to developing countries and thus may affect the medium-term supply capacity of the countries. Yet again the exchange rate effect has to be taken into consideration. As a result of massive capital inflows, the ECU would appreciate and improve the competitive position of those developing countries pegging to non-ECU currencies. This could help to initiate a process of channelling some investment funds towards developing countries.

5. Stronger competition, economies of scale and the harmonization of standards by competition (*ex post*) or by law (*ex ante*) within the Community will give rise to process innovations which accelerate labour-saving technological progress. In some industries factor intensities may be reversed and capacities be relocated in the EC. Episodical evidence in the clothing industry, for instance, does exist (Mody and Wheeler, 1987; Jungnickel, 1990). Temporarily, shifts in investment back to the Community could hamper exports of developing countries in those industries which are vulnerable to labour-saving techniques. Yet, in an aggregate view developing countries could also become hosts of sectors which Community suppliers would have to leave because of rising income levels and structural change.

6. Technological progress in the Internal Market will not only be labour-saving, but also resource-saving and less pollution-intensive (Siebert, 1990). Demand for mineral fuels and for other mineral commodities would then continue to delink from economic growth. Commodity exporters among the developing countries could become seriously affected as the short-run demand effect for commodities would be overshadowed by the medium-term effect of economizing on commodities. Countervailing effects are possible in the agricultural sector if the Community reduces its degree of market intervention in the agricultural sector under international pressure and budget constraints. However, in principle, the reform of the Common Agricultural Policy has to be dealt with separately from the Internal Market.

To summarize points 1-6, there is no universal answer on changing import propensities after 1992. Effects will differ by countries affected as well as by products. Most importantly, hypotheses on the income-dependent import propensity must be supplemented by those on the price-dependent import propensity. If the transmission process between EC-internal prices and international prices is allowed to run via flexible exchange rates as well as liberal trade policies, a short-run decline in the import propensity would remain a transitory problem.

4. Import market penetration in a large Internal Market

Import demand functions only allow for hints on determinants of one part of total demand satisfied by imports. Whether imports contribute more strongly to apparent consumption in a large internal market than in a 'not-so-perfect-customs union' (Donges, 1981) like the old EEC remains an open question. An historical comparison of import market penetrations ratios (IMPRs) in the EC as well as in the US/Canada (as a yardstick for an internal market)[3] may be helpful to discuss this question.

In concrete terms, should the Community have already moved towards an internal market, differences in import market penetration ratios between the two regions should have become smaller under a *ceteris paribus* assumption. To test this hypothesis, the deviation of average ratios between EC and US/Canada IMPRs from unity is taken as the relevant criterion (Table 2).[4] As a result it emerges that:

1. Total extra-EC imports as well as EC imports from developing countries always contributed more to apparent consumption than imports of the US and Canada;

2. Differences in the level of import market penetration between the EC and US/Canada varied considerably by individual industries so that IMPRs were not found to be statistically significantly higher in the EC than in US/Canada;

3. Levels of IMPRs in the two regions were more similar for imports from developing countries than for total imports;

4. During the early eighties IMPRs of the two regions converged, probably as a result of the real US$ appreciation rather than of converging levels of market integration.

Table 2   Relative Market Penetration Ratios, EC-US/Canada, 1968-1984/5.

	1968	1970/71	1972/73	1974/75	1976/77	1980/81	1982/83	1984/85
Total Imports								
Food, beverages, tobacco	1.84	2.04	1.97	1.56	1.79	1.48	1.68	1.50
Textiles	0.92	1.18	1.47	1.94	2.10	2.68	2.55	1.92
Clothing	0.70	0.96	1.10	1.24	1.20	1.28	1.21	1.01
Wood products, paper and printing	8.95	9.94	8.24	9.88	9.91	9.07	8.93	5.82
Rubber	1.37	1.38	0.89	0.94	0.89	0.99	1.25	0.95
Chemicals	3.07	3.33	2.50	2.06	2.16	2.23	2.25	1.91
Petroleum and coal products	0.85	0.75	0.60	0.72	1.00	1.95	2.19	1.93
Non-metallic mineral products	0.55	0.89	0.78	0.93	0.94	0.83	0.78	0.63
Ferrous and non-ferrous metals	1.60	1.86	1.61	1.32	1.71	1.98	1.34	1.34
Transport equipment	1.62	1.18	1.12	1.09	1.56	1.13	1.01	0.94
Machinery and other manufactured goods	1.50	1.80	1.57	1.58	1.59	1.74	1.70	1.46
Manufacturing sector	1.80	1.96	1.71	1.61	1.73	1.76	1.67	1.42
Average	2.09*	2.30*	1.99*	2.11*	2.26*	2.30*	2.26*	1.77*

Table 2 (continued)   **Relative Market Penetration Ratios, EC-US/Canada, 1968-1984/5.**

	1968	1970/71	1972/73	1974/75	1976/77	1980/81	1982/83	1984/85
Imports from developing countries								
Food, beverages, tobacco	1.59	2.03	2.20	1.43	2.09	1.66	2.13	1.87
Textiles	0.87	1.43	1.63	1.80	2.26	2.38	2.41	1.82
Clothing	0.97	0.99	0.98	0.96	1.05	0.99	0.99	1.83
Wood products, paper and printing	1.56	1.56	1.61	1.45	2.09	2.23	2.18	1.60
Rubber	2.20	1.88	1.07	0.96	0.98	0.90	0.83	0.58
Chemicals	2.21	2.66	2.20	1.63	1.75	2.09	2.03	1.60
Petroleum and coal products	0.40	0.27	0.20	0.28	0.41	1.01	1.07	1.01
Non-metallic mineral products	0.17	0.17	0.24	0.36	0.61	0.59	0.54	0.39
Ferrous and non-ferrous metals	3.37	3.51	2.44	2.14	1.94	1.90	1.58	1.14
Transport equipment	8.00	3.50	1.82	1.25	2.38	3.24	2.50	1.35
Machinery and other manufactured goods	0.59	0.55	0.48	0.47	0.60	0.72	0.63	0.58
Manufacturing sector	1.52	1.51	1.26	0.97	1.12	1.19	1.10	0.90
Average	1.99*	1.67*	1.35*	1.16*	1.47*	1.61*	1.53*	1.16*

Source: UNCTAD, *Handbook of International Trade and Development Statistics*, current issues.
Ratio between the shares of imports in apparent consumption in the EC and in US/Canada.
For the EC extra-regional imports are considered.
* Not significantly different from one at the 1 per cent level

In general, the comparison does not suggest dramatic changes in the level of import market penetration after 1992.

5. Remnants of national sovereignties in trade policies: possible consequences for developing countries

The completion of the Internal Market requires that remnants of national quantitative restrictions are fully abandoned. This condition is not yet fulfilled. In 1988, about 1,000 national quotas still existed outside the textile industry, but only 4 per cent of them were made effective by invoking Article 115 of the EC Treaty in order to control intra-EC trade in such products (Bundesverband, 1988, p.7). This low share suggests that the majority of national quotas is redundant. They will be removed without the major resistance of Member States until 1992 as recent evidence demonstrates (Leg. L 2429/89 of 28 July 1989). Yet, a hard core of national quotas exists in textile, clothing, entertainment electronics, and — as the major stumbling bloc to a common trade policy — in the car industry. Tables A 1 and A 2 provide a survey on measures under Article 115 mostly invoked by Ireland and France against Asian countries and NICs. In the agricultural sector national quotas are still very relevant for some tropical products like bananas (Cable, 1990; Davenport, 1988) while excise taxes in some Member States on products like coffee are looked upon as a further national barrier to imports.

Yet, the major relevant test case of whether remnants of national sovereignty in trade policies can be abandoned until 1992 is the car industry and the common treatment of Japanese car exports to the Community. Consensus is hampered by the different character of national measures. They comprise strict per unit quotas (Italy, Spain and Portugal) which are made effective by application of Article 115 of the EC Treaty, the surveillance of ceilings in terms of upper limits in percentage shares of imports in newly registered cars (France), privately organized voluntary export restraints (VERs) between importers and exporters (UK), as well as progressive national sales taxes (Denmark, Greece). It is very likely that controversies among EC Member States on a common policy in the car industry will affect advanced developing countries in future. This may occur either directly if low-cost car producers like South Korea and Malaysia try to penetrate the Community and then face local content requirements, or indirectly if suppliers of car components in developing countries suffer from barriers against Japanese car investments outside Japan. Globalization of production will increasingly include developing countries in the module-type of manufacturing and this trend will make trade policies redundant which still try to discriminate between final goods imports of different origins when the origin is defined in terms of a single producer country.

Where such remnants of national sovereignty exist, there are three scenarios of possible changes in order to comply with the 1992 target:

First, under a pessimistic *status quo* scenario, national competences in sensitive sectors (clothing, cars) cannot be abandoned until the end of 1992. There is no need to discuss this scenario in detail as it would mean failure to meet the deadline.

Secondly, under a neutral scenario national quotas are replaced by a common measure. Yet, to find a measure which is neutral in the sense that it does not imply a worsening of conditions of market access after 1992 is difficult, especially in industries with quota markets and non-quota markets and with widely differing national measures (quotas, ceilings, private VERs).

For developing countries, those product groups are of particular interest which hitherto are *de jure* subject to national quotas in all Member State markets, however, under very different conditions of quota controls. Cases in point are the sensitive categories of the MFA. How differently individual EC members have handled their quotas in the past has been demonstrated by Hamilton (1986, cited in Winters, 1988) who estimated tariff equivalents of national quotas for Hong Kong exports of jeans in the EC. Estimates ranged from 32 per cent for the UK to 11 per cent for France and 0 per cent for West Germany which did not apply its quota.[5]

A realistic assumption under the neutral scenario would be the introduction of a common quota as the sum of national quotas. Assuming that quotas would have been applied by all Members in the same way, the import volume would not change after 1992. The political economy background of consensus-building suggests a gloomier result, however. Restrictive partner countries are expected to agree to a common quota only under the binding commitment of all Members to apply the quota strictly. Such commitment could mean that relatively liberal Members would be disciplined under the Brussels-led administration of quotas, whereas in the past they were free to lift national quotas 'by revealed preference' because restrictive Members could resort to Article 115 and thus could protect their markets. Under such a scenario, a strict control of a common quota would deteriorate market access compared to the side-by-side of less restrictive and more restrictive national procedures and would have to pass the test of GATT conformity.

The extent of differently applied national quotas emerges from an MFA-example (Table 3). As quotas were politically negotiated *ex ante* in a case-by-case procedure, low and strictly controlled quotas for countries like France and Ireland led to incentives to exploit the potential of price arbitrage and to shift imports from open markets to restrictive markets. To discourage this, the latter countries invoked Article 115 and hence prevented prices falling in their markets. Under a common quota, prices would be expected to fall in the former restrictive markets and to rise in the relatively open markets, and this would affect export earnings of developing countries in individual EC Member States.

Table 3   Quota Utilization in Imports of Shirts (MFA-Category 8) of Individual EC Members from Developing Countries, 1986.

Export country affected by Article 115	Quota relation between EC Member invoking Article 115 and West Germany[a]	EC member invoking Article 115[b]	Quota utilization of EC member invoking Article 115[c] in percentages	Quota utilization in West Germany in percentages
Thailand	1 3.6	France	109.3	114.1
Hong Kong	1: 25.7	France	104.3	110.6
South Korea	1: 25.9	France	91.8	116.8
Indonesia	1: 2.5	France	113.4	73.9
India	1: 6.6	France	95.8	104.1
Taiwan	1: 45.7	France	15.6	112.6
India	1: 44.7	Ireland	148.9	104.1
Hong Kong	1: 327.7	Ireland	136.7	110.6
Pakistan	1: 16.5	Ireland	83.8	104.1
Indonesia	1: 56.8	Ireland	96.5	73.9
Macao	1: 75.3	Ireland	29.7	106.3

Sources: Official Journal of the European Communities, L 374, 31.12.1982; Eurostat, External Trade, Analytical Tables, NIMEXE 1986; own calculations
[a]Quotas of individual EC Members are defined towards individual export countries. West Germany is taken as a yardstick for a relatively liberal member as it did not apply Article 115
[b]EC member controlled intra-EC trade in shirts originating from the export country in 1986 according to Article 115
[c]Volume imports in per cent of national quota.

Apart from income effects which arise from changing export earnings, income effects may also become effective for suppliers acting under oligopolistic competition. The segmentation of EC markets by means of national quotas and the scope for price discrimination may have enabled foreign suppliers to exploit the consumer surplus better than would be possible under a common quota. In this respect a common quota could be instrumental to erode economic rents in the former restrictive markets, to intensify the competition between established suppliers and newcomers, but also to create new rents in the formerly open markets.

A transitory common quota seems to have been preferred by EC officials for those products in which quota markets and non-quota markets still exist side-by-side (Krenzler, 1988). How strong the incentives are which stem from price arbitrage depends on the speed of abandoning national quotas and Article 115 cases. As far as MFA products are concerned, the MFA IV (1986-91) comprises some adjustment measures, e.g. the lifting of non-utilized quotas or the partial transferability of quotas among Member States (Neundörfer, 1987, pp. 49-54). Yet, individual VERs between the Community and developing countries still include national quotas for sensitive products till the end of 1992. Thus, there is reason to assume that in such cases some members will try to insist on a transition period.

In general, it is this 'neutral' scenario of common measures which has given rise to concerns about 'fortress Europe'. In trade with manufacturers, for instance, national customs authorities which are the executive bodies of a common trade policy still have command over a large bundle of 'grey' administrative measures to discriminate against imports. Historically influenced perceptions pro or contra imports will remain different among EC countries beyond 1992.

The third scenario is called optimistic as it assumes that national quotas are abandoned without any substitute. As a compromise, a transitory rise of the common external tariff by the amount of the tariff equivalent of a common quota comes to mind. Under various assumptions the static trade effects of the optimistic scenario are assessed in Table 4. The magnitudes of trade creation and trade diversion mainly depend on the importance of national quotas in individual EC Member States, and thus imports are expected to increase, particularly in France, the UK and Italy. Yet, as in all empirical studies on static trade effects, magnitudes in terms of total trade are marginal because of both low tariff equivalents and low price elasticities of demand. This holds for trade creation (replacement of domestic production by imports) as well as for trade diversion (replacement of imports from OECD countries outside the EC by imports from developing countries), both 'once-and-for-all' effects. Compared to the income-induced increase of import demand, the price-induced increase of imports due to the dismantling of national quotas is estimated to be much lower. Yet, compared to the neutral scenario, the optimistic one would offer a unilateral improvement of market access and a true step forward towards a single market.

Table 4   **Static Trade Effects of Removing National Quotas Against Developing Countries.**

Exogenous parameter	Relevance of national quantitative restrictions[a]		Estimated trade creation (TC)[b] in ECU million under		Estimated trade diversion (TD)[c] in ECU million under	
			MFN rate	GSP rate	MFN rate	GSP rate
Average MFN tariff for semi-manufactures and manufactures from developing countries (in per cent)	7.1	FRG	1.1	1.2	1.0	1.0
		France 10.8	65.1	69.1	43.2	45.9
		Italy 6.1	35.9	38.1	24.2	25.7
Average GSP rate	0.9	United Kingdom 12.3	104.1	110.5	89.9	95.5
		Benelux-Countries 0.6	4.0	4.2	3.3	3.5
Tariff equivalent of national quota (in per cent)	10.0	Denmark 5.2	3.6	3.8	6.9	7.4
		Ireland 2.2	0.6	0.7	0.6	0.6
Price elasticity of import demand	-0.96	EC-9 —	214.4d	227.6	169.1d	179.6d

a Imports from developing countries subject to national quantitative restrictions as percentage of total EC Member State imports of semi-manufactures and manufactures (CCT 25-99) from developing countries (excluding fuels), in 1978 in per cent

b Estimated as follows

$$TC = M_E \quad \frac{\Delta t_Q}{(1 + t_Q)(1 + t)} \cdot e_m$$

where

M_E = initial imports according to footnote (a) in 1987

Δt_Q = reduction of tariff protection by the tariff equivalent of quota t_Q

t = tariff rate without the average tariff equivalent

e_m = price elasiticity of import demand

c Estimated by using the so-called non-restrictive Verdoorn concept:

$$TD = M_E [a(e_s - e_m)] \quad \left[\frac{\Delta t_Q}{(1 + t_Q)(1 + t)} \right]$$

Where

a = share of extra-regional imports from non-developing countries (M_{NE}) in total imports of the EC from non-Members ($a = M_{NE}/M_{E + NE}$) and

e_s = elasticity of substitution between imports from developing countries and non-developing countries. This elasticity is assumed to be -2.0. See for the various assumptions underlying the estimates of trade diversion Sawyer and Sprinkle (1989).

d The sum of trade creation and trade diversion amounts to 0.8 per cent (MFN rate) and 0.9 per cent (GSP rate) of EC-9 imports of semi-manufactures and manufactures from developing countries in 1987.

Sources: Langhammer (1981, Table 1); Borrman *et al.* (1985, Table 37); EC Foreign trade NIMEXE 1987; own calculations

6. Discrimination between developing countries: will unequal treatment become redundant after 1992?

The EC tradition of discrimination is deeply rooted as the Community itself is a preferential trading arrangement. There is no other actor in the international trading system who has deviated so widely from the principle of unconditional Most Favoured Nation (MFN) as the Community. Special treatment of developing countries under the Generalized System of Preferences (GSP) and the special Lomé and Mediterranean Preferences, special treatment of Eastern European countries, political preferences for sectoral arrangements, and safeguard protection on a selective basis within the GATT framework bear witness to this argument. With respect to developing countries, the EC has tried to use trade policies as a vehicle of resource transfer (by allowing developing countries to raise export prices by the amount of tariff revenues forgone). While objections in principle (Patterson, 1983; Wolf, 1987) as well as discouraging results (Agarwal *et al.*, 1985; Langhammer and Sapir, 1987) may have spurred reforms within the preferential trading arrangements, there has not been a basic revision towards separating trade policies from aid policies and returning to MFN treatment.

Whether this revision will be launched after 1992 cannot be answered because of the still open outcome of the four major events in the international trading system. Thus, the following hypotheses are not directly intertwined with the completion of the Single Market.

First, the EC will maintain the principle of unequal treatment of different groups of developing countries, mainly in order to avoid a further erosion of the ACP preference margins *vis-à-vis* better-off developing countries.

Secondly, within the ACP framework the trend from widely ineffective trade preferences to the transfer of resources will continue. Should the trade performance of ACP countries in EC markets deteriorate further, perhaps as an indirect result of accelerated structural change within the Single Market (e.g. enhanced resource-saving technological progress, full integration of Spain and Portugal into the Community, higher competition intensity), additional policy measures will be introduced (including the improvement of trade preferences where they are still restrictive).

Thirdly, non-EC Member States from the Mediterranean area will receive the special attention of the Community as their export structure shows a stronger overlap with that of the applicant countries than between the ACP countries and the applicants. Thus, the full integration of Spain and Portugal is likely to have a short-term negative impact on Maghreb and Mashreq countries and will require compensation payments if the *status quo ante is* to be guaranteed. Yet, should the currencies of the applicant countries appreciate in real terms because of rising unit labour costs and massive capital inflows, Mediterranean countries could improve their relative competitive position *vis-à-vis* Spain and Portugal.

Fourthly, advanced developing countries and especially the small group of Asian NICs will be graduated after 1992. That means that preferential treatment of their exports will not be improved but 'frozen', perhaps even diminished as an 'admission fee' levied by the Community for allowing access to a large Single Market (Krenzler, 1988).

Fifthly, unilateral tariff preferences, regardless of whether they are general or region-specific, will become less relevant simply because of MFN tariff cuts in the GATT framework. In trade policy issues where decisions have to be negotiated, the EC will continue to prefer bilateral over multilateral negotiations wherever possible.

Above all, what matters more is the question when the Community will pay tribute to the on-going globalization of production and new assembly types of manufacturing (just-in-time-procedures, module-type of assembly). Both make traditional selectivity and discrimination of individual countries as well as their implementation by rules of origin widely obsolete. Controversies between the Community, Member States and private investors on minimum local content requirements (such as in the case of Nissan cars produced in the UK and exported to France) support concerns about future disputes challenging the Commission and the European Court. The same holds for the recent decision of the Community to link free intra-EC trade in chips to the location of a specific production stage in the Community (diffusion process).

The legal framework of EC traditional trade policies has no guidelines to settle such disputes between investors operating world-wide and the EC authorities which try to enforce the fiction of an 'EC-originating' product or — in the investment field — of an 'EC-based' company. Three factors, however, give rise to hope that the Community will refrain from excessive interventions into flows of investments to keep investors *non grata* out of the Single Market. First, there is a large number of legal and illegal options to circumvent controls of local content and rules of origin; secondly, the potential of retaliatory actions in the Asian NICs and Japan as well as in the US is large; and, thirdly, challenge and response-games between investors circumventing restrictions and the Community face budget constraints on the Community side.

7. External effects of liberalizing intra-EC trade in services: looking briefly into the crystal ball

As mentioned above, the liberalization of services is one of the key tasks of the 1992 operation. It is strongly linked to the liberalization of intra-EC capital transactions as there will be no free trade in financial services without free movement of capital.

As trade in invisibles frequently escapes from statistical registration (Langhammer, 1989; 1990), there is very skimpy information on the competitive strength of developing countries as suppliers of services. Such information suggests that tourism, passenger transport (aviation), as well as merchandise transport are services in which a large number of developing countries have witnessed international competitiveness. Construction activities, engineering and financial services are relevant for only a few advanced developing countries.

Without going into the details and the speculative nature of this issue, the following hypotheses can be summarized.

Tourism

Relative prices of tourist services inside and outside the Community are expected to be influenced by two countervailing aspects of the EC Single Market. Internal prices will fall because of intensified competition in the aviation market and transborder mergers of tourist agencies. On the other hand, internal prices are feared to rise once-and-for-all if a VAT of 6.5 per cent is levied on intra-European travel as well as a fuel tax imposed on intra-EC shipping. Finally, it is argued that airport companies may try to raise their fees in order to compensate for the loss in earnings from duty-free shops which become redundant in the Single Market.

The net effect of both price movements is uncertain as changes in the real exchange rates relevant to the European tourist resort areas have to be taken into account. With rising unit labour costs in the Mediterranean Member States, there is room for the (*ceteris paribus*) assumption that the ratio between internal and extra-EC prices for tourist services will increase, thus providing chances for developing countries to attract tourists.

Aviation

The aviation market is of considerable export interest for low-cost carriers in developing countries. The market is characterized by an extremely high degree of bi-lateralism, and though the Commission has subjected aviation to the competition rules of the Rome Treaty, it is very likely that there will be no common policy until 1992. Capacities have been expanded because of lowered barriers to entry, but price competition is still very much restricted because of the so-called group exemption in the competition articles through which pool arrangements are sanctioned.

Recent decisions of the European Court (Nouvelles Frontières and Saeed) which would theoretically widen the scope for price competition have not yet been implemented. It remains open whether the Commission will make greater use of the competition rules in order to discourage concerted actions of EC carriers. As long as other Member States still have the right to protect their national flag carriers (e.g. in France and in Germany), price competition will be confined to few routes within the EC.

Developing countries assess the effects of the EC aviation market mainly under the concentration issue. Should intensified competition among EC carriers lead to a merger process with few remaining mega-carriers, negotiations on landing rights and slots are hypothesized to become more difficult than under the current situation because of changes in the relative bargaining power (Mathew, 1989). Fifth freedom rights are expected to be guaranteed for the period beyond 1992 so that the definition of intra-EC transport as 'domestic' transport would not mean to deny third countries the right to continue to supply such transport services. A further aspect of concern for developing countries is stronger competition from revitalized EC carriers outside the Community.

Maritime Transport

Unlike in the aviation market, the Commission has gained a mandate in maritime transport to act against third country suppliers if unfair pricing is alleged. In a case decided in early 1989 the Commission for the first time imposed a countervailing duty on an external supplier of services, a South Korean shipping company operating a liner service between EC ports and Australia (Leg. 15/89, L 4, 4 January 1989). The company allegedly received subsidies and thus underbid European companies which requested the 'unfair pricing' regulation to be imposed by the Commission. This regulation can be regarded as the nucleus of a common policy in maritime transport against third countries. A common policy is facilitated by the fact that most EC shipping agencies already jointly act in liner conferences and have established common institutions which lobby in Brussels.

Banking and Insurance Services

In banking and insurance third countries are confronted with the reciprocity clause in the so-called draft Second Banking Directive. Banking licences which are necessary to provide services in the Single Market are issued if EC banks and insurances do not notify discriminatory actions against their own business in the third country. The reciprocity debate became heated because of vague definitions in the first draft, but seems to have relaxed with a new draft through which licences are issued *bona fide* rather than after an examination of conditions in the applicant country market. For the majority of developing countries the reciprocity clause will be ineffective since their banks have only established funding offices or financing agencies of merchandise trade in EC countries, rather than branches offering the full scale of banking services.

8. Summary and outlook

The completion of the Single Market marks the third stage in the integration process. After finishing the free trade area and the customs union, the liberalization of services and of factor movement will bring the Community to the stage of a common market. The residual process of monetary integration would then mean advancing towards the level of an economic union.

It is important to note that the major effects in this third stage are transmitted through changes in internal prices for services and factors and not through changes in domestic prices for merchandise imports. Such changes should have been the task of the customs union stage.

Looking upon European integration from this 'stages approach', chances and risks for third countries can be sketched in a relatively clear way.

First, with respect to the chances, the completion of the third stage stimulates structural change in the Community and accelerates economic growth. This holds particularly for the tertiary sector which lags behind in its development because of massive barriers to market entry. Such growth impulse may prolong the upward side of the business cycle which itself is the most effective shelter against the emergence of protectionist lobby groups in the Community. Furthermore, as a result of becoming more competitive, EC suppliers may contribute to terms of trade gains for developing countries due to a downward pressure on world market prices of manufactures.

On the supply side, competition for risk capital within the Community between the core regions and the periphery will be enhanced, and the initial inflow of capital to the periphery will lead to rising prices for non-tradeables relative to tradeables (real appreciation) in these countries. Then labour costs would rise and the participation of the periphery countries in the European Monetary System would deny the option of fighting real appreciation by autonomous exchange rate adjustments. Rising labour costs could be furthered by political pressure towards 'social harmonization' within the

EC-12 so that differences in labour costs between the centre and the periphery would be levelled. Under this scenario, relatively labour-intensive production in the periphery would lose its competitiveness and would be shifted to countries outside the Community, mainly to developing countries.

On the demand side, import absorption can be expected to increase because of higher growth. In cumulative terms, this effect seems to weigh more than the expected 'once-and-for-all' decline of extra-EC imports (trade diversion).

Secondly, risks culminating in the 'fortress Europe' fear are based on three arguments:

1. In some so-called sensitive sectors the stage of the customs union has not been accomplished. This delay is evident in the car industry, the textiles and clothing sector, some steel products, some agricultural products, and in the entire service sector.

    Thus, there is an adjustment jam as liberalization steps of the second and third stage of integration coincide. This jam provokes political resistance in such Member States in which remaining protection in goods markets as well as in factor markets is relatively high (e.g. in France). Attempts are thus made to shift parts of the adjustment burden stemming from internal liberalization to third countries. Yet, in a Single Market such shifts can only be implemented if the relatively open EC Member States agree, and this will bring the Community into conflict with the targets of the Uruguay Round which runs parallel to the Single Market process.

2. As discussed above, it is probably the group of applicant Mediterranean countries which will claim for strategies to shift the burden of adjustment to third countries. Spain and Portugal which are still in the transition period towards full membership have to pass through all three stages simultaneously. Hence, it comes as no surprise that lobbying activities, for instance, to prolong the MFA beyond 1991 are strong in the two countries. In addition, there are pressures in the old Member States against 'social dumping' of the Mediterranean countries. Together with the political decision in these countries to join the EMS, rising real labour costs will aggravate adjustment problems just in those industries which compete with imports from developing countries.

3. The vague term 'reciprocity' is another source of concern as long as the Community uses it in the context of the Single Market. Third countries will interpret reciprocity as political leverage and as a bargaining chip in the sense that there is no free admission to a large Single Market. In this respect, it is important to note that the Single European Act does not reaffirm the obligation laid down in the EC Treaty to promote trade between Member States and third countries. In the White Paper the Commission argues that third countries should not benefit from the advantages of a larger common market unless they make concessions. As reciprocity is a criterion in multilateral trade negotiations only, and as the completion of the Single Market — with very few exceptions — has nothing to do with the change of the common external level of protection, the term should be dropped in the Single Market context.

To summarize, in a macroeconomic view the Single Market will give a new impulse to structural change and economic growth in the world economy. Developing countries will gain larger benefits from this impulse than they incur short-run losses because of trade diversion. Such benefits will be larger for middle-income countries exporting manufactures than for low-income countries relying on commodities. For the latter group, the need to remove home-made barriers to structural change will become more urgent. In a microeconomic view, however, some concerns about 'fortress Europe' could not yet he dissipated by the Community. Common policies in the textiles and clothing industry and particularly in the car industry are still pending, and it remains to be seen whether compromises on a common policy will offer developing countries better market access than the side-by-side of different national policies.

Table A1: Article 115 Cases by Product groups and EC Members (%).

Product groups	1981	1983	1985	1986	1987	1988a
By product groups						
Agricultural products	1.8	3.1	5.3	1.9	1.5	8.4
MFA products	74.6	74.4	70.2	74.1	69.5	57.8
Other products	23.7	22.5	24.6	24.1	29.0	33.7
Total	114	160	114	108	131	114
By EC Member States						
MFA products						
Benelux countries	17.6	12.6	2.5	0.0	1.1	0.0
France	37.6	27.7	38.8	55.0	45.1	39.6
Ireland	27.1	38.7	36.3	37.5	42.9	45.8
Italy	7.1	6.7	8.8	3.8	8.8	14.5
United Kingdom	9.4	10.9	13.8	3.8	1.1	0.0
All others	1.2	3.4	2.3	0.3	2.1	0.0
Total[b]	85	119	80	80	91	82
Other manufactures						
Benelux countries	3.7	11.1	3.5	0.0	0.0	0.0
France	37.0	27.7	35.7	26.9	36.8	35.7
Ireland	11.1	5.6	7.1	7.7	7.9	0.0
Italy	40.7	47.2	35.7	61.5	28.9	25.0
United Kingdom	7.4	8.3	14.3	0.0	0.0	0.0
All others	0.0	0.0	0.0	3.8	26.3	39.3
Total[b]	27	36	28	26	38	48

Source: Spinanger (1988)
[a] Until July, extrapolated to annual figures
[b] Number of cases

Table A2: **Article 115 Cases[a] by Regions/Countries Affected and by Product Groups, 1981-5 and 1986-8.**

Region/country	—1981, 1983, 1985—				—1986, 1987, 1988[b]—			
	Total	MRA	Other	Total clothing	Total	MFA	Other	Total clothing
PACRIM	64.6	62.0	62.6	72.4	76.0	75.0	77.4	78.3
East Asia	58.2	54.1	56.5	70.7	68.9	64.6	68.1	78.3
China, P. R.	9.2	7.6	3.1	13.8	12.8	13.5	8.6	11.4
China, R.	11.8	11.1	11.1	13.8	14.0	11.8	12.9	18.7
Hong Kong	17.5	21.2	29.4	6.5	18.3	26.6	34.1	—
Japan	7.7	—	—	30.9	12.1	0.3	—	38.0
Korea, R.	10.0	11.4	9.5	5.7	10.6	10.7	10.0	10.2
South East Asia	6.3	7.9	6.1	1.6	7.2	10.4	9.3	
Philippines	2.5	3.3	4.6	0.8	0.8	1.1	1.4	
Thailand	2.0	2.7	0.8	—	5.8	8.5	6.8	
South Asia	8.4	10.6	10.3	1.6	10.4	15.1	15.4	
India	4.7	6.0	5.7	0.8	7.0	10.2	11.8	
Pakistan	3.7	4.6	4.6	0.8	3.2	4.7	2.9	
Other countries	27.1	27.4	27.1	26.0	13.6	9.9	7.2	21.7
Total	491	368	262	123	530	364	279	166
Per cent	100.0	74.9	53.4	25.1	100.0	68.7	52.6	31.3

Source: Spinanger (1988)
[a] BTN 4-digit product groups affected by Article 115 cases
[b] For 1988 until July, extrapolated to annual figures
[c] Number of cases

References

Agarwal, J. P., Dippl, M. and Langhammer, R. J. (1985) *EC Trade Policies Towards Associated Developing Countries — Barriers to Success*, Kieler Studien, No. 193 (Tübingen: Mohr).

Amtsblatt der Europäischen Gemeinschaften, Mitteilungen und Bekanntmachungen, C 213, 25.8. 1989.

Bakhoven, A. F. (1990) 'An Alternative Assessment of Macroeconomic Effects of "Europe 1992". In H. Siebert, ed., *The Completion of the Internal Market. Symposium 1989* (Tübingen: Mohr), pp. 24-44.

Borrmann, A., Borrman, C., Langer, C. and Menck, K. W. (1985) *The Significance of the EEC's Generalised System of Preferences* (Hamburg: Verlag Weltarchiv).

Bundesverband des Deutschen Exporthandels e.V., Verband der Fertigwaren e.V. (1988) 'Auswirkungen des EG-Binnenmarktes auf die Drittländerbeziehungen', mimeo, September.

Cable, V. (1990) '1992 and its Implications for Developing Countries'. In H. Siebert, ed., *The Completion of the Internal Market. Symposium* 1989 (Tübingen: Mohr), pp.255- 72.

Cecchini, P. (1988) *The European Challenge, 1992: The Benefits of a Single Market* (Aldershot: Wildwood House).

Commission of the European Communities (1988) 'The Economics of 1992. An Assessment of the Potential Economic Effects of Completing the Internal Market of the European Community', *European Economy*, March.

Davenport, M. W. S. (1988) 'European Community Trade Barriers to Tropical Agricultural Products', ODI Working Paper 27 (London: Overseas Development Institute).

Davenport, M. (1990) 'The External Policy of the Community and its Effects upon the Manufactured Goods of the Developing Countries', *Journal of Common Market Studies*, Vol. XXIX, No. 2.

Donges, J. B. (1981) 'What is Wrong with the European Communities?' Eleventh Wincott Memorial Lecture, (London: Institute of Economic Affairs).

Hamilton, C. (1986) 'An Assessment of Voluntary Restraints on Hong Kong Exports to Europe and the USA', *Economica,* 53, pp. 339-50.

Hamilton, C. (1988) 'Follies of Policies for Textile Imports in Western Europe' in L.B.M. Mennes and J. Kol, eds., *European Trade Policies and the Developing World* (London: Croom Helm) pp. 224-45.

Jungnickel, R. (1990) *Neue Technologien und Produktionsverlagerungen.* (Hamburg: Verlag Weltarchiv).

Krenzler, H. G. (1988) 'Zwischen Protektionismus und Liberalismus. Europäischer Binnenmarkt fund Drittlandsbeziehungen', *Europa-Archiv*, 9, pp. 241-8.

Lächler, U. (1985) 'The Elasticity of Substitution Between Imported and Domestically Produced Goods in Germany', *Weltwirtschaftliches Archiv,* 121, pp. 74-96.

Langhammer, R. J. (1981) 'Nationaler Protektionismus im Rahmen der EG-Handelspolitik, dargestellt am Beispiel der Industriegüterimporte aus ASEAN-Ländern', *Die Weltwirtschaft*, 1 pp. 74-93.

Langhammer, R. J. (1989) 'North-South Trade in Services. Some Empirical Evidence'. In H. Giersch, ed., *Services in World Economic Growth. Symposium 1988* (Tübingen: Mohr), pp. 248-71.

Langhammer, R. J., (1990) *Patterns of Trade in Services Between ASEAN Countries and EC Member States. Case Studies for West Germany, France and Netherlands* (Singapore: Institute of Southeast Asian Studies).

Langhammer, R. J. and Sapir, A. (1987) *Economic Impact of Generalised Tariff Preferences*, Thames Essays 49, (London: Gower).

Lewis, W. A. (1980) 'The Slowing Down of the Engine of Growth', *American Economic Review*, 70, pp. 555-64.

Mathew, S. (1989) 'Air Transport in Europe After 1992: Implications and Responses'. Paper presented at the Colloquium on 'ASEAN and Europe 1992. Implications and Response', 10-11 July, Institute of Strategic and International Studies, Kuala Lumpur.

Matthews, A. and McAleese, D. (1990) 'LDC Primary Exports to the EC: Prospects Post 1992', *Journal of Common Market Studies*, Vol. XXIX, No. 2.

Mody, A. and Wheeler, D. (1987) 'Towards a Vanishing Middle: Competition in the World Garment Industry', *World Development,* 15, 10/11, October/November, pp. 1269-84.

Mutti, J. (1977-8) 'The Specification of Demand Equations for Imports and Domestic Substitutes', *Southern Economic Journal,* 44, pp. 68-73.

Neundörfer, K. (1987) 'Das vierte Welttextilabkommen', *Schriften zur Textilpolitik,* 4, (Frankfurt: Textil Service und Verlag GmbH).

Nicolaides, P. (1990) 'Responding to European Integration: Developing Countries and Services', *Journal of Common Market Studies*, Vol. XXIX, No. 2.

OECD (1986) 'The OECD Compatible Trade and Production Data Base 1970-1983', Working Paper, 31, (Paris: OECD) March.

OECD (1987) *The Costs of Restricting Imports. The Automobile Industry* (Paris: OECD).

Patterson, G. (1983) 'The European Community as a Threat to the System'. In W. L. Cline, ed., *Trade Policy in the 1980s* (Washington, D.C.: Institute for International Economics) pp. 223-42.

Pelkmans, J. (1986) *Completing the Internal Market for Industrial Products* (Luxemburg: OOPEC).

Republique Française, Conseil Economique et Social (1982) 'Le Devenir des Industries du Textile et de l'Habillement', *Journal Officiel de la République Française, Avis et Rapports du Consiel Economique et Social*, 5, 25 February.

Reidel, J. (1984) 'Trade as the Engine of Growth in Developing Countries, Revisited', *Economic Journal,* pp. 56-73.

Sawyer, W. C. and Sprinkle, R. L. (1989) 'Alternative Empirical Estimates of Trade Creation and Trade Diversion: A Comparison of the Baldwin-Murray and Verdoorn Models', *Weltwirtschaftliches Archiv,* 125, 1, pp. 61-73.

Siebert, H. (1990) 'The Harmonisation Issue in Europe: Prior Agreement or a Competitive Process?' In H. Siebert, ed., *The Completion of the Internal Market. Symposium 1989* (Tübingen: Mohr), pp. 53-75.

Spinanger, D. (1988) 'Die EG und Drittländer nach 1992 — Einige Implikationen des angekündigten Wegfalls des Artikels 115'. Paper prepared for the German-French Conference of the Friedrich-Ebert-Stiftung on 'Europäeische Außenhandels-politik in Zeichen des vollendeten Binnenmarktes, Paris, 12-13 December.

UN (1963) A *Study of Industrial Growth,* ST/ECA/74 (New York: UN).

Winters, L. A. (1988) 'Completing the European Internal Market. Somes Notes on Trade Policy', *European Economic Review,* 32. pp. 1477-99.

Wolf, M. (1987) 'An Unholy Alliance: the European Community and Developing Countries in the International Trading System'. *Aussenwirtschaft.* 42, 1, pp. 41-64.

World Development Report (1988) (World Bank (IBED): Washington D.C.).

Notes

The author appreciates helpful comments provided by participants, especially Ad Koekkoek, of the Expert Meeting on 'Europe 1992 and the Developing Countries'.

1　Compared to the equation form $\ln M = a_0 + a_1 \ln Y + a_2 \ln P_m + a_3 \ln P_d + a_4 \ln P$, this equation assumes that consumers do not have money illusions. That means that $a_2 + a_3 + a_4 = 0$. There is an additional advantage of the equation form applied in the sense that problems of multicollinearity are reduced. For a discussion see Mutti (1977-8) and Lächler (1985).

2　This estimate has been criticized as unduly optimistic as it is based on very high income elasticities of EC import demand towards developing countries (Table 1). It was argued that the base effect of low manufactured exports of the seventies biased the results upwards. However, it should be borne in mind that there are a number of pros and cons (including market access, accelerated structural change in the Community towards services and exchange rate effects) as to whether this elasticity can be expected to be relevant for the next decade too. The most relevant determinant is the sample of countries. Should the NICs and near-NICs be excluded from the sample, there is little hope in assuming that high income elasticities could be maintained. Contrary to the more pessimistic assessments, Ad Koekkoek argues that the estimate of trade diversion should be lower for developing countries because there were hardly any barriers between Member States in the traditional manufacturing sectors. However, national quotas are concentrated just in the traditional manufacturing sectors (see section 5) in which developing countries have strong export interests.

3　Though being not yet a strongly integrated region, the US and Canada had to be taken as a joint yardstick because of data constraints. Yet, the distorting effect is small since Canada as a minor trading partner does not significantly influence the level of IMPRs of the US and Canada together.

4　The test is right-tail. Thus, it is assumed that IMPRs are higher in a customs union like the EC than in an internal market like the US.

5　One may argue that the protective effects of national quotas are not significant as there are always substitutes from EC-internal production (Hamilton, 1988). The case of French and Italian protection in cars favouring German producers comes to mind. However, in the case of low-price clothing, for instance, such substitutes may have been more imperfect.

Part V

The Human Dimension of External Relations

16. Regulation of Immigration in 1993: Pieces of the European Community Jig-Saw Puzzle

Giuseppe Callovi

Migration and immigration issues illustrate better than most other subjects the challenge the European Community is facing, both in terms of doctrine and in practice. This article takes stock of past EC policy on migration, and covers some basic elements which are shaping a future common policy, carried out either through intergovernmental cooperation or community legislation or both. The regulation of immigration in 1993 is still at a crossroads with multiple possible outcomes. However, the most recent features and the vital impetus set up by the Intergovernmental Conference on Political Union provides some new institutional capacity for the EC to act in a strengthened juridical and political framework.

In the course of recent years, the institutions of the European Community, public opinion, governments and national parliaments have become increasingly aware of immigration issues and of the role played by migrants in the labor market and in society as a whole.

Significant changes have taken place both within the Community, where new countries of immigration have emerged, and outside, where new pressure points have produced prospective emigrants.

With 1993 in sight, the removal of restrictions on freedom of movement of persons enshrined in the Paris Charter, occasional misuse of the right of asylum, and the increasingly interdependent economies of the Community have caused immigration to move up the agenda.

Within the European Community, we are witnessing the shaping of a new political decision-making landscape which involves in some cases the sharing of sovereignty among member states. The redistribution of power among institutions, and between nation-states and the Community, is part of a subtle game where interests and aims do not always converge.

The work around the Intergovernmental Conference on Political Union which was completed in December 1991 and the slow implementation of the Single European Act on questions dealing with "persons," one of the four fundamental freedoms, provide clear evidence of the discrepancies and difficulties in adjusting and possibly increasing institutional powers and, above all, establishing a balance among rival objectives.

Giuseppe Callovi: 'Regulation of Immigration in 1993: Pieces of the European Community Jig-Saw Puzzle' in *INTERNATIONAL MIGRATION REVIEW* (1993), Vol. 26. No.2. pp. 353-372. Reprinted by permission of International Migration Review published by The Center for Migration Studies of New York, Inc.

The movement of persons and immigration illustrates better than most other subjects the challenge we are facing, both in terms of doctrine (share of national power) and in practice. We are taking part today in an intensive game being played at all levels, and the ongoing process moves very rapidly, seeking all possible paths. An external observer might have the impression he is walking on quicksand. But it is like producing a tapestry: the different speed in decision-making according to the subject and the different forums dealing with it hide the final design that should appear at the end. For instance, controls at a common external border affect not only travelers, immigrants, refugees and asylum seekers, but also drugs, firearms, works of art, smuggling, trade, public safety and public order. Some of the related obligations are already imposed under a Community law, particularly in the field of customs and duties; this has to do not only with repressive measures, but also with positive action in the field, and both are not always provided at one go.

The European Community must be able to develop both its internal solidarity, in particular with regard to its millions of unemployed and all resident workers whatever their nationality, and its capacity not to appear to the rest of the world to be turning in on itself.

This contribution will try, on one hand, to take stock of the past Community policy on migration and on the other hand to provide the basic elements which are shaping a future potentially common (or partly common) policy, carried out either through intergovernmental cooperation or community legislation or both.

The Community faces a challenge arising from necessity if not from political will.

The Treaty of Rome to the Single European Act (1957-1985/87)

Before the creation of the EEC under the Treaty of Rome, the principles of national sovereignty and of the priority for nationals to enter the domestic labor market were always stringently applied to foreign labor in Western Europe, apart from a few exceptions such as the easing of the rules for the issue of work permits, embodied in a Council Decision of 1953, amended in 1956, for member states of the Organization for Economic Cooperation and Development (OECD). Further exception at the regional level were the Nordic Employment Market in 1954 and the special relationship between Ireland and the United Kingdom.

It was basically the 1957 Treaty of Rome that was to give recognition of the subjective right of nationals of the six signatory states to have access to employment or self-employment throughout the territory covered by the Treaty.

The generalization of the geographical mobility of workers arose chiefly from the economic and political rationale of the movement: a common economic market could not do without the free movement of workers, at least as a support measure, when it wanted to introduce the free circulation of three other economic factors — goods, services and capital.

The economic link is evident considering that free movement was not guaranteed for persons as citizens, but for persons who move for an economic purpose, whether for self-employment or dependent employment, or as recipients or providers of services.

Rights for family members of the worker, for instance, appear only in secondary law (mainly Regulation No. 1612 of 1968 and Directive 68/360). It must be remembered, nevertheless, that Article 3(c) of the Treaty of Rome provided for the free movement of persons (without any nationality distinction or other conditions) but did not set out any obligation for implementing it, whereas it did make provisions for implementations in regard to workers (Arts. 48 to 51) and freedom of establishment (Arts. 52 to 58).

The gradual implementation of free movement of EEC workers kept pace with recruitment of labor from third countries. At the Community level, before 1974, there was practically no discussion on the migratory flow of nationals of third countries, regarded as the exclusive preserve of national sovereignty.

Under the pressure of events (accession of three new member states — Denmark, Ireland and the United Kingdom — effect on employment of price rises for several raw materials and recession, national decisions to stop recruiting labor from third countries), for the first time the question of migrant labor was identified by the Ministers in 1974 as a key factor of social policy, followed by the adoption in December of that year of an "Action Program in favor of migrant workers and their families."

In its Resolution of February 9, 1976, the Council of Ministers advocated a Community approach to the nationals of third countries, particularly through consultation among member states on migration policies. In fact, this consultation took the form of a communication by the Commission to the Council in March 1979 seeking more clearly defined terms of reference: in turn the Council merely confirmed its attachment to "appropriate" consultation, devoid however of any binding legal character.

At the same time, the "putting on ice" of a number of bilateral agreements that dealt with the material conditions for the selection and recruitment of workers and for their travel for purposes of taking up employment gave way to a new type of agreement between the European Community and third countries or groups of countries, containing provisions dealing with the treatment of migrants once admitted under national legislation. Within the bounds of the exercise of its extended powers, enabling it to make agreements with third countries, the Community used for the first time its capacity to bring the rights of the workers from a third country within the legal framework of the Community, based on Article 238 of the Treaty of Rome.

Agreements concluded between the Community and five third countries were not devised for recruitment of labor; nevertheless they contain non-discrimination clauses in regard to social security and to working conditions and pay (EEC/Turkey Association Agreement — Decision 1/80 of the association Council of 9/19/1980; Cooperation Agreements between EEC and Algeria, Morocco and Tunisia — entered into force in 1978; and between EEC and Yugoslavia — entered into force in 1983 and suspended November 1, 1991).

In accordance with a recent judgment by the Court of Justice in the Kziber Case Law, January 31, 1991), all social security benefits may henceforth be claimed by workers who are nationals of the above countries and members of their families on the same terms as Community nationals.

It is important to note that the European Court of Justice has drawn the curtains wide apart on the question of competences; to the Demirel, Sevince and Kziber cases should be added the Court arguments on a Commission's Decision case of July 9, 1987.

With the aim of updating its policy in the migration sphere, the Commission adopted and submitted to the Council a communication, on March 1, 1985, called "Guidelines for a Community Policy on Migration." For the first time, the term "Community" was found alongside "migration policy."

At the same time the Commission took a "Decision" based on Article 118 of the Treaty of Rome on July 8, 1985, introducing a procedure for "prior communication and consultation on migration policies in relation to non-member countries"

Following appeals to the European Court of Justice by Germany, France, the Netherlands, Denmark and the United Kingdom, the Court annulled the Commission's decision in a ruling handed down on July 9, 1987. A new decision was adopted by the Commission on June 8, 1988, taking account of the Court's objections.

Paradoxically, however, that annulment provided the opportunity for a major step forward toward involving the Community in responsibility for the situation of non-Community workers, since the Court gave the fullest recognition to the main goals assigned to the consultation procedure, namely: to facilitate the adoption of a common position by the member states; to achieve progress toward harmonization of national legislation on foreigners; to promote the inclusion of common provisions in bilateral agreements; and to improve the protection of Community nationals working and living in nonmember countries.

The Court argued that the employment situation and, in more general terms, living and working conditions in the Community are likely to be affected by the member states' policies with regard to labor from third countries, and therefore Article 118 allowed the Commission to adopt a binding decision in order to organize a consultation procedure.

In the mid-1980s, it seemed safe to sustain that national decisions regarding immigration from third countries had a bearing on the Community, that they had general implications for employment policy within the Community and, finally, that a joint response to a problem of common interest appeared to be feasible, including the Community's legal capacity to explore ways for a Community policy on migration. These developments coincided with an overall new spirit inspiring the construction of the European Community.

In spite of the idea of creating a single European economy by establishing a common market as defined by the Treaty of Rome in 1957, many of the original barriers to the internal market survived for 30 years. Many fundamental issues were left untackled.

In the early 1980s, the mood began to change, and the cost of non-Europe was felt to be a burden in both qualitative and quantitative terms. The European Parliament and "federalist" movements put pressure on member states and on the Commission and the Council to accelerate the implementation of the four fundamental freedoms and to improve the mechanism for institutional decisions.

The Single European Act and the completion of the internal market

In 1985, the heads of state or government of all the member states asked the Commission to put forward concrete proposals for the completion of the internal market. The Commission published, in June of the same year, a White Paper identifying all the existing physical, technical and fiscal barriers and setting out proposals as well as the necessary timetable to reach all the objectives by the end of 1992.

For the removal of physical barriers, the White Paper suggested a number of key areas upon which a common policy had to be adopted: the easing of controls and formalities at intra-Community frontiers as a first step toward the eventual elimination of frontier controls on people; the approximation of firearms legislation; the approximation of drugs legislation; the coordination of rules on the granting of asylum and refugee status; the coordination of visa policies; the coordination of rules on extradition; and the coordination of rules on the status of third-country nationals.

Following the Intergovernmental Conference held in the autumn of 1985, the heads of state or government reached agreement on institutional reform of the European Community at their meeting in Luxembourg in December 1985. This agreement is incorporated in the Single European Act (the first major amendment to the Treaty of Rome since its adoption in 1957) which entered into force on July 1, 1987.

The Single European Act states in its Article 8a that "the internal market comprises an area without internal frontiers in which the free movement of goods, persons, services and capital is ensured in accordance with the provisions of this Treaty." Furthermore, a policy declaration by the governments of the member states affirms that "in order to promote the free movement of persons, the Member States shall cooperate, without prejudice to the powers of the Community, in particular as regards the entry, movement and residence of nationals of third countries."

A link can be seen here between the abolition of frontiers within the Community and the necessity of strengthening controls at the external borders. However, cooperation should not be conceived of solely in its repressive meaning, but also in its dynamic requirement to have Community regulations introduced that activate immigration policy.

Nevertheless, for the Single European Act, the question of migration concentrates on the problems linked to the removal of physical controls. This is why another general declaration is not to be interpreted as a contradiction: "Nothing in these provisions shall affect the right of Member States to take such measures as they consider necessary for the purpose of controlling immigration from third countries."

A possible Community migration policy and the political opportunity is therefore left to the powers that the original Treaty of Rome gives the Community (*see* for instance, Articles 3c, 100, 117, 118, 235, 238 and the existing jurisprudence of the European Court of Justice). In practice, it seems technically possible and feasible *prima facie* to have a common policy on border controls between member states without having a common policy on migration (the Schengen Agreement is a good example), regardless of the legal aspects, intergovernmental or community approaches.

If we single out the question of "migration" and asylum seekers, we will recognize immediately that its scope is wider than that covered by the removal of internal frontier controls on people. Common external border controls can be agreed upon without solving the questions of national immigration policies (from restrictive to liberal), of the historical ties of each member state to certain third countries, of economic pull, of policy on family reunion and refugees, or bilateral agreements, of Community power to include third-country nationals among the people referred to in the Single European Act, and more generally of common Community policy on migration.

Common controls on external borders will, of course, have an indirect impact on immigration, but control machinery is not the answer to the need for an active policy on migration.

The obstacles result mainly from the politically and legally disputed Community power to operate such a policy. While the debate remained at this level, no doctrine has been developed on a gradual common policy on immigration nor on the way domestic immigration policies could fit into a coherent Community strategy. Each country has been trying to solve its own problems.

Implementation of the White Paper and of the Single European Act

Two initiatives were taken in 1985 and 1986, providing new vectors for thought and action.

First, in June 1985, Germany, France and the Benelux countries signed an agreement at Schengen on the removal of controls at their common frontiers by January 1, 1990. The Commission has regarded their initiative as a kind of testbed that can point the way to technical solutions for speeding up the removal of controls throughout the Community.

Secondly, under the UK presidency, in October 1986 an ad hoc Immigration Group was created within the Council's secretariat, setting the objective of "easing and ultimately abolishing the internal frontier controls," giving a significant start to "Intergovernmental" action.

A communication of the Commission of December 7, 1988 illustrates this new political situation. In order to organize work effectively for the achievement of an area without frontiers, two preliminary questions need answering. The first concerns the extent to which national policies and legislations need to be harmonized. Leaving aside the long-term desirability of the harmonization of member states legislation in this area, the immediate priority should be to determine what actions are indispensable in order to achieve the abolition of border controls at internal frontiers by 1992. For example, while it could be a long-term objective to reach a common policy on the rules governing the status and the right of residence of third-country nationals within the Community, the Commission believes that the abolition of frontiers for all persons can and should be achieved on the basis of a more limited program, which could include in particular a common visa policy, a common policy on refugees, and the strengthening of controls at the Community's external borders.

The second question concerns which actions should be taken at the Community level and which should be left to intergovernmental cooperation. The Commission is fully aware of the delicate nature of an exercise of this kind, and it considers that attention should be focused on practical effectiveness rather than on matters of legal doctrine. Therefore, without prejudging its interpretation of the Treaty as modified by the Single European Act, the Commission proposes that Community legislation in this field be applied only to those cases where the legal security and uniformity provided by Community law constitutes the best instrument to achieve the desired goal. This would mean, therefore, that large scope would be left, at this stage, to cooperation among member states.

The Commission would not, however, wish to rule out the possibility of coming forward with additional proposals, particularly if it becomes clear that intergovernmental cooperation is not the most efficient or cost-effective method, or if a consensus were to emerge among member states that further harmonization and coordination would be desirable.

The consequence of this situation has been the development of new or existing bodies dealing with different areas of concern — European political cooperation group, Ad hoc Immigration Group, TREVI Group, Mutual Assistance Group. The reason is simple: states rely on national border controls for their own security; if they loosen this instrument, they have to compensate through another mechanism that tightens up controls at the Community's external borders, and policy areas to be covered are quite wide.

The Rhodes European Council of December 2-3, 1988 felt that coordination was necessary among the various groups in order to avoid a dilution of the objective expressed by Article 8A of the Single European Act. Thus, the Rhodes Group of Coordinators came to life. Its role was mainly to ensure coherence in the material positions adopted by the representatives in the many different forums and to speed up work to be done by the end of 1992.

A document, called "Palma de Majorca" and addressed to the European Council of Madrid in June 1989 drew up a list of problems that need to be solved to achieve the target of free movement of people. A list of measures required divided into two categories (short-term and essential and long-term and desirable) as well the competent forums to deal with the questions. The titles may be sufficiently illustrative: actions at external borders, actions on the Community territory, action against drug trafficking, action against terrorism and international crime, visa policies, granting of asylum, rules on extradition, judicial cooperation.

Common policy on migration or the status of third-country nationals are considered as long-term and desirable items: the political obstacles would have hindered any quick advancement. The "early harvest" way seemed to draw a general consensus.

At the European Council that took place in Strasbourg December 8-9, 1989, the heads of state or government reiterated: "the progressive abolition of border formalities shall not affect the right of Member States to take such measures as they consider necessary for the purpose of controlling immigration from third countries."

Moreover, the European Council asked that an inventory be prepared of national positions on immigration so that a discussion on this issue within the Council (General Affairs) could be prepared. In the light of that debate, the European Council called upon the relevant bodies to conclude as soon as possible, and no later than the end of 1990, the conventions which were under examination on the right of asylum, the crossing of the Community's external frontiers, and visas.

At the same date, on the question of the "social dimension" of the Single Market, the heads of state and of government of eleven member states (the United Kingdom did not agree) adopted "the Community Charter of the fundamental social rights of workers."

It is interesting to note a recital contained in the preamble of the Charter: "Whereas it is for Member States to guarantee that workers from non-member countries and members of their families who are legally resident in a Member State of the European Community are able to enjoy, as regards their living and working conditions, treatment comparable to that enjoyed by workers who are nationals of the Member State concerned."

One can notice the insistence on avoiding the Community's powers and responsibilities and the will to embody any common decision in a series of intergovernmental agreements rather than in Community legally-binding instruments.

Border controls on people and migration is a key area where the EEC governments find it particularly hard to reconcile national sovereignty and security requirements with the commitment of Article 8a introduced by the Single European Act.

Starting off with discussions on the doctrine would have been suicidal. On the other hand, an advanced level of cooperation between states is essential, as mutual confidence is decisive for opening the internal borders. Thus, from a tactical standpoint, it appeared more appropriate to recall the objectives and commitments subscribed by the member states in signing the Single European Act and to let intergovernmental cooperation find its own solutions.

But let's follow again the calendar of developments. After the European Council of Strasbourg in December 1989, on December 15 the Schengen Group failed to agree the opening of the internal borders between the five countries on January 1, 1990.

On the same date, the Ministers of the twelve member states of the European Community made a declaration in Paris, stating *inter alia*:

> We are convinced that the work we have accomplished in the fields of immigration, the crossing of borders, visa policy and the determination of the Member State responsible for examining an application for asylum is an important step towards the construction of a People's Europe and the completion of the internal market. We solemnly declare that our objectives shall be achieved in accordance with the international commitments regarding asylum and the humanitarian traditions of our States. We affirm that our States have the right and duty to combat illegal immigration in their respective territories and in the territory of the Twelve as a whole. At the same time we undertake to uphold the rights and safeguards of foreigners whose presence there is valid. We believe that the overall concern about immigration necessitates appropriate policies in this area.

The task of establishing an inventory of national positions on immigration as a follow-up of the European Council of Strasbourg has been split into two main tasks: entry and movement of third-country citizens to be examined by the Immigration and Coordinators groups, and integration matters to be scrutinized by a Commission's appointed group of experts. (This report, dated September 28, 1990, came after a previous report drawn up at the request of the European Council in Hannover on June 27-28, 1988, and dated June 22, 1989).

From this exercise it emerges that there is no alternative policy but integration, and that a common control of migration flows is itself a prerequisite for integration (a debate on the outcome of the mandate of the European Council in Strasbourg took place during a general Affairs Council on December 4, 1990).

At the European Council of Dublin in June 1990, a first set of measures regarded as essential was adopted in an intergovernmental context: that is, the Dublin Convention of June 15, 1990, relating to the determination of the country responsible for examining an application for asylum (the examination procedures or, indeed, the situation of the applicant while his case is being handled are not affected by the Convention).

On June 19 of the same year, the Schengen Group (enlarged to Italy and subsequently to Spain and Portugal) signed its Application Convention, which embodies all the measures required (sufficient measures, however) to abolish checks on individuals at the internal borders.

The practical results achieved by the Schengen Group show that, once agreement is reached on the objectives, the goal of abolishing border checks on individuals is politically feasible and the technical problems which have to be solved for that purpose in order to maintain the current level of internal security are not insurmountable.

Even if some topics might be covered by both the Schengen Group Convention and the future instruments of the Twelve, this should not give rise to conflict. The instruments of the Twelve will legally "prevail" over the provisions of the Schengen Convention in the event of discrepancies.

Under the Italian presidency in the last semester of 1990, the opening on December 15, in Rome of two Intergovernmental Conferences, one on Economic and Monetary Union and one on Political Union, was a major event. The Commission adopted its opinion on the proposal for amendments of the Treaty on October 21, 1990. It argues strongly that revision of the Treaty is to integrate new objectives into a single Community; common foreign policy, free movement of persons and the notion of European citizenship as a supplement to national are recalled alongside the principle of subsidiarity, the broadening of the Community's powers, a better decision-making process and strengthening democractic legitimacy of the institutions. The outcome of these conferences should be ratified by the member states by the end of 1993.

The Rome European Council of December 14-15, 1990 called also for further deliberation in three areas — aid to countries of emigration, conditions for entry into the Community, and aid for the social integration of immigrants — and stressed the need of a harmonized policy on the right of asylum.

On the basis of the principle of subsidiarity, the Commission shares the view that some topics are identifiable on which consensus might be reached for a common approach, notably harmonized information on migration flows, the conditions governing the movements of legal immigrants, assistance for devlopment and economic cooperation with countries of emigration, and the integration of legally established immigrants, without prejudging the institutional aspects. A communication of the Commission to the Council and the European Parliament had to provide the necessary input for the deliberations, but it could not be adopted in the first semester of 1991.

The European Council in Luxembourg on June 28-29, 1991 "called *inter alia* for rapid agreement on the Convention between the Member States on the crossing of their external borders" (the Convention could not be signed owing to a problem still outstanding with regard to Gibraltar), and "agreed on the objectives underlying the German government's proposals on asylum, immigration and aliens and on the fight against international drug trafficking and organized crime." Ministers with responsibility for immigration had to submit proposals before the European Council in Maastricht in December.

It was thought, therefore, that in the context of the European Council of Maastricht, Treaty commitments to "formal and actual harmonization" could take place regarding policies on asylum, immigration and aliens, and activities currently carried on in an intergovernmental framework could be brought into the sphere of the Union. The Commission prepared, as a contribution, two communications, one dated October 11, 1991 on the right of asylum and another dated October 23, 1991 on immigration.

To complete the series of events important for forecasting what might be the regulation of migration after 1993, we may also note two new global accords: the political agreement reached in Luxembourg on October 22, 1991 with the seven EFTA countries (Austria and Sweden have already applied for full EC membership) creating a European Economic Area (EEA) where the four fundamental freedoms are to be in force by 1993 (under some conditions and temporary exceptions) after ratification of all nineteen countries, members of EEA; and the Association Agreements with Poland, Hungary and Czechoslovakia signed in mid-December 1991.

Migration policy in 1993: achievements of the Single European Act

The canvas sketched above is a necessary premise for understanding and predicting migration patterns in the European Community after 1992 at the institutional level, within the framework of the implementation of the Single European Act.

The most recent features and the vital impetus originated by the Intergovernmental Conference on Political Union providing new institutional capacity of the Community to act in a strengthened juridical framework will be briefly discussed at the end of this article. Although the outlines of the emerging context of political decision-making are still blurred, it may nonetheless be sustained that the Community will not be a self-contained and inward-looking fortress, if only because of its commitments to respect basic human rights (family reunion and humanitarian factors will be valid reasons for immigration, but so probably will employment factors, albeit via different channels from those of the past) and for foreign and trade policies.

For instance, if closer agreement between the member states in applying policies on access will mean that operations designed to reduce illegal immigration to the minimum will be increasingly coordinated, as a counterbalance there might be more openings for the right to seek employment throughout the Community territory for third-country nationals allowed permanent residence in a member state. The Community cannot just drop some of the citizens which it has allowed in, for a tense climate would be the ideal breeding ground for racism and xenophobia.

For the time being, we cannot say for sure what the migration issue will be on January 1, 1993, as most of the relevant and decisive elements are still under scrutiny, such as the removal of the Community's internal frontiers and the attached conditions.

However, the foregoing cannot be defined yet as a system of joint and active management of immigration. To achieve this, a fairly high political price would have to be paid because the matters of sovereignty and national identity still form the core of the discussion. The European Parliament gives strong support in the debate for a decisive step toward a unified and cohesive external and security policy centered on the Community institutions.

Movement of people, asylum seekers, and issues of immigration and border controls are areas where nationalism tends to survive, not ultimately for technical reasons, but for a "political culture" and the fear of introducing surreptitiously the concept of federation or confederation.

This explains the above mentioned efforts to find ways and means to create an "area without internal frontiers," without delivering supplementary power to the Community — the aim being to reconcile national sovereignty and requirements for security with a "reasonable" degree of free movement of people within the EEC territory that constitutes a major element of a "citizen's Europe."

The Community is not a state, though some sovereign powers have been conferred on the Community institutions in limited and specified areas. On the legal significance of Article 8a introduced by the Single European Act to the EEC Treaty and its associated declarations, for the time being there are divergences.

One could question the extent to which the member states are committed to remove border controls, the legal cover for third-party nationals, and the measures to be taken, either as part of the institutions' own legislative powers, or only as a mutual understanding based on a convention, or both. What if the creation of a single market (according to the European Court of Justice it means: "reproducing as closely as possible the conditions of a domestic market") introduces an obligation to abolish internal borders? Does Article 8a have direct effect? If not, is there an obligation to adopt the necessary measures so that the controls are no longer justified? If such measures are not taken (national or intergovernmental), is there an obligation to adopt Community legislation and therefore the necessity for the Commission to make a proposal?

The Commission has not formally expressed its view on Article 8a.[1] In practice, the ongoing activity at the intergovernmental level insures that the necessary conditions to abolish internal borders are fulfilled. It is to be expected thereafter that the decision for free EC borders will follow soon.

But even freedom of movement for people across internal borders will not by itself directly affect national policies on immigration. The abolition of internal borders may affect, nevertheless, some aspects of migration. What seems almost certain might be summarized as follows:

- third-country nationals who have entered the Community legally will be included in the right to cross internal borders (Convention);

- however, they will not acquire the right to seek a residence permit or to look for employment (if they have such rights in a member state, this territorial limitation will subsist; if they do not enjoy such rights in any country, their right to stay in the Community is limited in all countries to the visa period);

- the target is the creation of a common visa giving access to the whole Community;

- asylum seekers will have a guarantee that their request will be examined, and clear rules state which member state is responsible for processing an asylum request, as laid down by the Dublin Convention signed on June 15, 1990 (an act of international public law); for those already legally resident in the territory of the Community, the Ministers concerned with immigration declared on December 15, 1989, "we undertake to uphold the rights and safeguards of foreigners whose presence is valid"; but according to the different national laws, except for those under an EC agreement;

- the question of illegal immigration and of asylum seekers looking for a better economic life rather than seeking to escape from political, racial or religious persecution is not directly linked to frontier controls. This item is complex and for the purpose of the abolition of internal borders it is only dealt with under the form of nonadmission to the territory or of extradition outside the Community frontiers, or of re-admission by the first responsible state.

Bearing in mind these clarifications, we can see that under the heading of "area without frontiers" a common immigration policy and an approximation of national legislation on foreigners are not seen as part of the necessary political decisions to be taken with the approach of the 1993 deadline, but they are nonetheless seriously considered for future developments.

The Single European Act had been driven by an inner dynamic that found its actual peak in the Treaty on Political Union.

The prospects for a Community policy on migration

European countries are facing two challenges. On the one hand there is the situation of communities constituted in the last 40 years of ill-integrated immigrants and the more recent inflows in the southern European countries, and on the other hand there is possible future inflows due to economic, demographic and political differentials that separate the EEC members from a great many other states in the world.

To the first challenge concerning the integration of third-country migrants residing lawfully in the member states, the Community has responded by some initiatives. But here again Community initiatives may be jeopardized by the question of Community power versus national sovereignty. For example, should not the social dimension of the internal market without frontiers and a common labor market imply the right for every citizen living legitimately in the Community territory to seek employment anywhere in the Community, particularly if they are unemployed and vacancies exist in another member state? The obstacles are not technical (for refugees, for instance, Regulation 1408 is already in application) but exclusively political. Will not firms' competitiveness in a free economic and trade area be threatened if third-country labor does not enjoy, in all member states, equality of treatment with national labor? The establishment of a Community-wide market in services and, particularly, common rules providing for open and fair conditions of competition to cover the major part of public procurement will certainly increase the number of contracts with non-nationally based firms employing third-country nationals.

As regards the second challenge, concerning immigration, the Community has not yet developed a consolidated response; as a machinery of control is not the only answer to the need for an active policy on migration.

Most member states (some albeit reluctantly) are now conscious of the need for a real policy on the immigration issue at the level of the Twelve for five main reasons: 1) the fulfillment of their aim to remove internal borders checks, 2) the direct and indirect effects on the common labor market of domestic strategy on migration, 3) the challenge posed by the increasing influx of asylum seekers, 4) the implications of Community policy on foreign and trade relations particularly with developing countries, and 5) the issue of policies of adjustment and integration versus the marginalizing factors that become inexorably a subject of anxiety to the Twelve. Nevertheless, the widely acknowledged need for a Community strategy does not answer the question of how to build a flexible Community policy on migration that respects domestic interests and national sovereignty.

The adoption by Community insitutions of legal acts that will form the supporting pillars of a common strategy, setting up the margins of maneuver for member states, would be in accordance with the principle of "subsidiarity" whereby the Community acts when the set of objectives can be reached more effectively at its level than at that of the single member states. Such safeguards would not prevent the taking into account of particular domestic situations. Community law (for instance, Art. 13/3 and 42/3 of Reg. 1612/68) does not prejudge the obligations of member states arising from special relationships or from agreements based on institutional links already existing between them and non-European territories.

An active strategy at the Community level on migratory flows, at a steady but slow pace, seems to be better able to control the volume of migration and to integrate non-Community nationals within the social and economic fabric. However this would mean first, the strengthening of links within the Community, freely and loyally acknowledged; second, the making of a step forward toward a "common foreign policy"; and third, the acceptance of the consequences of an integrated labor market which cannot remain dependent on twelve different policies in regard to immigration.

The Commission Communication to the Council and to the European Parliament on immigration of October 23, 1991 (SEC/91/1855 final) suggests analyses and proposals for discussion on the "basis of dialogue through the competent channels (general Affairs Council and Conference of Immigration Ministers)," determining "the future institutional framework within which the immigration question will be pursued."

Taking action on migration pressure, controlling flows (including a new use of the right of asylum), and strengthening integration policies are the main pillars around which the Commission develops considerations and proposes initiatives. *Inter alia,* it underlines that migration has to be an integral issue of Community external policy, in particular in relation to Mediterranean policies, to ACP countries (Lomé IV agreement), and to Central and Eastern Europe.

Politically the Community is still crippled by a slow decision-making machinery; the alternative would mean trimming powers of national governments. Nation-states as descendants of the age of enlightenment and of the nineteenth century philosophers live a painful historical momentum. In a recent article,[2] Jacques Delors, President of the Commission, wrote, "The Community is the first institution of the post-national era . . . In this post-national era we are interdependent, so 'nations' have to find more integrated forms of cooperation; but it does not imply that they will disappear."

"Post-national era" is a concept to be defined more closely, as political unity would no longer correspond to cultural unity. Even the concept of "European citizenship" has a "functional" character that could easily, for the purpose of obligations and rights, include people residing permanently on the territory of the Community without being nationals of one of the member states. This movement toward a "post-national identity" will not be concluded immediately and at the level of twelve countries. A new rendezvous, both "political and institutional," has to be thought out to prepare a structure of 24 or 30 countries (J. Delors). The partial splitting of nation and state needs another definition of sovereignty; this will also be relevant to the question of priorities for admission to the Community, of movement of people, of treatment of residents who are nationals of a third country, of foreign policy. Professor A. Zolberg recalls the need for clarification of principles guiding admission policies and for exploring the implications of norms and ethics in this field;[3] this is a valid viewpoint. However, for the Community the debate is more complicated than for one single nation-state: national strategies, interests, history and needs do not necessarily coincide.

This is why regulation of immigration in 1993 and onward is still at a crossroads, with multiple exits and possibly variable speeds.

The outcome of the Maastricht Summit

The Maastricht European Council of December 9-10, 1991 reached agreement on a Treaty on European Union that will enter into force on January 1, 1993, provided that all the instruments of ratification have been deposited. It agreed also on the program of work laid down a week earlier by the Ministers for immigration and invited the Ministers to implement it according to set priorities.

Indeed, the Ministers for Immigration, on December 2-3, 1991, in the Hague, had endorsed the Commission's conclusions that "only a joint approach could meet challenges arising from immigration and asylum." In their report, they expressed the need to harmonize the migration and asylum policies of Member States with regard to third-country nationals. A work program has been established, listed in order of priority, to be carried out if possible before the entry into force of the Treaty on European Union. On migration policy, five main Titles have been set out: 1) harmonization of admission policies: 2) common approach to the question of illegal immigration, 3) policy on the migration of labor, 4) situation of third-country nationals, and 5) migration policy in the broad meaning of the term. On asylum policy the work program includes: 1) application and implementation of the Dublin Convention, 2) harmonization of substantive asylum law, 3) harmonization of expulsion policy, 4) setting up a clearing house, 5) legal examination, and 6) conditions for receiving applicants for asylum.

Nevertheless, the Ministers for immigration did not prejudge the institutional framework, as this was to be examined at the Intergovernmental Conference on Political Union. And indeed, Heads of State and Government sowed the seeds of significant institutional changes, although a quick reading of the Treaty seems like a journey through a labyrinth that needs Arianne's thread to find the right way out to the light.

The text that emerged from Maastricht is the result of a compromise. Three major building blocks can be identified. The first block concerns the award of clear legal competence to the Community in the area of "visas" (to determine those countries whose nationals need visas, which will have a uniform format), as laid down by Article 100c. But paragraph 7 of Article 100c provides for intergovernmental conventions to remain in force (such as, if ratified, the one on external borders as a result of the Single European Act) until their content is replaced by Community instruments. Paragraph 6 deserves specific mention, as it anticipates the mechanism of decision at the Community level on subjects other than visas if a transfer is decided from the field of intergovernmental cooperation to Article 100c of the Treaty.

The second building block establishes formal cooperation on justice and home affairs, and lists several areas of common interest (Title VI, Article K): 1) asylum policy; 2) crossing of the external borders of the Member States by persons; 3) immigration policy (conditions of entry, residence, movement and treatment of unauthorized immigration); 4) drugs; 5) fraud on an international scale; 6) civil matters; and 7) criminal matters; 8) customs; and 9) police cooperation (Europol).

For the first six topics, the Treaty envisages the Commission's initiating proposals, with a view to coordinating the action of the member states. For its part, the Council may handle such initiatives in a two-tier way: in one case, by adopting joint positions or joint action or by drawing up conventions (Art. K.3); in the second and stronger case, by deciding to apply Article 100c of the Treaty. An attached "Declaration on asylum" is worthy of mention here, where the Council is invited to consider member states' asylum policies as a matter of priority and to consider, by the end of 1993, asylum policy as a possible priority candidate for transfer to Article 100c.

The third building block is found in a "Protocol on Social Policy," and an annexed "Agreement" concluded between eleven member states, with the exception of the United Kingdom; by way of derogation from the Treaty, the Agreement and the acts thus adopted by the Council will not be applicable to the United Kingdom.

Article 2, paragraph 3 of the Agreement lists several areas where the Council will act unanimously on a proposal from the Commission, and, among others, it mentions "conditions of employment for third country nationals legally residing in Community territory."

In several existing Council and Commission documents, the usual sentence has been "living and working conditions." The expression used by the new Treaty seems to limit the scope of proposals to economic rights and to the working environment. More general topics linked to "integration" and living conditions, such as housing, education, health, equality of social rights and opportunities, seem hardly to be part of the expression "conditions of employment" and therefore subjects for proposals under this Article. In its Communication on immigration of October 23, 1991, the Commission advocated that action at the Community level in strengthening integration policies for the benefit of legal immigrants "can boost the chances of success of national integration policies, in themselves an essential element of guaranteeing democracy and solidarity."

Yet this step toward a Political Union is to be welcomed, as it can be considered an intermediate but a nevertheless more advanced stage. Article V, paragraph 2, announces a new Conference of representatives of the governments to be convened in 1996, to continue work in accordance with the objectives set out in Articles A and B.

Among others, Article B sets as objectives: the strengthening of economic and social cohesion; the implementation of a common foreign policy, and the development of cooperation on justice and home affairs.

All these objectives are very relevant to further promotion of harmonized migration policies and of a common integration process.

Notes

1   A communication of the Commission to the Council and to Parliament on "Abolition of Border Controls," May 8, 1992, concludes that the abolition of all physical frontiers must be achieved by the end of 1992, under the terms of Article 8a.

2   *Belvedere* (1991)

3   *Zolberg* (1989).

References

Belvedere

1991 "Calendrier pour l'Europe," *Belvedere*. October-November.

Zolberg, A.R.

1989   "The Next Waves: Migration Theory for a Changing World," *International Migration Review*, 23(3): 403-430.

17. The Immigration Policy of the European Union: The Inadequacy of Structural Explanations*

Mehmet Ugur

Introduction

From the mid-1980s onwards the issue of third-country immigration into the European Union (EU) has emerged as a major area of interest for both policy-makers and researchers. Looking at the themes around which the debate is unfolding, it can be seen that the revival of interest in this issue has been associated with two developments: the adoption of the Single European Act (SEA) in 1986 and the relative increase in the immigration pressure faced by Western Europe. The SEA provides, *inter alia*, for a single European market where not only goods and capital but also people would be allowed to move freely. This 'abolition' of internal borders, it is argued, has made the control of external borders a critical issue, the urgency of which has been amplified by the increase from the mid-1980s onwards in the number of illegal immigrants and asylum seekers. The events of 1989 and the following disintegration of the former socialist regimes in Eastern/Central Europe are presented as a catalyst in this process. In the context of European integration, the immediate question that these developments have posed is the level at which the EU's immigration policy should be defined. In other words, should immigration policy be defined at the European level with a certain degree of authority delegation to European institutions or should it be considered as a matter of national policy-making? In addition to this, and irrespective of the level at which the policy is defined, what should the stance of the policy be? Should Europe reinforce the control measures that have been in operation since the early 1970s, when foreign labour recruitment came to an end? Or, given the demographic trends in Europe, should policy-makers allow for the fact that Europe cannot manage without a permissive immigration policy designed to ensure a smooth operation of its labour markets?

Asking these questions is something like opening pandora's box. We are immediately faced with a barrage of related questions that need to be addressed simultaneously. If the externalities involved and the linkage between intra-EU freedom of movement and third-country immigration suggest that the policy should be determined at the European level, does the issue of immigration possess some special characteristics that could make the required authority delegation problematic? If the apparent insistence of the member states on treating the issue as a matter of national policy-making is to be taken as a reflection of the exceptional nature of the immigration problem, why have the same member states conceded to the regulation of intra-EU migration at the

* This chapter draws on data comiled for an article entitled 'Inclusion *vs* Exclusion: A Reinterpretation of the "Insider-Outsider" Divide in the European Union' due to appear in *INTERNATIONAL MIGRATION REVIEW*.

European level with some degree of authority delegation? Is the political economy of intra-EU immigration essentially different from that of third-country immigration? Or, are we faced with a superficial difference which is a result of policy decisions? Finally, what can the theory of international integration have to offer for predicting the likely outcome of the struggle for competence that the Commission and the member states have been caught in?

This article sets itself the task of developing a theoretical framework that would enable us to address such questions without having to resort to *ad hoc* explanations. In doing this, it begins with a brief review of the literature. The aim of this exercise is to highlight the relative strengths and shortcomings of the current debate in terms of its contribution to our understanding of the issues raised by the questions above. This is done in *Section I,* which describes the tone of the debate as structural because of its concerns with structural parameters such as immigration pressure, functional links between policy areas, the impact of immigration on marginal productivity of labour and welfare, etc. In *Section II,* the article proposes an alternative perspective based on the specific nature of the immigration issue and the implications of this for policy-making. The aim here is to develop a theoretical framework that would enable us to account for two obvious aspects of immigration policy-making in the European Union: the exclusionist and intergovernmental drive of the policy against third-country immigration and the co-existence of this stance with a fairly inclusive and liberal one concerning intra-EU migration. Following the development of this perspective, *Section III* examines the evidence on the EU's immigration policy-making so that the compatibility of the proposed perspective with actual developments can be gauged. Finally, the *Concluding Remarks* attempt at highlighting the main findings and pointing out some policy implications.

I. The European Union's immigration policy: an overview of the debate

One common feature of the debate on the European Union's immigration policy is its emphasis on the relative increase in immigration pressure from the mid-1980s onwards. Economic and political instability in the third world, coupled with high levels of population growth, is considered as a major 'push' factor that would generate large migratory movements. On the other hand, there is a 'pull' factor due to higher wage levels and a stagnating and ageing population in receiving countries. The combination of these factors is considered to be creating a fertile ground for increased immigration pressure, which the European Union will have to address (Straubhaar and Zimmerman, 1993: 229). Similar conclusions are arrived at by other students of immigration. As Gollini *et al* (1993: 79) conclude, social scientists envisage a "strong increase in migratory flows from the world's most backward areas toward the more developed ones" — with the inevitable implication that such flows would require some sort of regulation.[1]

There are, however, various problems with this push-pull analysis. First, there is no formal model used for estimating the size of migratory flows. This is not surprising given the difficulty involved in quantifying the factors that bear upon migratory movements. It is highly difficult to estimate the impact of factors such as networks, historical/cultural ties, social/economic imbalances, effectiveness/ineffectiveness of control measures, etc. Secondly, the predictions are based on the extrapolation of current trends into the future — an exercise that poses various problems as current trends are not independent of either past experience (for example, family reunion and network effects of the recruitment period) or existing policy frameworks. Under this condition even the development of a formal model might not be of great value as the estimated parameters are likely to change following policy announcements. The third problem with this approach is the lack of consensus about the optimal level of immigration compatible with equilibrium in the labour markets of receiving countries. For example, how can one determine whether or not the current levels of unemployment in the EU are too high to allow for recruitment of foreign labour if vacancies in at least some sectors of the labour market are too high? Even if a certain level of unemployment or vacancies can be taken as a threshold, is there any market mechanism that would induce the immigrants to adjust their quantity? Given the fact that forceful deportation of legal immigrants is not a feasible option, the only such mechanism would be financial incentives to encourage returns. This mechanism, however, has proved to be ineffective as the German experience with Turkish immigrants has clearly demonstrated. Another difficulty with devising some criteria for triggering control measures may be the segmentation of the labour market into formal and informal sections — a possibility that enables the immigrant population to engage in some informal activities that may not be attractive for the indigenous labour force.[2]

Therefore, despite its contribution to our understanding of the factors that may bear upon migratory flows, the pull-push approach remains highly problematic as a basis for either policy recommendations or policy analysis. As a result, what we observe is a clear divergence between the expectations raised by the model and the actual policies adopted by the governments of receiving countries. Not only that, the actual policy is in fact completely detached from what the existing data would suggest. As can be seen in Table I, recent attempts at reinforcing the control measures in the EU are in fact associated with very low rates of increase in the number of non-EU nationals immigrating into the EU. The rate of increase has been about one-tenth of one percentage point over the period from 1986 to 1992. In addition, this low rate should be considered in conjunction with the already low proportions of non-EU nationals to total population. With the exception of Germany, France and the United Kingdom, the ratio of non-EU nationals to total population is generally lower than 3 per cent, with the ratio in the EU being 2.87% in 1986 and 3.02% in 1992.

Table 1   **Non-EU Nationals in the European Union and Rates of Unemployment Stocks (000), Ratios (%) and Rate of Unemployment (%).**

| | 1986 | | | 1992 | | |
	Stock	Ratio	Unemployment (1985)	Stock	Ratio	Unemployment (1990)
Belgium	308.4	3.13	11.3	367.9	3.67	7.3
Denmark	91.1	1.78	7.8	141.1	2.73	8.3
France	2,285.7	4.30	10.3	2,357.7	4.14	9.4
Germany	3,022.3	4.95	6.9	4,395.0	6.82	4.9
Greece	185.3	1.86	7.8	174.9	1.73	7.0
Ireland	17.9	0.51	18.0	—	—	14.1
Italy	—	—	9.2	425.9	0.75	9.8
Luxembourg	—	—	2.6	13.9	3.56	1.6
Netherlands	391.0	2.69	10.5	557.4	3.68	7.8
Portugal	59.0	0.58	8.8	83.9	0.85	4.7
Spain	121.9	2.69	10.5	202.4	0.52	16.3
UK	1,052.1	1.88	11.5	1,207.2	2.12	7.0
EU	7,534.7	2.87	10.8	9,922.3	3.02	8.8

Source: Commission of the EC (1994: 66) and (1992: 36-40).

Another conclusion that can be derived from Table 1 is the fact that there is no meaningful relationship between the level of unemployment and the stance of immigration policy in EU member states. On the one hand, the relative decline in the level of EU unemployment from 10.8% in 1985 to 8.8% in 1992 has been accompanied by a frantic anxiety in the EU member states about immigration pressure. This response, however, is just the opposite of what a push-pull analysis would recommend. Such analysis would imply that a relaxed view of the immigration pressure should prevail as levels of unemployment tend to fall. On the other hand, if one is to consider the level of unemployment as still too high to justify such a relaxed view, the push-pull approach would have difficulty in providing an explanation as to why European governments have failed to stop the increase in immigration. Explaining the gap between restrictive policies and their outcomes requires elaboration on other factors that make the control of immigration difficult.[3] Once the analysis becomes involved with such factors, the policy recommendation that immigration flows should be managed in line with labour demand becomes unoperational.

To their credit, the proponents of the push-pull model are explicitly in favour of establishing an international framework for the management of migratory flows. In fact, they suggest that an international agreement on migration — a General Agreement on Migration Policy (GAMP) — should be concluded. This policy recommendation is made by pointing to the success of the General Agreement on Tariffs and Trade (GATT) in managing international trade. (Straubhaar and Zimmerman, 1993: 236-39). At the European level, they argue, a coherent policy is even more urgent as free markets for goods and labour are already established. Although this is a step in the right direction, it raises the question of why the EU member states have been extremely reluctant to agree to similar Commission proposals since the early 1970s. In the context of European integration, this reluctance becomes more interesting given the fact that the same member states have already established extensive arrangements for the regulation of external trade and intra-EU migration.

An alternative perspective for explaining this outcome may be derived from some theories of international relations. State-centric theories such as Realism and Neo-realism would suggest that states, as sovereign entities, should be able to decide on the control of their external borders. There are two aspects of this sovereignty thesis. On the one hand, state sovereignty implies strategic interaction between equally sovereign units of the international system. One possible outcome of this strategic interaction is the lack or temporary nature of inter-state co-operation. (Morgenthau, 1956 and Waltz, 1976). This general conclusion, applied to the specific case of migration, implies that governments would tend to be reluctant to engage in international regulatory arrangements that could compromise their sovereignty. Another possible outcome of the state-centric analysis is presented by the international regimes approach to international relations. According to this view, interdependence and the externalities it involves may push the states towards policy co-ordination and co-operation (Keohane, 1989 and 1984). Consequently, it is possible to envisage the emergence of regulatory frameworks for the management of international migration. The problem with this reasoning, however, is that the extent of authority delegation to international institutions and the change in state perceptions about the desirability of international co-operation are left undetermined. In other words, we are faced with a tautological explanation: EU member states may opt for policy co-ordination and even authority delegation, but we do not know when this option may be exercised and how the perceived benefits of such co-ordination may change over time or from one member state to the other.

The other aspect of this perspective relates to the implication of sovereignty for the differentiation between nationals and non-nationals. According to the state-centric view, the sovereign state should be capable of deciding on who is a 'national' and what privileges should be associated with nationality. The implication of this argument is that the state should also be capable of determining who is a 'foreigner' and how they should be excluded from the privileges that nationality entails. (Oppenheim, 1905: 378). This is by no means an outdated argument entertained by international lawyers only. Kelsen (1966: 366) argues that every sovereign state has the power "... to admit aliens only in such cases and upon such conditions" that it may regard as appropriate and "... to expel them at any time". Also, Weiner (1985) argues that sovereign states are bound to regulate international migration in accordance with their national interests. This inward-looking version of the sovereignty thesis implies that regulation of immigration at an international level, even if feasible or desirable, should be exclusionist. In other words, international arrangements should be based on discrimination in favour of nationals and against non-nationals.

Looked at from this perspective, the insistence of the EU member states on intergovernmental frameworks and the exclusionist stance of the current policy becomes understandable. Not only that, it becomes possible also to explain the failure of the push-pull approach in accounting for the lack of a European immigration policy. The crippling vagary of power politics springs up as an obstacle that prevents the development of a coherent policy based on rational criteria. There remains, however, a significant unresolved question: why have EU member states agreed to supranational arrangements providing for freedom of movement and equal treatment of non-nationals from other members of the European Union?

A possible explanation to this question can be derived from the neo-functionalist theory of integration. According to this theory, the expansion of the integrative framework is determined by the structural exigencies of the initial step towards integration. This is described as a 'spill-over' process that involves gradual integration of new policy areas as the policy-makers realise that the objectives of the preceding stages cannot be achieved unless new areas are also integrated (Haas, 1964; 1968). In the specific case of immigration, this perspective would predict that the initial integration of the policy on intra-EU migration would eventually lead to the emergence of an integrated EU policy on non-EU immigration. That is due to linkages between the two policy areas that make the achievement of the initial goal (intra-EU freedom of movement) conditional on the integration of the new area (non-EU immigration). Without an integrated policy on non-EU immigration, the EU member states would be faced with negative externalities. These may emerge for two reasons. First, nationals of some member states may find themselves incapable of benefiting from free movement as other member states happen to be pursuing permissive policies towards less costly non-EU immigrants. Secondly, uncoordinated immigration policies may have distorting effects on competition in trade, whereby member states with liberal immigration policies may be obtaining artificial competitiveness as a result of reduced labour costs. In either case, it is highly probable that the adversely-affected member states would tend to retaliate by restricting either free movement of EU-nationals or trade. Either type of retaliation is a move away from the preceding step of integration — i.e., freedom of movement or customs union.

As will be seen below, this perspective has been highly influential on the European Commission's approach to the formulation of an EU immigration policy towards non-EU nationals. In various policy documents the Commission has argued consistently that avoiding policy harmonization in this area would make it impossible to maintain freedom of movement for EU-nationals and free trade. Not only that, the legitimacy of the European Union would be also put at risk. How could European integration be legitimated if nationals of some member states find it impossible to have access to employment opportunities in some other member states as a result of the latter's permissive policy towards non-EU immigrants? Despite such attempts at linking the two policy areas, however, the Commission has been largely unsuccessful in convincing the member states to agree on a common immigration policy determined at the

European level. In other words, the EU experience has demonstrated that the neo-functionalist perspective is too optimistic and teleological to account for immigration policy-making.

II. Labour markets, states and immigration: an alternative perspective

The analysis above indicates that structural approaches to immigration, whether they focus on the structural causes of immigration, on the structural properties of the international system, or on exigencies of the integration process itself can go only some way towards explaining the dynamics of policy-making in this area. It is, therefore, necessary to develop an alternative theoretical framework that could redress the shortcomings of structural approaches. To do this, it is necessary to focus not on structural cause-effect explanations but on (i) the specific features of immigration as a policy area and (ii) the dynamics of legitimating policy outcomes in the context of state-constituent relations.

The argument in this section is fairly simple: a satisfactory account of EU immigration policy-making can be developed only if the specific features of the concepts of state, labour market and immigration are identified. If we begin with the labour market, one specific aspect that emerges is the relatively low degree of mobility of labour as a factor of production. This is the case not only across national boundaries, but also within national labour markets. Traditions, language, community ties, housing market conditions, etc., are the most obvious factors that tend to limit labour mobility. Another aspect of the labour market is closely linked to this and concerns the connection between labour market conditions and social/political stability. Because of low labour mobility, unanticipated shocks could result in the concentration of unemployment in certain regions or industries. This makes the re-absorption of the excess labour into other regions or industries a prolonged process. Given the inverse relationship between the duration of unemployment and the possibility of being re-employed, such shocks could have highly destabilising consequences. Under this condition there is an incentive for governments to minimise the occurrence of such adverse shocks. If restrictive measures on international trade is one instrument, the other is the restriction of immigration flows. Existing evidence, however, suggests that national governments tend to deploy such measures against immigration rather than international trade. Even if restrictive measures are introduced against international trade, they tend to be negotiated at international levels as has been the case in the Multi Fibre Agreement (MFA) that limits the import of textiles into industrialised countries.

The preference of national governments for adopting mainly unilateral restrictions on immigration requires an examination of state sovereignty and the issue of immigration. As far as state sovereignty is concerned, I would argue that the concept utilised by the state-centric approaches to international relations should be put upside down. Putting it simply, the concept of sovereignty should not be interpreted in a way that renders the state a closed entity interacting with similar units. On the contrary, one should also look at the constraining implications of sovereignty. The necessity of this exercise can be clearly seen when one examines the implications of the power to define nationality for policy options available to policy-makers. If sovereignty implies the state's ability to define who is national and what privileges are associated with nationality, then the legitimation of the state or its government becomes highly dependent on its ability to satisfy the demands of its nationals when the latter feel that the privileges associated with nationality are being eroded. Such demands will intensify as (i) the legitimacy of the state becomes increasingly dependent on the provision of welfare services and devising a macroeconomic framework conducive to economic prosperity, and (ii) societal security — i.e. the society's perception of itself as a viable entity emerges as an increasingly significant concern in addition to traditional concerns about external security.[4] Once this aspect of the state sovereignty is taken into account, it becomes clear that sovereignty should be seen as a source of constraint on policy-makers as much as a source of power.

In this context the issue of immigration emerges as a policy area with special characteristics. Immigration is not only an issue that involves the incoming of 'foreigners' with possible claims on existing employment and welfare resources, but it also represents a possible erosion of the privileges associated with nationality — hence a threat to societal security. In this sense, the immigration issue is both non-divisible and non-transparent. Immigration is a *non-divisible* policy issue because it makes the trading-off of group interests extremely difficult if not impossible. The non-divisibility of the policy issue stems from the basis on which immigrants are differentiated from the indigenous population: the concept of nationality. Once nationality is taken as the criteria for distinguishing foreigners from citizens, the policy-makers are faced with the special constraints of an *exclusive club,* the viability of which is dependent upon its provision of a club 'good' or 'service' to its members.[5] In addition, the issue of immigration is *non-transparent* too. The non-transparency of the issue is a result of the symbolic nature of identity and the possibility of xenophobic sentiments that make the construction of cost-benefit analysis highly difficult. This aspect reinforces the non-divisibility of the immigration policy and tends to exclude the possibility of including the immigration issue into package deals between national policy-makers, where concessions in one policy issue are compensated by returns in other areas. Faced with such constraints, national policy-makers would tend to be reluctant to engage in international frameworks with binding rules on the conduct of national immigration policy. On the contrary, they would be inclined to either stay away from international arrangements or to agree only to intergovernmental procedures without binding rules. It is only in this way that they can maintain a certain degree of 'autonomy' enabling them to bend the stance of the policy in line with constituent perceptions of the immigration phenomenon at a given time.

The usefulness of this perspective is that it enables us to explain not only the essentially intergovernmental and exclusionist aspects of the member states' policy against third-country immigration, but also the contrast between this stance and the degree of authority delegation with respect to intra-EU migration where a highly liberal and inclusive policy is at work. The key to this contrast is the re-definition of the social space over which the club 'good' associated with nationality is to be provided. European integration, by providing free movement and equal treatment for nationals of the member states, extends the boundaries of the exclusive club. This extension, in turn, generates two tendencies. On the one hand, intra-EU migration policy would be liberal and national policy-makers would tend to be willing to delegate authority to European institutions. On the other hand, however, EU immigration policy towards third-country nationals would be exclusionist, with the formulation of policy remaining as an essentially intergovernmental process. The essentially intergovernmental nature of the policy-making in the area of third-country immigration would prevail so long as the movement of non-EU nationals within the Union is still subject to restrictions as a result of the fact that intra-EU freedom of movement is based on the principle of nationality. Given that this is still the case in the EU, it can be conjectured that the efforts of the European Commission and those of the EP to expand their competence with respect to non-EU immigrants will yield very limited results. These limited results, in turn, will be dependent on these institutions' willingness to concur with national governments' emphasis on the exclusion of potential immigrants as a pre-condition for the improvement of the rights of already existing immigrants from third countries.

III. Exclusion and intergovernmentalism in the european union's immigration policy: the evidence

In the following paragraphs the article will examine the evidence on EU immigration policy from the mid-1970s onwards. The aim of this section is to draw attention to two interrelated processes: the establishment of intra-EU freedom of movement and the evolution of the exclusionist policies *vis-à-vis* non-EU immigrants. As the following account will hopefully reveal, understanding the way in which intra-EU freedom of movement has been established is a necessary first step in explaining the exclusionist and intergovernmental features of the policy on extra-EU immigration. This is the case for two reasons: first, intra-EU freedom of movement has been established only after member states have agreed on principles reducing the non-divisibility and non-transparency of intra-EU migration. Secondly, as a result of maintaining the non-transparent and non-divisible aspects of third-country immigration, the establishment of intra-EU freedom of movement has been accompanied by the erection of control measures against non-EU immigration within an essentially intergovernmental framework.

III.1. Freedom of movement and equal treatment with nationals: reducing the non-divisibility and non-transparency of intra-EU migration

Intra-EU freedom of movement is provided for in Article 48 (1) of the EEC Treaty, which states that freedom of movement for workers will entail the abolition of discriminatory measures based on nationality between the 'workers of the Member States.' Although the 'worker' of a member state does not always have to be a 'national' of that member state, the member states and national courts established later on that 'nationality' is the basis for eligibility to free movement. The first step in this direction was Regulation No. 15/61 of the Council, which stated that a 'Community worker' must be 'national' of a member state (J.O. des C.E., 1961: 1075).[6] Regulations 38/64 and 1612/68 adhered to the same interpretation (J.O. des C.E, 1964: 965 and O.J. of the E.C., 1968: 1), which was also shared by national courts (Goodwin-Gill 1978: 172), Consequently, by the time the free movement of workers was established in 1968, it became clear that this right was to be granted to EU nationals only, excluding the existing immigrants from Greece, Turkey, Yugoslavia and other countries. This gradual establishment of the freedom of movement for EU-nationals was accompanied by the principle of equal treatment.

413

According to this principle, a national of a certain member state will be treated equally with the nationals of the host country as far as employment and remuneration conditions are concerned.

Regulation 1612/68 stated that "Any *national* of a member state, irrespective of his place of residence, shall have 'the right' to take up employment and 'to pursue such activity within the territory of another member state...' " (Article 1(1)). This definite acceptance of the nationality principle as a basis for a worker's right to move freely within the Union finalised the gradual process of creating 'insiders' and 'outsiders' in the area of free movement. The way in which this divide was created can be seen in other articles of the Regulation. For example, Article 4(1) stipulated that a member state, although allowed to devise restrictions aimed at foreigners, could not extend such restrictions to nationals of other member states. Also, Article 3(2) stated that nationals of the member states would not have to go through the special recruitment procedures for third-country nationals which generally required medical checks, possession of work permits, restriction on the type of employment, etc. Finally, in terms of access to employment, Article 16(2) gave priority to EU nationals *vis-à-vis* non-EU nationals: vacancies would be offered to third-country nationals only if the member state having such vacancies considered that there was not sufficient supply from other member states. Under these conditions non-EU nationals were faced with double discrimination: they were forced to compete on an unequal footing under given labour market conditions and they were the ones who would be denied access should these conditions deteriorate.

One consequence of this process was the generation of perceptions about the desirability and feasibility of a European identity/citizenship. Freedom of movement was described by the Commission in 1968 as "an incipient form of European Citizenship" and not only an economic arrangement (Commission of the EC, 1968: 5-6). Not only that, the Commission proposed in 1975 the creation of a Community passport that would "emphasise the feeling of the *nationals of the nine member states* of belonging to the Community." (Commission of the EC, 1975: 23. Emphasis added). Although the Commission's emphasis on this nascent European identity might be exaggerated, some students of international migration have tended to concede that such a possibility exists if certain further steps are to be taken.[7] Irrespective of the extent to which one can speak of a European citizenship, the underlying message in this presentation is not difficult to detect: European policy-makers — the Commission and the member states who had called for the creation of a Union passport in the Paris Summit of 1974 — were engaged in devising new measures that would reinforce the creation of a new social/political space over which privileges associated with nationality can be enjoyed.

Another consequence of the principle of nationality, ironically, has been the separation of immigration policy issues from issues related to nationality. As soon as nationality was accepted as a basis for determining the beneficiaries of the free movement, the issue of immigration became more transparent and the member states were no longer in need of mixing intra-EU migration with nationality. In other words, the membership of the exclusive club is now composed of all nationals of the member states. As a result of expanding the membership, the perceived cost of belonging to the club may increase, but this increase in cost is balanced with an increase in club benefits that result from expanded club resources. Consequently, the free movement of EU nationals became essentially a transparent technical issue that reduced the possibility of some member-state nationals acting as veto groups against the presence of other member-state nationals. In other words, the presentation of the intra-EU free movement as a non-zero-sum game became more plausible. This opportunity is not missed in the Preamble to Regulation 1612/68, which states that intra-EU freedom of movement must be seen as a means of *improving* living and working conditions as well as the range of choice open to nationals of all member states.

The other principle of the free movement of labour — equal treatment with respect to working conditions and pay — made the regulation of intra-EU migratory flows a divisible policy issue too. Once equal treatment was in place, intra-EU migration became dependent on the demand for *rather than* supply of labour. Although there may be incentives for workers to move from one member state with high-unemployment /low-social protection to others with low-unemployment/high-social protection, potential emigrants may find it highly difficult to do so unless there is a shortage of labour in the country of destination. In other words, equal treatment of EU-nationals makes the employment decisions of employers biased towards their own nationals as the incentives implied by lower wages and/or social protection would no longer be available. Consequently, allowing for free entry of EU-nationals does not imply sacrificing the interests of the domestic labour force in favour of other EU nationals faced with high rates of unemployment in their own countries. This bias towards 'own nationals', in turn, enables the policy-makers to overcome the problem of non-divisibility as migratory flows into the domestic labour market will not imply displacement of nationals.

This imputed divisibility is, in turn, enhanced by the fact that EU-nationals are still able to enjoy privileges against third-country immigrants when there are asymmetries in labour markets of the member states — i.e. unemployment in some and labour shortage in others. Consequently, authority delegation to the Commission in the area of intra-EU migration becomes not only feasible, but desirable. The desirability of such authority delegation derives from the fact that the Commission can act as an impartial umpire ensuring adherence to the principle of equal treatment and preventing either competitive pre-emption (employers' hiring of cheap labour from countries of high unemployment and/or low social protection) or the exporting of unemployment. The feasibility of authority delegation, on the other hand, is enhanced by the fact that the imputed transparency and divisibility tend to dampen the intra-EU migratory flows.

Evidence on intra-EU migration lends support to this argument. For example, in the mid-1980s the proportion of EU-nationals migrating within the EU to the total number of documented immigrants was 39.2% for residents (wage/salary earners and their dependents) and 43.7% for wage and salary earners (ILO, 1990: 31-32). Evaluated against the restrictive measures imposed against non-EU nationals since 1973, it can be seen that freedom of movement and equal treatment has proved to be a more effective policy option in terms of preventing large migratory flows. The effectiveness of the policy can also be seen in the specific cases of EU nationals who acquired the right to free movement following their countries' accession to the EU. For example, following the establishment of the right for free movement in 1968 there was no unexpected or large-scale increase in the number of Italian workers who up to then had constituted the largest migrant community within the EU. More recent developments also reflect similar trends: the number of Greek nationals (who, after the Italians, constituted another major source of migrant labour in the EU) seeking employment in the Community did not increase after January 1989 when they became entitled to free movement. Similarly, no substantial increase has taken place in the number of migrant workers from Spain or Portugal even after the completion of the single market (ILO, 1990: 4-5).

III.2. Exclusion of non-EU nationals and intergovernmentalism in the EU's immigration policy-making

Contrary to what the recent wave of activity on immigration control would suggest, the exclusion of non-EU nationals has been a direct consequence of the freedom of movement established in 1968 for EU-nationals. As indicated above, Regulation 1612/68 provides ample evidence to this effect. According to the provisions of the Regulation, not only is freedom of movement limited to EU-nationals, but also the latter have priority in accessing employment in the face of potential competition from non-EU nationals. This, however, is not the only consequence of the 1968 arrangement. The Regulation 1612/68 has also contributed to the ability of the member states to pursue a national rather than an integrated EU policy vis-à-vis non-EU immigration. Under the nationality principle, the level of non-EU immigration into a particular member state does not pose a threat to others as non-EU immigrants are not allowed to move freely within the Union. Until the early 1970s this arrangement allowed member states to pursue relatively permissive immigration policies based on the recruitment of non-EU labour. From the early 1970s onwards, however, it allowed the same member states to introduce unilateral restrictive policies — this time as a result of emerging xenophobic sentiments among their constituents.[8]

Although sporadic interest in an EU immigration policy emerged in the early 1970s, it was not until 1973 that the Commission made its first attempt at proposing some policy guidelines.[9] The Commission, on 25 October 1973, put forward its proposal for a Social Action Programme (Commission of the EC, 1974). Because the Treaty of Rome did not provide for EU competence in the area of third-country immigration, the Commission was trying to derive some implied competence by referring to Article 118 of the Treaty. Article 118 provides for the Commission to promote co-operation between member states in the social field and to make studies, deliver opinions, and arrange consultations on problems arising both at national level and in international organizations.

The Social Action Programme of 1973 called for: (i) achievement of equality in living and working conditions, (ii) ensuring the participation of immigrant workers in Community life, and (iii) co-ordination of immigration policies of the member states as regards third-country immigration. The Commission, although aware of the legal constraints, seemed to entertain some degree of optimism about the feasibility of deriving implied competence by resorting to Article 118 of the EEC Treaty. The Council, under pressure from third countries following the introduction of restrictive policies by member states from 1973 onwards, adopted a resolution on the Social Action Programme on 21 January 1974 — only three months after the Commission's submission.[10] In the meantime, however, the Commission's proposal for equal treatment of third-country immigrants remained subject to existing legislation. This implied no improvement for those immigrants because existing EU provisions were already based on priority to EU-nationals. Partly to compensate for this lack of improvement and partly to contain the strong reactions from third-countries, the Council asked for the establishment of an action programme for migrant workers, to which the Commission would respond in the same year.

The Commission's response was the Action Programme in Favour of Migrant Workers and their Families (the Action Programme). The Committee on Social Affairs and Employment within the European Parliament found the Action Programme to be non-committal and lacking prioritization and timetabling.[11] This criticism, however, did not cause any change in the content of the proposed programme. The Commission, aware of the member states' reluctance to engage in developing an EU immigration policy, must have considered the Action Programme as a limited yet significant first step in getting the ball rolling. Therefore, the Commission proposed that the priority of EU-nationals in employment would be maintained, but the third-country nationals should be granted voting rights in local elections from 1980 onwards. Notwithstanding the limited nature of the concession to third-country immigrants, it was made conditional on successful restriction of further inflows, especially illegal immigration (Commission of the EC, 1976: 10-21). It was hoped that this presentation would be functional in striking a cord with the policy orientation in member states, most of whom had already stopped recruitment and begun to think about the integration problems of the existing immigrants.

It appeared at the time that this soft approach was likely to yield positive results. The Council adopted a resolution on 9 February 1976 on the Action Programme which, *inter alia,* considered it important to (i) engage in consultation on immigration policies against third countries and (ii) accelerate co-operation between member states "in the campaign against illegal immigration" (Commission of the EC, 1976: 7-8). But there was no indication about the mechanism through which consultation and co-operation would take place. Also, there was no instruction to the Commission about preparations for the establishment of such a framework. There were only two positive signs given by the Council: the directive it adopted on the same date in relation to the compilation of statistics on foreign workers; and the Directive of 28 June 1977 on the education of the children of immigrants. The compilation of statistics can be seen as one of the initial steps towards the formulation of an EU immigration policy, but later developments would prove that even this cautious interpretation was too optimistic. The Directive of 28 June 1977, on the other hand, was based on Article 49 EEC — which relates only to EU-nationals. Once more, third-country immigrants and their children were excluded. In his reply to a Parliamentary question, the President-in-Office of the Council, Mr Simonet, stated that inclusion of third-country immigrants would have required legislation on the basis of Article 235 which required unanimity, and that this was impossible to attain (O.J. of the E.C., 1977: 170).

417

The reluctance of the member states to develop an EU policy was to be observed once more following the Commission proposal of 1978 on the approximation of member state policies on illegal immigration. In that proposal, the Commission's linkage strategy was essentially the same as before: illegal immigration was considered to lead to conditions which jeopardised not only the stability of the national labour markets but also the realisation of free movement for EU nationals (Commission of the EC, 1978: 1-7, Annex). This linkage was made more explicit by the Vice-President of the Commission, Mr Vredeling, in his address to the Parliament. Mr Vredeling's stated that illegal immigration was impinging upon the freedom of movement of EU-nationals and detracting the Union from improving the working and living conditions of its workers (O.J. of the E.C., 1978: 49-50). The Commission's proposal was supported by most of the MEPs, with the exception of British MEPs (both Labour and Conservative) and some right-wing French MEPs. Nevertheless, the Council failed to agree on a directive to that effect. As the rapporteur of the Committee on Social Affairs and Employment indicated, the resistance was "...virtually tantamount to refusal in the case of the United Kingdom and partial refusal in the case of France" (O.J. of the E.C., 1978: 37).

Despite this resistance from member states, the Commission's push for establishing implied competence continued. Hoping that its emphasis on the priority of EU-nationals would strike a chord with national governments, it prepared a new document formulating the rationale for policy co-ordination and identifying the issues on which consultation should take place. This document was communicated to the Council on 23 March 1979. It invited the Council to engage in an exchange of views with the Commission to enable the Commission to "organize, within the existing Community institutions, ..., consultation with and between member states" (Commission of the EC, 1979). When asked about its opinion, the Economic and Social Committee (ESC) approved the Commission's communication in October of the same year. According to the Committee, "the problem of migrant workers from non-member countries has to be seen in the more general context of migrant workers as a whole, so that the broadest possible Community consensus can be attained" (Commission of the EC, 1979a: 112). Since the Commission's proposal was based on priority to EU-nationals, the ESC saw no reason for disagreeing with the Commission.

Faced with this alliance between the ESC and the Commission, the Council could not ignore the Commission's communication. It reacted on 22 November 1979 by adopting a Resolution calling for co-ordination efforts "... to be concentrated on (i) questions concerning priority to be given to workers who are nationals of the member states and (ii) current matters concerning labour from non-member countries in the context of Community relations with those countries" (Commission of the EC, 1979b: 45). Although this move seemed to be in line with the Commission's requests, in reality it constituted a fatal blow to the latter's efforts for establishing an EU competence in this area. In an entry in the Council minutes of the meeting in which the Resolution was adopted, the council stated that the aim of the consultation was "... to facilitate the adoption *not of Community instruments, but of a common attitude of the member states*." Prior negotiations at the Committee of Permanent Representatives (COREPER) were also along similar lines.[12]

Thus, towards the end of the 1970s, not only have the Commission's attempts at establishing derived competence failed, but also the resolution of the member states to keep the issue of third-country immigration within an intergovernmental framework seemed to be reinforced. In fact, until 1985, no further Commission initiatives took place. In 1985, the Commission came forward with a Decision aimed at overcoming the inertia that had lasted for so long. According to Article 1 of the Decision, the member states must give the Commission and other member states advance information on all draft measures and agreements that they intend to conclude, including their texts. This article was apparently seeking to form a pool of information and impute some degree of transparency on the complexity of the member states' immigration policies. Article 2 of the Decision, on the other hand, provided for consultation meetings following a request either by the Commission itself or by a member state. Article 3 of the Decision provided that one aim of the consultation procedures was to ensure that draft measures and agreements mentioned in Article 1 were in conformity with EU policies, in particular as regards the Union labour market (Commission of the EC, 1985: 25-26). This Decision proved to be the final straw that broke the camel's back: five member states, Denmark, France, Germany, the Netherlands and the United Kingdom challenged the Decision in the Court of Justice.

The Court ruled in 1987 that the Decision was void because it extended the scope of communication and consultation procedure to cover matters (such as cultural integration of workers from non-member states and their families) which were beyond the provisions of Article 118 EEC. No doubt, the ruling meant a major setback for the Commission. More importantly, however, the Court of Justice — the institution which had displayed a well-known eagerness about implied competence in other areas such as trade policy — felt it necessary to refrain from establishing such a competence in the area of immigration policy, which, in the view of the Attorney General, was both inescapable and conceded by the Council various times.

As the Commission was fighting its case in the Court of Justice and trying to marshall the support of Parliament, the member states' intergovernmental drive was gathering new steam. The major steps in this drive were the Schengen Agreement of 1985 and the 1986 London Summit of the European Council. Although the Schengen Agreement is an initiative outside the EU framework, the developments following its inception proved so important for the European Union that it is now impossible to examine the EU immigration policy without dealing with the Schengen Agreement and the Implementing Convention of 1990 (known as Schengen II) that followed it (Callovi, 1992). Schengen, through its provisions for removal of internal border checks, reinforcement of external border controls and intensive police co-operation among the signatory states proved to be "... not a try-out forerunner for more extensive and more elaborate instruments between the Twelve ... but rather the very realization of those objectives..." (Schutte 1991: 568)

The EU member states, by following the Schengen example, are now involved in intergovernmental negotiations at different levels and in relation to various issues. The most important platform for our purposes is the platform where immigration policy issues are being discussed: the Ad Hoc Immigration Group. This group was established on 20 October 1986 in London, following an agreement between the EU ministers in charge of immigration (mainly interior ministers). About two months later, at the 5-6 December Summit of the European Council in London, the heads of states and governments called on the interior ministers to, *inter alia*, "consider the role of co-ordinating and possibly harmonizing the visa regimes of the member states in tightening controls at the Community's external borders" and "intensify co-operation on measures to prevent illegal immigration" (Agence Europe, 1986: 5).

Following this instruction, the Ad Hoc Immigration Group reached preliminary agreement on various issues only four months after the London Summit, on 27 April 1987. The agreement concerned issues such as visa policies, control of external borders, repatriation of third-country citizens who are in an irregular situation in the Union, restrictive procedures concerning political asylum seekers, and reinforcement of controls on third-country nationals who are in an irregular situation (*Europe Documents*, 1987: 1-3). As far as visa policies were concerned, the Ad Hoc Immigration Group agreed on a gradual approach to a unified visa system, including the criteria for the issue of visas. In the case of external border controls, it agreed on a "modulated control of travellers" in accordance with whether or not they are citizens of one of the member states. This control is supposed to be "... organized without restricting the efficiency of the control concerning clandestine immigration from third countries ..." This principle links with the unified visa system and implies that third-country nationals are once more discriminated against, even if they have been residents in one of the member states for a long time. In some member states such as Germany, where application for naturalization is very low, those subject to discrimination could be even second or third generation young people.

In the area of political asylum applications the Ad Hoc Immigration Group established common principles concerning the two stages of the asylum process: the pre-arrival stage where transporters are to be held responsible for ensuring that their passengers possess the right documents; and the stage of examining the application, during which the aim is to fight against simultaneous and/or successive applications. The principles agreed upon in this meeting of 27 April 1987 led to the *Convention Determining the State Responsible for Examining Applications for Asylum Seekers in One of the Member States of the European Communities*, which was later on signed on 15 June 1990 in Dublin.[13]

The most important aspect of the Convention is the rules it establishes for determining the state responsible for the processing of an asylum application. The state responsible for the examination of the asylum application is either the state where the asylum seeker has family ties, or the one which initially issued him/her with a visa or a residence permit. The immediate implication of these principles is that member states with an already large number of political refugees, or the ones more easily accessible, will have to examine more asylum applications than others. Consequently, countries like the United Kingdom which scores well on these two counts will be in an advantageous situation, whereas countries with liberal asylum legislation like Germany are put under pressure to tighten its asylum policies. Given the political difficulties faced by the German government in relation to a change in asylum legislation, the EU ministers concerned managed to find a temporary solution which may alleviate the pressure on one of their partners. They invented the concept of 'host third country' in their London meeting just before the Edinburgh Summit of 1992. The 'host third country' essentially means a country on the periphery of the EU through which an asylum seeker has entered the Union and to which he/she can be returned (Mortimer, 1992). Apparently, encouraged by the positive results of the intergovernmental procedures, the EU member states have begun to externalise the cost of any migratory flows which could slip through the exclusionary net.

Another feature of the activities of the Ad Hoc Immigration Group is the stigmatization they imply for the immigrant population of the EU. The more emphasis is placed upon illegal immigration by the Ad Hoc Group, the more easily a link is established by the European public between illegal immigration and third-country nationals — even though the latter may have been residing in one of the member states for many years. This stigmatization further intensifies the non-transparent nature of the immigration issues. As a report prepared for the Commission indicates, the immigration issue is increasingly becoming a 'hot potato', a subject of "a political logic rather than a technical logic needed to help identify and solve important problems" (Matheson, 1991: 56).

Where do these developments leave the Commission? The Commission participates in all meetings of the Ad Hoc Group Immigration — generally at the Vice-President level. The role it plays, however, is far from clear. There is no evidence to indicate that the Commission is capable of influencing the agenda. It may, however, be able to express its views on the implications of the intergovernmental process for the Union's existing commitments towards third-countries — especially for those countries to which the Union is linked with co-operation/association agreements. It is also clear that participation in those meetings implies access to highly important information which may enable the Commission to play the role of an effective 'broker' when the member states fails to agree among themselves. This, however, is a far cry away from the role that the Commission was pushing for until 1985. It also implies that the relationship between the Commission and the European Parliament is deteriorating. As one MEP observed, "... the European Commission plays double towards the Parliament and there are constant doubts" about whether it is looking "after the Community's interests" (van Outrive, 1992: 5). On the other hand, the Council has increased its influence by putting itself both inside and then outside the Union framework — reflecting the gain made by the member states as we have argued above.

Concluding Remarks

The analysis above suggests that intergovernmental procedures and the exclusionist stance of the EU's immigration policy *vis-à-vis* third-country immigrants should be examined in the light of a contract between states and constituents. This contract is implied by the concept of nationality and the privileges associated with it. Member states of the Union managed to formalize and implement a liberal policy concerning the cross-border movement of their nationals by redefining the space over which the privileges associated with nationality can be enjoyed. The delegation of authority to supranational institutions in this area, therefore, becomes feasible and desirable. That is because, once the issue of immigration is made transparent in this manner, the member states are relieved of the risk of facing 'veto group' actions by their nationals and the incentives generating go-it-alone attitudes have diminished. In contrast to this outcome, the member states have always been vociferous about defending their 'sovereign rights' for controlling the movement of third-country nationals within both the Union and their own territories. This contrast cannot be explained by referring to structural factors. What is involved here is a specific manifestation of a state-society collusion that implies exclusion of non-nationals. This exclusion is determined by the exclusiveness of the rights associated with nationality as a basis for defining the insider group — i.e., nationals of the EU member states.

The examination of the evidence also suggests that the intergovernmental and exclusionist stance of the EU immigration policy cannot be considered as a recent development. This stance has existed throughout the process of establishing the freedom of movement on the basis of member-state nationality from 1968 onwards. The establishment of the Single Market must be seen only as a catalyst. In that sense, the heavy emphasis placed on the Single Market as an explanatory variable for the increased exclusionism and intergovernmentalism needs to be qualified. The analysis above would suggest that a more useful and effective explanation of the EU immigration policy should take into account the mutually-reinforcing dynamics that originate from both the state and society levels. Both the member states and their nationals will continue to be motivated to exclude non-nationals unless (i) the political élites are placed under some type of constraint emanating from a redefined concept of nationality and (ii) the nationals of the member states are prepared to embrace such a redefinition, which needs to be based on openness towards non-nationals.

Notes

1. For example, this is not an untypical description of the immigration pressure faced by developed countries: "Industrial countries are experiencing their highest ever levels of unwanted immigration, to which there is no end in sight" (Martin, 1993: 13). See also, Widgren (1994), Heisler and Layton-Henry (1993: 149-51), and Bohning (1991).

2. On the issue of dual labour market, see Piore (1979), and Berger and Piore (1980).

3. This issue has been dealt with extensively by Hollifield (1992). Hollifield argues that the rights-based political system in receiving countries imposes a serious constraint on policy-makers' ability to control immigration at levels compatible with labour market requirements.

4. The post-1945 period witnesses the emergence of these factors as essential elements in the legitimation of the European states. For the move towards a new legitimation strategy based on the satisfaction of welfare-related demands, see Milward (1992). On the other hand, see Waever *et al* .(1993) for the emergence of societal security in Europe.

5. On the theory of clubs, see Cornes and Sandler (1986: 157-243). It is important to note here that an exclusive club increases the members' claims on the club good which, in turn, increases the tendency to reinforce the exclusion of non-members. That is because the marginal benefit derived from club membership must be high enough to balance the marginal cost of membership, which includes not only the 'membership fee', but also the cost of exclusion.

6. Although critical of this change, Dummett and Nicol (1990: 9) concede that the term *ressortissant* used in that regulation "has the precise meaning of a 'national' " as it is described in public international law.

7. For example, Plender (1976: 48) argues that it may be possible to discern an incipient form of European citizenship if the principle of priority to EU-nationals is consolidated and the national courts give their support to the implementation of Articles 48-51 of the EEC Treaty.

8. At the time of suspending the recruitment of foreign labour, the OECD was of the view that Western European governments were forced to retreat against constituent pressures rather than acting in line with labour market requirements. (SOPEMI, 1974: 4-5).

9. The EU's interest in immigration policy was mainly limited to Parliamentary questions. See J.O des C.E (1972: 11) and O.J. of the EC (1973: 9) and (1974: 12).

10. In EU legislation a Resolution is not binding, therefore it does not give a clear indication of what the policy stance would be in the area that it covers. It does, however, imply a political commitment by the Council, which eventually could be used as a source of pressure by other EU institutions or as part of a compromise between them. For the text of the Resolution, see Commission of the EC (1974: 7-10).

11. These criticisms were raised in a speech by the rapporteur in the sitting of 24 September 1974. See (O.J. of the E.C., 1974a: 177-181).

12. According to the Advocate General of the European Court of Justice, Frederico Mancini, France was opposed to the idea of using the Advisory Committee created by Resolution 1612/68 as a platform for discussing the issue of third-country immigration. Also, France and Germany were against giving the Commission a leading role in discussions of such matters. See Mancini (1988: 23. Emphasis added).

13. Ministers Responsible for Immigration, *Press Release,* Dublin, (15 June 1990), No. 6941/90. As of December 1992, only four member states had ratified the Convention. However, given the fact that the Schengen Agreement and the Implementing Convention contain highly similar rules, the direction towards which the developments are heading is largely determined.

References

Berger, S. and Piore, Michael J. (1980) *Dualism and Discontinuity in Industrial Societies* (Cambridge, Cambridge University Press).

Bohning, W. R. (1991) 'Integration and Immigration Pressures in Western Europe' in *International Labour Review*, Vol. 130, No. 4, pp. 445-58.

Callovi, G. (1992) "Regulation of Immigration in 1993: Pieces of the European Community Jig-Saw Puzzle" in *International Migration Review*, Vol. 26, No. 2, pp. 353-72.

Commission of the EC (1968) *Bulletin of the EC, No. 11/68* (Luxembourg, Office for Official Publications of the EC).

Commission of the EC (1974) *The Social Action Programme* in *Bulletin of the EC, Supplement*, No. 2/74, February.

Commission of the EC (1975) *Implementation of Point 10 of the Final Communique Issued at European Summit Concerning a Passport Union*, COM(75)/322, Final.

Commission of the EC (1976) *Bulletin of the EC, Supplement*, No. 3/76, March.

Commission of the EC (1978) *Proposal for a Council Directive Concerning the Approximation of the Legislation of the Member States in Order to Combat Illegal Migration and Illegal Employment*, COM(78)/86, Final. 3 April.

Commission of the EC (1979) *Communication to the Council Concerning Consultations on Migration Policies vis-à-vis Third Countries*, COM(79)/115, Final. 23 March.

Commission of the EC (1979a) *Bulletin of the EC*, No. 10/79. October.

Commission of the EC (1979b) Bulletin of the EC, No. 11/79. November.

Commission of the EC (1985) 'Decision Setting Up a Prior Communication Procedure on Migration Policies in relation to Non-Member Countries' in *Official Journal of EC*, No. L217. 14 August.

Commission of the EC (1992) *Employment in Europe: 1992*, Com(92)/354 (Luxembourg, Office for Official Publications of the EC).

Commission of the EC (1994) Communication on Immigration and Asylum Policies, COM(94)/23, final. Brussels, 23 February.

Cornes, R. and Sandler, T. (1986) *The Theory of Externalities, Public Goods, and Club Goods* (Cambridge, Cambridge University Press).

Dummet, A. and Nicol, A. (1990) *Subjects, Citizens, Aliens and Others: Nationality and Immigration Law* (London, Weidenfield and Nicolson).

Gollini, A., Bonifazi, C. and Righi, A. (1993) 'A General Framework for the European Migration System in the 1990s' in King, R. (ed.), *The New Geography of European Migrations* (London, Belhaven Press), pp. 67-82.

Haas, Ernst B. (1964) *Beyond the Nation State* (Stanford, Stanford University Press).

Hass, Ernst B. (1968) *The Uniting of Europe* (2nd ed.) (Stanford, Stanford University Press).

Heisler, Martin O. and Layton-Henry, Z. (1993) 'Migration and the Links between Social and Societal Security' in Waever *et al*, pp. 148-66.

ILO (1990) *Informal Consultation Meeting on Migrants from Non-EEC Countries in the Single Market after 1992 — Informal Summary Record* (Geneva, ILO).

J.O. des C.E. (1972) *Journal Officiel des Communaute Europeennes*, No. C134, 27 December.

Kelsen, H. (1966) *Principles of International Law*. Quoted in (Plender, 1988), p.1.

Keohane, R.O. (1984) *After Hegemony Collaboration and Discord in the World Economy* (Princeton, N.J.: Princeton University Press).

Keohane, R.O. (1989) *International Relations and State Power: Essays in International Relations Theory* (London, Westview Press).

Mancini, F. (1988) 'Opinion on the Cases of 281/85, 283/85 and 287/85: Germany and Others vs. the Commission' in *Common Market Law Report*, No. 51, Part 636.

Martin, Philip (1993) "The Migration Issue" in Russel King (ed.) *The New Geography of European Migrations* (London, Belhaven Press), pp. 1-16.

Matheson, J.H.E. (1991) 'The Immigration Issue in the Community: An ACP View' in *The Courrier: ACP/EC*, No. 1298, September-October 1992.

Milward, A.S. (1992) *The European Rescue of the Nation-State* (London, Routledge).

Morgenthau, Hans, J. (1956) *Politics among Nations: The Struggle for Power and Peace* (3rd ed.) (New York, Alfred A. Knopf).

Mortimer, E. (1992) 'Pass the Human Parcel' in The Financial Times, 9 December, p. 17.

O.J. of the EC (1973) *Official Journal of the European Communities*, No. C106, 6 December.

O.J. of the EC (1974) *Official Journal of the European Communities*, No. C29, 18 March.

O.J. of the EC (1974a) *Official Journal of the European Communities*, No. 194, September.

O.J. of the EC (1977) *Official Journal of the European Communities*, No. 220, September.

Oppenheim, L. (1905): *International Law: Volume I, Peace*. (London: Longmans, Green & Co.).

Piore, Michael J. (1979) *Birds of Passage* (Cambridge, Cambridge University Press).

Plender, R. (1976) 'An Incipient form of European Citizenship?' in F. G. Jacobs (ed.), *European Law and the Individual* (Amsterdam, North Holland Publishing).

Plender, R. (1988) *International Migration Law* (2nd ed.) (Dordrecht, Martinus Nijhoff).

SOPEMI (1974) *Continuous Reporting System on Migration: 1974 Report* (Paris, OECD).

Straubhaar, T. and Zimmerman, K.F. (1993) "Towards of European Migraton Policy" in *Population Research and Policy Review*, Vol. 12, No. 3, pp. 225-41.

van Outrive, L. (1991) 'Legislation and Decision Making in Europe: International Police Co-operation and Human Rights', paper submitted to the Twentieth Annual Conference of the European Group for the Study of Deviance and Social Control, (3-6 September 1992), Padova, Italy.

Waever, Ole *et al* (1993) *Identity, Migration and the New Security Agenda in Europe* (London, Pinter Publishers).

Weiner, M. (1985) 'International Migration and International Relations' in *Population and Development Review*, Vol. 11, pp. 441-455.

Widren, Jonas (1994) 'Shaping a Multilateral Response to Future Migrations' in K. A. Hamilton (ed.), *Migration and the New Europe* (Washington, D.C., The Centre for Strategic and International Studies). pp. 37-55.